Lecture Notes in Computer Science 12689

More information about this subseries at http://www.springer.com/series/7407

Ying Tan · Yuhui Shi (Eds.)

Advances in Swarm Intelligence

12th International Conference, ICSI 2021
Qingdao, China, July 17–21, 2021
Proceedings, Part I

 Springer

Editors
Ying Tan (iD)
Peking University
Beijing, China

Yuhui Shi
Southern University of Science
and Technology
Shenzhen, China

ISSN 0302-9743 ISSN 1611-3349 (electronic)
Lecture Notes in Computer Science
ISBN 978-3-030-78742-4 ISBN 978-3-030-78743-1 (eBook)
https://doi.org/10.1007/978-3-030-78743-1

LNCS Sublibrary: SL1 – Theoretical Computer Science and General Issues

This Springer imprint is published by the registered company Springer Nature Switzerland AG
The registered company address is: Gewerbestrasse 11, 6330 Cham, Switzerland

Preface

This book and its companion volume, comprising LNCS volumes 12689 and 12690, constitute the proceedings of The Twelfth International International Conference on Swarm Intelligence (ICSI 2021) held during July 17–21, 2021, in Qingdao, China, both on-site and online.

The theme of ICSI 2021 was "Serving Life with Swarm Intelligence." The conference provided an excellent opportunity for academics and practitioners to present and discuss the latest scientific results and methods, innovative ideas, and advantages in theories, technologies, and applications in swarm intelligence. The technical program covered a number of aspects of swarm intelligence and its related areas. ICSI 2021 was the twelfth international gathering for academics and researchers working on most aspects of swarm intelligence, following successful events in Serbia (ICSI 2020, virtually), Chiang Mai (ICSI 2019), Shanghai (ICSI 2018), Fukuoka (ICSI 2017), Bali (ICSI 2016), Beijing (ICSI-CCI 2015), Hefei (ICSI 2014), Harbin (ICSI 2013), Shenzhen (ICSI 2012), Chongqing (ICSI 2011), and Beijing (ICSI 2010), which provided a high-level academic forum for participants to disseminate their new research findings and discuss emerging areas of research. ICSI 2021 also created a stimulating environment for participants to interact and exchange information on future challenges and opportunities in the field of swarm intelligence research.

Due to the ongoing COVID-19 pandemic, ICSI 2021 provided opportunities for both online and offline presentations. On the one hand, ICSI 2021 was held normally in Qingdao, China, but on the other hand, the ICSI 2021 technical team provided the ability for authors who were subject to restrictions on overseas travel to present their work through an interactive online platform or video replay. The presentations by accepted authors were made available to all registered attendees on-site and online.

The host city of ICSI 2021, Qingdao (also spelled Tsingtao), is a major sub-provincial city in the eastern Shandong province, China. Located on the western shore of the Yellow Sea, Qingdao is a major nodal city on the 21st Century Maritime Silk Road arm of the Belt and Road Initiative that connects East Asia with Europe, and has the highest GDP of any city in the province. It had jurisdiction over seven districts and three county-level cities till 2019, and as of 2014 had a population of 9,046,200 with an urban population of 6,188,100. Lying across the Shandong Peninsula and looking out to the Yellow Sea to its south, Qingdao borders the prefectural cities of Yantai to the northeast, Weifang to the west, and Rizhao to the southwest.

ICSI 2021 received 177 submissions and invited submissions from about 392 authors in 32 countries and regions (Algeria, Australia, Bangladesh, Belgium, Brazil, Bulgaria, Canada, China, Colombia, India, Italy, Japan, Jordan, Mexico, Nigeria, Peru, Portugal, Romania, Russia, Saudi Arabia, Serbia, Slovakia, South Africa, Spain, Sweden, Taiwan (China), Thailand, Turkey, United Arab Emirates, UK, USA, and Vietnam) across 6 continents (Asia, Europe, North America, South America, Africa, and Oceania). Each submission was reviewed by at least 2 reviewers, and had on average 2.5 reviewers. Based on rigorous reviews by the Program Committee members and additional reviewers, 104 high-quality papers were selected for publication in this proceedings, an acceptance rate of 58.76%. The papers are organized into 16 cohesive sections covering major topics of swarm intelligence research and its development and applications.

On behalf of the Organizing Committee of ICSI 2021, we would like to express our sincere thanks to the International Association of Swarm and Evolutionary Intelligence (IASEI), which is the premier international scholarly society devoted to advancing the theories, algorithms, real-world applications, and developments of swarm intelligence and evolutionary intelligence. We would also like to thank Peking University, Southern University of Science and Technology, and Ocean University of China for their co-sponsorships, and the Computational Intelligence Laboratory of Peking University and IEEE Beijing Chapter for their technical co-sponsorships, as well as our supporters including the International Neural Network Society, World Federation on Soft Computing, International Journal of Intelligence Systems, MDPI's journals Electronics and Mathematics, Beijing Xinghui Hi-Tech Co., and Springer Nature.

We would also like to thank the members of the Advisory Committee for their guidance, the members of the Program Committee and additional reviewers for reviewing the papers, and the members of the Publication Committee for checking the accepted papers in a short period of time. We are particularly grateful to Springer for publishing the proceedings in the prestigious series of Lecture Notes in Computer Science. Moreover, we wish to express our heartfelt appreciation to the plenary speakers, session chairs, and student helpers. In addition, there are still many more colleagues, associates, friends, and supporters who helped us in immeasurable ways; we express our sincere gratitude to them all. Last but not the least, we would like to thank all the speakers, authors, and participants for their great contributions that made ICSI 2021 successful and all the hard work worthwhile.

May 2021   Ying Tan
                                                                                           Yuhui Shi

Organization

General Co-chairs

Ying Tan   Peking University, China
Russell C. Eberhart   IUPUI, USA

Program Committee Chair

Yuhui Shi   Southern University of Science and Technology, China

Advisory Committee Chairs

Xingui He   Peking University, China
Gary G. Yen   Oklahoma State University, USA

Technical Committee Co-chairs

Haibo He   University of Rhode Island, USA
Kay Chen Tan   City University of Hong Kong, China
Nikola Kasabov   Auckland University of Technology, New Zealand
Ponnuthurai Nagaratnam   Nanyang Technological University, Singapore
  Suganthan
Xiaodong Li   RMIT University, Australia
Hideyuki Takagi   Kyushu University, Japan
M. Middendorf   University of Leipzig, Germany
Mengjie Zhang   Victoria University of Wellington, New Zealand
Qirong Tang   Tongji University, China
Milan Tuba   Singidunum University, Serbia

Plenary Session Co-chairs

Andreas Engelbrecht   University of Pretoria, South Africa
Chaoming Luo   University of Mississippi, USA

Invited Session Co-chairs

Andres Iglesias   University of Cantabria, Spain
Haibin Duan   Beihang University, China

Special Sessions Chairs

Ben Niu	Shenzhen University, China
Yan Pei	University of Aizu, Japan

Tutorial Co-chairs

Junqi Zhang	Tongji University, China
Shi Cheng	Shanxi Normal University, China

Publications Co-chairs

Swagatam Das	Indian Statistical Institute, India
Radu-Emil Precup	Politehnica University of Timisoara, Romania

Publicity Co-chairs

Yew-Soon Ong	Nanyang Technological University, Singapore
Carlos Coello	CINVESTAV-IPN, Mexico
Yaochu Jin	University of Surrey, UK
Rossi Kamal	GERIOT, Bangladesh
Dongbin Zhao	Institute of Automation, China

Finance and Registration Chairs

Andreas Janecek	University of Vienna, Austria
Suicheng Gu	Google, USA

Local Arrangement Chair

Gai-Ge Wang	Ocean University of China, China

Conference Secretariat

Renlong Chen	Peking University, China

Program Committee

Ashik Ahmed	Islamic University of Technology, Bangladesh
Rafael Alcala	University of Granada, Spain
Abdelmalek Amine	Tahar Moulay University of Saida, Algeria
Sabri Arik	Istanbul University, Turkey
Carmelo J. A. Bastos Filho	University of Pernambuco, Brazil
Sandeep Bhongade	G.S. Institute of Technology, India
Sujin Bureerat	Khon Kaen University, Thailand
Bin Cao	Tsinghua University, China

Abdelghani Chahmi	Universite des Sciences et Technologie d'Oran, Algeria
Junfeng Chen	Hohai University, China
Walter Chen	National Taipei University of Technology, Taiwan, China
Hui Cheng	Liverpool John Moores University, UK
Shi Cheng	Shaanxi Normal University, China
Prithviraj Dasgupta	U. S. Naval Research Laboratory, USA
Khaldoon Dhou	Texas A&M University, USA
Bei Dong	Shaanxi Nomal University, China
Haibin Duan	Beijing University of Aeronautics and Astronautics, China
Hongyuan Gao	Harbin Engineering University, China
Shangce Gao	University of Toyama, Japan
Ying Gao	Guangzhou University, China
Weian Guo	Tongji University, China
Changan Jiang	Osaka Institute of Technology, Japan
Mingyan Jiang	Shandong University, China
Liangjun Ke	Xian Jiaotong University, China
Germano Lambert-Torres	PS Solutions, USA
Xiujuan Lei	Shaanxi Normal University, China
Bin Li	University of Science and Technology of China, China
Zhetao Li	Xiangtan University, China
Jing Liu	Xidian University, China
Ju Liu	Shandong University, China
Qunfeng Liu	Dongguan University of Technology, China
Wenlian Lu	Fudan University, China
Chaomin Luo	Mississippi State University, USA
Wenjian Luo	Harbin Institute of Technology, China
Chengying Mao	Jiangxi University of Finance and Economics, China
Bernd Meyer	Monash University, Australia
Efrén Mezura-Montes	University of Veracruz, Mexico
Daniel Molina Cabrera	University of Granada, Spain
Sreeja N. K.	PSG College of Technology, India
Linqiang Pan	Huazhong University of Science and Technology, China
Quan-Ke Pan	Huazhong University of Science and Technology, China
Endre Pap	Singidunum University, Serbia
Mario Pavone	University of Catania, Spain
Yan Pei	University of Aizu, Japan
Mukesh Prasad	University of Technology Sydney, Australia
Radu-Emil Precup	Politehnica University of Timisoara, Romania
Robert Reynolds	Wayne State University, USA
Yuji Sato	Hosei University, Japan
Carlos Segura	Centro de Investigación en Matemáticas, Mexico
Kevin Seppi	Brigham Young University, USA

Zhongzhi Shi	Institute of Computing Technology, China
Joao Soares	GECAD, Portugal
Xiaoyan Sun	China University of Mining and Technology, China
Yifei Sun	Shaanxi Normal University, China
Ying Tan	Peking University, China
Qirong Tang	Tongji University, China
Mladen Veinović	Singidunum University, Serbia
Cong Wang	Northeastern University, China
Dujuan Wang	Sichuan University, China
Guoyin Wang	Chongqing University of Posts and Telecommunications, China
Rui Wang	National University of Defense Technology, China
Yong Wang	Central South University, China
Yuping Wang	Xidian University, China
Ka-Chun Wong	City University of Hong Kong, China
Shunren Xia	Zhejiang University, China
Ning Xiong	Mälardalen University, Sweden
Benlian Xu	Changsu Institute of Technology, China
Peng-Yeng Yin	National Chi Nan University, Taiwan, China
Jun Yu	Niigata University, Japan
Saúl Zapotecas Martínez	UAM Cuajimalpa, Mexico
Jie Zhang	Newcastle University, UK
Junqi Zhang	Tongji University, China
Tao Zhang	Tianjin University, China
Xingyi Zhang	Huazhong University of Science and Technology, China
Xinchao Zhao	Beijing University of Posts and Telecommunications, China
Yujun Zheng	Zhejiang University of Technology, China
Zexuan Zhu	Shenzhen University, China
Miodrag Zivkovic	Singidunum University, Serbia
Xingquan Zuo	Beijing University of Posts and Telecommunications, China

Additional Reviewers

Bao, Lin	Márquez Grajales, Aldo
Chen, Yang	Ramos, Sérgio
Cortez, Ricardo	Rivera Lopez, Rafael
Gu, Lingchen	Rodríguez de la Cruz, Juan Antonio
Han, Yanyang	Vargas Hakim, Gustavo Adolfo
Hu, Yao	Yu, Luyue
Lezama, Fernando	Zhou, Tianwei
Liu, Xiaoxi	

Contents – Part I

Swarm Intelligence and Nature-Inspired Computing

Swarm Unit Digital Control System Simulation 3
    Eugene Larkin, Aleksandr Privalov, and Tatiana Akimenko

Natural Emergence of Heterogeneous Strategies in Artificially Intelligent
Competitive Teams 13
    Ankur Deka and Katia Sycara

Analysis of Security Problems in Groups of Intelligent Sensors 26
    Karen Grigoryan, Evgeniya Olefirenko, Elena Basan, Maria Lapina,
    and Massimo Mecella

Optimization of a High-Lift Mechanism Motion Generation Synthesis
Using MHS 38
    Suwin Sleesongsom and Sujin Bureerat

Liminal Tones: Swarm Aesthetics and Materiality in Sound Art 46
    Mahsoo Salimi and Philippe Pasquier

Study on the Random Factor of Firefly Algorithm. 58
    Yanping Qiao, Feng Li, Cong Zhang, Xiaofeng Li, and Zhigang Zhou

Metaheuristic Optimization on Tensor-Type Solution via Swarm
Intelligence and Its Application in the Profit Optimization in Designing
Selling Scheme. 72
    Frederick Kin Hing Phoa, Hsin-Ping Liu,
    Yun-Heh (Jessica) Chen-Burger, and Shau-Ping Lin

An Improved Dragonfly Algorithm Based on Angle Modulation
Mechanism for Solving 0–1 Knapsack Problems. 83
    Lin Wang, Ronghua Shi, Wenyu Li, Xia Yuan, and Jian Dong

A Novel Physarum-Based Optimization Algorithm for Shortest Path 94
    Dan Wang and Zili Zhang

Traveling Salesman Problem via Swarm Intelligence 106
    Pei-Chen Yen and Frederick Kin Hing Phoa

Swarm-Based Computing Algorithms for Optimization

Lion Swarm Optimization by Reinforcement Pattern Search 119
    Falei Ji and Mingyan Jiang

Fuzzy Clustering Algorithm Based on Improved Lion Swarm
Optimization Algorithm   130
   Haiyan Yu, Mingyan Jiang, Dongfeng Yuan, and Miaomiao Xin

Sparrow Search Algorithm for Solving Flexible Jobshop
Scheduling Problem   140
   Mingliang Wu, Dongsheng Yang, Zhile Yang, and Yuanjun Guo

Performance Analysis of Evolutionary Computation Based on Tianchi
Service Scheduling Problem   155
   Jun Yu, Yuhao Li, Tianwei Zhou, Churong Zhang, Guanghui Yue,
   and Yunjiao Ge

An Intelligent Algorithm for AGV Scheduling in Intelligent Warehouses   163
   Xue Wu, Min-Xia Zhang, and Yu-Jun Zheng

Success-History Based Position Adaptation in Gaining-Sharing Knowledge
Based Algorithm   174
   Shakhnaz Akhmedova and Vladimir Stanovov

Particle Swarm Optimization

Multi-guide Particle Swarm Optimisation Control Parameter Importance
in High Dimensional Spaces   185
   Timothy G. Carolus and Andries P. Engelbrecht

Research on the Latest Development of Particle Swarm Optimization
Algorithm for Satellite Constellation   199
   Jia-xu Zhang and Xiao-peng Yan

Polynomial Approximation Using Set-Based Particle Swarm Optimization . . .   210
   Jean-Pierre van Zyl and Andries P. Engelbrecht

Optimizing Artificial Neural Network for Functions Approximation Using
Particle Swarm Optimization   223
   Lina Zaghloul, Rawan Zaghloul, and Mohammad Hamdan

Two Modified NichePSO Algorithms for Multimodal Optimization   232
   Tyler Crane, Andries Engelbrecht, and Beatrice Ombuki-Berman

VaCSO: A Multi-objective Collaborative Competition Particle Swarm
Algorithm Based on Vector Angles   244
   Libao Deng, Le Song, Sibo Hou, and Gaoji Sun

The Experimental Analysis on Transfer Function of Binary Particle
Swarm Optimization   254
   Yixuan Luo, Jianhua Liu, Xingsi Xue, Renyuan Hu, and Zihang Wang

Multi-stage COVID-19 Epidemic Modeling Based on PSO and SEIR   265
  Haiyun Qiu, Jinsong Chen, and Ben Niu

Particle Swarms Reformulated Towards a Unified
and Flexible Framework.   275
  Mauro Sebastián Innocente

Ant Colony Optimization

On One Bicriterion Discrete Optimization Problem and a Hybrid Ant
Colony Algorithm for Its Approximate Solution   289
  Yurii A. Mezentsev and Nikita Y. Chubko

Initializing Ant Colony Algorithms by Learning from the Difficult
Problem's Global Features   301
  Xiangyang Deng, Limin Zhang, and Ziqiang Zhu

An Ant Colony Optimization Based Approach for Binary Search   311
  N. K. Sreelaja and N. K. Sreeja

A Slime Mold Fractional-Order Ant Colony Optimization Algorithm
for Travelling Salesman Problems   322
  Ziheng Rong, Xiaoling Gong, Xiangyu Wang, Wei Lv, and Jian Wang

Ant Colony Optimization for K-Independent Average Traveling
Salesman Problem.   333
  Yu Iwasaki and Koji Hasebe

Differential Evolution

Inferring Small-Scale Maximum-Entropy Genetic Regulatory Networks
by Using DE Algorithm.   347
  Fu Yin, Jiarui Zhou, Zexuan Zhu, Xiaoliang Ma, and Weixin Xie

Variable Fragments Evolution in Differential Evolution   358
  Changshou Deng, Xiaogang Dong, Yucheng Tan, and Hu Peng

The Efficiency of Interactive Differential Evolution on Creation
of ASMR Sounds   368
  Makoto Fukumoto

Genetic Algorithm and Evolutionary Computation

Genetic Algorithm Fitness Function Formulation for Test Data Generation
with Maximum Statement Coverage   379
  Tatiana Avdeenko and Konstantin Serdyukov

A Genetic Algorithm-Based Ensemble Convolutional Neural Networks
for Defect Recognition with Small-Scale Samples   390
    Yiping Gao, Liang Gao, Xinyu Li, and Cuiyu Wang

Biased Random-Key Genetic Algorithm for Structure Learning.   399
    Baodan Sun and Yun Zhou

Fireworks Algorithms

Performance Analysis of the Fireworks Algorithm Versions   415
    Ira Tuba, Ivana Strumberger, Eva Tuba, Nebojsa Bacanin,
    and Milan Tuba

Using Population Migration and Mutation to Improve Loser-Out
Tournament-Based Fireworks Algorithm   423
    PengCheng Hong and JunQi Zhang

Region Selection with Discrete Fireworks Algorithm for Person
Re-identification   433
    Xuan Li, Tao Zhang, Xin Zhao, and Shuang Li

Fireworks Harris Hawk Algorithm Based on Dynamic Competition
Mechanism for Numerical Optimization   441
    Wenyu Li, Ronghua Shi, Heng Zou, and Jian Dong

Enhancing Fireworks Algorithm in Local Adaptation
and Global Collaboration   451
    Yifeng Li and Ying Tan

Brain Storm Optimization Algorithm

Multi-objective Brainstorming Optimization Algorithm Based on Adaptive
Mutation Strategy   469
    Yali Wu, Yulong Wang, and Xiaoxiao Quan

Brain Storm Optimization Algorithm Based on Formal Concept Analysis. . . .   479
    Fengrong Chang, Lianbo Ma, Yan Song, and Aoshuang Dong

An Improved Brain Storm Optimization Algorithm Based on Maximum
Likelihood Estimation   492
    Junfeng Chen, Xingsi Xue, and Bulgan Ninjerdene

Bacterial Foraging Optimization Algorithm

Reorganized Bacterial Foraging Optimization Algorithm for Aircraft
Maintenance Technician Scheduling Problem   505
    Ben Niu, Bowen Xue, Tianwei Zhou, Churong Zhang, and Qinge Xiao

A Bacterial Foraging Optimization Algorithm Based on Normal
Distribution for Crowdfunding Project Outcome Prediction.   513
   Yingsi Tan, Shilian Chen, and Shuang Geng

Bacterial Foraging Optimization with Leader Selection Strategy
for Bi-objective Optimization   523
   Hong Wang, Yixin Wang, Yikun Ou, and Ben Niu

DNA Computing Methods

Stability and Hopf Bifurcation Analysis of DNA Molecular Oscillator
System Based on DNA Strand Displacement   537
   Tao Sun, Hui Lv, and Qiang Zhang

Dynamic Behavior Analysis of DNA Subtraction Gate with Stochastic
Disturbance and Time Delay   547
   Huiwen Li, Hui Lv, and Qiang Zhang

Modeling and Analysis of Nonlinear Dynamic System with Lévy Jump
Based on Cargo Sorting DNA Robot.   557
   Hao Fu, Hui Lv, and Qiang Zhang

Stability and Hopf Bifurcation Analysis of Complex DNA Catalytic
Reaction Network with Double Time Delays   567
   Wei Chen, Hui Lv, and Qiang Zhang

Author Index   583

Contents – Part II

Multi-objective Optimization

A Multi-objective Evolutionary Algorithm Based on Second-Order
Differential Operator 3
    Ruizhi Wan, Yinnan Chen, and Xinchao Zhao

An Improved Evolutionary Multi-objective Optimization Algorithm Based
on Multi-population and Dynamic Neighborhood 13
    Shuai Zhao, Xuying Kang, and Qingjian Ni

A Multiobjective Memetic Algorithm for Multiobjective Unconstrained
Binary Quadratic Programming Problem 23
    Ying Zhou, Lingjing Kong, Lijun Yan, Shaopeng Liu, and Jiaming Hong

A Hybrid Algorithm for Multi-objective Permutation Flow Shop
Scheduling Problem with Setup Times. 34
    Cuiyu Wang, Shuting Wang, and Xinyu Li

Dynamic Multi-objective Optimization via Sliding Time Window
and Parallel Computing 45
    Qinqin Fan, Yihao Wang, Okan K. Ersoy, Ning Li, and Zhenzhong Chu

A New Evolutionary Approach to Multiparty Multiobjective Optimization . . . 58
    Zeneng She, Wenjian Luo, Yatong Chang, Xin Lin, and Ying Tan

Swarm Robotics and Multi-agent System

Immune System Algorithms to Environmental Exploration of Robot
Navigation and Mapping 73
    *Elakiya Jayaraman, Tingjun Lei, Shahram Rahimi, Shi Cheng,
    and Chaomin Luo*

Primitive Shape Recognition Based on Local Point Cloud
for Object Grasp. 85
    Qirong Tang, Lou Zhong, Zheng Zhou, Wenfeng Zhu, and Zhugang Chu

Odometry During Object Transport: A Study with Swarm
of Physical Robots 92
    Muhanad H. M. Alkilabi, Timoteo Carletti, and Elio Tuci

Active Disturbance Rejection Control of Underwater Manipulator. 102
    Qirong Tang, Daopeng Jin, Yang Hong, Jinyuan Guo, and Jiang Li

Distributed Position-Force Control for Cooperative Transportation with
Multiple Mobile Manipulators.   111
    Pengjie Xu, Jun Zheng, Jingtao Zhang, Kun Zhang, Yuanzhe Cui,
    and Qirong Tang

Real-Time Sea Cucumber Detection Based on YOLOv4-Tiny and Transfer
Learning Using Data Augmentation.   119
    Thao NgoGia, Yinghao Li, Daopeng Jin, Jinyuan Guo, Jiang Li,
    and Qirong Tang

Toward Swarm Robots Tracking: A Constrained Gaussian Condensation
Filter Method   129
    Shihong Duan, Hang Wu, Cheng Xu, and Jiawang Wan

Adaptive Task Distribution Approach Using Threshold Behavior Tree
for Robotic Swarm   137
    Li Ma, Weidong Bao, Xiaomin Zhu, Meng Wu, Yutong Yuan, Ji Wang,
    and Hao Chen

Map Fusion Method Based on Image Stitching for Multi-robot SLAM   146
    Qirong Tang, Kun Zhang, Pengjie Xu, Jingtao Zhang, and Yuanzhe Cui

Robotic Brain Storm Optimization: A Multi-target Collaborative Searching
Paradigm for Swarm Robotics   155
    Jian Yang, Donghui Zhao, Xinhao Xiang, and Yuhui Shi

Distributed Multi-agent Shepherding with Consensus.   168
    Benjamin Campbell, Heba El-Fiqi, Robert Hunjet, and Hussein Abbass

Non-singular Finite-Time Consensus Tracking Protocols for Second-Order
Multi-agent Systems˙.   182
    Yao Zou, Wenfu Yang, Zixuan Wang, Keping Long, and Wei He

UAV Cooperation and Control

Multi-UAV Cooperative Path Planning via Mutant Pigeon Inspired
Optimization with Group Learning Strategy   195
    Yueping Yu, Yimin Deng, and Haibin Duan

UAV Path Planning Based on Variable Neighborhood Search Genetic
Algorithm   205
    Guo Zhang, Rui Wang, Hongtao Lei, Tao Zhang, Wenhua Li,
    and Yuanming Song

An Improved Particle Swarm Optimization with Dual Update Strategies
Collaboration Based Task Allocation.   218
    Shuang Xia, Xiangyin Zhang, Xiuzhi Li, and Tian Zhang

Intelligent Intrusion Detection System for a Group of UAVs   230
Elena Basan, Maria Lapina, Nikita Mudruk, and Evgeny Abramov

Machine Learning

NiaAML2: An Improved AutoML Using Nature-Inspired Algorithms   243
Luka Pečnik, Iztok Fister, and Iztok Fister Jr.

Proof Searching in PVS Theorem Prover Using Simulated Annealing   253
M. Saqib Nawaz, Meng Sun, and Philippe Fournier-Viger

Deep Reinforcement Learning for Dynamic Scheduling of Two-Stage
Assembly Flowshop   263
Xin Lin and Jian Chen

A Hybrid Wind Speed Prediction Model Based on Signal Decomposition
and Deep 1DCNN.   272
Yuhui Wang, Qingjian Ni, Shuai Zhao, Meng Zhang, and Chenxin Shen

A Cell Tracking Method with Deep Learning Mitosis Detection
in Microscopy Images   282
Di Wu, Benlian Xu, Mingli Lu, Jian Shi, Zhen Li, Fei Guan,
and Zhicheng Yang

A Knowledge Graph Enhanced Semantic Matching Method for Plan
Recommendation   290
Rupeng Liang, Shaoqiu Zheng, Kebo Deng, Zexiang Mao, Wei Ma,
and Zhengwei Zhang

Classification of Imbalanced Fetal Health Data by PSO Based Ensemble
Recursive Feature Elimination ANN   300
Jun Gao, Canpeng Huang, Xijie Huang, Kaishan Huang,
and Hong Wang

Evolutionary Ontology Matching Technique with User Involvement   313
Xingsi Xue, Chaofan Yang, Wenyu Liu, and Hai Zhu

Sequential Stacked AutoEncoder-Based Artificial Neural Network
and Improved Sheep Optimization for Tool Wear Prediction   321
Fei Ding, Mingyan Jiang, Dongfeng Yuan, Falei Ji, and Haiyan Yu

Application of Internet Plus: TCM Clinical Intelligent Decision Making   331
Jun Xie, Sijie Dang, Xiuyuan Xu, Jixiang Guo, Xiaozhi Zhang,
and Zhang Yi

Parallel Random Embedding with Negatively Correlated Search   339
Qi Yang, Peng Yang, and Ke Tang

Value-Based Continuous Control Without Concrete State-Action
Value Function   352
   Jin Zhu, Haixian Zhang, and Zhen Pan

Exploring the Landscapes and Emerging Trends of Reinforcement Learning
from 1990 to 2020: A Bibliometric Analysis   365
   Li Zeng, Xiaoqing Yin, Yang Li, and Zili Li

Data Mining

NiaClass: Building Rule-Based Classification Models Using
Nature-Inspired Algorithms   381
   Luka Pečnik, Iztok Fister, and Iztok Fister Jr.

Mining Neighbor Frames for Person Re-identification by Global
Optimal Tracking   391
   *Kai Han, Jinho Lee, Lang Huang, Fangcheng Liu, Seiichi Uchida,
   and Chao Zhang*

Artificial Fish Swarm Algorithm for Mining High Utility Itemsets   407
   Wei Song, Junya Li, and Chaomin Huang

Ensemble Recognition Based on the Harmonic Information Gain Ratio
for Unsafe Behaviors in Coal Mines   420
   Jian Cheng, Botao Jiao, Yinan Guo, and Shijie Wang

Feature Selection for Image Classification Based on Bacterial
Colony Optimization   430
   Hong Wang, Zhuo Zhou, Yixin Wang, and Xiaohui Yan

Local Binary Pattern Algorithm with Weight Threshold
for Image Classification   440
   Zexi Xu, Guangyuan Qiu, Wanying Li, Xiaofu He, and Shuang Geng

Applying Classification Algorithms to Identify Brain Activity Patterns   452
   Marina Murtazina and Tatiana Avdeenko

An Improved El Nino Index Forecasting Method Based
on Parameters Optimization   462
   Chenxin Shen, Qingjian Ni, Shuai Zhao, Meng Zhang, and Yuhui Wang

Intrusion Detection System Based on an Updated ANN Model   472
   Yu Xue, Bernard-marie Onzo, and Ferrante Neri

Bayesian Classifier Based on Discrete Multidimensional
Gaussian Distribution   480
   Yihuai Wang and Fei Han

An Improved Spatial-Temporal Network Based on Residual Correction
and Evolutionary Algorithm for Water Quality Prediction   491
  Xin Yu, Wenqiang Peng, Dongfan Xue, and Qingjian Ni

Can Argumentation Help to Forecast Conditional Stock Market Crisis
with Multi-agent Sentiment Classification?   500
  Zhi-yong Hao and Peng-ge Sun

Stock Market Movement Prediction by Gated Hierarchical Encoder.   511
  Peibin Chen and Ying Tan

Other Applications

Spiking Adaptive Dynamic Programming with Poisson Process   525
  Qinglai Wei, Liyuan Han, and Tielin Zhang

Designing a Mathematical Model and Control System for the Makariza
Steam Boiler   533
  Taha Ahmadi and Sebastián Soto Gaona

Compositional Object Synthesis in Game of Life Cellular Automata Using
SAT Solver   543
  Haruki Nishimura and Koji Hasebe

Automatic Detection of Type III Solar Radio Burst   553
  Shicai Liu, Guowu Yuan, Chengming Tan, Hao Zhou, and Ruru Cheng

The Impact of Wechat Red Packet Feature at Achieving Users Satisfaction
and Loyalty: Wechat Users in China   563
  Kamal Abubker Abrahim Sleiman, Lan Juanli, Xiangyu Cai, Wang Yubo,
  Lei Hongzhen, and Ru Liu

Author Index   577

Swarm Intelligence and Nature-Inspired Computing

Swarm Unit Digital Control System Simulation

Eugene Larkin[1]([✉]), Aleksandr Privalov[2], and Tatiana Akimenko[1]

[1] Tula State University, Tula 300012, Russia
[2] Tula State Lev Tolstoy Pedagogical University, Tula 300026, Russia

Abstract. Physical swarm unit, as an object under digital control is analyzed. It is shown, that Von Neumann digital controller, as a physical device, has new properties in comparison with analogue controllers, namely due to sequentially interpretation of control algorithm there are time delays between quests to sensors and actuators, that cause influence on a swarm unit performance as a whole. Flowchart of digital control system is worked out and closed loops transfer function, which takes into account real properties of Von Neumann digital controller, is obtained. The method of time lags estimation, based on notion the interpretation of arbitrary complexity cyclic algorithm as semi-Markov process, is proposed. Theoretical postulates are confirmed by simulation of two-loop digital control system functioning. Results of simulation emphatically show how data skew and feedback lag affect on swarm unit control dynamics.

Keywords: Physical swarm unit · Object under control · Von Neumann controller · Semi-Markov process · Transfer function · Time delay · Data skew · Feedback lag

1 Introduction

Basic concept of modern swarm development is complication of tasks, which decide every unit, when solving common swarm aim problem [1–3]. When physical swarm units operate at the environment space, the problem is to minimize a time of units mutual control, that increase demands to units digital control systems [4]. As a rule, for control the unit onboard equipment Von Neumann computers are used. This device, in comparison with analogue controllers, possesses with new properties, which follows from sequential, operator-by-operator, interpretation of algorithm [5–7], embedded into controller. So it is necessary to spend any time to calculate action, transmitted to actuator after receiving data from sensors [8]. Time intervals emerging between input/output data vectors (data skew), and between input data from sensors and output data to actuators (pure lag) affect on quality characteristics of swarm unit control system as a whole [9, 10], so they should be taken into account when design the system.

There are no any difficulties in estimation of time intervals in simple case, when cyclic control algorithm include input-output-calculation-return operators only, but when structure of soft, involving transactions operators, is rather complicated, there is the problem to estimate time intervals between transactions at the stage of algorithm design. To solve the problem one should to take into account those facts, that data, forming on

© Springer Nature Switzerland AG 2021
Y. Tan and Y. Shi (Eds.): ICSI 2021, LNCS 12689, pp. 3–12, 2021.
https://doi.org/10.1007/978-3-030-78743-1_1

swarm unit sensors outputs, are random one; data may be processed by quite different algorithm branches, possessing quite different time complexities; algorithm includes decision operators at branching points. So to facilitate the problem solution semi-Markov processes theory [11–14] should be accepted as basic concept for control algorithm simulation. Methods of swarm unit digital control system simulation at the stage of its design in order to determine unit performance are not widespread, that confirms necessity and relevancy of investigation in the area.

2 Features of Von Neumann Computer Control

Multi, K-loop, digital control system (DCS) structure is shown on the Fig. 1. It is rather classic one, and includes two subsystems: linear Object Under Control (OUC) and Digital Controller (DC). OUC consists of K units, every of which is described with transfer function vector $\mathbf{W}_k(s) = [W_{k1}(s), \ldots, W_{kl}(s), \ldots, W_{kK}(s)]$ and feedback scalar transfer function $W_{0,k}(s)$, $1 \leq k \leq K$. Vectors $\mathbf{W}_k(s)$, and scalars $W_{0,k}(s)$, describe the dynamics of OUC k-th unit itself and feedback sensor, respectively. DC is real time Von Neumann type computer, which interprets control program, and in cycle generates quests both to actuators, and to sensors for organizing the managing procedure.

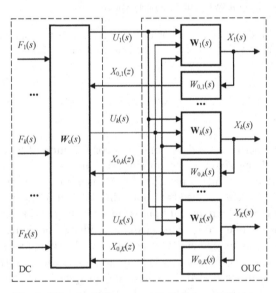

Fig. 1. Flowchart of swarm unit digital control system

System operates as follows. The control aim vector $\mathbf{F}(s) = [F_1(s), \ldots, F_k(s), \ldots, F_K(s)]$ is generated element-by-element by controller, or inputted element-by-element into DC from outside. On outputs of controller action vector $\mathbf{U}(s) = [U_1(s), \ldots, U_k(s), \ldots, U_K(s)]$ is generated by software, and is physically transformed into the swarm unit state $\mathbf{X}(s) = [X_1(s), \ldots, X_k(s), \ldots, X_K(s)]$ as follows:

$$\mathbf{X}(s) = \mathbf{U}(s) \cdot \mathbf{W}(s) = \mathbf{U}(s) \cdot \begin{bmatrix} \mathbf{W}_1(s) \\ \ldots \\ \mathbf{W}_k(s) \\ \ldots \\ \mathbf{W}_K(s) \end{bmatrix}, \tag{1}$$

where s is the Laplace operator [15].

OUC state is measured by K sensors, and vector signal $\mathbf{X}_0(s) = [X_{0,1}(s), \ldots, X_{0,k}(s), \ldots, X_{0,K}(s)]$ is inputted into DC back, sequentially, element-by-element. Due to time intervals between transactions are essential values for DC description, below is considered, that they are counted from moment of input of the first. All other data are input/output respectively element $F_1(s) \in \mathbf{F}(s)$ with lags, nominated as follows:

$F_k(s)$ are inputted respectively $F_1(s)$ with lags $\tau_{f,k}, 2 \le k \le K$;
$X_{0,k}(s)$ are inputted respectively $F_1(s)$ with lags $\tau_{0,k}, 1 \le k \le K$;
$U_k(s)$ are outputted respectively $F_1(s)$ with lags $\tau_{u,k}, 1 \le k \le K$.

In accordance with the theorem about shifting in the time domain [15, 16]

$$L[\varphi(t - \tau)] = \exp(-\tau s)\Phi(s), \quad \tau > 0, \tag{2}$$

where τ is the shifting value; t is the time; $\varphi(t)$ is a function; $L[\ldots]$ - direct Laplace transform: $\Phi(s)$ is the Laplace transform of $\varphi(t)$.

From (2) it follows, that

$$\mathbf{F}_{sh}(s) = \mathbf{F}(s) \cdot \mathbf{Q}_f(s); \tag{3}$$

$$\mathbf{X}_{sh}(s) = \mathbf{X}_0(s) \cdot \mathbf{Q}_0(s); \tag{4}$$

$$\mathbf{U}_{sh}(s) = \mathbf{U}(s) \cdot \mathbf{Q}_u(s), \tag{5}$$

where $\mathbf{F}_{sh}(s), \mathbf{X}_{sh}(s), \mathbf{U}_{sh}(s)$ are vectors $\mathbf{F}(s), \mathbf{X}_0(s), \mathbf{U}(s)$, elements of which are delayed on time; $\mathbf{Q}_f(s) = \lfloor Q_{f,kl}(s) \rfloor$, $\mathbf{Q}_0(s) = \lfloor Q_{0,kl}(s) \rfloor$, $\mathbf{Q}_v(s) = \lfloor Q_{u,kl}(s) \rfloor$ are diagonal lag matrices, in which

$$Q_{f,kl}(s) = \begin{cases} 0, & \text{when } k \ne l; \\ 1, & \text{when } k = l = 1; \\ \exp(-\tau_{f,k}s), & \text{when } 2 \le k = l \le K; \end{cases} \tag{6}$$

$$Q_{0,kl}(s) = \begin{cases} 0, & \text{when } k \ne l; \\ \exp(-\tau_{0,k}s), & \text{when } k = l; \end{cases} \tag{7}$$

$$Q_{u,kl}(s) = \begin{cases} 0, & \text{when } k \neq l; \\ \exp(-\tau_{u,k}s), & \text{when } k = l. \end{cases} \tag{8}$$

Data, processed in DC, are discrete one, so in strict sense, ordinary transfer function apparatus is not fit for description of $\mathbf{U}(s)$ vector elements calculation. But, when sampling period is approached to zero, then data processing in frequency domain may be described as ordinary transfer function matrix $\mathbf{W}_c(s)$. So, in the case, when, processing feedback signal, DC realizes a linear control law, on its outputs $\mathbf{U}(s)$ the following vector signal is generated [5, 6]:

$$\mathbf{U}(s) = \lfloor \mathbf{F}(s) \cdot \mathbf{Q}_f(s) - \mathbf{X}(s) \cdot \mathbf{W}_0(s) \cdot \mathbf{Q}_0(s) \rfloor \cdot \mathbf{W}_c(s) \cdot \mathbf{Q}_u(s), \tag{9}$$

where $\mathbf{W}_c(s) = \lfloor W_{c,kl}(s) \rfloor$ is the $K \times K$ matrix of linear transfer functions, which are embedded into DC as a software; $\mathbf{W}_0(s) = \lfloor W_{0,kl}(s) \rfloor$ is the $K \times K$ diagonal matrix, whose elements are as follows:

$$W_{0,kl}(s) = \begin{cases} 0, & \text{when } k \neq l; \\ W_{0,k}(s), & \text{when } k = l. \end{cases} \tag{10}$$

Simultaneous solution of (9) and (11) relatively to $\mathbf{X}(s)$ gives the following expression

$$\mathbf{X}(s) = [\mathbf{E} - \mathbf{W}_0(s) \cdot \mathbf{Q}_0(s) \cdot \mathbf{W}_c(s) \cdot \mathbf{Q}_u(s)]^{-1} \times \mathbf{F}(s) \cdot \mathbf{W}_c(s) \cdot \mathbf{Q}_f(s) \cdot \mathbf{W}(s) \cdot \mathbf{Q}_u(s), \tag{11}$$

where $\mathbf{E}$ is the $K \times K$ unit diagonal matrix;

Matrices $\mathbf{Q}_f(s) = \lfloor Q_{f,kl}(s) \rfloor$, $\mathbf{Q}_0(s) = \lfloor Q_{0,kl}(s) \rfloor$, $\mathbf{Q}_v(s) = \lfloor Q_{u,kl}(s) \rfloor$, characterizing lags, are situated both in the numerator, and in denominator of (12). Matrices situated at numerator, defines so called data skew and common lag of external commands execution. Matrices situated at denominator, defines common feedback lag, therefore changes qualitatively characteristics of transition process.

3   Semi-Markov Model of DC Operation

For estimation of time intervals the model of Von Neumann computer operation in time domain should be worked out. For simplicity it may be represented as including transaction operators only. Control process in such model is reduced to elements of vectors $\mathbf{F}(s)$, $\mathbf{X}_0(s)$ reading from interface and elements of vector $\mathbf{U}(s)$ writing to interface. The algorithm, generated quests, is the cyclic one, but in it absent a looping effect. The algorithm may generate transactions in an arbitrary sequence, with one exception; the same transaction can not be generated twice at a time. Also, due to the fact, that for control action $\mathbf{U}(s)$ calculation all element of vectors $\mathbf{F}(s)$ and $\mathbf{X}_0(s)$ should be used, the strong connectivity condition should be imposed [17, 18] on the graph, which, represents the structure of control algorithm. In common case such properties has the full oriented graph without loops, shown on the Fig. 2 a. In simplest case vectors $\mathbf{F}(s)$ and

$\mathbf{X}_0(s)$ elements are quested in turn, after that control action is calculated, and after that elements of $\mathbf{U}(s)$ are quested in turn (Fig. 2 b).

With taking into account randomness of time interval between transactions and stochastic transactions sequence for external observer, the adequate approach to algorithm simulation is semi-Markov process [11–14], which states are abstract analogues of algorithm operators. Semi-Markov process is represented by the semi-Markov matrix

$$\mathbf{h}(t) = [h_{kl}(t)] = \big[g_{kl}(t)\big] \otimes \big[p_{kl}(t)\big], \tag{12}$$

where $p_{kl}(t)$ is probability of the direct switching from the k-th state to the l-th state; $g_{kl}(t)$ is the time density of residence the process (17) in the k-th state before switching into the l-th state; $\otimes$ is the direct multiplication sign; t is the physical time.

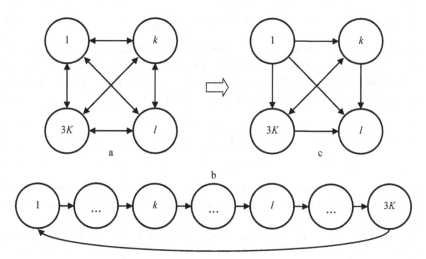

Fig. 2. Common structure of semi-Markov process (a), simplest case (b) and the model for time interval estimation (c)

Semi-Markov process (13) is ergodic one and does not include both absorbing, and partially absorbing states. Due to semi-Markov process ergodicity on densities $g_{k,l}(t)$ and probabilities $p_{k,l}(t)$ following restrictions are imposed:

$$0 < T_{kl}^{\min} \le \arg[g_{kl}(t)] \le T_{kl}^{\min} < \infty, \quad 1 \le k, l \le 3K; \tag{13}$$

$$\sum_{l=1}^{3K} p_{kl} = 1; \tag{14}$$

where $3K$ is common quantity of transaction operators; $T_{kl}^{\min}$ and $T_{kl}^{\max}$ are upper and lower bounds of density $g_{kl}(t)$ domain.

When estimation of time intervals between transactions it is no matter how semi-Markov process (13) gets l-th state from the first one. Determining in the case is that switch is the first, but not second, third, etc. For time interval estimation initial semi-Markov process should be transformed into the process with the structure, shown on the Fig. 2 c, in which first state is the starting one, and l-th state is the absorbing one. For getting such structure:

First column and l-th row of $\mathbf{h}(t)$ are reset to zeros;
Probabilities $p_{ki}(t)$ in all rows excluding the l-th, and in all columns, excluding the first, are recalculated as follows:

$$p'_{ki} = \frac{p_{ki}}{1 - p_{k1}}, \quad 1 \le k, i \le 3K, \quad k \ne l, \quad i \ne 1. \tag{15}$$

In such a way

$$\mathbf{h}(t) \to \mathbf{h}'(t) = \left[g_{kl}(t) \cdot p'_{kl} \right]. \tag{16}$$

After recalculation probabilities according (15), partially absorbing states are annihilated, and events of getting the l-th state from the first state begin to make up a full group of incompatible events. In such a way, time density of wandering from the first state to the l-th state may be estimated as follows [19]

$$g_{1,l}^{\Sigma}(t) = \mathbf{I}_1^r \cdot L^{-1} \left[\sum_{j=1}^{\infty} \{L[\mathbf{h}'(t)]\}^j \right] \cdot \mathbf{I}_l^c, \tag{17}$$

where $L^{-1}[...]$ is the inverse Laplace transform; $\mathbf{I}_1^r$ is the row-vector, first element of which is equal to one, and other elements are equal to zeros; $\mathbf{I}_l^c$ is the column-vector, l-th element of which is equal to one, and other elements are equal to zeros.

For time density (19) the expectation and the dispersion may be calculated, as usual [20]:

$$T_{1l}^{\Sigma} = \int_0^{\infty} t \cdot g_{1l}^{\Sigma}(t) dt; \tag{18}$$

$$D_{1l}^{\Sigma} = \int_0^{\infty} \left(t - T_{1l}^{\Sigma} \right)^2 \cdot g_{1l}^{\Sigma}(t) dt \tag{19}$$

In simplest case density, expectation and dispersion of reaching time the l-th state from the first, are as follows:

$$g_{1l}^{\Sigma}(t) = L^{-1} \left[\prod_{k=1}^{l-1} L[g_{k,k+1}(t)] \right], \tag{20}$$

$$T_{1l}^{\Sigma}(t) = \sum_{k=1}^{l} T_{k,k+1}; \tag{21}$$

$$D_{1l}^{\Sigma}(t) = \sum_{k=1}^{l} D_{k,k+1}; \tag{22}$$

where $g_{k,k+1}(t)$, $T_{k,k+1}$, $D_{k,k+1}(t)$ are density, expectation and dispersion of time of residence the process, shown on the Fig. 2 c, in the k-th state before switching into the $(k + 1)$-th state.

Expectations $T_{1l}^{\Sigma}(t) = \tau_{1l}$ give middle estimations of time delays. Also time intervals may be estimated with using "three sigma rule" [21], as follows:

$$\tau_{1l} = T_{1l}^{\Sigma} + 3\sqrt{D_{1l}^{\Sigma}}. \tag{23}$$

Estimations (17)–(23) define lags of input/output vectors $\mathbf{F}(s)$, $\mathbf{X}_0(s)$, $\mathbf{U}(s)$ elements with respect to input the element $F_1(s)$. All other delays may be obtained from these parameters. For example, delay between input of k-th element, $1 \leq l \leq 2K$ and output of l-th element $2K + 1 \leq m \leq 3K$ may be defined as

$$\tau_{kl} = \tau_{1l} - \tau_{1k}. \tag{24}$$

When obtaining swarm unit control system closed loop transfer function according (11) estimations (18), (21), or (23) may be used.

4 Example of Control System Analysis

As an example, swarm unit two-loop digital control system is considered (Fig. 3). Structure of algorithm, realized in DC, is shown on the Fig. 2 b.

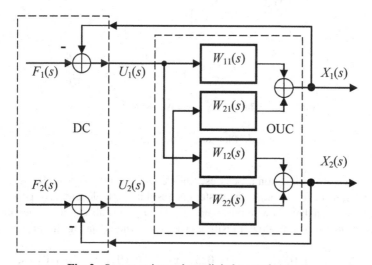

Fig. 3. Swarm unit two-loop digital control system

Transfer functions, which define OUC dynamics are as follows:

$$W_{11}(s) = W_{22}(s) = \frac{5}{0,2s+1}; \quad W_{12}(s) = W_{21}(s) = \frac{2}{0,2s+1}. \tag{25}$$

In the system proportional feedback is realized. Sensors, which measure state vector $[X_1(s), \ X_1(s)]$ of OUC, are characterized by transfer functions $W_{0,1}(s) = W_{0,2}(s) = 1$. Inputs $F_1(s)$ and $F_2(s)$ are Laplace transform of Heaviside functions $L^{-1}[F_1(s)] = 1 \cdot \eta(t), L^{-1}[F_2(s)] = 0.5 \cdot \eta(t)$. Values of Heaviside functions are established differently to divide plots on ordinate axis. Transition processes shown on the Fig. 4. Plots on all charts, shown on the Fig. 4 have the same nominations, namely $x_1(t) = L^{-1}[X_1(s)]$ $x_2(t) = L^{-1}[X_2(s)]$, when data skew of vector $[F_1(s), \ F_2(s)]$ is absent; $x_{1,\tau}(t), \ x_{2,\tau}(t)$ denote signals $x_1(t), \ x_2(t)$, when under experimental conditions signal $x_2(t)$ lag behind signal $x_1(t)$ at 0,5 s.

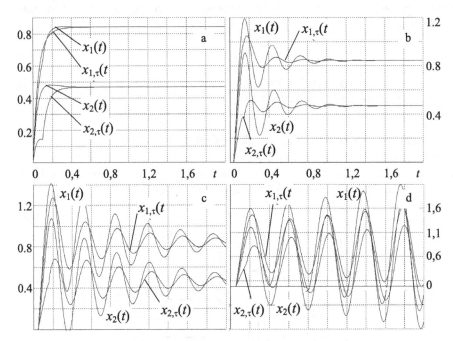

Fig. 4. Plots of transtion processes

Figure 4 a shows transition processes, when controller in the system is an analogue one. As one can see at the plots, the system is absolutely stable and have good performance, both when a data skew in the signals $F_1(s), \ F_2(s)$ is absent, and when the skew take place. Figure 4 b, c, d show transition processes, when data lags at interfaces are:

Figure 4 b - $\tau_{U,1} = 0, 02$ s, $\tau_{U,2} = 0, 025$ s, $\tau_{0,1} = 0, 01$ s, $\tau_{0,2} = 0, 015$ s;
Figure 4 c - $\tau_{U,1} = 0, 025$ s, $\tau_{U,2} = 0, 03$ s, $\tau_{0,1} = 0, 015$ s, $\tau_{0,2} = 0, 02$ s;
Figure 4 d - $\tau_{U,1} = 0, 03$ s, $\tau_{U,2} = 0, 035$ s, $\tau_{0,1} = 0, 02$ s, $\tau_{0,2} = 0, 025$ s.

At all named plots processes start with delays, which are defined by output lags of signals $U_1(s)$, $U_2(s)$. Figure 4 b demonstrates in general a stable system, but with increased overshooting and time of reaching the mode. Figure 4 c demonstrate the performance of system, close to stability border, and Fig. 4 c shows fully unstable system.

5 Conclusion

As a result, the mathematical model of physical swarm unit digital control system, which takes into account real characteristics of Von Neumann type controllers, is worked out. Method of estimation of time intervals between transactions, generated by digital controller algorithm of arbitrary complexity, to unit actuators and sensors, is proposed. It is shown, that time delays between input/output elements of the same vector (data skew), and between input of data from sensors and output data to actuators (feedback lag) causes deterioration of swarm unit performance characteristics, such as overshooting and time of reaching the mode. The results of investigation may be recommended for utilization in ingineering practice of swam unit soft design.

Further investigations in the domain may be directed to working out methods of practical swarm control algorithms synthesis, optimal to complexity-quality ratio.

The research was supported by the Foundation for Basic Research under the project 19-47-710004 r_a.

References

1. Bouallègue, S., Haggège, J., Ayadi, M., Benrejeb, M.: PID-type fuzzy logic controller tuning based on particle swarm optimization. Eng. Appl. Artif. Intell. **25**(3), 484–493 (2012). https://doi.org/10.1016/j.engappai.2011.09.018
2. Reyes-Sierra, M., Coello Coello, C.A.: Multi-objective particle swarm optimizers: a survey of the state-of-the-art. Int. J. Comput. Intell. Res. **2**(3), 287–308 (2006). https://doi.org/10.5019/j.ijcir.2006.68
3. Babishin, V., Taghipour, S.: Optimal maintenance policy for multicomponent systems with periodic and opportunistic inspections and preventive replacements. Appl. Math. Model. **40**(23), 10480–10505 (2016). https://doi.org/10.1016/j.apm.2016.07.019
4. Larkin, E., Antonov, M.: On assessing the temporal characteristics of reaching the milestone by a swarm. In: Tan, Y., Shi, Y., Tuba, M. (eds.) ICSI 2020. LNCS, vol. 12145, pp. 46–55. Springer, Cham (2020). https://doi.org/10.1007/978-3-030-53956-6_5
5. Landau, I.D., Zito, G.: Digital Control Systems, Design, Identification and Implementation, p. 484. Springer, Heidelberg (2006)
6. Aström, J., Wittenmark, B.: Computer Controlled Systems: Theory and Design, p. 557. Tsinghua University Press. Prentice Hall (2002)
7. Fadali, M.S., Visioli, A.: Digital Control Engineering: Analysis and Design, pp. 239–272. Elsevier Inc. (2013)
8. Larkin, E.V., Ivutin, A.N.: Estimation of latency in embedded real-time systems. In: 3rd Meditteranean Conference on Embedded Computing (MECO-2014), Budva, Montenegro, pp. 236–239 (2014)

9. Auslander, D.M., Ridgely, J.R., Jones, J.C.: Real-time software for implementation of feedback control. In: Levine, W.S. (ed.) The Control Handbook. Control System Fundamentals, pp. 16-1–16-32. CRC Press. Taylor and Francis Group (2017)
10. Karnopp, D.C., Margolis, D.L., Rosenberg, R.C.: System Dynamics: Modeling, Simulation and Control of Mechatronic Systems, p. 636. Hoboken, Willey (2012)
11. Bielecki, T., Jakubowski, J., Niewęgłowski, M.: Conditional Markov chains: properties, construction and structured dependence. Stochast. Process. Appl. **127**(4), 1125–1170 (2017). https://doi.org/10.1016/j.spa.2016.07.010
12. Ching, W.K., Huang, X., Ng, M.K., Siu, T.K.: Markov Chains: Models, Algorithms and Applications. International Series in Operations Research & Management Science, vol. 189, p. 241. Springer, New York (2013)
13. Howard, R.A.: Dynamic Probabilistic Systems, vol. 1: Markov Models. vol. II: Semi-Markov and Decision Processes. Courier Corporation (2012)
14. Janssen, J., Manca, R.: Applied Semi-Markov Processes, p. 310. Springer, Heidelberg (2006)
15. Schiff, J.L.: The Laplace Transform: Theory and Applications, p. 233. Springer, New York (1991)
16. Li, J., Farquharson, C.G., Hu, X.: Three effective inverse Laplace transform algorithms for computing time -domain electromagnetic responses. Geophysics **81**(2), E75–E90 (2015)
17. Arnold, K.A.: Timing analysis in embedded systems. In: Ganssler, J., Arnold, K., et al. (eds.) Embedded Hardware, pp. 239–272. Elsevier Inc. (2008)
18. Balsamo, S., Harrison, P., Marin, A.: Methodological construction of product-form stochastic Petri nets for performance evaluation. J. Syst. Softw. **85**(7), 1520–1539 (2012). https://doi.org/10.1016/j.jss.2011.11.1042
19. Larkin, E., Akimenko, T., Privalov, A.: Synchronized swarm operation. In: Tan, Y., Shi, Y., Tuba, M. (eds.) Advances in Swarm Intelligence, ICSI 2020, pp. 15–24. Springer, Cham (2020). https://doi.org/10.1007/978-3-030-53956-6_2
20. Kobayashi, H., Marl, B.L., Turin, W.: Probability, Random Processes and Statistical Analysis, p. 812. Cambridge University Press (2012)
21. Pukelsheim, F.: The three sigma rule. Am. Stat. **48**(2), 88–91 (1994)

Natural Emergence of Heterogeneous Strategies in Artificially Intelligent Competitive Teams

Ankur Deka$^{(\boxtimes)}$ and Katia Sycara

Robotics Institute, Carnegie Mellon University, Pittsburgh, PA 15213, USA
{adeka,katia}@cs.cmu.edu

Abstract. Multi agent strategies in mixed cooperative-competitive environments can be hard to craft by hand because each agent needs to coordinate with its teammates while competing with its opponents. Learning based algorithms are appealing but they require a competitive opponent to train against, which is often not available. Many scenarios require heterogeneous agent behavior for the team's success and this increases the complexity of the learning algorithm. In this work, we develop a mixed cooperative-competitive multi agent environment called FortAttack in which two teams compete against each other for success. We show that modeling agents with Graph Neural Networks (GNNs) and training them with Reinforcement Learning (RL) from scratch, leads to the co-evolution of increasingly complex strategies for each team. Through competition in Multi-Agent Reinforcement Learning (MARL), we observe a natural emergence of heterogeneous behavior among homogeneous agents when such behavior can lead to the team's success. Such heterogeneous behavior from homogeneous agents is appealing because any agent can replace the role of another agent at test time. Finally, we propose ensemble training, in which we utilize the evolved opponent strategies to train a single policy for friendly agents. We were able to train a large number of agents on a commodity laptop, which shows the scalability and efficiency of our approach. The code and a video presentation are available online (Code: https://github.com/Ankur-Deka/Emergent-Multiagent-Strategies, Video: https://youtu.be/ltHgKYc0F-E).

Keywords: Multi-Agent Reinforcement Learning (MARL) · Graph Neural Networks (GNNs) · Co-evolution

1 Introduction

Multi agent systems can play an important role in scenarios such as disaster relief, defense against enemies and games. There have been studies on various

Supported by organization ONR N00014-19-C-1070, AFOSR/AFRL award FA9550-18-1-0251, Darpa DARPA Cooperative Agreement No.: HR00111820051 and AFOSR FA9550-15-1-0442.

Y. Tan and Y. Shi (Eds.): ICSI 2021, LNCS 12689, pp. 13–25, 2021.
https://doi.org/10.1007/978-3-030-78743-1_2

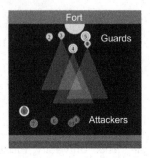

Fig. 1. The FortAttack environment in which guards (green) need to protect the fort (cyan semicircle at the top) from the attackers (red). The attackers win when any one of them reaches the fort. Each agent can shoot a laser which can kill an opponent.

aspects of it including task assignment [16], resilience to failure [12], scalability [1] and opponent modeling [23]. Multi agent systems become increasingly complex in mixed cooperative-competitive scenarios where an agent has to cooperate with other agents of the same team to jointly compete against the opposing team. It becomes difficult to model behavior of an agent or a team by hand and learning based methods are of particular appeal.

Our goal is to develop a learning based algorithm for decentralized control of multi agent systems in mixed cooperative-competitive scenarios with the ability to handle a variable number of agents, as some robots may get damaged in a real world scenario or some agents may get killed in a game. To be able to handle a variable number of agents and to scale to many agents, we propose to use a Graph Neural Networks (GNNs) based architecture to model inter-agent interactions, similar to [1] and [3]. This approach relies on shared parameters amongst all agents in a team which renders all of them homogeneous. We aim to study if heterogeneous behavior can emerge out of such homogeneous agents.

Our contributions in this work are:

– We have developed a mixed cooperative-competitive multi agent environment called FortAttack with simple rules yet room for complex multi agent behavior.
– We show that using GNNs with a standard off the shelf reinforcement learning algorithm can effectively model inter agent interactions in a competitive multi agent setting.
– To train strong agents we need competitive opponents. Using an approach inspired by self play, we are able to create an auto curriculum that generates strong agents from scratch without using any expert knowledge. Strategies naturally evolved as a winning strategy from one team created pressure for the other team to be more competitive. We were able to achieve this by training on a commodity laptop.
– We show that highly competitive heterogeneous behavior can naturally emerge amongst homogeneous agents with symmetric reward structure

(within the same team) when such behavior can lead to the team's success. Such behavior implicitly includes heterogeneous task allocation and complex coordination within a team, none of which had to be explicitly crafted but can be extremely beneficial for multi agent systems.

2 Related Work

2.1 Multi-agent Reinforcement Learning

The recent successes of reinforcement learning in games, [11,17] and robotics, [6, 15] have encouraged researchers to extend reinforcement learning to multi agent settings.

There are three broad categories of approaches used, centralized, decentralized and a mix of the two. Centralized approaches have a single reinforcement learning agent for the entire team, which has global state information and selects joint actions for the team. However, the joint state and action spaces grows exponentially with the number of agents rendering centralized approaches difficult to scale [5].

Independent Q-learning, [19,20] is a decentralized approach where each agent learns separately with Q-learning, [22] and treats all other agents as parts of the environment. Inter agent interactions are not explicitly modeled and performance is generally sub-par.

Centralized learning with decentralized execution has gained attention because it is reasonable to remove communication restrictions at training time. Some approaches use a decentralized actor with a centralized critic, which is accessible only at training time. MADDPG, [10] learns a centralized critic for each agent and trains policies using DDPG, [9]. QMIX, [13] proposes a monotonic decomposition of action value function. However, the use of centralized critic requires that the number of agents be fixed in the environment.

GridNet, [7] addresses the issue of multiple and variable number of agents without exponentially growing the policy representation by representing a policy with an encoder-decoder architecture with convolution layers. However, the centralized execution realm renders it infeasible in many scenarios.

Graphs can naturally model multi agent systems with each node representing an agent. [18] modeled inter agent interactions in multi agent teams using GNNs which can be learnt through back propagation. [8] proposed to use attention and [1] proposed to use an entity graph for augmenting environment information. However, these settings don't involve two opposing multi agent teams that both evolve by learning.

[3] explored multi agent reinforcement learning for the game of hide and seek. They find that increasingly complex behavior emerge out of simple rules of the game over many episodes of interactions. However, they relied on extremely heavy computations spanning over many millions of episodes of environment exploration.

We draw inspiration from [1] and [3]. For each team we propose to have two components within the graph, one to model the observations of the opponents and one to model the interactions with fellow team mates. Our work falls in the paradigm of centralized training with decentralized execution. We were able to train our agents in the FortAttack environment using the proposed approach on a commodity laptop. We believe that the reasonable computational requirement would encourage further research in the field of mixed cooperative-competitive MARL.

2.2 Multi-agent Environments

Although there are many existing multi-agent environments, they suffer from the following deficiencies:

- Multi-Agent Particle Environment (MAPE) [10] doesn't consider competitive scenarios (2 competiting teams).
- StarCraft II Learning Environment (SC2LE) [21] assumes a centralized controller for all agents in a team which is impractical for real world scenarios.
- Starcraft Multi-Agent Challenge (SMAC) [14] doesn't incorporate learning based opponents.
- RoboSumo [2] Doesn't scale to many agents (only contains 1 vs 1 scenarios).

Moreoever, SC2LE [21], SMAC [14] and SoboSumo [2] are computationally heavy environments.

To overcome these deficiencies, we design a new light-weight (can run on commodity laptop) mixed cooperative-competitive environment called FortAttack (Fig. 1) which can handle (1) Large number of agents, (2) Decentralized controllers, (3) Learning based opponents, (4) Variable number of agents within a single episode and (5) Complex multi-agent strategies as is evident from our results (Sect. 5.1).

3   Method

The agents in a multi-agent team can be treated as nodes of a graph to leverage the power of Graph Neural Networks (GNNs). GNNs form a deep-learning architecture where the computations at the nodes and edges of the graph are performed by neural networks (parameterized non-linear functions), [1]. Due to the presence of graph structure and multiple neural networks, they are called GNNs.

We describe our use of GNNs from the perspective of one team and use X_i to denote the state of ith friendly agent in the team, which in our case is its position, orientation and velocity. We use $XOpp_j$ to denote the state of the jth opponent in the opposing team. Let $S = \{1, 2, \ldots, N_1\}$ denote the set of friendly agents and $S_{Opp} = \{N_1 + 1, N_1 + 2, \ldots, N_1 + N_2\}$ denote the set of opponents. Note that a symmetric view can be presented from the perspective of the other team.

In the following, we describe how agent 1 processes the observations of its opponents and how it interacts with its teammates. Figure 2 shows this pictorially for a 3 agents vs 3 agents scenario. All the other agents have a symmetric representation of interactions.

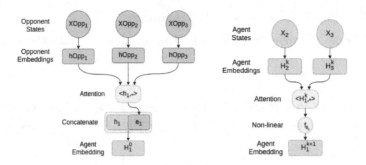

Fig. 2. Modeling of inter agent interactions with Graph Neural Networks (GNNs) from the perspective of agent 1, in a 3 friendly agents vs 3 opponents scenario. Left: agent 1's embedding, H_1^0 is formed by taking into consideration the states of all opponents through an attention layer. Right: agent 1's embedding gets updated, $(H_1^k \rightarrow H_1^{k+1})$ by taking into consideration its team mates through an attention layer.

3.1   Modeling Observation of Opponents

Friendly agent 1 takes its state, X_1 and passes it through a non-linear function, f_{θ_a} to generate an embedding, h_1. Similarly, it forms an embedding, $hOpp_j$ from each of its opponents with the function f_{θ_b}.

$$h_1 = f_{\theta_a}(X_1) \tag{1}$$

$$hOpp_j = f_{\theta_b}(XOpp_j) \quad \forall j \in S_{Opp} \tag{2}$$

Note that the opponents don't share their information with the friendly agent 1. Friendly agent 1 merely makes its own observation of the opponents. It then computes a dot product attention, ψ_{1j} which describes how much attention it pays to each of its opponents. The dimension of h_1 and $hOpp_j$ are d_1 each. This attention allows agent 1 to compute a joint embedding, e_1 of all of its opponents.

$$\hat{\psi}_{1j} = \frac{1}{d_1} < h_1, hOpp_j > \quad \forall j \in S_{Opp} \tag{3}$$

$$\psi_{1j} = \frac{\exp(\hat{\psi}_{1j})}{\sum_{m \in S_{Opp}} \exp(\hat{\psi}_{1m})} \tag{4}$$

$$e_1 = \sum_{j \in S_{Opp}} \psi_{1j} hOpp_j \tag{5}$$

In Eq. 3, $<,>$ denotes vector dot product. Note that $\sum_{j \in S_{Opp}} \psi_{1j} = 1$ which ensures that the net attention paid by agent 1 to its opponents is fixed. Finally, e_1 is concatenated with h_1 to form an agent embedding, H_1^0:

$$H_1^0 = \text{concatenate}(h_1, e_1) \tag{6}$$

3.2   Modeling Interactions with Teammates

Agent 1 forms an embedding for each of its team mates with the non-linear function, f_{θ_a}.

$$H_i^0 = f_{\theta_a}(X_i) \quad \forall i \in S, i \neq 1 \tag{7}$$

Dimension of $H_i^k, \forall i \in S$ is d_2. Agent 1 computes a dot product attention, ϕ_{1i} with all of its team mates and updates it's embedding with a non-linear function, f_{θ_c}.

$$\hat{\phi}_{1i} = \frac{1}{d_2} < H_1^k, H_i^k > \quad \forall i \in S, i \neq 1 \tag{8}$$

$$\phi_{1i} = \frac{\exp(\hat{\phi}_{1i})}{\sum_{m \in S, m \neq 1} \exp(\hat{\phi}_{1m})} \tag{9}$$

$$\hat{H}_1^{k+1} = \sum_{i \in S, i \neq 1} \phi_{1i} H_i^k \tag{10}$$

$$H_1^{k+1} = f_{\theta_c}(\hat{H}_1^{k+1}) \tag{11}$$

Equations, 8 to 11 can be run over multiple iterations for $k = \{0, 1, \ldots, K\}$ to allow information propagation to other agents if agents can perceive only its local neighborhood similar to [1].

3.3   Policy

The final embedding of friendly agent 1, H_1^K is passed through a policy head. In our experiments, we use a stochastic policy in discrete action space and hence the policy head has a sigmoid activation which outputs a categorical distribution specifying the probability of each action, α_m.

$$\pi(\alpha_m|O_1) = \pi'(\alpha_m|H_1^K) = \text{sigmoid}(f_{\theta_d}(H_1^K)) \tag{12}$$
$$\text{where, } O_1 = \{X_i : i \in S\} \cup \{XOpp_j : j \in S_{Opp}\}$$

Here, O_1 is the observation of agent 1, which consists of its own state and the states of all other agents that it observes. This corresponds to a fully connected graph. We do this for simplicity. In practice, we could limit the observation space of an agent within a fixed neighborhood around the agent similar to [1] and [3].

3.4   Scalability and Real World Applicability

Due to the use of GNNs, the learn-able parameters for a team are the shared parameters, $\theta_a, \theta_b, \theta_c$ and θ_d of the functions, $f_{\theta_a}, f_{\theta_b}, f_{\theta_c}$ and f_{θ_d}, respectively which we model with fully connected neural networks. Note that the number of learn-able parameters is independent of the number of agents and hence can scale to a large number of agents. This also allows us to handle a varying number of agents as agents might get killed during an episode and makes our approach applicable to real world scenarios where a robot may get damaged during a mission.

Table 1. Reward structure

Sl. No.	Event	Reward
1	Guard i leaves the fort	Guard i gets -1 reward.
2	Guard i returns to the fort	Guard i gets +1 reward.
3	Attacker j moves closer to the fort	Attacker j gets small +ve reward = $2[D_j(t-1) - D_j(t)]$. Where, $D_j(t)$ = distance between attacker and fort at time t.
4	Attacker j moves away from the fort	Attacker j gets small -ve reward = $-2[D_j(t-1) - D_j(t)]$.
5	Guard i shoots attacker j with laser	Guard i gets +3 reward and attacker j gets -3 reward.
6	Attacker j shoots guard i with laser	Guard i gets -3 reward and attacker j gets +3 reward.
7	Agent i shoots laser but doesn't hit any opponent	Agent i gets low -ve reward (-0.1 if guard, -1 if attacker).
8	All attackers are killed	All alive guards get high +ve reward (+10). Attacker(s) that just got killed gets high -ve (-10) reward.
9	Attacker j reaches the fort	All alive guards high -ve reward. Attacker j gets high +ve reward

3.5 Training

Our approach follows the paradigm of centralized training with decentralized execution. During training, a single set of parameters are shared amongst team-mates. We train our multi agent teams with Proximal Policy Optimization (PPO), [15]. At every training step, a fixed number of interactions are collected from the environment using the current policy for each agent and then each team is trained separately using PPO.

The shared parameters naturally share experiences amongst teammates and allow for training with fewer number of episodes. At test time, each agent maintains a copy of the parameters and can operate in decentralized fashion. We trained our agents on a commodity laptop with i7 processor and GTX 1060 graphics card. Training took about 1–2 days without parallelizing the environment.

4   Environment

We design a mixed cooperative-competitive environment called Fortattack with OpenAI Gym, [4] like interface. Figure 1 shows a rendering of our environment.

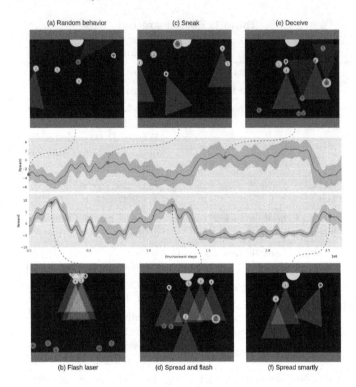

Fig. 3. Average reward per agent per episode for the teams of attackers and guards as training progresses. The reward plots have distinct extrema and corresponding snapshots of the environment are shown. The x-axis shows the number of steps of environment interaction. The reward is plotted after Gaussian smoothing.

The environment consists of a team of guards, shown in green and a team of attackers, shown in red, that compete against each other. The attackers need to reach the fort which is shown as a cyan semi-circle at the top. Each agent can shoot a laser beam which can kill an opponent if it is within the beam window.

At the beginning of an episode, the guards are located randomly near the fort and the attackers are spawned at random locations near the bottom of the environment. The guards win if they manage to kill all attackers or manage to keep them away for a fixed time interval which is the episode length. The guards lose if even one attacker manages to reach the fort. The environment is built off of Multi-Agent Particle Environment [10].

4.1 Observation Space

Each agent can observe all the other agents in the environment. Hence, the observation space consists of states (positions, orientations and velocities) of team mates and opponents. We assume full observability as the environment

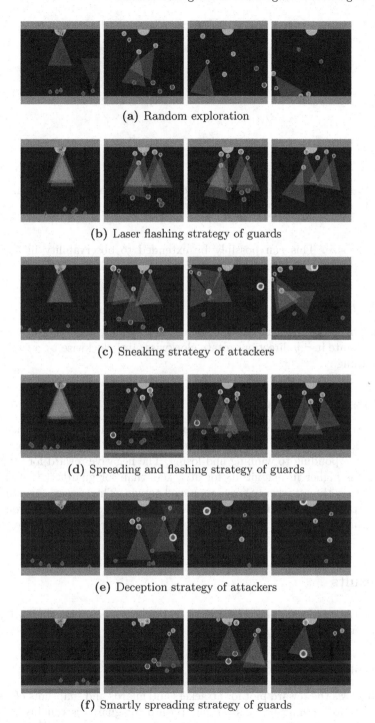

(a) Random exploration

(b) Laser flashing strategy of guards

(c) Sneaking strategy of attackers

(d) Spreading and flashing strategy of guards

(e) Deception strategy of attackers

(f) Smartly spreading strategy of guards

Fig. 4. Sample sequences for different strategies that evolved during training. Each row represents one sequence and time moves from left to right.

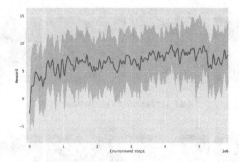

Fig. 5. Average reward per agent per episode for guards as ensemble training progresses. The reward is shown after Gaussian smoothing.

is small in size. This can possibly be extended to observability in the local neighborhood such as in [1] and [3].

4.2 Action Space

At each time step, an agent can choose one of 7 actions, accelerate in $\pm x$ direction, accelerate in $\pm y$ direction, rotate clockwise/anti-clockwise by a fixed angle or do nothing.

4.3 Reward Structure

Each agent gets a reward which has components of its individual and the team's performance as described in Table 1. The last two rows show the major reward signals corresponding to winning and losing. The negative reward for wasting a laser shot is higher in magnitude for attackers than for guards. Otherwise, we observed that the attackers always managed to win. This reward structure can also be attributed to the fact that attackers in a real world scenario would like to sneak in and wouldn't want to shoot too often and reveal themselves to the guards.

5 Results

We show the results for the 5 guards vs 5 attackers scenario in the FortAttack environment.

5.1 Evolution of Strategies

Figure 3 shows the reward plot for attackers and guards and snapshots of specific checkpoints as training progresses. The reward for guards is roughly a mirror image of the reward for attackers as victory for one team means defeat for the other. The rewards oscillate with multiple local extrema, i.e. maxima for one team and a corresponding minima for the other. These extrema correspond to increasingly complex strategies that evolve naturally - as one team gets better at its task, it creates pressure for the other team, which in turn comes up with a stronger and more complex strategic behavior.

1. *Random behavior*: At the beginning of training, agents randomly move around and shoot in the wild. They explore trying to make sense of the FortAttack environment and their goals in this world.
2. *Flash laser*: Attackers eventually learn to approach the fort and the guards adopt a simple strategy to win. They all continuously flash their lasers creating a protection zone in front of the fort which kills any attacker that tries to enter.
3. *Sneak*: As guards block entry from the front, attackers play smart. They approach from all the directions, some of them get killed but one of them manages to sneak in from the side.
4. *Spread and flash*: In response to the sneaking behavior, the guards learn to spread out and kill all attackers before they can sneak in.
5. *Deceive*: To tackle the strong guards, the attackers come up with the strategy of deception. Most of them move forward from the right while one holds back on the left. The guards start shooting at the attackers on the right which diverts their attention from the single attacker on the left. This attacker quietly waits for the right moment to sneak in, bringing victory for the whole team. Note that this strategy requires heterogeneous behavior amongst the homogeneous agents, which naturally evolved without explicitly being encouraged to do so.
6. *Spread smartly*: In response to this, the guards learn to spread smartly, covering a wider region and killing attackers before they can sneak in.

5.2   Being Attentive

In each of the environment snapshots in Fig. 3 and Fig. 4, we visualize the attention paid by one alive guard to all the other agents. This guard has a dark green dot at it's center. All the other agents have yellow rings around them, with the sizes of the rings being proportional to the attention values. Eg. in Fig. 4(e), agent 1 initially paid roughly uniform and low attention to all attackers when they were far away. Then, it started paying more attention to agent 8, which was attacking aggressively from the right. Little did it know that it was being deceived by the clever attackers. When agent 9 reached near the fort, agent 1 finally started paying more attention to the sneaky agent 9 but it was too late and the attackers had successfully deceived it.

5.3   Ensemble Strategies

To train and generate strong agents, we first need strong opponents to train against. The learnt strategies in Sect. 5.1 give us a natural way to generate strategies from simple rules of the game. If we wish to get strong guards, we can train a single guard policy against all of the attacker strategies, by randomly sampling one attacker strategy for each environment episode. Figure 5 shows the reward for guards as training progresses. This time, the reward for guards continually increases and doesn't show an oscillating behavior.

6   Conclusions

In this work we were able to scale to multiple agents by modeling inter agent interactions with a graph containing two attention layers. We studied the evolution of complex multi agent strategies in a mixed cooperative-competitive environment. In particular, we saw the natural emergence of deception strategy which required heterogeneous behavior amongst homogeneous agents. If instead we wanted to explicitly encode heterogeneous strategies, a simple extension of our work would be to have different sets of policy parameters (f_{θ_d}) within the same team, e.g. one set for aggressive guards and one set of defensive guards. We believe that our study would inspire further work towards scaling multi agent reinforcement learning to large number of agents in more complex mixed cooperative-competitive scenarios.

References

1. Agarwal, A., Kumar, S., Sycara, K.: Learning transferable cooperative behavior in multi-agent teams. arXiv preprint arXiv:1906.01202 (2019)
2. Al-Shedivat, M., Bansal, T., Burda, Y., Sutskever, I., Mordatch, I., Abbeel, P.: Continuous adaptation via meta-learning in nonstationary and competitive environments. arXiv preprint arXiv:1710.03641 (2017)
3. Baker, B., et al.: Emergent tool use from multi-agent autocurricula. arXiv preprint arXiv:1909.07528 (2019)
4. Brockman, G., et al.: Openai gym. arXiv preprint arXiv:1606.01540 (2016)
5. Bu, L., Babu, R., De Schutter, B., et al.: A comprehensive survey of multiagent reinforcement learning. IEEE Trans. Syst. Man Cybern. Part C (Appl. Rev.) **38**(2), 156–172 (2008)
6. Haarnoja, T., Zhou, A., Abbeel, P., Levine, S.: Soft actor-critic: off-policy maximum entropy deep reinforcement learning with a stochastic actor. arXiv preprint arXiv:1801.01290 (2018)
7. Han, L., et al.: Grid-wise control for multi-agent reinforcement learning in video game ai. In: International Conference on Machine Learning, pp. 2576–2585 (2019)
8. Hoshen, Y.: Vain: attentional multi-agent predictive modeling. In: Advances in Neural Information Processing Systems, pp. 2701–2711 (2017)
9. Lillicrap, T.P., et al.: Continuous control with deep reinforcement learning. arXiv preprint arXiv:1509.02971 (2015)
10. Lowe, R., Wu, Y., Tamar, A., Harb, J., Abbeel, P., Mordatch, I.: Multi-agent actor-critic for mixed cooperative-competitive environments. In: Neural Information Processing Systems (NIPS) (2017)
11. Mnih, V., et al.: Human-level control through deep reinforcement learning. Nature **518**(7540), 529–533 (2015)

12. Ramachandran, R.K., Preiss, J.A., Sukhatme, G.S.: Resilience by reconfiguration: Exploiting heterogeneity in robot teams. arXiv preprint arXiv:1903.04856 (2019)
13. Rashid, T., Samvelyan, M., De Witt, C.S., Farquhar, G., Foerster, J., Whiteson, S.: Qmix: monotonic value function factorisation for deep multi-agent reinforcement learning. arXiv preprint arXiv:1803.11485 (2018)
14. Samvelyan, M., et al .: The starcraft multi-agent challenge. arXiv preprint arXiv:1902.04043 (2019)
15. Schulman, J., Wolski, F., Dhariwal, P., Radford, A., Klimov, O.: Proximal policy optimization algorithms. arXiv preprint arXiv:1707.06347 (2017)
16. Shishika, D., Paulos, J., Kumar, V.: Cooperative team strategies for multi-player perimeter-defense games. IEEE Rob. Autom. Lett. **5**(2), 2738–2745 (2020)
17. Silver, D., et al.: Mastering the game of go without human knowledge. Nature **550**(7676), 354–359 (2017)
18. Sukhbaatar, S., Fergus, R., et al.: Learning multiagent communication with back-propagation. In: Advances in Neural Information Processing Systems, pp. 2244–2252 (2016)
19. Tampuu, A., et al.: Multiagent cooperation and competition with deep reinforcement learning. PLoS one **12**(4), e0172395 (2017)
20. Tan, M.: Multi-agent reinforcement learning: independent vs. cooperative agents. In: Proceedings of the tenth International Conference on Machine Learning, pp. 330–337 (1993)
21. Vinyals, O., et al.: Starcraft ii: a new challenge for reinforcement learning. arXiv preprint arXiv:1708.04782 (2017)
22. Watkins, C.J., Dayan, P.: Q-learning. Mach. Learn. **8**(3–4), 279–292 (1992)
23. Wen, Y., Yang, Y., Luo, R., Wang, J., Pan, W.: Probabilistic recursive reasoning for multi-agent reinforcement learning. arXiv preprint arXiv:1901.09207 (2019)

Analysis of Security Problems in Groups of Intelligent Sensors

Karen Grigoryan[1], Evgeniya Olefirenko[1], Elena Basan[1] (ID), Maria Lapina[2(✉)] (ID),
and Massimo Mecella[3] (ID)

[1] Southern Federal University, Chekova St., 2, 347922 Taganrog, Russia
[2] North-Caucasus Federal University, Pushkina St., 1, 355000 Stavropol, Russia
mlapina@ncfu.ru
[3] Sapienza University of Rome, via Ariosto 25, 00185 Rome, Italy

Abstract. Today, the creation of intelligent sensors became possible due to the development of the hardware base, the use of small boards, where the processor, memory, and network interfaces can be placed. Examples of such cards can be Raspberry Pi, Arduino, and others. These devices can be used to connect various sensors to them depending on the tasks. Today, there are many protocols for the exchange of messages between such sender devices, which ultimately leads to the creation of distributed networks with distributed functionality. Such systems can be decision-making and are like swarm intelligence, where each device performs its functions, but together they are a single system. This study will examine the information security issues of such systems. An analysis of threats and vulnerabilities for intelligent sensor systems was carried out. Demonstrated an attack on the secure ZigBee protocol, which is often used to create a network between smart sensors. The use of lightweight cryptography to minimize risks is proposed.

Keywords: Internet of Things (IoT) · Cipher · Cryptography · LWC · SPECK · Tiny encryption algorithm

1 Introduction

Today, the range of devices and technologies that can be attributed to the systems of the "Internet of Things" is actively expanding, first, these are systems such as: "Smart Home", "Smart City", "Smart Greenhouses", "Smart Farm", "Smart Plant" Etc., that is, such systems that can consist of sensors, cameras, actuators, in combination with information and telecommunication technologies and control systems. The use of such systems in various spheres of human life gives a positive economic effect and allows you to receive additional benefits from various points of view. Such devices usually work in a group and can use swarm intelligence to solve various problems. To solve problems with the Internet of things devices, it is necessary to exchange information. The IoT is a network of connected objects, each of which has a unique identity that can collect and exchange data via the Internet with or without human participation [1]. The market now includes many IoT devices and this means that there is a huge exchange of data between them.

© Springer Nature Switzerland AG 2021
Y. Tan and Y. Shi (Eds.): ICSI 2021, LNCS 12689, pp. 26–37, 2021.
https://doi.org/10.1007/978-3-030-78743-1_3

Experts predicted that by 2020 about 28 billion devices will be connected to the Internet, with only a third of them being computers, smartphones and tables [1, 2].

The expansion of the Internet of Things is facilitated by the proliferation of wireless networks, the active transition to IPv6, the growing popularity of clouds and the emergence of a group of technologies of machine-to-machine interaction (Machine to Machine, M2M) [3]. The NIC (National Intelligence Council) report lists IoT as one of six disruptive technologies. It is also noted that the ubiquitous and imperceptible transformation of such common things as commercial furniture and paper documents into Internet nodes for consumers, can significantly increase the risks in the field of national information security [4]. The vision of the IoT is to build a smart environment with interconnected elements that provide an autonomous service to users [5–7]. In other words, the IoT is valuable for providing intelligent environments with a distinct power of ambient intelligence and pervasive communication (this can also be called the pervasive power of omnipresent computing) [8].

Confidentiality, integrity, and availability are three important concepts for securing applications and services in intelligent IoT environments; thus, to solve these problems, information security in the systems of the Internet of Things requires closer attention of researchers [9]. For example, IoT smart homes face security and privacy issues that span all levels of the IoT architecture [10] especially from an industrial point of view [11]. IoT devices are easily accessible and susceptible to many security attacks directly [12] because they use sensitive data or manipulate variables in the physical environment, making them a desirable target for attackers [13]. Based on this, it can be concluded that Cybersecurity is a significant problem for IoT devices with requirements for confidentiality, data integrity, authentication and authorization, availability, confidentiality, and regulatory standards, as well as regular system updates. As with all areas of network computing, security and privacy are fundamental requirements for a reliable IoT system. Many of the principles that apply to critical enterprise security and safety systems are equally applicable to the security of the Internet of Things [14]. IoT security encompasses many areas, such as creating access control policies, protecting keys using hardware and software security mechanisms, installing key material during device production, and preparing a new addition at a later stage [15]. In this scheme, it is possible that cryptography will become one of the effective measures to ensure confidentiality, integrity and authentication and authorization of data transmission through IoT devices [16]. Cryptography can also be a solution to protect data stored or transmitted over a network. However, established cryptographic solutions based on a typical information system are not suitable for various IoT devices due to limited resources. A lighter version of these solutions might solve this problem. Lightweight versions of computational cryptography are known as lightweight cryptography (LWC).

2 Analysis of Information Security Problems of the Internet of Things as a Group with Swarm Intelligence

The first problem can be formulated as follows. Due to the growing popularity of information systems of the "Internet of Things" and the simultaneous increase in the number of threats, vulnerabilities and security requirements, as well as the constantly increasing level of knowledge about such systems, it becomes necessary to create natural language processing tools to create a knowledge base about threats and requirements for security for the "Internet of Things", as well as the use of intelligent technologies, expert systems to improve the accuracy and speed of identification and minimize information security risks of the "Internet of Things".

The second problem is formulated as follows. Due to the wide variety of software and hardware platforms, telecommunication equipment and communication standards for creating the information system of the "Internet of Things", and at the same time, significant computing and power resources spent on scanning the information system using standard tools, there is a problem of obtaining timely and reliable information about the structural and functional characteristics of the "Internet of Things".

Finally, the third problem that this project is aimed at is related to the need to improve the reliability of wireless communication networks of the Internet of Things by ensuring an adequate level of security by developing effective recommendations and information security requirements for the current information system.

Many researchers in this area, argue that the implementation of the Internet of Things without ensuring information security is unacceptable and will lead to significant negative consequences, as well as reduce the reliability and resiliency of the information system. For the information system of the "Internet of Things" to function stably and reliably, the user or the owner of the system must not only assess the possible damage and information security risks, but also take actions to minimize the risks. At the same time, users or owners usually want to avoid the additional costs and economic costs of purchasing equipment and paying for the work of an information security expert and often neglect the security system. It is important to note that in addition to the existing problem of the growing popularity of the "Internet of Things" and the increase in the number of threats to information security, there is another problem. The information system of the "Internet of Things" has a fundamental difference from a typical information system. This is expressed, first, in the fact that only information that is stored, processed, etc. is considered as objects of protection of a typical information system. in the information system, and a software and hardware complex, including technical means (including workstations, industrial servers, telecommunications equipment, communication channels, etc.). In the case of the "Internet of Things" information system, it is also necessary to consider the entity controlled by the information system as an object of protection. At the same time, violation of one of the properties of information security in relation to the object (entity) controlled by the information system can lead to significant negative consequences (economic). The point is that if an attacker, for example, attacks an intelligent sensor that regulates the pressure when the gas is supplied, then this can lead to an explosion and human casualties, that is, the impact will be exerted on the object and related entities (objects).

In addition, the information system of the "Internet of Things" is heterogeneous, consists of many sensors that perform different functions. Sensors can be stationary and mobile, and can be intelligent, some "Internet of Things" can have direct access to the Internet thanks to mobile communication modules, "Internet of Things" can include several different segments or be included in a segment of a typical information system. All this imposes certain conditions on the protection system and on a set of measures to assess and minimize risks. This is also due to the presence of significant differences between the structural and functional characteristics of a typical information system and the information system "Internet of Things".

The authors of the article [17] try to identify most of the known threats at different levels of the Internet of Things (IoT) architecture with an emphasis on the possibility of carrying out attacks using malicious programs. The authors present a detailed methodology for implementing attacks on the IoT, as well as a detailed scenario of a distributed denial-of-service attack through an IoT botnet, followed by the necessary measures to improve information security. The authors provide guidance on developing an IoT security methodology based on best foreign industry practices. The methodology includes a risk assessment, security measures that increase the confidentiality, integrity and availability of information, and a method for calculating the impact of identified risks. The authors also write that risk assessment and threat modeling is the first step in developing a security policy for any organization. It is also important to assess the risks for all processes, equipment - both hardware and software - at every level of the IoT, from the stage of production, transportation, installation and commissioning to the operation and management of the IoT system. The main purpose of this assessment is to identify all security incidents that can occur in the organization and subsequently initiate a risk treatment process to minimize the damage from such events. In addition, the risk assessment does not consider the risks associated with an object that is "managed" by the Internet of Things.

The authors of the article [18] offer a test bench that simulates the operation of the "Internet of Things" system for conducting security analysis. The authors analyzed the principles, basic architectures and material and technical base for building IoT systems and developed a universal stand that simulates various technologies, presented a method of security testing. At the same time, as part of the security analysis, the authors use standard port scanning and vulnerability scan tools and offer scenarios for implementing attacks. The authors argue that IoT devices can pose serious security and privacy risks due to their range of functionality and the variety of processes involved in their operation, including collecting, processing, storing, and transmitting data. In addition, these smart devices are integrated into corporate networks, deployed in public places, located in public, and can work continuously to collect information from the environment. The authors of [19] propose a threat model obtained by analyzing IoT use cases from a security point of view. This article recommends measures to help you keep your IoT secure. The authors propose a method that enables case-based security analysis and formulation of security and privacy properties for multi-user IoT systems. The threat model presented by the authors is described in general terms and does not consider the peculiarities of such systems. The authors provide attack analysis and security and privacy issues for each device with case studies. However, the range of attacks that are applicable to various components of the IoT architecture is not widely represented; there is no methodology for conducting attacks or a description of the toolkit.

The Industrial Internet Consortium, currently implementing the OpenFog program of the Object Management Group, Inc. ("OMG") have developed a document describing a security model for the Internet of Things [20]. In April 2018, the Industry Internet Consortium (IIC) published the first of two papers dealing with the IoT security maturity model. The first document, The IoT Security Maturity Model, contains the description and intended use of the IoT, intended for stakeholders to understand the need and purpose of the model. The second document, the practitioner's guide, provides details of the model and describes how it should be used. The IoT Security Maturity Model (SMM) enables Internet of Things (IoT) providers to set security goals and invest in security mechanisms that meet their requirements, without over-investing in unnecessary security mechanisms. Security maturity is a measure of understanding the current level of security, its need, benefits, and cost of support. SMM provides a conceptual framework to help organizations select and implement appropriate security controls from a variety of options. This helps an organization determine what their target security maturity state should be and assess their current state. The National Institute of Standards and Technology (NIST) presented the "Framework for Improving Critical Infrastructure Cybersecurity" standard - a standard for improving the Cybersecurity of critical information systems [21]. The document is divided into three parts: the core of the standard, the implementation levels and the profiles of the standard. The underlying core of the platform is a collection of Cybersecurity activities, outcomes and information guides that are shared across sectors and critical infrastructure. Thus, cryptographic protection methods can be applied to ensure security and minimize risks. In this case, the choice of an acceptable algorithm becomes a separate problem. In this work, the analysis of existing algorithms and their application to the Internet of Things will be carried out.

3   Exploitation Vulnerabilities

One of the popular solutions for creating a fully connected topology of the Internet of Things, mobile roots or UAVs is the ZigBee network. ZigBee networks, unlike other wireless data transmission networks, fully meet the following requirements:

1. Thanks to the mesh (mesh) network topology and the use of special routing algorithms, the ZigBee network provides self-healing and guaranteed packet delivery in cases of disconnection between individual nodes (obstacles), overload or failure of an element;
2. The ZigBee specification provides cryptographic protection for transmitted data over wireless channels and a flexible security policy;
3. ZigBee devices are characterized by low power consumption, especially end devices for which a "sleep" mode is provided, which allows these devices to work for up to three years on a single AA or even AAA battery;
4. ZigBee network is self-organizing, its structure is set by the parameters of the configurator stack profile and is formed automatically by attaching (re-attaching) to the network of its constituent devices, which ensures ease of deployment and ease of scaling by simply attaching additional devices;
5. ZigBee devices are low power consumption.
6. Communication in the ZigBee network is carried out by sequential packet retransmission from the source node to the destination node. The ZigBee network provides several alternative routing algorithms, which are automatically selected.

In order to monitor the ZigBee network, we applied the Wi-Fi network analysis method. To do this, you need to use a network card that switches to the "Monitor" mode and receives all traffic that passes through this network. For ZigBee, a CC2531 "stick" can be used as a network card, which is stitched to intercept protocols. Thus, the equipment required for sniffing and traffic analysis is presented in the following list: "sticks" ZigBee cc2531; CC-Debugger for firmware; firmware "stick" as a packet interceptor; Wireshark packet analyzer; Utility for working with ZigBee interceptor and packet translation in Wireshark "TiWsPc"; Encrypted data decoder built in Wireshark.

Therefore, the enemy intercepted the radio message and proceeded to analyze it, he can assume that known types of communication with their protocols, for example, Wi-Fi, MAVLink or ZigBee, were used to simplify control. Then, for each protocol, he uses a typical traffic analyzer and sees the next packet dump. Thus, the adversary realized that ZigBee communication was being used, but the intercepted information did not make any sense for him, since he needed two network encryption keys and an optional one. Accordingly, the adversary can find the network key by brute-force, knowing about the structure of the ZigBee protocol and its vulnerabilities. The vulnerability of the protocol is that the network key does not encrypt the entire packet, but only some of its bytes, for example, the name of the transmitted data: telemetry or an optional key (Transport key). Explanations in Fig. 1.

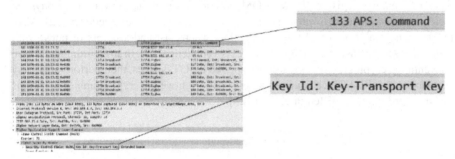

Fig. 1. Example of ZigBee vulnerability in open and closed text

After decryption, the "Command" network key will become "Transport Key".

In stage 3, we defined the actions and the search for which data will give us complete information about the network traffic. So, in order to read what kind of data is transmitted over the network, you need a network key, if the enemy tries to pick it up, then we had it. Wireshark has a built-in packet decoder, so you only need to specify the algorithm and encryption keys in the parameters. Now, all that remains for us and the enemy is to find the value of the optional key. One of the values of the packet fields, which is called "Command Frame", contains the key value (Fig. 2).

By adding, it by analogy with the network key in the Wireshark parameters, we and the adversary will be able to read the decrypted bytes of the payload.

```
∨ ZigBee Security Header
  › Security Control Field: 0x30, Key Id: Key-Transport Key, Extended Nonce
    Frame Counter: 0
    Extended Source: Jennic_00:04:4b:b0:04 (00:15:8d:00:04:4b:b0:04)
    Message Integrity Code: 5efb56c9
    [Key: 5a6967426565416c6c69616e63653039]
    [Key Label: Trust]
∨ Command Frame: Transport Key
    Command Identifier: Transport Key (0x05)
    Key Type: Standard Network Key (0x01)
    Key: 9cf1029f587d1e0bd4c9fa3710d59623
    Sequence Number: 1
    Extended Destination: Jennic_00:03:f4:7f:66 (00:15:8d:00:03:f4:7f:66)
```

Fig. 2. Found optional encryption key

4   Internet of Things and Lightweight Cryptography

Thus, the most common vulnerability due to which such systems are hacked is unreliable keys and passwords. In addition, a common problem is the use of default passwords and keys. Therefore, it is necessary to apply additional device protection schemes. It should be borne in mind that encryption can be resource intensive. Therefore, this paper proposes to evaluate several lightweight encryption algorithms. The main problems of implementing classical cryptography in groups of intelligent sensors are as follows: types of memory (registers, RAM, ROM); reduced computing power; small physical area for implementation; low battery level (or no battery); real-time feedback [22]. Also, IoT systems deal with a real-time application, where fast and accurate response with significant security using available resources is a challenge [23]. In an environment where conventional cryptography standards are applied to IOT devices, their performance may be unacceptable [24]. Three main characteristics of lightweight cryptographic algorithms and their proposals are listed in Table 1 [25].

Table 1. Characteristics of lightweight cryptographic algorithms

Characteristics		What LWS can offer
Physical (Cost)	Physical area	Smaller block size
	Memory	Smaller key size
	Battery power	Simple round logic
		Simple key scheduling
Performance	Computing power	
Security	Minimum security strength	Strong structure
	Attack model	
	Side channel attack	

The amount of memory is another important characteristic that characterizes the size of the executable program. Power consumption - characterizes the required energy required for the device to function.

5   The Tiny Encryption Algorithm Cipher Description

Further The Tiny Encryption Algorithm (TEA) was presented in 1994 at the Fast Encryption Algorithms Conference in Leuven, Belgium. The authors of the algorithm are Roger Needham and David Wheeler [26]. The advantage of the TEA cipher is its excellent resistance to linear cryptanalysis. In addition, TEA is simple to implement in a forehead programming language and can be optimized for 32-bit microcontrollers, since it is based on xor, shift and sum operations modulo 232. Since the algorithm does not use lookup tables and the round function is quite simple, the algorithm requires at least 16 cycles (32 rounds) to achieve effective diffusion, although complete diffusion is achieved already in 6 cycles (12 rounds) [26].

First, a key of length 128 is divided into 4 equal parts - K [0], K [1], K [2] and K [3]. Thus, the round keys are generated. In odd rounds the keyss K [1] and K [2] are used, and in even ones - K [2] and K [3]. The two rounds of the TEA cipher are depicted. Actions used in the algorithm:

$\boxplus$ – addition operation modulo 2^{32},
$\oplus$ – XOR operation,
$>>$ and $<<$ – shifts to the right t and left,
δ – constant derived from the golden ratio:

$$\delta = \left(\sqrt{5} - 1 \right) \cdot 2^{31} = 9e3779b9_{16} = 2654435769_{10}.$$

In each round, a constant is multiplied by the number of cycles i to protect the algorithm from round symmetry. A distinctive feature of the TEA crypto algorithm is its size. The disadvantage of the algorithm is some slowness caused by the need to repeat the Feistel cycle 32 times (this is necessary for careful "mixing of data" due to the lack of table substitutions).

6   Speck Cipher Description

Speck is a family of simple block ciphers that were published by the US NSA in June 2013 [27]. The Speck cipher is of the ARX (add, rotate, xor) cipher type. This cipher is optimized for software implementation for low-resource material base, for example, for microcontrollers. The round function of the Speck cipher is shown in Fig. 3. To obtain round keys, a similar scheme is used, only the round number is given in it as a key. This approach allows you to reuse the code of the round function and gives you additional flexibility—if you need to optimize the execution speed, you can count the round keys in advance, and if you want to save memory, you can count them on the go.

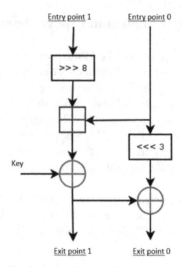

Fig. 3. Round Speck cipher function

Table 2 shows a comparison of the TEA and Speck ciphers.

Table 2. Comparison of tea and speck ciphers

Code	Block size	Key size	Number of rounds
TEA	64	128	64
Speck	2 × 32	4 × 16	22
	2 × 24	3 × 24	22
	2 × 24	4 × 24	23
	2 × 32	3 × 32	26
	2 × 32	4 × 32	27
	2 × 48	2 × 48	28
	2 × 48	3 × 48	29
	2 × 64	2 × 64	32
	2 × 64	3 × 64	33
	2 × 64	4 × 64	34

This table shows that the TEA cipher has a fixed block size, key and number of blocks, while a Speck is a family of ciphers and can have a different block size, key and number of blocks.

7 Experimental Research of Encryption Algorithms

The Arduino Uno controller and the STM32F401CC microcontroller were chosen for testing. Debugging of software implementations was performed in the AVR Studio 7 program and debugging of the STM32 microcontroller in the KEIL program uVision 5.

Arduino uno is based on the ATmega328P eight-bit controller [29]. STM32A401CC - This is a 32-bit microcontroller based on the Arm core. The clock frequency of the Arduino uno is 16 MHz, and that of the STM32 is 84 MHz. The Arduino's RAM and Flash memory are 2 and 32 KB, respectively. For STM32, these indicators are 64 and 256 KB, respectively. To test the TEA cipher, an implementation was taken from an article by David Wheeler and Roger Needham. The encryption time for 64 blocks with a 128-bit key was 9.213 ms. The SRAM was occupied by 70 bytes. On the STM32F401CC microcontroller, encryption took 6.738 μs. To test the Speck cipher, a reference implementation was taken [30, 31]. It shows an example of encrypting a 128-bit message with a 128-bit key:

```
#define ROR(x, r) ((x >> r) | (x << (64 - r)))
#define ROL(x, r) ((x << r) | (x >> (64 - r)))
#define R(x, y, k) (x = ROR(x, 8), x += y, x ^= k, y = ROL(y, 3), y
^= x)
#define ROUNDS 32

void encrypt(uint64_t pt[],
uint64_t ct[],
uint64_t K[])
{
   uint64_t y = pt[0], x = pt[1];
   uint64_t b = K[0], a = K[1];

   R(x, y, b);
   for (int i = 0; i < ROUNDS - 1; i++) {
     R(a, b, i);
     R(x, y, b);
   }
   ct[0] = y;
   ct[1] = x;
}
int setup(void)
{
    uint64_t pt[2] = { 11,22 };
    uint64_t ct[2];
    uint64_t K[2] = {33, 44};
    encrypt(pt, ct, K);
}
```

The encryption time for a 128 block with a 128-bit key was 18.447 ms. From SRAM memory was allocated 98 bytes. On the STM32F401CC microcontroller, encryption took 12.44 μs.

8 Conclusion

Research has shown that smart sensor systems are vulnerable to attacks that involve wireless networks. One of the considered attacks is related to the interception and analysis of key information in one of the standards, which is considered the most secure. Securing swarm intelligence systems should ensure not only confidentiality, integrity, and availability, but also low resource utilization. The TEA and Speck encryption algorithms were implemented on the Arduino Uno controller and the STM32F401CC microcontroller. Their implementation has shown that these ciphers are suitable for their use in different smart sensor devices based on the efficiency and performance of these reference algorithms. Further research may include implementing other ciphers across different IoT device platforms, test different implementations on messages of different sizes, load voltage testing for an IoT device.

References

1. Educational portal Geekbrains Homepage. https://geekbrains.ru/posts/what_is_iot. Accessed 02 Dec 2020
2. Yanovsky, G.: Assessment of voice quality in IP networks. Newsletter In **2**, 91–94 (2018)
3. Evans, D.: The Internet of Things. How the Next Evolution of the Internet Is Changing Everything
4. Chernyak, L.: Platform of the Internet of Things. Open systems. DBMS, No. 7 (2012). Open Systems. Accessed 05 Dec 2020
5. Quackenbush, S.R., Barnwell, T.P., Clements M.A.: Objective Measures of Speech Quality. Prentice Hall (1988)
6. Disruptive Civil Technologies. Six Technologies with Potential Impacts on US Interests out to 2025
7. Coetzee, L., Olivrin, G.: Inclusion through the Internet of Things. In: Cheein, A. (ed.) Assistive Technologies, IntechOpen, Rijeka (2012)
8. Baker, B., Xiang, W., Atkinson, I.: Internet of Things for smart healthcare: technologies, challenges, and opportunities IEEE Access **5**, 26521–26544 (2017)
9. Lin, H., Bergmann, N.W.: IoT Privacy and security challenges for smart home environments. Information **7**(3), 44 (2016). https://doi.org/10.3390/info7030044
10. Singh, S., Sharma, P.K., Moon, S.Y., Park, J.H.: Advanced lightweight encryption algorithms for IoT devices: survey, challenges and solutions. J. Ambient Intell. Humanized Comput. 1–18 (2017). https://doi.org/10.1007/s12652-017-0494-4
11. Weber, M, Boban, M.: Security challenges of the Internet of Things In: 39th International Convention on Information and Communication Technology, Electronics and Microelectronics (MIPRO), pp. 638–643. IEEE, Opatija (2016)
12. Ali, B., Awad, A.I.: Cyber and physical security vulnerability assessment for IoT-based smart homes. Sensors **18**(3), 1–17 (2018)
13. Forsström, S., Butun, I., Eldefrawy, M., Jennehag, U., Gidlund, M.: Challenges of securing the industrial internet of things value chain In: 2018 Workshop on Metrology for Industry 4.0 and IoT, pp. 218–223. IEEE, Brescia (2018)
14. Feng, W., Qin, Y., Zhao, S., Feng, D.: Aaot: lightweight attestation and authentication of low-resource things in IoT and cps. Comput. Netw. **134**, 167–182 (2018)
15. Keoh, S.L., Kumar, S.S., Tschofenig, H.: Securing the Internet of Things: a standardization perspective. IEEE Internet Things J. **1**(3), 265–275 (2014)

16. Mano, Y., Faial, B., Nakamura, V., Gomes, H., Libralon, L., Meneguete, I., et al.: Exploiting IoT technologies for enhancing Health Smart Homes through patient identification and emotion recognition. Comput. Sci. (2016). https://doi.org/10.1016/j.comcom.2016.03.010

17. Makhdoom, I., Abolhasan, M., Lipman, J., Liu, R.P., Ni, W.: Anatomy of threats to the Internet of Things. IEEE Commun. Surv. Tutor. 21(2), 1636–1675 (2019). SECOND QUARTER

18. Shachar, S., et al.: Security test bed for Internet-of-Things devices. IEEE Trans. Reliab. 68(1), 23–44 (2019)

19. Atamli, A.W., Martin, A.: Threat-based Security analysis for the Internet of Things. In: International Workshop on Secure Internet of Things, pp. 36–43 (2014)

20. Zhou, W., Yu, B.: A cloud-assisted malware detection and suppression framework for wireless multimedia system in IoT based on dynamic differential game. China Commun. 209–223 (2018)

21. Sandy Carielli (Entrust Datacard), Matt Eble (Praetorian), Frederick Hirsch (Fujitsu), Ekaterina Rudina (Kaspersky), Ron Zahavi (Microsoft). IoT Security Maturity Model: Practitioner's Guide Version 1.0 129 p. (2019)

22. National Institute of Standards and Technology. Framework for Improving Critical Infrastructure Cybersecurity .Version 1.1. 16 April (2018). 55 p

23. Jurafsky, D., Martin, J.: Speech and Language Processing, 2nd Edition, 2nd edn. Prentice Hall, Upper Saddle River (2008)

24. Mano, L.Y., Faiçal, B.S., Nakamura, L.H.V., Gomes, P.H., Libralon, G.L., et al.: Exploiting IoT technologies for enhancing Health Smart Homes through patient identification and emotion recognition. Comput Commun. 89–90, 178–190 (2016)

25. Mohd, B.J., Hayajneh, T.: Lightweight block ciphers for IoT: energy optimization and survivability techniques, IEEE Access 6, 35 966–35 978 (2018)

26. McKay, K., Bassham, L., Turan, M.S., Mouha, N.: Report on lightweight cryptography (nistir8114), National Institute of Standards and Technology (NIST), (2017)

27. Toshihiko, O.: Lightweight cryptography applicable to various IoT devices. NEC Tech. J. 12(1), 67–71 (2017)

28. Research Gate [Electronic resource], https://www.researchgate.net/publication/342434954_Lightweight_Cryptography_for_IoT_A_State-of-the-Art. Accessed 03 Dec 2020

29. Panasenko, S.: Encryption algorithms. Special reference book. SPb.: BHV-Petersburg (2009)

30. Federal Information Processing Standards Publication 197 (FIPS PUB 197). Specification for the Advanced Encryption Standard (AES). // Department of Commerce, National Institute of Standards and Technology, Information Technology Laboratory, 26 November (2001)

31. Perspectives of System Informatics: 12th International Andrei P. Ershov Informatics Conference, PSI 2019, Novosibirsk, Russia, 2–5 July 2019, Revised Selected Papers/Bjørner N., Virbitskaite I., Voronkov A. - Springer International Publishing, –P. 249. – (Theoretical Computer Science and General Issues). - ISBN 978-3-030-37486-0 (2019)

Optimization of a High-Lift Mechanism Motion Generation Synthesis Using MHS

Suwin Sleesongsom[1](✉) and Sujin Bureerat[2]

[1] Department of Aeronautical Engineering, International Academy of Aviation Industry, King Mongkut's Institute of Technology Ladkrabang, Bangkok 10520, Thailand
suwin.se@kmitl.ac.th

[2] Sustainable and Infrastructure Development Center, Department of Mechanical Engineering, Faculty of Engineering, KhonKaen University, KhonKaen 40002, Thailand

Abstract. The purpose of this paper is to synthesize a high-lift mechanism (HLM) of a transportation aircraft. In the past still lack in studying to synthesize of the HLM using a very recent technique. The device is an important mechanism to generate an addition lift to the wing of aircraft in take-off and landing condition. The crucial designing problem is to minimize the error between actual flap motion and target points. The optimum target points are positions and angles of flap at the take-off and landing condition. Designing constraints include the possibility of four-bar mechanism to work well, limiting position and includes workplace of mechanism. The optimizers are selected to tackle the problem is in a group of metaheuristics (MHs). The results show the propose method and MHs can synthesize the flap mechanism meet with the design targets.

Keywords: High-lift mechanism · Four-bar mechanism · Optimization technique · Motion generation · Metaheuristics

1 Introduction

The modern transportation aircraft can carry high payload that depends on plane form area and camber to develop lifting force. The high lift system (HLS) is one key of increasing lift in the modern large transportation aircraft, which is included high lift devices (HLD), support truss, drive mechanism or high lift mechanism (HLM), control system, and so on. The HLD can produce the addition lift to the wing, it focuses on increasing payload and increasing the performance of HLD and HLM. The system is very important for aircraft performance in takeoff and landing [1]. In many decades, the researcher tries to improve the performance of HLS, which expects to increase lift, reduce drag and noise, and to reduce the error of HLM. The improvements dramatically increase weight and operating cost [2]. The operating cost depends on complexity of mechanism that effect on manufacturing cost, maintenance cost and reliability of mechanism. Transportation flap normal can separate into plan flap, split flap, slotted flap, single-slot and double-slotted Fowler flap [3], while the HLM are separated into dropped-hinge, four-bar, link-track, and hooked-track [4]. Design the methodology of HLM aims to

© Springer Nature Switzerland AG 2021
Y. Tan and Y. Shi (Eds.): ICSI 2021, LNCS 12689, pp. 38–45, 2021.
https://doi.org/10.1007/978-3-030-78743-1_4

develop the designing process of mechanism synthesis. Traditional design process of HLM separately aerodynamics shape of flap from the mechanism synthesis by the way of finding optimum aerodynamic first and fit the mechanism for controlling is in the last step [4]. The aerodynamic step is based on data collecting from tabular or experimental and the mechanism synthesis is based on position parameters rather than the dimension of mechanism. Later this technique has been improved in process of design by combine both process to couple technique, which is performed the aerodynamic analysis of flap and mechanism synthesis at the same time by technique of iteration design simulation [2].The previous study still lacks in mechanism synthesis, which needs to improve HLM error. In our present study expects to increase the performance of HLM synthesizing and reducing HLM error.

From previous researches, there are any researches has been studied to synthesize the four-bar HLM [5], which was studied with the motion generation synthesis of HLM and penalty techniques. The study will be basic information for future research to study in designing this kind of mechanism. Due to the robustness, derivative-free and simplicity of meta-heuristics, this makes them to be more popular selection in the present for solving four-bar linkage motion generation problem [6, 7]. The work collects the metaheuristics (MHs) included the most popular and recently algorithm for solving the motion generation problem [7]. In their work presented the competition of MHs performance in solving the motion generation problem and also showed the TLBO outperformed the other MHs [7]. The result can extend to the present work and combine with [5] for solving HLM problem. The present work is different from previous research that solved the problem with only the best used MHs. Some of the best algorithms are the differential evolution (DE) [7], and teaching-learning based optimization (TLBO) [6]. As mention earlier, the present study expects to synthesize of four-bar HLM in viewing of motion generation synthesis using a penalty technique and MHs are optimizers.

The remaining of this paper is divided in four sections by starting from Sect. 2, the details of high lift mechanism, while the high-lift mechanism motion generation problem is performed in Sect. 3. The design results are detailed in Sect. 4 and the conclusions and discussion of the study are summarized in Sect. 5, respectively.

2 High-Lift Mechanism

High-lift mechanism attaches at trailing edge normally known as flap mechanism. A flap is a movable piece, which control a mechanism, that composes of actuator and support structure to produce addition lift to wing of aircraft. At the present, using mechanism type for HLM is that the four-bar linkage type, which is designed for Boeing B767, B777, and C-17. Due to advance of four-bar mechanism synthesis at present [5–7] causes our study focuses on this kind of mechanism and the model is shown in Fig. 1. Four-bar HLM is composed of four links, which has one frame, one crank, one rocker motion, and one is coupler link. The motion of the last link is combined between translation and rotation, causes this link usually attached with flap. The position of crank is installed at the rear spar to ensure that it can sustain the addition load lift and it simply supplies the input. All input motion drive with rotary actuators, and the driving actuator is mounted to the rear spar of the wing.

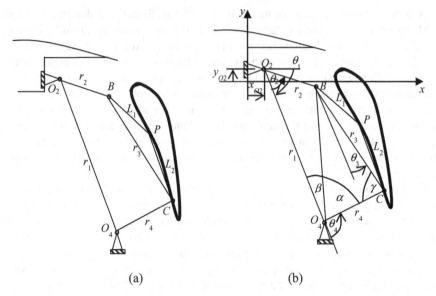

Fig. 1. Kinematic diagram of four-bar linkage for HLD and global coordinate system [5].

The occurred linkage needs only one input applying at link 1. The trigonometric is used to analyze the position analysis of four-bar linkage. The relation is in form of linkage lengths r_1, r_2, r_3, and r_4 and other parameters, which is proved in the previous work [5–7]. The coupler point (P) in the global coordinate in Fig. 2 is expressed as

$$x_P = x_{O2} + r_2 \cos(\theta_2 + \theta_1) + L_1 \cos(\phi_0 + \theta_3 + \theta_1) \tag{1.1}$$

$$y_P = y_{O2} + r_2 \sin(\theta_2 + \theta_1) + L_1 \sin(\phi_0 + \theta_3 + \theta_1)$$

where x_{O2} and y_{O2} are the global coordinate positions of O_2 [6]. The angle ϕ_0 can be obtained by considering the couple link BCP using law of cosine, which is expressed as

$$\phi_0 = \cos^{-1}\left[\frac{L_1^2 + r_3^2 - L_2^2}{2L_1 r_3}\right] \tag{1.2}$$

At input crank angle (θ_2) the values of angles θ_3, θ_4, and Γ for link lengths r_1, r_2, r_3, and r_4 are determined as follows [7]:

$$z^2 = r_1^2 + r_2^2 - 2r_1 r_2 \cos\theta_2, \quad z^2 = r_3^2 + r_4^2 - 2r_3 r_4 \cos\gamma$$

$$\gamma = \cos^{-1}\left[\frac{r_3^2 + r_4^2 - r_1^2 + 2r_1 r_2 \cos\theta_2}{2r_3 r_4}\right]$$

$$\gamma = \cos^{-1}\left[\frac{r_3^2 + r_4^2 - z^2}{2r_3 r_4}\right], \quad \alpha = \cos^{-1}\left[\frac{z^2 - r_3^2 + r_4^2}{2z r_4}\right] \tag{1.3}$$

$$\beta = \cos^{-1}\left[\frac{z^2 + r_1^2 - r_2^2}{2zr_1}\right], \quad \theta_3 = \pi - (\alpha + \beta + \gamma)$$

$$\theta_4 = \pi - (\alpha + \beta)$$

3 Optimization Problem and Constraint Handling

The conventional motion generation problem is different from the path generation problem as the desired angles of coupler link included in the objective function. The objective function has two parts, the first part is the position error between the target points $P_d(x_d, y_d)$ and the actual points $P(x_p, y_p)$ and the second part is the angular error between target angles (θ_{3d}) and actual angles (θ_{3p}). The design variables in this problem are included r_1, r_2, r_3, r_4, L_1, L_2, the coordinates of O_2 (x_{O2}, y_{O2}), and the angle of link 1(a frame) (θ_1). The motion generation problem in this research is called motion generation synthesis without prescribed timing. The input set of θ_2^i values also set as the design variables. A highlight in this study is weighting factor w that is scaled the position and the angle error in the objective function that is combined as one of design variables, which expects to improve the previous cumbersome in finding the proper weighting factor by varying the values [7]. Then, the optimization problem without prescribed timing is written as

$$\text{Min} f(x) = w \sum_{i=1}^{N}\left[(x_{d,i} - x_{p,i})^2 + (y_{d,i} - y_{p,i})^2\right] + (1 - w) \sum_{i=1}^{N}\left[(\theta_{3d,i} - \theta_{3p,i})^2\right] \quad (2)$$

subject to

$$\min(r_1, \ r_2, \ r_3, \ r_4) = \text{crank}(r_2) \tag{3}$$

$$2\min(r_1, \ r_2, \ r_3, \ r_4) + 2\max(r_1, \ r_2, \ r_3, \ r_4) < (r_1, \ r_2, \ r_3, \ r_4) \tag{4}$$

$$\theta_2^1 < \theta_2^2 \cdots < \theta_2^N \tag{5}$$

$$x_1 \leq x \leq x_u \tag{6}$$

where $x = \{r_1, \ r_2, \ r_3, \ r_4, \ L_1, \ L_2, \ \theta_0, \ x_{O2}, \ y_{O2}, \ \theta_2^i, \ w\}^T$, N is the number of points on the prescribed or target curve, and x_l and x_u are lower and upper bounds of design vector x, respectively. Furthermore, this synthesis problem can represent the behavior of HLM by applying proper constraints.

The external penalty can handle the design constraints by adding the term of constraints to the objective function (2). The difficulty occurs due to the additional two parts of penalty function value. The first part is assigned to control link lengths to meet Grashof's criterion (3–4), while the second part is assigned to ensure that input crank can rotate with a part or complete revolution in either a clockwise or counterclockwise direction (5). The working process of penalty function is to add enough high value to modify the objective function when some of constraints are violated. It promotes that adding value to the non-candidate solution and kicks it out of the design space; otherwise, the constant is zero. The constraints can be induced and approached a feasible solution. The proper adding value is rather than abstract causes this technique is inefficient for solving above design problem. The unknowns θ_2^i in (5) are removed and solved by another technique that is proved to increase the performance [6, 7].The constraint (4) and (5) are achieved, when the mechanism is a crank-rocker. The new idea has been tackled both constraints in new way [6], which instead of the traditional penalty technique. The process applies for solving a motion generation problem. At the present, the constraints (5) can write in a common form as $g_i(x) \leq g_{0,i}$.Then, a set of N input angle values (θ_2) is generated that are equally spaced from 0 to π radian. The higher intervals indicate higher efficiency, however, it needs more time consuming. Then the positions of point P corresponding to all targets are calculated, the objective function is

$$f(\mathbf{x}) = \sum_{i=1}^{N} \min\left(wd_{ij}^2 + (1 - w)\theta_{ij}^2\right) \qquad (7)$$

where $d_{ij}^2 = \left(x_{d,i} - x_{P,j}\right)^2 + \left(y_{d,i} - y_{P,j}\right)^2$ and $\theta_{ij}^2 = \left(\theta_{3d,i} - \theta_{3p,i}\right)^2$ for $j = 1,..., N$. The details of this technique can be seen in [6, 7].

From the motion generation problem formulation is applied to HLM, when position and angle of flap are known at each condition. The landing and take-off position of HLM is shown in Table 1. In design HLM at least two positions should define. In this research, the desired position and angular of HLM at both conditions are assigned following with the previous study by Liu [2] as shown in Table 1.

Table 1. Desired position and angular of HLM at take-off and landing conditions.

Case	Position (x$_i$, y$_i$)* 1.1173	Angle, $\delta_i(°)$
1. Take-off	(0.059, 0.0032), (0.0642, −0.0455)	0, 24.90
2. Landing	(0.059, 0.0032), (0.0703, −0.0454)	0, 43.52

From Table 1, the design optimization problems can summarize as follow: Design variables for $\mathbf{x}$ are

$$\mathbf{x} = \left[r_1, \ r_2, \ r_3, \ r_4, \ L_1, \ L_2, \ x_{O2}, \ y_{O2}, \ \theta_1\right]$$

Target points are showed in Table 1.
Limits of the variables:

$$0.01 \leq r_1 \leq 0.3$$

$$0.01 \leq r_2, \ r_3, \ r_4 \leq 0.5$$

$$-0.1 \leq L_1, \ L_2 \leq 0.2$$

$$x_{O2} = 0$$

$$-0.05 \leq y_{O2} \leq 0.05$$

$$-60 \leq \theta_1 \leq -45$$

In order to solve the design problems, some of MHs are selected due to high performance in solving the motion generation problem [5–7]. The used MHs are the differential evolutionary (DE), the teaching-learning based optimization (TLBO) and the self-adaptive population size teaching-learning based optimization (SAP-TLBO) [8]. All algorithms are coded in MATLAB commercial software. The population size is set $n_P = 100$ and the number of iterations is set at 500. To study statistical performance of present technique, the number of running times of simulation is set at 30 times.

4 The Design Results

Table 2. The best design results of HLM

Parameter	Case-1			Case-2		
	DE	TLBO	SAP-TLBO	DE	TLBO	SAP-TLBO
r_1	0.3000	0.3000	0.3000	0.2877	0.3000	0.2998
r_2	0.0292	0.0100	0.0100	0.0100	0.0100	0.0100
r_3	0.2634	0.0233	0.0233	0.0196	0.0231	0.0230
r_4	0.4055	0.2944	0.2944	0.2856	0.2994	0.2991
L_1	−0.0642	−0.0786	−0.0786	−0.0806	−0.0854	−0.0849
L_2	0.1999	−0.0560	−0.0560	−0.0633	0.0636	−0.0627
x_0	0	0	0	0	0	0
y_0	−0.0500	−0.0424	−0.0423	−0.0408	−0.0500	−0.0489
θ_1	−60.0000	−45.0551	−45.0053	−45.0000	−49.3926	−53.9316
w	0.5000	0.5000	0.5000	0.4999	0.5000	0.5000
Mean	**0.023194**	0.023221	**0.023194**	0.138108	**0.138061**	0.138115
Min	0.023188	**0.02297**	**0.02297**	0.137685	**0.137642**	**0.137643**
Max	0.023245	0.023425	0.023425	0.138634	0.138456	0.138438
Std	1.49E−05	7.21E−05	9.3E−05	0.000132	0.000243	0.00014

The design results of four-bar linkage synthesis for take-off and landing condition are showed in Fig. 2 and Fig. 3. The optimum path of each case is showed in the same figures. The descriptive statistics are mean, worst result (max), best result (min), and the standard deviation (std) of objective function values from 30 optimization runs that are in Table 2. In Case-1 (Take-off condition), there are two target points and angles. The result shows that SAP-TLBO and TLBO give the best min (error = 0.02297) while the worst in this case is DE (error = 0.023188). The most consistent methods are SAP-TLBO and DE based on mean and std. The result of Case-2 (Landing condition), there are two target points, but different position and angle as compare with the Case-1. The result shows that the recent case promotes SAP-TLBO and TLBO gives the best min (error = 0.13764), while the worst case is DE. The most consistent method is TLBO and DE based on mean and std.

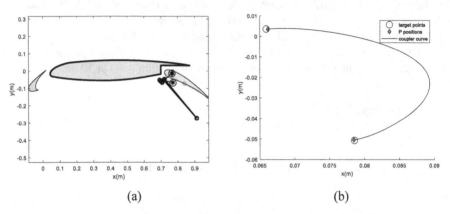

(a)   (b)

Fig. 2. (a) Optimum HLM for take-off condition (b) Optimum path HLM for take-off condition

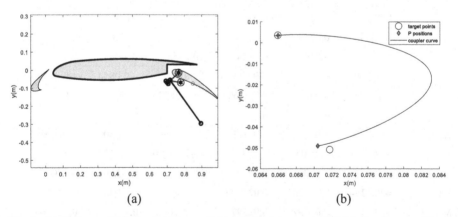

(a)   (b)

Fig. 3. (a) Optimum HLM for landing condition (b) Optimum path HLM for landing condition.

Moreover, the results show that the propose techniques also promote the moderate results in all cases due to its error are highly when compare with the previous study with the traditional testing problems [5–7]. The optimum design variable of weighting factor in both cases and all algorithms is w = 0.5, which is similar with our previous work [6, 7] that the designer recommended. Additionally, if another objective is more important than other one, the value can recommend by the designer rather than using the best compromise value from the simulation.

5   Conclusion and Discussion

This paper proposed the motion generation synthesis problems of high-lift mechanism. It is an extension of the motion generation technique in our previous study to design the high lift mechanism. The comparative results reveal that the employed meta-heuristics can be used to design HLM problems successfully. Overall, TLBO and the improvement of TLBO give the best solutions as well as the search consistency in both design cases. DE gives moderate efficient for this kind of optimization design. However, it still needs to improve the result with an efficient technique, which has been proved in performance for the motion generation problem. Nevertheless, this is a basic study of traditional technique for solving HLM motion generation problem without prescribed timing. The future works would use other techniques to increase the performance of design problem.

Acknowledgment. The authors are grateful for the financial support provided by King Mongkut's Institute of Technology Ladkrabang, and the Thailand Research Fund (RTA6180010).

References

1. Van Dam, C.P., Shaw, S.G., Vander Kam, J.C., Brodeur, R.R., Rudolph, P.K.C., Kinney, D.: Aero-mechanical design methodology for subsonic civil transport high-lift systems. In: RTO AVT Symposium on Aerodynamic Design and Optimization of Flight Vehicles in a Concurrent Multidisciplinary, Ottawa, Canada (1999)
2. Liu, P., Li, D., Qu, Q., Kong, C.: Two-dimensional new-type high-lift systems with link/straight track mechanism coupling downward defection of spoiler. J. of Aircr. **56**(4), 1524–1533 (2019)
3. Monte, A.D., Castelli, M.R., Benini, E.: A retrospective of high-lift device technology. Int. J. Aerosp. Mech. Eng. **6**(11), 2561–2566 (2012)
4. Zaccai, D., Bertels, F., Vos, R.: Design methodology for trailing-edge high-lift mechanisms. CEAS Aeronaut. J. **7**(4), 521–534 (2016). https://doi.org/10.1007/s13272-016-0202-7
5. Chabphet, P., Santichatsak, S., Thalang, T.N., Sleesongsom, S., Bureerat, S.: High-lift mechanism motion generation synthesis using a metaheuristic. Multidisc. Digit. Publ. Inst. Proc. **39**(1), Article no. 5 (2020)
6. Sleesongsom, S., Bureerat, S.: Alternative constraint handling technique for four-bar linkage motion generation. In: IOP Conf Series: Mater Science and Engineering, vol. 501, p. 012042 (2019)
7. Phukaokaew, W., Sleesongsom, S., Panagant, N., Bureerat, S.: Synthesis of four-bar linkage motion generation using optimization algorithms. Adv. Comput. Des. **4**(3), 197–210 (2019)
8. Sleesongsom, S., Bureerat, S.: Four-bar linkage path generation through self-adaptive population size teaching-learning based optimization. Knowl. Based Syst. **135**, 180–191 (2017)

Liminal Tones: Swarm Aesthetics and Materiality in Sound Art

Mahsoo Salimi$^{(\boxtimes)}$ and Philippe Pasquier

Metacreation Lab for Creative AI, Simon Fraser University, Surrey, BC V3T03, Canada
{salimi,pasquier}@sfu.ca

Abstract. The application of swarm aesthetic in music composition is not new. Artistic swarm application has resulted in complex soundscapes and musical compositions. However, sound composition using physical swarm agents has not been extensively studied. Using an experimental approach, we create a series of sound textures know as Liminal Tones (B/Rain Dream) based on swarming behaviours. We study the influence of different materials and emergent patterns and evaluate the acoustic properties of different materials such as wood, ceramic or granite, and effect of imperfections of the physical agents on the overall aesthetic quality. Finally, we consider the historical and theoretical foundation of swarm music, the role of materiality and actions in sound, and challenge the traditional perception of sound as an immaterial art form.

Keywords: Swarm aesthetic · Swarm intelligence · Sound objects · Random Walk · Brownian Motion · Emergence · Chaos · Bristlebots

1 Introduction

Swarm systems inspired by swarm intelligence and natural ecosystems (e.g., social insects) are a unique frontier for art. Many artists utilize swarm principles such as indirect communication, self-organization and emergent behaviours to create musical compositions, soundscapes and sonic environments. SWARMUSIC [3] is a system that uses swarm behaviour to create music. It is an interactive music improvisation tool with multiple swarms of particles as musical events that move in a virtual 3D space by utilizing Boids flocking algorithm [24]. Bisig et al. [2] created a series of experimental projects known as Interactive Swarm Orchestra (ISO) and Interactive Swarm Space (ISS). The ISO system explores flocking algorithms to control sound synthesis and sound spatialization. The ISS is a MIDI-based virtual orchestra involving meaningful interactions between artificial swarms and composers to generate artistic expression. Bisig et al. also have explored multi-modal feedback and audio-visual spatialization or creative engagement using swarm techniques.

© Springer Nature Switzerland AG 2021
Y. Tan and Y. Shi (Eds.): ICSI 2021, LNCS 12689, pp. 46–57, 2021.
https://doi.org/10.1007/978-3-030-78743-1_5

Expanding on previous work, Davis and Karamanlis [9] added a controllable leader to typical Boids simulations for musical swarms. The leader agent lets the user directly control the behaviour of the other agents and the overall movement of the flock. In a different approach, Jones [18] introduced AtomSwarm. This is a framework for sound-based performance that uses swarm dynamics with genetically-encoded behaviours, artificial pheromones and imitations. The result is a complex sonic ecosystem capable of sonic spatialization and self-organizing regulation. Flock to Music [6] is a real-time improvisation tool that simulates the behaviour of the Boids as compositions with musical parameters.

Despite the broad interest in swarm music, most experiments to date utilize artificial swarms and software simulations. To our knowledge, there has been little exploration of physical swarming agents. Blackwell [4] provides a comprehensive review of swarm music.

Self-organization is a unique and complex collective behaviour common in swarms. It results from simple and local interactions between agents (members of the group) and emerges at the colony level. Self-organization of social insects usually happens via stigmergy, an indirect communication strategy through the environment [16]. Stigmergy results in a complex emerging intelligence at the colony level without the need for planning, control or direct communication between agents. However, with no prior knowledge about the sources, systematic searches become less effective and social insects often use other searching mechanisms known as random walk. There are several random walk variants, including Stigmergic Random Walk (SRW), Correlated Random Walk (CRW) and Lévy Walk. Random Walks are commonly used for artistic experiments and in swarm robotics particularly if the robots have limited individual abilities (e.g., local sensing, memory or processing power). Considering the limitation of our BBots, we have leveraged stigmergic foraging behaviours and variations of random walks to create sound compositions.

Non-Human Sounds – Sound as Action. Using mechanical devices and computer-controlled sound objects is not new in sound art. However, there is a new series of work involving mechanical and glitch sounds. Such works have focused on exploring repetitive sonic processes and events with mechatronic mediation. Mechanical/rhythmic actions, sound experiences and the ontological properties of non-human sounds are more important than traditional interventions. The investigation of space as a compositional element, modulated by movement, offers new idiosyncrasies and aesthetic potentials for musical creation [7, 12].

Over the past two decades, robotic and mechatronic interventions have become prominent aesthetic elements in the work of composers and sound artists. These implications include electro-acoustic experimentation, sonic environments, sound sculptures and the use of drumming apparatuses. However, mechatronic systems used for musical creations can have many different aesthetic roles. Some artists use motion, direction and distance of sound as compositional means and sound spatialization. Composer and sound artist Trimpin employs the visual, spatial and kinetic properties of sound in his works (e.g., Conloninpurple, 1997; Sheng High, 2004). Other artists use them to evoke memories and imaginary environments and to stimulate different emotions [11].

Sound artists Peter Bosch and Simone Simons [5] explore the spatial characteristics of sound in their kinetic sound project Cantan un Huevo (2000). They use glass bottles, containers and metal springs as sound objects. The distribution of the sound sources in the space is an integral part of their work and results in different acoustic experiences in different parts of the space.

Other artists use similar sound objects distributed evenly across space in their work. Pe Lang and Zimoun [22, 32] create sound sculptures and installations with rhythms and flow, using basic mechanical components (as sound objects) in large numbers. In their practice, together and individually, they create analog rhythms, textures and flow to study the creation and degeneration of sonic spaces. Inspired by generative systems and swarm behaviours, their works display simplicity and complexity. The emergent and intricate behaviours of these sound objects (in sound and motion) appear to be organic or alive and sound like "the acoustic hum of natural phenomena" [27].

Building on our previous work [25] on swarming techniques and robotic interventions in sound art, and inspired by Pe Lang and Zimoun's artworks [22, 32] and Blackwell's SWARMUSIC [4], we introduce Liminal Tones (B/Rain Dream) as an experimental sound art project/tool. Our goal is to demonstrate the importance of actions, materials and acoustic media in sound texture, using multi-bodies (a swarm of physical agents) and challenging the traditional perception of music as an immaterial art form.

Previously we used digital mediation and PSO-PID controller to derive the movement of DC motors and generate sound, but here we use an analogue approach and swarming BBots to generate sound textures and further investigate the influence of materiality and robotic intervention to generate novel sound textures (acoustic aesthetics). So, we present Liminal Tones (B/Rain Dream) and show the results and analyze the influence of different materials on the aesthetic quality of sound textures in Sect. 2. Then, we follow up with a discussion of the relationship between order, chaos and emergent behaviours of Liminal Tones (B/Rain Dream) in Sect. 3. Finally, we explain the underlying concepts of swarm aesthetics for musical creation and discuss our future plans in Sect. 4.

2 Methods

2.1 Concept

Liminal Tones (B/Rain Dream) is a series of sound textures made by a group (5–10) of BBots (as sound objects) that move, twist and turn on the ground to generate sounds (BBot is a modified version of vibration-driven Bristlebot [1, 15] with no brush). Inspired by Pe Lang and Zimoun's sound sculptures [22, 32], we used DC vibrator motors, wires and electrical circuits to create the BBots and control their motion and sound. Liminal Tones (B/Rain Dream) demonstrate collective behaviours while embracing randomness and imperfections (due to battery degradation and DC perturbation). The resulting sound textures are both organized and chaotic. Liminal Tones (B/Rain Dream) can be viewed as an experimental tool for emergent behaviours and materiality in sound art [13] rather than an artwork. Using different materials (as surface) and tuning the initial conditions (placement, speed, direction), we were able to create different sound textures despite the identical shape and properties of BBots. Listening to the textures, one can recognize rhythms such as the clicking of a drum or natural sounds (e.g., raindrops on the metal roof). Audio samples can be found on our website [21].

2.2 Model

BBots (sound objects) exhibit complex movements similar to the stigmergic foraging behaviour of ants, in two phases. First, sound objects demonstrate Lévy Walk with high power and speed. Over time, the sound objects cycle to Brownian Motion as the battery degrades (with lower speed).

Phase 1 – Lévy Walk. At the start each BBot move quickly with large step-size similar to Lévy Walk motion – a modification of the standard random walk in which the step size has a heavy-tailed distribution [31]:

$$P(s) = s^{-\mu}. \tag{1}$$

where s is the step size with $1 < \mu \leq 3$. With increasing values of μ the movement becomes less super-diffusive (due to jumps with heavy-tail distribution) and more Brownian. Individual objects with super-diffusive movement paths will appear to move faster than those with normally diffusive (Brownian) or sub-diffusive movements [31]. Therefore, Lévy walks represent a spectrum of random walks, with ballistic motion at one extreme ($\mu > 1$) and Brownian Motion ($\mu \simeq 1$) at the other.

Formal Asymptotics. We used 5 BBots as sound objects with DC perturbation ranging between 1.5–3V. BBots move with a random heading and a step length selected from a power-law distribution with parameter μ. The periodic vibration of DC motors paired with a friction mechanism lead to a propulsion interaction between the sound objects and the environment, alternating between high friction in some parts and low friction in others. BBots have a body with a rotational spring of stiffness k and are in frictional contact with the surface without any legs.

The force (f_Ω) resulted from the body mass oscillation and frequency Ω drives the internal movement of the sound objects. The modulation of friction of BBots results from the oscillations of the normal forces and leads to a stick-slip motion. DeSimone and Tatone [10] modelled the tangential frictional force by:

$$F = -\mu N \dot{x}. \tag{2}$$

where N is the normal reaction force, $\dot{x}$ is the velocity (denoted with a dot with respect to time), and μ is a constant. For simplicity, we assume that rotations of the BBots are not allowed and they are always in contact with the ground with two degree of freedoms: horizontal movement and deviation ϕ from the rest angle $\alpha = 0$. Therefore, the motion equation is as follows [8]:

$$M\ddot{x} = -\mu N(t)\dot{x}. \tag{3}$$

$$M\ddot{y} = N(t) - M_g + f_\Omega(t). \tag{4}$$

$$k_\varphi = N(t)L\sin(\alpha + \varphi) - \mu N(t)\dot{x}L\cos(\alpha + \varphi). \tag{5}$$

where N is the normal reaction force ($N = \sum_{i=1}^{m} N_i$), and M_g is the body mass. We consider the following ansatz for the normal force:

$$N(t) = N^* + \tilde{N}\sin\Omega t. \tag{6}$$

$$N^* = M_g. \tag{7}$$

$$N^\sim/N^\wedge* = \eta \ll 1. \tag{8}$$

where η is the ratio between the amplitude of a harmonic ($\tilde{N}$) and the average normal force (N^*) and usually smaller than 1. To normalize the dynamic variables, we consider the following constants:

$$\sigma = \sin(\alpha). \tag{9}$$

$$\chi = \cos(\alpha). \tag{10}$$

$$f_\Omega(t) = N^* f(\Omega t). \tag{11}$$

$$\Omega = \sqrt{(k/M)}\omega/L\chi. \tag{12}$$

where f and ω are the normalized force and frequency. Applying all the definitions above we can rewrite Eqs. (3) and (5) as the equivalent system in respect to dynamical variables (θ, w).

$$\theta = n\tau\frac{\sin(\alpha + \theta)}{\sigma} - \xi n\tau\left(w + \dot{\theta}\frac{\cos(\alpha + \theta)}{\chi}\right)\cos(\alpha + \theta)/\chi. \tag{13}$$

$$w' = -\lambda n\tau\left(w + \left(\theta^\cdot\left(\cos(\alpha + \theta)\right)/\chi\right)'\right). \tag{14}$$

where $\tau = \Omega t$, $\xi = \frac{\mu N^* L^2 \cos\alpha\Omega}{k}$ and $\lambda = \frac{\mu N^*}{M\Omega}$.

Phase 2 – Brownian Motion. After a few minutes, BBots move slowly with smaller step sizes as the batteries degrade. In this phase each BBot acts as a particle with a normalized step-size distribution similar to Brownian motion and constantly moves in random directions.

The Brownian motion is a complex random process with noise. There are different methods to formulate the Brownian motion in terms of the evolution of a nonstationary probability and here we use Langevin and Fokker-Plank equation [19, 23] to study the evolution of the velocity distribution and interactions between the environment and Brownian agents. The dynamics and speed fluctuation of the Brownian particle are defined as:

$$x^{\cdot} = v. \tag{15}$$

$$\dot{v} = -\gamma(x, v)v + F(t) + \xi(t). \tag{16}$$

where $F(t)$ represents a random external force, m and v the mass and the velocity of the particle, $\xi(t)$ is a Gaussian noise, α is the friction constant and $\gamma = \frac{\alpha}{m}$.

For simplicity, we assume there is no external forces, and therefore $F(t) = 0$. The Brownian particle with the state space (x, v) has a distribution probability $\rho(x, v, t)$ as follows [23]:

$$\partial/\partial t \, \rho(x, v, t) = -\nabla(\rho(x, v, t)(x^{\cdot}, v^{\cdot}). \tag{17}$$

$$\partial/\partial t \, \rho(x, v, t) = -\partial/\partial x \left(\rho x^{\cdot}\right) - \partial/\partial v\left(\rho v^{\cdot}\right). \tag{18}$$

To simplify the equation, operators A and B are defined as:

$$A = v \, \partial/\partial x - \partial/\partial v \, (\gamma(x, v)v) - \gamma(x, v)v \, \partial/\partial v. \tag{19}$$

$$B = \xi(t)\frac{\partial}{\partial v}. \tag{20}$$

Hence:

$$\partial/\partial t \, \rho(x, v, t) = -A\rho - B\rho. \tag{21}$$

3 Results

In this section we present the initial results of Liminal Tones (B/Rain Dream) and step-length distributions for each phase of the model scheme. We analyze samples taken from different intervals and compare the sound quality of different motion (Lévy Walk or Brownian) and the surface material in Fig. 1 and Fig. 2. First, we show examples of movement trajectories of BBots of different surfaces (wood, ceramic, granite) and the dependence of those trajectories on control parameters $\varepsilon \to f(x, y)$ and DC motor speeds. When $\mu > 1$ and BBots have high turning angle and speed (interacting with the environment), the motion is ballistic with long, straight movements and many short steps as shown in Fig. 1. In contrast, when $\mu \simeq 1$ the motion is Brownian as shown in Fig. 2.

The movement trajectories (different μ) depends on the distribution of step lengths. With smaller and fixed μ, the step-length distribution is more stable (Cauchy distribution). With random or higher μ values, the step-length distribution becomes Gaussian. Moreover, the motions result from turning angles $\Delta\theta_t$ over time (t). When the value of $\Delta\theta_t$ is close to zero for a long time, BBots move in a straight line. In contrast, when $\Delta\theta_t$ fluctuates dynamically, BBots twist and turn many times.

To evaluate the quality of the generated sound textures, we compare them to natural ambient sounds with similar audio profiles. Usually, BBots generate rhythmic patterns with high jumps between different frequencies. This would be similar to the rhythmic pattern of heavy hail and the noisy profile and calming pattern of sleet, as illustrated in Fig. 3. To qualitatively assess the role of materiality in sound, we compare the spectrum of acoustic sound objects in relation to different materials, and their pitch and timbral aesthetic for 12 sound textures [21] as shown in Fig. 4. Here, vertical lines represent the rhythmic structures and horizontal lines represent the harmonic structures. For some sound categories, the audio samples are noisy, meaning most frequencies are present. Other categories have fewer frequencies and show step intervals and rhythmic cycles which resulted from vibrating patterns, turn and twist of motors, or errors (on-off interruptions). The speeding patterns can also be identified where the sound amplitudes vary due to power fluctuations of the batteries. Notably, each material shows different music signatures. For example, wood resonates at higher frequencies while ceramics absorb sounds and do not resonate as much (low, mid frequencies).

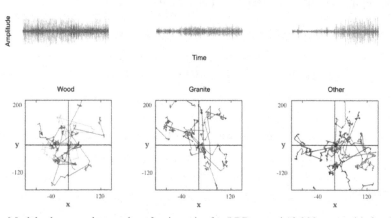

Fig. 1. Model scheme and examples of trajectories for 5 BBots and 10,000 steps with fixed step distribution and high-speed during Phase 1 which follows a ballistic Lévy Walk. Different colours correspond to each BBot and its initial conditions (placement, speed, direction). When the value of $\Delta\theta_t$ is close to zero for a long time, the BBots move in a straight line with short steps in between. (Color figure online)

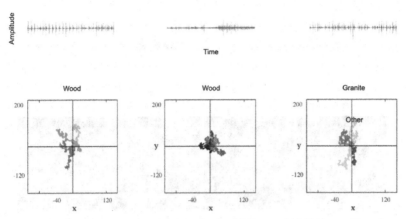

Fig. 2. Model scheme and examples of trajectories for 5 BBots and 10,000 steps. There is random step distribution and low-speed movement during Phase 2, similar to Brownian Motion. The internal dynamics x and y produce agent movements in 2D space. Movement is produced by turning angles $\Delta\theta_t$ over time (t). The trajectory of each BBot in a 2D space is represented by different colours corresponding to each BBot and its initial conditions (placement, speed, direction). (Color figure online)

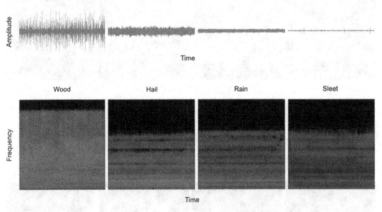

Fig. 3. Comparison of audio samples (left) with natural sounds (hail, rain, sleet). Examples were selected to be roughly similar in sound textures. The top row shows the waveforms. Note that our sample is more extremely periodic with high jumps compared to the other three. The bottom row shows the spectrograms. Here, the vertical lines represent step intervals. Note the constant tones around mid-levels in rain and the noisy profile of sleet sound.

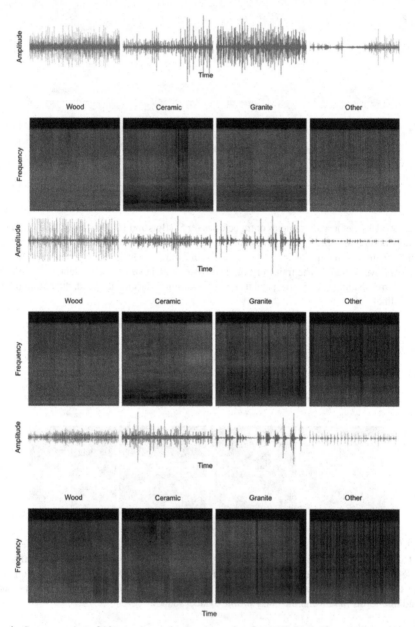

Fig. 4. Spectrograms of 12 sound samples (each ranging from 15–30 s). Note the constant noisy profile of wood and the mid-level frequencies and orders of ceramics, and resonance of granite. Some samples have different characteristics such as rhythmic patterns and high-low passes. Others are noisy with a wide range of pitch and timbral qualities, which creates unique sound textures [21].

4 Discussion and Future Works

Swarm intelligence is one of the most beautiful and unusual phenomena in nature. It is the product of the interaction between a group of decentralized agents and their environment. Widely recognized examples of swarms include but are not limited to bird flocking, bacterial growth, fish schooling, and the societal superorganisms of ant colonies (i.e., foraging). Due to their aesthetic qualities, swarm systems inspired by swarm intelligence and natural ecosystems present unique frontiers for art domains such as visual art [17, 28] and sound composition [2, 3, 6].

Swarm aesthetics are mostly concerned with form, the collective patterns of artificial swarm agents, and intuitive visual and sonic representations in digital forms. There is a gap in the research and practice of using swarm techniques to create sounds mediated by robotic actions and spatio-temporal processes resulting from: multiple interactions, amplification of fluctuations, or randomness between physical agents (sound objects). We propose Liminal Tones (B/Rain Dream) as a tool to create sounds from actions (of multiple sound objects) and explore swarm aesthetics in sound.

4.1 Order and Chaos – Sound as Emergence

Chaos theory and the study of complex systems (nonlinear dynamics), provide a framework for thinking about constant tensions and emergence from chaos and order. Deterministic and dynamic systems regardless of their subject matter have universal characteristics, including repetition, self-organization, emergence, feedback loop and unpredictability. Chaos theory focuses on simple systems with unpredictable and emergent behaviours. Complexity theory focuses on complex systems that have numerous interacting parts which are often self-organized and unexpected. In such systems, emergent patterns arise from simple rules, local interactions between the individual elements (or agents) and adaptive behaviours.

Not surprisingly, many artists use multi-agent systems and emergence in music improvisation, compositions and sound art. Despite the emergent behaviours of dynamic systems, artists can control the musical outputs subject to the complexity of the rule set and important variables. Manual control of interconnected systems such as music generative systems is almost impossible because each agents' every movement is affected by other agents. For more control, artists use simple computational models such as Cellular Automaton [5, 14], swarming techniques [3, 17, 18, 28, 30] or abstract constraints [2, 4, 20, 22, 32].

Throughout the past decades of sound art, there have been a few artists who applied emergence and chaos principles in their work without any digital mediation. Joe Jones, and more recently Zimoun and Pe Lang [29], use simple elements such as motors, wires and solenoids to create sound sculptures and installations. The rhythm and flow in these sonic environments result from repetition, randomness and imperfections or glitches. Zimoun and Pe Lang, together and individually, study the creation and degeneration of patterns. Inspired by generative systems and swarm behaviours, their works display both simplicity and complexity. Here complexity grows from simple rules with some randomness and emphasizes their oppositional position of order and chaos [26].

Inspired by current artistic applications and the rich aesthetic qualities of swarms, we explore robotic interventions and the role of materiality in sound art to create novel sound textures with different pitch and timbral qualities.

4.2 Future Works

While While experimenting with different setups for Liminal Tones (B/Rain Dream), we tested the use of physical swarming bodies to create sound. To achieve different aesthetic qualities, we explored chaotic and random behaviours, and embraced imperfections and error (due to battery degradation and DC perturbation). Liminal Tones (B/Rain Dream) that resulted are a critical reflection of a still-emergent field of work.

With respect to our future work, our plan is to investigate multi- swarms (with different sound qualities) and large numbers of BBots (50 or more) to explore collective behaviours, and swarm aesthetics with wide timbral and frequency range, and mechanical tones.

References

1. Becker, F., et al.: On the mechanics of bristle-bots-modeling, simulation and experiments. In: ISR/Robotik 2014; 41st International Symposium on Robotics. VDE (2014)
2. Bisig, D., Schacher, J.C., Neukom, M.: Flowspace-a hybrid ecosystem. In: NIME, pp. 260–263 (2011)
3. Blackwell, T.M., Bentley, P.: Improvised music with swarms. In: Proceedings of the 2002 Congress on Evolutionary Computation. CEC 2002 (Cat. No. 02TH8600), vol. 2, pp. 1462–1467. IEEE (2002)
4. Blackwell, T.: Swarming and music. In: Miranda, E.R., Biles, J.A. (eds.) Evolutionary Computer Music, pp. 194–217. Springer London, London (2007). https://doi.org/10.1007/978-1-84628-600-1_9
5. Bosch, P., Simons, S.: Our music machines. Organised Sound 10(2), 103 (2005)
6. Bouchard. https://www.livestructures.com/flock-to-music/. Accessed 20 Apr 2021
7. Candy, L., Edmonds, E., Poltronieri, F.: Explorations in art and technology. Springer, London (2002). https://doi.org/10.1007/978-1-4471-7367-0
8. Cicconofri, G., DeSimone, A.: Motility of a model bristle-bot: a theoretical analysis. Int. J. Non-Linear Mech. 76, 233–239 (2015)
9. Thomas, D., Karamanlis, O.: Gestural control of sonic swarms: Composing with grouped sound objects (2007)
10. DeSimone, A., Tatone, A.: Crawling motility through the analysis of model locomotors: two case studies. Eur. Phys. J. E 35(9), 1–8 (2012). https://doi.org/10.1140/epje/i2012-12085-x
11. Di Bona, E.: Towards a rich view of auditory experience. Philos. Stud. 174(11), 2629–2643 (2016). https://doi.org/10.1007/s11098-016-0802-4
12. Dorin, A.: Aesthetic fitness and artificial evolution for the selection of imagery from the mythical infinite library. In: Kelemen, J., Sosík, P. (eds.) ECAL 2001. LNCS (LNAI), vol. 2159, pp. 659–668. Springer, Heidelberg (2001). https://doi.org/10.1007/3-540-44811-X_76
13. Flø, A.B.: Materiality in Sound Art. Organised Sound 23(3), 225 (2018)
14. Gage, D., Laub, E., McGarry, B.: Cellular automata: is rule 30 random. In: Proceedings of the Midwest NKS Conference, Indiana University (2005)

15. Giomi, L., Hawley-Weld, N., Mahadevan, L.: Swarming, swirling and stasis in sequestered bristle-bots. In: Proceedings of the Royal Society A: Mathematical, Physical and Engineering Sciences, vol. 469, no. 2151, 20120637 (2013)

16. Grasse, P.-P.: Reconstruction of the nest and coordination between individuals in terms. bellicositermes natalensis and cubitermes sp. the theory of stigmergy: test interpretation of termite constructions. Soc. Insect **6**, 41–80 (1959)

17. Jacob, C.J., Hushlak, G., Boyd, J.E., Nuytten, P., Sayles, M., Pilat, M.: Swarmart: Interactive art from swarm intelligence. Leonardo **40**(3), 248–254 (2007)

18. Jones, D.: AtomSwarm: a framework for swarm improvisation. In: Giacobini, M., et al. (eds.) EvoWorkshops 2008. LNCS, vol. 4974, pp. 423–432. Springer, Heidelberg (2008). https://doi.org/10.1007/978-3-540-78761-7_45

19. Klimontovich, Y.L.: Nonlinear brownian motion. Phys. Usp. **37**(8), 737 (1994)

20. McCormack, J.: Evolving Sonic Ecosystems. Kybernetes (2003)

21. Metacreation. https://metacreation.net. Accessed 20 Apr 2021

22. Pe, L.: https://www.pelang.ch/pelang.html. Accessed 20 Apr 2021

23. Radpay, P.: Langevin Equation and Fokker-Planck Equation (2020)

24. Reynolds, C.W.: Flocks, herds and schools: A distributed behavioral model. In: Proceedings of the 14th Annual Conference on Computer Graphics and Interactive Techniques, pp. 25–34 (1987)

25. Salimi, M., Pasquier. P.: Exploiting Swarm Aesthetics in Sound Art, Art Machines 2: International Symposium on Machine Learning and Art 2021, Art Machines 2 (2021)

26. Satin, S., Gangal, A.D.: Random walk and broad distributions on fractal curves. Chaos, Solitons Fractals **127**, 17–23 (2019)

27. Schlatter, N.E., Waller, R., Matheson, S.: Flow, Just Flow: Variations on a Theme (2013)

28. Shiffman, D.: Swarm. In: ACM SIGGRAPH 2004 Emerging technologies, p. 26 (2004)

29. Stoddart, M.M.: Swiss/Mecha-Swiss: An Investigation Into the Kinetic, Sonic and Entropic Oeuvre of Zimoun. PhD diss., University of London (Courtauld Institute of Art) (2015)

30. Urbano, P.: Playing in the pheromone playground: experiences in swarm painting. In: Rothlauf, F., et al. (eds.) EvoWorkshops 2005. LNCS, vol. 3449, pp. 527–532. Springer, Heidelberg (2005). https://doi.org/10.1007/978-3-540-32003-6_53

31. Viswanathan, G.M., Buldyrev, S.V., Havlin, S., Da Luz, M.G.E., Raposo, E.P., Stanley, H.E.: Optimizing the success of random searches. Nature **401**(6756), 911–914 (1999)

32. Zimoun. https://www.zimoun.net. Accessed 20 Apr 2021

Study on the Random Factor of Firefly Algorithm

Yanping Qiao[1,2]([✉]), Feng Li[3], Cong Zhang[4], Xiaofeng Li[3], and Zhigang Zhou[3]

[1] School of Power and Energy, Northwestern Polytechnical University,
Xi'an 710072, China
[2] Science and Technology on Altitude Simulation Laboratory,
Mianyang 621700, China
[3] China Ship Scientific Research Center, Wuxi 214082, China
[4] AECC Sichuan Gas Turbine Establishment, Mianyang 621700, China

Abstract. The firefly algorithm (FA) is a swarm intelligence algorithm that mimics the swarm behaviour of the firefly in nature. The idea is simple, and FA is easy to realize. To improve its performance, a new method to control the random factor in FA is proposed in this paper, based on the design idea and mathematical model of FA and a simple experiment. Under the new method, the value of the random factor decreases according to a geometric progression sequence. Twenty common ratios of geometric progression sequences are used to optimize nine standard benchmark functions. The experimental results are analysed by the ANOVA and step-up methods. The analysis shows that the performance of FA improves under the new method to control the random factor.

Keywords: Firefly algorithm · Random factor · Swarm intelligence

1 Introduction

Swarm intelligence algorithm is an optimization algorithm constructed by simulating the swarm behavior of animals, which is mainly reflected by the characteristics of individuals in a group learning from each other and competing to evolve. Typical examples are the ant colony algorithm and particle swarm optimization (PSO), which have both been extensively researched in terms of algorithm theory, improvement, and application, and greatly reflect the ability of swarm intelligence to optimize solutions. Fireflies also have swarm behavior, mainly to locate, attract, and warn each other, and to feed by fluorescence, and the intensity of fluorescence and the distance between fireflies have a great influence on these characteristics. Yang proposed the firefly algorithm (FA) in 2009 after studying the swarm behavior of fireflies, whose luminescence intensity and distance from each other determine their direction [1,2]. Yang showed through numerical experiments that FA has better search performance than a genetic or particle swarm optimization algorithm, and can better solve complex optimization problems [1,3]. FA also has the characteristics of simplicity and ease of

© Springer Nature Switzerland AG 2021
Y. Tan and Y. Shi (Eds.): ICSI 2021, LNCS 12689, pp. 58–71, 2021.
https://doi.org/10.1007/978-3-030-78743-1_6

implementation. Researchers have gradually improved FA and its applications [4–10,17–31]. This paper points out the role of the random search term of the algorithm in optimization by analyzing the design of FA and its mathematical model and verifies the influence of the random factor in the random search term on the convergence performance of the algorithm through a simple numerical experiment. We propose a method to control the values of the random factor based on a geometric sequence in order to improve the algorithm's performance. We optimize and solve nine standard benchmark functions for different common ratios of the geometric sequence, and statistically analyze the optimization results, which show that the optimization performance of FA is improved with the new control method for the random factor. A common ratio is derived to optimize the overall performance of the algorithm. For comparison with the geometric decreasing control method, we investigate methods to control the random factor of FA by linearly and exponentially decreasing it. We also compare the performance of the improved FA, PSO, and improved PSO.

2   Review of FA

2.1   Algorithm Idea

There are more than 2000 known species of fireflies, and many reflect swarm behaviors through their own fluorescence. The two most basic behaviors are attracting fireflies of the opposite sex in the same species group and attracting and feeding on food; that is, the most basic swarm behaviors of fireflies are closely related to their own fluorescence, and this understanding is important to the construction of FA. The intensity of fluorescence decreases with the distance between the light source and object. At the same time, when fluorescence is transmitted in the air, its intensity is attenuated because it is absorbed by the air, and the degree of attenuation is necessarily related to the absorption coefficient of the air and the distance of transmission.

To design the group behavior of fireflies as a swarm intelligence algorithm for the solution of optimization problems, the location of a firefly is considered a feasible solution to the problem, and the fluorescence intensity of the fireflies is considered as the value of the objective function. For convenience of the algorithm design, the fireflies are considered homogeneous. Under this assumption, the attraction relationship between them does not need to consider their gender. The attraction between two fireflies is considered proportional to their fluorescence intensity. A firefly with lower fluorescence intensity will fly toward one with higher intensity, which means the firefly with higher intensity is more attractive to the firefly with lower intensity. The attraction behavior among fireflies corresponds to the convergence behavior of the algorithm, i.e., fireflies search for a region with a better value of the objective function.

2.2   Model Analysis of FA

Based on the above analysis, to implement FA, it is first necessary to determine a mathematical model between fluorescence intensity and distance. In the real world, the intensity of light decays with distance, so objects far from a light source become darker. The intensity of light is inversely proportional to the square of the distance between the object and the light source, so we can obtain the following model:

$$I(r) = I_s/r^2 \tag{1}$$

where r is the distance from the flashing firefly, I_s is the fluorescence intensity of the firefly at the source, and I is the fluorescence intensity at distance r.

Next, it is necessary to determine the model of fluorescence absorption and attenuation during transmission in the medium. If the absorption coefficient of fluorescence by the medium is γ, then at distance r, the fluorescence intensity decays as

$$I(r) = I_s \cdot e^{-\gamma r} \tag{2}$$

where r, I_s and I have the same meaning as in Eq. (1).

Considering the combined effect on fluorescence intensity by distance and absorption of the transmission medium, Eqs. (1) and (2) can be approximated by combining them as

$$I(r) = I_s \cdot e^{-\gamma r^2} \tag{3}$$

Next, the attraction model between fireflies must be determined. According to the previous assumption, the degree of attraction between two fireflies is proportional to their fluorescence intensity, so the attraction model can be defined by Eq. (3) as

$$\beta(r) = \beta_0 \cdot e^{-\gamma r^2} \tag{4}$$

where γ and r have their meanings in Eq. (3), β is the attraction between two fireflies, and β_0 is the attraction when the distance between two fireflies is zero, i.e., their maximum attraction.

Based on the above three models, when the fluorescence intensity of firefly i is lower than that of firefly j, then firefly i will be attracted to firefly j, i.e., firefly i will move toward firefly j so as to realize a position update,

$$\begin{aligned} x_i^k(t+1) = {}& x_i^k(t) + \beta_{ij}(t) \cdot (x_j^k(t) - x_i^k(t)) \\ & + \alpha(t) \cdot (rand_{ij}^k(t) - 0.5) \end{aligned} \tag{5}$$

$$\beta_{ij}(t) = \beta_0 \cdot e^{-\gamma r_{ij}^2(t)} \tag{6}$$

$$r_{ij}(t) = \|x_j(t) - x_i(t)\| = \sqrt{\sum_{k=1}^{D} (x_j^k(t) - x_i^k(t))^2} \tag{7}$$

where $x_i^k(t)$ and $x_j^k(t)$ are the positions of fireflies i and j, respectively, in the kth dimension of the tth iteration; $r_{ij}(t)$ is the distance between fireflies i and j in the tth iteration; D is the maximum dimension of the problem space; $rand$ is a random number uniformly distributed in $[0, 1]$; and α is a random factor. The evolution equation of the firefly position consisting of Eqs. (5)–(7) is the FA.

The position update equation of the firefly can be divided into three parts, where $x_i^k(t)$ is the flight inertia of the firefly itself; $\beta_{ij}(t) \cdot (x_j^k(t) - x_i^k(t))$ is the motion of firefly i by the attraction of firefly j, which is equivalent to the convergence behavior of the firefly in the evolutionary process; and $\alpha(t)\cdot(rand_{ij}^k(t)-0.5)$ is a random search term that is completely independent of fireflies i and j, by which a random disturbance can be generated to make a firefly reach a new search position.

Yang [1,3] proposed that when implementing and applying FA, $\beta_0 = 1$; the constant γ, where $\gamma \in [0.01, 100]$, is generally set to 1; and the constant α, where $\alpha \in [0,1]$, is generally set to 0.5.

If $\gamma = 0$, i.e., the medium does not absorb the fluorescence intensity, and the absorption coefficient $\beta = \beta_0 = 1$, then the position update equation of the firefly is

$$x_i^k(t+1) = x_j^k(t) + \alpha(t) \cdot (rand_{ij}^k(t) - 0.5) \tag{8}$$

If $\gamma \rightarrow \infty$, i.e., the medium completely absorbs the fluorescence and the absorption coefficient $\beta = 0$, then the position update equation of the firefly is

$$x_i^k(t+1) = x_i^k(t) + \alpha(t) \cdot (rand_{ij}^k(t) - 0.5) \tag{9}$$

From equations (5), (8), and (9), we can see that the random search term is an important component of the firefly position update regardless of whether the fluorescence is absorbed, and the ability of the random search is affected by the random factor α, so the study of the random factor can be used to improve the FA's search ability, which we do below. The algorithm flow of FA is shown in Fig. 1.

3 Research on the Random Factor Control Method of FA

3.1 Problem Analysis

As discussed in Sect. 2.2, the selection and control method of the random factor α in FA affects the optimization performance of the algorithm. The FA in the literature has a fixed value, but it varies. From Eqs. (5), (6), and (7), it can be seen that at the early stage of the operation of the algorithm, the distance between fireflies is large, and the attraction coefficient is small. At this point, the fireflies are expected to be highly random, which can make the algorithm optimize in a large search range; as the swarm evolves, the distance between fireflies gradually decreases, and the attraction coefficient gradually increases, which enables the algorithm to gradually converge, and the randomness of fireflies should also be reduced at this point to speed up convergence and improve the accuracy of the solution.

A two-dimensional multimodal function, whose mathematical expression is

$$\begin{aligned} y = &-(e^{(-(x-4)^2-(y-4)^2)} + e^{(-(x+4)^2-(y-4)^2)} \\ &+ 2 \cdot e^{(-x^2-(y+4)^2)} + 2 \cdot e^{(-x^2-y^2)}) \end{aligned} \tag{10}$$

is used to verify the above results. In the domain $[-5, 5]$, it has two positions with a global minimum of -2, at $(0, 0)$ and $(0, -4)$, and two with a local minimum of -1, at $(-4, 4)$ and $(4, 4)$.

We chose four ways to control the random factor α of FA. Two of these are to fix the value of α at 0.5 and 0.05, which is consistent with most of the literature; the other two are to set the values of α to 0.5 and 0.05, decreasing linearly with the number of iterations to zero. The settings of the experiments are shown in Table 1.

We recorded the positions of each firefly at the initialization, 20 iterations, 40 iterations, and the end of the algorithm, as shown in Figs. 2, 3, 4 and 5, respectively, from which we can see that the random factor with decreasing control can better control the convergence behavior of the algorithm.

Table 1. Parameter settings for the experiments on α

Population size	20	Control method 1	$\alpha = 0.5$
Maximum iteration	50	Control method 2	$\alpha = 0.05$
Maximum absorption coefficient	$\beta_0 = 1$	Control method 3	$\alpha = 0.5 \to 0$
Absorption coefficient	$\lambda = 1$	Control method 4	$\alpha = 0.05 \to 0$

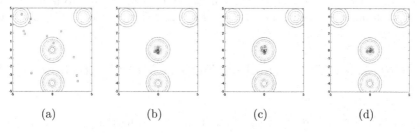

(a)   (b)   (c)   (d)

Fig. 1. $\alpha = 0.05$, positions of the population on different iterations (a) $t = 0$ (b) $t = 20$ (c) $t = 40$ (d) $t = 50$

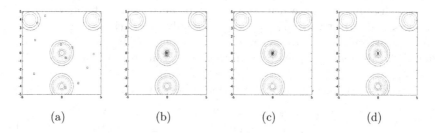

(a)   (b)   (c)   (d)

Fig. 2. $\alpha = 0.05 \to 0$, positions of the population on different iterations (a) $t = 0$ (b) $t = 20$ (c) $t = 40$ (d) $t = 50$

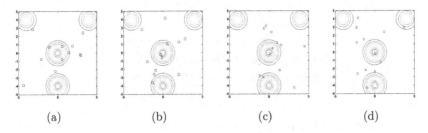

(a)   (b)   (c)   (d)

Fig. 3. $\alpha = 0.5$, positions of the population on different iterations (a) $t = 0$ (b) $t = 20$ (c) $t = 40$ (d) $t = 50$

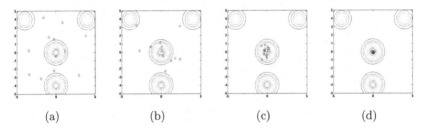

(a)   (b)   (c)   (d)

Fig. 4. $\alpha = 0.5 \to 0$, positions of the population on different iterations (a) $t = 0$ (b) $t = 20$ (c) $t = 40$ (d) $t = 50$

3.2   New Control Method for the Random Factor

The analysis and experimental results in Sect. 3.1 show the effect of the decreasing random factor α with iteration on the convergence process and accuracy of the solution. Therefore, for the random factor, we propose a control method that decreases geometrically, i.e.,

$$\alpha(t+1) = k \cdot \alpha(t), \alpha(0) = 0.5 \tag{11}$$

where t is the current number of iterations, and k is the common ratio. It is found from a previous study that a k value in the interval $[0.97, 0.998]$ can be optimized for the standard benchmark function to obtain more reasonable results. In this paper, the 20 sets of common ratios in Table 2 are used to investigate the optimization performance of FA. The effect of different k values on the random factor values depends on their rate of decrease. Figure 6 shows the decreasing curves for four k values, and the rate of decrease of the random factor decreases as k increases.

Table 2. Values of k

0.97	0.98	0.99	0.9901	0.9902
0.9903	0.9904	0.9905	0.9906	0.9907
0.9908	0.9909	0.991	0.992	0.993
0.994	0.995	0.996	0.997	0.998

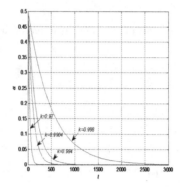

Fig. 5. Values of random factor on different values of k

4　Experimental Results

4.1　Experiment Design

Nine commonly used standard benchmark functions were used to analyze the effect of the proposed control method on the optimization ability of FA, and their mathematical expressions, search ranges, and global optimum values are listed in Table 3. All the standard benchmark functions were tested using FA and the improved FA with the proposed geometrically decreasing random factor. Each algorithm was randomly run 100 times for each function. The dimension of the benchmark function was 30, the population size of the algorithm was 20, the maximum number of iterations was 3000, the maximum attraction of the algorithm $\beta_0 = 1$, and the absorption coefficient $\lambda = 1$. The optimal solution obtained from each run was recorded, and the mean value of the optimal solutions after 100 runs was obtained, which is presented in Table 4 together with the standard variance statistics. The data in the first row corresponding to each algorithm in Table 4 are the mean values of the optimal solutions, and the data in the second row in parentheses are their standard variances.

Among them, $y_i = 1 + \frac{1}{4}(x_i+1)$, $u(x_i, a, k, m) = \begin{cases} k(x_i - a)^m & x_i > a \\ 0 & -a \le x_i \le a \\ k(-x_i - a)^m & x_i < -a \end{cases}$

Table 3. Nine benchmark functions

Functions	Search space	Global optimum
$f_1(x) = \sum_{i=1}^{D} x_i^2$	± 100	0
$f_2(x) = \sum_{i=1}^{D} \left(\sum_{j=1}^{i} x_j \right)^2$	± 100	0
$f_3(x) = \sum_{i=1}^{D} [100(x_{i+1} - x_i^2) + (x_i - 1)^2]$	± 30	0
$f_4(x) = \sum_{i=1}^{D} -x_i \sin(\sqrt{|x_i|})$	± 500	$-418.98D$
$f_5(x) = \sum_{i=1}^{D} [x_i^2 - 10\cos(2\pi x_i) + 10]$	± 5.12	0
$f_6(x) = -20\exp(-0.2\sqrt{(\frac{1}{D}\sum_{i=1}^{D} x_i^2)} - \exp(\frac{1}{D}\sum_{i=1}^{D} \cos 2\pi x_i) + 20 + e$	± 32	0
$f_7(x) = \frac{1}{4000}\sum_{i=1}^{D} x_i^2 - \prod_{i=1}^{D} \cos(\frac{x_i}{\sqrt{i}}) + 1$	± 600	0
$f_8(x) = \frac{\pi}{D}\{10\sin^2(\pi y_1) + \sum_{i=1}^{D-1} (y_i - 1)^2[1 + 10\sin^2(\pi y_{i+1})] + (y_D - 1)^2\}$ $+ \sum_{i=1}^{D} u(x_i, 10, 100, 4)$	± 50	0
$f_9(x) = 0.1\{\sin^2(3\pi x_1) + \sum_{i=1}^{D-1} \frac{(x_i - 1)^2\{1 + \sin^2(3\pi x_{i+1})\}}{+(x_D - 1)^2\{1 + \sin^2(2\pi x_D)\}} \}$ $+ \sum_{i=1}^{D} u(x_i, 5, 100, 4)$	± 50	0

4.2 Results Analysis

To determine whether a significant difference exists in the optimization performance of the algorithm's random factors when different common ratios are used,
we first tested for a significant difference between the algorithm's means for each
benchmark function using analysis of variance (ANOVA) at $p < 0.05$. The calculated F-values are given in the last row of Table 4. By querying the F-statistics
table and comparing them, it is clear that the algorithms differ significantly for
each benchmark function, indicating that the random factor of FA had an impact
on the performance of the algorithm after the new control method was adopted.
Therefore, it is necessary to further clarify the advantages and disadvantages of
the algorithms in terms of optimization performance at different common ratios.
The step-up method [11] was used to perform multiple comparisons to obtain the
priority relationship of the algorithm in each benchmark function. Specifically,
the algorithms were ranked in increasing order according to the mean values
in Table 4. The scoring of all the algorithms was set to 1; then the algorithms
were compared pairwise from the smallest two mean values, and if there was
a significant difference, the score of the algorithm with the larger mean value
was increased by 1. Otherwise, there was no change to the score, and the two
algorithms were included in the same group. After several pairwise comparisons,
the scoring results of each algorithm in each test function were obtained, and
the scoring results of each algorithm in each benchmark function were summed
to obtain the total score of each algorithm. The smaller the score the better the
overall optimization performance of the algorithm. The final scores are listed in
Table 5.

From the scores in Table 5, it can be seen that the optimization performance
of FA and improved FA showed significant differences in the optimal solution of

Table 4. Experimental results for nine benchmark functions (average values and standard deviations)

	f_1	f_2	f_3	f_4	f_5	f_6	f_7	f_8	f_9
FA	3.10E−04	2.11E−02	59.87	−7977.64	64.26	4.17E−03	4.47E−03	1.04E−03	1.44E−03
	(4.87E−05)	(7.44E−03)	(78.82)	(728.52)	(19.96)	(2.91E−04)	(6.02E−03)	(1.04E−02)	(3.72E−03)
$k = 0.97$	2.62E−75	3896.55	333.07	−7068.08	66.7	4.52E−02	1.38E−03	8.72E−03	3.50E−03
	(5.30E−76)	(1255.82)	(606.02)	(749.83)	(21.45)	(1.84E−01)	(3.27E−03)	(3.00E−02)	(5.57E−03)
$k = 0.98$	1.07E−48	1667.73	126.76	−7425.57	74.02	1.86E−02	4.43E−03	1.04E−02	3.06E−03
	(1.97E−49)	(821.48)	(240.61)	(738.13)	(21.55)	(1.32E−01)	(6.64E−03)	(3.14E−02)	(5.39E−03)
$k = 0.99$	2.33E−22	20.17	129.06	−7605.18	70.64	3.46E−12	3.55E−03	2.07E−03	1.98E−03
	(3.40E−23)	(22.47)	(262.39)	(704.26)	(21.99)	(3.62E−13)	(6.04E−03)	(1.47E−02)	(4.26E−03)
$k = 0.9901$	4.09E−22	21.54	140.22	−7643.76	69.89	4.81E−12	3.84E−03	1.46E−24	2.64E−03
	(6.96E−23)	(28.59)	(332.64)	(633.46)	(26.11)	(4.53E−13)	(5.81E−03)	(3.65E−25)	(4.74E−03)
$k = 0.9902$	7.68E−22	22.47	76.32	−7649.37	69.43	6.53E−12	2.37E−03	2.07E−03	1.52E−03
	(1.42E−22)	(36.26)	(108.63)	(727.43)	(23.4)	(4.92E−13)	(4.53E−03)	(1.47E−02)	(4.36E−03)
$k = 0.9903$	1.44E−21	16.38	137.48	−7533.51	66.52	8.77E−12	2.42E−03	4.80E−24	2.64E−03
	(2.41E−22)	(26.59)	(336.06)	(745.52)	(19.8)	(8.83E−13)	(4.55E−03)	(9.78E−25)	(4.74E−03)
$k = 0.9904$	2.52E−21	13.15	90.23	−7631.87	67.54	1.20E−11	3.06E−03	8.34E−24	1.74E−03
	(5.08E−22)	(16.42)	(172.94)	(673.97)	(21.56)	(1.17E−12)	(4.99E−03)	(2.07E−24)	(4.55E−03)
$k = 0.9905$	4.80E−21	13.71	78.83	−7592.86	69.29	1.59E−11	4.93E−03	4.15E−03	2.64E−03
	(8.16E−22)	(18.54)	(101.42)	(721.86)	(21.47)	(1.27E−12)	(5.52E−03)	(2.05E−02)	(4.74E−03)
$k = 0.9906$	8.38E−21	8.38	123.36	−7711.15	68.63	2.16E−11	4.93E−03	6.22E−03	2.20E−03
	(1.62E−21)	(14.77)	(204.99)	(700.13)	(20.59)	(1.64E−12)	(5.52E−03)	(2.49E−02)	(4.44E−03)
$k = 0.9907$	1.51E−20	13.04	190.31	−7817.81	68.59	2.93E−11	3.45E−03	2.07E−03	2.84E−03
	(2.16E−21)	(20.29)	(295.75)	(826.79)	(21.41)	(2.62E−12)	(5.95E−03)	(1.47E−02)	(5.28E−03)
$k = 0.9908$	2.91E−20	11.17	138.5	−7557.43	67.42	4.04E−11	4.04E−03	9.71E−23	2.60E−03
	(4.19E−21)	(22.65)	(281.6)	(702.82)	(21.77)	(2.94E−12)	(5.58E−03)	(2.44E−23)	(5.56E−03)
$k = 0.9909$	5.36E−20	7.49	164.25	−7722.41	73.55	5.33E−11	2.46E−03	4.15E−03	2.20E−03
	(9.68E−21)	(11.88)	(347.07)	(828.57)	(26.85)	(4.32E−12)	(4.37E−03)	(2.05E−02)	(4.44E−03)
$k = 0.991$	9.55E−20	7.09	128.84	−−.12	66.14	7.29E−11	3.74E−03	2.99E−22	2.86E−03
	(1.56E−20)	(12.71)	(281.43)	(773.43)	(17.84)	(5.75E−12)	(6.14E−03)	(5.58E−23)	(4.87E−03)
$k = 0.992$	3.95E−17	1.08	126.75	−7581.21	65.85	1.49E−09	2.86E−03	2.07E−03	2.20E−03
	(7.78E−18)	(3.87)	(171.99)	(744.42)	(22.37)	(1.21E−10)	(6.27E−03)	(1.47E−02)	(4.44E−03)
$k = 0.993$	1.60E−14	1.88E−02	108.23	−7765.53	60.63	2.92E−08	4.98E−03	5.03E−17	2.64E−03
	(2.29E−15)	(1.33E−01)	(213.89)	(704.13)	(15.74)	(2.87E−09)	(6.28E−03)	(8.75E−18)	(4.74E−03)
$k = 0.994$	6.25E−12	1.07E−10	108.45	−7816.91	63.92	5.80E−07	3.45E−03	4.15E−03	1.98E−03
	(1.11E−12)	(3.48E−11)	(198.8)	(734.81)	(21.34)	(4.96E−08)	(6.86E−03)	(2.05E−02)	(4.26E−03)
$k = 0.995$	2.44E−09	2.75E−08	45.33	−7759	65.17	1.17E−05	5.32E−03	2.07E−03	1.32E−03
	(3.90E−10)	(8.67E−09)	(43.62)	(818.12)	(19.1)	(8.15E−07)	(6.65E−03)	(1.47E−02)	(3.61E−03)
$k = 0.996$	9.79E−07	8.35E−06	66.27	−7917.3	72.09	2.31E−04	3.06E−03	2.68E−09	4.40E−04
	(1.37E−07)	(2.88E−06)	(84.41)	(704.1)	(20.07)	(1.86E−05)	(5.77E−03)	(5.23E−10)	(2.17E−03)
$k = 0.997$	3.77E−04	2.52E−03	42.62	−8257.41	63.8	4.58E−03	5.92E−03	1.02E−06	1.55E−03
	(5.62E−05)	(9.82E−04)	(39.71)	(729.71)	(22.41)	(3.70E−04)	(7.92E−03)	(1.70E−07)	(3.85E−03)
$k = 0.998$	1.30E−01	6.73E−01	58.22	−8159.73	66.36	1.12E−01	3.51E−01	3.54E−04	7.61E−03
	(1.81E−02)	(1.78E−01)	(61.42)	(801.51)	(19.91)	(8.27E−03)	(3.97E−02)	(6.67E−05)	(4.09E−03)
F	102988.23	15264.8	124.41	219.25	46.25	549.74	104578.97	70.29	176.32

f_1, f_2, f_6, and f_8, with the performance of improved FA better than that of FA. In the optimal solution of other functions, the improved FA showed no improvement for the solution of f_3, and obtained better optimization results than FA for f_4, f_5, f_7, and f_9. The improved FA had better optimization results than FA. Overall, when the coefficients of the geometric sequence were 0.9902, 0.9903, and 0.9904, the corresponding improved FA could achieve the best combined optimization results among all nine functions. Therefore, the optimization performance of FA with the decreasing geometric sequence was improved by the random factor control method. The new control method used for the random factor of FA only performs a simple constant multiplication operation on the random factor;

Table 5. Ranking of FA and improved FA based on ANOVA

	f_1	f_2	f_3	f_4	f_5	f_6	f_7	f_8	f_9	
FA	19	=4	=1	=3	=1	17	=12	=9	=2	68
k = 0.97	1	21	21	21	=1	20	=1	=9	=2	97
k = 0.98	2	20	=6	=12	=18	19	=12	=9	=2	100
k = 0.99	3	17	=6	=12	18	1	=1	=9	=2	69
k = 0.9901	4	18	=6	=12	=1	2	=12	1	=2	58
k = 0.9902	5	19	=6	=3	=1	3	=1	=9	=2	**49**
k = 0.9903	6	16	=6	=12	=1	4	=1	2	=2	50
k = 0.9904	7	14	=6	=12	=1	5	=1	3	=2	51
k = 0.9905	8	15	=6	=12	=1	6	=12	=9	=2	71
k = 0.9906	9	11	=6	=3	=1	7	=12	=9	=2	60
k = 0.9907	10	13	20	=3	=1	8	=1	=9	=2	67
k = 0.9908	11	12	=6	=12	=1	9	=12	4	=2	69
k = 0.9909	12	10	=6	=3	=18	10	=1	=9	=2	71
k = 0.991	13	9	=6	=12	=1	11	=1	5	=2	60
k = 0.992	14	8	=6	=12	=1	12	=1	=9	=2	65
k = 0.993	15	4	=6	=3	=1	13	=12	6	=2	62
k = 0.994	16	1	=6	=3	=1	14	=1	=9	=2	53
k = 0.995	17	2	=1	=3	=1	15	=12	=9	=2	62
k = 0.996	18	3	=1	=3	=18	16	=1	7	1	68
k = 0.997	20	=4	=1	=1	=1	18	=12	8	=2	67
k = 0.998	21	7	=1	=1	=1	21	21	=9	21	103

so, this improvement does not increase the computational complexity of the algorithm.

4.3 Comparison with Other Decreasing Control Methods

We compare the optimization performance using linearly decreasing and exponentially decreasing control methods with the control method using geometric decreases in the previous section. The mathematical form of these two control methods is

$$\alpha(t) = (\alpha_{\max} - \alpha_{\min}) \cdot (T - t)/T + \alpha_{\min} \tag{12}$$

$$\alpha(t) = \alpha_{\min} \cdot \left(\frac{\alpha_{\max}}{\alpha_{\min}}\right)^{(1/(1+10 \cdot \frac{t}{T}))} \tag{13}$$

where t is the current number of iterations, T is the maximum number of iterations, $\alpha_{\max} = 0.5$, and $\alpha_{\min} = 0$. Figure 6 depicts the graphs of the three control methods.

These two control methods were applied to FA, and the same parameters as in Sect. 4.2 were used to optimally solve the nine benchmark functions. The mean and standard deviation of the optimal solutions obtained after 100 random runs are shown in Table 6, from which shows the improved FA with a common ratio of 0.9902 achieves better optimization results than the other two control methods for the six benchmark functions, and shows a stronger optimization capability.

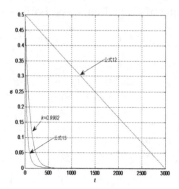

Fig. 6. Different decreasing control methods of k

Table 6. Experimental results based on three different control methods

	f_1	f_2	f_3	f_4	f_5	f_6	f_7	f_8	f_9
k $=0.9902$	**7.68E−22**	22.47	76.32	−7649.37	**69.43**	**6.53E−12**	**2.37E−03**	**2.07E−03**	**1.52E−03**
	(1.42E−22)	(36.26)	(108.63)	(727.43)	**(23.4)**	**(4.92E−13)**	**(4.53E−03)**	**(1.47E−02)**	**(4.36E−03)**
Eq. (12)	9.20E−04	**2.66E−03**	48.39	−7531.65	72.17	2.56E−02	6.53E−03	6.22E−03	1.79E−03
	(1.03E−04)	**(6.27E−04)**	**(67.12)**	(762.15)	(21.87)	(1.31E−01)	(7.08E−03)	(2.49E−02)	(4.07E−03)
Eq. (13)	1.76E−01	1.45E+02	286.1	**−7908.6**	75.29	2.56E−01	3.77E−01	2.79E−03	4.19E−02
	(5.46E−02)	(4.91E+01)	(551.3)	**(821.97)**	(22.42)	(1.45E−01)	(1.13E−01)	(1.25E−03)	(1.64E−02)

Table 7. Comparison among FA and PSO with variants

	f_1	f_2	f_3	f_4	f_5	f_6	f_7	f_8	f_9
FA with	7.68E−22	22.47	76.32	−7649.37	69.43	**6.53E−12**	**2.37E−03**	**2.07E−03**	**1.52E−03**
$k = 0.9902$	(1.42E−22)	(36.26)	(108.63)	(727.43)	(23.4)	**(4.92E−13)**	**(4.53E−03)**	**(1.47E−02)**	**(4.36E−03)**
FIPS	**2.81E−46**	10.9	39.76	−10445.25	54.96	2.27E−01	4.64E−03	3.94E−02	8.19E−02
	(1.30E−45)	(11.56)	(41.32)	(1038.95)	(14.92)	(4.68E−01)	(1.12E−02)	(7.52E−02)	(5.10E−01)
GBBPSO	2.00E+02	13809.09	11515.32	−8796.74	110.83	7.67E+00	5.06E+00	6.43E−02	1.10E−01
	(1.41E+03)	(8198.37)	(29305.68)	(622.49)	(36.46)	(8.85E+00)	(1.73E+01)	(9.34E−02)	(3.79E−01)
PSO_CO	3.51E−38	**0.05**	**27.78**	−18485.21	68.57	2.78E+00	9.56E−02	9.12E−02	1.23E−01
	(1.07E−37)	**(0.13)**	**(28.35)**	(2797.71)	(18.74)	(1.28E+00)	(2.44E−01)	(1.21E−01)	(5.26E−01)
PSO_IN	1.96E−13	766.51	88.42	**−33603.31**	**45.69**	4.87E−02	1.83E−02	7.94E+01	6.15E−03
	(3.47E−13)	(1076)	(92.11)	**(4117.75)**	**(32.28)**	(2.48E−01)	(2.76E−02)	(5.61E+02)	(1.04E−02)
PSO_LB	8.23E−10	2084.05	78.01	−31596.47	49.45	2.80E−01	1.17E−02	1.91E−02	3.75E−03
	(9.40E−10)	(952.14)	(52.5)	(3970.77)	(11.49)	(6.16E−01)	(1.59E−02)	(4.56E−02)	(9.32E−03)
SPSO	3.54E−26	41.51	37.4	−16766.27	63.96	1.69E−01	6.60E−03	2.90E−02	7.28E−02
	(4.92E−26)	(34.26)	(30.56)	(2386.1)	(14.44)	(4.45E−01)	(1.02E−02)	(5.94E−02)	(5.09E−01)

Table 8. Ranking of FA and the other compared algorithms

	f_1	f_2	f_3	f_4	f_5	f_6	f_7	f_8	f_9	Total
FA with k $=0.9902$	4	3	4	7	4	1	=1	1	1	**26**
FIPS	1	2	3	5	3	4	=1	4	=3	**26**
GBBPSO	6	7	7	6	7	7	7	5	=3	55
PSO_CO	2	1	1	3	4	6	6	6	=3	32
PSO_IN	5	5	6	1	1	2	5	6	=3	34
PSO_LB	6	6	5	2	1	5	4	2	2	33
SPSO	3	4	2	4	4	3	3	3	=3	29

4.4 Performance Comparison with Other Swarm Intelligence Algorithms

We compared FA with other PSO algorithms, including standard PSO (SPSO) [12], PSO with inertia weight (PSO-In) [13], PSO with constriction factor (PSO-Co) [14], Gaussian barE−bones PSO (GBBPSO) [15], PSO with lbest (PSO-Lb) [16], and fully-informed PSO (FIPS) [16], for optimization performance. These algorithms were also used to optimize the nine benchmark functions in 4.1, with the same experimental parameters as in Sect. 4.1. The experimental results are given in Table 7. The performance of the seven algorithms was scored and analyzed using the same statistical method as in Sect. 4.2, and the results are presented in Table 8. Tables 7 and 8 show that the combined optimization performance of the improved FA with a common ratio of 0.9902 is close to that of the FIPS optimization algorithm, and it can achieve better optimization results than several other algorithms.

5 Conclusion

We first analyzed the design idea and mathematical model of the firefly algorithm. We pointed out that the random search term of the algorithm is an important factor affecting optimization performance. Through numerical experiments, we analyzed the relationship between the optimization performance of an algorithm and the way the random factor takes values. Based on those results, we designed a method to control the values of the random factor by geometrically decreasing them. Using different common ratios for FA, we compared the optimization performance of nine standard benchmark functions and analyzed the optimization results by ANOVA and step-up statistical methods. The analysis results show that the improved FA has better optimization ability. We also compared linearly and exponentially decreasing controlling values for the random factor with geometrically decreasing it. The results of our numerical experiments show that the geometric method achieved better optimization results in most tested functions. The performance of the improved FA was compared with that of the PSO and improved PSO algorithms, and the results show that the improved FA was able to achieve better optimization results. In conclusion, the proposed geometric decreasing of controlling values for the FA random factor can improve the optimization effect of FA and is a feasible control method.

References

1. Yang, X.-S.: Firefly algorithms for multimodal optimization. In: Watanabe, O., Zeugmann, T. (eds.) Stochastic Algorithms: Foundations and Applications, pp. 169–178. Springer, Heidelberg (2009). https://doi.org/10.1007/978-3-642-04944-6_14

2. Yang, X.-S.: Nature-Inspired Metaheuristic Algorithms. Luniver Press, UK (2008)

3. Yang, X.-S.: Firefly algorithm, lévy flights and global optimization. In: Bramer, M., Ellis, R., Petridis, M. (eds.) Research and Development in Intelligent Systems XXVI, pp. 209–218. Springer, Heidelberg (2010). https://doi.org/10.1007/978-1-84882-983-1_15

4. Farahani, S.M., Abshouri, A.A., Nasiri, B., Meybodi, M.R.: A Gaussian firefly algorithm. Int. J. Mach. Learn. Comput. 1(5), 448–453 (2011)

5. Senthilnath, J., Omkar, S.N., Mani, V.: Clustering using firefly algorithm: performance study. Swarm Evol. Comput. 1, 164–171 (2011)

6. Yang, X.-S., Hosseini, S.S.S., Gandomi, A.H.: Firefly Algorithm for solving nonconvex economic dispatch problems with valve loading effect. Appl. Soft Comput. 12, 1180–1186 (2012)

7. Gandomi, A.H., Yang, X.-S., Talatahari, S., Alavi, A.H.: Firefly algorithm with chaos. Commun. Nonlinear Sci. Numer. Simul. 18(1), 89–98 (2012)

8. Gandomi, A.H., Yang, X.-S., Alavi, A.H.: Mixed variable structural optimization using Firefly Algorithm. Comput. Struct. 89, 2325–2336 (2011)

9. Abshouri, A.A., Meybodi, M.R.: New firefly algorithm based on multi swarm & learning automata in dynamic environments. In: Proceedings of the 5th Indian International Conference on Artificial Intelligence, pp. 1–5. IEEE (2011)

10. Horng, M.-H.: Vector quantization using the firefly algorithm for image compression. Expert Syst. Appl. 39, 1078–1091 (2012)

11. Dunnett, C.W., Tamhane, A.C.: A step-up multiple test procedure. J. Am. Stat. Assoc. 87(417), 162–170 (1992)

12. Bratton, D., Kennedy, J.: Defining a standard for particle swarm optimization. In: Proceedings of the 2007 IEEE Swarm Intelligence Symposium, pp. 120–127. IEEE, Honolulu (2007)

13. Shi, Y., Eberhart, R.C.: A modified particle swarm optimizer. In: Proceedings of the 1998 IEEE International Conference on Evolutionary Computation, pp. 69–73. IEEE, Anchorage (1998)

14. Clerc, M., Kennedy, J.: The particle swarm-explosion, stability and convergence in a multidimensional complex space. IEEE Trans. Evol. Comput. 6, 58–73 (2002)

15. Kennedy, J.: Probability and dynamics in the particle swarm. In: Proceedings of the 2004 Congress on Evolutionary Computation, pp. 340–347. IEEE, Portland (2004)

16. Mendes, R., Kennedy, J., Neves, J.: The fully informed particle swarm: simpler, maybe better. IEEE Trans. Evol. Comput. 2004(8), 204–210 (2004)

17. Shan, J., Pan, J.S., Chang, C.K., Chu, S.C., Zheng, S.G.: A distributed parallel firefly algorithm with communication strategies and its application for the control of variable pitch wind turbine. ISA Trans. (2021, in press)

18. Peng, H., Zhu, W., Deng, C., Wu, Z.: Enhancing firefly algorithm with courtship learning. Inf. Sci. 2021(543), 18–42 (2021)

19. Tian, M., Bo, Y., Chen, Z., Wu, P., Yue, C.: A new improved firefly clustering algorithm for SMC-PHD filter. Appl. Soft Comput. 2019(85), 105840 (2019)

20. Dhal, K.G., Das, A., Ray, S., Gálvez, J.: Randomly attracted rough firefly algorithm for histogram based fuzzy image clustering. Knowl.-Based Syst. 216 (2021)

21. Trachanatzi, D., Rigakis, M., Marinaki, M., Marinakis, Y.: A firefly algorithm for the environmental prize-collecting vehicle routing problem. Swarm Evol. Comput. 57 (2020)

22. Altabeeb, A.M., Mohsen, A.M., Ghallab, A.: An improved hybrid firefly algorithm for capacitated vehicle routing problem. Appl. Soft Comput. 84 (2019)

23. Ariyaratne, M.K.A., Fernando, T.G.I., Weerakoon, S.: Solving systems of nonlinear equations using a modified firefly algorithm (MODFA). Swarm Evol. Comput. **48**, 72–92 (2019)
24. Yelghi, A., Köse, C.: A modified firefly algorithm for global minimum optimization. Appl. Soft Comput. **62**, 29–44 (2018)
25. Wang, H., et al.: A hybrid multi-objective firefly algorithm for big data optimization. Appl. Soft Comput. **69**, 806–815 (2018)
26. Zhang, Y., Song, X.-F., Gong, D.-W.: A return-cost-based binary firefly algorithm for feature selection. Inf. Sci. **418–419**, 561–574 (2017)
27. He, L., Huang, S.: Modified firefly algorithm based multilevel thresholding for color image segmentation. Neurocomputing **240**, 152–174 (2017)
28. Wang, H., et al.: Firefly algorithm with neighborhood attraction. Inf. Sci. **382–383** (2017)
29. Kalantzis, G., Shang, C., Lei, Y., Leventouri, T.: Investigations of a GPU-based levy-firefly algorithm for constrained optimization of radiation therapy treatment planning. Swarm Evol. Comput. **26**, 191–201 (2016)
30. Xiao, L., Shao, W., Liang, T., Wang, C.: A combined model based on multiple seasonal patterns and modified firefly algorithm for electrical load forecasting. Appl. Energy **167**, 135–153 (2016)
31. Lei, X., Wang, F., Wu, F.-X., Zhang, A., Pedrycz, W.: Protein complex identification through Markov clustering with firefly algorithm on dynamic protein-protein interaction networks. Inf. Sci. **329**, 303–316 (2016)

Metaheuristic Optimization on Tensor-Type Solution via Swarm Intelligence and Its Application in the Profit Optimization in Designing Selling Scheme

Frederick Kin Hing Phoa[1]([✉]) [ID], Hsin-Ping Liu[2],
Yun-Heh (Jessica) Chen-Burger[3], and Shau-Ping Lin[2] [ID]

[1] Institute of Statistical Science, Academia Sinica, Taipei 115, Taiwan
fredphoa@stat.sinica.edu.tw
[2] National Taiwan University, Taipei 106, Taiwan
[3] Heriot-Watt University, Edinburgh EH14 4AS, UK

Abstract. Nature-inspired metaheuristic optimization has been widely used in many problems in industry and scientific investigations, but their applications in designing selling scheme are rare because the solution space in this kind of problems is usually high-dimensional, and their constraints are sometimes cross-dimensional. Recently, the Swarm Intelligence Based (SIB) method is proposed for problems in discrete domains, and it is widely applied in many mathematical and statistical problems that common metaheuristic methods seldom approach. In this work, we introduce an extension of the SIB method that handles solutions with many dimensions, or tensor solution in mathematics. We further speed up our method by implementing our algorithm with the use of CPU parallelization. We then apply this extended framework to real applications in designing selling scheme, showing that our proposed method helps to increase the profit of a selling scheme compared to those suggested by traditional methods.

Keywords: Swarm intelligence · Tensor-type particle · CPU parallelization · Selling scheme

1 Introduction

Inspired by the behavior of biological systems and physical or chemical systems in nature [1], nature-inspired metaheuristic algorithms have been widely recognized as a powerful tool for optimization problems that are usually extremely complex

This work is partially supported by the Academia Sinica grant number AS-TP-109-M07 and the Ministry of Science and Technology (Taiwan) grant numbers 107-2118-M-001-011-MY3 and 109-2321-B-001-013.

© Springer Nature Switzerland AG 2021
Y. Tan and Y. Shi (Eds.): ICSI 2021, LNCS 12689, pp. 72–82, 2021.
https://doi.org/10.1007/978-3-030-78743-1_7

and challenging in the real world. Swarm intelligence [2], which describes a collective intelligent behavior of self-organized and decentralized systems, is a major class of metaheuristics. Some well-known algorithms, such as Genetic Algorithms (GA) [3], Artificial Bee Colony [4], Particle Swarm Optimization (PSO) [5], the Swarm Intelligence Based (SIB) method [6], and many others, belong to this algorithm family. Among all, PSO is widely used in engineering problems and some scientific investigations in the past decades. It has been well-designed for solving high-dimensional optimization problems in various fields. [7] pointed out four distinctive features for the popularity of the use of PSO among engineers. There are many versions and variants of PSO after its first introduction in [8], we denote PSO as the traditional framework of PSO mentioned in [8] for the rest of this paper unless specified.

Similar to many metaheuristics, PSO works well in a continuous domain as its velocity and position are well-defined with physical meanings, but it may not be the best candidate for problems with solutions in a non-continuous domain, which is not necessarily a discrete domain but some domains with "holes". Such optimization methods are common in mathematics and statistics, especially when solutions are in the matrix form and full of categorical variables like choices or symbols. Even though [7] and many others suggest to tackle thiese discrete scenario via a simple round-off, it is not trivial to verify if the resulting solution is truely optimal. This leads to an introduction of the Swarm Intelligence Based (SIB) method proposed in [6] that works perfectly in a wide range of discrete optimization problems, such as the constructions of optimal experimental designs [9], the uniform distribution of testing points [10], target localization [11], supercomputing scheduling [12], hot spot determination [13], and many others. Details will be briefly reviewed in the next section.

Traditionally, a solution can be just a zero-dimensional number, an one-dimensional vector, or at most a two-dimensional matrix. A solution that has dimensions more than two is rare because the search becomes difficult in a huge solution domain, and the higher the dimensions, the larger the solution domain. As science and technology have advanced, practitioners attempt to perform complex optimization problems, and the computing power of searching high-dimensional solutions is available in the era of artificial intelligence. Not only do high-dimensional solutions test the feasibility of computation in both hardware and software, but additional cross-dimensional constraints, like some interactive quantities among several dimensions, create additional complexity in the optimization procedure. If cross-dimensional constraints do not exist, one may decompose the high-dimensional solution into layers of low-dimensional components and optimizes them one-by-one, but the existence of cross-dimensional quantities, which commonly exist in the real applications, break this layer independency assumption.

A real example of complex optimization with high-dimensional solution space exists in supply chain management, which was first termed in 1982 by Keith Oliver, a consultant at Booz Allen Hamilton. Supply chain management is the flow of goods and services management, and it includes all processes that transform raw materials into final products [14]. It can also be considered as the connection of a business's supply-side from suppliers to customers. Good supply chain management helps a company gain a competitive advantage in the marketplace. Readers who are interested in the basics of supply chain management are referred to [15] and [16]. It is of great interest to coordinate all parts of a supply chain from supplying raw materials to delivering products under the purpose of minimizing total costs and maximizing net profits in the process. Surprisingly, many optimization problems in supply chain management employ traditional methods like linear programming and others [17]. In the era of big data and artificial intelligence, there are many advanced optimization techniques that can greatly reduce the computational complexity and include many complicated problem constraints into consideration. This growing gap of optimization methods becomes an obstacle for researchers in supply chain management to develop large-scale data analysis techniques for better optimization schemes like the multi-channel selling scheme where products and services are sold and delivered to customers via different means.

In this work, we consider the optimization of the multi-channel selling scheme via a modern optimization technique in swarm intelligence. In Sect. 2, we briefly review optimization techniques in swarm intelligence. In Sect. 3, we implement the swarm intelligence based method for the optimization of the multi-channel selling scheme. Two real-life examples are used to demonstrate the efficiency of the proposed optimization method in Sect. 4. Some concluding remarks are stated in the last section.

2   A Brief Review of PSO and SIB

In this section, we review the basics of PSO and SIB, which are the two main algorithms used in this work. Readers who are interested in the details and theories of these algorithms are referred to [5] and [6].

Particle Swarm Optimization (PSO) Algorithm. Particle Swarm Optimization (PSO) is one of the most representative swarm intelligence algorithms in the past decades, and it has been widely applied in many industrial and scientific optimization problems. It is popular because of its easy implementation, and it is highly efficient in terms of memory and speed. In a PSO algorithm, we first initialize a swarm or a number of random particles, each of which represents a possible solution to the objective problem in the search space. The position of a particle is expressed as a vector consisting of values in every dimension. In addition to a position, each particle is given a velocity to determine its movement. At the end of every iteration, the position of every particle is updated based on its own velocity.

To make the swarm results in a good solution, an objective function has to be defined for evaluating the performance of a solution. With this definition, we are able to determine the Local Best (LB) particle and the Global Best (GB) particle. LB is the best solution a particle has encountered so far, and GB is the best one among all LB or the best solution that the whole swarm has encountered so far. In each iteration, each particle's position is influenced by its LB and GB position through its velocity, which can be expressed as the following equations:

$$v_i^{t+1} \leftarrow \alpha v_i^t + b(x_i^{*,t} - x_i^t) + c(x_i^{+,t} - x_i^t)$$

$$x_i^{t+1} = x_i^t + v_i^t,$$

where i denotes the number of the iteration, v_i is the velocity of the particle, $alpha$ is the inertia weight, b is the weight given to the cognitive/individual aspect, c is the weight given to the social aspect, x_i is the particle's position, x_i^* is the LB position of the particle, and x_i^+ is the GB position of the swarm. The determinations of b and c are generally user-defined or based on expert's experience.

Swarm Intelligence Based (SIB) Algorithm. Although PSO does not have any assumptions for the objective function, the search space is assumed to be continuous in the standard framework. There exist some variants of PSO to modify non-continuous domains, such as a simple round-off of velocities or using a probabilistic approach, but they may not be as good as in the Swarm Intelligence Based (SIB) method, which can be viewed as a hybrid method that some of SIB components can be viewed as a discretized version of PSO.

Similar to PSO, there is a swarm consists of several particles, LB particles, and a GB particle in the SIB algorithm. The objective function is also defined for evaluating the performance of particles. The main difference comes in the velocity update process. Rather than a linear combination formula of inertia and information from the two best particles in PSO, SIB extracts some important information from LB and GB particles by "mixing" particle units in the MIX operation. In addition, instead of only one choice of position updates in PSO, SIB picks the best of the three candidates to update in the MOVE operation. Below are the details of the two operations.

In the MIX operation, every particle has to be mixed with their own LB and GB, respectively, which returns two new positions called *mixwLB* and *mixwGB*. To mix a particle with a best particle, a given proportion, called q_{LB} and q_{GB} for mixing with LB and GB respectively, of entries in the particle is modified based on the corresponding values in the best particle. For example, we may simply replace the entry with the value in the best particle, or we may choose a random number in the range of two values to be the new value from the entry. Although there are no theoretical derivations to set the optimal values of q_{LB} and q_{GB}, our experience suggests setting $q_{LB} > q_{GB}$ to avoid premature convergence towards a relative good particle without an adequate exploration of the search space.

The MOVE operation is undertaken after all MIX operations are completed in an iteration. The performances of *mixwLB* and *mixwGB* are compared with the original position based on the objective function. If the best one among these three positions is one of the *mixwLB* and *mixwGB*, then it will be the new position of the particle. If none of the modified particles perform better than the original particle, we randomly alter some units in the original particle to create a new particle, so the particle can escape from the trap of a local optimum and explore unknown search space near original positions. The algorithm is ceased at some pre-defined stopping criteria, such as reaching the assigned maximum number of iterations or achieving convergence towards a pre-defined threshold range of GB.

3   Method and Implementation

Multi-channel selling is a process of selling products on more than one sales channel. This sale strategy is popular in the E-commerce world nowadays, but the optimization of such a sale strategy can be very complicated with the existence of a middleman for product centralization between suppliers and customers. For example, a selling scheme of farm products may involve products gathering to a middleman company from multiple suppliers (farmers) and reselling to customers from the middleman company. On the other hands, a direct sale skips the middleman and connects the selling relationship between farmers and customers. It is obvious that if a direct sale is considered, the multi-channel selling scheme may not only increase the revenues of farmers and decrease the prices of products sold to customers, but also simplifies the complexity of the optimization and thus shortens the computational time.

Due to its high-dimensional and discrete natures of the selling scheme, we choose to use the SIB algorithm to tackle this important supply chain management problem. We consider a scenario that there are M suppliers supplying K types of products to N customers. The overall selling scheme is a three-dimensional matrix or a tensor with dimensions $N \times K \times M$. Before we propose the SIB algorithm for this problem, we state several underlying assumptions behind this scenario. First, we assume that all products are delivered directly from suppliers to customers, and there are no further complications on resale, buy-back, or others. Second, we assume that the quantities of supply and demand are known in prior. This assumption is possibly valid nowadays as the selling information can be collected online and analyzed via big data analytics. Third, we assume that every product has a constant price for customers and a constant cost for buying from suppliers, and the transportation cost per mile for a specific product is constant. This assumption makes the optimization simpler, and it is not difficult to implement price and cost variations in the optimization.

Table 1. The SIB algorithm.

1: Initialize a swarm of particles.
2: Evaluate the objective function values of each particle.
3: Determine the Local Best (LB) and the Global Best (GB) for each particles.
4: while STOPPING CRITERIA NOT FULFILLED
5:     Do MIX operation.
6:     Do MOVE operation.
7:     Update all LB particles and the GB particle.
8:     Check the conditions of convergence.

To implement the SIB method for the multi-channel selling scheme, we follow the standard framework in [6] with pseudo-codes stated in Table 1. It consists of an initialization part and an iteration part. In short, we first randomly generate a set of different schemes that are feasible to exist under the constraints. By evaluating the objective function values, we define the LB schemes as the initial schemes and the GB scheme as the one with maximum profit. Then in the iteration part, each scheme is mixed with its own LB scheme and the GB scheme respectively and results in two mixed schemes (MIX operation). Two newly created schemes are compared wth the original scheme in terms of profits, and the particle is updated if the mixed scheme creates a higher profit (MOVE operation), or a perturbed scheme from the original scheme is used for update. Iteration contines until the pre-defined terminal criteria are fulfilled. The details about the implementation of the operations and the strategies for preserving the feasibility are specified as follows.

Initialization. We define a particle in SIB as a three-dimensional tensor X with dimensions $N \times K \times M$ for N customers, K product types, and M suppliers. Each entry x_{nkm} in X stands for the number of the kth product suggested to be sold to the nth customer from the mth supplier. Each column with K entries represents a selling scheme between a supplier and a customer, and each slice of size $M \times K$ represents a selling scheme towards a specific customer of interest. In a supply chain optimization problem, the objective function is generally the profit that a selling scheme is able to earn. The profit is the difference between sales and costs. To simplify our problems, we only consider the cost of packaging from suppliers and the cost of delivery to customers as the only two costs in the objective function, and the sale is simply product prices and quantities that a customer purchases. Mathematically speaking, we have

$$Profit = Sale - Cost, \tag{1}$$

where $Cost = \Sigma(Delivery + Package)$ and $Sale = \Sigma(Price \times Quantity)$.

There are constraints in supply and demand in this problem, and we implement these constraints in the particle generation step. In specific, we generate each column separately and combine these columns into a particle. To make sure the availability of products in both supply and demand, we record the remaining supply and demand after generating each slice of the particle. We randomly choose integers from 0 to the minimum between the remaining supply and demand to the available entry. In case of no remaining supply or demand, the entry will set to be zero. Moreover, we shuffle the generating order in both column level and slice level to increase variations among particles. Once the particle initialization is done, then their objective function values are evaluated, and the best particles are defined accordingly.

Iteration and Update. Every particle is mixed with its own LB and GB of the swarm respectively in an iteration step and results in two outcomes denoted as mixwLB and mixwGB. The MIX operation is done via mixing two particles in a column-by-column fashion and shuffling the order of columns in each slice. We deal with a pair of columns in each MIX operation, one from the original particle and another from either the LB or the GB particle. To ensure the availability of output positions, we calculate the remaining demand and supply and update them after every MIX operation of a pair of columns is completed. For each pair of columns, we first identify entry indices that their values are larger in the best particle, and both demand and supply constraints are still fulfilled. In other words, we do not do anything if there are no remaining counts in the demand or supply constraints. Then, we randomly choose a specific proportion of those selected indices and replace values in the original particle with the values corresponding best particle, where the proportion is equal to q_{LB} or q_{GB}; we set q_{LB} to be 0.6 and q_{GB} to be 0.4. Since we only select entries with larger values in the best particle, the objective function values will only increase in this process, and we determine to add this condition for achieving convergence faster.

After the MIX operation, we have three tensor particles: the original particle, the mixwLB particle, and the mixwGB particle. The MOVE operation in this algorithm is the same as the standard SIB algorithm. If either the mixwLB or the mixwGB particle has a better objective function value, then the original particle will be updated with a better choice. If the original particle still has the best objective function value, we first count the number of elements that corresponds to the non-zero demand in each column, then we randomly choose half of them and assign new integers that are randomly generated from the range between 0 and the minimum within the remaining demand and supply. This step ensures that the particle is out of the local-attractive trap while fulfills demand and supply constraints.

The procedure continues until the stopping criteria are reached. The criteria can be the maximum number of iterations, the achievement of a pre-defined profit value, or a convergence of a large proportion of tensor particles towards GB. Once the procedure is completed, the GB particle is the outcome, which is the optimal multi-channel selling scheme suggested by our proposed SIB algorithm.

Acceleration by CPU Parallelization. The computation among tensors is time-consuming, so we use the CPU parallelization technique to accelerate the whole process. Using the python package Multiprocessing, the data of the global best particle is stored in the shared memory while pairs of particles and their local best particles are stored in different CPUs. The MIX and MOVE operations for every particle are run in different CPUs, and the new positions are compared with the GB particle separately. If an output particle performs better than the GB particle, we modify the GB particle in the shared memory. To keep the process synchronous, Barriers are used to hold the complete sub-processes until all particles are completed. Moreover, a Lock is used to protect a shared resource from being modified by two or more concurrently running processes at the same time to make sure that the correct information is recorded.

Since our SIB algorithm contains a lot of for-loop and basic numerical functions, it is essential for the success of our program to implement efficiently. Numba [18], which translates Python functions to optimize machine code at runtime using the industry-stand LLVM compiler library, is a suitable choice for our SIB algorithm. Numba-compiled numerical algorithms in Python is claimed to approach the speeds of C or FORTRAN. The source code of Numba can be found in Github at github.com/numba/numba.

Numba translates Python functions to optimize machine code at runtime using the industry-standard LLVM compiler library. Numba-compiled numerical algorithms in Python can approach the speeds of C or FORTRAN. Our program contains a lot of for-loop and basic numerical functions, which makes it suitable for applying Numba.

4   Applications

In this section, we apply our SIB algorithm in two examples. The first example is the real data from the layer industry in Taiwan with one dealer playing the only supplier in the supply chain. We can neither find any data with multiple suppliers (without dealer) nor find other data with a larger number of customers and products, so we randomly generate data as an extended example with additional suppliers based on this real data in order to demonstrate the capability of handling high-dimensional data of our SIB algorithm.

A Real Example in Layer Industry in Taiwan. In this example, we have 30 farmers, 82 customers, 78 products, and one dealer. We consider the dealer as the only supplier in this supply chain. Our data consists of the supply amount of each product, the cost of purchasing eggs from farmers, distances between customers and the dealer, the transport cost per mile for each product, and product prices that are different among customers due to quantities. To compare the performance of the SIB method on this data, we implement the GA algorithm and the PSO algorithm (with feasible initial particles, constrained velocities and a random back strategy).

In the first experiment, the simulations are performed about 100 times for each algorithm. The swarm size is set at 50 particles, and the stopping criterion is fulfilled after 50 iterations. Figure 1 shows the boxplots of the profits of the final GBs suggested by the algorithms. The SIB algorithm achieves a better position and deviates in a smaller range than the other two algorithms. The profit of the best selling scheme by the SIB algorithm is $2,071,885, and those of the PSO and GA algorithms are only $ 1,629,555 and $1,622,400 respectively.

It is possible that the PSO and GA algorithms might not achieve their convergence with small number of iterations, so we rerun the same experiemnts for the PSO and the GA algorithms for 100 times with the stopping criterion fulfilled after 1000 iterations. Figure 2 shows the profits of the selling scheme suggested by the two algorithms, and we also plot the result of SIB algorithm with 50 iterations for comparison. The highest final profits are $1,643,027 and $1,712,644 suggested by the PSO and GA algorithms respectively. It is obvious that even after 1000 iterations, the performance of the output selling schemes are still underperformed by the one suggested by the SIB algorithm with less iterations.

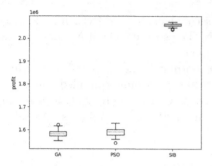

Fig. 1. Final GBs after 50 iterations.

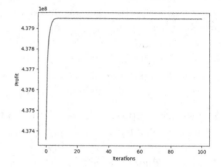

Fig. 2. Final GBs after 1000 iterations.

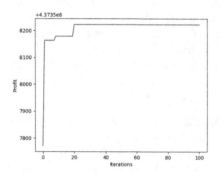

Fig. 3. Profit trend of GA.   **Fig. 4.** Profit trend of SIB.

An Example of Multi-channel Selling. The first example is not "multi-channel" because there is only one dealer on the supply side of the selling scheme. In addition, the numbers of customers and products are quite small when we consider standard e-commerce. Therefore, we artificially generate extended data based on the real data in the first example, with 1000 customers, 100 kinds of products, and 100 different suppliers. We set the swarm size at 20, and the maximum number of iterations are set at 100 steps. Since each particle in this example is a tensor of size $1000 \times 100 \times 100$, and the computation is time-consuming, thus CPU parallelization is employed. As a comparison, the whole procedure is completed in roughly an hour with CPU parallelization instead of 20 h without CPU parallelization. In this case, we only compare the SIB algorithm with the GA algorithm since the PSO algorithm cannot deal with multi-supplier cases.

Figures 3 and 4 show how the profits of the multi-channel selling scheme are improved through the iterations in the GA and SIB algorithms. We discard the potential unfairness in this comparison by setting the initial swarm for both algorithm the same. Notice that the range of the y-axises are different. The resulting profits given by SIB algorithm is \$437,947,645 and that of GA is \$437,358,222 while the best selling scheme in the initial swarm can only earn \$437,357,771.

The significant increase in the profit from the initial swarm to the final swarm shows that the SIB algorithm has greatly improved the multi-channel selling scheme. In specific, it modifies the scheme by creating a better configuration between the sellers and buyers, so that the selling scheme produces a very good profit as a result.

5   Conclusion

In the era of big data and artificial intelligence, a multi-channel selling scheme is an important advancement in supply chain management and e-commerce. However, computations on the optimization of the multi-channel selling scheme are infeasible if one employs traditional optimization techniques instead of parallelization. In this work, we propose the use of the SIB method to tackle this highly computational intensive problem. We introduce the high-dimensional tensor particle to be a solution particle in the SIB method with the consideration of demand and supply constraints and a new MIX operation to handle the information exchange between two particles with the preservation of the particle validity under these constraints. The simulation shows that the SIB method helps to increase the profits of these multi-channel selling schemes.

Extended from the current works, there are many practical considerations in multi-channel selling that we simplified in our assumptions. Some of them are easy to implement as additional constraints, and they can be handled similarly to supply and demand constraints in our SIB method. If one considers the variations of price and cost due to the change of demand and supply, which is valid in the common sense of microeconomics, we may need advanced marketing models to perform predictions prior to the optimization. If one considers any buy-back or resale actions, we may need to consider the sale dynamics rather than a static model.

References

1. Mifjalili, S.: The art lion optimizer. Adv. Eng. Softw. **83**, 80–98 (2015)
2. Ab Wahab, M.N., Nefti-Meziani, S., Atyabi, A.: A comprehensive review of swarm optimization algorithms. PLoS ONE **10**(5), e0122827 (2015)
3. Goldberg, D.: Genetic Algorithms in Optimization. Search and Machine Learning. Addison Wesley, New York (2003)
4. Karaboga, D., Basturk, B.: A powerful and efficient algorithm for numerical function optimization: artificial bee colony (ABC) algorithm. J. Global Optim. **39**(3), 459–471 (2007)
5. Kennedy, J.: Particle swarm optimization. In: Sammut, C., Webb, G.I. (eds.) Encyclopedia of Machine Learning, vol. 10, pp. 760–766. Springer, Heidelberg (2010). https://doi.org/10.1007/978-0-387-30164-8_630
6. Phoa, F.K.H.: A Swarm Intelligence Based (SIB) method for optimization in designs of experiments. Nat. Comput. **16**(4), 597–605 (2016). https://doi.org/10.1007/s11047-016-9555-4

7. Kim, T.H., Maruta, I., Sugie, T.: A simple and efficient constrained particle swarm optimization and its application to engineering design problems. Proc. Inst. Mech. Eng. Part C: J. Mech. Eng. Sci. 389–400 (2010)
8. Kennedy, J., Eberhart, R.: Particle swarm optimization. In: Proceedings of ICNN 1995 - International Conference on Neural Networks, pp. 1942–1948 (1995)
9. Phoa, F.K.H., Chen, R.B., Wang, W.C., Wong, W.K.: Optimizing two-level super-saturated designs using swarm intelligence techniques. Technometrics 58(1), 43–49 (2016)
10. Phoa, F.K.H., Chang, L.L.N.: A multi-objective implementation in swarm intelligence and its applications in designs of computer experiments. In: 12th International Conference on Natural Computation, Fuzzy Systems and Knowledge Discovery (ICNC-FSKD) 2016 on Proceedings, pp. 253–258. IEEE (2016)
11. Lin, F.P.C., Phoa, F.K.H.: An efficient construction of confidence regions via swarm intelligence and its application in target localization. IEEE Access 6, 8610–8618 (2017)
12. Lin, F.P.C., Phoa, F.K.H.: Runtime estimation and scheduling on parallel processing super-computers via instance-based learning and swarm intelligence. Int. J. Mach. Learn. Comput. 9, 592–598 (2019)
13. Hsu, T.-C., Phoa, F.K.H.: A smart initialization on the swarm intelligence based method for efficient search of optimal minimum energy design. In: Tan, Y., Shi, Y., Tang, Q. (eds.) ICSI 2018. LNCS, vol. 10941, pp. 78–87. Springer, Cham (2018). https://doi.org/10.1007/978-3-319-93815-8_9
14. Kozlenkova, I., Hult, G.T.M., Lnd, D., Mena, J., Kekec, P.: The role of marketing channels in supply chain management. J. Retail. 91, 05 (2015)
15. Fredendall, L.D., Hill, E.: Basics of Supply Chain Management, 1st edn. CRC Press, USA (2000)
16. Mentzer, J.T., DeWitt, W., Keebler, J.S., Min, S., Nix, N.W., Smith, C.D., Zacharia, Z.G.: Defining supply chain management. J. Bus. Logist. 22(2), 1–25 (2001)
17. Delloite: Supply chain leadership: Distrinctive approaches to innovation, collaboration, and talent alignment. Deloitte Consulting LLP, Technical Report (2014). Accessed 30 Mar 2020. https://www2.deloitte.com/content/dam/Deloitte/us/Documents/process-and-operations/us-cons-supply-chain-leadership-report-040914.pdf
18. Numba Homepage. https://numba.pydata.org/. Copyright at 2018 Anaconda

An Improved Dragonfly Algorithm Based on Angle Modulation Mechanism for Solving 0–1 Knapsack Problems

Lin Wang, Ronghua Shi, Wenyu Li, Xia Yuan, and Jian Dong[✉]

School of Computer Science and Engineering, Central South University, Changsha, China
dongjian@csu.edu.cn

Abstract. Dragonfly Algorithm (DA) is a new intelligent algorithm based on the theory of dragonfly foraging and evading predators. DA exhibits excellent performance in solving multimodal continuous problems. To make DA work in the binary spaces, this paper introduces an angle modulation mechanism on DA (called AMDA) to generate bit strings, that is, to give alternative solutions to binary problems. Instead of running on the original high-dimensional binary spaces, the original AMDA utilizes the four-dimensional trigonometric function. However, the original AMDA has certain limitations, such as poor algorithm stability and slow convergence speed. Therefore, an improved AMDA called IAMDA is proposed. Based on the original generating function, a variable coefficient is added to control the vertical displacement of the cosine function. In this paper, seven high-dimensional zero-one knapsack problems are considered. Experimental results prove that IAMDA has superior convergence speed and quality of solution as compared to AMDA, BDA and BPSO.

Keywords: Angle modulation mechanism · Trigonometric generating function · Dragonfly algorithm · Binary optimization · 0–1 knapsack problem

1 Introduction

Over the years, more and more algorithms based on artificial intelligence, sociality of biological swarms, or the laws of natural phenomena have emerged. Many complex optimization problems are difficult to solve by traditional optimization algorithms, and various studies have proved that nature-inspired optimization algorithms are good alternative tools for solving complex computing problems. This type of optimization algorithms can be roughly divided into the following five categories: (i) evolutionary algorithms (EAs), (ii) swarm intelligence, (iii) simulated annealing [1], (iv) tabu search [2, 3], and (v) neural networks. EAs includes genetic algorithms (GA) [4, 5], differential evolution (DE) [6] and immune system [7]. Among these three algorithms, GA is based on the concept of survival of the fittest mentioned in Darwin's theory of evolution, GA and DE can be considered as the most standard form of EAs. The swarm intelligence algorithms such as classic particle swarm optimization (PSO) [8], bat algorithm (BA) [9], artificial bee colony [10], ant colony algorithm [11], firefly algorithm [12], artificial

© Springer Nature Switzerland AG 2021
Y. Tan and Y. Shi (Eds.): ICSI 2021, LNCS 12689, pp. 83–93, 2021.
https://doi.org/10.1007/978-3-030-78743-1_8

fish-swarm algorithm [13] and fruit fly optimization algorithm [14]. These algorithms mentioned above are based on social activities of birds, bats, honey bees, ants, fireflies, fish and fruit flies, respectively. Intelligent optimization algorithms are technically random search algorithms based on biological intelligence or physical phenomena, they are far less perfect in theory than the traditional optimization algorithms at present, and often fail to ensure the optimality of the solution. Considering the perspective of practical applications, this type of budding algorithm generally does not require the continuity and convexity of the objective function and constraints, and it also has excellent ability to adapt to data uncertainty.

Dragonfly algorithm (DA) is a new type of swarm intelligence optimization algorithm proposed by Seyedali Mirjalili [15] in 2015. Since the principle of DA is simple, easy to implement, and possesses certain optimization capabilities, it has shown promising results when applied to multi-objective optimization [15], image segmentation problem [16], and parameter optimization of support vector machines [16]. And a binary version of DA (BDA) was proposed by Mirjalili [15], which was successfully applied in the feature selection problem [17]. Traditional binary algorithms were developed by using transfer functions, which may be limited in applications for optimization problems, owing to poor algorithm stability and slow convergence speed.

To avoid such problems, Zakaria et al. proposed an angle modulated bat algorithm called AMBA in 2015 [18]. Inspired by AMBA, an angle modulated dragonfly algorithm (AMDA) is proposed in this paper to make DA work more efficiently in binary-valued optimization spaces, which can generate n-dimensional bit strings by applying a 4-dimensional trigonometric function. AMDA is observed to have better performance as compared to BDA and BPSO. Nevertheless, the limitation of the original four-dimensional trigonometric function is that there is no dynamically scalable parameter for adjusting the vertical displacement of the cosine function. Accordingly, this limitation may lead AMDA to produce a relatively large standard deviation when dealing with some problems.

To mitigate the shortcomings and improve the performance of AMDA, this paper proposes an improved AMDA, called IAMDA. Based on the original generating function, a variable coefficient is added to control the vertical displacement of the cosine function in the generating function. According to seven 0–1 knapsack problems, the experimental results have proven that as compared to AMDA, BDA and BPSO, IAMDA performs better in terms of optimization ability, convergence speed, stability and calculating time.

2 Dragonfly Algorithm

Every swarm in DA follows the principle of survival, and each dragonfly exhibits two separate behaviors: looking for food and avoiding the enemies in the surrounding. The positioning movement of dragonflies consists of the following five behaviors:

(1) Separation. The separation between two adjacent dragonflies is calculated as follows:

$$S_i = -\sum_{j=1}^{N} (X_i - X_j) \tag{1}$$

where X_i is the location of the *i-th* individual, X_j indicates the location of the *j-th* neighboring individual, and N is the number of neighborhoods.

(2) Alignment. The alignment of dragonflies is calculated as follows:

$$A_i = \frac{\sum_{j=1}^{N} V_j}{N} \tag{2}$$

where V_j indicates the velocity of the *j-th* neighboring individual.

(3) Cohesion. The cohesion is derived as follows:

$$C_i = \frac{\sum_{j=1}^{N} X_j}{N} - X_i \tag{3}$$

where X_i is the location of the *i-th* individual, N represents the number of neighboring individuals, and X_j shows the location of the *j-th* neighboring individual.

(4) Attraction. The attraction toward the source of food is calculated as follows:

$$F_i = X^+ - X_i \tag{4}$$

where X_i is the location of the *i-th* individual, and X^+ represents the location of the food source.

(5) Distraction. The distraction from an enemy is derived as follows:

$$E_i = X^- + X_i \tag{5}$$

where X_i is the location of the *i-th* individual, and X^- indicates the location of the natural enemy.

To update the location of dragonflies in a search space and to simulate their movements, two vectors are considered: step vector (ΔX) and position vector (X). The step vector suggests the direction of the movement of dragonflies and can be formally defined as follows:

$$\Delta X_i^{t+1} = (sS_i + aA_i + cC_i + fF_i + eE_i) + w\Delta X_i^t \tag{6}$$

where s is the separation weight, S_i is the separation of the *i-th* individual, a shows the alignment weight, A_i indicates the alignment of *i-th* individual, c is the cohesion weight, C_i indicates the cohesion of the *i-th* individual, f represents the food factor, F_i shows the food source of the *i-th* individual, e indicates the enemy factor, E_i represents the position of an enemy of the *i-th* individual, w represents the inertia weight, and t represents the iteration count.

According to the calculation of the above step vector, the position vector can be updated by using Eq. (7):

$$X_i^{t+1} = X_i^t + \Delta X_i^{t+1} \tag{7}$$

where t indicates the current iteration.

3   Improved Angle Modulated Dragonfly Algorithm (IAMDA)

3.1   AMDA

In this paper, the AM technique is used for the homomorphic mapping of DA to convert the complex binary optimization problem into a simpler continuous problem. And the angle modulated dragonfly algorithm (AMDA) is derived the original DA that uses a trigonometric function to generate bit strings. The trigonometric function comes from angle modulation technology, which was firstly applied in signal processing [19]. The value of trigonometric function can be calculated by the following formula:

$$g(x) = sin(2\pi(x - a) \times b \times \cos(2\pi(x - a) \times c)) + d \qquad (8)$$

where x represents a single real number element, which indicates evenly spaced intervals, and a bit string value can be generated by Eq. (9), and the four parameters a, b, c, and d are in $[-1, 1]$ at initialization. The corresponding candidate binary solutions are composed of these generated bit strings. If the output value $g(x)$ is negative, the result corresponding to the bit value is bit 0; otherwise, the result is bit 1. This mapping method can be explained by the following formula:

$$g(x) = \begin{cases} 0, g(x) \leq 0 \\ 1, g(x) > 0 \end{cases} \qquad (9)$$

The main steps of AMDA are simplified as the pseudo-code shown in Algorithm 1.

Algorithm 1: Pseudo code of AMDA

Initialize the continuous algorithm DA in $[-1,1]^4$
Initialize the dragonflies' population X_i (i=1, 2, ..., popsize)
Initialize the step vectors ΔX_i (i=1, 2, ..., popsize)
while the end condition is not satisfied
    Calculate the objective values of all dragonflies
    Update the food source and enemy
    Update w, s, a, c, f, and e
    Calculate S, A, C, F, and E using Eqs. (1) to (5)
    Calculate the output value $g(x)$ using Eq. (8) to generate bit strings
    Update the position vectors using Eq. (9)
end while
Return the best bit string as the solution;

Alg. 1. Pseudo-codes of AMDA.

3.2 IAMDA

AMDA's generating function is a combination of a sine wave and a cosine wave. The parameter d can control the vertical displacement of the sine wave but the vertical displacement of the cosine wave cannot be corrected, which results in a large variance of the entire generating function value. This defect, coupled with a small initialization range of DA, will encounter some difficulties while searching for a binary solution consisting of the majority of bit 0 or bit 1.

To alleviate the problem of the inability to control the vertical displacement of the cosine wave in the original AMDA generating function, this paper introduced an improved AMDA, called IAMDA. The proposed IAMDA uses a variable coefficient k to modify the generating function. which controls the degree of disturbance of the generating function in the transformation space, and gives the following generating function:

$$g(x) = sin(2\pi(x - a) \times b \times cos(2\pi(x - a) \times c) + k) + d \tag{10}$$

When the dragonfly individual is initialized in the dragonfly algorithm, the dragonflies are initialized randomly in the domain $[-1, 1]^5$. Therefore, the five parameters $a, b, c, d,$ and k are also in $[-1, 1]$ at initialization. Then, the standard DA is used for evolving a quintuple that is composed of (a, b, c, d, k), and this leads the position of each dragonfly to become a 5-dimensional vector. Therefore, the optimization procedure only generates the tuple values, which are substituted back to the Eq. (10), bit strings are generated.

The original generating function has one limitation, if the value of d is not large enough, the generating function will always be above or below 0, which will make the bit string only contain 0 or 1 bit. Hence, a variable parameter k is added to IAMDA to generate a bit string composed of 0's and 1's. The effect of parameter k is to compensate for the insufficient disturbance in trigonometric function as well as adjust vertical displacement of cosine function. Compared with the original method, the advantage of this improved method is that, even if the vertical displacement is not large enough, the generating function can still lie in the region of 0 and 1. In this manner, it is easier to generate solutions that are mostly 0' s or 1's. Moreover, the displacement coefficient k can increase the diversity of the solutions, so that IAMDA may achieve better solutions in certain adverse problem situations.

In order to demonstrate the mapping procedure, Fig. 1 shows the procedure of using the improved trigonometric function to map a continuous 5-dimensional search space to a discrete n-dimensional search space. The main process of IAMDA can be described as the following pseudo-code given in Algorithm 2.

Algorithm 2: Pseudo code of IAMDA

Initialize the continuous algorithm DA in $[-1,1]^5$
Initialize the dragonflies' population X_i (i=1, 2, ..., popsize)
Initialize the step vectors ΔX_i (i=1, 2, ..., popsize)
while the end condition is not satisfied
        Calculate the objective values of all dragonflies
        Update the food source and enemy
        Update w, s, a, c, f, and e
        Calculate S, A, C, F, and E using Eqs. (1) to (5)
        Calculate the output value $g(x)$ using Eq. (10) to generate bit strings
        Update the position vectors using Eq. (9)
end while
Return the best bit string as the solution;

Alg. 2. Pseudo-codes of IAMDA.

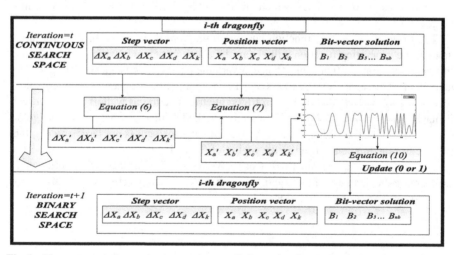

Fig. 1. The process of mapping a continuous 5-dimensional search space to a discrete n-dimensional search space.

4 Experimental Results and Discussion

In this paper, the population size of IAMDA, AMDA, BDA and BPSO is set to 30 and the number of iterations is set to 500. To avoid the resulting bias caused by chance, the algorithm runs independently on each function 30 times.

Table 1 represents k_6–k_{12} [20], which are high-dimensional 0–1 knapsack problems, after applying a random number generator. In the tables, 'D' indicates the dimension of a knapsack problem, 'C' denotes the capacity of a knapsack, 'Total values' in Table 1 represents overall profits of all items. Table 2 shows the best, worst and average solutions for 0–1 knapsack problems, besides, the average calculation time and the standard deviation (SD) are also listed.

Table 1. Related parameters of seven randomly generated zero-one knapsack problems.

No.	D	C	Total values
k_6	200	1948.5	15132
k_7	300	2793.5	22498
k_8	500	4863.5	37519
k_9	800	7440.5	59791
k_{10}	1000	9543.5	75603
k_{11}	1200	11267	90291
k_{12}	1500	14335	111466

Table 2 indicates that IAMDA and AMDA can always find better results in less computing time, suggesting the strong global optimization capabilities and computational robustness of IAMDA and AMDA in discrete spaces. Besides, it can also be observed that the higher the dimensionality of the 0–1 knapsack problem, the more obvious the advantages of IAMDA and AMDA. Moreover, as compared to AMDA, the standard deviation of IAMDA is much smaller, which suggests that in some cases, IAMDA is more stable and effective than AMDA for solving the 0–1 knapsack problems.

Table 2. Result comparisons between IAMDA, AMDA, BDA and BPSO on 0–1 knapsack problems in various dimensions.

No.	Alg.	Best	Worst	Mean	SD	time
k_6	IAMDA	**1.3075e+04**	**1.2300e+04**	**1.2632e+03**	**207.7428**	0.4770
	AMDA	1.2801e+04	1.1921e+04	1.2498e+03	211.4083	**0.4631**
	BDA	1.2820e+04	1.1501e+04	1.2316e+03	315.2521	1.6793
	BPSO	1.1640e+04	1.0951e+04	1.1174e+06	213.5035	0.6185
k_7	IAMDA	**1.8386e+04**	**1.6408e+04**	**1.7800e+04**	413.3773	0.6500
	AMDA	1.8220e+04	1.6107e+04	1.7595e+04	594.7544	**0.6137**
	BDA	1.7979e+04	1.6227e+04	1.7554e+04	370.3743	2.8821
	BPSO	1.6084e+04	1.5385e+04	1.5717e+04	**181.8523**	0.8482
k_8	IAMDA	**3.1266e+04**	**2.8010e+04**	**3.0387e+04**	713.8203	0.9952
	AMDA	3.0763e+04	2.7902e+04	3.0134e+04	816.0871	**0.9457**
	BDA	2.9598e+04	2.6478e+04	2.8067e+04	848.2838	3.6978
	BPSO	2.5404e+04	2.3997e+04	2.4656e+04	**328.1345**	1.3125
k_9	IAMDA	**4.7364e+04**	**4.1702e+04**	**4.5928e+04**	1.4190e+03	1.7125
	AMDA	4.7078e+04	4.0453e+04	4.5502e+04	1.6564e+03	**1.7014**
	BDA	4.5734e+04	4.1055e+04	4.2988e+04	1.2721e+03	5.3235
	BPSO	3.8119e+04	3.6775e+04	3.7448e+04	**355.7410**	2.0791
k_{10}	IAMDA	**5.9952e+04**	**5.5335e+04**	**5.8646e+04**	1.3125e+03	2.5047
	AMDA	5.9566e+04	5.3099e+04	5.7783e+04	1.8917e+03	**2.5023**
	BDA	5.7356e+04	5.0011e+04	5.3727e+04	2.3538e+03	6.2211
	BPSO	4.6572e+04	4.5209e+04	4.5749e+04	**362.8049**	2.6863
k_{11}	IAMDA	**7.1022e+04**	**6.3479e+04**	**6.8977e+04**	1.9784e+03	3.2814
	AMDA	7.0417e+04	5.9200e+04	6.7161e+04	3.0546e+03	**3.0616**
	BDA	6.7241e+04	5.5492e+04	6.3396e+04	3.0978e+03	7.6517
	BPSO	5.5506e+04	5.3168e+04	5.4227e+04	**552.3881**	3.0838
k_{12}	IAMDA	**8.8872e+04**	**8.1067e+04**	**8.7179e+04**	2.1245e+03	3.5053
	AMDA	8.8691e+04	7.8917e+04	8.6422e+04	2.5499e+03	**3.3711**
	BDA	8.2644e+04	6.9772e+04	7.6970e+04	3.9042e+03	8.5147
	BPSO	6.7097e+04	6.5470e+04	6.6496e+04	**648.1773**	3.7690

Figure 2 indicates the average convergence curves of the four algorithms on the selected large-scale problems in 30 independent runs. As denoted in the figure, (i) the purple curve representing IAMDA is always on the top of the other curves and the effect becomes more obvious with increasing the problem dimension; (ii) the red and blue curves representing BDA and BPSO are slowly climbing, or even stagnating. In other words, IMADA has the strongest convergence, while BDA and BPSO converge prematurely to solve large-scale testing problems.

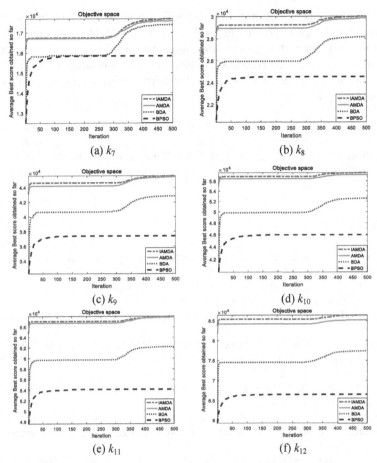

Fig. 2. Average convergence graphs of IAMDA, AMDA, BDA and BPSO on some selected large-scale problems over 30 independent runs. (a) - k_7. (b) - k_8. (c) - k_9. (d) - k_{10}. (e) - k_{11}. (f) - k_{12}.

It can be summarized from the above simulation results that when IAMDA solves the 0–1 knapsack problems, it decreases the computational time while ensuring the accuracy of the solution. IAMDA has a smaller variance than AMDA and the original BDA, indicating better robustness of the IAMDA algorithm.

5   Conclusions

To make the dragonfly algorithm work efficiently in the binary space, this paper applies an angle modulation mechanism to the dragonfly algorithm. The original AMDA applies the four-dimensional trigonometric function instead of running on the high-dimensional binary spaces. Hence, using AMDA can decrease the computational cost as compared to BDA. However, AMDA also has some limitations, such as poor algorithm stability and slow convergence speed.

To deal with the limitations and to improve the performance of AMDA, this paper proposes an improved angle modulated dragonfly algorithm (IAMDA) which runs on a continuous 5-parameter tuple through a five-dimensional trigonometric function. According to high-dimensional zero-one knapsack problems, it can be concluded that IAMDA outperforms AMDA, BDA and BPSO in terms of stability, convergence rate, quality of the solution and computational time.

Acknowledgement. This research was funded in part by the National Natural Science Foundation of China under grant number 61801521 and 61971450, in part by the Natural Science Foundation of Hunan Province under grant number 2018JJ2533, and in part by the Fundamental Research Funds for the Central Universities under grant number 2018gczd014 and 20190038020050.

References

1. Kirkpatrick, S., Gelatt, C.D., Vecchi, M.P.: Optimization by simulated annealing. Science **220**(4598), 671–680 (1983)
2. Glover, F.: Tabu search: part I. ORSA J. Comput. **1**(3), 190–206 (1989)
3. Glover, F.: Tabu search: part II. ORSA J. Comput. **2**(1), 4–32 (1990)
4. Holland, J.H.: Adaptation in Natural and Artificial Systems. University of Michigan Press, Ann Arbor (1975)
5. Mitchell, M.: An Introduction to Genetic Algorithms. MIT Press, Cambridge (1998)
6. Das, S., Suganthan, P.N.: Differential evolution: a survey of the state-of-the-art. IEEE Trans. Evol. Comput. **15**(1), 4–31 (2011)
7. Farmer, J.D., Packard, N.H., et al.: The immune system, adaptation, and machine learning. Phys. D **22**, 187–204 (1986)
8. Kennedy, J., Eberhart, R.: Particle swarm optimization. In: Proceedings of International Conference on Neural Networks (ICNN), Perth, WA, Australia, November/December 1995, pp. 1942–1948 (1995)
9. Yang, X.-S.: A new metaheuristic bat-inspired algorithm. In: González, J.R., Pelta, D.A., Cruz, C., Terrazas, G., Krasnogor, N. (eds.) Nature Inspired Cooperative Strategies for Optimization (NICSO 2013), vol. 284, pp. 65–74. Springer, Berlin (2010). https://doi.org/10.1007/978-3-642-12538-6_6
10. Liu, X.F., Zhan, Z.H., Deng, J.D., Li, Y., Gu, T., Zhang, J.: An energy efficient ant colony system for virtual machine placement in cloud computing. IEEE Trans. Evol. Comput. **22**(1), 113–128 (2018)
11. Chen, Z.G., et al.: Multi-objective cloud workflow scheduling: a multiple populations ant colony system approach. IEEE Trans. Cybern. **PP**(99), 1–15 (2018)
12. Yang, X.-S.: Firefly algorithms for multimodal optimization. In: Watanabe, O., Zeugmann, T. (eds.) SAGA 2009. LNCS, vol. 5792, pp. 169–178. Springer, Heidelberg (2009). https://doi.org/10.1007/978-3-642-04944-6_14
13. Li, X.: A new intelligent optimization-artificial fish swarm algorithm. Doctor thesis, Zhejiang University of Zhejiang, China (2003)
14. Pan, W.-T.: A new fruit fly optimization algorithm: taking the financial distress model as an example. Knowl. Base Syst. **26**, 69–74 (2012)
15. Mirjalili, S.: Dragonfly algorithm: a new meta-heuristic optimization technique for solving single-objective, discrete, and multi-objective problems. Neural Comput. Appl. **27**(4), 1053–1073 (2015). https://doi.org/10.1007/s00521-015-1920-1

16. Tharwat, A., Gabel, T., Hassanien, A.E.: Parameter optimization of support vector machine using dragonfly algorithm. In: Hassanien, A., Shaalan, K., Gaber, T., Tolba, M. (eds.) Advanced Intelligent Systems and Informatics, vol. 639, pp. 309–319. Springer, Heidelberg (2017). https://doi.org/10.1007/978-3-319-64861-3_29

17. Mafarja, M.M., Eleyan, D., Jaber, I., Hammouri, A., Mirjalili, S.: Binary dragonfly algorithm for feature selection. In: 2017 International Conference on New Trends in Computing Sciences (ICTCS), pp. 12–17. IEEE (2017)

18. Dahi, Z.A.E.M., Mezioud, C., Draa, A.: Binary bat algorithm: On the efficiency of mapping functions when handling binary problems using continuous-variable-based metaheuristics. In: Amine, A., Bellatreche, L., Elberrichi, Z., Neuhold, E., Wrembel, R. (eds.) Computer Science and its Applications, vol. 456, pp. 3–14. Springer, Heidelberg (2015). https://doi.org/10.1007/978-3-319-19578-0_1

19. Proakis, J.G., Salehi, M., Zhou, N., Li, X.: Communication Systems Engineering, vol. 2. Prentice Hall, New Jersey (1994)

20. Kulkarni, A.J., Shabir, H.: Solving 0–1 knapsack problem using cohort intelligence algorithm. Int. J. Mach. Learn. Cybern. 7(3), 427–441 (2016)

A Novel Physarum-Based Optimization Algorithm for Shortest Path

Dan Wang and Zili Zhang[✉]

College of Computer and Information Science, Southwest University,
Chongqing 400715, China
zhangzl@swu.edu.cn

Abstract. As a new bio-inspired algorithm, the Physarum-based algorithm has shown great performance for solving complex computational problems. More and more researchers try to use the algorithm to solve some network optimization problems. Although the Physarum-based algorithm can figure out these problems correctly and accurately, the convergence speed of Physarum-based algorithm is relatively slow. This is mainly because many linear equations have to be solved when applying Physarum-based algorithm. Furthermore, many iterations are required using Physarum-based algorithm for network optimization problems with large number of nodes. With those observations in mind, two new methods are proposed to deal with these problems. By observing the traffic network data, there are many redundant nodes, which don't need to be computed in practical applications. The calculation time of the algorithm is reduced by avoiding these special nodes. The convergence speed of Physarum-based algorithm can then be accelerated. Two real traffic networks and eighteen random sparse connected graphs are used to verify the performance of the proposed algorithm.

Keywords: Physarum-based algorithm · Network optimization · Redundant nodes · Traffic networks

1 Introduction

Physarum-based algorithm, as a bio-inspired algorithm, has caused widespread concern. Physarum polycephalum is a multinucleated single-celled organism, which shows high intelligent behavior in maze experiment. Physarum polycephalum can spontaneously form a shortest protoplast tube connecting the starting and exit nodes in the labyrinth tube. Tero [20] first proposed a mathematical model for the adaptive dynamics of the transport network in an amoeba-like organism with the Physarum. They used agar to make a labyrinth [17], placing two food sources at the beginning and exit nodes of the labyrinth. If the food source was placed in towns' locations in Tokyo by the relative geographical information, the road network was established by Physarum polycephalum had a better performance than the real Tokyo railway transportation network [18].

© Springer Nature Switzerland AG 2021
Y. Tan and Y. Shi (Eds.): ICSI 2021, LNCS 12689, pp. 94–105, 2021.
https://doi.org/10.1007/978-3-030-78743-1_9

Most existing methods adopted by some researchers in the network optimization problems. Here, several categories were proposed. Tero constructed mathematical models with Poiseuille's law and Kirchhoff's Law to solve the shortest path in the maze. In the perspective of non-traditional computer models, Adamatzky analyzed the foraging behavior of Physarum polycephalum [2] and realized the Oregonator model by the BZ reaction. The multi-agent model established by Jones had simulated the dynamic evolution process and characteristics of Physarum polycephalum network [3,6–8]. In the cellular automata model, Gunji modified the morphology of Physarum polycephalum [4,5]. In addition, Pershin leveraged a new physical memristors [15] to model the learning behavior and explore the predictive ability to the periodic signal in the Physarum polycephalum. Tsompanas designed the amoeba-like cellular automaton (ALCA) of Physarum polycephalum with software and hardware methods, and simulated Physarum polycephalum [21] to manufacture the railway network in Tokyo. Tusda performed a Boolean gate as a biological device made of slime mold Physarum polycephalum to achieve self-repairing computation [22]. Many scholars took the intelligent behavior of Physarum polycephalus as the research object and established mathematical models, such as, the Oregon equation model, Agent-based bionic model, and positive feedback mechanism model (hereinafter referred to as PMM). The PMM model first proposed by Tero was widely developed since its excellent fault tolerance and performance. In the positive feedback mechanism of Physarum polycephalum, the intelligent behavior of Physarum polycephalus was simulated by the combination of flow conservation theory and Poiseuille formula. The PMM model was first applied to the maze problem and a series of network problems, such as, fuzzy shortest path [25] , multi-objective shortest path problem [14,26], 0–1 knapsack problem [24], etc. Tero also described how the network of tubes expanded and contracted depending on the flux of protoplasmic streaming, and reproduced experimental observations of the behavior of the organism [19]. This model constructed a multi-object shortest path network with a great fault tolerance. In the complex network problem, Zhang used the Physarum polycephalum algorithm to calculate the centrality of the complex network [28]. In addition to solve the shortest path problem, the Physarum algorithm can also figure out other NP-hard problems, for instance, the classic TSP problem [9] and constrained shortest path [23,27]. Of course, Physarum algorithms can not only solve NP-hard problems, but also optimize some existing algorithms. Especially, the positive feedback mechanism in the PMM model of physaum solver can optimize some heuristic algorithms, such as, Ant Clony Optimization [12,16], genetic algorithm [11], random walks [13], etc. Physarum algorithm can enhance the robustness of original algorithm, accelerate the convergence speed of the original algorithm. In the past decade, researches have shown that the physarum solver with good performance to solve complex network problems, there are still some shortcomings limiting the development of the algorithm. The shortcomings of Physarum algorithm are mainly reflected in the following: when we utilize the physarum algorithm to solve some NP-hard problems, we need to solve a large number of linear equations to obtain the pressure value of each node. While the problem scale is large enough, each iteration requires a lot of calculation to solve those linear equations and cost a lot of computing time. According to the standard incomplete Cholesky conjugate gradient scheme [10], if the graph we need to solve is sparse and undirect, the time complexity of the physarum algorithm is $O(n^2)$, where n is the number of the nodes in the graph. As a result, the time of the entire algorithm has been greatly increased when n is big enough. In this paper, we propose two effective improvement methods to improve the calculation efficiency of Physarum algorithm, and increase the convergence speed for the problems raised above. In order to verify the optimization of the algorithm, we select two real traffic networks, and randomly generated eighteen sparse and connected networks. After that, we employ the novel Physarum-based algorithm and the traditional Physarum algorithm to detect the shortest path for the total networks.

The rest of this paper is organized as follows. In the Sect. 2, we briefly introduce the classical concepts and notations of the classic Physarum algorithm. In the Sect. 3, we give a detailed overview and demonstration of our novel methods. In the Sect. 4, we prove the feasibility of the proposed methods through specific experiments. Finally, in the Sect. 5, we draw conclusions and some future works.

2   Classical Physarum Algorithm

In this section, we elaborate on the basic principles of the Physarum algorithm and some basic notations. In addition, the shortest path convergence of the physarum polycephalum are proposed and analysed.

2.1   Basic Notations

$G(V, E)$ represents an undirected graph G and $S = \{s, v_{a1}, v_{a2}, v_{a3}, \ldots, v_{ak-1}, t\}$ represents a series of nodes sequences on the path from node s to node t, and all nodes are sorted in the order from s to t. Then the total length of this path

Table 1. Mathematical Notations.

Symbols	Description	Symbols	Description
G	Graph	D_{ij}	Conductivity along edge e_{ij}
V	Set of nodes in G	L_{ij}	Length of edge e_{ij}
E	Set of edges in G	p_i	Pressure of node v_i
s	Starting node	Q_{ij}	Flux through edge e_{ij}
t	Exit node	D_{next}	Conductivity in the next time
$S*$	The shortest path	D_{diff}	Current conductivity gap
e_{ij}	Edge between v_i and v_j	Bi	The degree of v_i
S	One path from s to t	D_{min}	A predefined conductivity gap

is $\sum_{i=0}^{k-1} L_{v_{ai}v_{ai+1}}$, where v_{a0} and v_{ak} denote the starting node s and exit node t. In particular, the shortest path between s and t is represented by $S*$. All the mathematical notations used in the rest of this paper are summarized in Table 1.

2.2 Physarum Algorithm

In the labyrinth experiment [17], the phytoplasma tube of Physarun covers the entire maze firstly. Then, the longer tube disappears. Finally, the protoplasm tube converges to the shortest path. Tero analyzed the convergence process of physarum in detail fistly. The radius of the protoplasmic pipeline and the flow in the pipeline show a positive feedback relationship, that is, an increase in the flow stimulate the increase in the radius of the pipeline, and an increase in the radius of the pipeline also stimulate an increase in the flow in the pipeline. On this basis, Tero used the Poiseuille equation to describe the relationship between the pipe's radius and the flux, and established a positive feedback mechanism based on Kirchhoff's law to modify the intelligent behavior presented by Physarum polycephalum. Here, we briefly introduce the PMM.

In the Physarum algorithm, the flow in the protoplasmic tube roughly obeys the Poiseuille flow, so the relationship among the flux Q and the conductivity D and the pressure value p can be expressed as Eq.(1).

$$Q_{ij} = \frac{\pi r_{ij}^4}{8w} \frac{p_i - p_j}{L_{ij}} = \frac{p_i - p_j}{L_{ij}} D_{ij} \tag{1}$$

where r_{ij} represents the radius of the tube between v_i and v_j, and the w represents the viscosity coefficient of flow. According to the above formula, it is shown that the conductivity D_{ij} is related to r and w. But w is the viscosity coefficient of the fluid, which is only related to the fluid. So here, the value of w is a fixed value, then D_{ij} can be obtained only positively related to p and Q_{ij}. Considering that the flow in the protoplasmic pipeline is regarded as a fluid, so the flow need to follow the law of conservation of flow in the Physarum algorithm. Two nodes as the starting node s and the exit node t are setted respectively. Then the flow flows in from the starting node and flows out from the exit node, so the flow at the starting node is set to -1 and the flow at the exit node is set to $+1$. The flow at other nodes must match the flow conservation, so the flow in other nodes is zero. The flow conservation of Physarum algorithm is described in Eq. (2):

$$\sum_{i \neq j} = \begin{cases} -1, for\ i = s \\ 0, for\ i \neq i, j \\ +1, for\ i = j \end{cases} \tag{2}$$

In the initial stage of the algorithm, all edges have an initial conductivity $D = 1$, and then the pressure value of the exit node is zero. Combining the above Eq. (1) with Eq. (2), the pressure value p_i of each node and the flow value Q_{ij} of each edge are obtained. Next, the algorithm starts to iterate. According to the adaptive behavior of Physarum, the flow is the larger in the pipe, the thicker the pipe become larger. On the contrary, the pipes gradually disappear with smaller flow. Therefore, the conductivity D_{ij} changes with the flow Q_{ij}. In order to describe the adaptive behavior of Physarum, the following equation is leveraged to establish an mathematical model to calculate the change of the conductivity D_{ij} during the convergence process of Physarum.

$$\frac{d}{dt}D_{ij} = f(|Q_{ij}|) - rD_{ij} \tag{3}$$

In the above equation, r is the decay rate of the conductivity. Since the conductivity of the pipelines increases with the increase of the flow, it is obvious that the function f is a monotonically increasing continuous function. It means and when the flow is zero, the conductivity is also zero. So the function satisfies $f(0) = 0$. In order to simplify the calculation of the algorithm, Eq. (4) is ususlly leveraged instead of Eq. (3).

$$\frac{d}{dt}D_{ij} = |Q_{ij}| - D_{ij} \tag{4}$$

3   Novel Physarum-Based Algorithm

The proposed Physarum Algorithm is summarized in the Sect. 3. First of all, we initialize all pipelines. The initial conductivity of all the pipelines is set to 1, and the flow of starting node is set to -1. What's more, we set up a conductivity differential D_{diff}, a threshold value of the minimum conductivity D_{min} and the conductivity D_{next}. When the conductivity of an edge is less than the threshold, it basically means that the edge has no flux passing through. We can remove such edge from the network. Furthermore, when the D_{diff} between the conductivity of a certain iteration and the previous iteration is less than an initial set value D_{min}, it means the iterative process of the algorithm is terminated and the network is converged to the shortest path.

In the above section, we briefly introduce some basic principles of classical Physaum algorithm. It can be shown that the essence of Physaum algorithm is to continuously delete nodes and edges that not exist in the shortest path. In the end, all the flow concentrates on the shortest path, so as to reach the purpose of the algorithm: filtering the shortest path. In order to achieve this goal, we need to delete these nodes and edges from algorithm to form the shortest path quickly. A large quantity of experiments show that removing nodes ande edges with too many iterations slowly is not enough efficiency.

As a result, the algorithm cannot achieve the desired effect to search the shortest path. In order to accelerate the efficiency of eliminating redundant nodes in the Physarum algorithm, two novel methods are proposed to accelerate the convergence speed of physarum algorithm.

In the classical Physarum algorithm, those edges with conductivity below a certain threshold are removed with continuous iteration. The above contents are mentioned, the way to delete the nodes is obviously not enough efficiency. In

---

Algorithm 1: Classical Physarum Algorithm

Input: G,s,t
Output: The shortest $s-t$ path $S*$
1 $D_{diff} \leftarrow \infty, D_{min} \leftarrow 10^{-5}, D \leftarrow 1, and\ itr \leftarrow 0;$
2 **while** $D_{diff} \geq D_{min}$ **do**
3      $itr \leftarrow itr + 1;$
4   obtain node pressure p with Eq. (2);
5   update Q according to Eq.1;
6   calculate the new conductivity D_{next} using Eq. (4);
7      $D_{diff} \leftarrow sum(|D_{next} - D|);$
8      $D \leftarrow D_{next};$
9 **end**
10 **return** $S*;$

---

order to accelerate the convergence speed, we optimize the process to remove the nodes and edges in the graphs and propose two methods. The first method can quickly delete redundant edges to accelerate the convergence speed. The other method can effectively reduce the computation of the algorithm. It can reduce the each iterative time in the algorithm to enhance the performance.

3.1 Method 1: Quickly Removing Redundant Edges

To explain the proposed method, there is a special path in the original graph or algorithm process, as shown in the Fig. 1(2) and Fig. 1(3). There are two paths between v_a and v_b, respectively, path 1 and path 2. And the lengths of path 1 and path 2 are different. If v_a and v_b are in the shortest path, then either path 1 or path 2 must be in the shortest path. Obviously, we search the shortest

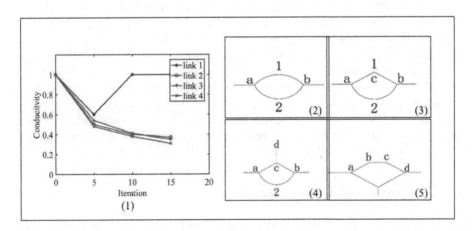

Fig. 1. (1) Variation of conductivity of non-redundant and redundant edges, Link 1 represent non-redundant edge, and others represent different redundant edges. (2) redundant nodes and redundant edges in different networks.

path between two nodes and delete the longer path 2 from the graph without multiple iterations. We call the similar edge as a redundant edge. However, it is important to notice that paths 1 and 2 are non-bifurcated paths. For example, in the Fig. 1(4), there is two paths $v_a\ v_c\ v_b$ and $v_a\ v_b$ between v_a and v_b, but v_c in the path has additional path to v_d. Therefore, edges such as e_{ac} and e_{cb} cannot be called redundant edges. In the example, on the path 1, there is only one node v_c between v_a and v_b. There may be multiple such nodes between v_a and v_b. If none of these nodes has a bifurcation path, these edges are regarded as redundant edges. In the method, those redundant edges are removed directly from the graph. In order to illustrate the correctness of the redundant edges deletion, we conduct several experiments to test the variables in the conductivity of the redundant edges we need to delete in the classical Physarum algorithm.

The experimental results are shown in the Fig. 1(1), we can show that the conductivity of the redundant edges continue to decrease, reach the thresholds and these redundant edges are removed by the algorithm eventually. With the variable rates in the conductivity become slower and slower as the process of the algorithm, it leads to redundant edges staying in the network for long time. It requires many iterations to delete those redundant edges, significantly affecting the efficiency of the algorithm. Therefore, the running time are decreased greatly by removing redundant edges in advance.

3.2   Method 2: Merging Redundant Nodes

The classical physarum algorithm needs to deal with a large number of linear equations to obtain pressure value of each node. If other factors remain unchanged and the scale of the linear equation is smaller, the algorithm will cost shorter running time. We hope to reduce the scale of the algorithm during the process of the algorithm. So, a method is proposed to reduce the number of nodes. In the Fig. 1(5), it is discovered that a lot of redundant nodes appear in the graph while the redundant edges are deleted. At the beginning and running stages of the algorithm, some edges gradually disappear in the iterative process, and finally forming a path similar to the structure.

We can realize that the degree of v_b and v_c is two without additional branch in the undirected graph. And the feature of v_b and v_c are retained. In next iteration, instead of analysing of v_b and v_c, $v_a\ v_b\ v_c\ v_d$ are combined into an edge e_{ad}. And $L_{ad} = L_{ab} + L_{bc} + L_{cd}$. In this way, we can greatly reduce the computation of the algorithm to achieve the purpose of accelerating the algorithm in each iteration. The novel physarum-based algorithm is described in the Algorithm 2 in details.

4   Computational Experiments

In this section, two real traffic networks and eighteen randomly generated graphs are selected to examine the effects of proposed methods. We compare the experiomental result of the classical physarum algorithm (PA) with the proposed novel physarum-based algorithm (NPA). All the computations are performed using the

---

Algorithm 2: Novel Physarum-Based Solver

    Input: G, s, t

    Output: The shortest $s - t$ path $S*$

1 $D_{diff} \leftarrow \infty, D_{min} \leftarrow 10^{-5}, D \leftarrow 1, and \, itr \leftarrow 0;$

2 **while** $D_{diff} \geq D_{min}$ **do**

3 | **if** $B_k = 2$ *and* $k \neq s, t$ **then**

4 | | **if** e_{ij} *exist and* $L_{ij} > L_{ik} + L_{jk}$ **then**

5 | | | Delet $e_{ij};$

6 | | **else**

7 | | | Delet $e_{jk}, e_{ik};$

8 | | | $L_{ij} \leftarrow L_{jk} + L_{ik}$;

9 | | **end**

10 | **end**

11 | $itr \leftarrow itr + 1;$

12 | obtain node pressure p with Eq.(2);

13 | update Q according to Eq.1;

14 | calculate the new conductivity D_{next} using Eq.(4);

15 | $D_{diff} \leftarrow sum(|D_{next} - D|);$

16 | $D \leftarrow D_{next};$

17 **end**

18 **return** $S*;$

MATLAB 2016b in Windows 10 with an Inter Core I7-6700 CPU (3.40 GHz) and 16 GB of memory.

In the experiment, different starting and exit nodes are extracted in the same graphs many times. The shortest path between two nodes has been tested at least ten times and pick up the average results in total. In addition, we perform the same training as above with the PA algorithm, and then make a detailed comparison of the results. In the following, we respectively test the time required by different algorithms to find the shortest path with the same starting node, exit node and the iterations. In order to simulate the real traffic network, all graphs are sparse and connected. The feature of sparse and normal graphs is represented in Table 2 and Table 3.

Table 2. The feature of sparse graphs.

Items	RG-1	RG-2	RG-3	RG-4	RG-5	RG-6	RG-7	RG-8	RG-9	RG-10
V	100	200	300	400	500	600	700	800	900	1000
E	255	542	788	1001	1341	1531	1780	2189	2357	2771

The results of the NPA and the PA algorithm in randomly generated graphs are shown in Fig. 3. Among all the comparisons, NPA algorithm always takes the shortest time to find the shortest path and spend the least iterations. Moreover, we can detect that the optimization effect of NPA is very well compared

Table 3. The feature of normal graphs.

Items	BRG-1	BRG-2	BRG-3	BRG-4	BRG-5	BRG-6	BRG-7	BRG-8
V	100	200	300	400	500	600	700	800
E	387	804	1229	1784	2261	2589	3681	4007

with PA, which greatly decrease the running time. Different with PA, the NPA algorithm can be reduced by 10% running time in the normal graphs and can even reach the highest reduction 90% in the sparse graphs. In addition, we analysis that average degree of network graph is the smaller and the optimization effect is the better in the NPA algorithm, since the more redundant nodes can be found in the sparse graphs. Even though the real traffic network exist without high average degree, eight random graphs are utilized and the average degree is in the interval of [4.0, 5.0] from some relative experiments. It can be shown in Fig. 3 (normal) that the improvement of NPA has over 10% than the PA. Therefore, the NPA algorithm proposed is more suitable to select the shortest path of the network graphs with low average degree. Compared with PA, two real traffic network graphs are leveraged in the NPA algorithm, such as, Berlin Mitte Prenzlauerberg Friedrichshain Center Network (BMPF), Chicago Area Transportation Network [1]. Here, the BMPF network contians 2184 edges and 975 nodes, especially, there is one isolated node (node 105). In Chicago area transportation network, there are 933 nodes and 2950 edges. The starting and exit nodes are selected randomly, and four different pairs of nodes are adopted in two real traffic network graphs.

Table 4 reveals that the proposed NPA algorithm shows obvious advantages that have the shorter running time and less iterations than PA in the real traffic network graphs. Also, we can indicate that the change of the starting and exit

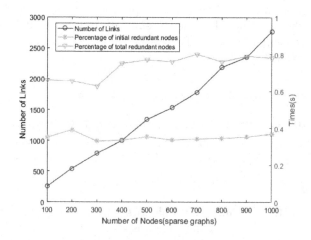

Fig. 2. Change in the number of redundant nodes over time.

nodes for NPA has little effect on the running time. The overall number of iterations and consuming time maintain stable basically. However, we discover that the consuming time and the number of iterations have the connection in the distance between two nodes in the PA. Therefore, NPA algorithm has excellent robustness compared with PA.

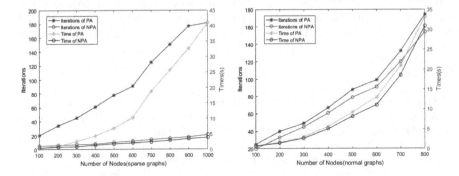

Fig. 3. Performance of PA and NPA in sparse and normal graphs

Table 4. Performance comparison of PA and NPA in real traffic networks.

Items	s	t	Iterations (PA)	Time(s) (PA)	Iterations (NPA)	Time(s) (NPA)
BMPF	78	515	30	20.57	10	6.67
BMPF	1	900	11	12.61	10	6.18
BMPF	31	789	19	16.21	10	6.28
BMPF	50	511	14	13.91	10	6.07
Chicago	2	900	13	12.11	9	9.45
Chicago	5	614	11	11.92	9	9.53
Chicago	4	893	12	12.01	9	9.81
Chicago	200	900	25	14.82	9	9.93

5 Conclusions

In this paper, two novel optimization methods are combined with the PA, which quickly remove redundant edges and merge redundant nodes. The performance of the classical physarum algorithm is improved greatly by proposed methods. The NPA can greatly reduce the number of iterations and the time required for each iteration, and finally achieve the goal of optimizing the algorithm. Finally, eighteen random graphs and two real traffic networks are leveraged in the experiments. The experimental results are compared with PA, and the performance of computation time is pretty great in the proposed methods.

In the future, the NPA algorithm can be further developed to some NP-hard problems, such as, Steiner minimum tree problem, TSP problem, path optimization problem, transportation problem, 0–1 backpack problem and so on. In addition, we can analysis the Physarum algorithm combined with other optimization algorithms. And the combined algorithm may combine the advantages of different algorithms, while try to avoid some weakness, so as to solve some NP-hard problems more efficiently. Of course, we can also devote to develop other models of physarum polycephalum, such as the multi-agent model, ALCA and Oregonator model, etc. So that the physarum can solve more NP-hard problems.

References

1. Transportation networks. https://github.com/bstabler/TransportationNetworks
2. Adamatzky, A.: If bz medium did spanning trees these would be the same trees as physarum built. Phys. Lett. A **373**(10), 952–956 (2009)
3. Adamatzky, A., Jones, J.: Towards physarum robots: computing and manipulating on water surface. J. Bionic Eng. **5**(4), 348–357 (2008)
4. Gunji, Y.P., Shirakawa, T., Niizato, T., Haruna, T.: Minimal model of a cell connecting amoebic motion and adaptive transport networks. J. Theor. Biol. **253**(4), 659–667 (2008)
5. Gunji, Y.P., Shirakawa, T., Niizato, T., Yamachiyo, M., Tani, I.: An adaptive and robust biological network based on the vacant-particle transportation model. J. Theor. Biol. **272**(1), 187–200 (2011)
6. Jones, J.: Characteristics of pattern formation and evolution in approximations of physarum transport networks. Artif. Life **16**(2), 127–153 (2010)
7. Jones, J.: A morphological adaptation approach to path planning inspired by slime mould. Int. J. Gen Syst **44**(3), 279–291 (2015)
8. Jones, J.: Applications of multi-agent slime mould computing. Int. J. Parallel Emergent Distrib. Syst. **31**(5), 420–449 (2016)
9. Jones, J., Adamatzky, A.: Computation of the travelling salesman problem by a shrinking blob. Nat. Comput. **13**(1), 1–16 (2013). https://doi.org/10.1007/s11047-013-9401-x
10. Kershaw, D.S.: The incomplete cholesky–conjugate gradient method for the iterative solution of systems of linear equations. J. Comput. Phys. **26**(1), 43–65 (1978)
11. Liang, M., Gao, C., Liu, Y., Tao, L., Zhang, Z.: A new physarum network based genetic algorithm for bandwidth-delay constrained least-cost multicast routing. In: Tan, Y., Shi, Y., Buarque, F., Gelbukh, A., Das, S., Engelbrecht, A. (eds.) ICSI 2015. LNCS, vol. 9141, pp. 273–280. Springer, Cham (2015). https://doi.org/10.1007/978-3-319-20472-7_29
12. Liu, Y., et al.: Solving np-hard problems with physarum-based ant colony system. IEEE/ACM Trans. Comput. Biol. Bioinf. **14**(1), 108–120 (2015)
13. Ma, Q., Johansson, A., Tero, A., Nakagaki, T., Sumpter, D.J.: Current-reinforced random walks for constructing transport networks. J. R. Soc. Interface **10**(80), 20120864 (2013)
14. Masi, L., Vasile, M.: A multi-directional modified physarum algorithm for optimal multi-objective discrete decision making. In: Schuetze O. et al. (eds) EVOLVE-A Bridge between Probability, Set Oriented Numerics, and Evolutionary Computation III, pp. 195–212. Springer, Heidelberg (2014). https://doi.org/10.1007/978-3-319-01460-9_9

15. Pershin, Y.V., Di Ventra, M.: Solving mazes with memristors: a massively parallel approach. Phys. Rev. E **84**(4), 046703 (2011)
16. Qian, T., Zhang, Z., Gao, C., Wu, Y., Liu, Y.: An ant colony system based on the physarum network. In: Tan, Y., Shi, Y., Mo, H. (eds.) ICSI 2013. LNCS, vol. 7928, pp. 297–305. Springer, Heidelberg (2013). https://doi.org/10.1007/978-3-642-38703-6_35
17. Tero, A., Kobayashi, R., Nakagaki, T.: Physarum solver: a biologically inspired method of road-network navigation. Phys. A **363**(1), 115–119 (2006)
18. Tero, A., et al.: Rules for biologically inspired adaptive network design. Science **327**(5964), 439–442 (2010)
19. Tero, A., Yumiki, K., Kobayashi, R., Saigusa, T., Nakagaki, T.: Flow-network adaptation in physarum amoebae. Theory Biosci. **127**(2), 89–94 (2008)
20. Toth, A., Nakagaki, T.: Intelligence: maze-solving by an amoeboid organism. Nature **407**(28), 470 (2000)
21. Tsompanas, M.A.I., Sirakoulis, G.C.: Modeling and hardware implementation of an amoeba-like cellular automaton. Bioinspiration Biomim. **7**(3), 036013 (2012)
22. Tsuda, S., Aono, M., Gunji, Y.P.: Robust and emergent physarum logical-computing. Biosystems **73**(1), 45–55 (2004)
23. Wang, H., Lu, X., Zhang, X., Wang, Q., Deng, Y.: A bio-inspired method for the constrained shortest path problem. Sci. World J. **2014**, 1–12 (2014)
24. Zhang, X., Huang, S., Hu, Y., Zhang, Y., Mahadevan, S., Deng, Y.: Solving 0–1 knapsack problems based on amoeboid organism algorithm. Appl. Math. Comput. **219**(19), 9959–9970 (2013)
25. Zhang, X., Wang, Q., Adamatzky, A., Chan, F.T., Mahadevan, S., Deng, Y.: A biologically inspired optimization algorithm for solving fuzzy shortest path problems with mixed fuzzy arc lengths. J. Optim. Theory Appl. **163**(3), 1049–1056 (2014)
26. Zhang, X., Wang, Q., Chan, F.T., Mahadevan, S., Deng, Y.: A physarum polycephalum optimization algorithm for the bi-objective shortest path problem. Int. J. Unconv. Comput. **10**, 143–162 (2014)
27. Zhang, X., Zhang, Y., Hu, Y., Deng, Y., Mahadevan, S.: An adaptive amoeba algorithm for constrained shortest paths. Expert Syst. Appl. **40**(18), 7607–7616 (2013)
28. Zhang, Y., Zhang, Z., Wei, D., Deng, Y.: Centrality measure in weighted networks based on an amoeboid algorithm. J. Inf. Comput. Sci. **9**(2), 369–376 (2012)

Traveling Salesman Problem via Swarm Intelligence

Pei-Chen Yen and Frederick Kin Hing Phoa[✉]

Institute of Statistical Science, Academia Sinica, Taipei, Taiwan
{lornayen,fredphoa}@stat.sinica.edu.tw

Abstract. Traveling Salesman Problem (TSP) is one of the most classic combinatorial optimization problems. It can be widely applied in many real-world applications. In this paper, we propose an efficient method via swarm intelligence to handle the traveling salesman problem, which may not be suitable for the standard particle swarm optimization due to its domain's discrete nature. Compared to the classic Ant Colony Optimization method, the SIB method performs well in terms of efficiency and accuracy in the TSP problem. For TSP with cities size between 15 to 25, SIB has a significantly lower average executing time to obtain an adequate solution with close distance.

Keywords: Traveling Salesman Problem · Swarm intelligence · Ant Colony Optimization · Combinatorial optimization problems · Metaheuristic method

1 Introduction

With the rapidly-growing technological development and innovation nowadays, real-world search and optimization problems in various sectors have become highly complex. Many optimization problems belong to the category of combinatorial optimization problems, which is nonlinear and usually consists of multi-objective scopes. Addressing these problems through traditional methods is challenging since traditional methods are mainly local search, problem-specific and difficult to solve nonlinear or discontinuity problems, leading the range of solutions to be easily stuck in local regions. Moreover, traditional methods mostly search through all possible solutions for a correct answer, which leads to an exponential growth in the whole process time.

In order to tackle these challenges, recent research in solving combinatorial optimization problems has been toward metaheuristic methods. In contrast to traditional methods, the metaheuristic methods result in an approximate global solution through processes of group searching and information sharing to improve local candidate solutions. Moreover, most metaheuristic methods employ stochastic techniques to escape from the local optima to avoid trapping [1]. Thus, for most modern combinatorial optimization problems that are intractable and with non-mathematically-defined objective functions, the metaheuristic methods are suitable for building solution systems or algorithms within an affordable execution time.

© Springer Nature Switzerland AG 2021
Y. Tan and Y. Shi (Eds.): ICSI 2021, LNCS 12689, pp. 106–115, 2021.
https://doi.org/10.1007/978-3-030-78743-1_10

Among all metaheuristic methods, the nature-inspired methods, especially methods based on swarm intelligence [2], are popular. The main idea of swarm intelligence is to mimic natural, physical or biological phenomena and immerse them to build optimization procedures [3]. Decision making for solutions is generated by agents such as ants or bees through interacting with other agents and updating local information among their own community. Representative swarm intelligence-based algorithms include Ant Colony Optimization (ACO) [4], Particle Swarm Optimization (PSO) [5], Artificial Bee Colony (ABC) [6], and many others. In addition to these representative methods, the number of new algorithms based on swarm intelligence, like Bat Algorithm (BA) [7], Cuckoo Search (CS) [8], and others, have increased remarkably over the last decade. They showed more supreme performance than the existing methods in the literature, and they are effective for solving combinatorial optimization problems in various real-world applications such as Traveling Salesman Problem (TSP), Vehicle Routing Problem (VRP), and integrated circuit design. Among these application areas, TSP is the most studied one. Due to its NP-hard nature, it is viewed as a highlighted application of meta-heuristic algorithms to show how they can be a powerful alternative solution. It can be extensively applied to many practical applications in the industry.

In this paper, we propose a new optimization approach for the TSP problem, based on swarm intelligence called the Swarm Intelligence Based (SIB) method, to find an optimal route passing through a defined number of destinations. The SIB method was first introduced by Phoa [9], which is widely considered as the discrete version of the PSO with some variants to tackle optimization problems with discrete solution domains. The SIB method has demonstrated good performances for problems with discrete or continuous domains in experimental designs [10, 11], target localization [12], scheduling [13], and others. This paper is structured as follows: In Sect. 2, we propose a modified framework of SIB for solving TSP. In Sect. 3, a test of SIB for TSP is presented for practical data. We draw some concluding remarks in the last section.

2 The Swarm Intelligence Based Method for Solving TSP

The traveling salesman problem is to find the shortest distance route for individuals to visit all target stations exactly once with returning to the starting station. It can be defined by a graph $G = (V, E)$, where $V = \{1, 2, ..., N\}$ is a group of nodes and E is a group of edges. Each node represents a target station, and each edge represents the path between station pairs if the path exists. Each edge $(i, j) \in E$ is assigned a distance d_{ij}, which is the distance between target stations i and j. The main goal is to find an order of target stations in one route such that the total distance of the route is minimum.

The most representative metaheuristic methods for solving TSP include Simulated Annealing (SA), Tabu Search (TS), Ant Colony Optimization (ACO), Particle Swarm Optimization (PSO) and Genetic Algorithm (GA). Readers who are interested in the introduction and implementation of these methods towards TSP are referred to [14–19]. In this paper, we describe how the SIB method is modified for implementing the TSP problem.

A standard SIB method consists of three main parts: initialization, iteration and output. After the initialization step for particle generations and parameter definitions, one enters an iterative process to improve the particle status according to the user-defined objective function. This iterative process consists of two operators: MIX and MOVE. The MIX operator can be viewed as an information exchange process between the current particle and its (local or global) best particle. The process is similar to the crossover step in the genetic algorithm. After the MIX operator is completed, three candidate particles, including the current particle and two mixed particles with the local and global best particles, are compared in the MOVE operator. The current particle is then updated to the best of three if some components of the particle change, or several randomly chosen components of the current particle are randomly assigned from the pool to create the slight alteration. After the iteration process is done, the global best particle becomes the solution of the problem suggested by the SIB method.

It is not trivial to directly implement the SIB method to the TSP problem. Table 1 shows the modified framework of SIB and some detailed descriptions are provided in the rest of this section.

Table 1. The SIB algorithm

Input	Distance matrix, number of particles N, number of iterations (N_loop), q_{LB} and q_{GB} .
Output	The optimal GB particle
1:	Randomly generate a set of N routes (particles) with m stations as initial particles
2:	Evaluate value of objective function for each particle, i.e., the total distance of each route
3:	Initialize LB for all routes
4:	Initialize GB
5:	For each N_loop
6:	For each particle, perform MIX operation
7:	For each particle, perform MOVE operation
8:	Evaluate value of objective function for each particle
9:	Update the LB for all particles
10:	Update GB
11:	end loop

2.1 Initialization Step

The initialization step can be viewed as the zeroth iteration of the SIB algorithm procedure. Users are required to input initial parameters as follows:

1. *Distance Matrix.* The distance matrix shows the distance between pairs of target stations.
2. *Number of particles (N).* The number of randomly generated particles in the SIB algorithm. These particles represent the routes with stations in TSP. Note that the

larger the N is, the smaller number of iterations are required to reach optimization, but it requires more time to execute in each iteration. As a rule of thumb, if we set a number of particles to be 100 as there are less than 11 stations in the TSP, we can get an accurate result within few seconds. When the number of target stations reaches 20 or higher, we recommend N to be at least 200.

3. *Number of iterations (N_loop).* The number of iterations executed in the SIB algorithm. The larger the N_loop is, the more accurate the value of an objective function towards optimization, but it generally requires more time to execute. As a rule of thumb, an accurate result can be obtained within a few seconds if N_loop is set to be 100 and N is set to be 100 for a TSP with less than 11 stations. We recommend to set N to be 300 if there are more than 25 stations in a TSP.

4. *Number of discrete units being exchanged with LB and GB particles (q_{LB} and q_{GB}).* The SIB algorithm is expected to converge to optimal value by exchanging q units with LB or GB consistently in every iteration. A large value of q_{LB} or q_{GB} will accelerate particles towards the best particles with a probability of overlooking the potentially good particles in between the current particle and the best particle. We suggest that setting $q_{LB} = [m/3]$ or $[m/4]$ and $q_{GB} = [m/2]$, respectively. Here $[x]$ refers to the rounded positive integer at least as large as x, m is the number of target stations (Fig. 1).

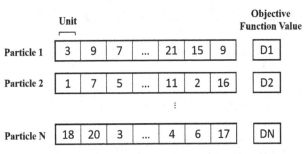

Fig. 1. A set of particles with N size

We begin with randomly generating N tours as a set of N particles named "initial particles". Each tour is represented by a single particle, and there are m stations in one single particle. A station is considered as a unit in a particle. Then we evaluate the value of an objective function for each particle, i.e., the total distance for each tour from a distance matrix. As a result, there will be N values of objective functions in one set of particles. Then we can define the Local Best (LB) particle for each particle and the Global Best (GB) particle for all particles according to these objective function values. This ends the initialization step of the SIB algorithm.

2.2 Iteration Step

We have a set of initial particles, a set of initial LB particles, and a GB particle prior to the iteration step. The goal of this iteration step is to obtain a particle with an approximate minimum value of an objective function after N_loop iteration. The resulting particle, i.e., the GB particle, describes the best tour for m target stations suggested by the SIB algorithm with an order and an approximate minimum value of objective function, or the shortest distance of the suggested best tour.

Although the SIB algorithm is similar to the PSO, a fundamental difference between two algorithms appears in the information sharing step. In PSO, the LB and GB information are shared to the current particle via the velocity update formula, which can also be considered as a weighted linear combination of the two best particles plus the inertia. In contrast, the LB and GB particles are mixed with the current particle separately to create two new particles in the MIX operation, and the MOVE operation serves as a decision maker to pick the best of three. This difference helps the SIB to preserve the information sharing and domain searching properties of the PSO but it can converge to the optimum more efficiently.

Below is the detailed implementation of the MIX and MOVE operations in TSP.

2.2.1 MIX Operation

The MIX operation consists of mixing with LB and GB respectively (Fig. 2).

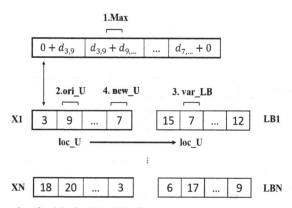

Fig. 2. MIX operation for LB for X1: This figure just shows one-time swapping - ori_U and new_U will be swapped.

In the MIX operation with the LB, we change unit order based on the LB particle information. Consider a candidate particle X from an initial particle set and its LB particle. We first evaluate the distance value between two consecutive units in X. Then we find a unit with the biggest value of a sum of distance values from its two adjacent sides. We consider this unit too far from its two adjacent stations in that order and thus we change its location. We denote this unit be ori_U and its location of this unit be loc_U. We refer to the same loc_U location in its LB particle, and then find the unit on loc_U, denoted as var_LB. Next, we go back to X and find the unit value equivalent to var_LB in X denoted as new_U. Then, we proceed to swap the ori_U units and the new_U unit in X. The same swap procedure is performed qLB times. We obtain a new particle called mixwLB from the original X after this procedure is completed. Similar procedures are done in other particles X in the original particles set and we get a set of mixwLB as the result of the MIX operation for LB.

We perform the same procedure for an initial particle to swap with a GB particle, except only that we use qGB instead of qLB, and we find units in the loc_U location in the GB particle instead of LB. After applying the MIX operations for LB and GB, we obtain both mixwLB set for LB and mixwGB set for GB, which are the mixed particles set based on LB information and GB information, respectively.

2.2.2 MOVE Operation

The MOVE operation comes after the MIX operations. We get three candidates, mixwLB, mixwGB and X. The MOVE operation is a decision-making procedure to select the best particle among all candidates with the optimal value of objective functions. First, we compare the value of objective function among mixwLB, mixwGB and X. Then we choose the best one with a minimum value of an objective function and replace X with it. However, if both mixwLB and mixwGB are worse than X, two units of X are randomly chosen and then swapped with each other as an update of X. We perform this random swap several times to escape from the local optimum trap, but we suggest not to perform these random swap more than qLB times.

2.2.3 Update Procedure

After each X has been updated from either mixwLB, mixwGB or a random swap of X from the MOVE operation, we obtain a new set of particles. For each particle in the set, we evaluate the value of an objective function again, and compare it with its LB's objective function value, and update LB if its objective function value is smaller than the original LB's. After all particles update their LB, we can get a new GB particle among all update LB particles. After all current particles, all LB particles and the GB particle are updated, the search continues to the next iteration in the same way until the pre-defined N_loop is reached. The final GB particle and its objective function value are considered as the outputs of the SIB algorithm.

3 Performance of SIB for TSP

3.1 Implementations

This experiment aims at determining an optimal tour that passes all cities and backs to the original station using the proposed SIB algorithm and evaluate its performance. We use the ACO algorithm as a method comparison to the SIB algorithm in a small city size. We use data provided by a logistic company in our experiments as an input data source, but one may use any types of address data for similar comparisons. We select the number of cities ranging from 10 to 30. The data contains two columns: target station name and its location. The location is in coordinate format for each station. Then we obtain the distance between each pair of cities and get a distance matrix as input data for the objection function calculating in SIB procedure.

Both algorithms are executed 10 times and the average distance is served as the comparison metric. The parameters for both algorithms are listed in Table 2. We obtain the average execution time and the average distance of the tour generated by each algorithm for the specified number of cities. All implementations were executed on a MacBook Pro with Intel Core i7 2.6 GHz.

Table 2. Iteration parameters set-up for both algorithms

Iteration parameters	ACO	SIB
10 cities	ant = 30, N_loop = 200	particle = 100, n_loop = 200
15 cities	ant = 30, N_loop = 200	particle = 100, n_loop = 200
20 cities	ant = 30, N_loop = 200	particle = 200, n_loop = 200
25 cities	ant = 30, N_loop = 300	particle = 200, n_loop = 300
30 cities	ant = 30, N_loop = 300	particle = 300, n_loop = 300

3.2 Results

Figure 3 shows that the average executing times of both algorithms among 10 times executions tested for 10 cities, 15 cities, 20 cities, 25 cities and 30 cities. The SIB algorithm performs significantly efficient in terms of executing time in the tests of 15 cities, 20 cities and 25 cities. For example, for the test with 25 cities, the average executing time and average best distance for ACO is 15.6 s and 100 km, while it only needs 10.8 s for SIB to find an optimized solution of 104 km. Figure 4 shows the corresponding distance. The total distances of the tests in 10 cities, 15 cities, 20 cities and 25 cities are very close for both algorithms. However, in the test in TSP with 30 cities, the ACO obtains a shorter distance then the SIB and the difference in average distance is about 10 km. Still, the SIB algorithm has the significant advantage of a short execution time to

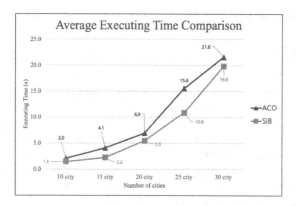

Fig. 3. Average executing time comparison

solve TSP, and it can obtain almost the same quality of solution in the problems under 25 cities and an adequately good solution in 30 cities.

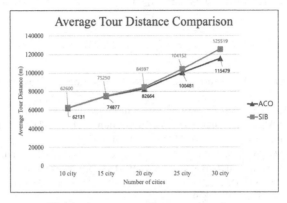

Fig. 4. Average tour distance comparison

3.3 Discussion

From the previous section, we know the SIB algorithm has good performance for solving a small number of destinations ranging from 10 to 25 destinations. We expect that the SIB method for TSP can be efficiently find optimal solutions in various practical fields of small-size TSP, which has a wide range of applications because a route with less than 25 destinations is close to common practice in the real-world problems. If the number of destinations exceed 25, conventional wisdom suggests to group these destinations into clusters first before executing optimization for groups with smaller number of destinations. This kind of TSP problem is called generalized TSP (GTSP) and their framework usually comes with a clustering stage of large number of destinations and a TSP optimization of small number of destinations in a cluster. See [20, 21] for details.

4 Conclusion

We present the SIB algorithm for addressing small-size Traveling Salesman Problem. The experiment result shows that it works excellent with better efficiency than the traditional ACO method in a number of cities ranging from 15 to 25 cities. In reality, it is seldom to schedule a daily route with more than 25 destinations due to the 24-h limit and the driver's working hours, so we expect the SIB algorithm for small size TSP can be widely applied to solve various related problems efficiently and provide adequately good solutions. We only propose the basic framework in this work and there are many potential modifications to this framework to improve its practicality and feasibility.

Acknowledgement. The authors would like to thank Ms. Ula Tzu-Ning Kung to provide English editing service in this paper. This work is partially supported by the Academia Sinica grant number AS-TP-109-M07 and the Ministry of Science and Technology (Taiwan) grant numbers 107-2118-M-001-011-MY3 and 109-2321-B-001-013.

References

1. Bandaru, S., Deb, K.: Metaheuristic techniques. In: Decision Sciences, pp. 693–750. CRC Press (2016)
2. Yang, X.-S.: Mathematical analysis of nature-inspired algorithms. In: Yang, X.-S. (ed.) Nature-Inspired Algorithms and Applied Optimization. SCI, vol. 744, pp. 1–25. Springer, Cham (2018). https://doi.org/10.1007/978-3-319-67669-2_1
3. Biswas, A., Biswas, B.: Swarm intelligence techniques and their adaptive nature with applications. In: Zhu, Q., Azar, A. (eds.) Complex System Modelling and Control Through Intelligent Soft Computations. STUDFUZZ, vol. 319, pp. 253–273. Springer, Cham (2015). https://doi.org/10.1007/978-3-319-12883-2_9
4. Dorigo, M., Birattari, M., Stutzle, T.: Ant colony optimization. IEEE Comput. Intell. Mag. **1**(4), 28–39 (2006)
5. Kennedy, J., Eberhart, R.: Particle swarm optimization. In: Proceedings of ICNN 1995-International Conference on Neural Networks, vol. 4, pp. 1942–1948. IEEE, November 1995
6. Karaboga, D.: An idea based on honey bee swarm for numerical optimization. Technical report-tr06, Erciyes University, Engineering Faculty, Computer Engineering Department, vol. 200, pp. 1–10 (2005)
7. Yang, X.S.: A new metaheuristic bat-inspired algorithm. In: González, J.R., Pelta, D.A., Cruz, C., Terrazas, G., Krasnogor, N. (eds.) Nature Inspired Cooperative Strategies for Optimization: NICSO 2010. SCI, vol. 284, pp. 65–74. Springer, Heidelberg (2010). https://doi.org/10.1007/978-3-642-12538-6_6
8. Yang, X.S., Deb, S.: Cuckoo search via Lévy flights. In: 2009 World Congress on Nature & Biologically Inspired Computing (NaBIC), pp. 210–214. IEEE (2009)
9. Phoa, F.K.H.: A Swarm Intelligence Based (SIB) method for optimization in designs of experiments. Nat. Comput. **16**(4), 597–605 (2016). https://doi.org/10.1007/s11047-016-9555-4
10. Phoa, F.K.H., Lin, Y.-L., Wang, T.-C.: Using swarm intelligence to search for circulant partial hadamard matrices. In: Tan, Y., Shi, Y., Coello, C.A.C. (eds.) ICSI 2014. LNCS, vol. 8794, pp. 158–164. Springer, Cham (2014). https://doi.org/10.1007/978-3-319-11857-4_18
11. Phoa, F.K.H., Chen, R.B., Wang, W.C., Wong, W.K.: Optimizing two-level supersaturated-designs using swarm intelligence techniques. Technometrics **58**(1), 43–49 (2016)
12. Lin, F.P.C., Phoa, F.K.H.: An efficient construction of confidence regions via swarm intelligence and its application in target localization. IEEE Access **6**, 8610–8618 (2017)
13. Lin, F.P.C., Phoa, F.K.H.: Runtime estimation and scheduling on parallel processing super-computers via instance-based learning and swarm intelligence. Int. J. Mach. Learn. Comput. **9**, 592–598 (2019)
14. Osaba, E., Yang, X.S., Del Ser, J.: Traveling salesman problem: a perspective review of recent research and new results with bio-inspired metaheuristics. In: Nature-Inspired Computation and Swarm Intelligence, pp. 135–164. Academic Press (2020)
15. Wang, K.P., Huang, L., Zhou, C.G., Pang, W.: Particle swarm optimization for traveling salesman problem. In: Proceedings of the 2003 International Conference on Machine Learning and Cybernetics (IEEE Cat. No. 03ex693), vol. 3, pp. 1583–1585. IEEE (2003)

16. Dorigo, M., Maniezzo, V., Colorni, A.: The ant system: an autocatalytic optimizing process. Technical report 91-016 Revised, Dipartimento di Elettronica, Politecnico di Milano, Italy (1991)
17. Dorigo, M., Maniezzo, V., Colorni, A.: Ant system: optimization by a colony of cooperating agents. IEEE Trans. Syst. Man Cybern. Part B (Cybern.) **26**(1), 29–41 (1996)
18. Stützle, T., Hoos, H.: MAX–MIN ant system. Future Gener. Comput. Syst. **16**(8), 889–914 (2000). https://doi.org/10.1016/S0167-739X(00)00043-1
19. Dorigo, M., Gambardella, L.M.: Ant colony system: a cooperative learning approach to the traveling salesman problem. IEEE Trans. Evol. Comput. **1**(1), 53–66 (1997)
20. Shi, X.H., Liang, Y.C., Lee, H.P., Lu, C., Wang, Q.X.: Particle swarm optimization-based algorithms for TSP and generalized TSP. Inf. Process. Lett. **103**(5), 169–176 (2007)
21. Shin, K., Han, S.: A centroid-based heuristic algorithm for the capacitated vehicle routing problem. Comput. Inform. **30**(4), 721–732 (2012)

Swarm-Based Computing Algorithms
for Optimization

Lion Swarm Optimization by Reinforcement Pattern Search

Falei Ji and Mingyan Jiang$^{(\boxtimes)}$

School of Information Science and Engineering, Shandong University,
Qingdao 266237, China
jiangmingyan@sdu.edu.cn

Abstract. Lion swarm optimization (LSO) is a swarm intelligence algorithm that simulates lion king guarding, lioness hunting, and cub following. However, there are problems that lions are easily out of bounds when the range of activity is large and the position update formulas are not universal, which affect the performance of LSO. Aiming at above problems, a swarm intelligence algorithm, lion swarm optimization by reinforcement pattern search (RPSLSO) is proposed. The algorithm is based on the proposed modified lion swarm optimization (MLSO) and reinforcement pattern search (RPS) algorithm. The former solves above two problems, and the latter enhances the local search capability of MLSO, making the search more directional. In order to test the performance of RPSLSO, RPSLSO was compared with MLSO, LSO and the other two algorithms on the CEC2013 test function set. The experimental results show that the performance of RPSLSO is better, and the modifications to LSO and the proposed RPS in this paper are also effective.

Keywords: Modified lion swarm optimization · Reinforcement pattern search · Q-learning · Pattern search

1 Introduction

Swarm intelligence algorithm is a kind of optimization algorithm by simulating intelligent behaviors of biological population. Particle swarm optimization (PSO) proposed by Kennedy in 1995 is a classic swarm intelligence algorithm [1]. Later, swarm intelligence algorithms such as artificial fish swarm algorithm [2] and artificial bee colony algorithm [3] appeared one after another. In recent years, some scholars have proposed swarm intelligence algorithms such as marine predators algorithm [4] and artificial jellyfish search optimizer [5].

As animals at the top of the food chain, lions are inseparable from the intelligent behaviors of lions such as cooperative hunting. At the same time, the efficient hunting behavior of lions is worth learning. In recent years, some scholars have proposed swarm intelligence algorithms based on the behaviors of lions [6–10], with better results.

Lion swarm optimization (LSO) is a swarm intelligence algorithm proposed by S. Liu in 2018 [11]. The algorithm simulates the intelligent behaviors of lion

ⓒ Springer Nature Switzerland AG 2021
Y. Tan and Y. Shi (Eds.): ICSI 2021, LNCS 12689, pp. 119–129, 2021.
https://doi.org/10.1007/978-3-030-78743-1_11

king guarding, lioness hunting, and cub following. The lion king guards territory and possesses the priority of food, lionesses cooperate in hunting, and lion cubs fall into eating, learning to hunt, and being expelled after entering adulthood. LSO has a fast convergence speed, but there are problems that lions are easily out of bounds when the range of activity is large and the position update formulas are not universal. In response to above problems, a modified lion swarm optimization(MLSO) is proposed in Sect. 2. In order to enhance the local search capability of MLSO, the paper proposes a reinforcement pattern search (RPS) algorithm in Sect. 3, which uses Q-learning to guide the pattern search to make the local search more directional. In Sect. 4, the lion swarm optimization by reinforcement pattern search (RPSLSO) is proposed. In order to verify the performance of RPSLSO, the paper compares RPSLSO with MLSO, LSO, PSO, and Gaussian bare bones particle swarm optimization (GBBPSO) [12] on the CEC2013 test function set in terms of error and convergence curve in Sect. 5. Experimental results show that RPSLSO performs better, and MLSO and RPS are also effective.

2   Modified Lion Swarm Optimization

2.1   Lion Swarm Optimization

The locations of lion king, lioness and lion cub are updated as follows.

The lion king moves around the best food area to ensure his own privileges, and the location is updated:

$$x_i^{k+1} = g^k \left(1 + \gamma \|p_i^k - g^k\|\right), \tag{1}$$

where g^k represents the optimal position of the k-th generation group, γ is a standard normal random number, p_i^k represents the historical optimal position of the k-th generation of the i-th lion.

A lioness is also known as a hunting lion. It needs to cooperate with another lioness to hunt, and the position is updated:

$$x_i^{k+1} = \frac{p_i^k + p_c^k}{2} \left(1 + \alpha_f \gamma\right), \tag{2}$$

where p_c^k is the historical optimal position of a lioness randomly selected in the k-th generation. α_f is defined as:

$$\alpha_f = step \cdot \exp\left[-30 \left(\frac{t}{T}\right)^{10}\right],$$

where

$$step = 0.1 \left(\overline{high} - \overline{low}\right)$$

indicates the maximum step size that the lion can move within the range of activity. $\overline{low}$ and $\overline{high}$ are the minimum mean and maximum mean of each dimension in the range of lion activity space, respectively. T is the maximum number of iterations, and t is the current number of iterations.

The position of lion cub is updated:

$$x_i^{k+1} = \begin{cases} \frac{g^k + p_i^k}{2}(1 + \alpha_c \gamma), & q \leq \frac{1}{3} \\ \frac{p_m^k + p_i^k}{2}(1 + \alpha_c \gamma), & \frac{1}{3} \leq q \leq \frac{2}{3} \\ \frac{\bar{g}^k + p_i^k}{2}(1 + \alpha_c \gamma), & \frac{2}{3} \leq q < 1 \end{cases} \tag{3}$$

where p_m^k is the k-th historical optimal position of lioness followed by lion cub. q is a uniformly distributed random number. α_c is a parameter that decreases linearly with the number of iterations and it is defined as:

$$\alpha_c = step\left(\frac{T - t}{T}\right),$$

$$\bar{g}^k = \overline{low} + \overline{high} - g^k$$

is the i-th lion cub being driven away from the lion king.

LSO converges fast, but it is easy to fall into the local optimum, and the local search ability is not strong enough.

2.2 Problems with LSO

Problem 1: In LSO, if the search range of the optimized problem is large, that is, the range of the lion's activity space is large, so that the *step* and the parameters α_f and α_c in the early stage of the algorithm operation are relatively large. Observing the update formula (2) and (3) of lionesses and cubs, we can find that when the search range of the optimized problem is large, $1 + \alpha_f \gamma$ and $1 + \alpha_c \gamma$ in parentheses will be very large, so the positions of lionesses and cubs will frequently cross the boundary. After crossing the boundary, they are initialized randomly, which makes the directionality and search efficiency of LSO worse, and tends to be random. This problem can be summarized as lions are easily out of bounds when the range of activity is large.

Problem 2: Suppose the minimum point of a test function is at the origin, that is, all dimensions are 0. In the lioness's update formula (2) and the cub's update formula (3), once $1 + \alpha_f \gamma$ and $1 + \alpha_c \gamma$ in parentheses are equal to 0 or approach 0, LSO will quickly approach the minimum point, and the fitness curve appears as a jump. Taking into account the number of lions and the number of iterations, the probability of the above occurrence is relatively high. In addition, LSO is easy to fall into local optimum when the function with local minimum at the origin is optimized by LSO. This problem can be summarized as non-universal position update formulas.

It can be seen that the above two problems are caused by $1 + \alpha_f \gamma$ and $1 + \alpha_c \gamma$ in parentheses, so we can start from here.

2.3   Modifications to LSO

The original paper of LSO obtains the position update distribution of lion through normal distribution sampling, and illustrates it with a one-dimensional distribution. The location update distribution of the lion king is:

$$x_i(t+1) \sim N\left(g, |p_i - g|^2\right). \tag{4}$$

The location update distribution of the lioness is:

$$x_i(t+1) \sim N\left(\frac{p_i + p_c}{2}, \alpha_f^2\right). \tag{5}$$

The location update distribution of the cub is:

$$x_i(t+1) \sim \begin{cases} N\left(\frac{g+p_i}{2}, \alpha_c^2\right), & q < \frac{1}{3} \\ N\left(\frac{p_i+p_c}{2}, \alpha_c^2\right), & \frac{1}{3} \le q < \frac{2}{3} \\ N\left(\frac{\bar{g}+p_i}{2}, \alpha_c^2\right), & \frac{2}{3} \le q < 1 \end{cases}. \tag{6}$$

From above three normal distributions, we can see that the standard deviations of the location update distribution of lion king, lioness and cub are $|p_i - g|$, α_f and α_c respectively, and the maximum values of the latter two are only $1/10$ of the lion's range of activity, and the three distributions are not close to 0, which better avoid the two problems mentioned in Sect. 2.2. Then we can redesign the position update formula of the lion swarm according to the three distributions. For the sake of simplification, let each dimension obey the above distribution, as shown below.

Given $X \sim N(0, 1)$, then $Y = \mu + \sigma X \sim N(\mu, \sigma^2)$.

According to (4), the position update formula of the lion king is rewritten as:

$$x_i^{k+1} = g^k + |p_i^k - g^k| \odot \gamma, \tag{7}$$

where γ is a D-dimensional standard normal distribution random number vector, $\odot$ represents the Hardman product, and other symbols have the same meanings as above.

According to (5), the update formula for lioness is rewritten as:

$$x_i^{k+1} = \frac{p_i^k + p_c^k}{2} + \alpha_f \gamma. \tag{8}$$

According to (6), the position update formula of cub is rewritten as:

$$x_i^{k+1} = \begin{cases} \frac{g^k + p_i^k}{2} + \alpha_c \gamma, & q \le \frac{1}{3} \\ \frac{p_m^k + p_i^k}{2} + \alpha_c \gamma, & \frac{1}{3} \le q \le \frac{2}{3} \\ \frac{\bar{g}^k + p_i^k}{2} + \alpha_c \gamma, & \frac{2}{3} \le q < 1 \end{cases}. \tag{9}$$

Through above modifications, MLSO is obtained. By comparing the position update formulas in LSO, we can clearly see the differences between them.

3   Reinforcement Pattern Search

In order to strengthen the local search ability of the lion king in MLSO, the time complexity of the algorithm is required to increase slightly, which requires the local search to be directional. For this reason, RPS is introduced, and the idea of Q-learning is used in pattern search.

3.1   Pattern Search

The pattern search algorithm is an improved search method based on the coordinate search method proposed by Hooke and Jeeves [13]. The algorithm includes two important steps: axial search and pattern movement, which are performed alternately to achieve the purpose of search. The pseudo code of the algorithm is shown in Algorithm 1.

Algorithm 1. Pattern Search

1: **Initialization:** initial point x_1, step δ, dimension D, acceleration factor α, deceleration factor β, accuracy ε, orthonormal basis $\{e_j, \ j = 1, 2, \cdots, D\}$, $y_1 = x_1$, $k = 1$, $j = 1$;
2: **while** $\delta > \varepsilon$ **do**
3:   **for** $j \in [1, D]$ **do**
4:    **if** $f\left(y_j + \delta e_j\right) < f\left(y_j\right)$ **then**
5:     $y_{j+1} = y_j + \delta e_j$;
6:    **else if** $f\left(y_j - \delta e_j\right) < f\left(y_j\right)$ **then**
7:     $y_{j+1} = y_j - \delta e_j$;
8:    **else**
9:     $y_{j+1} = y_j$;
10:    **end if**
11:   **end for**
12:   **if** $f\left(y_{D+1}\right) < f\left(x_k\right)$ **then**
13:    $x_{k+1} = y_{D+1}$, $y_1 = x_{k+1} + \alpha\left(x_{k+1} - x_k\right)$;
14:   **else**
15:    $\delta = \beta\delta$, $y_1 = x_k$, $x_{k+1} = x_k$;
16:   **end if**
17:   $k = k + 1$;
18: **end while**
19: Return the point x after the search.

3.2   Q-learning

The main components of reinforcement learning include a learning agent, an environment, states, actions and rewards. Q-learning is a typical and commonly used reinforcement learning algorithm [14]. Let $S = [s_1, s_2, \cdots, s_n]$ be a set of states of the learning agent, $A = [a_1, a_2, \cdots, a_n]$ be a set of actions that the learning agent can execute, r_{t+1} be the immediate reward acquired from executing action a, γ be the discount factor within [0,1], α be the learning rate within [0,1], $Q(s_t, a_t)$ be the total cumulative reward that the learning agent has gained at time t, then the updated Q value is:

$$Q_{t+1}(s_t, a_t) = Q(s_t, a_t) + \alpha \left[r_{t+1} + \gamma \max_a Q(s_{t+1}, a) - Q(s_t, a_t) \right]. \quad (10)$$

3.3   Reinforcement Pattern Search Algorithm

The RPS algorithm is shown in Algorithm 2. Algorithm 2 performs a one-dimensional pattern search according to the dimension selected by random or Q table, and the Q table update formula is simplified by (10). Use the Q-learning guidance mode to search for better directionality.

Algorithm 2. Reinforcement Pattern Search(RPS)

1: **Initialization:** initial point x_1, step δ, dimension D, acceleration factor α, deceleration factor β, accuracy ε, K, $p \in [0,1]$, immediate reward r, learning rate α_Q, Q table $Q = zeros(1, D)$, orthonormal basis $\{e_j, \ j = 1, 2, \cdots, D\}$, $y = x_1$, $k = 1$;
2: **while** $\delta > \varepsilon$ && $k \le K$ **do**
3:     **if** $rand < p$ **then** //$rand \sim U(0, 1)$
4:         Random choose $d \in [1, D]$;
5:     **else**
6:         Select the dimension d where $Q(d) = \max(Q)$;
7:     **end if**
        /*If the following two if conditions are out of bounds, initialize randomly*/
8:     **if** $f(y + \delta e_d) < f(y)$ **then**
9:         $y = y + \delta e_d$, $r = 1$;
10:    **else if** $f(y - \delta e_d) < f(y)$ **then**
11:        $y = y - \delta e_d$, $r = 1$;
12:    **else**
13:        $r = -1$;
14:    **end if**
15:    $Q(d) = Q(d) + \alpha_Q(r - Q(d))$; //Update Q table
16:    **if** $f(y) < f(x_k)$ **then**
        /*Initialize randomly if $y(d)$ is out of bounds*/
17:        $x_{k+1} = y$, $y(d) = x_{k+1}(d) + \alpha(x_{k+1}(d) - x_k(d))$, $k = k + 1$;
18:    **else**
19:        $\delta = \beta\delta$;
20:    **end if**
21: **end while**
22: Return the point x after the search.

---

4 Lion Swarm Optimization by Reinforcement Pattern Search

In this paper, the proposed RPS algorithm (Algorithm 2) is introduced into MLSO, and the local search ability of MLSO is improved by strengthening the local search ability of lion king. The proposed RPSLSO is shown in Algorithm 3.

Algorithm 3. Lion Swarm Optimization by Reinforcement Pattern Search (RPSLSO)

1: **Initialization:** the number of lions N, the maximum number of iterations T, the proportion of adult lions;
2: Initialize the position of the lion swarm randomly, and calculate the *fitness*;
3: Get the historical optimal position *pBest* and historical optimal value *pValue* of each lion;
4: Obtain the historical optimal position *gBest* and the optimal value *gValue* of the lion swarm;
5: $t = 1$;
6: **while** $t < T$ **do**
7:     Compute the Q learning rate $\alpha_Q = 1 - 0.9\frac{t}{T}$;
8:     Update the position of the lioness by (8);
9:     Assign g^k to the lion king, and use Algorithm 2 on the lion king;
10:     Update the position of the cub by (9);
11:     **for** $i \in [1, N]$ **do**
12:         **if** $fitness(i) < pValue(i)$ **then**
13:             $pValue(i) = fitness(i)$;
14:             $pBest(i) = lion(i)$;
15:         **end if**
16:         **if** $pValue(i) < gValue$ **then**
17:             $gValue = pValue(i)$;
18:             $gBest = pBest(i)$;
19:         **end if**
20:     **end for**
21:     $t = t + 1$;
22: **end while**
23: Return *gBest* and *gValue*.

---

5 Experiment and Analysis

In order to verify the performance of the RPSLSO proposed in this paper, including the modifications to LSO and the proposed RPS, the proposed algorithm is compared with MLSO, LSO and PSO. In addition, the original LSO paper mentioned that the basic update method of the algorithm comes from GBBPSO, so GBBPSO is also added to the comparison.

5.1 Experimental Setup

The CEC2013 test function set [15] is selected as the experimental test function, which includes 5 unimodal functions, 15 multimodal functions and 8 composition functions, a total of 28 test functions, which are rich in types and widely used. The domain of each dimension of 28 functions is $[-100, 100]$, and function dimension is set to 30.

The experiment was carried out on the Matlab2019a platform of Windows10. The population size of the five algorithms is set to 100, and the number of iterations is set to 5000. In the PSO algorithm, the acceleration constant $c_1 = c_2 = 2$, and the inertia weight ω linearly decreases from 0.9 to 0.4. The proportion factors of adult lions in the three lion swarm optimization algorithms are all 0.2. In the RPSLSO, the acceleration factor $\alpha = 1$, the deceleration factor $\beta = 0.5$, the accuracy $\varepsilon = 10^{-6}$, the number of searches $K = 10$, and the initial step size $\delta = 1$. Each algorithm runs independently 30 times to obtain the errors of 30 results, then the mean error is calculated.

5.2 Comparison of Experimental Results

The average error of each algorithm is shown in Table 1. Sort the error of each algorithm under each test function from small to large, then give an evaluation of 1 to 5 respectively, and give the same evaluation if the error is the same, and finally accumulate the evaluations of all test functions to get Rank. The smaller the Rank value, the smaller the mean error on the 28 test functions, and the better the result.

From the Rank value in Table 1, it can be seen that the proposed RPSLSO has the best result on the CEC2013 function set, followed by MLSO, the result of LSO is the worst, and PSO and GBBPSO are in the middle. It shows that RPSLSO and MLSO are better than the other three algorithms, which proves that the modifications to LSO in this paper is effective, and RPSLSO is better than MLSO, which proves that RPS is also effective. The above conclusions can also be seen from the number of functions that achieve the smallest error in several algorithms. RPSLSO has the smallest error on 15 functions, which is more than half of the total number of functions. MLSO performs best on 7 functions, four of which are combination functions. PSO and GBBPSO perform best on 6 and 4 functions respectively. The error of LSO is the smallest on only one function. Dividing Table 1 into three parts: unimodal functions, multimodal functions, and combination functions, RPSLSO performs best on unimodal functions and slightly worse on multimodal functions, but it is also better than the other four. RPSLSO is slightly worse than MLSO in combination functions. This may be due to the slightly higher complexity of the combination functions, which weakens the local search ability of RPS.

In order to compare the performance of the five algorithms intuitively, select F2, F6, F16, F27 among the 28 test functions, and draw the logarithmic error curves of five algorithms as shown in Fig. 1. F2 is an unimodal function, F6 and

F16 are multimodal functions, F27 is a combination function. All three functions are selected. It can be seen from Fig. 1 that RPSLSO converges fast on F2, F6 and F16 functions, with relatively small errors. It shows that RPSLSO has more advantages when optimizing unimodal functions and multimodal functions. RPSLSO and MLSO have similar curves on F27. Although the initial convergence speed is not as good as GBBPSO, the final error is smaller than GBBPSO, and GBBPSO quickly stagnated. Although MLSO performs generally on unimodal and multimodal functions, slightly better than PSO, it performs better on combination functions, which can also be seen from Table 1.

Table 1. Mean errors of five algorithms.

Function	RPSLSO	MLSO	LSO	PSO	GBBPSO
F1	**0.00E+00**	2.27E−13	5.78E+03	2.27E−13	**0.00E+00**
F2	**1.68E+05**	6.35E+06	1.11E+08	9.66E+06	1.73E+06
F3	**3.39E+06**	5.72E+06	3.79E+10	7.45E+07	4.37E+07
F4	**2.89E+03**	1.36E+04	4.09E+04	3.46E+03	4.97E+03
F5	1.53E−06	3.91E−02	1.69E+03	3.41E−13	**2.27E−13**
F6	**8.42E+00**	3.54E+01	4.29E+02	6.54E+01	3.48E+01
F7	**5.09E+00**	5.85E+00	1.63E+02	3.00E+01	7.26E+01
F8	**2.09E+01**	**2.09E+01**	**2.09E+01**	**2.09E+01**	2.10E+01
F9	**1.11E+01**	1.24E+01	3.85E+01	2.18E+01	2.60E+01
F10	2.08E−01	2.79E−01	9.25E+02	**1.63E−01**	1.73E−01
F11	2.68E+01	1.57E+01	2.72E+02	**1.54E+01**	4.19E+01
F12	2.45E+01	**1.76E+01**	2.94E+02	8.07E+01	9.94E+01
F13	5.10E+01	**4.05E+01**	2.74E+02	1.42E+02	1.82E+02
F14	4.56E+03	6.17E+03	7.49E+03	7.20E+02	**6.76E+02**
F15	**4.50E+03**	5.28E+03	7.30E+03	6.47E+03	5.06E+03
F16	**1.61E+00**	2.35E+00	2.34E+00	2.15E+00	2.34E+00
F17	1.01E+02	1.78E+02	3.34E+02	**5.01E+01**	6.95E+01
F18	**1.16E+02**	1.86E+02	3.16E+02	2.29E+02	1.59E+02
F19	6.07E+00	5.80E+00	8.22E+02	**2.70E+00**	3.87E+00
F20	**1.05E+01**	1.14E+01	1.30E+01	1.35E+01	1.12E+01
F21	3.33E+02	3.04E+02	1.75E+03	**2.93E+02**	2.99E+02
F22	3.98E+03	3.38E+03	7.73E+03	8.12E+02	**6.75E+02**
F23	4.59E+03	**3.61E+03**	7.79E+03	6.74E+03	4.94E+03
F24	**2.04E+02**	**2.04E+02**	3.06E+02	2.66E+02	2.65E+02
F25	2.19E+02	**2.07E+02**	3.25E+02	2.84E+02	2.91E+02
F26	2.21E+02	**2.00E+02**	2.05E+02	3.37E+02	2.46E+02
F27	**3.43E+02**	3.45E+02	1.17E+03	8.82E+02	9.57E+02
F28	**2.80E+02**	3.00E+02	2.41E+03	4.03E+02	3.00E+02
Rank	**56**	73	132	80	77

In short, RPSLSO has better optimization performance and higher convergence accuracy than the other four algorithms. The performance of MLSO is also much better than LSO. It proves that both the modifications to LSO and the proposed RPS are more effective, which improve the performance of LSO.

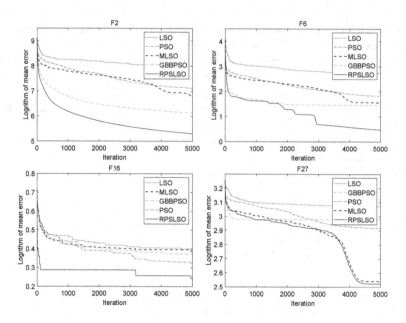

Fig. 1. Logarithmic error curves of five algorithms.

6   Conclusion

This paper proposes a lion swarm optimization by reinforcement pattern search (RPSLSO). Firstly, a modified lion swarm optimization (MLSO) is proposed, which solves the problems of the basic lion swarm optimization (LSO) that lions are easily out of bounds when the range of activity is large and the position update formulas are not universal. Secondly, based on the pattern search algorithm and Q-learning algorithm, a new local search algorithm-reinforcement pattern search (RPS) algorithm is proposed. The advantages are that the local search is more directional and the time complexity is slightly increased. Finally, RPSLSO is proposed based on MLSO and RPS. In order to test the performance of RPSLSO, the CEC2013 test function set was used to compare RPSLSO with MLSO, LSO, particle swarm optimization and Gaussian bare bones particle swarm optimization. Comparing the mean error and convergence curve of each algorithm, it is found that RPSLSO has the best performance, higher accuracy, and faster convergence speed. The performance of MLSO is also much better than LSO, and MLSO and RPS are both effective.

Acknowledgement. This study is supported by the Shandong Province Science Foundation of China (Grant No. ZR2020MF153) and Key Innovation Project of Shandong Province (Grant No. 2019JZZY010111).

References

1. Kennedy, J., Eberhart, R.: Particle swarm optimization. In: Proceedings of ICNN 1995-International Conference on Neural Networks, vol. 4, pp. 1942–1948. IEEE (1995)
2. Jiang, M., Yuan, D.: Artificial Fish Swarm Algorithm and its Application. Science Press, Beijing (2012)
3. Jiang, M., Yuan, D.: Artificial Bee Colony Algorithm and its Application. Science Press, Beijing (2014)
4. Faramarzi, A., Heidarinejad, M., Mirjalili, S., Gandomi, A.: Marine predators algorithm: a nature-inspired metaheuristic. Expert Syst. Appl. **152**, 113377 (2020)
5. Chou, J., Truong, D.: A novel metaheuristic optimizer inspired by behavior of Jellyfish in ocean. Appl. Math. Comput. **389**, 125535 (2021)
6. Kaveh, A., Mahjoubi, S.: Lion pride optimization algorithm: a meta-heuristic method for global optimization problems. Scientia Iranica **25**(6), 3113–3132 (2018)
7. Boothalingam, R.: Optimization using lion algorithm: a biological inspiration from lion's social behavior. Evol. Intel. **11**(1), 31–52 (2018)
8. Yazdani, M., Jolai, F.: Lion optimization algorithm (LOA): a nature-inspired meta-heuristic algorithm. J. Comput. Des. Eng. **3**(1), 24–36 (2016)
9. Rajakumar, B.: Lion algorithm for standard and large scale bilinear system identification: a global optimization based on lion's social behavior. In: 2014 IEEE Congress on Evolutionary Computation (CEC), pp. 2116–2123. IEEE (2014)
10. Rajakumar, B.: The lion's algorithm: a new nature-inspired search algorithm. Procedia Technol. **6**, 126–135 (2012)
11. Liu, S., Yang, Y., Zhou, Y.: A swarm intelligence algorithm-lion swarm optimization. Pattern Recogn. Artif. Intell. **31**(5), 431–441 (2018)
12. Kennedy, J.: Bare bones particle swarms. In: Proceedings of the 2003 IEEE Swarm Intelligence Symposium, SIS 2003 (Cat. No. 03EX706), pp. 80–87. IEEE (2003)
13. Wei, M., Sun, Z.: A global cuckoo optimization algorithm using coarse-to-fine search. Acta Electron. Sin. **43**(12), 2429–2439 (2015)
14. Samma, H., Lim, C., Saleh, J.: A new reinforcement learning-based memetic particle swarm optimizer. Appl. Soft Comput. **43**, 276–297 (2016)
15. Liang, J., Qu, B., Suganthan, P., Hernández-Díaz, A.: Problem definitions and evaluation criteria for the CEC 2013 special session on real-parameter optimization. Computational Intelligence Laboratory, Zhengzhou University, Zhengzhou, China and Nanyang Technological University, Singapore, Technical Report **201212**(34), 281–295 (2013)

Fuzzy Clustering Algorithm Based on Improved Lion Swarm Optimization Algorithm

Haiyan Yu[1], Mingyan Jiang[1(✉)], Dongfeng Yuan[1], and Miaomiao Xin[2]

[1] School of Information Science and Engineering, Shandong University,
Qingdao 266237, China
jiangmingyan@sdu.edu.cn

[2] School of Mechanical and Electrical Engineering, Qilu Institute of Technology,
Jinan 250200, China

Abstract. Aiming at the shortcomings of fuzzy C-means (FCM) clustering algorithm that it is easy to fall into local minima and sensitive to initial values and noisy data, this paper proposes a fuzzy clustering algorithm based on improved lion swarm optimization algorithm. Aiming at the problem that lion swarm optimization (LSO) algorithm is easy to fall into the local optimum, this paper improves lion swarm optimization algorithm by introducing sin cos algorithm and elite opposition-based learning. In addition, the introduction of a supervision mechanism enhances the lions' ability to jump out of local optimum and improves the local search ability of lion swarm optimization algorithm. The optimal solution obtained by improved lion swarm optimization algorithm is used as the initial clustering center of FCM algorithm, then FCM algorithm is run to obtain the global optimal solution, which effectively overcomes the shortcomings of FCM algorithm. The experimental results show that, compared with original FCM clustering algorithm, FCM clustering algorithm based on improved lion swarm optimization algorithm has improved the algorithm's optimization ability and has better clustering results.

Keywords: Fuzzy C-mean clustering · Lion swarm optimization algorithm · Sin cos algorithm · Data mining

1 Introduction

Cluster analysis is an important part of data mining technology. It can discover new and meaningful data distribution patterns from potential data. Clustering is to group data according to its own characteristics. The important feature is that things are clustered, that is, the larger the gap between different groups of data, the more obvious, the better, and the data in each group should be as similar as possible, and the smaller the gap, the better. Therefore, the boundaries of different categories are clear. But in the real world, there are many practical problems

Y. Tan and Y. Shi (Eds.): ICSI 2021, LNCS 12689, pp. 130–139, 2021.
https://doi.org/10.1007/978-3-030-78743-1_12

without strict attributes. Therefore, people have proposed a soft division of the objects to be processed. The fuzzy set theory proposed by L.A. Zedeh provides a powerful analysis tool for soft partitions. The use of fuzzy methods to deal with clustering problems is called fuzzy clustering. The fuzzy C-means (FCM, where C represents the number of clustering categories) clustering algorithm was established by Dunn [1] and Bezdek [2]. In summary, there are mainly the following aspects: (1) The number of initial centers needs to be given in advance, and there are no guidelines to follow; (2) Only clumpy clusters can be identified, irregular clusters and ribbon clusters cannot be identified, and they are sensitive to noise in many cases; (3) Sensitive to the initial clustering center, it is easy to fall into the local optimum, it is difficult to obtain the global optimum, or the entire clustering process takes a long time to converge to the global optimum, which affects the clustering effect.

In recent years, many documents have proposed improved methods for problem (3), which can be summarized as: combining the improvement of genetic algorithm, the improvement of cuckoo optimization algorithm, the improvement of bat algorithm, etc., such as fuzzy clustering based on improved genetic algorithm [3], fuzzy clustering based on cuckoo optimization algorithm [4], fuzzy clustering based on bat algorithm [5]. These algorithms use different methods to improve FCM algorithm, and improve the performance of the FCM algorithm to a certain extent. With the advent of the intelligent era, swarm intelligence algorithm is an important branch of intelligent optimization methods. Because of its distributed, self-organizing, cooperative, robust and easy to implement, swarm intelligence algorithm has good performance in many optimization problems. The commonly used algorithms include ABC [6], AFSA [7], IA [8], PSO [9] and LSO [10] algorithm, etc. This paper introduces improved lion swarm optimization (ILSO) algorithm into FCM algorithm to improve FCM algorithm's shortcomings that it is easy to fall into the local optimum and sensitive to the initial clustering center. Tested on a classic data set, the experimental results show that this improvement is effective.

2   The Basic Theory

2.1   Fuzzy C-Mean Clustering

The fuzzy C-means clustering algorithm is an iterative optimization algorithm, which can be described as minimizing the exponential function. Suppose set $X = \{x_1, x_2, ..., x_n\}$ is a finite data set on the feature space R^n, then X is divided into c categories $(2 \leq c \leq n)$, and suppose cluster centers c is $V = \{v_1, v_2, ..., v_n\}$. $n \times c$-dimensional matrix $U = (u_{ij}), u_{ij} \in [0,1]$ represents the membership matrix of each sample, where: $i = 1, 2, ...n; j = 1, 2, ...c$.

The objective function of FCM algorithm is as follows, the minimum value is obtained under the constraints of formula (2):

$$J_{FCM}(U,V) = \sum_{i=1}^{n} \sum_{j=1}^{c} u_{ij}^m \|x_i - v_j\|^2, \tag{1}$$

$$\sum_{j=1}^{c} u_{ij} = 1, \quad u_{ij} \in [0,1] . \tag{2}$$

Applying Lagrangian multiplication and combining the constraints of formula (2) to derive formula (1), we get:

$$v_j = \frac{\sum_{i=1}^{n} u_{ij}^m x_i}{\sum_{i=1}^{n} u_{ij}^m}, \tag{3}$$

$$u_{ij} = \frac{1}{\sum_{k=1}^{c} \left[\frac{\|x_i - v_j\|^2}{\|x_i - v_k\|^2} \right]^{\frac{2}{m-1}}}, \tag{4}$$

where: m is a fuzzy weighted index, and a suitable m value has the effects of suppressing noise and smoothing the membership function, but how to optimize the parameter m is still lacking theoretical guidance.

FCM algorithm obtains fuzzy clustering of the data set by iterative optimization of the objective function. The objective function is decreasing in the iterative process. This method depends to a large extent on the selection of the initial clustering center. The unreasonable selection of the central matrix will cause false clustering, increase the complexity of the system and reduce the efficiency of the algorithm. The pseudo code of FCM algorithm is as follows:

Algorithm 1. FCM

1: **Input:** The number of clusters c and the data set.
2: **Out:** The cluster center set v_j minimizes $J_{FCM}(U,V)$.
3: According to the number of clusters c, randomly give the cluster center $V_0 = (v_1, v_2, ..., v_c)$ and the termination error ε, and set the current iteration number as $t = 0$.
4: Find the membership matrix U_t according to formula (3).
5: According to formula (4), find the cluster center V_{t+1} of the next iteration.
6: If $\|U^{t+1} - U^t\| < \varepsilon$, end the iteration, otherwise set $t = t + 1$ and return to 4.

2.2   Lion Swarm Optimization Algorithm

According to a certain proportion, lion group is divided into three categories: lion king, lioness and cub. The lion king is responsible for the distribution of food, the protection of territory and the protection of the cub. The lioness is mainly responsible for hunting and taking care of the cub. Update the lioness position according to formula (5).

$$x_i^{t+1} = \frac{p_i^t + p_c^t}{2} (1 + \alpha_f \gamma), \quad \alpha_f = step \cdot \exp\left[-30 \left(\frac{t}{T}\right)\right]^{10}, \tag{5}$$

where p_i^t is the i lioness of the t generation. p_c^t is the lioness randomly selected from the t generation of lioness. γ is the random number generated by normal distribution. α_f is perturbation factor. $step$ is the step size of the lioness. T is the population iteration number. t is the current iteration number.

The activities of cub are mainly divided into three situations: when they are hungry, they eat close to the lion king; when they are full, they learn to hunt with the lioness; when they grow up, they will be driven out of the group by the lion king and come back to challenge the status of the lion king after growing up. Update the cub position according to formula (6).

$$
x_i^{t+1} = \begin{cases} \frac{g^t + p_i^t}{2}\left(1 + \alpha_c\gamma\right), & q \le \frac{1}{3} \\ \frac{p_m^t + p_i^t}{2}\left(1 + \alpha_c\gamma\right), & \frac{1}{3} \le q \le \frac{2}{3} \\ \frac{\bar{g}^t + p_i^t}{2}\left(1 + \alpha_c\gamma\right), & \frac{2}{3} \le q < 1 \end{cases} ,
\tag{6}
$$

where g^t is the global optimal lion of the generation. p_m^t is the history optimal position of lioness. α_c is perturbation factor. $\bar{g}^t$ is the position far away from the lion king.

2.3 Sin Cos Algorithm

Sin cos algorithm (SCA) [11] is optimized by using the oscillation characteristics of sine function and cosine function. Its advantages are good convergence and easy implementation.

$$
\begin{aligned}
&[\min] f\left(x\right) = \min f\left(x_1, x_2, ..., x_n\right) \\
&s.t \ \ L_i \le X_i \le U_i, i = 1, 2, ..., n
\end{aligned} ,
\tag{7}
$$

where X_i is the i-th variable to be optimized, L_i and U_i are the upper and lower boundaries of X_i, respectively.

SCA first randomly generates N search individuals, calculates the fitness of each individual according to the fitness function, and records the individual with the best fitness as the optimal individual X^*. The individual position update formula in the optimization process is:

$$
X_i^{t+1} = \begin{cases} X_i^t + r_1 \sin\left(r_2\right)\left|r_3 X_i^* - X_i^t\right|, r_4 < 0.5 \\ X_i^t + r_1 \cos\left(r_2\right)\left|r_3 X_i^* - X_i^t\right|, r_4 \ge 0.5 \end{cases} ,
\tag{8}
$$

$$
r_1 = a\left(1 - \frac{t}{t_{\max}}\right).
\tag{9}
$$

Among them, X_i^t is the position of the i-th individual in the t-th generation population, X_i^* is the current optimal individual position. a is a constant greater than 1, and is assigned a value of 2 in this article, t is the number of previous iterations and $t_{\max}$ is the maximum number of iterations. $r_2 \in (0, 2\pi)$ is a random number subject to uniform distribution, $r_3 \in (0, 2)$ is a random number subject to uniform distribution, $r_4 \in (0, 1)$ is a random number subject to uniform distribution.

2.4 Elite Opposition-Based Learning

Opposition-Based Learning (OBL) is a new strategy that has emerged in the field of computational intelligence in recent years. Studies have shown that the probability that the reverse solution is closer to the global optimal solution is 50% higher than the current solution. This strategy can effectively enhance the diversity of the population and prevent the algorithm from falling into local optimums. Elite Opposition-Based Learning (EOBL) [12] is proposed for the problem that the reverse learning strategy is not necessarily easier to find the global optimal solution than the current search space. This strategy uses dominant individuals to construct the reverse population, in order to increase the diversity of the population.

Assuming that $X_i = (x_{i1}, x_{i2}, ..., x_{iD})$ is an ordinary particle, and the corresponding extreme is the elite particle $X_i^e = (x_{i1}^e, x_{i2}^e, ..., x_{iD}^e)$, the elite reverse solution can be defined as:

$$X_i^e = \mu \left(da_j + db_j \right) - x_{ij}^e, \tag{10}$$

where $x_{ij}^e \in [a_j, b_j]$, $k \in (0,1)$ are random numbers that obey a normal distribution, and $[da_j, db_j]$ is the dynamic boundary of the j-th dimensional search space, which can be calculated according to formula (11):

$$da_j = \min \left(x_{ij} \right), \ db_j = \max \left(x_{ij} \right). \tag{11}$$

Using dynamic boundaries to replace the fixed boundaries of the search space can accumulate search experience, so that the generated inverse solution is located in the gradually reduced search space and accelerate the algorithm convergence. When the generated reverse solution lies outside the boundary, use a randomly generated method to reset. As shown in formula (12):

$$X_i^e = rand \left(da_j, db_j \right). \tag{12}$$

3 The Improved Lion Swarm Optimization Algorithm

3.1 The Improved Lion Swarm Optimization Algorithm

The improvement of lion swarm optimization is to update the positions of lioness and cub.

Improvement of Lioness Position Updating Method. For the location update method of lioness, introduce the sine part of sin cos optimization algorithm. Update the position of the lioness according to formula (13).

$$X_i^{t+1} = X_i^t + r_1 \sin \left(r_2 \right) \left(r_3 g^t - X_i^t \right) \tag{13}$$

Improvement of Position Updating Method for Cub. For the position update mode of cub, introduce sin cos optimization algorithm. Update the position of the cub according to formula (14).

$$
\begin{aligned}
&if\ r_5 < 0.5 \\
&\quad if\ r_4 < 0.5 \\
&\qquad X_i^{t+1} = X_i^t + r_1 \sin{(r_2)}\,(r_3 g^t - X_i^t) \\
&\quad else \\
&\qquad X_i^{t+1} = X_i^t + r_1 \cos{(r_2)}\,(r_3 g^t - X_i^t) \\
&else \\
&\quad if\ r_4 < 0.5 \\
&\qquad X_i^{t+1} = X_i^t + r_1 \sin{(r_2)}\,(r_3 p_m^t - X_i^t) \\
&\quad else \\
&\qquad X_i^{t+1} = X_i^t + r_1 \cos{(r_2)}\,(r_3 p_m^t - X_i^t)
\end{aligned}
\tag{14}
$$

The Introduction of Supervision Mechanism. In the iterative process, when the difference between the two adjacent global optimal values is less than the set threshold, the algorithm falls into the local optimum. At this time, a Gaussian random walk strategy is used to generate new individuals to help the algorithm jump out of the local optimum. The position generating formula is as follows:

$$
X_i^{t+1} = Gaussian\left(X_i^t, \sigma\right),
\tag{15}
$$

$$
\sigma = \cos\left(\pi \frac{t}{2t_{\max}}\right)\left(X_i^t - X_r^*\left(t\right)\right),
\tag{16}
$$

where X_r^* is a random individual in the discoverer population. The cosine function is used to adjust the step size. As the number of iterations increases, the disturbance is gradually reduced, which is beneficial to balance the algorithm's global and local search capabilities.

3.2 Algorithm Process

The pseudo code of improved lion swarm optimization algorithm is in Algorithm 2.

3.3 Performance Comparison and Analysis

Four benchmark functions are selected to test the performance of the algorithm.
Rosenbrock

$$
f\left(x\right) = \sum_{i=1}^{d-1}\left[100\left(x_{i+1} - x_i^2\right)^2 + \left(x_i - 1\right)^2\right]
$$

Shifted-Rastrigin

$$
f\left(x\right) = 10d + \sum_{i=1}^{d}\left[\left(x_i - 2\right)^2 - 10\cos\left(2\pi\left(x_i - 2\right)\right)\right]
$$

Algorithm 2. Improved Lion Swarm Optimization

1: **Input: N,D,T,epsilon**
2: **Out: Optimal Solution**
3: Initialization and generate an elite opposition-based lion group. Calculate the fitness values of all lions and distribute the male lion, lioness and cubs in proportion.
4: **while** the iteration is not termination **do**
5:　　Update position of the male lion, lioness and cubs and generate an elite opposition-based lion group.
6:　　Calculate the fitness values of all lions, distribute the male lion, lioness and cubs in proportion and record the optimal fitness value of this iteration.
7:　　**if** difference between the optimal values of two adjacent iterations<epsilon **then**
8:　　　　Implementation monitoring mechanism.
9:　　**end if**
10: **end while**

Levy

$$f(x) = \sin^2(\pi w_1) + \sum_{i=1}^{d-1} (w_i - 1)^2 \left[1 + 10\sin^2(\pi w_i - 1)\right] + (w_d - 1)\left[1 + \sin^2(2\pi w_d)\right]$$

$$where\ w_i = 1 + \frac{x_i - 1}{4}\ for\ all\ i = 1, 2, ..., d$$

Shifted-Sphere

$$f(x) = \sum_{i=1}^{d} (x_i - 2)^2$$

PSO, LSO and ILSO algorithms are used to verify the four test functions. The parameters are set as follows: population size $N = 50$, function dimension $D = 40$, maximum iteration number $T = 6000$. PSO takes inertia weight $w = 0.8$ and learning factor $c1 = c2 = 1.5$. Each algorithm runs independently for 30 times. From (a), (b), (c) and (d) in Fig. 1, it can be seen that the optimization result of ILSO algorithm has higher solution accuracy than PSO and LSO algorithm, and the fitness value decreases and converges faster.

4　Experimental Results and Analysis

4.1　FCM Algorithm Based on ILSO Algorithm

Suppose the sample space $X = \{x_1, x_2, ..., x_n\}$, where x_i is a d-dimensional vector. A lion in LSO algorithm represents a cluster center set $V = \{v_1, v_2, ..., v_c\}$, where v_j is a vector of the same dimension as x_i. For the evaluation of each solution (clustering center) in the lion group, define an individual fitness function:

$$fit_i = \frac{1}{[1 + J_{FCM}(U, V)]}. \tag{17}$$

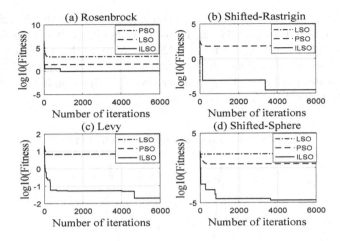

Fig. 1. Evolution curves of different test functions.

Among them: $J_{FCM}(U, V)$ is the objective function defined in formula (1), the better the clustering effect, the smaller the $J_{FCM}(U, V)$, the higher the fit_i.

The main idea of ILSO-FCM algorithm is: first use ILSO algorithm to obtain the optimal solution (clustering center) as the initial clustering center of FCM algorithm, then use FCM algorithm to optimize the initial clustering center, and finally find the optimal solution. The algorithm is a fast clustering algorithm, so the algorithm has good time performance and shortens the convergence time of FCM algorithm.

4.2 Database

The experimental data uses Ecoli data set [13,14] in UCI standard database, which describes the use of amino acid sequences in cell location sites to classify Ecoli proteins, that is, the chemical composition of the protein before folding to predict how the protein interacts with the cell Combine. The data set consists of 336 Ecoli protein data, each of which is described using 7 input variables calculated from the amino acid sequence of the protein, and is divided into 8 categories in total.

4.3 Experimental Results and Analysis

In order to verify the effectiveness and feasibility of ILSO-FCM algorithm, FCM, LSO-FCM and ILSO-FCM algorithm were used to cluster Ecoli data set, and minimum allowable error in each algorithm $\varepsilon = 10^{-3}$, fuzzy weighting index $m = 2$. The parameters of LSO-FCM and ILSO-FCM algorithm are set as: population size $N = 20$, maximum number of iterations $T = 200$, function dimension $D = 7 \times 30$. Run the three algorithms respectively and the experimental results are shown in the Fig. 2.

From Fig. 2, it can be seen that optimal clustering results of ILSO-FCM algorithm are better than FCM and LSO-FCM algorithm. It can be seen from Table 1 that the average correct rate of ILSO-FCM algorithm is higher than the other two algorithms. Therefore, it is concluded that the final optimization result of ILSO algorithm is better than the other two algorithms, and ILSO algorithm converges faster and has higher accuracy.

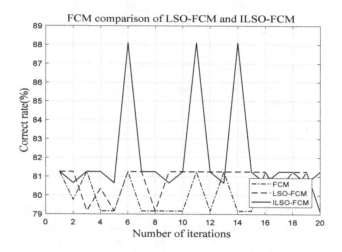

Fig. 2. FCM comparison of LSO-FCM and ILSO-FCM.

Table 1. Average accuracy rate(%) of FCM, LSO-FCM and ILSO-FCM.

Algorithm	[13] data	[14] data
FCM	80.01	52.70
LSO-FCM	80.74	52.70
ILSO-FCM	82.10	54.49

5 Conclusion

This paper introduces sin cos algorithm and elite opposition-based learning to improve lion swarm optimization algorithm and obtains improved lion swarm optimization algorithm, which improves local and global optimization capabilities. In the function test, the optimization result of ILSO algorithm is better than that of PSO and LSO algorithms, which reflects the superiority of ILSO algorithm in the optimization result. The ILSO algorithm is combined with

FCM algorithm then obtain ILSO-FCM algorithm, which not only overcomes the shortcoming of FCM algorithm that is easy to fall into the local optimal solution, but also makes up for the shortcoming of FCM algorithm that is sensitive to initial values and noisy data. Experiments show that ILSO-FCM algorithm has strong global search capabilities, and it is less sensitive to the initial values and significantly improves the clustering effect.

Acknowledgement. This study is supported by the Shandong Province Science Foundation of China (Grant No. ZR2020MF153) and Key Innovation Project of Shandong Province (Grant No. 2019JZZY010111).

References

1. Dunn, J.: A fuzzy relative of the ISODATA process and its use in detecting compact well separated cluster. J. Cyber-Net **3**, 32–57 (1974)
2. Bezdek, J.: Pattern Recognition with Fuzzy Objective Function Algorithms. Plenum, New York (1981)
3. Zhao, Q.: Research on personalized recommendation algorithm of chemical product ecommerce based on genetic fuzzy clustering. Bonding **44**(11), 86–89 (2020)
4. Yi, T., He, S., Zheng, G.: Medical image segmentation based on fuzzy C-means and improved cuckoo optimization. Intell. Comput. Appl. **10**(08), 144–147 (2020)
5. Chang, X.: Research on fuzzy clustering algorithm based on bat algorithm optimization. Shenyang University of Technology (2020)
6. Jiang, M., Yuan, D.: Artificial Fish Swarm Algorithm and its Applications. Science Press, Beijing (2012)
7. Jiang, M., Yuan, D.: Artificial Bee Colony Algorithm and its Applications. Science Press, Beijing (2014)
8. Yang, Z., Yang, Y., Luo, T.: A hybrid immune algorithm for solving dynamic optimization problems. In: China Control and Decision Conference, pp. 1174–1180 (2018)
9. Kennedy, J., Eberhart, R.: Particle swarm optimization. In: International Conference on Neural Networks, ICNN 1995 pp. 1942–1948. IEEE (1995)
10. Liu, S., Yang, Y., Zhou, Y.: A swarm intelligence algorithm - lion swarm algorithm. Pattern Recogn. Artif. Intell. **31**(05), 431–441 (2018)
11. Chegini, S., Bagheri, A., Najafi, F.: PSOSCALF: a new hybrid PSO based on sine cosine algorithm and levy flight for solving optimization problems. Appl. Soft Comput. J. **73**, 697–726 (2018)
12. Wang, W., Li, W., Wang, Z., Li, L.: Opposition-based multi-objective whale optimization algorithm with global grid ranking. Neurocomputing **314**(5), 41–59 (2019)
13. https://www.kaggle.com/kannanaikkal/ecoli-uci-dataset
14. https://www.qlit.edu.cn/datasets/

Sparrow Search Algorithm for Solving Flexible Jobshop Scheduling Problem

Mingliang Wu[1], Dongsheng Yang[1], Zhile Yang[2(✉)], and Yuanjun Guo[2]

[1] Intelligent Electrical Science and Technology Research Institute,
Northeastern University, Boston, USA
wuml@siat.ac.cn
[2] Shenzhen Institute of Advanced Technology, Chinese Academy of Sciences,
Beijing, China
{zl.yang,yj.guo}@siat.ac.cn

Abstract. With the global development of the third industrial revolution, intelligent manufacturing has received attention from many countries and regions since it was first proposed. In the next ten years, intelligent manufacturing has become an important factor in determining international status, and it is imminent for traditional manufacturing to switch to intelligent manufacturing. Flexible job-shop scheduling is a key research problem in the field of intelligent manufacturing. In this paper, we uses a novel swarm intelligence optimization algorithm-Sparrow Search Algorithm to solve the problem of the longest processing time of workshop scheduling. The experimental results show that compared with other advanced meta-heuristic algorithms, the Sparrow Search Algorithm (SSA) can not only achieve ideal optimization accuracy in the test function, but also can achieve acceleration effects and solving capabilities that other algorithms do not have in actual shop scheduling problems.

Keywords: Sparrow search algorithm · Flexible job shop scheduling problem · Makespan · Global convergence

1 Introduction

JSP is not only a difficult problem in the field of manufacturing, but also a key issue [1]. It is a key link that affects the production efficiency of manufacturing enterprises or production units. The production of a product requires a series of key links such as raw material collection, transportation, processing, and packaging. Today's workshop scheduling problem is not only limited to the processing link, but also permeates other production links [2]. Moreover, with the improvement of production efficiency requirements and the continuous progress of production levels, many machines can be set to process multiple types of workpieces, which makes the production process extremely rich in scheduling

Supported by organization x.

margin, that is, flexibility [3]. This gives rise to a new problem that needs to be solved urgently: flexible job shop scheduling. Compared with the traditional inflexible workshop scheduling problem, FJSP is more complicated and difficult to obtain a better solution because it adds an additional machine selection problem [4]. Therefore, in FJSP, there are two problems we need to solve, one is operation sequence problem that is also exist in the JSP, another is machine selection problem that is additional compared to FJSP machine selection problem is more difficult to solve compared to JSP in the case of the controlled variable method. In other words, the complexity of we solve the machine selection problem when the operation sequence is determined is bigger than we solve the operation sequence problem when machine selection is determined [4]. Because for the machine selection problem, the operation of the job can be processed on many machines (usually greater than two or three machines) in the most scenes. FJSP is different from most conventional optimization problems, In the FJSP, the process of optimizing is not inherited, in other words, The optimal solution obtained in the previous iteration has no decisive guiding significance for the next solution process as local optimal solutions are irregularly distributed in the search space. People have also tried different types of algorithms to solve FJSP problems that main includes two categories: exact and approximate algorithms. About the exact algorithm, it is more expensively spend time but more precise, most of which are formulated by integer linear programming (ILP) or mixed ILP (MILP) models [5].

About the approximate algorithm, Meta-heuristic algorithm is a major solver for FJSP that is design by summarizing the habits and behavior characteristics of creatures in nature compared to exact algorithm, Meta-heuristic algorithm is more random and uncertain when solving problems, and has the ability to jump out of local optimal solutions [6]. Therefore, in view of the characteristics of the FJSP problem, the meta-heuristic algorithm is a more suitable and convenient method compared to other types of algorithms [7]. Although emerging artificial intelligence algorithms such as deep learning or reinforcement learning have achieved rapid development, as far as FJSP is concerned, this machine learning method is still not suitable, because in FJSP, the top 20% of the scheduling scheme will directly affect The last 80% of the scheduling results. However, there are many types of meta-heuristics. Each meta-heuristic has its own characteristics in its search capabilities and search process. As one of the meta-heuristic algorithms, the sparrow search algorithm is a new swarm intelligence algorithm that was just proposed this year [8–10]. The sparrow search algorithm has a fast solution response capability, and the solution mechanism is simple and clear. Compared with most meta-heuristic algorithms, each iteration of SSA saves more time, This is particularly critical for time-critical FJSP problems. Moreover, its solving ability and final optimization effect are not inferior to most other algorithms, so this paper intends to use SSA to solve some actual FJSP. In order to test the performance of the SSA algorithm, we introduced six other algorithms as comparison algorithms, they are DA cfPSO, Jaya, SCA,SSA,DE [11–16]. The remaining structure of the article is arranged as follows: firstly, introduce the characteristics of FJSP, including its classification, constraints, and solution goals in Sect. 2. Next, the principles and mathematical formulas of the algorithm we used are discussed in Sect. 3. Thirdly, show the experiment results (that includes actual FJSP and test functions) and make the corresponding discussions in the Sect. 4. Finally, Sect. 5 concludes the paper.

2   Problem Formulation

FJSP is a scheduling and planning problem that mainly occur in manufacture field, a $N \times M$ can be described as: there are N jobs (each job contains several operations) and M machines [5,17]. In a job shop, our task is to arrange the machining machines of each operation of each job reasonably to best meet our expected requirements [18,19]. The different operation of different job own unique processing information. In other words, the set of optional machines and correspond process time of each operation is independent. For example, in the Fig. 1, operation O_{11} can be processed on the Machine M_1 and M_3. operation O_{12} can be processed on the Machine M_1 and M_2 yet.

2.1   T-FJSP and P-FJSP

Mentioned in the previous chapter, Compared with JSP, FJSP additionally added the "machine selection" problem, that breaking the constraint that one machine can only process one process. The job has a margin of choice when choosing a processing machine, that is, flexibility. In many literatures, flexibility is defined as the number of machines that can be selected for each of each job on average, as shown in the equation below:

$$flexibility = \frac{\sum_{i=1}^{i=n} \sum_{j=1}^{j=m} m\_s_{ij}}{n * m} \tag{1}$$

In the Eq. (1), n represents the number of jobs, m represents the number of operations, m_s_{ij} represents the number of available machines of the operation j of the job i. To illustrate the calculation process of flexibility more vividly, we introduce a actual workshop problem. There are 3 jobs and 3 machines in a workshop, each jobs has 2 operation The detailed processing information is shown in the following table: so the flexibility can be calculated as:

$$flexibility = \frac{2+2+1+2+2+1}{2*3}$$
$$= 1.6667 \; machines/operation$$

Flexibility directly reflects the margin of machine selection. Although it is numerically continuous, FJSP can be divided into two main types according to the problem-solving needs,that is total FJSP (T-FJSP) and partial FJSP (P-FJSP). T-FJSP has the highest flexibility, each operation of each job can

Job	Operation	Machine			Available machines
		M_1	M_2	M_3	
J_1	O_{11}	✓	✗	✓	2
	O_{12}	✓	✓	✗	2
J_2	O_{21}	✗	✓	✗	1
	O_{22}	✓	✗	✓	2
J_3	O_{31}	✗	✓	✓	2
	O_{32}	✗	✓	✗	1

Fig. 1. The 3×6 scale FJSP

be processed on all machines, P-FJSP has general flexibility, each operation of each job can be processed on partial machines. In order to elaborate the relationship between T-FJSP and P-FJSP, we introduce a actual 3×6 FJSP and corresponding detail of production are shwon in the below table:

Job	Operation	Machine			
		Z_1	Z_2	Z_3	Z_4
X_1	xy_{11}	3	2	6	7
	xy_{12}	4	7	9	5
X_2	xy_{21}	2	1	4	3
	xy_{22}	5	2	1	9

Fig. 2. The 3×6 scale T-FJSP

Figure 2 and Fig. 3 both show the actual processing information of the actual jobshop, but differently, each operation of each job can be processed on all machines in Fig. 2 and this situation belong to T-TJSP, each operation of each job can be processed on partial machines in Fig. 3 and this situation belong to P-TJSP.

2.2   The Relationship Between JSP and FJSP

According to the difference of resources constraints, FJSP can be divided into two categories: P-FJSP and T-FJSP [20]. In order to describe the differences between them, a 3×6 FJSP is introduced in detail in the Fig. 1.

In the Fig. 1, x_i denotes the ith job, $\forall i \in [1,3]$; xy_{ij} denotes the jth operation of ith job, $\forall j \in [1,3]$; z_k denotes the k machine, $\forall k \in [1,6]$, $z_k \in Z$. Assume Z_{ij} denotes the optional machine set for operation xy_{ij}, the difference can be summarized as follows:

Job	Operation	Machine			
		Z_1	Z_2	Z_3	Z_4
X_1	xy_{11}	3	2	6	7
	xy_{12}	-	7	-	5
X_2	xy_{21}	2	-	4	-
	xy_{22}	5	-	-	9

Fig. 3. The 3 × 6 scale P-FJSP

Job	Operation	Machine and Time					
		z_1	z_2	z_3	z_4	z_5	z_6
x_1	xy_{11}	1	3	6	-	9	9
	xy_{12}	4	2	-	3	3	6
	xy_{13}	-	7	-	4	6	1
x_2	xy_{21}	5	-	6	2	-	4
	xy_{22}	3	1	2	-	5	3
	xy_{23}	-	3	-	4	2	7
x_3	xy_{31}	3	2	-	7	-	6
	xy_{32}	1	-	3	2	6	1
	xy_{33}	2	3	7	-	-	2

Fig. 4. The 3 × 6 scale FJSP

- case one that each operation xy_{ij} of each x_i can be processed by all the machines, which represents $Z_{ij} = Z$, is called total FJSP.
- case two that each operation xy_{ij} of each x_i can be processed by partial machines, which represents $Z_{ij} \in Z$, is called partial FJSP (Fig. 4).

2.3 Symbol Definition and Description

Before describing the mathematical model of FJSP, defining some symbols and instructions is necessary, which are showed:

n: the number of job
ℓ: the set of all jobs, $\ell = \{D_i | i = 1, 2, ..., n\}$
D_i: the ith job
m: the number of machine
$\wp$: the set of all machines, $\wp = \{E_k | k = 1, 2, ..., m\}$
E_k: the kth machine
F_{ij}: the jth operation of D_i
N_i: the operation number of D_i
m_{ij}: the optional machine number of F_{ij}

$\wp_{ij}$: the optional machine set of F_{ij}
w_{ijk}: the processing time of F_{ij} on E_k
b_{ijk}: the beginning time of F_{ij} on E_k
f_{ijk}: the finishing time of F_{ij} on E_k
F_i: the completion time of D_i
C_{max}: the maximum completion time of all jobs
b_{ij}: the beginning time of F_{ij}
f_{ij}: the finish time of F_{ij}

2.4   The Mathematical Model of FJSP

The mathematical model can generally be boiled down to a set of constraints and objective functions, In the FJSP, constraints affect the selection rule of machines for corresponding operation, it can been described as follow:

(1) Pre-booking or cancellation is not allowed during processing, and it is not allowed to cancel during processing

$$b_{ijk} + w_{ijk} = f_{ijk} \qquad (2)$$

(2) When time is 0, all jobs can be processed and all machines are optional.

$$b_{ijk} \geq 0 \qquad (3)$$

$$f_{ijk} \geq 0 \qquad (4)$$

(3) Operations of the same job exist sequence:

$$f_{ij} \leq b_{i(j+1)} \qquad (5)$$

where $\forall i \in [1, n]$, $\forall j \in [1, N_i - 1]$
(4) Only one machine can be selected for each operation:

$$\sum_{k=1}^{m} x_{ijk} = 1 \qquad (6)$$

where $\forall i \in [1, n]$, $\forall j \in [1, N_i]$, $\forall k \in [1, m]$
(5) Each machine can only process one operation at a time:

$$f_{ij} \leq b_{i'j'} \qquad (7)$$

where $x_{ijk} = 1$, $x_{i'j'k} = 1$, $y_{ijk} = r$, $y_{i'j'k} = r + 1$, $\forall i \in [1, n]$, $\forall j \in [1, N_i]$.

There are many kinds of objective functions of FJSP, that mainly include maximum completion time, maximum machine load, processing cost. But because the maximum completion time can best represent the company's benefit, many documents regard the maximum completion time as the main goal of the research. Similarly, In this paper, maximum completion time is also used for testing algorithm performance, the following is the objective function of algorithm:

$$minC_{max} = min(\max_{i=1}^{n} F_i) \qquad (8)$$

3   Sparrow Search Algorithm

In recent years, with the development of swarm intelligence algorithms, meta-heuristic algorithm has become a hot research method to solve FJSP. As one of the meta-heuristic algorithm, SSA is proposed by researcher Jiankai Xue et al. in 2020. Practice and simulation have proved that SSA has fast iteration speed and good search ability, and can achieve better solution effects than most other algorithms. Let us describe the details of SSA below.

3.1   Biological Basis

The selection effect of nature gives animals the reason for survival, as a species in the biological kingdom, sparrows are distributed all over the world. Sparrows live in groups, their life behaviors are carried out by group activities, and they are a common group living animal. In the entire group of sparrows, there are mainly two identities, one is the producer, also called the explorer; the other is the scrounger, also called the follower. The producer is responsible for finding food in the population and providing foraging areas and directions for the entire sparrow population, while the scrounger uses the discoverer to obtain food. In order to obtain food, sparrows can usually forage for food using two behavioral strategies: producer and scrounger. Individuals in the population will monitor the behavior of other individuals in the population, and the attackers in the population will compete with high-intake companions for food resources to increase their predation rate. In addition, when sparrow populations are aware of danger, they will act against predation.

The foraging process of sparrows is very similar to the algorithmic optimization process, by summarizing the behavioral characteristics of sparrow foraging, Jiankai Xue et al. proposed the sparrow search algorithm in 2020. In order to verify the effectiveness of the algorithm, the author of the algorithm uses the Sphere function and Rosenbrock function to verify SSA, experiments prove that the SSA algorithm has fast convergence speed and search accuracy, and is a scientifically advanced meta-inspired swarm intelligence algorithm.

3.2   Algorithm Description of SSA

Similar to smart algorithms in many groups, the location update strategy of the SSA group is always carried out in steps. The producer is responsible for finding food for the entire sparrow population and providing directions for all those who join, Therefore, the producer can obtain a larger foraging search range than the joiner. The location update strategy of producer is as follows:

$$X_{ij}^{t+1} = \begin{cases} X_{i,j}^t * exp(\frac{-i}{a*iter_{max}}) & if \quad P_2 < ST \\ X_{i,j}^t + Q * L & if \quad P_2 \geq ST \end{cases} \tag{9}$$

In the above equation, $a * iter_{max}$ represents the maximum number of iterations, i represents the ith dimension, Q describes a normal distributed random number, L represents a d-dimension vector for which each element inside is $1(d$ represents the dimension of solution), P_2 is the random number range in the $[0, 1]$, ST denotes the warning value that is setted generally to the random number range in $[0.5, 1]$.

When $P_2 < ST$, which denotes there is no danger around, the producer carried out the fast and extensive search activity. In contrast, if $P_2 \geq ST$, producers are aware of the dangers of the surrounding environment and flee quickly and search for the next foraging place.

Different scroungers perform different actions according to their own characteristics. The location update strategy of all scroungers is shown in the following equation:

$$X_{i,j}^{t+1} = \begin{cases} Q * exp\left(\frac{X_{worst}^t - X_{i,j}^t}{i^2}\right) & otherwise \\ X_p^{t+1} + \left|X_{i,j}^t - X_p^{t+1}\right| * A^+ * L \ if & i < n/2 \end{cases} \tag{10}$$

Where X_P is the optimal position occupied by the producer. X_{worst}^t represents the global worst solution under current iteration conditions, A signifies a matrix of $1 * d$ for which each element inside is randomly assigned 1 or -1 (d represents the dimension of solution), and $A^+ = A^T * (A * A^T)^{-1}$.

When $i < n/2$, each scrounger has a higher fitness value and they will compete with followers for food. Otherwise, it suggests that the ith scrounger with the worse fitness value is most likely to be starving.

Among the whole sparrow group, there are always some sparrows in danger zone and those sparrows will quickly move toward the safe area to get a better position when they are aware of danger. while the sparrow in a safe zone will do a random walk strategy to prey efficiently. the mathematical model can be expressed as follows:

$$X_{i,j}^{t+1} = \begin{cases} X_{best}^t + \beta * \left|X_{i,j}^t - X_{best}^t\right| & if \quad f_i > f_g \\ X_{i,j}^t + K * \left(\frac{\left|X_{i,j}^t - X_{worst}^t\right|}{(f_i - f_w) + \varepsilon}\right) & if \quad f_i = f_g \end{cases} \tag{11}$$

where X_{best} is the current global optimal location, X_{worst} is the current global worst solution location. β is a step size control parameter that is setted to a normal distribution of random numbers with a mean value of 0 and a variance of 1. K represents a random number between 0 and $1.f_i$ represents the fitness value of the present sparrow, f_g and f_w are the current global best and worst fitness values, ε is the smallest constant so as to avoid zero-division-error.

When $f_i > f_g$ that indicates the current sparrow in a relatively dangerous position in the entire sparrow group, X_best represents the location of the centre of the population and is safe around it. Otherwise, which indicates the sparrow in the middle of the population, are aware of the danger and need to move closer to the others. K denotes the direction in which the sparrow moves and is also the step size control coefficient.

Through the above sparrow behavior analysis and specific algorithm description, the pseudo code of SSA can be summarized as shown in Fig. 5, and the algorithm flow chart of SSA is shown in Fig. 6.

Algorithm The pseudo code of SSA

Initialization stage

Iter_max: the maximum iterations

SD: the number of sparrows who perceive the danger

PD: the number of producers

N: the number of sparrows

D: the dimension of each sparrows

Iter: record the number of iterations

Generate a population of n sparrows

Calculate the fitness of all sparrows

Rank present population from high to low by fitness

Iteration stage

While *Iter< Iter_max*

Update the location of the producer

R_2=rand(1)

Select the *PD* best sparrow from the current population as producer

For i=1:*PD*

Using equation (9) update the location of producers

End for

Update the location of scoungers

Set the remaining sparrows as scoungers

For i=(*PD*+1):*N*

Using equation (10) update the location of scroungers

End for

Anti-predation behavior

Select randomly the *SD* sparrow to carry out following for_end circulation

For i =1:*SD*

Using equation (11) update the sparrow's location

End for

Rank present population from high to low by fitness

t=t+1

End while

Output result

Fig. 5. The flowchart of the SSA

4   Validation and Comparison

In this paper, in order to verify the effectiveness of the algorithm and further test the performance of the algorithm, we introduced several simple test functions and use SSA algorithm to solve. The information of these functions is shown in the Fig. 7.

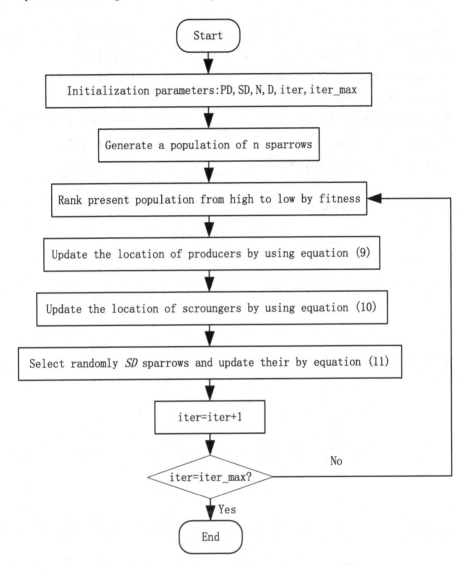

Fig. 6. The flowchart of the SSA

We introduce 6 other algorithms to compare with SSA, they are DA, cfPSO, Jaya, SSA, SCA, DE, The convergence curves of the optimization process of unimodal function and multimodal function are shown in the Fig. 8 and Fig. 9 respectively.

The iterative convergence curve is the average result obtained after running ten times, so this comparative analysis of the results is very representative. The six functions are divided into two types, which respectively test the exploration and exploitation capabilities of SSA. Experiments show that SSA has good con-

Function	Properties
Rotated_High_Conditioned_Elliptic_Function	Unimodal
Rotated_Bent_Cigar_Function	Unimodal
Rotated_Discus_Function	Unimodal
Rotated_Ackleys_Function	Multimodal
Schwefels_Function	Multimodal
Rotated_Schwefels_Function	Multimodal

Fig. 7. The details of the test function

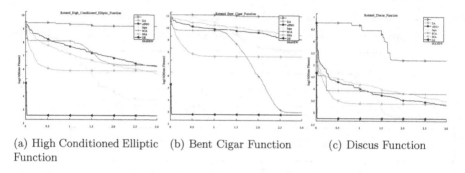

(a) High Conditioned Elliptic   (b) Bent Cigar Function   (c) Discus Function
Function

Fig. 8. The convergence curves of unimodal functions

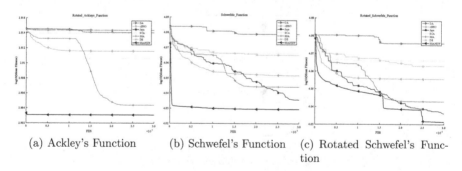

(a) Ackley's Function   (b) Schwefel's Function   (c) Rotated Schwefel's Function

Fig. 9. The convergence curves of multimodal functions

vergence ability and global optimization ability. Therefore, after comprehensive consideration, in the seven algorithms of the appeal, through the test of the test function, it can be concluded that SSA can achieve the best optimization effect.

In this paper, the objective function aims of FJSP to minimize the total processing time, where several famous benchmark data set is selected to evaluate the optimization ability of SSA. These algorithms are compared on ten medium and ten small size benchmarks. The algorithm terminates when the number of iteration reaches to the maximum generation count. Corresponding parameters of algorithms in the experiment are shown in Table 1.

Table 1. The parameters settings of optimization algorithms

Parameters	Value
Size of population	200
Total generation number	200
P_2 of SSANEW (warning value)	$P_2 \in [0,1]$
ST of SSANEW (safety value)	$ST \in [0.5, 1]$
C1 of cfPSO (individual learning factor)	2
C2 of cfPSO (society learning factor)	2
W of cfPSO (inertia weight)	$0.9 - iter * ((0.9 - 0.4)/Max\_iter)$
S1 of SSA (exploration coefficient)	$2e^{-(\frac{4i}{L})^2}$
r_1 of SCA (Balance parameter)	$r_1 = a - t * \frac{a}{T}$
r of DA (radius of ne)	$(ub - lb) * (1/4 + (iter/Max\_iter) * 2))$
s of DA (separation weight)	0.1
a of DA (alignment weight)	0.1
c of DA (cohesion weight)	0.7
f of DA (food factor)	1
e of DA (enemy factor)	1
w of DA (inertia weight)	$0.9 - iter * ((0.9 - 0.4)/Max\_iter)$

The FJSP experimental results of the comparison of the seven algorithms are placed in Table 2. The data with * indicates the optimal result, MFJS indicates the medium-scale FJSP, and SFJS indicates the small-scale FJSP. Since the difficulty of solving SFJS is relatively small, the optimization results of the seven algorithms are comparable, among which DA, Jaya, DE, and SSANEW can reach the complete optimal. In MFJS, SSANEW can achieve the best on nine scales of FJSP, and Jaya can achieve the best on MFJS08. Therefore, it can be seen from the experimental results that in practical applications, the application ability of SSANEW is stronger and more stable.

Figure 10 and Fig. 11 illustrate the Gantt charts of the optimal solution obtained by SSA algorithm on problem MFSJ02 and MFSJ10 respectively, it can conclude that for MFJS02, the shortest processing time obtained by SSA is 446 and for MFSJ10, the shortest processing time obtained by SSA is 1340, the result is better than other compared algorithms.

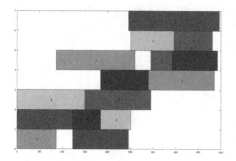   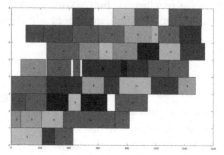

Fig. 10. Gantt chart of MFSJ01   **Fig. 11.** Gantt chart of MFSJ10

Table 2. The statistical results obtained by algorithms

Algorithms	MFJS01	MFJS02	MFJS03	MFJS04	MFJS05	MFJS06
DA	469*	456	517	650	610	722
Jaya	469*	465	533	656	662	728
SSA	469*	507	610	745	707	870
cfPSO	477	530	599	638	662	897
DE	469*	457	520	627	612	725
SCA	469*	512	614	745	701	872
SSANEW	469*	446*	491*	581*	519*	642*
Algorithms	MFJS07	MFJS08	MFJS09	MFJS10	SFJS01	SFJS02
DA	1080	1122	1262	1513	66*	107*
Jaya	1081	1064*	1296	1520	66*	107*
SSA	1190	1342	1406	1737	66*	107*
dfPSO	1186	1194	1368	1739	66*	107*
DE	1088	1099	1352	1536	66*	107*
SCA	1152	1366	1401	1710	66*	107*
SSANEW	910*	1159	1167*	1340*	66*	107*
Algorithms	SFJS03	SFJS04	SFJS05	SFJS06	SFJS07	SFJS08
DA	221*	355*	119*	320*	397*	253*
Jaya	221*	355*	119*	320*	397*	253*
SSA	221*	355*	119*	320*	397*	253*
cfPSO	221*	355*	119*	320*	397*	266
DE	221*	355*	119*	320*	397*	253*
SCA	221*	355*	119*	320*	397*	253*
SSANEW	221*	355*	119*	320*	397*	253*
Algorithms	SFJS09	SFJS10	Best num			
DA	210*	533*	11			
Jaya	210*	533*	12			
SSA	215	533*	10			
cfPSO	227	533*	08			
DE	210*	533*	11			
SCA	215	533*	10			
SSANEW	215*	533*	19*			

5 Conclusion

SSA is a swarm intelligence optimization algorithm, which is mainly inspired by the foraging behavior and anti-predation behavior of sparrows. SSA has not been put forward for a long time, it has a good potential for mining, and is suitable for a variety of application scenarios, such as path planning, image processing, and numerical optimization. A large number of literature experiments have proved that SSA has good convergence speed and convergence accuracy. Therefore, this paper uses SSA to solve FJSP. In order to prove the optimization effect of SSA, six test functions will be used to verify the performance indicators of the algorithm and compare with the six meta-heuristic algorithms. The experimental results show the excellent optimization ability of SSA. Finally, we use the SSA algorithm to get the result of FJSP. The experimental results prove that the optimization result of SSA is much better than other compared algorithms. On the basis of the excellent exploration and exploitation ability of SSA, the improved SSA will show superior optimization ability, and the future research will combine the advantages of various algorithms to solve different problems in accordance with different conditions to achieve better optimization result.

Acknowledgement. This research work is supported by the National Key Research and Development Project under Grant 2018YFB1700500, Shenzhen Technology Research Project under Grant JSGG20180507182901552, and Natural Science Foundation of China (No. 52077213 and 62003332).

References

1. Pezzella, F., Morganti, G., Ciaschetti, G.: A genetic algorithm for the flexible job-shop scheduling problem. Comput. Oper. Res. **35**(10), 3202–3212 (2008)
2. Kacem, I., Hammadi, S., Borne, P.: Pareto-optimality approach for flexible job-shop scheduling problems: hybridization of evolutionary algorithms and fuzzy logic. Math. Comput. Simul. **60**(3–5), 245–276 (2014)
3. Karthikeyan, S., Asokan, P., Chandrasekaran, M.: A hybrid discrete firefly algorithm for multi-objective flexible job shop scheduling problems with maintenance activity. Appl. Mech. Mater. **575**, 922–925 (2014). https://doi.org/10.1007/s00170-014-5753-3
4. Xing, L.N., Chen, Y.W., Wang, P., Zhao, Q.S., Xiong, J.: A knowledge-based ant colony optimization for flexible job shop scheduling problems. Appl. Soft Comput. **10**(3), 888–896 (2010)
5. Vallikavungal Devassia, J., Salazar-Aguilar, M.A., Boyer, V.: Flexible job-shop scheduling problem with resource recovery constraints. Int. J. Prod. Res. **56**(9–10), 3326–3343 (2018)
6. Beheshti, Z., Shamsuddin, S.M.H.: A review of population-based meta-heuristic algorithm. Int. J. Adv. Soft Comput. Appl. **5**(1), 1–35 (2013)
7. Tarantilis, C., Kiranoudis, C.: A meta-heuristic algorithm for the efficient distribution of perishable foods. J. Food Eng. **50**(1), 1–9 (2001)
8. Lei, Y., De, G., Fei, L.: Improved sparrow search algorithm based DV-Hop localization in WSN. In: 2020 Chinese Automation Congress (CAC) (2020)

9. Liu, G., Shu, C., Liang, Z., Peng, B., Cheng, L.: A modified sparrow search algorithm with application in 3D route planning for UAV. Sensors **21**(4), 1224 (2021)
10. Zhu, Y., Yousefi, N.: Optimal parameter identification of PEMFC stacks using adaptive sparrow search algorithm. Int. J. Hydrogen Energy **46**, 9541–9552 (2021)
11. Mirjalili, S.: Dragonfly algorithm: a new meta-heuristic optimization technique for solving single-objective, discrete, and multi-objective problems. Neural Comput. Appl. **27**(4), 1053–1073 (2016). https://doi.org/10.1007/s00521-015-1920-110.1007/s00521-015-1920-1
12. Qian, B., Wang, L., Huang, D.X., Wang, X.: An effective hybrid PSO-based algorithm for flow shop scheduling with limited buffers. Comput. Oper. Res. **33**(1), 2960–2971 (2009)
13. Chen, P., You, C., Ding, P.: Event classification using improved salp swarm algorithm based probabilistic neural network in fiber-optic perimeter intrusion detection system. Opt. Fiber Technol. **56**, 102182 (2020)
14. Wang, J., Yang, W., Pei, D., Tong, N.: A novel hybrid forecasting system of wind speed based on a newly developed multi-objective sine cosine algorithm. Ener. Convers. Manag. **163**, 134–150 (2018)
15. Chen, Y., Wang, C.-F.: Synthesis of reactively controlled antenna arrays using characteristic modes and de algorithm. IEEE Antennas Wirel. Propag. Lett. **11**, 385–388 (2012)
16. Warid, W., Hashim, H., Norman, M., Noor, A.W.: Optimal power flow using the jaya algorithm. Energies **9**(9), 678 (2016)
17. Ham, A.: Flexible job shop scheduling problem for parallel batch processing machine with compatible job families. Appl. Math. Model. **45**(May), 551–562 (2017)
18. Demir, Y., Isleyen, S.K.: Evaluation of mathematical models for flexible job-shop scheduling problems. Appl. Math. Modell. **37**(3), 977–988 (2013)
19. Liang, J., Wang, Q., Xu, W., Gao, Z., Yan, Z., Yu, F.: Improved Niche GA for FJSP. In: 2019 IEEE 6th International Conference on Cloud Computing and Intelligence Systems (CCIS) (2019)
20. Sun, L., Lin, L., Gen, M., Li, H.: A hybrid cooperative coevolution algorithm for fuzzy flexible job shop scheduling. IEEE Trans. Fuzzy Syst. **27**(5), 1008–1022 (2019)

Performance Analysis of Evolutionary Computation Based on Tianchi Service Scheduling Problem

Jun Yu[1], Yuhao Li[2], Tianwei Zhou[3(✉)], Churong Zhang[3], Guanghui Yue[4], and Yunjiao Ge[5]

[1] Institute of Science and Technology, Niigata University, Nigata, Japan
[2] ChengDuGuoYiDianZi Co., Ltd., Sichuan, China
[3] College of Management, Shenzhen University, Shenzhen, China
tianwei@szu.edu.cn
[4] School of Biomedical Engineering, Health Science Centre, Shenzhen University, Shenzhen, China
[5] Hubei Aerospace Vehicle Research Institute, Hubei, China
https://www.eng.niigata-u.ac.jp/ yujun

Abstract. We choose the well-known evolution strategy (ES) in the evolutionary computation (EC) community to solve the large-scale scheduling problem provided by Alibaba cloud services. Since the problem is accompanied by multiple strong constraints, we design two additional strategies for improving the search efficiency with a given limited computational cost. Compared with widely used numerical benchmark test suits, this problem arises from the requirements of real-world applications and has strict constraints that cannot be violated, such as processing time, response timeout, load balance, and so on. The main contribution of this paper is to establish a bridge between EC algorithms and the characteristics of real-world problems so that EC algorithms can solve real-world problems more effectively and smoothly. Based on the difficulties encountered in the experiment, we summarize some of our experiences and insights, and hope that they may bring new enlightenment to the latecomers.

Keywords: Evolutionary computation · Evolution strategy · Scheduling optimization · Large-scale optimization

1 Introduction

Optimization has always been a hot topic, and practitioners are committed to reducing consumption costs while obtaining higher returns. With the continuous growth of customers' personalized demand and the advent of the era of big data, real-world applications arising from industry have become quite complicated, so that many traditional optimization methods, such as linear programming [1] and nonlinear programming [2], are difficult to deal with these emerging large-scale

ⓒ Springer Nature Switzerland AG 2021
Y. Tan and Y. Shi (Eds.): ICSI 2021, LNCS 12689, pp. 155–162, 2021.
https://doi.org/10.1007/978-3-030-78743-1_14

optimization problems. As a new branch of finding the global optimal solution, evolutionary computation (EC) algorithms have attracted extensive attention [3] and solved many industrial problems successfully [4] thanks to their various advantages, such as robustness, parallelism, and usability.

EC algorithms have similar optimization framework and usually maintain a population composed of multiple individuals (candidate solutions). They borrow the idea of survival of the fittest to improve the quality of individuals and gradually converge to the global optimum. Since the pioneering genetic algorithm [5] started the upsurge of heuristic optimization, various novel EC algorithms have been proposed after decades of development [6]. Among them, many powerful EC algorithms have received lots of attention, e.g. evolution strategy (ES) [7], particle swarm optimization (PSO) [8], differential evolution (DE) [9] and others [10,11]. Besides, many researchers also focus on how to introduce new strategies into existing EC algorithms to further improve their performance [12,13]. For example, some use the model of fitness landscape to reduce the number of fitness evaluations [14] and accelerate EC search [15,16]. Owing to their continuous contribution, EC algorithms show excellent performance on various optimization problems, e.g., multimodal optimization [17], multi-objective optimization [18], and constrained optimization [19].

The main objective of this paper is to establish a bridge between EC algorithms and the characteristics of real-world problems so that EC algorithms can solve real-world problems more effectively and smoothly. Specifically, we try to analyze the match between the EC algorithms' performance and the problem characteristics by using the competition problem derived from real application scenarios, so as to take them away from the laboratory and better serve the industry.

Following this introductory Section, the Tianchi service scheduling problem is described in Sect. 2, and we present our proposal comprehensively in Sect. 3. The parameter configuration of our proposal used in the competition is given in Sect. 4. Although the results submitted to the organizer are not public, we still give a detailed analysis of our proposal and offer several potential topics in Sect. 5, and Sect. 6 summarizes our work.

2   Tianchi Service Scheduling Problem

As one of the most important global cloud service providers, Alibaba cloud provides full-cycle technical services for numerous enterprises, government agencies and developers. Every day, a large number of new technical problems (tasks) from customers are submitted to the service system and need to be assigned to technical experts for processing. Due to the rapid increase in demand, traditional rule-based scheduling schemes cannot meet the growing demand and may cause some new contradictions, such as uneven dispatch and continuous dispatch. Thus, it is necessary to rely on new scheduling algorithms that can meet the large-scale needs of customers and balance various factors well [20]. This is also why the competition is held.

Before explaining the competition problem, we first give some definitions to avoid confusion in the subsequent description.

Task: a task refers to a problem to be solved raised by a customer. The system will produce a task when the customer submits a problem to the cloud service system.

Expert: the person who handles the tasks produced by the system.

Problem classification: the category of a problem is specified by a customer when submitting the task.

Skill set: the corresponding relationship between the time required to solve different problem classification and the experts.

The competition problem can be described as follows. There are I experts and J tasks, each task belongs to only one problem classification and each expert has his own dedicated skill set to show his field of expertise. All unfinished tasks are needed to be assigned to experts and must meet the constraints mentioned below. The organizer (Alibaba cloud service) uses three factors, i.e., (1) average response timeout $\bar{M}$, (2) average processing efficiency $\bar{R}$, and (3) standard deviation of experts' working time σ_L, to evaluate the submitted solutions. Here, the Eq. (1) is used to calculate the score of a submitted solution in the preliminary stage. The higher the score, the better the performance.

$$score = \frac{c \times \bar{R}}{a \times \bar{M} + b \times \sigma_L} \tag{1}$$

where a, b, and c are constants, and they are set to 3, 2, and 3000, respectively.

When a task is submitted to the system, the timestamp is marked as the generation time. The period from the generation time of a task to the first processed timestamp is called the response time, and the period from the start timestamp of processing to the end timestamp of the processing is called the processing time. To ensure the customers' service experience, each task has a maximum response time limit T, that is, a task needs to be processed within the time T after it is generated, otherwise it will be regarded as a service response timeout. Besides, the processing time for an expert to complete a task depends on his skill set, i.e., the processing time of an expert for different tasks is different.

A task that is being processed but not completed can be reassigned to another expert, but the total number of task transfer is no more than five. Once a task is transferred, the task must stay at least one time unit (one minute) in the assigned expert, i.e., a task can only be assigned once within a minute, and the previous processing progress is cleared and needs to start all over again. Naturally, a completed task will not be reassigned again regardless of whether the maximum number of allocations is reached. Besides, each expert is not allowed to handle more than 3 tasks at the same time, and assumes that each task will be processed immediately after it is assigned to an expert.

3 Proposed Solution

Although a variety of powerful EC algorithms have been proposed, we choose ES as the baseline algorithm on account of the better local search ability, and propose two mutation methods to further customize our proposal. Besides, we also design corresponding mechanisms to deal with the above constraints so that our proposal can match the nature of the problem well.

The conventional ES algorithm mainly consists of mutation and selection operations. The mutation operation uses normally distributed random vectors to perturb μ parent individuals and then generate new λ offspring individuals. Based on the fitness rankings, top μ individuals are selected to the next generation from λ offspring individuals or the mixed group of μ parent individuals and λ offspring individuals. The above two operations are repeated to gradually optimize candidate solutions until a termination condition is satisfied. Although a large number of literatures show that the conventional ES plays an important role in real number optimization, the competition problem can be classified as a large-scale discrete problem. We thus propose the following two new mutation methods to replace the original mutation operation, but retain the original greedy selection operation.

Random variation: randomly select k genes and change their values.
Random exchange: randomly select k genes and exchange their values.

where k is a predetermined constant to determine the number of modified genes. Figure 1 is an example to show the process of the proposed two mutations.

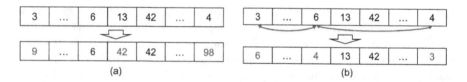

Fig. 1. Subgraphs (a) and (b) show the process of random variation and random exchange, respectively. The red parts indicate where the genes have changed. (Color figure online)

We virtualize a real expert into three fictitious experts to solve the constraint that an expert cannot handle more than three tasks at the same time. Figure 2 shows the effect of virtualization experts. Three virtual experts have exactly the same skill set as the original real expert before virtualization, but can only handle one task instead of multiple tasks at the same time. In other words, we transform the original constraint into whether there are free virtual experts to accept tasks.

Since a task can be transferred up to five times between different experts, we use the back-to-front order to assign virtual experts for handling tasks. Specifically, we first decide the last expert to complete the task, and then determine whether it is necessary to assign other experts to take over the task in turn from back to front. Suppose that the assigned sequence of experts dealing with a given task is A, B, and C, which means that the task is handled by three

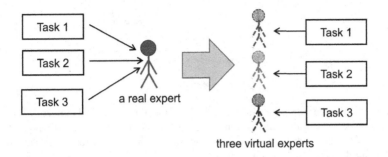

Fig. 2. A real expert is virtualized as three virtual experts, and all tasks are handled by virtual experts instead of real experts.

experts in total and experts A and C are the last and the first to deal with the task respectively. First, expert C handles the task but does not complete it, the task is then taken over by expert B. Similarly, expert B also does not complete the task and transfers it to expert A. Finally, expert A successfully completes the task, and the task is no longer assigned. Although we use a back-to-front allocation method, the actual processing order of tasks is the opposite of the allocation order. Besides, the task transfer is not mandatory, and no more than 5 transfers are allowed.

4 Experimental Evaluation

The organizer provides different data set in the preliminary and semifinal, however, only the data set for the preliminary round can be accessed freely, and another undisclosed data set is used in the semifinal. Unfortunately, we cannot know the implementation details of the other competitors, and only know the ranking information of the submitted results. Here, we give a brief introduction to the data set used in the preliminary round. The total number of tasks is 8840, but there are only 107 types of tasks, i.e., a task belongs to only one task type, but a task type may contain multiple different tasks. Compared to the number of tasks, the number of experts is very small and set to 133. We thus can say that the competition problem can be regarded as a large-scale discrete NP-hard problem.

Based on the characteristics of the competition problem, an individual (candidate solution) is encoded into the structure shown in Fig. 3, which contains $5J$ genes. The first J genes represent the sequence of experts who finally completed tasks, and the following four J genes indicate the order of experts who take over transferred tasks according to the back-to-front configuration method. Since the organizer only allows the proposed algorithm to run for four hours and output the optimal solution found, we thus use a two-stage search strategy to determine the sequence of experts to handle tasks. Specifically, we first optimize the experts who are most suitable to handle tasks in the first two hours based on the three factors mentioned above, and then optimize whether tasks need to be

Fig. 3. The data structure of an individual. The first J genes record experts who finally completed tasks, and following $4J$ genes record the sequence of experts who take over tasks accord to the back-to-front order assignment. Only when tasks are transferred, the following $4J$ genes will be configured.

transferred in the remaining time to get a better score. Based on the perspective of calculating cost and keeping feasible solutions, we only use one individual and set the number of mutated genes, k, to 100.

5   Discussions

We start the discussion by analyzing the new benefits of our proposal. Since the competition problem is a large-scale discrete problem with strong constraints, we choose the conventional ES as the baseline algorithm since it has strong local search ability, and customize two new mutation methods to better solve to the competition problem. Generally, changing too many genes at once may easily destroy the feasibility of individuals. We thus set the number of mutated genes, k, to a smaller number to maintain the feasibility as much as possible and gradually improve the quality of individuals.

Since constraint processing can improve search efficiency significantly and avoid invalid search in infeasible areas, we design two strategies, i.e., virtualization experts and back-to-front configuration, to deal with constraints. The first strategy, virtualization experts, can simplify the original constraint but keep the exactly same restriction effect. In other words, the constraint is transformed into whether there are available virtual experts to handle tasks, which can reduce the cost of detecting constraint violations and improve operational efficiency.

The other strategies, back-to-front configuration, is to emphasize different optimization indicators at different stages. Here, we are first committed to improving the efficiency of task processing, that is, let suitable experts finish the task as much as possible in the first two hours, then determine whether to add experts between task generation and final processing time to trigger task transfer in the remaining optimization time, which aims to reduce the response time and balance the working time of experts. Fortunately, our proposal won the 16th place among all 1382 participants.

Next, we would like to discuss the potential of our proposal. Not limited to the ES selected as baseline algorithm, we can also choose other EC algorithms to combine our proposed strategies without drastically changing their original optimization framework. As a first attempt, we fixed all the parameters in the entire search process instead of adjusting them dynamically. Actually, we firmly believe that the same problem may have different characteristics in different optimization periods, and the search strategy should be changed accordingly. Thus, how to use the information collected in evolution to tune parameters in real-time may be a topic worthy of further study.

Different from manually constructed benchmark functions, real-world problems often have various inviolable constraints, and usually cannot use a large number of fitness evaluations to optimize the problem. How to use a small amount of fitness evaluations to obtain satisfactory feasible solutions is an urgent problem that needs to be solved. Since every fitness evaluation may consume high computational costs, we should make full use of the existing individuals even if their fitness is poor. Thus, another potential topic is how to efficiently guide the subsequent search using existing information.

Finally, we want to give some insights about the practicality of EC algorithms. As stated by the no free lunch theorem, no one algorithm can be applied to all problems well. However, once we know the characteristics of the problem to be optimized, we can customize EC algorithms so that they can show stronger performance on the problem. We thus believe that establishing the connection between EC algorithms and real-world problems will be an important means to promote the practicality of EC algorithms.

6   Conclusion

We designed two constraint processing strategies and customized the ES algorithm to solve the competition problem provided by Alibaba Cloud. Although our proposal has achieved good results according to the submitted ranking, there is still much room to further improve our proposal.

In future work, we will try to use historical information to extract the characteristics of real-world problems, and use them to improve the performance of EC algorithms.

Acknowledgments. This work was supported in part by Natural Science Foundation of China under Grant 62001302, in part by Guangdong Basic and Applied Basic Research Foundation under Grant 2019A1515110401, 2019A1515111205, 2021A1515011348, and in part by Natural Science Foundation of Shenzhen under Grant JCYJ20190808145011259, and in part by Shenzhen Science and Technology Program under Grant RCBS20200714114920379.

References

1. Votaw, D.F.: Methods of solving some personnel-classification problems. Psychometrika **17**(3), 255–266 (1952). https://doi.org/10.1007/BF02288757
2. Wolfe, P.: Recent developments in nonlinear programming. Adv. Comput. **3**, 155–187 (1962)
3. Back, T., Hammel, U., Schwefel, H.P.: Evolutionary computation: comments on the history and current state. IEEE Trans. Evol. Comput. **1**(1), 3–17 (1997)

4. Xiao, Q.G., Li, C.B., Tang, Y., Pan, J., Yu, J., Chen, X.Z.: Multi-component energy modeling and optimization for sustainable dry gear hobbing. Energy **187**, 1–16 (2019)

5. Holland, J.H.: Outline for a logical theory of adaptive systems. J. ACM **9**(3), 297–314 (1962)

6. Kicinger, R., Arciszewski, T., Jong, K.D.: Evolutionary computation and structural design: a survey of the state-of-the-art. Comput. Struct. **83**(23–24), 1943–1978 (2005)

7. Beyer, H.G., Schwefel, H.P.: Evolution strategies: a comprehensive introduction. Nat. Comput. **1**(1), 3–52 (2002). https://doi.org/10.1023/A:1015059928466

8. Kennedy, J., Eberhart, R.: Particle swarm optimization. In: IEEE International Conference on Neural Networks, pp. 1942–1948 (1995)

9. Storn, R., Price, K.: Differential evolution: a simple and efficient heuristic for global optimization over continuous spaces. J. Glob. Optim. **11**, 341–359 (1997). https://doi.org/10.1023/A:1008202821328

10. Dervis, K., Bahriye, B.: A powerful and efficient algorithm for numerical function optimization: artificial bee colony (ABC) algorithm. J. Glob. Optim. **39**(3), 459–471 (2007). https://doi.org/10.1007/s10898-007-9149-x

11. Gandomi, A.H., Alavi, A.H.: Krill herd: a new bio-inspired optimization algorithm. Commun. Nonlinear Sci. Numer. Simul. **17**(12), 4831–4845 (2012)

12. Yu, J., Takagi, H.: Acceleration for fireworks algorithm based on amplitude reduction strategy and local optima-based selection strategy. In: Tan, Y., Takagi, H., Shi, Y. (eds.) ICSI 2017. LNCS, vol. 10385, pp. 477–484. Springer, Cham (2017). https://doi.org/10.1007/978-3-319-61824-1_52

13. Yu, J., Takagi, H., Tan, Y.: Accelerating the fireworks algorithm with an estimated convergence point. In: Tan, Y., Shi, Y., Tang, Q. (eds.) ICSI 2018. LNCS, vol. 10941, pp. 263–272. Springer, Cham (2018). https://doi.org/10.1007/978-3-319-93815-8_26

14. Jin, Y., Markus, O., Bernhard, S.: A framework for evolutionary optimization with approximate fitness functions. IEEE Trans. Evol. Comput. **6**(5), 484–494 (2002)

15. Yu, J., Pei, Y., Takagi, H.: Accelerating evolutionary computation using estimated convergence points. In: IEEE Congress on Evolutionary Computation, pp. 1438–1444 (2016)

16. Pei, Y., Yu, J., Takagi, H.: Search acceleration of evolutionary multi-objective optimization using an estimated convergence point. Mathematics **7**(2), 129–147 (2019)

17. Yu, J., Takagi, H., Tan, Y.: Fireworks algorithm for multimodal optimization using a distance-based exclusive strategy. In: IEEE Congress on Evolutionary Computation, pp. 2215–2220 (2019)

18. Niu, B., Wang, H., Wang, J., Tan, L.: Multi-objective bacterial foraging optimization. Neurocomputing **116**, 336–345 (2013)

19. Niu, B., Wang, J., Wang, H.: Bacterial-inspired algorithms for solving constrained optimization problems. Neurocomputing **148**, 54–62 (2015)

20. The homepage of the competition problem (in Chinese) (2020). https://tianchi.aliyun.com/competition/entrance/531831/information

An Intelligent Algorithm for AGV Scheduling in Intelligent Warehouses

Xue Wu[1], Min-Xia Zhang[1], and Yu-Jun Zheng[2(✉)] ⓘ

[1] College of Computer Science and Technology, Zhejiang University of Technology,
Hangzhou, China
[2] School of Information Science and Engineering, Hangzhou Normal University,
Hangzhou, China
yujun.zheng@computer.org

Abstract. In today's intelligent warehouses, automated guided vehicles (AGVs) are widely used, and their scheduling efficiency is crucial to the overall performance of warehouse business. However, AGV scheduling is a complex problem, especially when there are a large number of tasks to be undertaken by multiple AGVs in a large warehouse. In this paper, we present a problem of scheduling multiple AGVs for order picking in intelligent warehouse, the aim of which is to minimize the latest completion time of all orders. After testing a variety of algorithms, we propose a hybrid water wave optimization (WWO) and tabu search (TS) algorithm for efficiently solving the problem. We test the algorithm on a set of problem instances with different sizes, and the results show that the proposed algorithm exhibits significant performance advantages over a number of popular intelligent optimization algorithms.

Keywords: Automated Guided Vehicle (AGV) · Intelligent scheduling · Water Wave Optimization (WWO) · Tabu Search (TS) · Routing

1 Introduction

In today's supply chains, order picking is a key operation that accounts for about 55% to 75% of the total warehouse operational cost [1]. That is why more and more warehouses employ intelligent picking and delivery machines, particularly automated guided vehicles (AGVs), to improve their operational efficiencies. AGVs are self-propelled, driver-less vehicles that can pick goods from shelves and transport goods to the designated locations. Compared to traditional goods handling systems, AGVs have many advantages such as better controllability, flexibility, and accuracies. However, with the increase of the number of picking orders, scheduling multiple AGVs to handle these orders is a complex problem.

Supported by National Natural Science Foundation of China (Grant 61872123) and Natural Science Foundation of Zhejiang Province (Grant LR20F030002).

© Springer Nature Switzerland AG 2021
Y. Tan and Y. Shi (Eds.): ICSI 2021, LNCS 12689, pp. 163–173, 2021.
https://doi.org/10.1007/978-3-030-78743-1_15

In this paper, we present an AGV scheduling problem, which is to allocate order picking tasks to AGVs and route each AGV, such that the maximum completion time among all AGVs is minimized. After testing a variety of optimization algorithms, we propose a hybrid intelligent algorithm, which adapts water wave optimization (WWO) [18] for task allocation and employs tabu search (TS) [3] for routing each AGV. We test the algorithm on a set of problem instances, and the results show that the proposed algorithm exhibits significant performance advantages over a number of popular intelligent optimization algorithms.

2   Related Work

With the increasing usage of AGVs in logistics, AGV scheduling and routing problems have attracted much attention in recent years. Qiu et al. [8] proposed a particle swarm optimization (PSO) algorithm to solve a heterogeneous AGV routing problem considering energy consumption. Pinkam et al. [6] presented a greedy method to find the optimal route for AGV, where Dijkstrg's algorithm is used to plan the path and avoid obstacles, and local search is introduced to find nearby target items. Zhang et al. [17] proposed a collision free path planning method, using an improved Dijkstrg's algorithm [7] to create initial paths and classifying three collision solutions. Vivaldini et al. [15] presented three algorithms, including a global routing algorithm based on Dijkstrg's algorithm, a local path planning algorithm based on A^* algorithm, and an AGV auto-localization algorithm based on Extended Kalman Filter. Vivaldini et al. [14] proposed a method to determine the number of AGVs required to execute a given transportation order within a specific time window, and evaluated greedy and TS algorithms for task assignment and Dijkstrg's algorithm for AGV routing. Saidi-Mehrabad et al. [9] proposed a problem combining job shop scheduling and conflict free routing for AGVs, and proposed a two-stage ant colony algorithm to solve the problem. Smolic-Rocak et al. [11] proposed a dynamic routing method that uses time windows to supervise and control multiple AGVs, in which a path depends on the number of currently active AGVs' missions and their priorities. To solve the conflicts happened when multiple AGVs working in parallel, Xing et al. [16] proposed a TS algorithm, where relocation and exchange operations were designed for the neighborhood search. In [13] Umar et al. proposed a hybrid genetic algorithm (GA) based integrated scheduling, dispatching, and conflict-free routing for AGVs in FMS environment. However, to our knowledge, there are few studies on integrated scheduling of multiple AGVs for goods picking and transportation with consideration of collision avoidance.

3   Problem Description

The considered problem is to schedule a set A of m AGVs to complete a number of picking orders in an intelligent warehouse. The warehouse has R rows and C columns of storage locations; the entrance w_s is the top left corner at location $(0, 0)$, and the exit w_e is the bottom right corner at location $(C + 1, R + 1)$, as illustrated by Fig. 1. As is the case in most warehouses [5], for convenience, it is assumed that each storage location stores only one type of goods. The orders involve a set G of n types of goods, the total required amount of each goods $g \in G$ is q_g, and the storage location of g is denoted by l_g. The distances between w_s and l_g, between w_e and l_g, and between each pair of locations of g and g' are $d(w_s, g)$, $d(g, w_e)$, and $d(g, g')$, respectively. Here we use Manhattan distances, i.e., the distance between two locations (x, y) and (x', y') is $|x - x'| + |y - y'|$. The capacity of each AGV is Q, the AGV speed is v, and the average time for an AGV to pick up one unit of goods g is $\triangle t_g$. The initial location of each AGV $a \in A$ is denoted by p_a (in most cases $p_a = (0, 0)$, but not always).

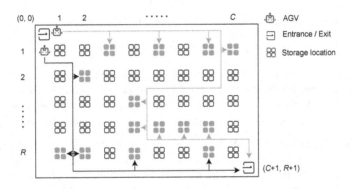

Fig. 1. Illustration of an AGV scheduling problem instance.

The problem is to allocate the picking tasks to the AGVs, and then determine the route of each AGV. As is the case in most warehouse operations, for each goods g, if $q_g \leq Q$, then the goods should be picked by only one AGV; otherwise, the goods should be picked by multiple AGVs, each of which being fully loaded of g until the remaining amount of g is less than Q. For those fully loaded AGVs, their tasks are just to directly move to l_g to load the goods and then directly moves to the exit. Therefore, we can simplify the problem by, for each goods g whose required amount $q_g \geq Q$, performing the following procedure:

1) Let $k = \lceil q_g/Q \rceil$ and q'_g be the remainder of q_g modulo Q;
2) If $q'_g = 0$, arrange k AGVs to fully load the goods, remove them from the AGV set A, and remove g from the goods set G;
3) Else, arrange $k - 1$ AGVs to fully load the goods, remove them from the AGV set A, and set $q_g = q'_g$.

As a result, we have $q_g < Q$ for each $g \in G$. After this simplification, the decision variables of the problem are as follows:

- The subset X_j of goods allocated to each jth AGV ($\forall 1 \leq j \leq m$).
- The route Y_j of each jth AGV; as the starting point is p_a and the ending point is the exit, we represent the route as the sequence of $n_j = |X_j|$ storage locations of goods, denoted by $\{y_{j_1}, y_{j_2}, \dots, y_{j_{n_j}}\}$ ($\forall 1 \leq j \leq m$).

For each jth AGV, the time at which it arrives the first storage location is:

$$t_j(1) = d(p_a, y_{j_1})/v \tag{1}$$

And the time at which it leaves the first storage location is:

$$t'_j(1) = t_j(1) + q_{y_{j_1}} \Delta t_{y_{j_1}} \tag{2}$$

For each kth storage location in Y_j, the arrive time and leaving time are as follows ($1 < k \le n_j$):

$$t_j(k) = t'_j(k-1) + d(y_{j_{k-1}}, y_{j_k})/v \tag{3}$$
$$t'_j(k) = t_j(k) + q_{y_{j_k}} \Delta t_{y_{j_k}} \tag{4}$$

Finally, the time at which the AGV completes its task is:

$$T_j = t_j(n_j) + d(y_{j_{n_j}}, w_e)/v \tag{5}$$

Equations (1)–(5) assume that an AGV can directly move to any storage location. However, in practice, we should consider possible collisions of AGVs. Assume that each aisle allows two AGVs to stop or pass through side by side, we use the following procedure to adjust the AGV routes for collision avoidance:

1) Initially, suppose that all AGV routes are row-first, i.e., a route from (x, y) to (x', y') first moves from (x, y) to (x', y), and then from (x', y) to (x', y');
2) Find all collision points and sort them in increasing order of collision time;
3) For each collision point c, if AGV a is obstructed by another AGV a' working on the point, then perform the following steps (if a and a' meets at the collision point at the same time, then we randomly select an AGV as a):
   3.1) let $c^\dagger$ be the most recent crossroads before c in the route of a;
   3.2) If there is no other AGV obstructing a in the segment from $c^\dagger$ to c aligned in the column-first manner, changing the segment to the column-first manner in the route of a;
   3.3) Else, let $c^\dagger$ be the previous recent crossroads: if $c^\dagger$ traces back to the initial location p_a, let a wait for a' to free the segment; otherwise go to step 3.2);
4) Repeat step 3) until all collision points have been processed.

The problem objective is to minimize the maximum completion time among all AGVs (equivalent to minimize the latest completion time of all orders), subject to AGV capacity constraint (7) and task allocation constraints (8) and (9):

$$\min \ f(X, Y) \max_{1 \le j \le m} T_j \tag{6}$$

$$\text{s.t.} \ \sum_{k=1}^{n_j} q_{y_{j_k}} \le Q, \quad 1 \le j \le m \tag{7}$$

$$X_j \cap X_{j'} = \emptyset, \quad \forall j \ne j', 1 \le j, j' \le m \tag{8}$$

$$\bigcup_{j=1}^{m} X_j = A \tag{9}$$

4   A Hybrid Intelligent Algorithm for the Problem

To efficiently solve the problem, after testing a variety of optimization algorithms, we propose a hybrid intelligent algorithm, which adapts the WWO metaheuristic to optimize task allocation and employs the TS algorithm to optimize the route of each AGV. The flowchart of the algorithm is shown in Fig. 2.

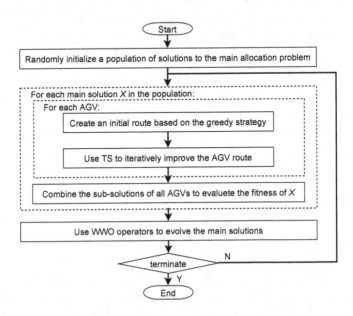

Fig. 2. The flow of the hybrid algorithm for the AGV Scheduling problem.

4.1   Tabu Search for AGV Routing

For each jth AGV, when the set X_j of goods allocated to the AGV is fixed, the subproblem of AGV routing is to find an optimal sequence of goods in X_j to minimize the completion time T_j. First, we use a greedy strategy to produce an initial route Y_j by always selecting a closest unvisited point as the next point until all points have been in the route. Next, we use TS to iteratively improve Y_j. At each iteration, the TS generates *NbSize* neighboring solutions, each being obtained by randomly swapping two adjacent points in Y_j. The best neighbor, if better than the current Y_j, or the swapping is not forbidden, will replace Y_j. A tabu list is used to record the forbidden moves, and the most recent position selected for swapping is always added to the end of the tabu list so as to prevent cycling during the search process. If the number of elements in the tabu list exceeds an upper limit *TabuSize*, the first element in the tabu list is released. Algorithm 1 presents the pseudocode of the TS algorithm.

Algorithm 1: The tabu search algorithm for AGV routing.

---

1 Initialize a path Y_j for AGV based on the greedy strategy and let $Y_j^* = Y_j$;
2 Create an empty tabu list;
3 **while** *the stopping condition is not met* **do**
4   **for** $i = 1$ *to NbSize* **do**
5   Randomly select a point p in Y_j;
6   Generate a neighboring solution Y_j' by swapping p and $p + 1$ in Y_j;
7   Let $Y^\dagger$ be the best neighbor among the *NbSize* ones and $p^\dagger$ be the corresponding selected point;
8   **if** $p^\dagger$ *is not in the tabu list or* $Y^\dagger$ *is better than* Y_j **then**
9   Add $p^\dagger$ to the tabu list;
10   **if** *The tabu length exceeds TabuSize* **then**
11   Remove the first element from the tabu list;
12   **if** $Y^\dagger$ *is better than* Y_j **then**
13   Update Y_j to $Y^\dagger$;
14   **if** $Y^\dagger$ *is better than* Y_j^* **then**
15   Update Y_j^* to $Y^\dagger$;

16 return Y_j^*.

4.2 WWO for Allocating Tasks to AGVs

A main allocation solution $X = \{X_1, X_2, \ldots, X_m\}$ is represented by an $n \times m$ dimensional 0–1 vector, where each component $x_{i,j} = 1$ denotes that goods g_i is allocated to AGV a_j and $x_{i,j} = 0$ otherwise. Each row has exactly one 1-element. In such an encoding, constraints (8) and (9) have been satisfied. To handle constraint (7), we add a constraint violation value to the objective function (6):

$$f(X) = f(X, Y^*) + M \sum_{j=1}^{m} \max\left(\left(\sum_{g \in X_j} q_g \right) - Q, 0 \right); \qquad (10)$$

where Y^* is the combination of all Y_j^* produced by the TS algorithm and processed by the collision avoidance process, and M is a large positive constant.

For optimizing task allocation, we employ WWO where each solution X is analog to a water wave with a wavelength λ_X that is inversely proportional to the solution fitness, such that low-fitness (high-fitness) solutions to explore large (small) spaces to balance global and local search. WWO first initializes a population of *NP* solutions to the problem, and then iteratively evolves the solutions using propagation and breaking operators (the original WWO has an additional refraction operator, which is abandoned in its improved version [21]. The propagation operator propagates each solution to a new position by moving each dimension d within a range proportional to its wavelength. As the original WWO is proposed for continuous optimization, we adapt the operators to this combinatorial optimization problem. Guided by the strategies from [20], we redefine the propagation operation on a solution X as performing K steps of local search, where K is proportional to the wavelength λ_X, and each local search step is conducted by randomly reversing a component $x_{i,j}$ from 0 to 1 and then reversing the corresponding component $x_{i,j'}$ (where $a_{j'}$ is the AGV to which goods g_i is originally allocated) from 1 to 0.

We also adapt the wavelength calculation method for our problem as follows:

$$\lambda_X = n^{(f(X)-f_{\min}+\epsilon)/(f_{\max}-f_{\min}+\epsilon)} \tag{11}$$

where $f_{\min}$ and $f_{\max}$ are the minimum and maximum fitness value among the population, respectively, and ϵ is a small number to avoid division-by-zero.

Whenever a new best solution X^* is found, the breaking operator generates a set of N_b neighboring solutions around X^*. Each neighboring solution is generated by perform a one-step local search on X^*.

We also adopt the population size reduction strategy in [21] to remove low-quality or static solutions:

$$NP = NP_{min} + (NP_{max} - NP_{min})\frac{g}{g_{max}} \tag{12}$$

where g and g_{max} are the current number and maximum allowable number of the generations (or function evaluations), and NP_{max} and NP_{min} are the upper and lower limits of the population size, respectively. Whenever the population size is decreased by one, the worst solution in the population is removed. Algorithm 2 presents the discrete WWO algorithm for the AGV scheduling problem.

5   Computational Experiments

We use a set of 15 test instances generated based on three real-world intelligent warehouses. We compare the proposed algorithm (denoted by S-WWO) with basic WWO (that uses refraction instead of population size reduction) and the following five popular metaheuristics (with parameters tuned on the test set):

- GA [2], for which we set crossover rate $p_c = 0.8$, and mutation rate $p_m = 0.2$.
- Bogeography-based optimization (BBO) [10] , for which we set $p_m = 0.1$.
- Ecogeography optimization (EBO) [19], for which we set the initial immaturity to 0.7, and the ending immaturity to 0.4.
- Differential Evolution (DE) [12], for which we set scale factor $F = 0.5$, and crossover rate $CR = 0.9$.
- PSO [4], for which we set $c_1 = 2$, $c_2 = 2$, $w_{max} = 0.9$, and $w_{min} = 0.4$.

For WWO and S-WWO, we set $NP_{max} = 50$, $NP_{min} = 6$, and $N_b = 12$. For basic WWO, we set $h_{max} = 12$. The population sizes of other algorithms are all set to 50. For fairness, we set the stopping condition as the number of function evaluations (NFEs) to $500m$ for all algorithms. Each algorithm is run 30 times on each instance. For the TS algorithm invoked, we $TabuSize = 10$, $Nbsize = 15$, and the maximum number of iteration to 100.

Algorithm 2: WWO algorithm for the AGV scheduling problem.

---

1 Randomly initialize a population of *NP* main allocation solutions;
2 **while** *the stopping condition is not met* **do**
3   **foreach** *solution X in the population* **do**
4   Call Algorithm 1 to plan the route for each AGV;
5   Combine the routes and apply the collision avoidance procedure;
6   Evaluate X based on the results;
7   Update the current best solution X^*;
8   Calculate the wavelengths of the solutions based on Eq.(11);
9   **foreach** *solution X in the population* **do**
10   Let $K = rand(1, \lambda_X)$;
11   Propagate X to a new X' by performing K reversal of components;
12   Evaluate the fitness of X' according to Lines 4–6;
13   **if** $f(X') < f(X)$ **then**
14   Replace X with X' in the population;
15   **if** $f(X) < f(X^*)$ **then**
16   Produce the N_b neighboring solution of X;
17   Let X' be the best neighbor;
18   **if** $f(X') < f(X^*)$ **then**
19   Replace X^* with X';

20   Update the population size based on Eq.(12);
21 return X^*.

Table 1 presents the medians and standard deviations of the results of the comparative algorithms, where the minimum median value among the algorithms on each instance is shown in bold. We use the nonparametric Wilcoxon rank sum test to compare the results of S-WWO and other algorithms, and use a superscript [†] before a median value to show that the result of the algorithm is significantly different from that of S-WWO (at a confidence level of 95%).

On each instance, S-WWO always achieves the best median value and best minimum value, and its performance advantages increases with the instance size. According to the statistical test, the result of S-WWO is statistically significantly better than those of the other six algorithms on each instances. Among the other six algorithms, the overall performance of WWO is the best. This demonstrates that the adapted WWO metaheuristic is efficient in solving this problem, and the removal of the refraction operator of the orginal WWO and inclusion of the population size reduction strategy problem can further improve the search performance. In summary, the results validate that the propose hybrid S-WWO and TS algorithm is efficient for solving the AGV scheduling problem compared to the other well-known metaheuristic algorithms.

Table 1. Experimental results on the 15 test instances

Ins	scale($R \times C$)	$m \times n$	Metric	GA	BBO	EBO	DE	PSO	WWO	S-WWO
1	50 × 50	5 × 30	Median	†481.5	†504	†504	†450	†473	†445.5	**429**
			Std	11.41	7.46	8.66	7.86	13.09	13.13	10.96
2		5 × 50	Median	†613.5	†647	†614	†586.5	†613.5	†569	**519**
			Std	13.56	12.75	12.22	8.47	15.09	15.45	11.07
3		8 × 60	Median	†881	†931	†854.5	†852.5	†905.5	†784	**719**
			Std	25.59	16.60	14.55	12.80	14.01	20.50	18.40
4		8 × 80	Median	†876.5	†962.5	†943	†882.5	†929	†862	**794.5**
			Std	24.49	15.00	17.15	9.28	15.82	20.69	13.99
5	100 × 100	5 × 30	Median	†833	†883	†828	†785.5	†827	†761.5	**722**
			Std	22.77	21.16	19.61	11.64	30.52	27.79	16.17
6		5 × 50	Median	†1022.5	†1078	†1020	†980.5	†1014	†950	**853.5**
			Std	19.70	20.64	24.49	15.30	27.94	26.71	19.67
7		8 × 60	Median	†1398.5	†1251.5	†1464	†1357	†1448	†1314.5	**1189.5**
			Std	51.84	33.58	28.64	29.46	31.14	46.05	28.31
8		8 × 80	Median	†1501.5	†1635.5	†1578.5	†1493	†1558	†1440.5	**1319**
			Std	49.71	27.78	28.27	16.80	23.24	34.50	18.89
9		10 × 100	Median	†2003.5	†2188.5	†2138	†2008.5	†2108.5	†1989	**1787**
			Std	66.12	42.21	25.33	27.66	34.82	47.89	27.89
10	200 × 200	5 × 40	Median	†1401.5	†1512.5	†1412.5	†1311.5	†1411.5	†1240	**1132.5**
			Std	60.82	50.38	45.56	30.10	59.84	70.28	40.80
11		5 × 50	Median	†1993	†2110	†1971	†1882	†1966	†1866	**1569.5**
			Std	41.74	54.57	43.67	43.22	78.75	72.75	39.73
12		8 × 60	Median	†2478	†2754	†2651	†2478	†2593	†2365.5	**2150.5**
			Std	106.28	63.38	56.47	37.65	76.78	72.03	54.2
13		8 × 80	Median	†2876	†3164	†3069.5	†2888.5	†3026.5	†2814	**2487.5**
			Std	89.71	52.42	58.47	22.78	44.40	82.76	43.47
14		8 × 100	Median	†3244.5	†3551	†3488	†3257.5	†3410	†3221.5	**2813.5**
			Std	113.90	81.77	81.77	45.47	79.29	103.10	60.86
15		10 × 120	Median	†4067	†4504	†4426	†4123.5	†4371.5	†4043	**3616.5**
			Std	162.65	80.68	89.99	45.98	67.48	112.23	85.25

6 Conclusion

This paper proposes a intelligent algorithm for AGV scheduling in warehouse. We adapt WWO to optimize the allocation of picking orders to AGVs, where each allocation is evaluated by using TS to route each AGV and then combining all routes while resolving collisions among them. Experimental results demonstrate the performance of the algorithm that compare to other popular metaheuristics. Our future work will study AGV scheduling for dynamically arriving orders.

References

1. Chiang, D.M.H., Lin, C.P., Chen, M.C.: The adaptive approach for storage assignment by mining data of warehouse management system for distribution centres. Enterp. Inf. Syst. **5**(2), 219–234 (2011)

2. Chu, P.C., Beasley, J.E.: A genetic algorithm for the multidimensional knapsack problem. J. Heuristics **4**(1), 63–86 (1998)
3. Glover, F.: Tabu search - part I. ORSA J. Comput. **1**(3), 190–206 (1989)
4. Hembecker, F., Lopes, H.S., Godoy, W.: Particle swarm optimization for the multidimensional knapsack problem. In: Beliczynski, B., Dzielinski, A., Iwanowski, M., Ribeiro, B. (eds.) ICANNGA 2007. LNCS, vol. 4431, pp. 358–365. Springer, Heidelberg (2007). https://doi.org/10.1007/978-3-540-71618-1_40
5. Ling, H.F., Su, Z.L., Jiang, X.L., Zheng, Y.J.: Multi-objective optimization of integrated civilian-military scheduling of medical supplies for epidemic prevention and control. Healthcare **9**(2), 126 (2021)
6. Pinkam, N., Bonnet, F., Chong, N.Y.: Robot collaboration in warehouse. In: 16th International Conference on Control, Automation and Systems, pp. 269–272. IEEE (2016)
7. Qing, G., Zheng, Z., Yue, X.: Path-planning of automated guided vehicle based on improved dijkstra algorithm. In: 29th Chinese Control and Decision Conference, pp. 7138–7143. IEEE (2017)
8. Qiu, L., Wang, J., Chen, W., Wang, H.: Heterogeneous AGV routing problem considering energy consumption. In: IEEE International Conference on Robotics and Biomimetics, pp. 1894–1899. IEEE (2015)
9. Saidi-Mehrabad, M., Dehnavi-Arani, S., Evazabadian, F., Mahmoodian, V.: An ant colony algorithm (ACA) for solving the new integrated model of job shop scheduling and conflict-free routing of AGV. Comput. Ind. Eng. **86**, 2–13 (2015)
10. Simon, D.: Biogeography-based optimization. IEEE Trans. Evol. Comput. **12**(6), 702–713 (2008)
11. Smolic-Rocak, N., Bogdan, S., Kovacic, Z., Petrovic, T.: Time windows based dynamic routing in multi-AGV systems. IEEE Trans. Autom. Sci. Eng. **7**(1), 151–155 (2009)
12. Tasgetiren, M.F., Pan, Q.K., Kizilay, D., Suer, G.: A differential evolution algorithm with variable neighborhood search for multidimensional knapsack problem. In: IEEE Congress on Evolutionary Computation,pp. 2797–2804. IEEE (2015)
13. Umar, U.A., Ariffin, M.K.A., Ismail, N., Tang, S.H.: Hybrid multiobjective genetic algorithms for integrated dynamic scheduling and routing of jobs and automated-guided vehicle (AGV) in flexible manufacturing systems (FMS) environment. Int. J. Adv. Manuf. Technol. 2123–2141 (2015). https://doi.org/10.1007/s00170-015-7329-2
14. Vivaldini, K., Rocha, L.F., Martarelli, N.J., Becker, M., Moreira, A.P.: Integrated tasks assignment and routing for the estimation of the optimal number of agvs. Int. J. Adv. Manuf. Technol. **82**(1–4), 719–736 (2016)
15. Vivaldini, K.C., et al.: Robotic forklifts for intelligent warehouses: routing, path planning, and auto-localization. In: IEEE International Conference on Industrial Technology, pp. 1463–1468. IEEE (2010)
16. Xing, L., Liu, Y., Li, H., Wu, C.C., Lin, W.C., Chen, X.: A novel tabu search algorithm for multi-AGV routing problem. Mathematics **8**(2), 279 (2020)
17. Zhang, Z., Guo, Q., Chen, J., Yuan, P.: Collision-free route planning for multiple AGVS in an automated warehouse based on collision classification. IEEE Access **6**, 26022–26035 (2018)
18. Zheng, Y.J.: Water wave optimization: a new nature-inspired metaheuristic. Comput. Oper. Res. **55**, 1–11 (2015)
19. Zheng, Y.J., Ling, H.F., Xue, J.Y.: Ecogeography-based optimization: enhancing biogeography-based optimization with ecogeographic barriers and differentiations. Comput. Oper. Res. **50**, 115–127 (2014)

20. Zheng, Y.J., Lu, X.Q., Du, Y.C., Xue, Y., Sheng, W.G.: Water wave optimization for combinatorial optimization: Design strategies and applications. Appl. Soft Comput. **83**, 105611 (2019)
21. Zheng, Y.J., Zhang, B.: A simplified water wave optimization algorithm. In: 2015 IEEE Congress on Evolutionary Computation (CEC), pp. 807–813. IEEE (2015)

Success-History Based Position Adaptation in Gaining-Sharing Knowledge Based Algorithm

Shakhnaz Akhmedova$^{(\boxtimes)}$ ⓘ and Vladimir Stanovov ⓘ

Reshetnev Siberian State University of Science and Technology, "Krasnoyarskiy Rabochiy" Avenue 31, 660037 Krasnoyarsk, Russian Federation

Abstract. This paper introduces a modification of the recently developed Adaptive Gaining Sharing Knowledge (AGSK) algorithm. The AGSK algorithm simulates the process of human gaining and sharing knowledge using two main phases to solve optimization problems: junior and senior. AGSK's efficiency was proved; however, there are still various approaches that can be used to improve its workability. In this study a new technique for generating potential solutions for the AGSK algorithm is proposed. This technique uses a historical memory of successful positions found by individuals stored in the external archive to guide those individuals in different directions and thus to improve the exploration and exploitation abilities of the AGSK algorithm. At first, the size of the external archive was fixed, but later in order to improve the performance of AGSK, a reduction technique was applied to decrease its size during the optimization process. Moreover, three different approaches were used to update the external archive after each algorithm's iteration. The modified algorithm (as well as its original variant) was evaluated on a set of test functions taken from the CEC 2021 competition. The obtained experimental results are presented and compared. It was established that the proposed modification of the AGSK algorithm allows finding better solutions with the same computational effort. Thus, proposed position adaptation technique's usefulness was demonstrated.

Keywords: Optimization · Gaining-sharing information · External archive · Nature-inspired algorithms · Evolutionary algorithms · Linear reduction

1 Introduction

Solving single objective unconstrained optimization problems can be found in the various disciplines and real-life applications, including computer science, engineering and many others. In the context of single-objective unconstrained real-valued problems, the optimization task is to find the values of decision variables by optimizing an objective function. This objective function may possess difficult mathematical properties (it can be non-linear, multimodal or rotated, for example), and in this case the standard optimization methods are usually not able to solve them.

Recently researchers use more frequently use the computational intelligence approaches, including evolutionary algorithms [1, 2], to solve complex optimization

© Springer Nature Switzerland AG 2021
Y. Tan and Y. Shi (Eds.): ICSI 2021, LNCS 12689, pp. 174–181, 2021.
https://doi.org/10.1007/978-3-030-78743-1_16

problems. Evolutionary algorithms are nature-inspired methods which use operators adapted from the biological systems: for example, operators that simulate mutation, recombination and selection in the nature are used in differential evolution (DE) or genetic algorithms (GA) [3, 4]. Besides, evolutionary algorithms have the capability to self-organize, do not require particular mathematical characteristics to be satisfied and can evaluate several solutions in parallel.

In this study, a new nature-inspired algorithm called Gaining-Sharing Knowledge algorithm or GSK is considered [5]. The GSK algorithm is inspired from the human life span and the process of sharing and gaining the knowledge. It has two main phases: junior and senior gaining-sharing knowledge phases. The GSK approach's performance has been evaluated on a set of test functions and its workability was demonstrated. Later this algorithm was improved by applying a new adaption technique to its control parameters. Mentioned modification was called Adaptive Gaining-Sharing Knowledge or AGSK, which is more efficient than the original algorithm according to the conducted experiments [6].

Thus, in this study additionally an adaptation has been proposed for the AGSK algorithm to enhance its ability to seek the balance between exploration and exploitation [7]. This adaptation was originally proposed for the DE algorithm in [8] and its main idea consists in the usage of an archive of potentially good solutions, which is limited in size and updated as the search proceeds.

The advantage of the archive is that it contains promising solutions that appear to have valuable information about the search space and its promising regions, therefore indicating the history of algorithms' successful search. The idea of using such information could be applied to any nature-inspired algorithm. In this paper the idea of applying the success-history based archive of potentially good solutions was explored in two stages, resulting in six potential versions of that modification. Namely, at first archive size was fixed and didn't change during the optimization process, besides, there were three different approaches to update archive on each step (the first three versions). Additionally, three versions of the proposed AGSK modification with reduction technique applied to decrease the archive size were considered.

Therefore, in this paper firstly the AGSK algorithm is described, and then the description of its modification, proposed in this study, is presented. In the next section the experimental results obtained by all versions of the proposed modification as well as results obtained by the original AGSK algorithm are discussed and demonstrated. Finally, some conclusions are given in the last section.

2   Gaining-Sharing Knowledge Based Algorithm

The gaining-sharing knowledge optimization algorithm or GSK has two main stages, the: first stage is called the junior gaining and sharing phase and the second stage is called the senior gaining and sharing phase [5]. Firstly, the initial population for a given problem is randomly generated. Namely, the set of potential NP solutions called individuals and defined as real-valued vectors with length D (where D is the number of dimensions for a given optimization problem) is randomly generated in a given search space.

Then, the number of gained and shared dimensions for each individual using both junior and senior stages will be determined at initialization phase. To be more specific, the number of the desired number of variables that will be updated using junior scheme and the other number of dimensions that will be updated using senior scheme during generations must be determined for each individual at the beginning of the search, which is done by using a nonlinear formula presented in [5]. The first control parameter of the GSK algorithm is used in this formula: k or knowledge rate.

During the junior phase, firstly, all individuals are arranged in ascending order according to their objective function value. Then, two different individuals (the nearest better and worsen) are selected for each individual. Additionally, the third individual is randomly selected among the rest of the population. After that all three selected individuals are used to calculate the new values for dimensions that use the junior scheme according to the rule described in [5]. It should be noted, that the best and worst individuals are updated by using the closest best two individuals and the closest worsen two individuals, respectively.

During the senior phase all individuals again are sorted in ascending order according to their objective function. After that they are divided into three categories: best individuals, better or middle individuals, worst individuals. Then, for each individual, the senior scheme uses two random chosen vectors of the top and bottom $100p\%$ individuals in the current population of size NP. The third individual is selected randomly from the middle $NP - (2 * 100p\%)$ individuals. Here p is the value from [0, 1]. Finally all three selected individuals are used to calculate the new values for dimensions that use the senior scheme according to the rule described in [5].

Both schemes use two additional control parameters [5]. The first one is k_f or knowledge factor, it controls the total amount of gained and shared knowledge that will be added from others to the current individuals during generations. The second parameter is k_r or knowledge ratio, it controls the ratio between the current and acquired experience.

In the study [6] an adaptation technique was proposed for each mentioned control parameter (knowledge rate, knowledge factor and knowledge ratio). Besides, the population size was also reduced during the optimization process. The modification described in [6] was called Adaptive Gaining-Sharing Knowledge or AGSK.

3 Proposed Adaptation

In this study the success-history based position adaptation of potential solutions for improving the search diversity of the nature-inspired AGSK algorithm and its efficiency is introduced. The key concept of the proposed technique can be described as follows.

First of all, in addition to the initial population, the external archive for best found positions is created. At the beginning the external archive is empty. If later the improved position for any individual from the population will be discovered, then its previous position will be stored in the external archive. Three different approaches to update the external archive are considered in this study. The only difference between them consists in the way the archive is updated when it is already full. To be more specific, let us assume that the archive is full and it is the archive update phase, then:

- the first approach – replace random individual from archive;
- the second approach – choose random individual from archive and replace it if its function value is worse than the value of a given individual from the population;

- the third approach – choose 3 random individuals from archive and repeat steps of the second approach until either one of the chosen individuals is replaced or it's proved that neither of them should be replaced.

Similar schemes for archive update have been previously proposed in [9]. The process of the external archive update can be described with the following pseudo-code for a minimization problem:

```
For each individual P_j (j = 1:NP)
   If f(P_j) < f(Q_j) and (k + 1) ≤ |A|
       A_{k+1} = Q_j and k = k + 1
   End If
   If f(P_j) < f(Q_j) and (k + 1) > |A|
       If approach 1
           Randomly choose r from [1, |A|] and A_r = Q_j
       Else If approach 2
           Randomly choose r from [1, |A|]
           If f(Q_j) < f(A_r)
               A_r = Q_j
           End If
       Else if approach 3
           Randomly choose r1, r2, r3 from [1, |A|]
           For i = 1:3
               If f(Q_j) < f(A_{ri})
                   A_{ri} = Q_j and break
               End If
           End For
       End If
   End If
End For
```

In this pseudo-code A is the external archive, $|A|$ is the archive size (it should be noted, that the size is fixed here), k is the current number of individuals stored in A, thus, A_i ($i = 1, ..., k$) are individuals stored in the archive. Besides, NP is the population size, P_j ($j = 1, ..., NP$) are the current coordinates of individuals in the population, while Q_j ($j = 1, ..., NP$) are the previous coordinates of individuals in the population; and finally f is the objective function.

Later to improve algorithm's efficiency the archive size was reduced during the optimization process. Therefore, the archive size will be decreased according to the following function:

$$|A| = round\left((N_{init} - N_{min}) \cdot \left(\frac{NFE}{NFE_{max}} \right)^{\frac{1-NFE}{NFE_{max}}} + N_{init} \right) \tag{1}$$

where $|A|$ is the archive size, N_{init} is the initial archive size, $N_{min} = 12$ is the minimum archive size, NFE is the current number of function evaluations and NFE_{max} is the maximum number of objective function evaluations. It should be noted that the initial archive size is equal to the initial population size.

Finally, individuals stored in the external archive are used during the junior and senior phases of the AGSK algorithm with some probability p_a.

4   Experimental Results

4.1   Benchmark Functions and Experimental Setup

Benchmark functions taken from the CEC 2021 competition on bound constrained numerical optimization [10] are used to test the performance of the proposed modification of the AGSK algorithm. To be more specific 6 versions of this modification were tested:

- the external archive with fixed size and three different approaches to update it (AGSK_f1, AGSK_f2, AGSK_f3);
- the external archive with reduced size and three different approaches to update it (AGSK_r1, AGSK_r2, AGSK_r3).

The mentioned benchmark set consists of 10 optimization problems, including basic, hybrid and composition functions. In this competition, the benchmark functions are considered by applying the different transformations such as bias, rotation and shift and their combinations. Thus, there are 80 test functions, which were used for tests with 10 and 20 dimensions. More details can be found in [10].

The idea was to check the workability of the proposed modification; therefore, the probability of using the external archive during both junior and senior phases was the same. Moreover, no adjustments were applied to this parameter and p_a was set to 0.2. For the first 3 versions of the proposed modification with fixed archive size $|A|$ was equal to the population size.

4.2   Numerical Results

The maximum number of function evaluations, or the terminal criteria, was set to 200000 and 1000000 for $D = 10$ and $D = 20$, respectively. All experiments for each function and each algorithm run 30 times independently. As an example, results obtained by the standard AGSK algorithm and its modifications for benchmark functions with bias, rotation and shift ($D = 20$) are presented in the Table 1. It includes the obtained mean values and the standard deviations of the obtained results.

The search process for all tested algorithms on the mentioned functions is presented in the Fig. 1. Here one can see how the results from Table 1 were achieved.

In Table 2 the results of comparison between the original AGSK algorithm and 6 versions of the proposed modification according to the Mann-Whitney statistical test with significance level $p = 0.01$ are presented. It should be noted that the standard AGSK approach was used as baseline.

Table 1. Results obtained for test functions with shift, bias and rotation ($D = 20$).

		AGSK	AGSK_f1	AGSK_f2	AGSK_f3	AGSK_r1	AGSK_r2	AGSK_r3
1	Mean	0	0	0	0	0	0	0
	Std	0	0	0	0	0	0	0
2	Mean	2,725E+01	9,769E+00	9,330E+00	1,087E+01	8,212E+00	1,268E+01	1,364E+01
	Std	1,682E+01	4,939E+00	3,630E+00	4,761E+00	3,603E+00	4,059E+00	6,819E+00
3	Mean	2,245E+01	2,185E+01	2,141E+01	2,182E+01	2,187E+01	2,177E+01	2,155E+01
	Std	9,106E−01	5,480E−01	5,164E−01	6,661E−01	6,844E−01	5,974E−01	6,640E−01
4	Mean	1,298E+00	1,307E+00	1,385E+00	1,326E+00	1,355E+00	1,385E+00	1,407E+00
	Std	1,184E−01	1,356E−01	1,098E−01	1,331E−01	1,192E−01	1,660E−01	1,425E−01
5	Mean	1,726E+02	1,697E+02	1,634E+02	1,450E+02	1,590E+02	1,408E+02	1,380E+02
	Std	7,848E+01	6,032E+01	7,507E+01	7,996E+01	7,884E+01	7,887E+01	6,123E+01
6	Mean	7,153E−01	4,547E−01	4,757E−01	4,722E−01	4,620E−01	4,600E−01	4,398E−01
	Std	1,744E−01	1,439E−01	1,250E−01	1,405E−01	1,008E−01	1,392E−01	1,375E−01
7	Mean	1,127E+01	1,032E+01	7,323E+00	7,819E+00	8,260E+00	8,568E+00	4,593E+00
	Std	1,017E+01	1,056E+01	8,252E+00	8,653E+00	8,297E+00	7,223E+00	6,147E+00
8	Mean	1,000E+02	1,000E+02	1,000E+02	1,000E+02	1,000E+02	1,000E+02	1,000E+02
	Std	0	0	0	0	0	0	0
9	Mean	1,236E+02	3,209E+02	3,168E+02	3,405E+02	3,242E+02	2,765E+02	3,292E+02
	Std	7,196E+01	1,433E+02	1,498E+02	1,387E+02	1,493E+02	1,592E+02	1,438E+02
10	Mean	4,137E+02	4,137E+02	4,137E+02	4,137E+02	4,137E+02	4,137E+02	4,137E+02
	Std	0	0	0	0	0	0	0

Table 2. Results of the Mann-Whitney statistical test with $p = 0.01$.

	D	AGSK_f1	AGSK_f2	AGSK_f3	AGSK_r1	AGSK_r2	AGSK_r3
+	10	11	10	9	17	12	8
	20	30	31	28	33	27	31
=	10	69	70	71	63	68	72
	20	42	39	44	39	45	39
−	10	0	0	0	0	0	0
	20	8	10	8	8	8	10
Total	10	11	10	9	17	12	8
	20	22	21	20	25	19	21

Thus, the following notations are used in Table 2: "+" means that considered modification was better compared to AGSK, similarly, "−" means that proposed algorithm was statistically worse, and "="means that there was no significant difference between their results.

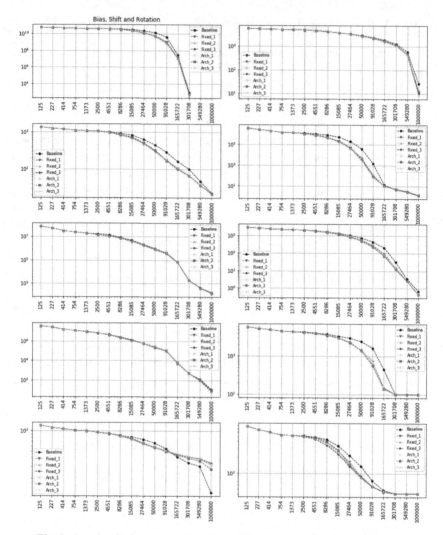

Fig. 1. Results obtained for test functions with shift, bias and rotation ($D = 20$).

Results showed that success-history based position adaptation with decreasing archive size and the first approach to update the external archive (the AGSK_r1 modification) improves the workability of the AGSK algorithm the most. Therefore, it can be used for solving the optimization problems instead of the original AGSK algorithm and other versions of the proposed modification.

5 Conclusions

In this study, a new modification of the nature-inspired AGSK algorithm is proposed for solving real-valued unconstrained optimization problems. Mentioned modification, uses success-history based position adaptation, or in other words, the external archive with size, which is reduced during the search process, and update technique based on random selection. This algorithm is compared with the original AGSK approach and other versions of the proposed modification by using the set of test functions taken from the CEC 2021 competition. The experimental results show that the performance of the proposed algorithm is superior to other algorithms mentioned in this study: it is better in exploiting the search space and also has advantages in exploration.

In the future research, the parameters of the introduced modification will be adjusted. This algorithm could also be considered for usage for multi-objective and constrained optimization problems.

Acknowledgments. This research was funded by the Council for grants of the President of the Russian Federation for young researchers, grant number MK-1579.2020.9 in 2020–2022.

References

1. Kumar, S., Chauhan, E.A.: A survey on image feature selection techniques. Int. J. Comput. Sci. Inf. Technol. **5**(5), 6449–6452 (2014)
2. Yoshida, M., et al.: Using evolutionary algorithms and machine learning to explore sequence space for the discovery of antimicrobial peptides. Chem **4**(3), 533–543 (2018)
3. Schmitt, L.M.: Theory of genetic algorithms II: models for genetic operators over the string-tensor representation of populations and convergence to global optima for arbitrary fitness function under scaling. Theoret. Comput. Sci. **310**(1–3), 181–231 (2004)
4. Storn, R., Price, K.: Differential evolution – a simple and efficient heuristic for global optimization over continuous spaces. J. Global Optim. **11**(4), 341–359 (1997)
5. Mohamed, A.W., Hadi, A.A., Mohamed, A.K.: Gaining-sharing knowledge based algorithm for solving optimization problems: a novel nature-inspired algorithm. Int. J. Mach. Learn. Cybern. **11**(7), 1501–1529 (2019). https://doi.org/10.1007/s13042-019-01053-x
6. Mohamed, A.W., Hadi, A.A., Mohamed, A.K., Awad, N.H.: Evaluating the performance of adaptive gaining sharing knowledge based algorithm on CEC 2020 benchmark problems. In: 2020 IEEE Congress on Evolutionary Computation, pp. 1–8 (2020)
7. Črepinšek, M., Liu, S., Mernik, M.: Exploration and exploitation in evolutionary algorithms: a survey. ACM Comput. Surv. **45**(3), Article no. 35 (2013)
8. Zhang, J., Sanderson, A.: JADE: adaptive differential evolution with optional external archive. IEEE Trans. Evol. Comput. **13**(5), 945–958 (2009)
9. Akhmedova, S., Stanovov, V., Semenkin, E.: Success-history based position adaptation in co-operation of biology related algorithms. In: Tan, Y., Shi, Y., Niu, B. (eds.) ICSI 2019. LNCS, vol. 11655, pp. 39–49. Springer, Cham (2019). https://doi.org/10.1007/978-3-030-26369-0_4
10. Mohamed, A.W., Hadi, A.A., Mohamed, A.K., Agrawal, P., Kumar, A., Suganthan P.N.: Problem definitions and evaluation criteria for the CEC 2021 special session and competition on single objective bound constrained numerical optimization. Technical report. https://github.com/P-N-Suganthan/2021-SO-BCO. Accessed 18 Apr 2021

Particle Swarm Optimization

Multi-guide Particle Swarm Optimisation Control Parameter Importance in High Dimensional Spaces

Timothy G. Carolus[1] and Andries P. Engelbrecht[1,2]([⊠])

[1] Department of Industrial Engineering, Stellenbosch University,
Stellenbosch, South Africa
engel@sun.ac.za
[2] Division of Computer Science, Stellenbosch University, Stellenbosch, South Africa

Abstract. This article presents an investigation into the effects of the search space dimension on the control parameter importance of the multi-guide particle swarm optimization (MGPSO) algorithm over time. The MGPSO algorithm is a multi-objective optimization algorithm that uses multiple swarms, each swarm focusing on an individual objective. This relative control parameter importance of the MGPSO is identified using functional analysis of variance (fANOVA). The fANOVA process quantifies the control parameter importance through analysing variance in the objective function values associated with a change in control parameter values. The results indicate that the inertia component value is the most influential control parameter to tune when optimizing the MGPSO throughout the run time. The relative importance of the inertia weight remains dominant with an increase in the search space dimensions.

Keywords: Particle swarm optimization · Multi-objective optimization · Multi-guide particle swarm optimization · Control parameter tuning · Functional analysis of variance

1 Introduction

The importance of understanding the impact of control parameter importance on algorithm performance allows for optimal resource allocation in control parameter tuning processes. Control parameter importance analysis is done through evaluating an algorithm under various control parameter configurations and comparing the fluctuations in the algorithm's performance [8]. The optimal control parameter configurations for low dimensional search spaces cannot be applied and assumed best for a high dimensional search space. Application of the algorithm to higher dimensional search spaces requires retuning of the algorithm's control parameters values [5].

Control parameter importance analysis has seen little application for meta-heuristics. Harrison et al. [3] were the first to study control parameter importance analysis of a meta-heuristic, specifically particle swarm optimisation (PSO). The

© Springer Nature Switzerland AG 2021
Y. Tan and Y. Shi (Eds.): ICSI 2021, LNCS 12689, pp. 185–198, 2021.
https://doi.org/10.1007/978-3-030-78743-1_17

analysis was done using functional analysis of variance (fANOVA) [8], which analyses the variance in performance relative to each input control parameter configuration. Carolus and Engelbrecht [1] followed on this research with the first control parameter importance analysis of the multi-guide PSO (MGPSO) [7].

The MGPSO control parameter importance was analysed through the evaluation of the algorithm across the walking fish group (WFG) [4] benchmark suite in a 10-dimensional search space. Carolus and Engelbrecht [1] found that the inertia component value is of greatest influence on the MGPSO performance. However, this investigation was applied to a limited number of benchmark problems and applied at a low dimensional space. The MGPSO performance was analysed on the final archive, which does not provide information on how the control parameter importance change during the search process.

Oldewage et al. [5] showed that the best control parameter values for a low dimensional problem does not necessarily best for a high dimensional problem. Therefore, this paper extends the MGPSO control parameter importance analysis to larger dimensional multi-objective optimisation problems (MOOPs) to determine if control parameter importance changes with an increase in problem dimensionality. Changes in control parameter importance over time is also studied. The analysis is also done on more MOOPs. The results show fluctuations in control parameter importance throughout the duration of the search process. Furthermore, the control parameter importance present with changes contrary to [1] when increasing the search dimensions.

The remainder of the paper is structured as follows: Sect. 2 provides background on multi-guide particle swarm optimisation. Section 3 outlines the experimental procedure, followed by a discussion of the results in Sect. 4. Section 5 provides concluding remarks.

2   Background

Background knowledge is presented in this section. Section 2.1 defines multi-objective optimization. Section 2.2 describes the MGPSO algorithm, and Sect. 2.3 provides a description of the fANOVA process.

2.1   Multi-objective Optimization

A MOOP, assuming minimization and only boundary constraints, is defined as

$$\min_{\mathbf{x}} (f_1(\mathbf{x}), f_2(\mathbf{x}), \cdots, f_m(\mathbf{x})) \text{ s.t. } x_j \in [x_{j,\min}, x_{j,\max}], \forall j = 1, \cdots, n \quad (1)$$

where m is the number of objectives and $\mathbf{x}$ is a particular solution within the boundaries of the solution space of dimension n.

The goals of a MOA are to find solutions as close to the true Pareto-optimal front (POF) as possible, with as many non-dominated solutions as possible, whilst obtaining an even spread of these solutions.

2.2 Multi-guide Particle Swarm Optimization

The MGPSO is a multi-swarm algorithm of the inertia weight PSO, that assigns a sub-swarm to each objective of the MOOP. Particles in each sub-swarm are evaluated with respect to their corresponding objective function. The velocity update equation of the MGPSO is defined as

$$
\begin{aligned}
\mathbf{v}_i(t+1) = {} & w\mathbf{v}_i(t) + c_1\mathbf{r}_1(t)(\mathbf{y}_i(t) - \mathbf{x}_i(t)) + \lambda_i c_2\mathbf{r}_2(t)(\hat{\mathbf{y}}_i(t) - \mathbf{x}_i(t)) \\
& + (1 - \lambda_i)c_3\mathbf{r}_3(t)(\hat{\mathbf{a}}_i(t) - \mathbf{x}_i(t))
\end{aligned}
\tag{2}
$$

w is the inertia weight, $\mathbf{c}_1$ and $\mathbf{c}_2$ are the cognitive and social acceleration coefficients, $\mathbf{y}_i(t)$ and $\hat{\mathbf{y}}_i(t)$ are respectively the personal and neighbourhood best position vectors at time t, and $\mathbf{r}_1, \mathbf{r}_2$ and $\mathbf{r}_3$ are vectors of random values, with each random value sampled from a uniform distribution between 0 and 1.

The fourth component of the velocity update includes an archive component to facilitate exchange of information about best positions with respect to all the objectives, between the sub-swarms. Here, $\hat{\mathbf{a}}_i(t)$ is the archive guide and the archive acceleration coefficient, c_3, controls the contribution of the archive component to the movement of the particles. The archive balance coefficient, λ, balance the exploitation of the neighbourhood best and the archive guide. The MGPSO initialises the archive balance coefficient to a random value sampled from a uniform distribution between 0 and 1.

At each iteration, new non-dominated solutions are stored in a bounded archive using the crowding distance [6]. The size of the archive is set to the total number of particles in the sub-swarms. At each iteration, the archive guide, $\hat{\mathbf{a}}_i(t)$, is selected from the archive using tournament selection, usually with a tournament size of 2 or 3 [7]. The solution with the largest crowding distance in the tournament is selected as the archive guide.

Particle positions, $\mathbf{x}_i$, are updated using

$$
\mathbf{x}_i(t+1) = \mathbf{x}_i(t) + \mathbf{v}_i(t+1)
\tag{3}
$$

The MGPSO algorithm is provided in Algorithm 1, where f_k refers to the k-th objective function.

2.3 Functional Analysis of Variance

Control parameter importance can be determined using functional analysis of variance (fANOVA) [8]. fANOVA aims to quantify the variance of the performance metric $m(\boldsymbol{\theta}_i, \pi_j)$ for a given problem π_j, in terms of a subset of control parameters. For more details on how the fANOVA process is applied, the reader is referred to [1,3]. Control parameters with higher variances are of greater importance, and consequently should have a higher priority in control parameter tuning of the algorithm in question.

Algorithm 1. Multi-guide Particle Swarm Optimization (MGPSO)

$t = 0$
for each objective $k = 1, \cdots, m$ **do**
    Create and initialize a swarm, S_k, of size n_{S_k}
    for each particle $i = 1, \cdots, S_k \cdot n_{S_k}$ **do**
        Let f_k be the objective function
        Initialise the personal best position be $S_k \cdot y_i(0) = S_k \cdot x_i(0)$
        Determine the neighbourhood best position, $S_k \cdot \hat{y}_i(0)$
        Initialise the velocity to $S_k \cdot v_i(0) = \mathbf{0}$
        Initialize $S_k \cdot \lambda_i \sim U(0, 1)$
    end for
end for
repeat
    for each objective $k = 1, \cdots, m$ **do**
        for each particle $i = 1, \cdots, S_k \cdot n_{S_k}$ **do**
            if $f_k(S_k \cdot x_i(t)) < f_k(S_k \cdot y_i(t))$ **then**
                $S_k \cdot y_i(t+1) = S_k \cdot x_i(t)$
            end if
            for particles j with particle i in their neighbourhood **do**
                if $f_k(S_k \cdot y_i) < f_k(S_k \cdot \hat{y}_j)$ **then**
                    $S_k \cdot y_j = S_k \cdot y_i$
                end if
            end for
            Update the archive with the solution $S_k \cdot x_i$
        end for
    end for
    for each objective $k = 1, \cdots, m$ **do**
        for each particle $i = 1, \cdots, S_k \cdot n_{S_k}$ **do**
            Select a solution, $S_k \cdot \hat{a}_i(t)$, from the archive using tournament selection
            $v_i(t+1) = wv_i(t) + c_1 r_1(y_i(t) - x_i(t))$
                $+\lambda_i c_2 r_2(\hat{y}_i(t) - x_i(t)) + (1 - \lambda_i) c_3 r_3(\hat{a}_i(t) - x_i(t)));$
            $x_i(t+1) = x_i(t) + v_i(t+1);$
        end for
    end for
until stopping condition is True

---

3 Experimental Procedure

The objectives of this investigation is to study the effects of larger dimensions on MGPSO control parameter importance, and the changes in control parameter importance throughout the duration of the search processes.

The MGPSO control parameters were initialised through sampling in increments of $\frac{1}{30}$ in the following ranges: $w \in [-1.0, 1.0]$, $c_1 \in [0.0, 2.0]$, $\phi_1 = \lambda c_2$ and $\phi_2 = (1 - \lambda)c_3$ such that $\lambda \in [0.0, 1.0]$ and $c_2 = c_3 = 2$. The archive balance coefficient, λ, balances the contribution of the social and archive components to update equation (2). It is the product of λc_2 and $(1 - \lambda)c_3$ that controls the weighting of the social and archive component to the movements of the particles and cannot be decoupled. Therefore, the products $\phi_1 = \lambda c_2$ and $\phi_2 = (1 - \lambda)c_3$ are analysed as weighted social and archive coefficients, since their contribution to equation (2) are not dependent on a single variable.

This produced 31744 control parameter configurations, of which 19168 control parameter configurations were within the region of stability derived in [7]. Of the generated control parameter configurations, only those within the theoretical region of stability were evaluated. This selection criterion is enforced as control parameter values outside the stability region generally leads to a performance worse than that of a random walk [2].

The MGPSO were evaluated on the two-objective Walking Fish Group (WFG) [4] and Zitzler-Deb-Thiele (ZDT) [9] benchmark suites (refer to Table 1) in 10, 30, and 100 dimensions.

Table 1. Properties of the ZDT and WFG problems

Name	Separability	Modality	Geometry
ZDT1	Separable	Unimodal	Convex
ZDT2	Separable	Unimodal	Concave
ZDT3	Separable	Unimodal/multimodal	Disconnected
ZDT4	Separable	Unimodal/multimodal	Convex
ZDT6	Separable	Multimodal	Concave
WFG1	Separable	Unimodal	Convex, mixed
WFG2	Non-separable	Unimodal/multimodal	Convex, disconnected
WFG3	Non-separable	Unimodal	Linear, degenerate
WFG4	Separable	Multimodal	Concave
WFG5	Separable	Multimodal	Concave
WFG6	Non-separable	Unimodal	Concave
WFG7	Separable	Unimodal	Concave
WFG8	Non-separable	Unimodal	Concave
WFG9	Non-separable	Multimodal, deceptive	Concave

Each control parameter configuration was evaluated for 30 independent runs per benchmark problem. Each run was executed for 1000 iterations. The performance measures considered are the IGD and the HV. The HV is calculated with the nadir vector as the reference point.[1] To evaluate the performance throughout the run, the performance measure was calculated at time intervals of 10% of the total run-time. The average performance measure across the 30 runs, at each time interval, is used to determine the control parameter importance using the fANOVA method.

---

[1] The nadir vector is a vector with components consisting of the worst objective values in the Pareto-optimal set.

4   Results

This section discusses the results of this study. Section 4.1 investigates the effects of larger dimensions on the control parameter importance. Section 4.2 studies the change in control parameter importance during the search processes.

4.1   Control Parameter Importance for Higher Dimensional Problems

Tables 2 and 3, contains the results for control parameter importance at 10, 30 and 100 dimensions. Across all benchmark problems, performance measures and dimensions, the inertia weight, w, accounted for the greatest proportion of variance. An increase in the proportion of variance arises for the inertia weight when applied to multi-modal, concave problems, such as WFG 4,9 and ZDT 6 with respect to HV. There is a general trend towards a decrease in control parameter importance of w with an increase in dimensions.

Similar to the inertia weight, the relative importance of the cognitive coefficient, c_1, changes with the modality and geometry of the problem as the dimension increase. The relative importance increases for uni-modal problems and decrease in importance for concave problem. The cognitive acceleration coefficient is the second most important control parameter to tune across all problems, except ZDT 2.

Contrary to the results by [1], the weighted social component, ϕ_1, is of greater importance than the archive component, ϕ_2, when increasing the dimensions, with respect to IGD. Alternatively, the relative importance of ϕ_1 and ϕ_2 becomes indistinguishable as the dimensions increase with respect to the HV. Implying that lower priority should be given to these components when control parameter tuning is considered.

4.2   Control Parameter Importance over Time

For each independent run of the MGPSO, the archive was stored at time intervals of 10 % and used to calculate the IGD and HV. The average IGD and HV, at each time interval, over the 30 independent runs were used within the fANOVA process. Figures 1, 2, 3, 4, 5, 6, 7, 8, 9, 10, 11, 12, 13 and 14 present the relative control parameter importance as a function of run-time for the 30D problems.

All the problems showed a high importance in the inertia weight, w, within the first 20% of the run, with the acceleration coefficients presenting with low importance in this period, for both IGD and HV. Most problems illustrate an increasing importance of the inertia weight in the first 20% of the iterations. Although the relative control parameter importance of the inertia weight is dominant throughout the run, the proportion of variance attributed to w generally peaks after 60% run time. The 2 most influence control parameters throughout the duration of the run are the inertia weight, w and the social acceleration coefficient, c_1.

Table 2. The proportion of Variance in IGD at 10D, 30D, and 100D

	n	c_1	ϕ_1	ϕ_2	w
wfg1	10	0.010338	0.005814	0.008457	0.049322
	30	0.010692	0.009932	0.009145	0.035651
	100	0.012314	0.011923	0.006686	0.029457
wfg2	10	0.014449	0.009283	0.005665	0.041766
	30	0.008568	0.008155	0.006562	0.021736
	100	0.012917	0.010078	0.008683	0.024468
wfg3	10	0.012384	0.008313	0.010789	0.031181
	30	0.010021	0.005302	0.007312	0.025119
	100	0.010596	0.006106	0.006240	0.019963
wfg4	10	0.013607	0.010366	0.007656	0.029092
	30	0.010504	0.004617	0.012989	0.018535
	100	0.011323	0.008379	0.008026	0.019355
wfg5	10	0.014423	0.011089	0.008180	0.029438
	30	0.014266	0.011149	0.008903	0.027062
	100	0.010742	0.010141	0.005778	0.027359
wfg6	10	0.008541	0.009025	0.009025	0.042318
	30	0.014376	0.005143	0.006818	0.011099
	100	0.014071	0.008708	0.009667	0.018873
wfg7	10	0.012572	0.008268	0.009570	0.040248
	30	0.012190	0.015746	0.006447	0.021688
	100	0.011594	0.011464	0.010457	0.047155
wfg8	10	0.011585	0.013803	0.005199	0.018879
	30	0.013435	0.007736	0.010032	0.031019
	100	0.010737	0.012131	0.010320	0.020276
wfg9	10	0.009969	0.006453	0.008996	0.021227
	30	0.011399	0.006491	0.009872	0.017915
	100	0.010231	0.008780	0.009283	0.041084
zdt1	10	0.011471	0.010660	0.009626	0.031351
	30	0.010481	0.010994	0.010551	0.027234
	100	0.010449	0.007651	0.007582	0.017027
zdt2	10	0.008170	0.008968	0.009859	0.017667
	30	0.008405	0.008608	0.009571	0.041801
	100	0.009352	0.010267	0.008302	0.049784
zdt3	10	0.008134	0.013607	0.011575	0.031963
	30	0.011560	0.009857	0.010064	0.022256
	100	0.011052	0.008249	0.012012	0.021287
zdt4	10	0.008258	0.009655	0.006635	0.022004
	30	0.010973	0.010164	0.008383	0.027489
	100	0.010482	0.009356	0.009368	0.030538
zdt6	10	0.012360	0.006237	0.008246	0.028341
	30	0.011527	0.010261	0.007603	0.030507
	100	0.012155	0.006396	0.006603	0.016431

Table 3. The proportion of Variance in HV at 10D, 30D, and 100D

c_1	ϕ_1	ϕ_2	w
0.009925	0.005174	0.006862	0.030629
0.013008	0.005693	0.009333	0.027992
0.009265	0.016173	0.009437	0.024282
0.010825	0.009987	0.007648	0.023400
0.010857	0.009355	0.010829	0.023924
0.013929	0.010759	0.006904	0.036403
0.009756	0.007365	0.009742	0.023252
0.014354	0.008718	0.011380	0.026553
0.008858	0.012245	0.007276	0.030449
0.010888	0.003467	0.007822	0.032223
0.011501	0.007194	0.007759	0.030531
0.010349	0.007658	0.008171	0.012540
0.012039	0.011680	0.008557	0.031422
0.008968	0.008292	0.007148	0.039820
0.011802	0.007273	0.007525	0.030190
0.012243	0.011366	0.007387	0.024050
0.009666	0.011745	0.010737	0.032641
0.010179	0.007773	0.011195	0.036260
0.010550	0.008557	0.008876	0.037149
0.009638	0.011629	0.009911	0.020874
0.011652	0.011715	0.013051	0.021824
0.010337	0.011546	0.008014	0.024821
0.012732	0.007769	0.008844	0.025232
0.009821	0.011145	0.010006	0.023210
0.009670	0.006925	0.010060	0.031003
0.010925	0.007180	0.006019	0.032193
0.011960	0.008116	0.004991	0.029861
0.012688	0.009528	0.012860	0.033321
0.011010	0.008369	0.008598	0.023686
0.011931	0.007444	0.005370	0.027588
0.009083	0.011609	0.006507	0.030648
0.008132	0.007304	0.010008	0.035430
0.010274	0.008632	0.007843	0.027236
0.007347	0.011424	0.010770	0.037996
0.014408	0.011047	0.004354	0.025680
0.008210	0.011067	0.007910	0.022667
0.008760	0.008478	0.009494	0.020543
0.014495	0.012847	0.006046	0.028266
0.010550	0.010133	0.007641	0.024943
0.011130	0.007808	0.006763	0.022569
0.011289	0.006473	0.009814	0.017399
0.009369	0.007988	0.009872	0.021797

For 9 of the 14 problems, the weighted archive component, ϕ_2, is of greater influence than the weighted social component, ϕ_1, in the first 60% of the runtime. The control parameter importance of ϕ_1 and ϕ_2 fluctuates to the end of the run, with problem specific changes.

Problems with uni-modality, such as WFG 1, 3, and 6, present an increase in the importance of the inertia weight as the search progress. The increasing importance of the inertia weight indicates a greater need for controlling the influence of the previous search direction. Most of the changes in the control parameter importance occurs between the 20% to 60% with respect IGD and between 60% to 100% with respect HV. Control parameter tuning should therefore in the first 60% of the search aims to achieve a solution closer the true POF. For the last 40% of the run improves the diversity of the obtained solutions and the volume of the objective space covered.

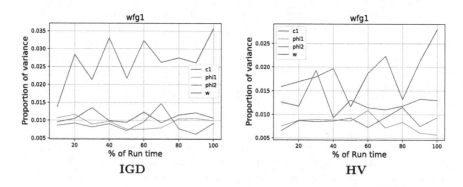

Fig. 1. WFG1 control parameter importance over time.

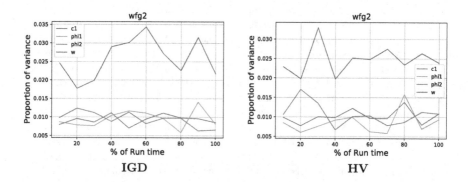

Fig. 2. WFG2 control parameter importance over time.

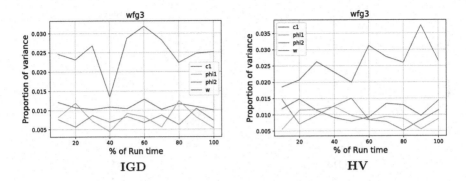

Fig. 3. WFG3 control parameter importance over time.

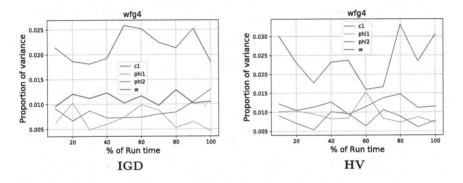

Fig. 4. WFG4 control parameter importance over time.

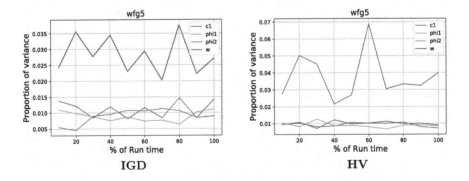

Fig. 5. WFG5 control parameter importance over time.

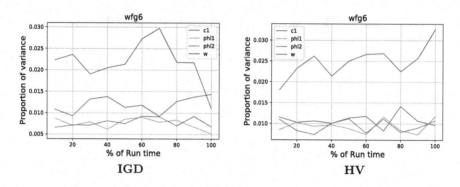

Fig. 6. WFG6 control parameter importance over time.

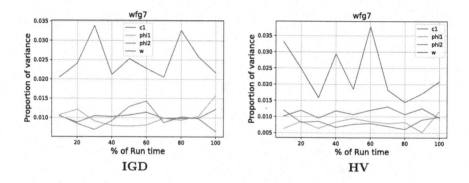

Fig. 7. WFG7 control parameter importance over time.

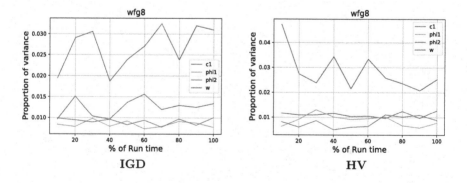

Fig. 8. WFG8 control parameter importance over time.

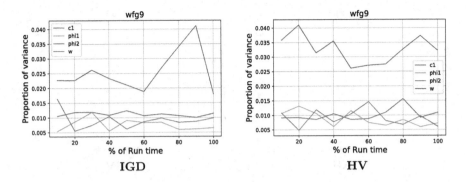

Fig. 9. WFG9 control parameter importance over time.

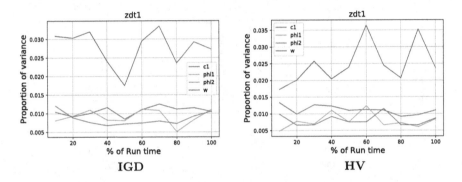

Fig. 10. ZDT1 control parameter importance over time.

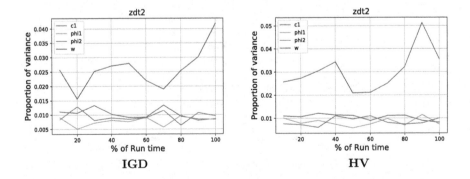

Fig. 11. ZDT2 control parameter importance over time.

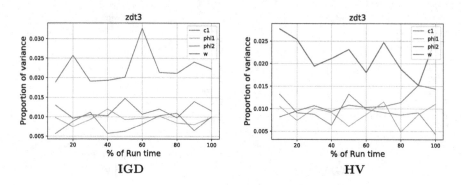

Fig. 12. ZDT3 control parameter importance over time.

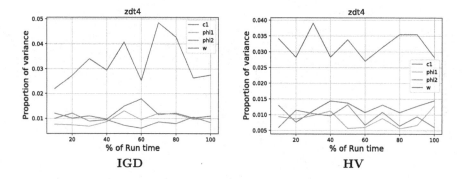

Fig. 13. ZDT4 control parameter importance over time.

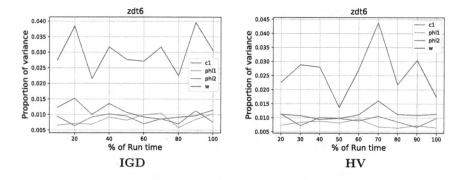

Fig. 14. ZDT6 control parameter importance over time.

5   Conclusions

This study investigated the relative importance of the multi-guide particle swarm optimization (MGPSO) algorithm control parameters in high dimensional problem spaces. The control parameter configuration space was initialised with 31744 different configurations. Configurations within the region of stability as proposed by [7] were used in the evaluation of the MGPSO on the Walking Fish Group (WFG) [4] and Zitzler-Deb-Thiele (ZDT) [9] benchmark functions. The relative control parameter importance was calculated at 10% intervals of the total runtime using function analysis of variance (fANOVA).

The inverted generational distance (IGD) and the hypervolume (HV) were used as performance measures. Both performance measures indicate that the inertia weight, w is of greatest importance to the MGPSO performance throughout the run. At the initialisation of the control parameters, greater emphasis should be placed on the selection of the inertia weight.

When control parameter tuning is considered for the MGPSO, resources should be targeted towards tuning the inertia weight, followed by the social component. The importance w increase for multi-modal, concave problems when increasing the dimensions. Lower priority should be placed on the weighted social, ϕ_1 and archive components, ϕ_2, when considering control parameter tuning in high dimensional problems spaces.

Significant fluctuations in the control parameter importance occurs within the the the first 60% of the run. Emphasis of tuning during this period drives the MGPSO to focus on finding solutions closer to the true POF. Tuning in the last 40% of the run time, improves the diversity of the solutions obtained.

Future research will investigate the development of explorative landscape analysis methods for multi-objective optimization and its use in understanding the periodic changes in control parameter importance.

References

1. Carolus, T.G., Engelbrecht, A.P.: Control parameter importance and sensitivity analysis of the multi-guide particle swarm optimization algorithm. In: Dorigo, M., et al. (eds.) ANTS 2020. LNCS, vol. 12421, pp. 96–106. Springer, Cham (2020). https://doi.org/10.1007/978-3-030-60376-2_8
2. Cleghorn, C.W., Engelbrecht, A.: Particle swarm optimizer: the impact of unstable particles on performance. In: 2016 IEEE Symposium Series on Computational Intelligence (SSCI), pp. 1–7. IEEE (2016)
3. Harrison, K.R., Ombuki-Berman, B.M., Engelbrecht, A.P.: An analysis of control parameter importance in the particle swarm optimization algorithm. In: Tan, Y., Shi, Y., Niu, B. (eds.) ICSI 2019. LNCS, vol. 11655, pp. 93–105. Springer, Cham (2019). https://doi.org/10.1007/978-3-030-26369-0_9
4. Huband, S., Hingston, P., Barone, L., While, L.: A review of multiobjective test problems and a scalable test problem toolkit. IEEE Trans. Evol. Comput. **10**(5), 477–506 (2006)
5. Oldewage, E.T., Engelbrecht, A.P., Cleghorn, C.W.: Movement patterns of a particle swarm in high dimensional spaces. Inf. Sci. **512**, 1043–1062 (2020)

6. Raquel, C.R., Naval Jr., P.C.: An effective use of crowding distance in multiobjective particle swarm optimization. In: Proceedings of the 7th Annual Conference on Genetic and Evolutionary Computation, pp. 257–264 (2005)
7. Scheepers, C., Engelbrecht, A.P., Cleghorn, C.W.: Multi-guide particle swarm optimization for multi-objective optimization: empirical and stability analysis. Swarm Intell. **13**(3-4), 245–276 (2019)
8. Sobol, I.M.: Sensitivity estimates for nonlinear mathematical models. Math. Model. Comput. Exp. **1**(4), 407–414 (1993)
9. Zitzler, E., Thiele, L.: Multiobjective optimization using evolutionary algorithms—a comparative case study. In: Eiben, A.E., Bäck, T., Schoenauer, M., Schwefel, H.-P. (eds.) PPSN 1998. LNCS, vol. 1498, pp. 292–301. Springer, Heidelberg (1998). https://doi.org/10.1007/BFb0056872

Research on the Latest Development of Particle Swarm Optimization Algorithm for Satellite Constellation

Jia-xu Zhang[✉] and Xiao-peng Yan

Science and Technology on Electromechanical Dynamic Control Laboratory, School of
Mechatronical Engineering, Beijing Institute of Technology, Beijing 100081, China
yanxiaopeng@bit.edu.cn

Abstract. As a huge space system, satellite constellation is developing rapidly.
Satellite constellation design is a basic problem in the design of multi spacecraft
space system. It is the premise of building constellation of earth observation, satellite navigation, satellite communication and various scientific exploration satellites. According to the characteristics of modern satellite constellation design, this
paper investigates the design and application of particle swarm optimization algorithm in satellite constellation, and the latest research progress of various research
institutions in satellite constellation maintenance and control, autonomous navigation and space real-time monitoring, and discusses the latest strategies and
technical methods of satellite constellation operation and management.

Keywords: Satellite constellation · Particle Swarm Optimization · Localization ·
Mapping · Position precision

1 Introduction

With the increasingly prominent position of space strategy, satellite constellation presents
a trend of rapid development and attracts widespread attention [1]. Satellite constellations
are widely applied for earth observation [2, 3], global navigation [4, 5], and communications [6, 7]. But as a huge space system, the operation and management of satellite
constellation is a big problem. [8] The design of satellite constellation is the premise
and key to the establishment of satellite system. The goal is to obtain the number of
satellites in the constellation and six orbit parameters of each satellite, i.e. semi major
axis r, eccentricity e, inclination i, perigee argument ω, right ascension of ascending
node (RAAN) Ω and mean anomaly f [9]. Satellite system tasks involve multiple objectives and constraints, such as coverage performance, communication performance, inter
satellite links, system cost, fault tolerance, stability, etc. [10]. Therefore, satellite constellation design is a multi-objective and multi-constraint optimization problem, that
is, to find the constellation configuration parameters that satisfy various constraints to
optimize the objective function. Particle swarm optimization (PSO) algorithm, which is
commonly used in science and engineering, can be used for complex optimization of

© Springer Nature Switzerland AG 2021
Y. Tan and Y. Shi (Eds.): ICSI 2021, LNCS 12689, pp. 199–209, 2021.
https://doi.org/10.1007/978-3-030-78743-1_18

nonlinear, non differentiable and multimodal. Compared with other optimization algorithms, the implementation of the algorithm is relatively simple, and there is no need to adjust the parameters, but its disadvantages are slow convergence speed and poor local search capability [11].

This paper investigates the design and application of particle swarm optimization algorithm in satellite constellation, as well as the latest research progress of various institutions in satellite constellation positioning and maintenance, autonomous navigation, etc., and discusses the latest strategies and technical methods of satellite constellation operation management. It also points out the shortcomings of the existing researches on constellation design. Finally, the development direction of communication satellite constellation design is pointed out.

2 Particle Swarm Optimization (PSO)

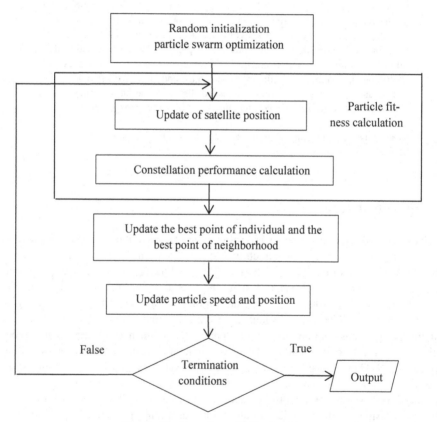

Fig. 1. The flow chart of PSO algorithm.

Kennedy and Eberhart proposed particle swarm optimization (PSO) in 1995. The flow chart of the algorithm is shown in Fig. 1. The basic particle swarm optimization

(PSO) is mainly based on the predatory behavior of birds in nature [12]. It puts forward the method of individual exploration and group cooperation to realize the search and optimization of the solution space. Each bird in the bird group is called a "particle", and each particle has a velocity and a position. The fitness value of the particle is determined by the fitness function defined by the problem. The historical optimal solution of the particle itself and the global optimal solution of the group affect the flight velocity and the next position of the particle, so that the particle can repeatedly explore and develop in the search space, and finally find the global optimal solution. To detect global most favorable, the velocity and position of each particle are upgraded repeatedly with help of succeeding equations [13, 14]:

$$vel_{id}^{t+1} = w * vel_{id}^t + c_1 * rand * \left(pbest_{id}^t - p_{id}^t\right) + c_2 * rand * \left(gbest_{gd}^t - pop_{id}^t\right) \tag{1}$$

$$p_{id}^{t+1} = p_{id}^t + vel_{id}^{t+1} \tag{2}$$

$$w = (w_{min} - w_{max}) * \frac{\text{Iter}^{\text{Max}} - t}{\text{Iter}^{\text{Max}}} + w_{max} \tag{3}$$

Where t is the repetition (generation) figure, vel_{id}^t and p_{id}^t are the velocity and population of ith particle in d dimension. w is the inertia constant, w_{min} and w_{max} are the coefficients of acceleration, and are the minimum and maximum value of inertia constants. $rand \in [0,1]$ is the uniformly distributed random number. $pbest_{id}^t$ and $gbest_{id}^t$ are the local and global best of ith particle in dimension. Kennedy has referred $c_1 * rand * (pbest_{id}^t - pop_{id}^t)$ as the cognitive component and $c_2 * rand * (gbest_{gd}^t - pop_{id}^t)$ as the social component respectively.

Particle swarm optimization algorithm is easy to implement, the parameter space is small, and the real number coding method can solve the real value optimization problem. It has good effect on continuous optimization problem and discrete optimization problem, but it is easy to fall into local optimization. Therefore, it has high requirements for the initial population and learning factor setting. The advantage of particle swarm optimization is very obvious. The real number coding is especially suitable for dealing with the optimization problems in constellation design, but the algorithm is easy to fall into the local optimal solution, which affects the optimization efficiency and optimization results. Therefore, the mutation operator similar to genetic algorithm can be introduced, so that the particles can accept other changes with a certain probability when they change their position and speed, so as to increase the efficiency. The diversity of candidate solutions is added to avoid falling into the local optimal solution [15].

In reference [16], the multi-objective particle swarm optimization (MOPSO) algorithm was used to optimize the design of navigation constellation. The number of satellites, number of orbital planes, orbital height, inclination angle and phase in the constellation were taken as design variables, the navigation performance and satellite production cost were taken as objective functions, and medium earth orbit (MEO) and geostationary orbit (GEO) were adopted (The MEO constellation uses walker model for global navigation, and the GEO satellite is used to enhance the navigation performance of China and its surrounding areas, which has a certain reference value for practical engineering applications.

In reference [17], a hybrid satellite constellation composed of low orbit and elliptical orbit is studied. The optimization objective is the minimum number of satellites to meet the coverage requirements, and the constraint condition is at least single coverage in the target area. An efficient particle swarm optimization algorithm with adaptive mutation is proposed to optimize the design. It is concluded that the performance of the algorithm is better than that of genetic algorithm and traditional particle swarm optimization algorithm.

To sum up, particle swarm optimization algorithm has the advantages of easy implementation, less parameters, high search efficiency, and its real coding characteristics are particularly suitable for constellation optimization problems, and has gradually become a research hotspot.

3 Binary Particle Swarm Optimization (BPSO)

The concept of binary particle swarm optimization (BPSO) is also given by Kennedy and Eberhart which allows BPSO to operate in binary space. In BPSO, a new approach is suggested to update the position of particle which takes either 0 or 1 in d^{th} dimension as:

$$p_{id}^{t+1} = \begin{cases} 0, \ if \ \mathrm{rand}() > Sig\left(vel_{id}^{t+1}\right) \\ 1, \ if \ \mathrm{rand}() < Sig\left(vel_{id}^{t+1}\right) \end{cases} \tag{4}$$

Where $Sig(\cdot)$ is the sigmoidal function which is used to transform the velocity into probability between [0, 1]. The sigmoidal function can be expressed as:

$$Sig\left(vel_{id}^{t+1}\right) = \frac{1}{1 + e^{-vel_{id}^{t+1}}} \tag{5}$$

Figure 2 shows the pseudo-code of BPSO. It must be taken care of that the BPSO is responsive to sigmoid function congestion, which occurs in case values of velocity are either too huge or too small. When the velocity of the particle approaches the lower bound, the probability in the change in value comes near to zero, thereby limit exploration. On the other hand, when the velocity of the particle approaches the upper bound, the probability in the change in value comes near to one, thereby limit exploitation. A probability of 0.5 returns by the sigmoidal function when the velocity of the particle comes near to zero, it means there is 50% chances for the bit to flip. However, velocity clamping will delay the occurrence of the sigmoid function saturation. Hence, the optimal selection of velocity is important for faster convergence [18, 19].

4 Modified Binary Particle Swarm Optimization (MBPSO)

They consider one planning period (such as 280s–300s) to facilitate the problem description and algorithm performance analysis. Figure 3 shows the performance analysis of

BPSO and MBPSO. All the parameters are the same to ensure a fair comparison [20]. As can be seen from Fig. 3, the algorithm of BPSO has slower convergence speed and is easily trapped in local minima. On the contrary, the MBPSO requires less number of iterations than BPSO to get converged to the global best value.

f	Fitness function given in equation ()
$Iter^{Max}$	Maximum number of iteration
$c1, c2$	Acceleration coefficients
$pbest$	Local best solution of particle p
$gbest$	Global best solution
d	Dimension of search space
$rand$	Uniformly distributed random numbers between (0 and 1)

1. Input image

2. Input optimization parameters

3. $vel=$ Velocity_Initialization ();

4. $pop=$ Particle_Initialization ();

5. for $i = 1$ to $Iter^{Max}$

    for each particle p in pop

        $obj = f(p)$

        if obj is better than $f(pbest)$

            $pbest = p$

        End if

        if obj is better than $f(gbest)$

            $gbest = p$

        End if

        update velocity using equation (4)

        update position using equation (7)

        end for

end for

Fig. 2. Algorithm for edge detection using BPSO

Still taking the algorithm performance between 280s and 300s as an example, they explain why the population size is set to be 40 and the iteration number is set to be 20. The performance of MBPSO is analyzed with varying population size and iteration number. Figure 4 shows the optimization history of MBPSO using 20, 30, 40 and 100 particles respectively. According to Fig. 4, it is clear that when the population size is small, the MBPSO algorithm is easily trapped in local minima with a slower convergence speed. This is due to the fact that larger population size can bring in larger area of search space. When the population size exceeds 40, the increase of population size would have little impact on the performance improvements but would significantly increase the computation time. So, a population size of 40 is finally selected in MBPSO for the sensor management problem. Figure 5 shows the optimal fitness value of MBPSO using 10, 20, 30 and 40 iterations respectively when the population size is 40. According to Fig. 5, it is clear that when the iteration number is small, the algorithm is more likely to be trapped in local minima. When the iteration number exceeds 20, the increase of iteration number would have little impact on the performance improvements but would significantly increase the computation time. So, an iteration number of 20 is finally selected in MBPSO for the sensor management problem [21].

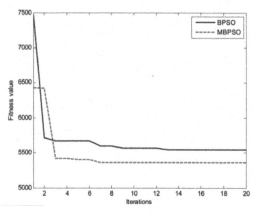

Fig. 3. Performance comparison of BPSO and MBPSO when the population size is 40 and the iteration number is 20.

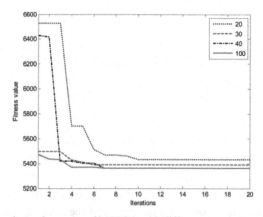

Fig. 4. Performance of MBPSO with different population size.

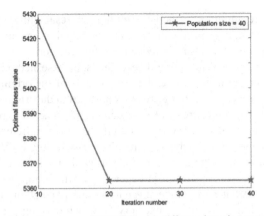

Fig. 5. Performance of MBPSO with different iteration number.

5 Hybrid-Resampling Particle Swarm Optimization (HRPSO)

The PSO algorithm has been successfully applied to high dimensional complex optimization problems and achieved good results [22]. However, due to the inherent properties of the PSO algorithm, there are still some shortcomings, which mainly manifest in two aspects: premature convergence and moving lag. A new optimization method is proposed by Wang et al.--the Hybrid-Resampling Particle Swarm Optimization (HRPSO). It provides higher efficiency for constellation design. Simulation results show that HRPSO is more efficient than standard particle swarm optimization (PSO) and other improved resampling particle swarm optimization (RPSO).

There are three key issues here: calculating particle weights, choosing the resampling methods, and determining the speed of particles after resampling.

First, calculating the weights of the particles. In the optimization algorithms, the weight of one particle should be related to its corresponding objective function or fitness value. Taking the minimum value optimization as an example, the smaller the objective value or the greater its contribution to the population is, the larger its weight should be. On the contrary, when the objective value is larger or its contribution to the population is lower, its weight should be smaller. According to this principle, the calculation method of the particle weight is given as follows:

$$q_i = \frac{1}{\sqrt{2\sigma\pi}}\exp\left(-\frac{\left(F(x_i) - p_g\right)^2}{2\sigma}\right) \tag{6}$$

Where q_i is the ith particle's weight, $F(\cdot)$ is the fitness value corresponding to the particle, p_g is the current optimal position of the group, and σ is the variance based on $F(x_i) - p_g$. In practice, normalized weights are used:

$$Q_i = \frac{q_i}{\sum_{i=1}^{N} q_i} \tag{7}$$

There are six resampling methods: multinomial resampling; stratified resampling; systematic resampling; residual resampling; residual-systematic resampling and reallocation resampling, which can be divided into two categories [23].

The first category contains the former five methods. In these methods, the resampling process will not generate new particles but only copies of the original particles. The speeds of the particles after resampling are also copied from the original particles. After resampling, all particle weights return to the same level. When one particle is copied multiple times, it will actually search from the same position in different directions even though its position and velocity are the same. This is due to the difference between the random factor and the optimal value of the particle in the velocity update formula. In this way, more particles can search in better areas, which improves the movement lag to a certain extent but reduces the diversity of the population at the same time. Reallocation resampling is in another category, in which existing particles are copied and new particles are generated. Particles with small weights will be eliminated and replaced by new particles. The positions of the new particles are randomly generated, and the speeds of the new particles are obtained by the following formula:

$$v_i^t = \frac{T_{max} + t}{2T_{max}} \bar{v}_i^t + \frac{T_{max} - t}{2T_{max}} v_i^t \tag{8}$$

Where T_{max} is the maximum number of iterations, and $\bar{v}_i^t$ is the randomly generated speed. In this way, the diversity of the population can be significantly increased, which will help overcome premature convergence. However, this method will reduce the efficiency of exploring local areas.

The two types of resampling methods have their own advantages and disadvantages [24]. To combine their advantages, the particle population is divided into two subpopulations. One subpopulation uses the first type of resampling method to quickly explore a local area, while the other subpopulation uses the second type of resampling method to maintain diversity of the population. At the same time, it is necessary to ensure that the information exchange between the two sub-populations is unobstructed. In this paper, this kind of PSO algorithm using multiple resampling methods at the same time is called the hybrid-resampling particle swarm optimization algorithm, i.e., HRPSO. The process of the HRPSO algorithm is shown as follows:

Step 1. Set the basic parameters of the algorithm, including the population size N, the sizes of the two subpopulations with different resampling methods N_1N_2, the dimension D, the maximum number of iterations T_{max}, and the acceleration factors c_1, c_2. Set the current count of the iterations to $t = 0$.

Step 2. Initialize the positions and velocities of the particles, calculate the particle fitness value, and initialize the individual optimal positions as well as the group optimal positions of the particles.

Step 3. Let $t = t + 1$. If $t\%5 \neq 0$, performing Step 4; otherwise, assign a weight to each particle using Eqs. (7) and (6), and resample based on the weights.

Step 4. Update the speed of each particle and limit it to the maximum speed if the speed is out of range. Update the position of each particle. If the position is out of range, correct the position and speed according to certain rules.

Step 5. Calculate the fitness value of each particle, update the individual optimal position of the particle based on the fitness, and then select the group optimal position from the individual optimal positions.

Step 6. If $t \geq T_{\max}$, return the optimal position of the current group as the final result; otherwise, go back to Step 3.

6 Conclusions and Future Work

With the rapid development of satellite constellation, in order to ensure the long-term high reliability, high performance, high precision and stable operation of satellite constellation, perfect operation management strategy and optimization algorithm are essential. The design of satellite constellation has entered a new stage. Traditional satellite constellation design methods have shown their shortcomings, and a new generation of constellation design method based on particle swarm optimization is emerging. Because satellite constellation is a very complex space system, satellite constellation design is also a very complex system optimization design problem, the understanding of its mission requirements, constraints, performance evaluation and other aspects is still in the process of deepening and improving.

This paper mainly investigates the achievements of satellite constellation positioning, maintenance and operation management at home and abroad in recent years, including traditional Particle Swarm Optimization, Binary Particle Swarm Optimization, Modified Binary Particle Swarm Optimization, Hybrid-Resampling Particle Swarm Optimization and so on. The advantages and disadvantages of each algorithm are analyzed:

1. Similar to genetic algorithm, PSO is an optimization algorithm based on iteration. The system is initialized as a set of random solutions, and the optimal value is searched by iteration. Compared with genetic algorithm, PSO is simple and easy to implement. Performance is not particularly good on some issues. The coding of network weights and the selection of genetic operators are sometimes troublesome.
2. BPSO is based on the discrete particle swarm optimization algorithm, the position vector and velocity vector are composed of 0 and 1 values. BPSO has strong global search ability, but it can't converge to the global optimal value. With the increasing randomness of iterative search, BPSO lacks local search ability;
3. The proposed MBPSO algorithm can effectively improve the tracking performance of Leo infrared constellation. Simulation results show that MBPSO algorithm is superior to BPSO algorithm in performance and convergence speed.
4. Compared with standard PSO algorithm and other improved PSO algorithm, HRPSO algorithm can achieve better coverage performance with less computing time. Therefore, HRPSO algorithm is expected to be a practical choice for constellation design.

The next step is to establish an accurate constellation design optimization model according to the actual objective requirements and constraints, comprehensively evaluate the constellation performance, and adjust the constellation scheme according to the evaluation results.

Acknowledgement. This research has been funded in 61973037 by the National Natural Science Foundation of China.

References

1. del Portillo, I., Cameron, B., Crawley, E.: A technical comparison of three low earth orbit satellite constellation systems to provide global broadband. Acta Astronautica **159**, 123–135 (2019)
2. Urata, K., Sri, J., Sumantyo, C., Santosa, T.: A compact C-Band CP-SAR microsatellite antenna for earth observation. Acta Astronautica **159**, 517–526 (2019)
3. Buzzi, P.G., Selva, D., Hitomi, N., et al.: Assessment of constellation designs for earth observation: application to the TROPICS mission. Acta Astronaut. **161**, 166–182 (2019)
4. Wang, D.G., Guo, R., Zhang, T.Q., Hu, X.G.: Timing performance evaluation of radio determination satellite service (RDSS) for Beidou system. Acta Astronaut. **156**, 125–133 (2019)
5. Zhang, T.J., Shen, H.X., Li, Z., et al.: Restricted constellation design for regional navigation augmentation. Acta Astronaut. **150**, 231–239 (2018)
6. Buinhas, L., Peytaví, G.G., Förstner, R.: Navigation and communication network for the Valles Marineris Explorer (VaMEx). Acta Astronaut. **160**, 280–296 (2019)
7. Bradbury, L.M., Diaconu, D., Laurin, S.M., et al.: NorSat-2: enabling advanced maritime communication with VDES. Acta Astronaut. **156**, 44–50 (2019)
8. Zhao, N., Dong, Z.: Study on satellite constellation management method. Radio Eng. **40**(06), 62–64 (2010)
9. Mo, Y., Yan, D., You, P., Yong, S.: A survey of constellation optimization design for satellite communications. Telecommun. Eng. **56**(11), 1293–1300 (2016)
10. Xiao, N., Liang, J., Zhang, J.: Design and planning of LEO satellite constellation network in China. Telecommun. Eng. **50**(12), 14–18 (2010)
11. Chen, F., Deng, W-D., Cheng, F.: Design of communication satellite constellation based on particle swarm optimization algorithm. Guidance Fuze (1), 40–43 (2016)
12. Kennedy, J.: Particle swarm optimization. In: Proceedings of 1995 IEEE International Conference on Neural Networks, Perth, Australia, 27 Nov–Dec 2011, vol. 4, no. 8, pp. 1942–1948 (2011)
13. Sharifi, M., Fathy, M., Tayefeh Mahmoudi, M.: A classified and comparative study of edge detection algorithms (2002)
14. Tan, H.L., Gelfand, S.B.: A comparative cost function approach to edge detection. IEEE Trans. Syst. Man Cybern. **19**(6), 1337–1349 (1989)
15. Meng, B., Yi, C., Han, C.: Optimization of navigation satellite constellation by multi-objective particle swarm algorithm. Acta Aeronauticaet Astronautica Sinica **30**(7), 1284–1291 (2009)
16. Meng, B., Han, C.: Optimization of hybrid constellation by modified particle swarm algorithm. Aerospace Shanghai AER **27**(1), 36–39 (2010)
17. Rocco, E.M., Souza, M.L.D.O.E., Prado, A.F.B.D.A.: Multi-objective optimization approach applied to station keeping of satellite constellations. Adv. Astronaut. Sci. **109**, 641–656 (2002)
18. Wang, X., Zhang, H., Bai, S., et al.: Design of agile satellite constellation based on hybrid-resampling particle swarm optimization method. Acta Astronaut. **178**, 595–605 (2021)
19. Kennedy, J., Kennedy, J.F., Eberhart, R.C., et al.: Swarm Intelligence, pp. 8–35. Morgan Kaufmann, San Francisco (2001)
20. Whittecar, W.R., Ferringer, M.P.: Global coverage constellation design exploration using evolutionary algorithms. In: AIAA/AAS Astrodynamics Specialist Conference (2014)

21. Qin, Z., Liang, Y.G.: Sensor management of LEO constellation using modified binary particle swarm optimization. Optik **172**, 879–891 (2018)
22. Kennedy, J., Eberhart, R.C.: A discrete binary version of the particle swarm algorithm. In: 1997 IEEE International Conference on Systems, Man, and Cybernetics. Computational Cybernetics and Simulation. IEEE (1997)
23. Mirjalili, S., Lewis, A.: S-shaped versus V-shaped transfer functions for binary particle swarm optimization. Swarm Evol. Comput. **9**, 1–14 (2013)
24. Naeem, M.: Swarm intelligence for sensor selection problems. IEEE Sens. J. **12**(8), 2577–2585 (2012)

Polynomial Approximation Using Set-Based Particle Swarm Optimization

Jean-Pierre van Zyl[1(✉)] and Andries P. Engelbrecht[1,2]

[1] Division of Computer Science, Stellenbosch University, Stellenbosch, South Africa
{20706413,engel}@sun.ac.za
[2] Department of Industrial Engineering, Stellenbosch University,
Stellenbosch, South Africa

Abstract. This paper introduces a new approach to solving regression problems by using a particle swarm optimization algorithm to find optimal polynomial regressions to these problems. Polynomial regression is defined as a multi-objective optimization problem, with the goals to find both an optimal combination of terms in the polynomial and optimal values of the coefficients of the terms, in order to minimize the approximation error. This paper shows that a set-based PSO works well to find the optimal term structure of the target polynomials in low dimensions, and holds promise for improved performance in higher dimensions. The results of the set-based PSO are compared to the results of a Binary PSO on the same problems. Finally, this paper explores possible solutions to create a hybrid algorithm that can find both the optimal term structure and the coefficients of the found terms.

Keywords: Particle swarm optimization · Polynomial regression · Adaptive coordinate descent · Set-based particle swarm optimization

1 Introduction

A polynomial is a functional mapping, $f : \mathbb{R}^{n_x} \to \mathbb{R}$, relating an n_x-dimensional input space to a one-dimensional output space. Polynomial regression refers to the process of finding an optimal polynomial that accurately approximates an arbitrary functional mapping. While a number of approaches exist, this paper develops a novel set-based optimization approach to find polynomial mappings.

Polynomial regression is here defined as a multi-objective optimization problem, using a set-based solution representation. The objectives are to find: (1) the smallest number of terms and lowest polynomial order, and (2) optimal coefficient values for these terms in order to minimize the approximation error.

This paper determines the viability of using a set-based particle swarm optimization (SBPSO) algorithm to find an optimal term set in order to achieve the first objective. As a precursor to future improvements to this approach, in order to meet the second objective, the suitability of an interleaved, dual optimization process is investigated to find both optimal term architecture and coefficients.

© Springer Nature Switzerland AG 2021
Y. Tan and Y. Shi (Eds.): ICSI 2021, LNCS 12689, pp. 210–222, 2021.
https://doi.org/10.1007/978-3-030-78743-1_19

This is achieved in a preliminary study by applying adaptive coordinate descent (ACD) [10] to find the coefficients of the found term sets' components. To the knowledge of the authors, this a first approach to polynomial regression using a set-based optimization algorithm.

The SBPSO algorithm is empirically evaluated on a number of problems to determine its ability to select optimal combination of terms, and is compared to a binary particle swarm optimization (BPSO) [7] algorithm's ability to select terms. The combined algorithm with ACD is compared to a standard non-set based particle swarm optimization (PSO) [6] algorithm. SBPSO is shown to be able to find an optimal set of terms by itself, and the preliminary results of the proposed hybrid algorithm shows that it is also able to find an optimal set of terms and optimal coefficients.

It is shown that the SBPSO and ACD hybrid algorithm performs well when applied on low dimensional problems and hold promise for improvement in higher dimensions. The hybrid algorithm is able to approximate the source polynomial from the input data both in structure and in coefficients.

Section 2 discusses the concepts needed to implement the work in this paper, and Section 3 outlines how existing optimization algorithms can be combined to approximate polynomial mappings. Section 4 contains the empirical procedure, while Section 5 discusses the results followed by the conclusion in Section 6.

2   Background

This section outlines background information on polynomial regression, PSOs, SBPSOs, and ACD as used in this paper.

2.1   Polynomial Regression

Polynomials are made of constituent parts called terms or monomials. These monomials are defined as the product of one or more input variables, each raised to a power and preceded by a coefficient:

$$a_i \prod x_j^n \tag{1}$$

The goal of polynomial regression is to find the best possible polynomial to accurately approximate a functional mapping, $f : \mathbb{R}^{n_x} \to \mathbb{R}$, embedded in a data-set, $D = \{(\boldsymbol{x}_p, y_p) | p = 1, \ldots, n_p\}$; where $\boldsymbol{x}_p = (x_{1p}, x_{2p}, \ldots, x_{n_x p})$ is a vector of input variables, y_p is the corresponding desired output value, p refers to a specific data point in D, n_x is the number of input variables, and $n_p = |D|$ is the total number of data points.

Univariate polynomials have $n_x = 1$, and are presented in the general form:

$$f(x) = \sum_{j=0}^{n_o} a_j x_j = a_0 + a_1 x + a_2 x^2 + \cdots + a_{n_o} x^{n_o} \tag{2}$$

where n_o is the order of the polynomial. Multivariate polynomials have $n_x > 1$, and have the general form:

$$f(\boldsymbol{x}) = a_0 + \sum_{t=1}^{n_t} a_t \prod_{q=1}^{n_q} x_q^{\lambda_q} \tag{3}$$

where n_t is the number of monomials, a_t is the coefficient of the tth monomial, n_q is the number of variables in the tth monomial, and λ_q is the order of the corresponding variable.

The goal of finding the best polynomial approximation can be broken down into the following sub-goals: (1) to find optimal monomials, (2) to find the smallest number of monomials, (3) to minimize the order of the monomials, and (4) to find the best coefficient values of these monomials.

The rationale of these sub-goals is to produce a polynomial that minimizes the approximation error and the complexity of the polynomial. The structure of the polynomial is minimized to prevent overfitting, while underfitting is prevented by minimizing the approximation error. Approximation error is estimated using the mean squared error (MSE), defined as

$$\mathcal{E} = \frac{1}{n_p} \sum_{p=1}^{n_p} (y_p - \hat{y}_p)^2 \tag{4}$$

Polynomial approximation is a multi-objective optimization problem, defined as:

$$\text{minimize } F(f(\boldsymbol{x}), D) = \mathcal{E}(f(\boldsymbol{x}), D) + \lambda P(f(\boldsymbol{x})) \tag{5}$$

where $f(\boldsymbol{x})$ is a polynomial from the universe, $\mathcal{U}$, of possible polynomials, D is the data-set of points, $\mathcal{E}$ is the MSE, P is a polynomial complexity penalty function, and λ is a penalty coefficient. An example penalty function is

$$P(f(\boldsymbol{x})) = \sum_{i=0}^{n_t} a_i^2 \tag{6}$$

referred to as ridge regression, or weight decay in neural network terminology [8].

Polynomial regression is a commonly performed task in model induction and machine learning in general and, as a result, various approaches have been tested. Notably, neural networks (NN) have been used for polynomial regression [15] and have been shown to be universal approximators capable of learning any non-linear mapping [5]. However, the output of a NN is not the target polynomial itself, but an uninterpretable list of tuned weights.

2.2 Particle Swarm Optimization

Particle swarm optimization is a well-established swarm-based optimization method [6]. Since its inception, many modifications have been proposed to improve its performance and its application on different problem types. Modifications for discrete environments include the BPSO or the angle modulated PSO [12].

Basic Particle Swarm Optimization. The first PSO, proposed by Kennedy and Eberhart [6], is a swarm-based optimization algorithm that makes use of stochastic optimization techniques inspired by the flocking behaviour of birds. The population of a PSO is called a swarm, and each agent in the swarm is known as a particle. Each particle represents a candidate solution to the optimization problem. These potential solutions are changed to explore the search landscape and attempt to exploit any potential optima that have been found in the process.

In the PSO algorithm, let n_s denote the swarm size, and n_x denote the dimensionality of the problem. Each particle i has a position $\boldsymbol{x}_i(t)$, a velocity $\boldsymbol{v}_i(t)$, a personal best position $\boldsymbol{y}_i(t)$, and a neighbourhood best position $\hat{\boldsymbol{y}}_i(t)$, with each variable being n_x-dimensional vectors. The personal best position is the best optimum discovered by particle i up to iteration t, and the neighbourhood best is the best optimum discovered by any particle in particle i's neighbourhood. Particle positions are updated in each iteration using:

$$x_{ij}(t+1) = x_{ij}(t) + v_{ij}(t+1) \tag{7}$$

where $v_{ij}(t)$ is the velocity, calculated for each dimension j using [13]:

$$v_{ij}(t+1) = \omega v_{ij}(t) + c_1 r_{1j}(t)[y_{ij}(t) - x_{ij}(t)] + c_2 r_{2j}(t)[\hat{y}_{ij}(t) - x_{ij}(t)] \tag{8}$$

where ω is the inertia weight, c_1 and c_2 are the acceleration coefficients and $r_{1j}(t) \sim U(0,1)$ and $r_{2j}(t) \sim U(0,1)$ are uniformly distributed random variables for all $i \in \{1, \ldots, n_s\}$ and $j \in \{1, \ldots, n_x\}$.

The control parameters ω, c_1 and c_2 control the exploration-exploitation trade-off in PSOs. This trade-off is adjusted to determine whether the goal of the swarm is to discover new potential solutions or to refine already found optima.

Binary Particle Swarm Optimization. While PSOs were initially developed for continuous search spaces, the binary PSO (BPSO) variant was developed by Kennedy and Eberhart to solve binary problem spaces [7].

The BPSO has a structure similar to the standard PSO, with its velocities still being defined by Eq. (8) in continuous space. However, the velocities are not interpreted as a spatial change in $\mathbb{R}^{n_x}$ space, but as probabilities of bit flips. The position vector is changed to consist of bits, *i.e.* each $\boldsymbol{x}_i \in \mathbb{B}^{n_x}$, and the position update equation is defined as:

$$x_{ij}(t+1) = \begin{cases} 1 & \text{if } r_{3j}(t) < S(v_{ij}(t+1)) \\ 0 & \text{otherwise} \end{cases} \tag{9}$$

where $S(v_{ij}(t)) = \frac{1}{1+e^{-v_{ij}(t)}}$ and $r_{3j}(t) \sim U(0,1)$.

Set-Based Particle Swarm Optimization. The set-based PSO, as implemented in this paper, was developed to solve the multi-dimensional knapsack problem [9]. This is a discretised version of the standard PSO which makes use of a set-based search space instead of a n_x-dimensional continuous search space. Particle positions consist of elements from the universal set, $\mathcal{U}$, while the velocity is a set of operation pairs which add to or remove from elements in the position. The set-based representation allows for candidate solutions of various dimensions (a variable number of components), contrary to the basic PSO where all candidate solutions have to be of the same dimension. This optimization algorithm has been successfully applied to real-world problems like portfolio optimization and feature selection [2,3], and performs well in discrete search spaces.

Because there is no concept of spatial structure for a set-based representation, analogies of the velocity and position update equations were developed by Langeveld and Engelbrecht [9]. These new equations contain operators to calculate the attraction to the global best position and to each particle's personal best position as seen in the standard PSO. There is also an operator to add unexplored terms to the position and an operator to remove possibly poorly selected terms. For more detail on the SBPSO and its position and velocity update equations, the reader is referred to [9].

A brief description of the important control parameters follows: Coefficient c_1 controls the particle's attraction to its own previous personal best position, while c_2 controls its attraction to the neighbourhood (global) best position up to iteration t. The additional acceleration coefficients, c_3 and c_4, manage the effect of the operators designed to improve exploration of the search space. The number of terms added to a position is controlled by c_3, and the number of terms from a position is controlled by c_4.

2.3 Adaptive Coordinate Descent

Adaptive coordinate descent (ACD) [10] is an improvement to the covariance matrix adaptation evolutionary strategy (CMA-ES). ACD adds adaptive encoding (AE), developed by Hansen [4], to the coordinate descent (CD) optimization algorithm. AE is applied to an optimization algorithm in a continuous domain to make the search independent from the coordinate system. This allows for performance improvements in non-separable problems and in problems where traditional CD fails. ACD utilises AE to perform its optimization process. For more detail on ACD, the reader is referred to [10].

3 Set-Based Particle Swarm Optimization Polynomial Regression

A BPSO can be used to learn polynomial structure by letting the position vector represent all possible terms in the universal set. A position entry where $x_{ij} = 1$ means that particle i has selected term j to form part of the polynomial structure. However, if the universal set contains n_t terms, the BPSO particles' positions and velocities are fixed at size $n_x = n_t$, which is expected to scale poorly [11].

The proposed solution to this dimensionality problem is to use a SBPSO, outlined in Algorithm 1, with its variable position size to represent the selected terms from the universal set. This allows only the necessary terms to be added to the position set, meaning that particle position sizes are not fixed to be of size n_t, allowing particle dimensions to be kept to a minimum. Positions are initialised from the universal set by selecting a small collection of terms, and velocities are initialised to the empty set. SBPSO velocities are interpreted as the terms which need to be added or removed in order to change the current set to a given target set which is calculated from the personal best, global best, or a randomly chosen set. Therefore, the attractions to the personal and global bests create pressure for position sets to add terms from the personal and global bests, and to remove possibly unnecessary terms. The SBPSO velocities also create pressure to explore the search space by adding terms not currently in the particle position, personal best or global best; while also removing terms from the position that are potentially unnecessary.

The size of the universal set increases exponentially as the number of input dimensions are increased, and linearly as the maximum power of the target polynomial is increased:

$$|U| = 1 + \sum_{p=1}^{n_o} \sum_{i=1}^{n_x} \binom{n_x}{i} \tag{10}$$

where n_o is the maximum order, n_x is the number of input variables and the constant of one accounts for the bias term of a_0.

Algorithm 1. Set-Based Particle Swarm Optimization

Generate the universal set
Create a swarm containing n_s particles
Initialise particle positions as random subsets of U
Initialise local and global best values
while Stopping conditions not true **do**
    for each particle $i = 1, \ldots, n_s$ **do**
        Use an optimization algorithm to find the coefficient values of the selected terms, and evaluate the quality of this solution.
        if $f(X_i) < f(Y_i)$ **then**
            Update local best: $Y_i = X_i$
        end if
        if $f(Y_i) < f(\hat{Y}_i)$ **then**
            Update global best: $\hat{Y}_i = Y_i$
        end if
    end for
    for each particle $i = 1, \ldots, n_s$ **do**
        Update particle i's velocity and position.
    end for
end while

SBPSO and BPSO algorithms both find only the optimal term structure, and not the coefficients; hence the following approaches are proposed.

A PSO can be used to find the coefficients of a polynomial by setting the position vector to refer to all the possible terms from the universal set. The value of each x_{ij} refers to the coefficient of the jth term, with coefficients close to 0 indicating that the corresponding term does not contribute to the polynomial structure. However, this approach has many drawbacks. The position vectors are fixed to size $n_x = n_t$ and, as with the BPSO, will suffer from poor performance in high dimensions [11]. Additionally, the threshold of when a coefficient is "close to 0" has to be defined and tuned as an additional control parameter.

In a preliminary feasibility study, this paper proposes a hybrid algorithm which uses SBPSO to find the polynomial structure and a separate optimization algorithm to find the optimal coefficients, with preliminary investigations conducted using ACD. This hybrid algorithm will have the advantage of minimizing the dimensionality of the problem using the SBPSO and the ability to find the coefficients of the polynomial using ACD.

The basic overview is as follows: the main concepts of the standalone SBPSO algorithm are still present in the hybrid algorithm; this includes the position and velocity update equations, as well as the additional set operators used to increase exploration. The interleaved optimization process using ACD is achieved in the fitness function of the SBPSO. By using the terms currently being evaluated as the input dimensions for ACD, coefficients can be found for each of the target terms. The whole optimization process, as outlined in [10], is completed for each fitness function evaluation of a SBPSO position.

4 Empirical Process

This section outlines the processes followed to evaluate the proposed polynomial regression algorithms and to compare it to existing regression algorithms.

4.1 Benchmark Problems

The main aim of this paper is to illustrate the feasibility of the SBPSO for inducing optimal polynomial structures and its secondary aim is to illustrate the need for a second optimization algorithm to find both the term structure and coefficients.

In order to test the ability of the SBPSO to find optimal polynomial structures and to compare these results to that of a BPSO, seven benchmark problems with varying characteristics were created. These test functions, f_1 to f_7, have coefficients of 1 to allow the SBPSO and BPSO algorithms to be tested in isolation and to accurately measure their term-choosing abilities. The polynomials for these problems have a known order, allowing this information to be used to calculate the universal set. A further three test functions, f_8 to f_{10}, were created with non-unit coefficients to test and compare the regression abilities of the proposed combined SBPSO and ACD algorithm, as well as a standard PSO algorithm. Table 1 outlines the test functions generated and their universal set characteristics.

Table 1. Proposed test functions and their generated universal set characteristics

Function	Max degree	Universe size
$f_1(x) = x_1^3 + x_2^2 + x_2 + 1$	5	16
$f_2(x) = x^3 + x^2 + x$	5	6
$f_3(x) = x^7 + x^5 + x^4 + 1$	9	10
$f_4(x) = x^8 + x^7 + x^6 + x^5 + x^4 + x^3 + x^2 + x + 1$	10	11
$f_5(x) = x_1^2 + x_2^2 + x_1^2 x_3^2 + x_3$	4	29
$f_6(x) = x_1^6 + x_2^5 + x_3^4 + x_1 + x_2^2 x_3^2 + x_3 + 1$	8	57
$f_7(x) = x_1 + x_2^2 + x_3^2 + x_4^2 + x_5^2 + x_1 x_2 x_4 x_5 + x_3 x_4 + 1$	4	125
$f_8(x) = 0.5x^3 + 2x^2 - x$	5	6
$f_9(x) = x_1^2 - 2x_2^2 + 3x_1^2 x_3^2 - 1.5x_3$	4	29
$f_{10}(x) = -3x_1 - 3x_2^2 - 3x_3^2 - 3x_4^2 - 3x_5^2 + 2x_1 x_2 x_4 x_5 + 5x_3 x_4 - 6.2$	4	125

4.2   Tuning Algorithm Configurations

Each of the control parameters of the algorithms used were tuned using quasi-randomly generated Sobol sequences [14]. These sequences are generated to provide good coverage of the hypercube generated by the control parameter search space.

The control parameters of each algorithm were tuned per problem. This was done by sampling values for the control parameters as specified in Table 2. For each algorithm, on each test problem, 128 Sobol sequences were generated by sampling from the specified ranges and tuned for 500 iterations, with 30 particles in the swarm. The PSO control parameters were sampled to also satisfy the stability conditions as outlined in [1]. The obtained optimal parameters are outlined in Table 3 and Table 4, rounded to four (4) decimal places for brevity. The best parameter combination was selected as the one that had the best generalizable approximation ability, as represented by the lowest MSE over the test set.

Table 2. Table of the parameters tuned for each implemented algorithm

SBPSO		BPSO		ACD		PSO	
Parameter	range	Parameter	range	Parameter	range	Parameter	range
c_1	$[0,1]$	ω	$[0,1]$	k_{succ}	$\{2\}$	ω	$[0,1]$
c_2	$[0,1]$	c_1	$[0,2]$	k_{unsucc}	$\{0.5\}$	c_1	$[0,2]$
c_3	$[0.5,5]$	c_2	$[0,2]$	λ	$[0,1]$	c_2	$[0,2]$
c_4	$[0.5,5]$	v_{max}	$[0,6]$			λ	$[0,1]$

Table 3. Optimal control parameters for SBPSO, BPSO on f_1 to f_7

Function	SBPSO c_1, c_2, c_3, c_4	BPSO $\omega, c_1, c_2, v_{max}$
f_1	$0.0683, 0.5605, 0.9130, 0.9306$	$0.5249, 1.0498, 0.2548, 5.4755$
f_2	$0.9648, 0.5351, 3.5410, 3.5410$	$0.2758, 1.0478, 1.4716, 3.3603$
f_3	$0.7226, 0.6523, 4.8417, 3.2246$	$0.5063, 0.7431, 0.5107, 3.4306$
f_4	$0.5166, 0.5498, 3.8793, 4.1782$	$0.3706, 0.4912, 1.6259, 0.6123$
f_5	$0.8105, 0.8183, 2.7060, 4.9736$	$0.9243, 1.0322, 0.3935, 4.2509$
f_6	$0.8916, 0.9248, 2.1918, 4.7407$	$0.9858, 0.4091, 1.7392, 4.5849$
f_7	$0.8564, 0.6787, 2.2797, 1.1372$	$0.9936, 1.2373, 0.6923, 3.7880$

Table 4. Optimal control parameters for Hybrid, PSO on f_8 to f_{10}

Function	Hybrid $c_1, c_2, c_3, c_4, \lambda$	PSO $\omega, c_1, c_2, \lambda$
f_8	$0.5830, 0.5146, 1.6118, 0.8208, 0.2998$	$0.7631, 0.9169, 1.7158, 0.0883$
f_9	$0.2041, 0.3623, 0.7856, 4.4594, 0.8818$	$0.7109, 1.4218, 1.2656, 0.9921$
f_{10}	$0.3720, 0.8818, 0.8032, 0.6450, 0.0576$	$0.6909, 0.3818, 1.8291, 0.2973$

4.3 Performance Measures

For each problem, 10000 n_x-dimensional data points were created by calculating the Cartesian product of n_x generated real-valued axes to form the complete data-set. These sets were split into training and test sets with the training set being 70% of the total and the test 30%. In order to quantify the performance of the algorithm, the MSE over the train and test set is reported on, as well as the average size of the found polynomial.

The final tests were run with the selected parameter combinations, with the results summarised in Section 5. For SBPSO and BPSO 2000 iterations over 30 independent runs were used; for the hybrid and PSO algorithms, 500 iterations over 30 independent runs were used due to the high computational complexity of the hybrid algorithm. For the final tests, all algorithms had 30 particles in their swarms.

5 Results

This section outlines the results obtained from applying the SBPSO to the problem of finding the optimal term structure, followed by the preliminary investigation into the feasibility of a hybrid algorithm to find both the optimal term structure and coefficients.

5.1 SBPSO and BPSO Results

Table 5 shows the performance of SBPSO and BPSO on test functions f_1 to f_7 by reporting on the train and test MSEs. Table 6 shows how many independent runs induced the correct target polynomial structure; this was calculated by comparing, term by term, the structure of the found polynomial with the known structure of the target polynomial. For each problem, the found polynomial that was most similar to the target polynomial is reported on, as well as how many of the independent runs induced the correct polynomial. In all test problems, except f_4, all 30 independent runs induced the correct polynomial term structure.

Table 9 compares the average size of the found optimum over the 30 independent runs with the target polynomial size for both the SBPSO and the BPSO. Specifically, the number of terms in the SBPSO global best positions, and the number of one's in the BPSO global best positions were averaged over the 30 independent runs to calculate the induced polynomial size.

Table 5. MSE values achieved by SBPSO and BPSO on problems f_1 to f_7

Problem	SBPSO		BPSO	
	Train MSE	Test MSE	Train MSE	Test MSE
f_1	0.99 ± 0.01	0.99 ± 0.02	0.99 ± 0.01	0.99 ± 0.03
f_2	1.00 ± 0.01	0.99 ± 0.02	1.00 ± 0.01	1.0 ± 0.03
f_3	0.99 ± 0.01	1.0 ± 0.02	0.99 ± 0.01	0.99 ± 0.02
f_4	1.02 ± 0.19	1.03 ± 0.17	0.99 ± 0.01	1.00 ± 0.02
f_5	1.00 ± 0.01	1.00 ± 0.02	1.00 ± 0.01	1.00 ± 0.02
f_6	1.00 ± 0.01	0.99 ± 0.03	0.99 ± 0.01	1.00 ± 0.02
f_7	0.99 ± 0.01	1.00 ± 0.02	9353.03 ± 41904.74	9263.03 ± 41475.77

Table 6. Polynomials induced by SBPSO for problems f_1 to f_7

Function	Best induced polynomial	# correct
f_1	$x_1^3 + x_2^2 + x_2 + 1$	30
f_2	$x^3 + x^2 + x$	30
f_3	$x^7 + x^5 + x^4 + 1$	30
f_4	$x^8 + x^7 + x^6 + x^5 + x^4 + x^3 + x^2 + x + 1$	29
f_5	$x_1^2 + x_2^2 + x_1^2 x_3^2 + x_3$	30
f_6	$x_1^6 + x_2^5 + x_3^4 + x_1 + x_2^2 x_3^2 + x_3 + 1$	30
f_7	$x_1 + x_2^2 + x_3^2 + x_4^2 + x_5^2 + x_1 x_2 x_4 x_5 + x_3 x_4 + 1$	30

The results show that SBPSO performed very well when inducing the optimal term. The SBPSO performs better than BPSO in higher dimensions, as seen for f_7 where BPSO failed and SBPSO succeeded. The results f_4 indicate that SBPSO tends to keep position sizes smaller, as it was unable to induce the correct structure in one run.

5.2 Hybrid and PSO Results

Table 7 shows the performance of the hybrid SBPSO and PSO on test functions f_8 to f_{10} by reporting on the train and test MSEs. Table 8 shows how many independent runs induced the correct target polynomial structure. For each problem, the found polynomial that was most similar to the target polynomial is reported on, as well as how many of the independent runs induced the correct polynomial. The hybrid algorithm often did not induce the exact polynomial term structure of the target polynomial, but was still able to minimize the MSE by compensating for incorrectly chosen terms by varying the coefficients.

Table 10 compares the average size of the found optimum over the 30 independent runs with the target polynomial size. Specifically, the number of terms in the hybrid algorithm's global best positions, and the number of dimensions in the PSO's global best positions were averaged over the 30 independent runs to calculate the induced polynomial size. In the case of the PSO, the particles' dimensionality is always the same as the size of the universal set, but it was added for consistency.

Table 7. MSE values achieved by the hybrid algorithm and PSO on problems f_8 to f_{10}

Problem	Hybrid		PSO	
	Train MSE	Test MSE	Train MSE	Test MSE
f_8	1.00 ± 0.01	1.00 ± 0.03	466018.07 ± 1045346.24	474531.68 ± 1073162.36
f_9	3.22 ± 4.82	17.06 ± 56.73	$3.56e21 \pm 5.75e21$	$3.46e21 \pm 5.58e21$
f_{10}	1.01 ± 0.04	1.08 ± 0.11	$2.56e28 \pm 7.25e28$	$2.47e28 \pm 7.06e28$

Table 8. Polynomials induced by the hybrid algorithm for problems f_8 to f_{10}

Function	Best induced polynomial	# correct
f_8	$0.50x^3 + 1.99x^2 - 0.99x + 0.02$	27
f_9	$x_1^2 - 2x_2^2 + 3x_1^2x_3^2 - 1.5x_3 - 0.04$	0
f_{10}	$-2.99x_1 - 3.00x_2^2 - 2.99x_3^2 - 3.0x_4^2 + 1.99x_5^2$ $+1.99x_1x_2x_4x_5 + 0.0x_1x_2x_3 + 4.99x_3x_4 + 0.00x_1x_4 - 4.78$	0

The hybrid algorithm performed considerably better than the PSO when searching for optimal coefficients. For each of the problems f_8 to f_{10}, the hybrid algorithm was able to minimize the MSE to an acceptable range. However, the hybrid algorithm did not find the optimal term structure, as ACD was able to minimize the contribution of these incorrectly chosen terms with coefficients close to zero. The PSO algorithm was unable to approximate the correct coefficient values, as seen by the poor MSE results.

Table 9. SBPSO and BPSO induced polynomial sizes

Problem	Target size	Average size	
		SBPSO	BPSO
f_1	4	4.0	4.0
f_2	3	3.0	3.0
f_3	4	4.0	4.0
f_4	9	8.96	9.0
f_5	4	4.0	4.0
f_6	7	7.0	7.0
f_7	8	8.0	8.5

Table 10. Hybrid and PSO induced polynomial sizes

Problem	Target size	Average size	
		Hybrid	PSO
f_8	4	4.1	6.0
f_9	4	8.03	29.0
f_{10}	8	11.57	125.0

6   Conclusions and Future Work

The purpose of this paper was to propose a novel set-based approach to inducing optimal polynomial structures using a well-established optimization algorithm, and to lay the foundation for future improvements and additions to be made to this approach.

The proposal of using a set-based optimization algorithm holds promise for future work, as the SBPSO performed well when tasked with selecting optimal term combinations and showed that it scales better than the existing BPSO method. Because the SBPSO is grounded in set-theory, it holds even more promise to be improved to perform better on the high dimensional problems in which it failed.

The proposed hybrid algorithm consists of the SBPSO algorithm to find an optimal combination of monomials in the polynomial, and the ACD algorithm to find optimal coefficients of these monomials. The application of the SBPSO and ACD shows promise as a well-suited set-based solution for polynomial regression problems. Preliminary results show good performance on low dimensional and low order polynomials where the universal set size remains relatively small, but with some performance drawbacks with larger search spaces. The proposed algorithm also provides the advantage over existing algorithms that it has easily interpretable results and the most potential for improvement. However, this paper's results are not sufficient to draw conclusions about the SBPSO or hybrid SBPSO algorithm's performance on high dimensional problems. More complex polynomials need to be tested to understand how the algorithms will behave in high dimensional spaces.

Future work includes further testing the capabilities of the SBPSO algorithm when applied to real-world data-sets and to investigate the possibility of using computationally cheaper methods to find optimal the coefficients. The algorithm can also be extended to work in dynamic environments by introducing quantum-PSO inspired effects.

Acknowledgements. The authors acknowledge the Centre for High Performance Computing (CHPC), South Africa, for providing computational resources for this research paper.

References

1. van den Bergh, F., Engelbrecht, A.P.: A study of particle swarm optimization particle trajectories. Inf. Sci. **176**(8), 937–971 (2006)
2. Engelbrecht, A.P., Grobler, J., Langeveld, J.: Set based particle swarm optimization for the feature selection problem. Eng. Appl. Artif. Intell. **85**, 324–336 (2019)
3. Erwin, K., Engelbrecht, A.P.: Set-based particle swarm optimization for portfolio optimization. In: Proceedings of the Twelfth International Conference on Swarm Intelligence, pp. 333–339 (2020)
4. Hansen, N.: Adaptive encoding: how to render search coordinate system invariant. In: Proceedings of the International Conference on Parallel Problem Solving from Nature, pp. 205–214 (2008)
5. Hornik, K., Stinchcombe, M., White, H.: Multilayer feedforward networks are universal approximators. Neural Netw. **2**(5), 359–366 (1989)
6. Kennedy, J., Eberhart, R.: Particle swarm optimization. In: Proceedings of the International Conference on Neural Networks, vol. 4, pp. 1942–1948 (1995)
7. Kennedy, J., Eberhart, R.C.: A discrete binary version of the particle swarm algorithm. In: Proceedings of the IEEE International Conference on Systems, Man, and Cybernetics. Computational Cybernetics and Simulation, vol. 5, pp. 4104–4108 (1997)
8. Krogh, A., Hertz, J.A.: A simple weight decay can improve generalization. In: Advances in Neural Information Processing Systems, vol. 4, pp. 950–957. Morgan-Kaufmann (1992)
9. Langeveld, J., Engelbrecht, A.P.: Set-based particle swarm optimization applied to the multidimensional knapsack problem. Swarm Intell. **6**, 297–342 (2012)
10. Loshchilov, I., Schoenauer, M., Sebag, M.: Adaptive coordinate descent. In: Proceedings of the Genetic and Evolutionary Computation Conference, pp. 885–892 (2011)
11. Oldewage, E.T.: The perils of particle swarm optimization in high dimensional problem spaces. In: MSc thesis, University of Pretoria (2019)
12. Pampara, G., Franken, N., Engelbrecht, A.P.: Combining particle swarm optimisation with angle modulation to solve binary problems. In: Proceedings of the IEEE Congress on Evolutionary Computation, vol. 1, pp. 89–96 (2005)
13. Shi, Y., Eberhart, R.: A modified particle swarm optimizer. In: Proceedings of the IEEE International Conference on Evolutionary Computation, pp. 69–73 (1998)
14. Sobol, I.M.: On the distribution of points in a cube and the approximate evaluation of integrals. USSR Comput. Math. Math. Phys. **7**(4), 86–112 (1967)
15. Specht, D.F.: A general regression neural network. IEEE Trans. Neural Netw. **2**(6), 568–576 (1991)

Optimizing Artificial Neural Network for Functions Approximation Using Particle Swarm Optimization

Lina Zaghloul[1], Rawan Zaghloul[2] (iD), and Mohammad Hamdan[1(✉)] (iD)

[1] Heriot Watt University, 38103 Dubai, United Arab Emirates
m.hamdan@hw.ac.uk
[2] Al-Balqa Applied University, Amman 11954, Jordan

Abstract. Artificial neural networks (ANN) are commonly used in function approximation as well as classification problems. This paper shows a configurable architecture of a simple feed forward neural network trained by particle swarm optimization (PSO) algorithm. PSO and ANN have several hyperparameters that have impact on the results of approximation. ANN parameters are the number of layers, number of neurons in each layer, and neuron activation functions. The hyperparameters of the PSO are the population size, the number of informants per particle, and the acceleration coefficients. Herein, this work comes to spot the light on how the PSO hyperparameters affect the ability of the algorithm to optimize ANNs weights in the function approximation task. This was examined and tested by generating multiple experiments on different types of input functions such as: cubic, linear, XOR problem. The results of the proposed method show the superiority of PSO compared to backpropagation in terms of MSE.

Keywords: Artificial Neural Network (ANN) · Particle Swarm Optimization (PSO) · Mean Square Error (MSE) · Function Approximation · Backpropagation

1 Introduction

Function approximation can be thought as a mapping problem where such input and output are only available without having an explicit equation or function to generate such outputs from the existed inputs [1]. Indeed, this is a core problem in various real world applications including image recognition, restoration, enhancement, and generation.

Formally, assume the inputs are denoted by the vector x, and the outputs are denoted by the vector y. The problem is to seek for a function f that maps x to y. The best f is that fits the actual output y with the lowest error rate. Herein, the main issue is to minimize the error to obtain more accurate approximation.

Function approximation using ANN has a long record in the literature [2], it is used effectively to search for a mapping that can approximate a function using a set of input-output pairs, classically using backpropagation learning algorithm [3]. However, backpropagation is widely used in training ANN, it suffers from lower efficiency in some cases, and it can easily being trapped in local minima [4]. On the other hand, as a

© Springer Nature Switzerland AG 2021
Y. Tan and Y. Shi (Eds.): ICSI 2021, LNCS 12689, pp. 223–231, 2021.
https://doi.org/10.1007/978-3-030-78743-1_20

global searching algorithm, PSO is well known for its simplicity compared with genetic algorithms (GA) [5, 6].

In [1], multiple activation functions were tested on different cases of functions' approximation. The authors applied two models of NN: The Radial Basis Function Network (RBFN), and the Wavelet Neural Network (WNN). They achieved better results when applying the RBFN in approximating the exponential function. However, the WNN showed better accuracy in approximating the periodic functions.

The authors in [7] focused on the approximation of four known cases including the XOR problem (one of the examined functions in this study). They applied different NN models, starting by backpropagation. The results revealed low performance compared with other models.

The aim of this study is to investigate the impact of different configurations of PSO hyperparameters on its ability to optimize the ANNs weights for the function approximation task. In parallel with testing different ANNs architectures.

The remaining of this paper is organized as follows: methodology in Sect. 2 which is divided in two subsections. Starting by building the ANN and followed by the implementation of the PSO. In Sect. 3, the results are analyzed, and limitations are discussed. Finally, Sect. 4 concludes the paper.

2 Methodology

This section illustrates the main steps that are adopted to build a testing model by which we can study and analyze how the hyperparameters (of both PSO and ANN) affect the ability of PSO to optimize ANNs. They are two main steps, first is to build a multilayer feed forward ANN, while the second is to implement the PSO algorithm to optimize the ANN's parameters as shown in Fig. 1.

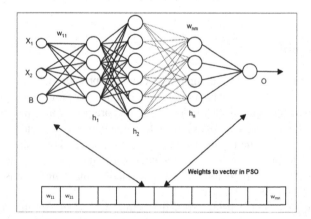

Fig. 1. Feedforward NN (weights and biases are optimized using PSO)

2.1 Building a Feed Forward ANN

In this work, a one input-output ANN is instantiated with fully connected hidden layers. The implemented is a dynamic architecture that enables the user to configure the number of hidden layers, the number of neurons in each layer, and the activation function at the hidden layers.

The NN is defined as a class called FNN that has the parameters: a. Number of input features, b. Number of neurons in each layer, which is defined as an array. The array size reflects the number of hidden layers and its members denote the number of neuros in each hidden layer, c. Number of outputs, and d. The name of the activation function to be employed at the hidden layers. For simplicity, the hidden layers were assumed to share the same activation function. However, linear activation function is fixed for the output layer.

Our implementation has assumed random values for initial weights and biases. They are set randomly since they will be optimized later using the PSO algorithm. Both, the number of neurons in each layer, and the number of layers are configurable. At this step, we did not implement any classical training algorithms–such as backpropagation, because the PSO will be used for the training task. The list of examined activation functions in this study was shown in Table 1.

Table 1. Activation functions used in this study.

Activation function	Equation
None	–
Sigmoid	$\frac{1}{1+e^{-x}}$
Hyperbolic Tangent	$tanh(x)$
Cosine	$cos(x)$
Gaussian	$e^{\left(-\frac{x^2}{2}\right)}$

2.2 Implementing the PSO Algorithm

The particle swarm optimization is an evolutionary algorithm, which is modeled to emulate the coordinated behavior of swarm [8]. In PSO, each particle has a position which denotes a possible solution for a minimization problem. The algorithm starts by initializing a set of random solutions. Thereafter, searching for the optimal solution iteratively. In PSO, the optimal solution (position) is achieved by tracking the best particles in the swarm.

In this work (of function approximation task), particle's position denotes the weights and biases of the ANN. The aim is to find the set of weights and biases by which the network can generate outputs that are approximately match the actual outputs of the function of interest.

PSO is an iterative algorithm, in each iteration particles move to new positions which, hopefully, better problem solutions. The movement is based on the velocity of the particle, the best position recorded by the particle, and the best position that is recorded globally on the swarm.

Each particle updates its velocity using Eq. 1, where the new velocity is v'. v is the current velocity of the particle. ω denotes the inertia weight. $c1$ and $c2$ are constants they called the acceleration coefficients –our experiments spot the light on the impact of population size [9] and these parameters on the overall accuracy of the model. Here, *pbest* denotes the best position recorded by the particle at any time and *gbest* denotes the best position recorded by any particle in the swarm. Where, x denotes the current position of the particle. Also, $r1$ and $r2$ are randomly generated variables in range [0,1) [10, 11].

$$v' = (\omega * v) + (c1 * r1 * (pbest - x)) + (c2 * r2 * (gbest - x)) \tag{1}$$

Thereafter, the updated position x' is defined as depicted in Eq. 2.

$$x' = x + v' \tag{2}$$

Briefly, the main steps of the PSO algorithm are:

1. Initialize particles of all populations and store them in matrix (xx) of size [n × k]; where n is the population size, and k is the particle size.
2. Find the fitness for each particle such that: *fitness = MSE*, where *MSE* is the mean square error between the target and the predicted output and defined as depicted in Eq. 3.

$$MSE = \frac{1}{n}\sum_{i=1}^{n}(target - output)^2 \tag{3}$$

3. Check the fitness value for each particle. If it is greater than the personal best (*pbest*), continue to step 4 otherwise skip to step 5.
4. Set the values of the current fitness as the new personal best then go to step 6.
5. Maintain the value of the previous personal best then go to step 7.
6. Set the global best (*gbest*) as the personal best of the best particle.
7. Find the velocity (*v*) for each particle, as defined in Eq. 1.
8. Update the position of (x) of each particle as defined in Eq. 2.
9. Check if the target reached continue to step 10 otherwise repeat steps 2–9.
10. End the process and return the best particle which gain the minimum fitness value.

Figure 1, summarizes the implemented learning model. The learning model is divided into four phases: (1) Defining the hyperparameters of the feedforward NN. (2) Initializing and configuring the NN. (3) Initializing PSO algorithm. (4) Starting the PSO learning algorithm. At the end, a vector of weights and biases is generated by the model to be used for approximating the function of interest (Fig. 2).

Input: NN architecture (*no_of_inputs, number_of_hlayers, number_hidden_neurons, Act_func*)
Output: (*gbest*) – a vector that contains the best weights and biases for the selected NN architecture.
Phase 1: Define the hyperparameters of the feed forward neural
    1. Define number of inputs to your NN, it equals to one in out case: (*no_of_inputs* = 1)
    2. Ask the user to enter the number of hidden layers: (*number_of_hlayers*)
    3. Ask the user to enter the number of hidden neurons in each layer (*number_hidden_neurons*)
    4. Define the number of outputs of your NN, it equals one in our case (*no_of_output_neurons*)
    5. Ask the user to enter the name of the activation function to be applied in the hidden layers. (*Act_func*)
Phase 2: Initialize and configure the NN
    6. Define an object of your feedforward NN such that it takes the parameters defind in steps (1-5)
Phase 3: Initialize PSO
    7. Initialize the particle size (*p_size*) to be equals to the total number of weights and biases in your NN
    8. Generate set of initial populations for the required parameters (weights and biases). The generated populations named (*x*) are random numbers in range [0 – 1]
    9. Set the initial velocity as: $v = 0.1 * x$.
    10. For each population do the following:
        a. Set the weights and biases according to poputaion values generated by the PSO
        b. Compute the cost function (*MSE*), between the outputs and the actual targets of the NN
        c. Store the results in a list called *f0*. So *f0[i]* is the *i*th element in the list and it contains the cost of the *i*th population
    11. Store the minimum cost (*fmin0*) and its index (*index0*)
    12. Define *pbest = x*
    13. Define the initial global best (*gbest*) to be the population of *x0* whose index is (*index0*)
Phase 4: Start the PSO algorithm
    14. Set the PSO accelaration coeffecients (*c1, c2*)
    15. Define the maximum number of iterations for the PSO (*maxite*)
    16. Apply the following until reach *maxite*:
        a. Set the weight of inertia.
        b. For each population in *x*, update the velocity according to Eq. 1
        c. For each population in *x*, update the position as depicted in Eq. 2, this step will produce a new set of populations (*x'*)
        d. For each population in *x'*, compute the cost function, and store the resulted costs in a list called (*f*)
        e. For each population in *x*, if the cost function of the ith population *f[i]* is less than *f0[i]* then update *x[i] = x'[i]* and *f0[i] = f[i]*
        f. For the minimum of *f0*, store its value and index in *fmin* and *index*, respectively
        g. For each iteration, store *fmin* in a list called *ffmin*. This list will store the minimal cost at each iteration
        h. Update *gbest* and best fitness such that if *fmin<fmin0* then *gbest = pbest[index]* and *fmin0 = fmin*

Fig. 2. Pseudocode of the implemented model.

3   Results and Analysis

This section discusses the conducted experiments and analyzes the obtained results.

3.1   Experimental Environment and Parameter Settings

Experiments in this study were performed using Python programing language on Intel Core i5 machine with 8GB of RAM and processor running at 1.60 GHz.

For all the conducted experiments, to simplify the architecture of the ANN, we assumed that all hidden layers share the same activation function for their neurons, however we apply linear activation function for the output layer.

3.2 Experimental Results

Multiple experiments were conducted by applying different values of PSO hyperparameters (population size, inertia weight, acceleration coefficients), and different NN architectures (*i.e.* varying the number of hidden layers and the number of neurons in hidden layers), this is to compare and examine the accuracy achieved by applying different activation functions.

A variety of function types are examined in this study including linear, nonlinear, classification, and complex functions. The selected functions are shown in Table 2. For each function, three main experimental scenarios were conducted to choose the number of hidden layers, the number of neurons per hidden layer, the population size, the inertia weight (ω), and the acceleration coefficients ($c1$, $c2$). Table 3 shows an example of the results for approximating the XOR function. Referring to the same table, the first scenario assumes an ANN with one hidden layer which contains two neurons, where $c1 = 0.5$, $c2 = 3$, $\omega = 0.2$. This scenario is tested for different population sizes (10, 20, 50) and different activation functions. The underline denotes the minimal MSE in each scenario, the bold underlined denotes the minimal MSE among the three scenarios for a specific activation function. The grey shaded cell denotes the overall minimal MSE among all the tested activation functions. As shown in the table, applying the cosine activation function on the hidden layer neurons obtained the best result in its third scenario for an ANN with three hidden layers and (4, 6, 9) neurons for each hidden layer respectively, where ($c1 = 0.7$, $c2 = 2.1$, $\omega = 0.5$). It is worth noting that MSE values in the table are the average of five runs per experiment. Likewise, Table 4. shows the results of the remaining functions. To avoid lengthy results and to save space, for each approximation function, it shows the results of only the best scoring scenario with its parameter settings.

Table 5 shows the results of the same ANN architectures trained by backpropagation with learning rate 0.01. By comparing the results in Tables 4 and 5, it can be noticed that the PSO has obtained better results in approximating all functions.

Table 2. Functions to be approximated.

Function	Equation
Linear	$y = x$
Cubic	$y = x^3$
Sine	$y = sin(x)$
Tanh	$y = tanh(x)$
XOR	$y = x_1 \oplus x_2$
Complex	$y = 1.9[1.35 + e^{x_1 - x_2} sin\left(13(x_1 - 0.6)^2\right) sin(7x_2)]$

Table 3. Average MSE for approximating the XOR function by varying the hyperparameters of the ANN and the PSO. ANN architecture is described in brackets, the number before the slash denotes the number of hidden layers while the number/s after the slash denote/s the number of neurons in each hidden layer.

	ANN Architecture: [1/2]			ANN Architecture: [1/9]			ANN Architecture: [3, {4,6,9}]		
	c1 = 0.5	c2 = 3	w = 0.2	c1 = 1.5	c2 = 2.5	w = 0.4	c1 = 0.7	c2 = 2.1	w = 0.5
	Population size			Population size			Population size		
Act.Fun	10	20	50	10	20	50	10	20	50
None	0.253605	0.276773	0.288392	0.263440	0.250477	**0.249867**	0.251875	0.275954	0.254363
Sigmoid	0.134012	0.049246	0.049872	0.037974	0.029498	**0.002504**	0.238960	0.112409	0.028918
Tanh	0.078690	0.025935	0.024623	0.005743	**0.000533**	0.000882	0.125313	0.067031	0.022191
Cosine	3.05E-08	1.20E-09	3.88E-11	3.62E-03	7.82E-04	9.34E-05	9.32E-11	4.45E-10	**4.32E-12**
Gaussian	8.88E-06	4.18E-07	**1.46E-11**	1.26E-03	9.72E-04	8.07E-04	1.37E-02	1.21E-10	1.72E-10

Table 4. Average MSE for approximating the functions in Table 2 (except the XOR). The best activation function which obtained the lowest MSE denoted in bold.

Linear	ANN Architecture: [1/2]		Population Size: 50	c1, c2, w: 0.5, 3, 0.2	
	Activation Functions				
	None	Sigmoid	Hyperbolic Tangent	Cosine	Gaussian
	2.26E-32	1.76E-06	4.96E-07	2.67E-06	1.64E-06
Cubic	ANN Architecture: [3, {4, 6, 3}]		Population Size: 50	c1, c2, ω: 0.7, 2.1, 0.5	
	Activation Functions				
	None	Sigmoid	Hyperbolic Tangent	**Cosine**	Gaussian
	0.012	7.32E-06	1.05E-05	**3.66E-06**	4.30E-05
Sine	ANN Architecture: [1/2]		Population Size: 50	c1, c2, w: 0.5, 3, 0.2	
	Activation Functions				
	None	Sigmoid	**Hyperbolic Tangent**	Cosine	Gaussian
	0.0003	1.22E-06	**4.83E-07**	8.41E-07	1.73E-06
Tanh	ANN Architecture: [3/ {4, 6, 3}]		Population Size: 50	c1, c2, w: 0.7, 2.1, 0.5	
	Activation Functions				
	None	Sigmoid	**Hyperbolic Tangent**	Cosine	Gaussian
	0.0006	8.19E-07	**2.47E-07**	8.72E-07	4.83E-07
Complex	ANN Architecture: [3/ {4, 6, 3}]		Population Size: 50	c1, c2, w: 0.7, 2.1, 0.5	
	Activation Functions				
	None	Sigmoid	Hyperbolic Tangent	**Cosine**	Gaussian
	0.102	0.028	0.029	**0.008**	0.011

3.3 Limitations

Due to hardware specifications, a small number of epochs (500 iteration) was applied in our experiments. In addition, five runs were applied to determine the average MSE score, however higher number of runs may produce more reliable results. And more measures could be used for comparisons in addition to the MSE.

Table 5. NN models trained by backpropagation, average MSE for approximating the functions in Table 2. The best activation function which obtained the lowest MSE denoted in bold.

Linear	ANN Architecture: [1/9]		Learning rate = 0.01		
	Activation Functions				
	None	Sigmoid	Hyperbolic Tangent	Cosine	Gaussian
	0.004971	0.048026	0.005462	0.079253	0.078026
Cubic	ANN Architecture: [1/9]		Learning rate = 0.01		
	Activation Functions				
	None	Sigmoid	**Hyperbolic Tangent**	Cosine	Gaussian
	0.018487	0.059585	**0.016164**	0.082899	0.072443
Sine	ANN Architecture: [1/9]		Learning rate = 0.01		
	Activation Functions				
	None	Sigmoid	**Hyperbolic Tangent**	Cosine	Gaussian
	0.00558	0.039814	**0.004323**	0.058145	0.057912
Tanh	ANN Architecture: [1/2]		Learning rate = 0.01		
	Activation Functions				
	None	Sigmoid	**Hyperbolic Tangent**	Cosine	Gaussian
	0.009825	0.064234	**0.007036**	0.051839	0.056086
XOR	ANN Architecture: [1/9]				
	Activation Functions				
	None	**Sigmoid**	Hyperbolic Tangent	Cosine	Gaussian
	0.196123	**0.120555**	0.17832	0.132438	0.121469
Complex	ANN Architecture: [1/2]		Learning rate = 0.01		
	Activation Functions				
	None	Sigmoid	**Hyperbolic Tangent**	Cosine	Gaussian
	0.104736	0.116643	**0.104106**	0.136408	0.121425

In this study, a set of activation functions (Sigmoid, Hyperbolic Tangent, Cosine, and Gaussian) were included in our comparisons, however other functions such as (ReLU) may produce comparable results.

Furthermore, we assumed that all hidden layers share the same activation function, for simplifying the comparisons. However, variating activation functions on the hidden layers was not tested and might have a remarkable effect on the learning capacity of the system.

4   Conclusion

For function approximation task, this study highlights: a. the influence of different settings of the PSO hyperparameters in training a simple feedforward NN, and b. the impact of the ANN parameters (the activation functions, number of hidden layers and number of neurons) on the resulted accuracy.

We observed impressive results when using PSO for training the ANN compared to the traditional backpropagation. In addition, it is noticed that PSO is highly sensitive to its hyperparameters.

As a future work, more complex functions can be examined with different ANN models. Deep NNs can be experimented, and their results can be compared with the achieved results.

References

1. Zainuddin, Z., Pauline, O.: Function approximation using artificial neural networks. WSEAS Trans. Math. **7**(6), 333–338 (2008)
2. Elbrächter, D., Perekrestenko, D., Grohs, P., Bölcskei, H.: Deep neural network approximation theory. arXiv preprint arXiv:1901.02220 (2019)
3. Rumelhart, D.E., Hinton, G.E., Williams, R.J.: Learning representations by back-propagating errors. Nature **323**(6088), 533–536 (1986)
4. Örkcü, H.H., Bal, H.: Comparing performances of backpropagation and genetic algorithms in the data classification. Expert Syst. Appl. **38**(4), 3703–3709 (2011)
5. Han, F., Zhu, J.S.: Improved particle swarm optimization combined with backpropagation for feedforward neural networks. Int. J. Intell. Syst. **28**(3), 271–288 (2013)
6. Rahmani, M.: Particle swarm optimization of artificial neural networks for autonomous robots. Master of Science in Complex Adaptive Systems Thesis, Department of Applied Physics, Chalmers University of Technology, Sweden (2008)
7. Dhar, V.K., Tickoo, A.K., Koul, R., Dubey, B.P.: Comparative performance of some popular artificial neural network algorithms on benchmark and function approximation problems. Pramana **74**(2), 307–324 (2010). https://doi.org/10.1007/s12043-010-0029-4
8. El-Shorbagy, M.A., Aboul, E.H.: Particle swarm optimization from theory to applications. Int. J. Rough Sets Data Anal. (IJRSDA) **5**(2), 1–24 (2018)
9. Piotrowski, A.P., Napiorkowski, J.J., Piotrowska, A.E.: Population size in particle swarm optimization. Swarm Evol. Comput. **58**, 100718 (2020)
10. Abhijit Suresh, K.V., Harish, N.: Particle swarm optimization over back propagation neural network for length of stay prediction. Procedia Comput. Sci. **46**, 268–275 (2015)
11. Yu, H., Gao, Y., Wang, L., Meng, J.: A hybrid particle swarm optimization algorithm enhanced with nonlinear inertial weight and Gaussian mutation for job shop scheduling problems. Mathematics **8**(8), 1355 (2020)

Two Modified NichePSO Algorithms
for Multimodal Optimization

Tyler Crane[1]([⊠]), Andries Engelbrecht[2], and Beatrice Ombuki-Berman[1]

[1] Department of Computer Science, Brock University, St. Catharines, ON, Canada
{tcrane2,bombuki}@brocku.ca
[2] Department of Industrial Engineering and Computer Science Division,
Stellenbosch University, Stellenbosch, South Africa
engel@sun.ac.za

Abstract. Multimodal function optimization (MMO) has seen a lot of interest and research over the past several years due to its many real world applications, and its complexity as an optimization problem. Several niching techniques proposed in past research have been combined with popular meta heuristic search algorithms such as evolutionary algorithms (EA), genetic algorithms (GA) and particle swarm optimization (PSO). The NichePSO algorithm was one of the first PSO algorithms proposed for utilizing niching methods and parallel swarms to apply PSO to MMO problems effectively. In this paper, two modified versions of the NichePSO algorithm are proposed, the NichePSO-R and NichePSO-S algorithms, in an attempt to improve its performance. Experimental results show that both proposed algorithms are able to locate more global optima on average than the NichePSO algorithm across several popular MMO benchmark functions.

1 Introduction

Over the past several years, the field of multimodal function optimization (MMO) has received considerable interest from researchers. Many real world problems have arisen that have proven too complex for traditional unimodal optimization algorithms to solve [1–4]. For a multimodal problem, it is often not enough to find a single global best solution. MMO algorithms and techniques focus on locating multiple strong solutions to a single problem concurrently, returning a set of solutions as opposed to a single solution.

Particle swarm optimization (PSO) is a unimodal function optimization algorithm proposed in [5]. PSO is a stochastic, population based algorithm that utilizes a swarm of particles to search the landscape. The traditional PSO algorithm showed strong results for many unimodal optimization problems, but was shown to be ineffective when applied to MMO problems [6]. Traditional niching techniques such as function stretching and neighbourhood clustering were applied to PSO [7,8], but they are limited in performance due to only being able to locate solutions sequentially as opposed to concurrently.

© Springer Nature Switzerland AG 2021
Y. Tan and Y. Shi (Eds.): ICSI 2021, LNCS 12689, pp. 232–243, 2021.
https://doi.org/10.1007/978-3-030-78743-1_21

The NichePSO algorithm was proposed in [9] as an extension of the traditional unimodal PSO algorithm. Instead of a single swarm of particles, the NichePSO algorithm uses multiple subswarms that each traverse the landscape in parallel, with the goal of each subswarm converging to a unique optimum. This allows the algorithm to search for multiple solutions concurrently, and return several strong solutions in a single run.

The NichePSO algorithm showed strong results across several tested MMO functions [9]. A follow up scalability study was done in [10] which showed that the NichePSO algorithm can perform well on MMO functions up to five dimensions. Further research was done in [11] which proposed several possible modifications to the NichePSO merging strategies with the goal of improving exploration and performance. Additional research was done in [12] which showed the existence of a major issue with the NichePSO algorithm, referred to as the merging subswarm problem. The impact of the alternative merging strategies discussed in [11] on the merging subswarm problem was analyzed, and a few more possible strategies were proposed that were shown to overcome this issue. An extensive analysis of the NichePSO algorithm was done in [13], along with empirical studies aimed to find optimal values for many of the control parameters.

The algorithms proposed in this paper utilize the work done in [11]-[13] to design two modified NichePSO algorithms. These two variants are shown through experimental results to track more global optima on average than the original NichePSO algorithm across multiple MMO benchmark functions.

Section 2 provides a detailed overview of the NichePSO algorithm. Section 3 presents the NichePSO-R algorithm, and Sect. 4 presents the NichePSO-S algorithm. Section 5 provides experimental setup and results that compare the three algorithms discussed on a variety of benchmark MMO functions.

2   The NichePSO Algorithm

This section describes the NichePSO algorithm in detail, along with all of its components. An overview of the NichePSO algorithm is given in Algorithm 1.

2.1   Cognitive Velocity Update

The velocities of main swarm particles are updated using Eq. 1, and the positions are updated using Eq. 2. These formulas match the traditional PSO update formulas, except that the social component has been removed. Social information is not shared between the particles so that they each act like an independent hill-climber. Each particle performs a local search of their immediate area in the search space with the goal of converging to a local optimum.

$$\mathbf{v}_i(t+1) = w\mathbf{v}_i(t) + c_1\mathbf{r}_{1i}(t)(\mathbf{y}_i(t) - \mathbf{x}_i(t)) \tag{1}$$

$$\mathbf{x}_i(t+1) = \mathbf{x}_i(t) + \mathbf{v}_i(t+1) \tag{2}$$

Initialize particles in main swarm;
while *stopping criteria not met* **do**
  Update position of all particles in main swarm;
  Evaluate fitness of particles in main swarm;
  for *each subswarm S* **do**
    Update position of all particles within S;
    Evaluate fitness of all particles within S;
    Recalculate the radius of S;
  end
  if *any subswarms intersect* **then**
    Merge subswarms;
  end
  for *each particle p in the main swarm* **do**
    if *p intersects with radius of a subswarm S* **then**
      Particle p is absorbed by subswarm S;
    end
    if *partitioning criteria for p is met* **then**
      Create new subswarm from particle p;
    end
  end
end

Algorithm 1: The NichePSO Algorithm

2.2 Social Velocity Update

Particles that are part of a subswarm use a velocity update formula based on the guaranteed convergence PSO (GCPSO) algorithm [14]. The GCPSO algorithm uses both a cognitive and social aspect to the particles' velocity update, and each subswarm shares social information amongst all particles within the subswarm. The velocities of particles within a subswarm are updated using the traditional PSO velocity update formula shown in Eq. 3, and the positions are updated using Eq. 2.

$$\mathbf{v}_i(t+1) = w\mathbf{v}_i(t) + c_1\mathbf{r}_{1i}(t)(\mathbf{y}_i - \mathbf{x}_i(t)) + c_2\mathbf{r}_{2i}(t)(\bar{\mathbf{y}}_\mathbf{i}(t) - \mathbf{x}_i(t)) \quad (3)$$

The GCPSO formula modifies the way that the subswarm best particles are updated, where the velocity of the strongest particle in each subswarm is updated using Eq. 4, and the position is updated using Eq. 5. The GCPSO algorithm has been proven to always converge to a local optimum given sufficient time [15]. Further details regarding the GCPSO algorithm can be found in [14].

$$\bar{\mathbf{v}}_i(t+1) = -\mathbf{x}_i(t) + \bar{\mathbf{y}}_\mathbf{i}(t) + w\bar{\mathbf{v}}_i(t) + \rho(t)(1 - 2\mathbf{r}_{1,i}) \quad (4)$$

$$\mathbf{x}_i(t+1) = \bar{\mathbf{y}}_\mathbf{i}(t) + w\bar{\mathbf{v}}_i(t+1) + \rho(t)(1 - 2\mathbf{r}_{2,i}) \quad (5)$$

2.3   Initialization

When initializing the particles in the main swarm, it is important that they are spread out throughout the search space to try and maximize exploration and to increase the total number of unique optima that can be found. Particles are initialized using *Faure*-sequences [16], which distribute the particles uniformly within an n-dimensional cube. Particle velocities are initialized to a value between $[-0.5, 0.5]$, but not to 0 [13].

2.4   Partitioning Criteria

The fitness of each particle is monitored each iteration, and a particle in the main swarm is considered to be converged when the variance of its change in fitness over the past three iterations is less than some threshold parameter $\delta = 0.0001$. When a particle converges, it is removed from the main swarm and creates a new subswarm. This new subswarm will consist of two particles, the converged particle and its closest (spatial) neighbour within the main swarm.

2.5   Merging Subswarms

To promote diversity amongst the particles and subswarm, each subswarm maintains a radius that defines the area in the search space it is currently exploring. A subswarm's radius is calculated as the greatest Euclidean distance between each particle in the subswarm and the subswarm's best position. If a particle in the main swarm moves inside the radius of a subswarm, that particle is absorbed by the subswarm and shares social information with its neighbours. If the radii of two subswarms intersect, then the subswarms are merged into one larger subswarm.

3   The NichePSO-R Algorithm

The NichePSO-R algorithm modifies the way that subswarms and particles interact with each other when they intersect. Instead of merging subswarms together, the radii of each subswarm is treated as an out of bounds area to particles not within the subswarm. In a traditional PSO algorithm, when a particle travels out of bounds it is unable to update its personal best position or the global best position of the swarm. This behaviour is replicated for when a particle travels within the radius of a subswarm that they are not a part of. This technique is referred to as the radius out of bounds (radiusOOB) method in this paper.

Another aspect that is modified is the way subswarms are created when a particle in the main swarm converges. Subswarms are no longer created by combining the converged particle with its closest neighbour. Instead, a subswarm is formed by creating κ particles and adding them to the subswarm along with the converged particle.

The originally proposed closest neighbour method has a few drawbacks that this modified creation method overcomes. The first issue is that there is no guarantee that the two particles that create the subswarm are actually close to each other. It is possible that by chance the closest neighbour to a particle is far away in the search space, which would result in a subswarm that contains a very large radius. This large radius would intersect with other subswarm's radii and trigger the radiusOOB method from applying, even though the subswarms are not searching the same area of the search space.

Along with the potential for particles to be located far away from each other, it is undesirable to modify the behaviour of a particle that could be tracking a unique optimum of its own. An advantage of this alternative subswarm creation method is that particles in the main swarm are free to converge and search their local neighbourhood to completion, without being forced to abandon their search to converge to another optimum already discovered by another particle. Pseudocode for the NichePSO-R algorithm is shown in Algorithm 2. Only the differences between the NichePSO and NichePSO-R algorithms are shown.

Initialize particles in main swarm;
while *stopping criteria not met* **do**
> ...
> **foreach** *subswarm S* **do** { ... }
> **foreach** *particle P* **do**
> > **foreach** *subswarm S* **do**
> > > **if** *P intersects with S & P is not a subset of S* **then**
> > > > Flag *P* as out of bounds;
> > > **end**
> > **end**
> > **if** *P is not within any subswarm radius* **then**
> > > Remove out of bounds flag from *P*;
> > **end**
> **end**
> **foreach** *particle P in the main swarm* **do** { ... }
end

Algorithm 2: The NichePSO-R Algorithm

4 The NichePSO-S Algorithm

The NichePSO-S algorithm uses several small subswarms that are regularly reinitialized to new areas of the search space when either intersection occurs or convergence is reached. This approach gives the algorithm a high exploration ability, while also allowing particles that find favourable positions sufficient time to explore their local neighbourhood before being moved to a new area of the search space.

The NichePSO-S algorithm utilizes the scatter merge modification proposed in [11]. When two subswarms intersect, the particles in the weaker subswarm are reinitialized back into the main swarm with a new location. This improves the exploration ability of the algorithm by allowing particles that are searching close to each other to move to a new area of the search space that may have not been searched.

Along with the scatter merge modification, the diversity merge modification proposed in [12] is also utilized. This modification changes the way that radii are calculated for each subswarm. The radius of a subswarm is determined by calculating the median distance between the subswarm best location and each particle within the subswarm. Using the median distance as opposed to the max distance used by the traditional NichePSO prevents radii from growing large if a particle was to travel far away from the rest of the swarm.

Another modification that the NichePSO-S algorithm uses is a reinitialization strategy, where particles within a subswarm are reinitialized back into the main swarm when the subswarm has existed for a long period of time. The length of time that a subswarm exists for is ι iterations. Empirical tests performed found that an ι value of ι = number of dimensions $* 300$ provides a sufficient amount of time for subswarms to converge fully. Once a subswarm has existed for ι iterations, the particle that originally created the subswarm is placed back into the main swarm with a new random position in the search space.

The NichePSO-S algorithm also utilizes the alternative subswarm creation method described previously for the NichePSO-R algorithm. To combine this method with the scatter merge and reinitialization modifications, when a subswarm is reinitialized the additional κ particles created from the creation strategy are removed from the search. This prevents more and more particles from being created exponentially as the run progresses. Pseudocode for the NichePSO-S algorithm is described in Algorithm 3. Only the differences between the NichePSO and NichePSO-S algorithms are shown.

Initialize particles in main swarm;
while *stopping criteria not met* **do**

   ...

   foreach *subswarm S* **do** { ... }
   foreach *subswarm S* **do**

      if *subswarm S meets convergence test* **then**
       | Reinitialize particles in subswarm S;
      end
      foreach *subswarm T* **do**

         if *S and T intersect* **then**
          | Reinitialize particles in weaker subswarm;
         end

      end

   end
   foreach *particle P in the main swarm* **do** { ... }

end

Algorithm 3: The NichePSO-S Algorithm

5   Experimental Results

This section compares the performance of the two proposed algorithms against the NichePSO algorithm using several benchmark functions. The functions selected were from the CEC 2013 competition on niching methods for multimodal function optimization. All twenty functions outlined in [17] are used, with the goal of detecting the most global optima over several runs. For each test, the peak ratio of detected global optima is recorded and averaged over 30 runs. The peak ratio of a run is the percentage of total global optima located for a function, calculated by the number of global optima found divided by the total number of global optima. A summary of the functions used is given in Table 1.

In order to effectively test whether a global optimum has been detected or not, an accuracy threshold is used. Each benchmark function has a global best score known beforehand, shown in Table 1. At the end of a run, a set of solutions is returned, one for each existing subswarm. A global optimum is considered located if the fitness evaluation of a subswarm's best position is greater than the global best score minus the accuracy threshold. A smaller accuracy threshold means that the subswarms will need to be closer to the global best score in order to have the optimum counted and located. For each experiment, an accuracy threshold of 0.0001 is used. This threshold matches the smallest threshold used in the CEC niching competitions, and provides a strict environment for detecting global optima for each algorithm.

The NichePSO-R and NichePSO-S algorithms are evaluated against the NichePSO algorithm using the diversity merge modification described in [12]. The original NichePSO algorithm was shown in [12] to suffer from a major problem where the subswarms created throughout a run do not isolate as intended, and instead merge into a single large subswarm. The diversity merge modification is applied to the NichePSO algorithm as it is shown to overcome the merging subswarm problem, while also modifying the original algorithm only a small amount.

Each algorithm uses the parameters $w = 0.7$ and $c_1 = c_2 = 1.2$ to match that of the original NichePSO. The NichePSO and NichePSO-R algorithms use 250 particles per run. The NichePSO-S algorithm requires less particles due to its use of a reinitialization strategy, and uses 80 particles per run. The NichePSO-R and NichePSO-S algorithms use the alternative subswarm creation strategy that creates κ particles, and for each run a value $\kappa = 1$ is used. These values were empirically shown in [13] to provide strong results with respect to the computational resources required.

5.1   Results

Experimental results are shown in Table 2. To verify the results shown, Mann-Whitney U-tests were performed for each pair of results, and the p-values returned are shown in Table 3. P-values that are statistically significant using a confidence level of $p < 0.05$ are shown in bold.

Table 1. A summary of the twenty benchmark functions described in [17].

Function	# of dimensions	# of global optima	Total function evaluations	Global peak fitness
Five uneven peak Trap	1	2	50 K	200
Equal maxima	1	5	50 K	1
Uneven decreasing maxima	1	1	50 K	1
Himmelblau	2	4	50 K	200
Six-hump camel back	2	2	50 K	1.031628453
Shubert	2	18	200 K	186.7309088
Vincent	2	36	200 K	1
Shubert	3	81	400 K	2709.093505
Vincent	3	216	400 K	1
Modified rastrigin	2	12	200 K	−2
Composite function 1	2	6	200 K	0
Composite function 2	2	8	200 K	0
Composite function 3	2	6	200 K	0
Composite function 3	3	6	400 K	0
Composite function 4	3	8	400 K	0
Composite function 3	5	6	400 K	0
Composite function 4	5	8	400 K	0
Composite function 3	10	6	400 K	0
Composite function 4	10	8	400 K	0
Composite function 4	20	8	400 K	0

The NichePSO-R algorithm outperformed the original NichePSO algorithm on nine out of the twenty benchmark functions used. Out of those nine functions, eight performances were statistically significant improvements over the original algorithm. The original NichePSO algorithm outperformed the NichePSO-R algorithm on two benchmark functions, but only one was statistically significant. All remaining results for both algorithms are either equal, or too similar to be considered a significant difference.

The NichePSO-S algorithm outperformed the original NichePSO algorithm on eleven out of twenty benchmark functions. Out of these eleven functions, nine showed an improvement that was statistically significant. The original NichePSO algorithm outperformed the NichePSO-S algorithm on three functions, two of which were statistically significant. All remaining results are either equal, or too similar to be considered a significant difference.

Overall both the NichePSO-R and NichePSO-S algorithm show a considerable improvement over the NichePSO algorithm. This improvement becomes more pronounced when one considers that the NichePSO algorithm being tested uses the diversity merge modification to mitigate the impact of the merging sub-swarm problem. Compared to the vanilla NichePSO algorithm proposed in [9], both modified versions greatly outperform the original.

The differences between the NichePSO-R and NichePSO-S algorithms are much less noticeable. Out of the twenty functions used, the NichePSO-R algorithm performed better than the NichePSO-S on six of the problems. Out of these six performances, four were a statistically significant improvement. The NichePSO-S algorithm outperformed the NichePSO-R algorithm on four of the twenty functions, three of which were statistically significant. All other results were either even or too similar to be considered a significant difference.

Table 2. The peak ratio of each Algorithm across all benchmark functions.

Function	NichePSO	NichePSO-R	NichePSO-S
Five-uneven-peak trap	1	1	1
Equal maxima	0.86	1	1
Uneven decreasing maxima	1	1	1
Himmelblau	1	1	1
Six-hump camel back	0.5667	1	1
Shubert	0.8241	1	1
Vincent	0.5565	0.6778	0.8472
Shubert	0.649	0.8852	0.8317
Vincent	0.2025	0.2769	0.3377
Modified rastrigin	0.4972	1	1
Composite function 1	0.9944	0.9944	0.7556
Composite function 2	0.7625	0.9833	0.85
Composite function 3	0.8944	0.7667	0.6778
Composite function 3	0.6667	0.6667	0.6667
Composite function 4	0.6292	0.6583	0.6417
Composite function 3	0.6667	0.6667	0.6667
Composite function 4	0.3	0.4167	0.4
Composite function 3	0	0	0.3833
Composite function 4	0	0	0.0125
Composite function 4	0	0	0

When comparing the NichePSO-R and NichePSO-S algorithms to each other, both have their own strengths and merits. The NichePSO-R algorithm performed the best consistently and on the most function used. The NichePSO-S algorithm also performed well, and was the only algorithm to be able to locate any optima on the functions with ten dimensions. Overall, both the NichePSO-R

Table 3. P-values comparing each algorithms results using mann-whitney U tests.

Function	NichePSO to NichePSO-R	NichePSO to NichePSO-S	NichePSO-R to NichePSO-S
Five uneven peak trap	0.9999	0.9999	0.9999
Equal maxima	**0.0271**	**0.0271**	0.9999
Uneven decreasing maxima	0.9999	0.9999	0.9999
Himmelblau	0.9999	0.9999	0.9999
Six-hump camel back	**0.0001**	**0.0001**	0.9999
Shubert	**0.0001**	**0.0001**	0.9999
Vincent	**0.0001**	**0.0001**	**0.0001**
Shubert	**0.0001**	**0.0001**	**0.0001**
Vincent	**0.0001**	**0.0001**	**0.0001**
Modified rastrigin	**0.0001**	**0.0001**	0.9999
Composite function 1	0.9999	**0.0001**	**0.0001**
Composite function 2	**0.0001**	0.05	**0.0001**
Composite function 3	**0.0003**	**0.0001**	**0.0017**
Composite function 3	0.9999	0.9999	0.9999
Composite function 4	0.2757	0.6384	0.5419
Composite function 3	0.9999	0.9999	0.9999
Composite function 4	**0.0001**	**0.0001**	0.6031
Composite function 3	0.9999	**0.0001**	**0.0001**
Composite function 4	0.9999	0.5093	0.5093
Composite function 4	0.9999	0.9999	0.9999

and NichePSO-S algorithms show a considerable improvement over the original NichePSO algorithm.

6   Conclusions

This paper proposed two variants of the NichePSO algorithm, referred to as the NichePSO-R and NichePSO-S algorithms. The NichePSO-R algorithm removes the ability for subswarms to merge, and instead treats them as out of bounds to particles not within the subswarm. The NichePSO-S algorithm implements the scatter merge approach proposed in [11] along with a reinitialization strategy to greatly improve the exploration and efficiency of the algorithm. Both proposed variants were shown to locate more global optima on average than the original NichePSO algorithm across several benchmark MMO functions.

Future work involves improving the performance and robustness for each proposed algorithm. The NichePSO-R algorithm would benefit from an alternative method of calculating subswarm radii that defines the area the subswarm is searching using the fitness landscape as opposed to the particle positions. The NichePSO-S algorithm would benefit from the use of a convergence test that accurately determines when a subswarm has fully converged before reinitialization. Using a convergence test instead of a set number of iterations would allow subswarms that converge quickly to reinitialize faster without wasting iterations, while also allowing subswarms that converge slower more time to fully explore the local neighbourhood.

Further analysis is needed into the scalability of the NichePSO algorithm and its variants. All three algorithms performed strongly on lower dimensional functions, but failed in most cases to find a single optimum on problems of ten dimensions or higher. Further analysis into the causes of the poor scalability of the algorithms, along with additional modifications aimed to improve performance on higher dimensional problems would benefit the NichePSO algorithms greatly.

References

1. Ward, A., Liker, J.K., Cristiano, J.J., Sobek, D.K.: The second toyota paradox: how delaying decisions can make cars faster. Sloan Manag. Rev. **36**(3), 43–61 (1995)
2. Wong, K.C., Leung, K.S., Wong, M.H.: Protein structure prediction on a lattice model via multimodal optimization techniques. In: Proceedings of the 12th Annual Conference on Genetic and Evolutionary Computation (GECCO), Portland, OR, USA, pp. 155–162 (2010)
3. Rivera, C., Inostroza-Ponta, M., Villalobos-Cid, M.: A multimodal multi-objective optimisation approach to deal with the phylogenetic inference problem. In: 2020 IEEE Conference on Computational Intelligence in Bioinformatics and Computational Biology (CIBCB), Viña del Mar, pp. 1–7 (2020)
4. Ren, H., Shen, X., Jia, X.: Research on multimodal algorithms for multi-routes planning based on niche techniques. In: 2020 International Conference on Culture-oriented Science & Technology (ICCST), Beijing, China, pp. 203–207 (2020)
5. Kennedy, J., Eberhart, R.: Particle swarm optimization. In: Proceedings of IEEE International Conference on Neural Networks, vol. IV, pp. 1942–1948 (1995)
6. Engelbrecht, A.P., Masiye, B.S., Pampard, G.: Niching Ability of Basic Particle Swarm Optimization Algorithms IEEE Swarm Intelligence Symposium (SIS), pp. 397–400. Pasadena, CA, USA (2005)
7. Parsopoulos, K.E., Plagianakos, V.P., Magoulas, G.D., Vrahitis, M.N.: Stretching technique for obtaining global minimizers through particle swarm optimization. In: Proceedings of the Particle Swarm Optimization Workshop (2001)
8. Brits, R., Engelbrecht, A.P., van den Bergh, F.: Solving systems of unconstrained equations using particle swarm optimization. In: IEEE Conference on Systems, Man, and Cybernetics, Yasmine Hammamet, Tunisia, vol. 3, p. 6 (2002)
9. Brits, R., Engelbrecht, A.P., van den Bergh, F.: A Niching Particle Swarm Optimizer. In: Proceedings of the 4th Asia-Pacific Conference on Simulated Evolution and Learning (SEAL), Singapore, pp. 692–696 (2002)
10. Brits, R., Engelbrecht, A.P., van den Bergh, F.: Scalability of niche PSO. Swarm Intelligence Symposium (SIS) (2003)
11. Engelbrecht, A.P., van Loggerenberg, L.N.H.: Enhancing the NichePSO, pp. 2297–2302. IEEE Congress on Evolutionary Computation, Singapore (2007)

12. Crane, T., Ombuki-Berman, B., Engelbrecht, A.P.: NichePSO and the merging subswarm problem. In: Proceedings 7th International Conference on Soft Computing & Machine Intelligence (ISCMI). Stockholm, Sweden, pp. 17–22 (2020)
13. Crane, T.: Analysis of the Niching Particle Swarm Optimization Algorithm M.Sc. Thesis. Brock University, St. Catharines, Canada (2021)
14. van den Bergh, F.: An Analysis of Particle Swarm Optimizers Ph.D. Dissertation. University of Pretoria, Pretoria, South Africa (2002)
15. van den Bergh, F., Engelbrecht, A.P.: A convergence proof for the particle swarm optimizer. Fundam. Inf. **105**(4), 341–374 (2010)
16. Thiémard, E.: Economic Generation of Low-Discrepancy Sequences with a b-ary Gray Code. Department of Mathematics, Ecole Polytechnique Fédérale de Lausanne, CH-1015, Lausanne, Switzerland
17. Li, X., Engelbrecht, A.P., Epitropakis, M.: benchmark functions for CEC 2013 special session and competition on niching methods for multimodal function optimization. Evolutionary Computation Machine Learning Group, RMIT University, Melbourne, VIC, Australia, Tech. Rep. (2013)

VaCSO: A Multi-objective Collaborative Competition Particle Swarm Algorithm Based on Vector Angles

Libao Deng[1(✉)], Le Song[1], Sibo Hou[2], and Gaoji Sun[3]

[1] School of Information Science and Engineering, Harbin Institute of Technology, Weihai, China
[2] Department of Automatic Test and Control, Harbin Institute of Technology, Harbin, China
[3] College of Economic and Management, Zhejiang Normal University, Jinhua 321004, China

Abstract. Recently, particle swarm algorithm (PSO) has demonstrated its effectiveness in solving multi-objective optimization problems (MOPs). However, due to rapid convergence, PSO has poor distribution when processing MOPs. To solve the above problems, we propose a multi-objective collaborative competition particle swarm algorithm based on vector angles (VaCSO). Firstly, in order to remove the influence of global or individual optimal particles, the competition mechanism is used. Secondly, in order to increase the diversity of solutions while maintaining the convergence, the population is clustered into two groups which use different learning strategies. Finally, a three-particle competition and co-evolution mechanism is proposed to improve the distribution and diversity of particle swarms. We set up comparative experiments to test the performance of VaCSO compared with the current popular multi-objective particle swarm algorithm. Experimental results show that VaCSO has excellent performance in convergence and distribution, and has a significant effect in optimizing quality.

Keywords: Multi-objective optimization · Co-evolution mechanism · Three-particle competition

1 Introduction

In engineering practice and scientific research, we often need to pursue multiple optimization goals. In optimization problems, multiple optimization goals

This work is supported by National Natural Science Foundation of China (Grant Nos. 71701187 and 61401121), the Fundamental Research Funds for the Central Universities (Grant No. HIT. NSRIF. 2019083) and Guangxi Key Laboratory of Automatic Detecting Technology and Instruments (Grant No. YQ19203).

Y. Tan and Y. Shi (Eds.): ICSI 2021, LNCS 12689, pp. 244–253, 2021.
https://doi.org/10.1007/978-3-030-78743-1_22

are contradictory [7]. This type of problem is called multi-object optimization problem (MOP).

In the past two decades, multi-objective optimization has attracted increasing interests in the evolutionary computation community. Some population-based meta-heuristic algorithms have been successfully applied to multi-objective optimization. As a result, various multi-objective optimization algorithms have evolved. Among them, the rapid convergence of PSO configured with reasonable control parameters on single-objective optimization problems [6] has caused more and more scholars to pay attention to the research of PSO on multi-objective optimization problems. Generally speaking, the existing multi-objective particle swarm algorithm can be divided into two categories. The first one is based on Pareto dominance, which determines the level of the global optimal particle and the individual optimal particle. The second category is the use of decomposition ideas, mainly decomposing multiple goals into single goals.

Competitive swarm optimizer (CSO) [1] is a variant of PSO. The main difference is that the search process is guided by competitors in the current group, rather than individual individual best particles and global best particles. Both theoretical analysis and empirical results show that by adopting a competition mechanism, the competitive group optimizer can achieve a better balance between convergence and diversity than the original PSO. There are also many studies applying CSO to MOPs. In CMOPSO [13], two particles are randomly selected from non-dominated individuals to compete to optimize the particles to be optimized. In LMOCSO [10], an accelerated speed update formula is used. In CMaPSO [11], a new environment selection mechanism different from CMOPSO is adopted. The above algorithms still have the shortcoming of a relatively simple offspring generation strategy. In order to overcome the problems of traditional CSO on MOPs, while considering the requirements of MOPs for convergence and distribution, we propose VaCSO.

In VaCSO, in order to comprehensively consider the two indicators of convergence and distribution in multi-objectives, the following measures are designed.

1. A cluster optimization strategy is proposed. The first population is mainly responsible for the convergence of the population, and the second population conducts collaborative learning based on the convergence, taking into account the distribution of the population.
2. A competitive particle strategy based on angle is proposed. In the proposed strategy, the competing winner particles enter the "winner set", and at the same time, the winning particles guide the losing particles towards the PF frontier, which improves the convergence of the algorithm.
3. A three-particle competition strategy is proposed. In the proposed strategy, the intermediate particles are drawn. We make the intermediate particles learn from the winning particles of the adjacent population to optimize the gap between the winning particles.

The rest of this paper is organized as follows. The details of the proposed VaCSO are given in Sect. 2 and the performance of VaCSO is verified in Sect. 3 by comparing it with existing multi-objective PSO algorithms. Finally, conclusion and future work are presented in Sect. 4 .

2   The Proposed VaCSO

2.1   General Framework

VaCSO is similar to the overall framework of other multi-objective optimization algorithms. The basic structure diagram is shown in Fig. 1. Firstly, randomly initialize a particle swarm with N solutions in the entire decision space. Then the particles are sorted according to the fitness value of each particle. The particles with the higher sorting show that they have better adaptability. Next, the particles are divided into two populations, and a set of offspring solutions are generated through particle learning based on the competition mechanism. Then put the generated offspring particles and the better individual particles into the selection pool, and obtain a round of better solution sets through the environment selection operator. Continue this step until the exit condition is met or the loop ends. Next, we introduce these steps in detail.

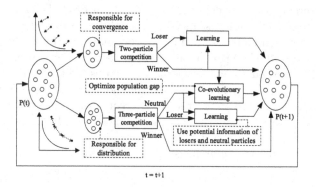

Fig. 1. Framework of the Proposed VaCSO

2.2   Clustering Based on Indicators

In the multi-objective optimization problem, the two issues we care about are the convergence and the distribution of the algorithm. According to these two directions, we divide the population into two populations. Population 1 is mainly responsible for generating more individuals with better convergence, and population 2 is responsible for generating individuals with better distribution.

We need to consider the impact of convergence indicators on algorithm performance for Population 1. Through the research of scholars, a variety of convergence indicators have also evolved [8]. Here we discuss four convergence indicators and analyze their pros and cons. The four methods are: the sum of all objectives (abbreviated as Sum), the Chebyshev distance to the ideal reference point (abbreviated as CdI), the Euclidean distance to the ideal reference point (abbreviated as EdI), and the Euclidean distance based on Nadir point (abbreviated as EdN).

Sum is one of the simplest and most famous aggregation functions that convert multiple goals into one goal. Since the shape of the optimal frontier of the Pareto to be optimized is unknown, it is unreasonable to use EdI or EdN directly. This algorithm is not a decomposition strategy, and CdI is not applicable. In addition, when calculating EdI and EdN, the ideal reference point or Nadir reference point must be found first. Sum only needs to sum the target value, which is simple and easy, so we use Sum as the convergence index.

Above we chose Sum as the convergence index, and then we choose the distribution index. At present, most of the distribution indicators are based on Euclidean distance, but this method has a big defect: when the target dimension increases, the amount of calculation increases greatly and the performance of the distribution evaluation deteriorates. Since we compete based on angle in the offspring generation strategy, in order to continue to use angle information, we use cosine similarity as our distribution index.

Cosine similarity uses the cosine value of the angle between two vectors as a measure. The calculation formula is as Eq. 1. Here, we use cosine distance as our distribution indicators.

$$\cos(\theta_{ij}) = \frac{\sum_{m=1}^{M} (f_m(x_i) - z_m^*) \cdot (f_m(x_j) - z_m^*)}{\sqrt{\sum_{m=1}^{M} (f_m(x_i) - z_m^*)^2} \cdot \sqrt{\sum_{m=1}^{M} (f_m(x_j) - z_m^*)^2}} \tag{1}$$

2.3   Competitive Learning Based on Elite Archive Sets

Our competition mechanism adopts the CSO framework, and use two small populations to pursue the convergence and the distribution of the algorithm. In order to ensure the convergence of the algorithm, we first obtain the elite particle set, and use the particles in the elite particle set to guide the particles to be optimized. Then in the two populations according to the CSO framework, conduct competitive learning.

When the elite particle swarm is initialized, here we use non-dominated sorting and crowding distance to obtain our elite particle swarm. In the later stage of evolution, the individuals in the elite particle swarm are the winning particles in the competitive particle swarm optimizer. The purpose of using the elite particle swarm is to use the winning particles in the elite particle swarm to guide the losing particles to the frontier.

In population 1, we use the competitive particle swarm optimizer to compete with the individuals in the elite particle swarm, and use the winning particles to guide the individuals in the non-elite particle swarm to improve convergence. The particles in the elite particle swarm compete with the particle to be optimized according to the angle, and the smaller angle is regarded as the winning particle, otherwise it is regarded as the losing particle.

We obtain the velocity formula and position formula of the particle to be optimized according to Eq. 2 and Eq. 3, respectively. R_1, R_2 is randomly generated by a uniform distribution in $[0, 1]$. w represents the victory particle, and p represents the particle to be optimized.

$$V_{p,k}(t + 1) = R_1(k, t)V_{p,k} + R_2(k, t)(X_{w,k}(t) - X_{p,k}(t)) \tag{2}$$

$$X_{p,k}(t + 1) = X_{p,k}(t) + V_{p,k}(t + 1) \tag{3}$$

2.4 Co-Evolution Based on the "Three-Particle Competition" Mechanism

When the basic CSO framework is directly used for multi-objective optimization, it has the following problems: the offspring generation strategy is single, and only one competition mechanism is used; only the information of the winning particles is used, so that the useful information hidden by the failed particles is not mined. In response to the above problems, we proposed a three-particle competition mechanism.

Algorithm 1. co-evolution based on the "three-particle competition".

Input: P (current position), V(current velocities), N(swarm size), D(Optimization target number)
Output: Offspring (Offspring individuals)
1: B ← According to Euclidean distance, get the adjacent distance between two population particles;
2: **for** each particle p_i in P2 **do**
3:     Use tournament selection rules to select individuals a, b, c from P2;
4:     Calculate the angle θ_1 between a and p_i , θ_2 between b and p_i , and θ_3 between c and p_i ;
5:     p_w, p_n, p_l ← Sort angles;
6:     Generate offspring;
7:     /* three-particle competition */
8:     p_w^* ← According to the adjacency matrix B, get the nearest victorious particle in population 1;
9:     Off_v2, Off_v3 ← The velocity vectors of the two offspring particles are obtained by Equation 4 and Equation 5;
10:    Off_p2, Off_p3 ← Obtain the position vectors of the two offspring particles by Equation 3;
11:    Offspring ← Individual offspring
12: **end for**
13: **return** Offspring

In the three-particle competition, in order to make full use of the information between particles and maximize the use of particle information, we now design two two speed update formulas, as shown in we now design two two speed update formulas 4 and we now design two two speed update formulas 5. The thought is further explained.

$$V_{p,k}(t+1) = R_1(k,t)V_{p,k}$$
$$+ R_2(k,t)((X_{n,k}(t) + X_{l,k}(t))/2 - X_{p,k}(t)) \tag{4}$$

$$V_{p,k}(t+1) = R_1(k,t)V_{p,k}$$
$$+ R_2(k,t)((X_{n,k}(t) + X_{w,k}^*(t))/2 - X_{p,k}(t)) \tag{5}$$

For population 2, in order to avoid the singularity of the offspring speed update strategy, we use Eq. 4 and Eq. 5 to generate two new velocity vectors, and the position vector uses Eq. 3.

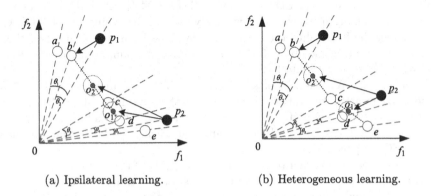

(a) Ipsilateral learning.   (b) Heterogeneous learning.

Fig. 2. Schematic diagram of co-evolution.

Figure 2 shows the schematic diagram of three-particle competition co-evolution in a two-dimensional target space. Among them, in the elite particle swarm, a and b are in population 1, and c, d, and e are in population 2. In population 1, the result of using the particle competition optimizer is that the particle P_1 to be optimized learns from the winning particle b with a smaller angle value, which improves the convergence of the algorithm.

In population 2, due to the use of the three-particle competition strategy, we mainly use the information of the failed particle and the intermediate particle. At this time, it will be divided into two cases: the same side and the opposite side of the failed particle and the intermediate particle.

The situation on the same side is shown in (a) in Fig. 2, p_2 will produce two possible offspring solutions o_1 and o_2. The generation of o_1 mainly uses Eq. 4 and Eq. 3, p_2 is optimized to the gap between the intermediate particle and the failed particle to expand the two The gap between particles. The generation of o_2 mainly uses Eq. 5 and Eq. 3, and p_2 advances in the middle direction between the intermediate particle and the nearest victory particle in the group 1. The occurrence of o_2 greatly improved the possibility of opening up the gap between the two populations.

The situation on the opposite side is shown in (b) in Fig. 2, which also produces two possible forward directions. The offspring o_2 produced by Eq. 5 and Eq. 3 is also used to optimize the gap between the two populations. The offspring o_1 produced by Eq. 2 and Eq. 3 may be closer to the victory particle, so we added a polynomial mutation strategy at the end to make o_1 fluctuate within a certain range.

3   Experimental Studies

3.1   Experimental Parameter Settings

In order to compare the performance of the algorithm, we used 9 WFG questions (WFG1-WFG9), and four ZDT questions (ZDT1-ZDT4) [12]. IGD [3] is a comprehensive evaluation index, which is widely used in the evaluation of MOEAs. The smaller the IGD value, the better the overall performance of the algorithm. For each test problem, about 5000 points uniformly sampled at the front of Pareto are used to calculate IGD.

Besides, the Wilcoxon rank sum test [5] with a significance level of 0.05 is adopted to perform statistical analysis on the experimental results, where the symbols "+", "−" and "≈" indicate that the result by another MOEA is significantly better, significantly worse, and statistically similar to that obtained by VaCSO, respectively.

In this research, in order to verify the effectiveness of the proposed algorithm, we compare with five multi-objective particle swarm optimization algorithms. It contains two multi-objective particle swarm optimization algorithms based on competition mechanisms: CMOPSO [13] and LMOCSO [10]. The other three multi-objective particle swarm algorithms include: MOPSO [2], MOPSOCD [9] and MPSO/D [4]. Table 1 shows the standard value and standard deviation of the IGD index of the algorithm on ZDT and WFG issues. In order to make the data more accurate, we run the data 30 times here.

In terms of experimental parameter setting, the number of each target division in MOPSO is 10. In MPSO/D, the parameters $C1$ and $C2$ for updating the particle velocity are both 2, the differential evolution parameter F is set to 0.5, and CR is set to 0.5. In MPSOCD, CMOPSO, LMOCSO and VaCSO, the expected number of mutations $proM$ is set to 1, and the distribution index of the polynomial mutation $disM$ is set to 20. The population size is set to 100, a total of 10,000 evaluations. In order to make the data more accurate, we run the data 30 times here, and take the average of the data as the IGD value.

3.2   Experimental Results and Analysis

From Table 1, we can clearly find that the VaCSO algorithm we proposed is better than the compared algorithms in terms of IGD indicators. Among them, VaCSO is significantly better than MOPSO and MPSO/D in terms of ZDT, but its performance is similar to that of LMOCSO and MOPSOCD, but slightly worse than CMOPSO. On the WFG problem, VaCSO has an absolute advantage over the compared algorithms. Among them, on the WFG1 issue, LMOCSO has the best performance, which may be because it is mainly suitable for large-scale optimization problems, which makes its distribution on the WFG1 issue better. CMOPSO also uses a particle swarm optimizer, and its performance on the WFG problems is gradually worse than VaCSO as the number of targets increases, which also proves the effectiveness of the three-particle competition strategy adopted in VaCSO.

Table 1. Median and IQR (in brackets) of IGD metric on the ZDT and all the WFG test instances

Problem	M	MOPSO	MOPSOCD	MPSO/D	CMOPSO	LMOCSO	VaCSO
ZDT1	2	4.1778e+1 (7.03e+0) −	4.1856e-3 (2.70e-4) +	3.2019e+0 (3.40e+0) −	4.4023e-3 (3.26e-4) +	6.7247e-3 (3.18e-3) +	7.8148e-3 (1.34e-3)
ZDT2	2	4.3674e+1 (9.64e+0) −	7.4947e-2 (1.89e-1) −	4.3791e+0 (4.23e+0) −	4.0492e-3 (1.55e-4) +	4.7076e-3 (8.18e-4) ≈	4.7953e-3 (5.89e-4)
ZDT3	2	3.9994e+1 (7.62e+0) −	2.0566e-1 (1.10e+0) −	4.8278e+0 (3.32e+0) −	1.2855e-1 (1.81e-1) ≈	1.4458e-1 (1.16e-1) −	4.5582e-2 (1.05e-1)
ZDT4	2	1.9745e+1 (8.21e+0) ≈	1.3855e+1 (6.21e+0) +	3.3712e+1 (7.29e+0) −	7.9530e+0 (5.68e+0) +	4.1246e-1 (2.40e-1) +	1.8097e+1 (5.43e+0)
WFG1	2	1.2253e+0 (7.04e-2) +	1.6796e+0 (3.87e-2) −	1.5412e+0 (5.22e-2) −	1.2424e+0 (4.56e-2) +	1.1706e+0 (6.15e-2) +	1.3260e+0 (4.45e-2)
	3	1.9551e+0 (6.87e-2) −	2.1160e+0 (2.65e-2) −	1.8661e+0 (8.37e-2) −	1.6338e+0 (4.32e-2) +	1.5726e+0 (3.89e-2) +	1.6619e+0 (3.22e-2)
	5	2.4268e+0 (7.00e-2) −	2.5634e+0 (2.67e-2) −	2.3139e+0 (4.85e-2) −	2.2220e+0 (3.75e-2) ≈	2.0673e+0 (5.19e-2) +	2.2237e+0 (5.03e-2)
	10	3.3886e+0 (9.83e-2) −	3.4103e+0 (3.55e-2) −	3.1803e+0 (2.79e-2) +	3.2508e+0 (3.62e-2) −	3.1284e+0 (5.66e-2) +	3.2122e+0 (2.79e-2)
WFG2	2	1.3418e-1 (2.69e-2) −	9.2168e-2 (2.14e-2) −	1.2087e-1 (1.58e-2) −	2.0572e-2 (2.13e-3) ≈	5.3130e-2 (1.41e-2) −	2.1518e-2 (3.77e-3)
	3	3.2488e-1 (4.22e-2) −	3.5691e-1 (2.73e-2) −	2.7035e-1 (1.62e-2) −	1.8651e-1 (6.82e-3) −	2.2475e-1 (2.06e-2) −	1.6949e-1 (4.29e-3)
	5	2.4341e+0 (9.62e-1) −	1.1056e+0 (1.02e-1) −	6.0474e-1 (1.80e-2) −	7.3783e-1 (2.42e-2) −	5.9159e-1 (2.65e-2) −	4.8673e-1 (7.88e-3)
	10	9.5223e+0 (1.83e+0) −	2.6106e+0 (9.40e-2) −	1.4166e+0 (4.26e-2) −	1.8852e+0 (9.68e-2) −	1.5997e+0 (3.99e-1) −	1.2088e+0 (7.64e-2)
WFG3	2	1.1414e-1 (2.74e-2) −	7.0699e-2 (1.18e-2) −	5.8759e-2 (9.39e-3) −	1.7997e-2 (8.79e-4) −	3.0116e-2 (5.46e-3) −	1.6695e-2 (7.83e-4)
	3	3.8832e-1 (8.14e-2) −	3.3790e-1 (4.25e-2) −	3.4200e-1 (2.29e-2) −	1.7139e-1 (1.42e-2) −	2.4798e-1 (2.73e-2) −	1.5421e-1 (1.31e-2)
	5	2.4556e+0 (8.41e-1) −	8.6330e-1 (1.00e-1) −	8.5910e-1 (4.21e-2) −	9.6669e-1 (9.43e-2) −	1.1568e+0 (1.10e-1) −	6.7039e-1 (8.92e-2)
	10	5.2002e+0 (9.27e-1) ≈	1.6121e+0 (1.39e-1) ≈	1.8904e+0 (1.23e-1) −	2.8452e+0 (3.30e-1) −	4.2248e+0 (1.46e+0) −	1.5964e+0 (3.30e-1)
WFG4	2	7.8633e-2 (7.28e-3) −	1.1940e-1 (8.71e-3) −	8.8641e-2 (7.23e-3) −	7.3051e-2 (5.63e-3) ≈	4.8903e-2 (4.65e-3) +	7.2310e-2 (5.65e-3)
	3	4.1395e-1 (4.23e-2) −	3.8760e-1 (1.78e-2) −	2.9576e-1 (9.66e-3) −	2.6888e-1 (5.73e-3) −	2.7562e-1 (6.56e-3) −	2.6211e-1 (5.79e-3)
	5	4.6722e+0 (3.92e-1) −	1.5000e+0 (3.80e-2) −	1.5978e+0 (3.51e-2) −	1.2221e+0 (1.77e-2) −	1.3654e+0 (1.45e-2) −	1.1971e+0 (1.19e-2)
	10	1.5538e+1 (6.56e-1) −	5.2612e+0 (4.90e-2) −	6.1486e+0 (2.65e-1) −	4.8903e+0 (6.23e-2) ≈	6.1074e+0 (2.05e-1) −	4.9099e+0 (6.25e-2)
WFG5	2	8.4917e-2 (8.44e-3) −	6.9996e-2 (1.44e-3) ≈	7.0960e-2 (1.71e-3) −	6.8998e-2 (2.38e-3) ≈	6.8342e-2 (1.84e-3) +	6.9127e-2 (2.13e-3)
	3	4.3794e-1 (7.86e-2) −	2.9738e-1 (1.34e-2) −	2.6617e-1 (8.19e-3) −	2.5140e-1 (7.26e-3) ≈	2.4578e-1 (2.35e-3) ≈	2.5272e-1 (1.54e-2)
	5	4.0059e+0 (6.12e-1) −	1.5552e+0 (3.88e-2) −	1.4362e+0 (2.86e-2) −	1.2322e+0 (3.65e-2) ≈	1.3245e+0 (8.68e-3) −	1.2390e+0 (5.06e-2)
	10	1.1093e+1 (8.00e-1) −	5.7343e+0 (1.04e-1) −	5.2567e+0 (7.12e-2) −	4.9480e+0 (8.48e-2) −	5.8189e+0 (1.63e-1) −	4.9700e+0 (7.12e-2)
WFG6	2	1.1050e-1 (2.40e-2) −	1.1837e-1 (4.89e-2) −	8.8136e-2 (2.68e-2) −	2.6005e-2 (9.73e-3) ≈	5.4579e-2 (1.69e-2) −	2.5630e-2 (7.82e-3)
	3	4.8528e-1 (3.97e-2) −	3.9377e-1 (2.02e-2) −	3.4912e-1 (2.01e-2) −	2.5339e-1 (1.13e-2) −	3.1164e-1 (2.00e-2) −	2.3988e-1 (9.96e-3)
	5	4.6054e+0 (3.92e-1) −	1.6368e+0 (4.28e-2) −	1.5489e+0 (2.38e-2) −	1.3165e+0 (4.09e-2) −	1.4541e+0 (4.80e-2) −	1.2086e+0 (2.27e-2)
	10	1.4431e+1 (4.50e-1) −	5.3088e+0 (5.84e-2) −	6.0739e+0 (2.52e-1) −	5.0485e+0 (6.15e-2) −	6.7209e+0 (6.60e-1) −	4.9086e+0 (5.88e-2)
WFG7	2	9.5939e-2 (2.24e-2) −	4.2870e-2 (8.38e-3) −	4.8391e-2 (8.68e-3) −	1.6809e-2 (8.47e-4) ≈	2.4804e-2 (2.31e-3) −	1.6724e-2 (7.22e-4)
	3	4.5871e-1 (4.35e-2) −	3.8667e-1 (1.97e-2) −	2.9634e-1 (9.47e-3) −	2.3650e-1 (4.10e-3) −	2.9675e-1 (2.11e-2) −	2.2513e-1 (2.94e-3)
	5	4.6796e+0 (2.45e-1) −	1.5465e+0 (3.53e-2) −	1.5758e+0 (3.44e-2) −	1.2604e+0 (3.16e-2) −	1.4098e+0 (2.41e-2) −	1.1861e+0 (1.63e-2)
	10	1.4044e+1 (4.88e-1) −	5.2650e+0 (6.03e-2) −	5.6609e+0 (1.81e-1) −	4.8550e+0 (4.49e-2) −	7.4325e+0 (2.79e+0) −	4.8077e+0 (3.28e-2)
WFG8	2	2.6151e-1 (2.53e-2) −	1.6339e-1 (1.37e-2) −	1.5922e-1 (1.17e-2) −	1.2600e-1 (5.69e-3) +	1.2990e-1 (1.04e-2) ≈	1.3271e-1 (8.27e-3)
	3	6.3536e-1 (5.48e-2) −	5.5580e-1 (1.70e-2) −	4.0112e-1 (1.06e-2) −	3.6556e-1 (9.30e-3) −	3.6932e-1 (1.82e-2) −	3.6639e-1 (1.19e-2)
	5	4.5986e+0 (3.98e-1) −	1.8097e+0 (4.56e-2) −	1.5182e+0 (2.09e-2) ≈	1.5404e+0 (6.15e-2) −	1.5583e+0 (5.40e-2) −	1.5037e+0 (5.86e-2)
	10	1.4427e+1 (4.33e-1) −	5.4528e+0 (6.22e-2) −	5.6601e+0 (8.74e-2) −	5.3514e+0 (5.65e-2) −	7.0812e+0 (2.54e+0) −	5.2545e+0 (3.91e-2)
WFG9	2	7.5531e-2 (1.96e-2) −	1.0364e-1 (6.11e-2) −	4.1279e-2 (4.35e-3) −	3.0851e-2 (1.92e-3) ≈	4.3027e-2 (3.63e-2) −	3.1617e-2 (2.51e-3)
	3	3.7027e-1 (3.56e-2) −	3.9860e-1 (1.68e-2) −	2.6639e-1 (8.27e-3) −	2.2633e-1 (5.53e-3) −	2.5988e-1 (9.21e-3) −	2.2523e-1 (5.74e-3)
	5	3.5757e+0 (6.09e-1) −	1.7392e+0 (5.41e-2) −	1.4693e+0 (2.49e-2) −	1.2227e+0 (4.05e-2) −	1.3581e+0 (1.76e-2) −	1.1682e+0 (3.21e-2)
	10	1.0972e+1 (9.45e-1) −	6.0271e+0 (1.88e-1) −	5.4366e+0 (1.06e-1) −	5.1758e+0 (7.47e-2) −	5.9593e+0 (2.39e-1) −	4.9273e+0 (1.00e-1)
+/−/≈		1/38/1	2/36/2	1/38/1	6/20/14	8/29/3	

Regarding the WFG series, whether the number of targets is 2, 3, 5 or 10, VaCSO has shown its good performance. Figure 3 shows the IGD convergence curves of the algorithm on WFG2, respectively. Take WFG2 as an example for discussion. In Fig. 3 (a), the number of targets is 3, and in (b), the number of targets is 10. In the case of three goals, VaCSO has the fastest convergence speed. At the same time, it is stable around the 40th generation, and the convergence speed and solution quality are better. As the dimensionality increases, the performance of CMOPSO and LMOCSO based on the competition mechanism declines faster in 10 dimensions. And the effect of MPSOD based on decomposition idea gradually becomes better as the target dimension increases. As the dimensionality increases, the convergence speed of VaCSO further increases, and it stabilizes around 30 generations, while the IGD value is the smallest.

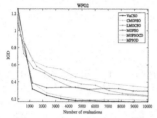
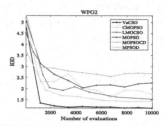

(a) WFG2 problem with two objectives. (b) WFG2 problem with ten objectives.

Fig. 3. Graphs of IGD value changes of 6 comparison algorithms on the WFG2 problem.

4   Conclusion and Remark

This paper proposes an angle-based multi-objective competitive particle swarm optimization algorithm (VaCSO). In VaCSO, groups are divided into groups 1 and 2 according to indicators. The population 1 is mainly responsible for improving the convergence of the algorithm and the competitive particle swarm optimizer is used in the population. In population 2, a three-particle cooperative competition mechanism is added. By learning from the victory particles in the population 1, the performance of the algorithm for optimizing the gaps between the population particles is improved. Experimental results show that our proposed VaCSO has better performance than the current main multi-objective particle swarm optimization on basic test problems, and the convergence speed and solution distribution performance are outstanding.

In the future, our three-particle competition mechanism and the maximum angle priority mechanism will be used to solve large-scale multi-objective algorithms, because the idea of three-particle co-evolution can make the particle distribution more widely, thus providing the possibility for later exploration of blank areas.

References

1. Cheng, R., Jin, Y.: A competitive swarm optimizer for large scale optimization. IEEE Trans. Cybern. **45**(2), 191–204 (2015)
2. Coello, C.C., Lechuga, M.S.: Mopso: a proposal for multiple objective particle swarm optimization. In: Proceedings of the 2002 Congress on Evolutionary Computation. CEC 2002 (Cat. No. 02TH8600), vol. 2, pp. 1051–1056. IEEE (2002)

3. Coello, C.A.C., Cortes, N.C.: Solving multiobjective optimization problems using an artificial immune system. Genet. Programm. Evolvable Mach. **6**(2), 163–190 (2005). https://doi.org/10.1007/s10710-005-6164-x
4. Dai, C., Wang, Y., Ye, M.: A new multi-objective particle swarm optimization algorithm based on decomposition. Inf. Sci. **325**, 541–557 (2015)
5. Derrac, J., García, S., Molina, D., Herrera, F.: A practical tutorial on the use of nonparametric statistical tests as a methodology for comparing evolutionary and swarm intelligence algorithms. Swarm Evol. Comput. **1**(1), 3–18 (2011)
6. Houssein, E.H., Gad, A.G., Hussain, K., Suganthan, P.N.: Major advances in particle swarm optimization: theory, analysis, and application. Swarm Evol. Comput. **63**, 100868 (2021)
7. Liefooghe, A., Daolio, F., Verel, S., Derbel, B., Aguirre, H., Tanaka, K.: Landscape-aware performance prediction for evolutionary multiobjective optimization. IEEE Trans. Evol. Comput. **24**(6), 1063–1077 (2020)
8. Liu, Y., Gong, D., Sun, J., Jin, Y.: A many-objective evolutionary algorithm using a one-by-one selection strategy. IEEE Trans. Cybern. **47**(99), 2689–2702 (2017)
9. Raquel, C.R., Naval Jr, P.C.: An effective use of crowding distance in multiobjective particle swarm optimization. In: Proceedings of the 7th Annual Conference on Genetic and Evolutionary Computation, pp. 257–264 (2005)
10. Tian, Y., Zheng, X., Zhang, X., Jin, Y.: Efficient large-scale multiobjective optimization based on a competitive swarm optimizer. IEEE Trans. Cybern. **50**(8), 3696–3708 (2020)
11. Yang, W., Chen, L., Wang, Y., Zhang, M.: Multi/many-objective particle swarm optimization algorithm based on competition mechanism. Comput. Intell. Neurosci. **2020**, 1–26 (2020)
12. Zapotecas-Martinez, S., Coello, C.A.C., Aguirre, H.E., Tanaka, K.: A review of features and limitations of existing scalable multiobjective test suites. IEEE Trans. Evol. Comput. **23**(1), 130–142 (2018)
13. Zhang, X., Zheng, X., Cheng, R., Qiu, J., Jin, Y.: A competitive mechanism based multi-objective particle swarm optimizer with fast convergence. Inf. Sci. **427**, 63–76 (2018)

The Experimental Analysis on Transfer Function of Binary Particle Swarm Optimization

Yixuan Luo[1,2], Jianhua Liu[1,2(✉)], Xingsi Xue[1,2], Renyuan Hu[1,2], and Zihang Wang[1,2]

[1] School of Information Science and Engineering, Fujian University of Technology, Fuzhou 350108, China
[2] Fujian Provincial Key Laboratory of Big Data Mining and Applications, Fujian University of Technology, Fuzhou 350108, China
jhliu@fjnu.edu.cn

Abstract. Binary Particle Swarm Optimization (BPSO) has extended the capacity of the conventional particle swarm optimization (PSO) for optimizing the discrete combinational optimization problems. The transfer function of BPSO is key for its capacity to search solution. This paper discuss the weight setting of two variants called the S-Shaped and the V-Shaped transfer functions in BPSO. The experimental results indicate that the increasing weight setting is beneficial to the performance of BPSO with the S-shaped transfer function, while the decreasing weight setting is flavorful for that of BPSO with the V-shaped transfer function. The Multi dimension Knapsack Problem (MKP) are used in the experiment for testing the discussable conclusions. The experimental results illustrate that the transfer function can be adjusted to improve the performance of BPSO, and the recommended weight setting is obtained, accordingly.

Keywords: Binary Particle Swarm Optimization · Transfer function · Weight setting · Knapsack problem

1 Introduction

Particle Swarm Optimization (PSO) is an evolutionary computation algorithm based on Swarm intelligence developed by R.Eberhart and J.Kennedy in 1995 [1]. In order to utilize PSO to solve the problems of discrete values, Binary Particle Swarm Optimization (BPSO) was developed in 1997 [2]. The BPSO has extended the functionality of PSO and is applied to many combinatorial problems in the discrete space [3,4], In order to gain more advantage for BPSO to optimize combinatorial problems, there are many methods to improve BPSO [3,4].

BPSO has rarely been analyzed in theory. [5] defined a conception of the bit change rate to analyze and find that BPSO is lack of the local searching

© Springer Nature Switzerland AG 2021
Y. Tan and Y. Shi (Eds.): ICSI 2021, LNCS 12689, pp. 254–264, 2021.
https://doi.org/10.1007/978-3-030-78743-1_23

ability; The runtime of BPSO is investigated and the lower bound for swarm polynomial size has been presented, but the results are hardly used to improve the BPSO [6]. One of the key components in BPSO is the transfer function. The original BPSO's transfer function is sigmoid function which increases over the velocity like the S shape which is called the S-shaped function. [7] provided a set of V-shaped functions and verified their effects. The different transfer functions may show diverse behaviors and have different impacts on the performance of algorithms [8].

In this paper, based the analysis on the velocity of BPSO with the different transfer functions [9], the setting of BPSO's weight is discussed and some experiments on Knapsack Problem are conducted to test the performance. In terms of the theory of the velocity on the BPSO, the different weight settings for the different transfer function of BPSO are proposed. The experimental results show that the transfer function can be adjusted to improve its performance.

The rest of the paper is composed as follows: in Sect. 2, BPSO is introduced and both of the S-shaped and the V-shaped transfer functions are discussed. Section 3 introduces the analysis on the velocity of BPSO, some theoretical results are introduced. In Sect. 4, the weight and the parameter of transfer function are investigated and the rule of weight and parameter setting is discussed. In Sect. 5, Knapsack Problem is used to compare with some variants of BPSO with different transfer function; Sect. 6 is the conclusion of the paper.

2   The Transfer Function of the BPSO

2.1   The Conventional BPSO

Unlike the PSO, the position updating of BPSO switches its values between "0" and "1" based on the velocity of each dimension, which is a binary bit, of a particle. At the beginning, each particle in BPSO consists of a string of binary code, and each binary bit uses Eq. (1) to generate the velocity.

$$v_{id} = w \cdot v_{id} + c_1 \cdot r_1 \cdot (p_{id} - x_{id}) + c_2 \cdot r_2 \cdot (p_{gd} - x_{id}) \tag{1}$$

where $0 < w \leq 1$ that is the inertia weight, v_{id} denotes the dth bit velocity of the ith particle, p_{id} is the dth bit of the best position found so far by the ith particle, p_{gd} is the dth bit of the best position found so far by all particles, c_1 and c_2 are the acceleration factors and r_1 and r_2 are random variables following the uniform distribution within the interval $[0, 1]$. After being updated by Eq. (1), the velocity v_{id} is bounded by a threshold v_{max} as follows:

$$v_{id} \begin{cases} v_{max} & if \ v_{id} > v_{max} \\ -v_{max} & if \ v_{id} < -v_{max} \end{cases} \tag{2}$$

The velocity of BPSO is mapped to the value in the range of $[0, 1]$ with a sigmoid function as Eq. (3), which is the so called transfer function.

$$s(v_{id}) = \frac{1}{1 + exp(-v_{id})} \tag{3}$$

The bits of a particle switch their binary value using the following equation Eq. (4).

$$x_{id} \begin{cases} 1 & if \ rand() < s(v_{id}) \\ 0 & otherwise \end{cases} \qquad (4)$$

where $rand()$ is a stochastic value sampled in the interval $[0, 1]$ in uniform distribution. The particle changes each bit value of its binary string using Eq. (4), so $s(v_{id})$ represents the probability of the bit x_{id} being 1 and is called as transfer function which controls the probability that each bit of BPSO switches from 1 to 0 and vice versa.

2.2   The Transfer Function of BPSO

In terms of BPSO, the velocity indicates the distance of a particle from the optimal position. The transfer function of BPSO must map the velocity to the probability of bit changing. For selecting transfer function, some rules are listed as follows which are considered [10]:

(1) A large absolute value of velocity must provide a high probability of changing the bit position with respect to its previous position (from 1 to 0 or vice versa).
(2) A small absolute value of velocity must provide a small probability of changing the position. In other words, a zero value of the velocity represents that the bit position is good and should not be changed.

The above ideas can make particle swarm slowly get close to the global optimal particle; and the searching behavior can be shifted from the exploration to the exploitation in the solution space. The curve of the transfer function in the conventional BPSO, Eq. (2), is shown in Fig. 1. We call the transfer function S-shaped transfer function. Based on Eq. (3), it can be found that the transfer function of conventional BPSO is not in accordance with the above ideas.

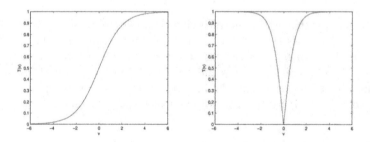

Fig. 1. The new transfer function of S-shape and V-shape

Another type of the transfer function was proposed with a different position updating rule [7], which is called the V-shaped transfer function. One of these new transfer functions is Eq. (5) and its figure is shown in Fig. 2. According to Eq. (5) and the Fig. 2, the new transfer function basically complies with the above ideas on the transfer function.

$$T(v_{id}) = |tanh(v_{id})| \tag{5}$$

Based on the V-shaped function, a new position updating scheme was designed in the [7], where the bit updating equation was changed as the follows:

$$x_{id} \begin{cases} 1 - x_{id} & if \; rand() < T(v_{id}) \\ x_{id} & otherwise \end{cases} \tag{6}$$

where $rand()$ is a stochastic number which is sampled from the distribution of interval $[0, 1]$, $1\text{-}x_{id}$ denotes that the bit value should be changed.

2.3   The Analysis on the Velocity of BPSO

In the analysis of BPSO, each dimension of a particle is one bit which switches its value between "0" and "1" [9]. For analyzing the velocity by just considering one bit, Eq.(1) can be simplified as follows:

$$v_{t+1} = w \cdot v_t + c_1 \cdot r_1 \cdot (p - x_t) + c_2 \cdot r_2 \cdot (p_{gd} - x_t) \tag{7}$$

where w is the weight. In the following section, $E[v_t]$ indicates the expected value of the velocity vt. In [9], theory conclusions are obtained as follows.

Lemma 1. *If $w = 1$ and $p = g = 1$, then $\forall v_{max} > v_0, \exists T > 0$,*

$$E[v_t] > v_{max}, \forall t > T \tag{8}$$

Lemma 2. *If $w = 1$ and $p = g = 0$, then $\forall v_{min} > v_0, \exists T > 0$,*

$$E[v_t] < v_{min}, \forall t > T \tag{9}$$

Lemma 3. *Given $0 < w < 1$, $p = g = 1$ and $v_0 \geq 0$, it can be deduced that*

$$w^t v_0 < E[v_t] < w^t v_0 + \frac{c_1 + c_2}{2} \cdot \frac{1 - w^t}{1 - w} \tag{10}$$

Lemma 4. *Given $0 < w < 1$, $p = g = 0$ and $v_0 \leq 0$, it can be deduced that*

$$w^t v_0 - \frac{c_1 + c_2}{2} \cdot \frac{1 - w^t}{1 - w} < E[v_t] < w^t v_0 \tag{11}$$

3   The Discussion of Transfer Function on BPSO

In this section, we discuss the V-shaped transfer function of BPSO with the weight based on the theory of the velocity in the above section. For the V-shaped transfer function, the bit updating formula Eq. (6) is different from the conventional BPSO updating formula Eq. (4). In terms of Eq. (3), (4), (5) and (6), the property of the two sets of transfer functions of BPSO can be obtained as the follows.

(1) For the original BPSO with S-shaped function, the bigger the absolute of velocity is, the smaller the probability is for the bit to keep fixed. On the contrary, the bit becomes random when the velocity approaches the zero.
(2) For the BPSO with V-shaped function, the results are contrary with that of the original BPSO. If the absolute value of velocity is bigger, the bit will be more random, while the bit will be more constant.

In terms of the Lemma 1 and Lemma 2, when $p = g$ and $w = 1$, the $E[v_t]$ will reach the maximum threshold (when $p = g = 1$) or minimal threshold (when $p = g = 0$), so the $|E[v_t]|$ will approach the largest value at the end. Under this case, the bit becomes random and switches between "0" and "1" by random for the V-shaped transfer function. However, for the S-shaped transfer function or original BPSO, the bit will become constant and approach 1 or 0 under this case.

In terms of the Lemma 3 and Lemma 4, when $p = g$ and $0 < w < 1$, $|E[v_t]| \in [0, \frac{c_1+c_2}{2} \cdot \frac{1}{1-w}]$ is a monotonically increasing of w. The bigger the w is, the wider the interval $[0, \frac{c_1+c_2}{2} \cdot \frac{1}{1-w}]$. The smaller the w is, the closer the interval $[0, \frac{c_1+c_2}{1-w}]$ is to the zero. Under this condition, for V-shaped transfer function, the smaller the w is, the nearer the value of function is to zero, so the more constant the bit becomes. However, for S-shaped transfer function, the bit will be random. When $p \neq g$, the v_t will vary randomly, so the bit will change by random.

The higher random degree of bit changing implies that the power of exploration is stronger while the bit being constant denotes that exploitation should be taken on. According to the rule of exploration changing to exploitation over time, the inertia weight w of BPSO with V-shaped transfer function should decrease over the time, and that with S-shaped transfer function increases over the time. Therefore, the BPSO with S-shaped transfer function should take on the increasing weight over time like Eq. (12), while that with V-shaped transfer function should use the decreasing inertia weight over the time like Eq. (13).

$$w = w_{min} + (w_{max} - w_{min})\frac{t}{t_{max}} \tag{12}$$

$$w = w_{max} - (w_{max} - w_{min})\frac{t}{t_{max}} \tag{13}$$

where w_{min} and w_{max} denotes the minimum and maximum of inertia weight respectively, t_{max} means the maximum iteration time of the algorithm running.

4   Experiment Test with 0/1 Knapsack Problem

In order to compare the effectiveness of different schemes of BPSO with different transfer functions, we solve the combination optimization problem – the Multi-dimensional 0/1 Knapsack Problem (MKP) with the different schemes. MKP has been used in the wide application fields. However, it is a NP problem in the computation theory. MKP can be denoted with 0/1 code and solved by the BPSO. Hence, MKP is commonly used as the benchmark problem for test binary optimization algorithms.

In the section, the transfer function and the position updating equation of S-shaped BPSO are defined in Eq. (3) and Eq. (4), while that of V-shaped BPSO are shown in Eq. (5) and Eq. (6). The weight increasing and weight decreasing are described as Eq. (12) and Eq. (13) respectively.

4.1   The Description of MKP

Multi-dimension 0/1 Knapsack Problem (MKP) considers $m(m > 1)$ resources to be consumed. Each resource has a capacity $C_j(j = 1, ..., m)$. MKP is about how to produce the n goods with the m resources which each capacity is confined as constant value. The MKP aims to maximize total profit of goods under the case of the confined resources capacity. Each good i has a profit p_i and a quantity of the consumption of resource $C_{ij}(i = 1, ..., n)$. The problem is formulated as the following equations.

$$max \sum_{i=1}^{n} p_i x_i \tag{14}$$

$$s.t. \sum_{i=0}^{n} c_{ij} x_i \leq C_j, j = 1, ..., m. \tag{15}$$

$$x_i \in \{0, 1\}, i = 1, ..., n. \tag{16}$$

where $x = (x_1, x_2, ..., x_n)$ can be represented as a scheme of Knapsack Problem, which $x_i \in 0, 1$ denotes whether the good x_i is produced. The value x denotes a particle position and a candidacy solution. The number n is the total dimensions of a particle and the total number of goods in knapsack problem. The value x_j represents whether the jth goods is selected in a particle. If $x_i = 1$, the jth goods is loaded in knapsack. Otherwise, the jth goods is not loaded in the knapsack.

Because MKP is a constraint optimization problem, MKP is tracked as the constraint problem using the penalty faction, which the objective function is described as follows:

$$f(x) = \sum_{i=1}^{n} p_i x_i + \beta \cdot \sum_{j=1}^{m} (Q \sum_{i=1}^{n} min(0, C_j - c_{ij} x_i)) \tag{17}$$

where Q is penalty factor. The value of Q is a positive constant number which is set as $1e+100$. So, the constrained optimization problem Eq. (16) is transformed into the non-constraint problem Eq. (17). It needs to note that the maximum of objective function will be computed, not minimum.

The test datasets of MKP are selected from the website of University of Nottingham (http://www.cs.nott.ac.uk/jqd/mkp/index.html), that are called as Sento, Weing and Weish which include 2, 8 and 30 instances respectively. Table 1 describes the parameter settings in the experiments in detail. Note that the number of particles is set as the number of goods of each instance, n.

Table 2 shows the results about the Sento and Weing instances. By observing the results collected in the table, it presents an obvious advantage of "SBPOSIW" over "SPBSODW", and "VBPSODW" over "VBPSOIW". For every instance, the t-test with significance level of 0.05 is carried out between "SBPODW" and "SBPSOIW", and between "VBPSODW" and "VBPSOIW". "SBPSOIW" obtains significantly better results than "SBPSODW" on 7 out of the total 10 instances (1 Sento instance and 6 outof 8 Weing instances), while "VBPSODW" is significantly better than "VBPSOIW" on all 10 instances. Moreover, "SBPSOIW" performs significantly best among four variants of BPSO which shows that "SPBOSP" is better than "VBPSODW". In terms of success rate of Table 4, "SPSOIW" performs better than "SPSODW", obtaining the higher success rate on 9 out of the total 10 instances. "VPSODW" obviously performs the better than "VPSOIW" for all instances.

Table 1. Parameter settings of the experiments.

Parameter	Description	Value
w_{max}	Upper bound of w	1
w_{min}	Lower bound of w	0.4
Q	Penalty coefficient in Eq. (17)	10^{100}
N	Number of particles in the BPSO	n
t_{max}	Maximal number of iterations	3000

The position of particle is initialized by the following equation:

$$x_{id} \begin{cases} 1 & if \ rand() < 0.5 \\ 0 & otherwise \end{cases} \tag{18}$$

where $rand()$ is the number which is generated in interval $[0, 1]$. The initial velocity v_{ij} is initialized by following equation:

$$v_{ij} = v_{min} + rand()(v_{max} - v_{min}) \tag{19}$$

where v_{max} and v_{min} represent the maximum and minimum of velocity respectively.

4.2 Experiment and Analysis

In order to compare four variants of BPSO algorithm using MKP instances, 100 independent runs are conducted for each instance with each BPSO algorithm, and the mean and standard deviation of the 100 corresponding results are calculated. Tables 2 and 3 present the mean and standard deviation of the results of the compared algorithms in 100 independent runs on the MKP instances. The columns "m" and "n" denote the number of resources and goods respectively. The larger m and n all is, the more complex the instance is. The column "Opt" indicates the optimal value of each instance, which is given in the datasets.

Table 2 shows the results about the Sento and Weing instances. By observing the results collected in the table, it presents an obvious advantage of "SBPOSIW" over "SPBSODW", and "VBPSODW" over "VBPSOIW". For every instance, the t-test with significance level of 0.05 is carried out between "SBPODW" and "SBPSOIW", and between "VBPSODW" and "VBPSOIW". "SBPSOIW" obtains significantly better results than "SBPSODW" on 7 out of the total 10 instances (1 Sento instance and 6 out of 8 Weing instances), while "VBPSODW" is significantly better than "VBPSOIW" on all 10 instances. Moreover, "SBPSOIW" performs significantly best among four variants of BPSO which shows that "SPBOSP" is better than "VBPSODW". In terms of success rate of Table IV, "SPSOIW" performs better than "SPSODW", obtaining the higher success rate on 9 out of the total 10 instances.

Table 3 presents the results on the Weish instances like the Table 2, in which the similar effect can be observed to the results listed in Table 2. In terms of both mean profit and standard deviation, "SBPSOIW" performs the better than "SBPSODW", and "VBPSODW" is better than "VBPSOIW". The statistical test shows that "SBPSOIW" is significantly better than "SBPSODW" in 27 out of the total 30 instances except 3 instances that the optimal is obtained, while "VBPSODW" embodies significantly better than "VBPSOIW" for all instances. Similarly, "SBPSOIW" presents better effectiveness than "VBPSODW".

Table 2. Mean and standard deviation of the results of the compared algorithms in 100 runs on the Sento and Weing datasets.

MKP	m	n	Opt	Mean (STD)			
				SBPODW	SBPSOIW	VBPSODW	VBPSOIW
Sent01	30	60	7.77E+03	7.71E+03 (5.23E+01)	**7.74E+03 (3.02E+01)**	7.65E+03 (8.55E+01)	7.17E+03 (3.82E+02)
Sent02	30	60	8.72E+03	8.68E+03 (2.48E+01)	**8.70E+03 (1.50E+01)**	8.65E+03 (4.92E+01)	8.53E+03 (9.28E+01)
Weing1	2	28	1.41E+05	1.41E+05 (1.33E+02)	1.41E+05 (7.03E+01)	1.41E+05 (6.28E+01)	1.38E+05 (3.79E+03)
Weing2	2	28	1.31E+05	1.31E+05 (3.94E+01)	1.31E+05 (4.36E+01)	1.30E+05 (8.38E+02)	1.24E+05 (5.59E+03)
Weing3	2	28	9.57E+04	9.51E+04 (6.01E+02)	**9.53E+04 (4.27E+02)**	9.44E+04 (1.32E+03)	8.38E+04 (7.61E+03)
Weing4	2	28	1.19E+05	1.19E+05 (9.01E+02)	**1.19E+05 (2.74E+02)**	1.18E+05 (1.57E+03)	1.13E+05 (4.76E+03)
Weing5	2	28	9.88E+04	9.79E+04 (1.52E+03)	**9.86E+04 (8.83E+02)**	9.69E+04 (2.05E+03)	9.14E+04 (5.70E+03)
Weing6	2	28	1.31E+05	1.30E+05 (1.99E+02)	1.30E+05 (1.93E+02)	1.30E+05 (6.67E+02)	1.24E+05 (5.37E+03)
Weing7	2	105	1.10E+06	1.09E+06 (2.00E+03)	**1.10E+06 (1.12E+03)**	1.09E+06 (3.92E+03)	1.08E+06 (7.47E+03)
Weing8	2	105	6.24E+05	6.04E+05 (1.36E+04)	**6.18E+05 (4.95E+03)**	5.94E+05 (1.91E+04)	5.36E+05 (3.55E+04)

Table 3. Mean and standard deviation of the results of the compared algorithms in 100 runs on the Weish datasets.

MKP	m	n	Opt	Mean (STD)			
				SBPODW	SBPSOIW	VBPSODW	VBPSOIW
Weish01	5	30	4.55E+03	4.54E+03 (2.64E+01)	**4.55E+03 (1.11E+01)**	4.52E+03 (4.79E+01)	4.37E+03 (1.76E+02)
Weish02	5	30	4.54E+03	4.53E+03 (8.09E+00)	**4.53E+03 (3.58E+00)**	4.50E+03 (3.97E+01)	4.38E+03 (1.75E+02)
Weish03	5	30	4.12E+03	4.09E+03 (2.99E+01)	**4.11E+03 (1.17E+01)**	4.07E+03 (4.47E+01)	3.90E+03 (1.71E+02)
Weish04	5	30	4.56E+03	4.56E+03 (0.00E+00)	**4.56E+03 (0.00E+00)**	4.55E+03 (3.76E+01)	4.24E+03 (3.23E+02)
Weish05	5	30	4.51E+03	4.51E+03 (0.00E+00)	**4.51E+03 (0.00E+00)**	4.49E+03 (8.04E+01)	4.11E+03 (3.57E+02)
Weish06	5	40	5.56E+03	5.53E+03 (2.34E+01)	**5.54E+03 (1.00E+01)**	5.51E+03 (4.22E+01)	5.37E+03 (1.19E+02)
Weish07	5	40	5.57E+03	5.56E+03 (1.60E+01)	**5.56E+03 (8.50E+00)**	5.53E+03 (5.60E+01)	5.37E+03 (1.43E+02)
Weish08	5	40	5.60E+03	5.59E+03 (2.14E+01)	**5.60E+03 (6.67E+00)**	5.57E+03 (4.16E+01)	5.42E+03 (1.23E+02)
Weish09	5	40	5.25E+03	5.24E+03 (2.26E+01)	5.24E+03 (9.70E+00)	5.20E+03 (7.00E+01)	4.94E+03 (2.35E+02)
Weish10	5	50	6.34E+03	6.31E+03 (3.19E+01)	**6.33E+03 (1.97E+01)**	6.28E+03 (6.56E+01)	6.05E+03 (2.17E+02)
Weish11	5	50	5.64E+03	5.60E+03 (4.95E+01)	**5.61E+03 (4.34E+01)**	5.56E+03 (7.75E+01)	5.33E+03 (2.23E+02)
Weish12	5	50	6.34E+03	6.32E+03 (3.79E+01)	**6.33E+03 (1.78E+01)**	6.26E+03 (8.90E+01)	6.00E+03 (2.72E+02)
Weish13	5	50	6.16E+03	6.13E+03 (4.50E+01)	**6.16E+03 (1.87E+01)**	6.08E+03 (7.85E+01)	5.82E+03 (2.26E+02)
Weish14	5	60	6.95E+03	6.92E+03 (3.57E+01)	**6.94E+03 (2.10E+01)**	6.85E+03 (8.98E+01)	6.59E+03 (1.86E+02)
Weish15	5	60	7.49E+03	7.47E+03 (2.49E+01)	**7.48E+03 (1.97E+01)**	7.43E+03 (7.54E+01)	7.11E+03 (3.08E+02)
Weish16	5	60	7.29E+03	7.26E+03 (3.09E+01)	**7.27E+03 (1.84E+01)**	7.22E+03 (6.90E+01)	7.00E+03 (1.77E+02)
Weish17	5	60	8.63E+03	8.62E+03 (1.09E+01)	**8.63E+03 (6.16E+00)**	8.61E+03 (2.40E+01)	8.49E+03 (1.04E+02)
Weish18	5	70	9.58E+03	9.54E+03 (2.80E+01)	**9.56E+03 (1.86E+01)**	9.51E+03 (5.56E+01)	9.33E+03 (1.47E+02)
Weish19	5	70	7.70E+03	7.64E+03 (4.72E+01)	**7.68E+03 (2.92E+01)**	7.58E+03 (9.25E+01)	7.25E+03 (2.33E+02)
Weish20	5	70	9.45E+03	9.42E+03 (3.04E+01)	**9.44E+03 (1.70E+01)**	9.37E+03 (6.81E+01)	9.06E+03 (2.11E+02)
Weish21	5	70	9.07E+03	9.03E+03 (3.40E+01)	**9.06E+03 (2.71E+01)**	8.99E+03 (6.54E+01)	8.65E+03 (2.50E+02)
Weish22	5	80	8.95E+03	8.87E+03 (4.86E+01)	**8.91E+03 (3.37E+01)**	8.79E+03 (1.22E+02)	8.45E+03 (2.44E+02)
Weish23	5	80	8.34E+03	8.26E+03 (5.95E+01)	**8.32E+03 (2.92E+01)**	8.19E+03 (1.07E+02)	7.84E+03 (1.93E+02)
Weish24	5	80	1.02E+04	1.02E+04 (3.26E+01)	**1.02E+04 (2.36E+01)**	1.01E+04 (6.03E+01)	9.95E+03 (1.23E+02)
Weish25	5	80	9.94E+03	9.90E+03 (2.31E+01)	**9.92E+03 (1.26E+01)**	9.86E+03 (6.47E+01)	9.58E+03 (1.70E+02)
Weish26	5	90	9.58E+03	9.48E+03 (6.22E+01)	**9.54E+03 (2.58E+01)**	9.44E+03 (1.07E+02)	8.94E+03 (2.72E+02)
Weish27	5	90	9.82E+03	9.70E+03 (8.05E+01)	**9.78E+03 (5.98E+01)**	9.61E+03 (1.45E+02)	9.16E+03 (2.17E+02)
Weish28	5	90	9.49E+03	9.37E+03 (8.94E+01)	**9.47E+03 (3.72E+01)**	9.32E+03 (1.22E+02)	8.89E+03 (2.32E+02)
Weish29	5	90	9.41E+03	9.28E+03 (7.20E+01)	**9.36E+03 (4.08E+01)**	9.23E+03 (1.10E+02)	8.76E+03 (2.43E+02)
Weish30	5	90	1.12E+04	1.11E+04 (2.35E+01)	**1.12E+04 (1.69E+01)**	1.11E+04 (4.67E+01)	1.08E+04 (1.76E+02)

From four tables, it can be found that the increasing weight setting is better than the decreasing weight setting for the original BPSO which utilizes the S-shaped transfer function. However, the decreasing weight setting is better than the increasing weight setting for BPSO with V-shaped transfer function.

Furthermore, one can obtain that the BPSO with S-shaped transfer function has better performance than that with V-shaped transfer function, which can be derived from the comparisons between "SBPSOIW" and "VBPSODW" in terms of four tables whether observing the mean profit or the success rate of 100 run times.

In order to compare the efficiency of different algorithms, the normalized deviation $\Delta(Mean, Opt)$ of mean profit to optima of each instance is defined in Eq. (20), and then the mean $\Delta(Mean, Opt)$ of difference algorithms on each MKP Dataset can be calculated.

$$\Delta(Mean, Opt) = \frac{Opt - Mean}{Opt} \tag{20}$$

Figure 2 shows the boxplots of $\Delta(Mean, Opt)$ for the compared algorithms over 100 runs of a subset of instances selected from the Sento, Weing and Weish MKP datasets, which are representative instances in terms of problem size.

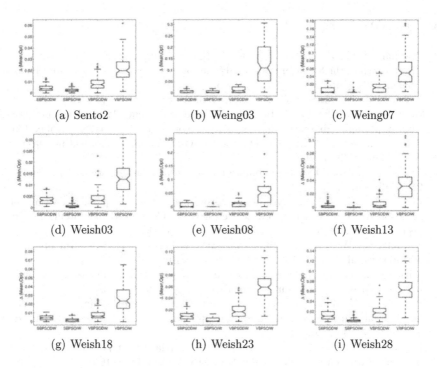

Fig. 2. The normalized deviation of the mean profit of the compared algorithms to the optimal profit on some MKP instances selected from the datasets.

The figures clearly show that the distribution of the normalized deviation of "SPSOIW" are below that of "SPSODW" and "VBPSODW" is lower than that of "VBPSOIW" for these instances. For Weish03, weish08 and Weish13, the median of "SBPSOIW" reaches zero, indicating that "SBPSOIW" is more likely to achieve the optimal solutions than the other algorithms on these instances. These figures can further show the same results as that of the previous tables with more visual method.

5   Conclusion

In this paper, in terms of the theory of the velocity on the BPSO, the S-shaped transfer function and V-shaped transfer function are analyzed. It is obvious that the different weight setting is appropriate to the different transfer function. The increasing weight setting is suit for the S-Shaped transfer function, while decreasing weight setting is favor for the V-shaped transfer function. Although the experimental results show that BPSO with S-shaped transfer function performs better than BPSO with V-Shape transfer function, the transfer function can be adjusted to improve its performance. It is important that the weight setting should imply with the conclusion obtained in the paper.

References

1. Eberhart, R.C., Kennedy, J.: A new optimizer using particle swarm theory. In Proceedings of the Sixth International Symposium on Micro Machine and Human Science, vol. 1, pp. 39–43, October 1995

2. Kennedy, J., Eberhart, R.C.: A discrete binary version of the particle swarm algorithm. In: 1997 IEEE International Conference on Systems, Man, and Cybernetics, Computational Cybernetics and Simulation, vol. 5, pp. 4104–4108, October 1997

3. Kumar, L., Bharti, K.K.: A novel hybrid BPSO-SCA approach for feature selection. Nat. Comput. **20**, 39–61 (2021)

4. Beheshti, Z.: A novel x-shaped binary particle swarm optimization. Soft. Comput. **25**, 3013–3042 (2021)

5. Liu, J., Fan, X.: The analysis and improvement of binary particle swarm optimization. In: International Conference on IEEE Computational Intelligence and Security, CIS 2009, vol. 1, pp. 254–258, December 2009

6. Sudholt, D., Witt, C.: Runtime analysis of a binary particle swarm optimizer. Theoret. Comput. Sci. **411**(21), 2084–2100 (2010)

7. Mirjalili, S., Lewis, A.: S-shaped versus V-shaped transfer functions for binary particle swarm optimization. Swarm Evol. Comput. **9**, 1–14 (2013)

8. Saremi, S., Mirjalili, S., Lewis, A.: How important is a transfer function in discrete heuristic algorithms. Neural Comput. Appl. **26**(3), 625–640 (2014). https://doi.org/10.1007/s00521-014-1743-5

9. Liu, J., Mei, Y., Li, X.: An analysis of the inertia weight parameter for binary particle swarm optimization. IEEE Trans. Evol. Comput. 1–16 (2016)

10. Rashedi, E., Nezamabadi-Pour, H., Saryazdi, S.: BGSA: binary gravitational search algorithm. Nat. Comput. **9**(3), 727–745 (2010)

Multi-stage COVID-19 Epidemic Modeling Based on PSO and SEIR

Haiyun Qiu[1], Jinsong Chen[2], and Ben Niu[1(✉)]

[1] College of Management, Shenzhen University, Shenzhen 518060, China
[2] Department of Industrial Engineering and Management, National Yunlin University of Science and Technology, Douliu 64002, Yunlin, Taiwan

Abstract. In this study, based on the characteristics and the transmission mechanism of COVID-19, SEIR epidemiological model is employed for modeling and analysis, utilizing the data of Hubei Province. To optimize the key epidemic parameters of the proposed SEIR model, a stochastic computational intelligence approach, the Particle Swarm Optimization (PSO) is introduced. To better analyze the epidemic, the data between January 20, 2020 to March 25, 2020 is selected and divided into four stages. The parameters are dynamically changeable at different stages of the epidemic, which shows the effectiveness of public health prevention and control measures. Moreover, the Genetic Algorithm (GA) and the Bacterial Foraging Optimization (BFO) are also executed for comparison. The experimental results demonstrate that all swarm intelligence algorithms mentioned above can help forecast COVID-19, and PSO shows the advantages of faster convergence speed and the capability of finding a better set of solutions in fewer iterations, particularly.

Keywords: COVID-19 · SEIR Model · Swarm Intelligence · Particle Swarm Optimization · Prevention and Control Measures

1 Introduction

A novel coronavirus disease (COVID-19) has rapidly spread, attracting worldwide attention since late 2019. Since the outbreak of the epidemic, three methods, i.e., curve fitting [1, 2], epidemic dynamics modeling and artificial intelligence algorithms [3] have been widely employed for prediction [4].

Epidemic dynamics modeling is a basic mathematical method in infectious disease research. In particular, the compartment model [5] is largely applied. It defines several states and tells the spread mechanism by simulating the transformation between different states. At present, the SEIR model, one of the classic compartment models, is frequently used to study COVID-19. Wu et al. [6] estimated the initial infected cases imported from Wuhan in the baseline scenario through an SEIR epidemiological model. Peng et al. [7] proposed a generalized SEIR model, introducing a new quarantined state to analyze the epidemic. Wang et al. [8] set the parameters of the SEIR model based on previous experimental results, which shows the limitation that these static parameters is

© Springer Nature Switzerland AG 2021
Y. Tan and Y. Shi (Eds.): ICSI 2021, LNCS 12689, pp. 265–274, 2021.
https://doi.org/10.1007/978-3-030-78743-1_24

unsuitable to analyze the situation at different stages. To avoid the limitation mentioned above, Fang et al. [9] revised the parameters artificially through grid search, which might inevitably cause deviations.

Via simulation of herd animals such as birds, Kennedy and Eberhart introduced PSO [10], which is now a classic computational intelligence algorithm. And it has become a popular optimization method in medical research by virtue of its high convergence speed, simple mathematics and good accuracy. For instance, Zeng et al. [11] developed PSO with switching delay, then applied it for optimization of the support vector machine (SVM) model's parameters, developing an effective method to diagnose the Alzheimer's disease. Navaneeth and Suchetha [12] put forward a combined architecture and also introduced PSO for parameter optimization, which help detect and classify diseases.

Motivated by above discussion, our major objective is model modification based on the characteristics and transmission mechanism of COVID-19. Meanwhile, we try to use the PSO algorithm as an available stochastic approach to optimize a set of model solutions. The goal of the optimization solver is to minimize the errors between the actual data and the predicted data by varying the improved SEIR model's parameters. The PSO algorithm provides a stochastic method instead of the standard deterministic method in solving SEIR model. Then, impact of public health initiatives on the epidemic can be further analyzed through the changes of key parameters. Moreover, the Genetic Algorithm (GA) and the Bacterial Foraging Optimization (BFO) are also executed for comparison.

2   SEIR Modeling of COVID-19

2.1   Data Sources

Data of Hubei Province are gathered from the National Health Commission of the People's Republic of China (abbreviated as NHC) [13], including current quarantined cases and cumulative cases of infection, death and cure. It is noteworthy that the Wuhan Municipal Health Commission has released two statements [14]: The number of newly confirmed cases on February 20, 2020 has been revised to 631, and the cumulative number of confirmed, recovered and dead cases on April 16, 2020 have been revised to 50333, 46335, 3869 respectively.

2.2   Modified SEIR Model of COVID-19

The classical SEIR model [15] simulates the dynamic transformation of people between four different states of an epidemic phenomenon (see Fig. 1), i.e., susceptible (S), exposed (E), infectious (I) and removed (R). The constant $N = S + E + I + R$ means the entire local population. The classic SEIR model does not consider the changes in the mobility, birth and mortality rate of the population, providing a basic model for the study of infectious diseases [15].

According to transmission mechanism and characteristics of COVID-19, we improved the classic SEIR model to better study the epidemic (see Fig. 2), introducing six different states to generalize the classical model, i.e., $S(t)$, $E(t)$, $I(t)$, $H(t)$, $R(t)$

and $D(t)$. These six different states denote the respective number of the susceptible cases, exposed cases, infectious and unconfirmed cases (with infectious capacity and without intervention), hospitalized cases (confirmed and treated), recovered cases and death cases at time t. The major parameters of the improved model are defined as Table 1. Details are as followed.

- January 19th, 2020, human-to-human transmission was confirmed. Since then, the Chinese government has applied rigorous isolation measures, including centralized isolation and self-isolation, to stem the spread of the virus from person to person. Thus, another new state of the exposed category is considered in the improved model, stimulating the situation where the uninfected people re-convert into the susceptible category after a prescribed quarantine period.
- The symptoms of COVID-19 are similar to some common cold, so it is difficult for patients to detect the bad condition in time. Besides, the epidemic is highly contagious, and if medical resources fail to meet the needs, it would also be difficult for the infected person to be diagnosed and treated in time. Referring to Peng et al. (2020) [7], the modified model adds the category of confirmed and hospitalized people, which is supposed not to contact with others. It is linked to the infective category through a parameter of the time reciprocal from infection to treatment.
- As COVID-19 has a certain fatality rate, the modified model separates the original R state into the recovered category and the death category. The two new states are linked to the confirmed and hospitalized category through the cure rate and the mortality rate respectively.
- With the continuous improvement of prevention and control measures, the domestic epidemic has gone through several stages, which means that the parameters of the model should be dynamically changeable.

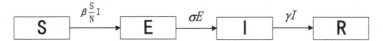

Fig. 1. The classic SEIR compartment model.

The prospective evolution is: under a certain probability (β), the susceptible category (S) is distinctly possible to turn into the exposed (E) after contacting with the infectious and unconfirmed cases (I). The exposed category has two states. Individuals with a probability (P_E) pass into the infectious and unconfirmed category after an incubation time ($1/\sigma_1$), while the rest ($1 - P_E$) goes back to the susceptible category after a quarantine time (λ). The infective persons are hospitalized and treated (become H) after being detected (normally in a time lag $1/\sigma_2$). Then they involve into the recovered category or the death category through the recovery rate (μ) or the mortality rate (κ), respectively. The mathematical description of the improved SEIR model is shown below:

$$\frac{dS(t)}{dt} = -\beta I(t) \cdot \frac{S(t)}{N} + \frac{1}{\lambda}(1 - P_E)E(t) \tag{1}$$

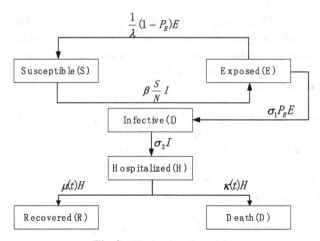

Fig. 2. The improved model.

Table 1. Definition of parameters.

Parameters	Meaning of parameters
β	Social contact transmission rate
λ	Quarantine time
σ_1	Inverse of the average incubation period
P_E	Proportion of virus carriers among exposed persons
σ_2	Inverse of the time lag from infection to treatment
μ	Recovery rate
κ	Mortality rate

$$\frac{dE(t)}{dt} = \beta I(t) \cdot \frac{S(t)}{N} - \frac{1}{\lambda}(1 - P_E)E(t) - \sigma_1 P_E E(t) \tag{2}$$

$$\frac{dI(t)}{dt} = \sigma_1 P_E E(t) - \sigma_2 I(t) \tag{3}$$

$$\frac{dH(t)}{dt} = \sigma_2 I(t) - \mu(t)H(t) - \kappa(t)H(t) \tag{4}$$

$$\frac{dR(t)}{dt} = \mu(t)H(t) \tag{5}$$

$$\frac{dD(t)}{dt} = \kappa(t)H(t) \tag{6}$$

3 Parameter Estimation of the Model

3.1 The PSO Algorithm

In PSO, particles reach the searching space with random initialized locations. Then, in order to find the optimal positions of the population and the particle itself, each particle keeps moving around. For each iteration, by tracking the determined optimal positions, position and velocity of each particle are prepared to be updated. The formulas of the update behavior are defined by:

$$V_{id}(t+1) = \omega(t)V_{id}(t) + c_1 r_1 [P_{b,id} - X_{id}(t)] + c_2 r_2 [P_{g,d} - X_{id}(t)] \tag{7}$$

$$X_{id}(t+1) = X_{id}(t) + V_{id}(t+1) \tag{8}$$

At iteration t, in dimension d of the particle i, the position and velocity can be respectively described by $X_{id}(t)$ and $V_{id}(t)$. As previously introduced, $P_{g,d}$ and $P_{b,id}$ are the optimal positions of the population and particle i, respectively. c_1 and c_2 are coefficients, which are generally considered as learning factors. Besides, in each update of velocity, r_1 and r_2 are randomly generated from interval [0,1]. In order to regulate the search process, $\omega(t)$ is introduced as inertia weight. $\omega(t)$ is determined by Eq. (9) below, where ω_{max} is 0.9 and ω_{min} is 0.4 [16], and $iter$ and $itmax$ respectively represent the number of current and maximum iteration.

$$\omega(t) = \omega_{max} - (\omega_{max} - \omega_{min}) \times \frac{iter}{it\,max} \tag{9}$$

3.2 Modified SEIR Model Optimized by PSO Algorithm

Root Mean Square Error (RMSE) is regularly employed in prediction problems for evaluation. The objective function is set as the sum of the RMSE between the actual data and the predicted data of S, E, I, H, R and D in this paper. The calculation formula of RMSE is as follows, where $Actual_i$ and $Predict_i$ respectively represent the actual data and the predicted data of a certain category on the i-th day in a certain stage, and T represents the total number of days in a certain stage.

$$RMSE = \sqrt{\frac{\sum_{i=1}^{T} Actual_i - Predict_i}{T}} \tag{10}$$

The PSO-SEIR algorithm is described as follows, with the goal of minimizing the objective function.

- Step 1. Initialize particles' positions and velocities. Both of them are $n \times d$ matrices, where n and d represent the number of individuals and model's dimensions, respectively. Particularly, d can also be considered as the four main output parameters, i.e., β, P_E, σ_1, σ_2 of the modified SEIR model.
- Step 2. For each particle with all dimensions, calculate the objective function value.

- Step 3. Update the best personal position.
- Step 4. Update the best global position.
- Step 5. Update each of the particles' position and velocity using the Eqs. (7) and (8). Importantly, make sure that the updated positions and velocities are all within the limitation.
- Step 6. Repeat Step 2–5 until the end condition is satisfied, which happens when the iteration reaches the maximum number or the fitness value is less than the previously determined value.
- Step 7. Each dimension of the final global position $P_{g,d}$ is corresponding to β, P_E, σ_1 and σ_2. Substitute them into the model to calculate data series $\{S, E, I, H, R, D\}$.

3.3 Parameter Estimation and Analysis

On January 23, 2020, to stem the virus from spreading, Wuhan City was decided to seal off. Afterwards, the same initiative was followed by several cities in Hubei Province. And in late March, outbound travel restrictions in Hubei were lifted. To avoid the influence of population mobility, data between Jan. 20 and Mar. 25 are selected to study COVID-19. The epidemic process is divided into four stages according to the epidemic prevention measures. The first stage is the outbreak period between Jan. 20 and Jan. 31; the second stage is the rapid spread period between Feb. 1and Feb. 11; the third stage is the initial containment period between Feb. 12 and Feb. 25; the fourth stage is the orderly recovery period between Feb. 26 and Mar. 25.

Initial value of each category is set to execute the modified SEIR model. N is set to 59170000, which is the population of Hubei Province. The calculation of E_0 is based on the infectious cases and their daily effective number of contacts. Yang et al. [3] proposed that the number of contacts is 3 after Jan. 23 and 10 after Mar. 1. I_0 is calculated based on the newly confirmed cases over a period of time. Besides, the settings of H_0, R_0 and D_0 can be determined from the actual data.

As previously introduced, $\{\beta, P_E, \lambda, \sigma_1, \sigma_2, \mu, \kappa\}$ are major parameters of the model. According to the requirements of epidemic prevention, the λ parameter is set to 14. Parameters μ and κ can be calculated based on actual data, and the fitting results of them are shown in Fig. 3 respectively.

The initial setting of PSO algorithm is: population size $PN = 40$, dimension $Di = 4$, learning factors $c_1 = c_2 = 2$, maximal velocity $vmax = 0.2$, maximal iteration $itmax = 1000$ and the search space is [0,1]. Utilizing the PSO algorithm, the system parameters are calculated, see Table 2.

In Table 2, it could be observed that the range of $1/\sigma_1$ (the inverse of the average incubation period) is approximately from 1.4 to 6.8, which is basically in line with reality. β (social contact transmission rate) and P_E (the proportion of the virus carriers in the exposed) are greatly reduced while $1/\sigma_2$ (the inverse of the time lag from infection to treatment) is increased, which can be explained by the prevention and control measures proposed at each stage. At the first stage, government issued public health first-level response and cancel mass gatherings, which help to reduce the possibility of healthy people coming into contact with the infected people. With the medical support from other regions and two newly built hospitals at the second stage, the time lag of infected people to be diagnosed and hospitalized could significantly decrease. What's more, people have

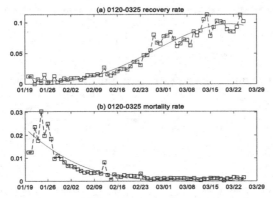

Fig. 3. Actual recovery rates, mortality rates and their fitting results.

Table 2. System parameters at different stages.

Stage	β	P_E	σ_1	σ_2
Jan. 20 to Jan. 31	0.9984	0.9901	0.1461	0.1648
Feb. 1 to Feb. 11	0.3230	0.3668	0.2667	0.2394
Feb. 12 to Feb. 25	0.0653	0.2725	0.6935	0.3940
Feb. 26 to Mar. 25	0.0014	0.2089	0.2855	0.4959

an obligation to improve their self-protection capabilities, such as minimizing outings, wearing masks when traveling and keeping hands clean, etc., which can significantly help stem the virus from human-human transmission. The third stage is the most critical stage, where experts predicted that the epidemic was about to reach its peak. Since then, the implementation of epidemic prevention and control strategies has gradually normalized.

With all the required parameters, data series $\{S, E, I, H, R, D\}$ can be predicted by the modified SEIR model. The prediction results of the current confirmed cases, recovered cases and death cases at each stage are shown in Fig. 4. In the same time, the GA-SEIR model and the BFO-SEIR model are also executed for comparison. The predictive ability is evaluated utilizing the Mean Absolute Error (MAE) function. The comparison results are presented in Table 3, and the fitness curves at each stage are shown in Fig. 5.

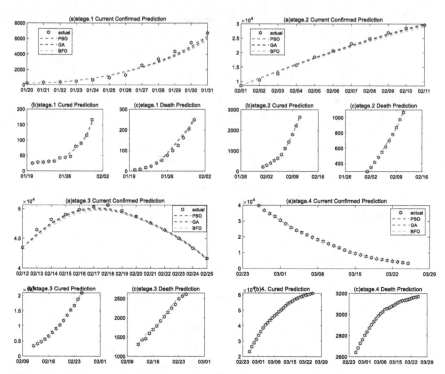

Fig. 4. Prediction results of the current confirmed, recovered and death cases at each stage.

Table 3. MAE values of each model at each stage.

	Jan. 20 to Jan. 31			Feb. 1 to Feb. 11			Feb. 12 to Feb. 25			Feb. 26 to Mar. 25		
	PSO	GA	BFO	PSO	GA	BFO	PSO	GA	BFO	PSO	GA	BFO
H	321.4	**262.0**	380.6	419.5	**343.6**	672.0	305.3	**202.4**	427.9	**232.0**	240.5	234.3
R	3.78	**3.10**	3.84	**12.46**	14.64	23.58	92.90	**90.60**	97.08	586.1	**552.3**	617.4
D	**6.25**	9.52	8.62	10.20	10.17	**7.29**	32.08	33.89	**30.42**	4.65	**4.19**	5.06

Note: The bold value represents the minimum MAE of a certain category in a certain stage

Figure 4 shows that PSO, GA, BFO are capable to be implemented for the epidemic prediction based on the proposed SEIR model. Meanwhile, from Table 3, it is intuitive to see that the predictive abilities of PSO-SEIR and GA-SEIR are better than BFO-SEIR overall. And the PSO algorithm also shows the advantages of faster convergence speed and accuracy (see Fig. 5).

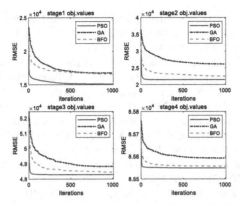

Fig. 5. Fitness curve of each model at each stage.

4 Conclusion

In this study, with a focus on Hubei Province, China, an SEIR epidemiological model is proposed to analyze COVID-19, a novel coronavirus disease spread across the world at the beginning of December 2019. Data from January 20, 2020 to March 25, 2020 are selected to avoid the impact of the population mobility rate on the epidemic model.

Based on the classic SEIR model, this model properly considers the intrinsic impact of isolation measures, taking into account the quarantine period. Thus, another new state of the exposed category is considered in the improved model to simulate the situation where the uninfected people re-convert into the susceptible category after a prescribed quarantine period.

Moreover, PSO is introduced for optimization of the key parameters of the improved model, providing a stochastic method instead of the standard deterministic method to solve SEIR model. The parameters are dynamically changeable at different stages of the epidemic, which shows the effectiveness of prevention and control initiatives.

The GA and the BFO algorithm based on the proposed SEIR model are also executed for comparison. The experimental results demonstrate that based on the proposed SEIR model, the PSO, GA and BFO can be applied for COVID-19 prediction. Particularly, the PSO algorithm shows the advantages of faster convergence speed and the ability to find the best set of model solutions in less iteration.

Acknowledgement. The work described in this paper was supported by The Natural Science Foundation of China (Grant No.71971143, 71571120); Natural Science Foundation of Guangdong Province (Grant No. 2020A1515010749); Key Research Foundation of Higher Education of Guangdong Provincial Education Bureau (Grant No. 2019KZDXM030), and Guangdong Province Postgraduate Education Innovation Research Project (Grant No. 2019SFKC46).

References

1. Zhao, S., Lin, Q., Ran, J., et al.: Preliminary estimation of the basic reproduction number of novel coronavirus (2019-nCoV) in China, from 2019 to 2020: a data-driven analysis in the early phase of the outbreak. Int. J. Infect. Dis. **92**, 214–217 (2020)

2. Zhao, S., Musa, S., Lin, Q., et al.: Estimating the unreported number of novel coronavirus (2019-nCoV) cases in China in the first half of january 2020: a data-driven modelling analysis of the early outbreak. J. Clin. Med. **9**(2), 388 (2020)

3. Yang, Z., Zeng, Z., Wang, K.: Modified SEIR and AI prediction of the epidemics trend of COVID-19 in China under public health interventions. J. Thorac. Dis. **12**(3), 165 (2020)

4. Huang, L., Wei, Y., Shen, S., et al.: Evaluation of predictive models for novel coronavirus pneumonia. Chin. J. Health Stat. **37**(03), 322–326 (2020)

5. Kermack, W.O., McKendrick, A.G.: Contribution to the mathematical theory of epidemics. Proc. R. Soc. Lond. Ser. B-Contain. Papers Abiological Char. **115**(772), 700–721 (1927)

6. Wu, J.T., Leung, K., Leung, G.M.: Nowcasting and forecasting the potential domestic and international spread of the 2019-nCoV outbreak originating in Wuhan, China: a modelling study. Lancet **395**(10225), 689–697 (2020)

7. Peng, L., Yang, W., Zhang, D., et al.: Epidemic analysis of COVID-19 in China by dynamical modeling (2020). arXiv:2002.06563

8. Wang, H., Wang, Z., Dong, Y., et al.: Phase-adjusted estimation of the number of Coronavirus Disease 2019 cases in Wuhan. China. Cell Discov. **6**(1), 10 (2020)

9. Fang, Y., Nie, Y., Penny, M.: Transmission dynamics of the COVID-19 outbreak and effectiveness of government interventions: a data-driven analysis. J. Med. Virol. **92**(6), 645–659 (2020)

10. Kennedy, J., Eberhart, R.: Particle swarm optimization. In: 1995 IEEE International Conference on Neural Networks Proceedings, pp. 1942–1948 (1995)

11. Zeng, N., Qiu, H., Wang, Z., et al.: A new switching-delayed-PSO-based optimized SVM algorithm for diagnosis of Alzheimer's disease. Neurocomputing **320**, 195–202 (2018)

12. Navaneeth, B., Suchetha, M.: PSO optimized 1-D CNN-SVM architecture for real-time detection and classification applications. Comput. Biol. Med. **108**, 85–92 (2019)

13. The National Health Commission of the People's Republic of China (NHC). http://www.nhc.gov.cn/. Accessed 25 Feb 2021

14. Wuhan Municipal Health Commission., http://wjw.hubei.gov.cn/. Accessed 25 Feb 2021

15. Aron, J.L., Schwartz, I.B.: Seasonality and period-doubling bifurcations in an epidemic model. J. Theor. Biol. **110**(4), 665–679 (1984)

16. Shi, Y., Eberhart, R.C.: Empirical study of particle swarm optimization. In: Proceedings of the 1999. Congress on Evolutionary Computation-CEC99, pp. 1945–1950 (1999)

Particle Swarms Reformulated Towards a Unified and Flexible Framework

Mauro Sebastián Innocente[(⊠)] [iD]

Autonomous Vehicles & Artificial Intelligence Laboratory (AVAILab),
Coventry University, Coventry, UK
Mauro.S.Innocente@coventry.ac.uk
https://www.availab.org/

Abstract. The Particle Swarm Optimisation (PSO) algorithm has undergone countless modifications and adaptations since its original formulation in 1995. Some of these have become mainstream whereas others have faded away. A myriad of alternative formulations have been proposed raising the question of what the basic features of an algorithm must be to belong in the PSO family. The aim of this paper is to establish what defines a PSO algorithm and to attempt to formulate it in such a way that it encompasses many existing variants. Therefore, different versions of the method may be posed as settings within the proposed unified framework. In addition, the proposed formulation generalises, decouples and incorporates features to the method providing more flexibility to the behaviour of each particle. The closed forms of the trajectory difference equation are obtained, different types of behaviour are identified, stochasticity is decoupled, and traditionally global features such as sociometries and constraint-handling are re-defined as particle's attributes.

Keywords: Particle Swarm Optimisation · Coefficients' settings · Types of behaviour · Trajectory · Learning strategy · Unstructured neighbourhood

1 Introduction

Proposed in 1995 [20], the Particle Swarm Optimisation (PSO) method is a global optimiser in the sense that it is able to escape poor suboptimal attractors by means of a parallel collaborative search. The overall system behaviour emerges from a combination of each particle's individual and social behaviours. The former is manifested by the trajectory of a particle pulled by its attractors, governed by a second order difference equation with three control coefficients. In the classical (and in most) versions of the algorithm, there is one individual attractor given by the particle's best experience, and one social attractor given by the best experience in its neighbourhood. The social behaviour is governed by the way the individually acquired information is shared among particles and therefore propagated throughout the swarm, which is controlled by the neighbourhood topology. The individual and social behaviours interact through the

© Springer Nature Switzerland AG 2021
Y. Tan and Y. Shi (Eds.): ICSI 2021, LNCS 12689, pp. 275–286, 2021.
https://doi.org/10.1007/978-3-030-78743-1_25

update of the social attractor. Thus, the two main features of the algorithm are the *trajectory difference equation* (and the setting of its coefficients) and the *neighbourhood topology* (a.k.a. *sociometry*).

In the early days, numerous empirical studies were carried out to investigate the influence of the coefficients in the *trajectory difference equation* on the overall performance of the method, and to provide guidelines for their settings [21,28]. Early theoretical work [5,25,30] provided insight into how the method works and interesting findings of practical use such as constriction factor(s) [5] to ensure convergence. These pioneering studies were a source of inspiration and set the foundations for an explosion of theoretical work [2–4,9,10,14,17,22,27].

1.1 Trajectory Difference Equation

In *classical PSO* (CPSO), three forces govern a particle's trajectory: the inertia from its previous displacement, the attraction to its own best experience, and the attraction to the best experience in its neighbourhood. The importance awarded to each of them is controlled by three coefficients: the inertia (ω), the individuality (iw), and the sociality (sw) weights. Stochasticity is introduced to enhance exploration via random weights applied to iw and sw. The behaviour of a particle, and by extension of the PSO algorithm as a whole, is very sensitive to the settings of these control coefficients. The system of two 1st-order difference equations for position and velocity updates in the CPSO algorithm proposed in [29] is rearranged in (1) as a single 2nd-order *Trajectory Difference Equation*:

$$
\begin{aligned}
x_{ij}^{(t+1)} = x_{ij}^{(t)} + \omega_{ij}^{(t)} \left(x_{ij}^{(t)} - x_{ij}^{(t-1)} \right) \\
+ iw_{ij}^{(t)} U_{(0,1)} \left(xb_{ij}^{(t)} - x_{ij}^{(t)} \right) + sw_{ij}^{(t)} U_{(0,1)} \left(xb_{kj}^{(t)} - x_{ij}^{(t)} \right)
\end{aligned}
\tag{1}
$$

where $x_{ij}^{(t)}$ is the coordinate j of the *position* of particle i at time-step t; $xb_{ij}^{(t)}$ is the coordinate j of the *best experience* of particle i by time-step t; k is the index identifying the particle with the best experience in the neighbourhood of particle i at time-step t; ω, iw and sw are the inertia, individuality, and sociality weights, respectively (which may depend on i, j, t); and $U_{(0,1)}$ is a random number from a uniform distribution within $[0, 1]$ resampled anew every time it is referenced.

In the original formulation [20], $\omega = 1$ and $iw = sw = 2$. This leads to an unstable system, as particles tend to diverge. The first strategy to prevent this was to bound the size of each component of a particle's displacement, which helps prevent the so-called *explosion* but does not ensure convergence or a fine-grain search. Instead, the coefficients in (1) can be set to ensure that.

1.2 Neighbourhood Topology

The original PSO algorithm [20] presented a global topology in which every particle has access to the memory of every other particle in the swarm. Local

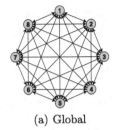 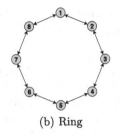 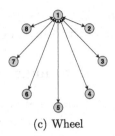

(a) Global   (b) Ring   (c) Wheel

Fig. 1. Three classical neighbourhood topologies in PSO.

topologies were proposed soon thereafter [8]. Since then, a plethora of sociometries have been proposed [1,23,24]. Three classical ones are shown in Fig. 1.

The global topology tends to lead to a rapid loss of diversity, which may lead to premature convergence to a poor suboptimal solution. Whilst this can be controlled to some extent by the settings of the coefficients in the trajectory equation, numerous neighbourhood topologies have been proposed reducing connectivity to delay the propagation of information throughout the swarm.

1.3   Other Features

Other important features of the PSO algorithm are the initialisation of the particles [11,18,19], the synchrony of the memory updates, the size of the swarm [7,26], and the handling of constraints [16].

The PSO algorithm is an unconstrained search method, therefore requiring an external constraint-handling technique (CHT) to be integrated to handle these types of problems. A straightforward CHT is the *Preserving Feasibility Method* [12], in which infeasible experiences are banned from memory. Another one is the *Penalty Method*, in which infeasible solutions are penalised by augmenting the objective function and treating the problem as unconstrained. Some authors propose adaptive penalties by using adaptive coefficients in the penalty function [6] or by adapting the tolerance relaxation [15]. Innocente et al. [13] propose using a *Preserving Feasibility with Priority Rules Method*, in which the objective function values and the constraint violations are treated separately.

Since its original formulation in 1995, countless PSO variants have been proposed. Some of them have become mainstream whereas many others have faded away. Thus, a myriad of alternative formulations have been proposed raising the question of what the basic features of an algorithm must be to belong in the PSO family. The aim of this paper is to establish what defines a PSO algorithm, and to attempt to formulate it in such a way that it encompasses many existing variants so that different versions may be posed as settings within the proposed unified framework. In addition, the proposed formulation generalises, decouples and incorporates new features providing more flexibility to the behaviour of each particle. The remainder of this paper is organised as follows: the overall proposed *Reformulated PSO* is introduced in Sect. 2, with the *Global Features*, the

Individual Behaviour Features and the *Social Behaviour Features* discussed in more details in Sects. 3, 4 and 5, respectively. Conclusions are provided in Sect. 6.

2   Reformulated Particle Swarm Optimisation

The proposed *Reformulated Particle Swarm Optimisation* (RePSO) method is structured in three sets of features: 1) *Global Features* (GFs), 2) *Individual Behaviour Features* (IBFs), and 3) *Social Behaviour Features* (SBFs). Figure 2 shows a high-level description of RePSO, where IBFs and SBFs are both viewed as individual attributes of a particle (*Particle Attributes*).

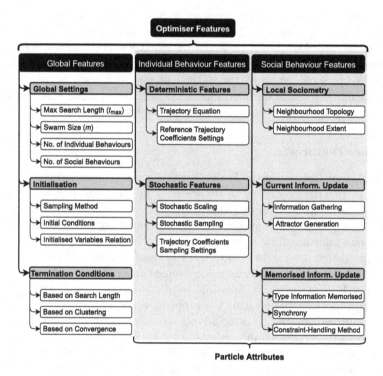

Fig. 2. High-level description of the proposed Reformulated PSO (RePSO).

3   Global Features

Despite being a swarm-intelligent method, some characteristics must still be defined at the swarm level. We define here three main subsets of global features: 1) *Global Settings*, 2) *Initialisation*, and 3) *Termination Conditions*. The first one consists of scalar settings like maximum search length (t_{max}) and swarm size (m), whereas the other two involve methods.

3.1 Initialisation

It is important to identify two aspects of the initialisation in PSO: 1) the *sampling method* to place m points over the search-space, and 2) what *variables* are to be initialised. Note that the particle's position update in RePSO is a 2nd order difference equation as opposed to the classical system of two 1st order difference equations (position and velocity). Therefore, the *variables* potentially involved in the initialisation are the initial, the previous, and the memorised positions $(\mathbf{x}^{(1)}, \mathbf{x}^{(0)}, \mathbf{xm}^{(1)})$ instead of two positions and one velocity $(\mathbf{x}^{(1)}, \mathbf{xm}^{(1)}, \mathbf{v}^{(1)})$.

Sampling Method. Originally, initialisation was purely random from uniform distributions: $x_{ij}^{(1)} = x_{\min\ ij} + U_{(0,1)}\,(x_{\max\ ij} - x_{\min\ ij})$. *Random Sampling* is easy to implement but does not usually result in good coverage of the search-space. More advanced sampling methods may be used, such as *Latin Hypercube Sampling*, *Orthogonal Sampling* or a range of different *Tesselations*.

Initial Conditions. Four types are proposed here:

1. *Stagnation*: $\mathbf{x}^{(1)} = \mathbf{x}^{(0)} = \mathbf{xm}^{(1)}$
   This requires the *sampling* of each particle's position at the initial time-step ($\mathbf{x}^{(1)}$). Stagnation implies that the previous position $\mathbf{x}^{(0)} = \mathbf{x}^{(1)}$, and that the particle has converged to its attractor: $\mathbf{xm}^{(1)} = \mathbf{x}^{(1)}$. Thus, movement starts purely due to cooperation (no inertia, no individual attractor).
2. *Two Positions*: $\mathbf{x}^{(1)} \neq \mathbf{x}^{(0)}$ and either $\mathbf{xm}^{(1)} = \mathbf{x}^{(1)}$ or $\mathbf{xm}^{(1)} = \mathbf{x}^{(0)}$
   Two positions per particle are *sampled* and compared, with the better one becoming $\mathbf{x}^{(1)}$, the other becoming $\mathbf{x}^{(0)}$, and $\mathbf{xm}^{(1)} = \mathbf{x}^{(1)}$. Thus, movement starts both due to cooperation and to inertia (no individual attractor).
3. *One Position and One Memory*: $\mathbf{x}^{(1)} = \mathbf{x}^{(0)} \neq \mathbf{xm}^{(1)}$
   Two positions per particle are *sampled* and compared, with the better one becoming $\mathbf{xm}^{(1)}$ and the other $\mathbf{x}^{(1)} = \mathbf{x}^{(0)}$. Movement starts due to both cooperation and acceleration towards its individual attractor (no inertia).
4. *Two Positions and One Memory* $\mathbf{x}^{(1)} \neq \mathbf{x}^{(0)} \neq \mathbf{xm}^{(1)} \neq \mathbf{x}^{(1)}$
   Three positions per particle are *sampled* and compared, with the best one becoming $\mathbf{xm}^{(1)}$. Thus, movement starts both due to all three sources: cooperation, inertia, and acceleration towards its individual attractor.

Initialised Variables Relation. For all *initial conditions* other than *stagnation*, more than one position is to be *sampled* per particle. The question is then whether these should be somehow related. Three alternatives are proposed here:

1. *Perturbation*: $\mathbf{x}^{(0)}$ is generated from controlled perturbations on $\mathbf{x}^{(1)}$. If applicable, $\mathbf{xm}^{(1)}$ is also generated from perturbations on $\mathbf{x}^{(1)}$.
2. *Independent*: Each population of positions is sampled independently.
3. *Simultaneous*: All populations of positions are sampled at once. For instance, if using the Latin Hypercube Sampling, there would be one single sampling with as many points as twice or three times the swarm size, as applicable.

3.2   Termination Conditions

The population-based nature of the method enables termination conditions different from the classical ones in numerical optimisation: 1) maximum number of iterations, and 2) convergence. Three types of conditions are identified here: 1) *based on search length* (or maximum number of iterations), 2) *based on clustering measures* (diversity loss), and 3) *based on measures of convergence*.

4   Individual Behaviour Features

These are the features of the algorithm which control the individual behaviour of a particle. Each particle has its own set of IBFs, which are viewed as particle attributes. The individual behaviour of a particle is materialised by its trajectory as it is pulled by its attractor. This is governed by a second order difference equation and the setting of its coefficients. The IBFs are grouped here in two main families, namely *Deterministic Features* and *Stochastic Features*.

4.1   Deterministic Features

Instead of viewing PSO as a *guided random search method*, it is viewed as a *randomly-weighted deterministic search method*. Thus, its desired deterministic behaviour is defined, adding only as much stochasticity as deemed beneficial.

By formulating the position update as in (5), it is clear that any given particle at any given time is pulled by a single attractor which results from a randomly weighted average of the components of the individual and social attractors. Thus, the *Trajectory Difference Equation* in (1) may be expressed as in (5).

$$iw_{ij}^{(t)} U_{(0,1)} \left(xb_{ij}^{(t)} - x_{ij}^{(t)} \right) + sw_{ij}^{(t)} U_{(0,1)} \left(xb_{kj}^{(t)} - x_{ij}^{(t)} \right) = \phi_{ij}^{(t)} \left(p_{ij}^{(t)} - x_{ij}^{(t)} \right) \quad (2)$$

$$\phi_{ij}^{(t)} = \iota_{ij}^{(t)} + \sigma_{ij}^{(t)} = iw_{ij}^{(t)} U_{(0,1)} + sw_{ij}^{(t)} U_{(0,1)} \quad (3)$$

$$p_{ij}^{(t)} = \frac{\iota_{ij}^{(t)} xb_{ij}^{(t)} + \sigma_{ij}^{(t)} xb_{kj}^{(t)}}{\phi_{ij}^{(t)}} \quad (4)$$

$$x_{ij}^{(t+1)} = x_{ij}^{(t)} + \omega_{ij}^{(t)} \left(x_{ij}^{(t)} - x_{ij}^{(t-1)} \right) + \phi_{ij}^{(t)} \left(p_{ij}^{(t)} - x_{ij}^{(t)} \right) \quad (5)$$

Trajectory Equation. Since we are dealing with a single particle, sub-index i is dropped. For simplicity, let us assume (ω, ϕ) constant in every dimension and $\forall t$, dropping sub-index j and super-index (t). If stochasticity is removed, the deterministic coefficients $(\hat{\omega}, \hat{\phi})$ are referred to as *Reference Trajectory Coefficients*.

CPSO Recurrence Formulation. The *CPSO Recurrence Formulation* is as in (6), which is the deterministic version of (5). The generation of the overall attractor $\mathbf{p}_i^{(t)}$ is now decoupled, comprising a *Social Behaviour Feature* (SBF).

$$x_{ij}^{(t+1)} = x_{ij}^{(t)} + \hat{\omega}\left(x_{ij}^{(t)} - x_{ij}^{(t-1)}\right) + \hat{\phi}\left(p_{ij}^{(t)} - x_{ij}^{(t)}\right) \tag{6}$$

CPSO Closed-Form Formulation. This is obtained by solving the difference equation in (6). The roots of the characteristic polynomial are as in (7) and (8). The solution is per dimension and per particle (therefore dropping indices i and j), and the attractor $\mathbf{p}$ is stationary.

$$r_1 = \frac{1 + \hat{\omega} - \hat{\phi}}{2} + \frac{\gamma}{2} \quad ; \quad r_2 = \frac{1 + \hat{\omega} - \hat{\phi}}{2} - \frac{\gamma}{2} \tag{7}$$

$$\gamma = \sqrt{\hat{\phi}^2 - (2\hat{\omega} + 2)\,\hat{\phi} + (\hat{\omega} - 1)^2} \tag{8}$$

Case 1 ($\gamma^2 > 0$). The two roots of the characteristic polynomial are real-valued and different ($r_1 \neq r_2$). Therefore the closed-form for *Case 1* is as in (9).

$$x^{(t)} = p + \frac{r_2\left(p - x^{(0)}\right) - \left(p - x^{(1)}\right)}{\gamma}r_1^t + \frac{-r_1\left(p - x^{(0)}\right) + \left(p - x^{(1)}\right)}{\gamma}r_2^t \tag{9}$$

Case 2 ($\gamma^2 = 0$). The two roots of the characteristic polynomial are the same ($r_1 = r_2$), as shown in (10). Therefore the closed-form for *Case 2* is as in (11).

$$r = r_1 = r_2 = \frac{1 + \hat{\omega} - \hat{\phi}}{2} \tag{10}$$

$$x^{(t)} = p + \left[-\left(p - x^{(0)}\right) + \left(\left(p - x^{(0)}\right) - \frac{2\left(p - x^{(1)}\right)}{1 + \hat{\omega} - \hat{\phi}}\right)t\right]\left(\frac{1 + \hat{\omega} - \hat{\phi}}{2}\right)^t \tag{11}$$

Case 3 ($\gamma^2 < 0$). The two roots are complex conjugates.

$$r_1 = \frac{1 + \hat{\omega} - \hat{\phi}}{2} + \left(\frac{\gamma'}{2}\right)i \quad ; \quad r_2 = \frac{1 + \hat{\omega} - \hat{\phi}}{2} - \left(\frac{\gamma'}{2}\right)i \tag{12}$$

$$\gamma' = \sqrt{-\gamma^2} = \sqrt{-\hat{\phi}^2 + (2\hat{\omega} + 2)\,\hat{\phi} - (\hat{\omega} - 1)^2} \tag{13}$$

Using polar coordinates (ρ, θ), the closed-form for *Case 3* is as in (16).

$$\rho = \sqrt{\hat{\omega}} \quad ; \quad \theta = \text{acos}\left(\frac{1 + \hat{\omega} - \hat{\phi}}{2\sqrt{\hat{\omega}}}\right) \tag{14}$$

$$\cos(\theta) = \frac{1}{\sqrt{\hat{\omega}}}\left(\frac{1 + \hat{\omega} - \hat{\phi}}{2}\right) \quad ; \quad \sin(\theta) = \frac{1}{\sqrt{\hat{\omega}}}\left(\frac{\gamma'}{2}\right) \tag{15}$$

$$\boxed{\begin{aligned} x^{(t)} = {}& p - \sqrt{\hat{\omega}}^{t}\left(p - x^{(0)}\right)\cos(\theta t) + \\ & \sqrt{\hat{\omega}}^{t}\left(\frac{\left(1 + \hat{\omega} - \hat{\phi}\right)\left(p - x^{(0)}\right) - 2\left(p - x^{(1)}\right)}{\gamma'}\right)\sin(\theta t) \end{aligned}} \tag{16}$$

Thus, the chosen trajectory equation in RePSO may be given by the *Recurrence Formulation* in (6) or by the *Closed-Form Formulations* in (9), (11) and (16). Other recurrence formulations as well as some considerantions to be taken into account for the closed-form formulation are left for future work.

Reference Trajectory Coefficients Settings. An analysis of the trajectory closed-forms shows that the magnitude of the dominant root $r = \max(\|r_1\|, \|r_2\|)$ controls convergence. Fastest convergence occurs for $(\hat{\phi}, \hat{\omega}) = (1, 0)$, where $r = 0$ (see Fig. 3(a)). The resulting convergence conditions are shown in (17), which define the area inside the convergence triangle ($r < 1$) shown in Fig. 3.

$$\boxed{\begin{aligned} & 1 > \hat{\omega} > \frac{\hat{\phi}}{2} - 1 \\ & \hat{\phi} > 0 \end{aligned}} \tag{17}$$

Whilst the magnitude of the dominant root controls the speed of convergence, the existence and sign of the dominant root controls the *Type of Behaviour*:

1. *Oscillatory*: Roots are complex conjugates (no dominant root).
2. *Monotonic*: Dominant root is real-valued and positive.
3. *Zigzagging*: Dominant root is real-valued and negative.

These *Types of Behaviour* are bounded within specific *Sectors* in the $(\hat{\omega}, \hat{\phi})$ plane, each associated with one edge of triangular isolines (same r). These three *Sectors* are shown in Fig. 3(b), where the white triangle separates the *Convergence* (inside) and *Divergence* regions. The settings of $(\hat{\omega}, \hat{\phi})$ can be chosen so as to achieve the desired behaviour and convergence speed. For example:

1. Choose *Type of Behaviour*: e.g. *Oscillatory*.
2. Set *Convergence Speed*: $\sqrt{\hat{\omega}} \in [0, 1]$, with fastest convergence for $\sqrt{\hat{\omega}} = 0$.
3. Set *Reference Acceleration Coefficient*: $\hat{\phi} \in \left(\left(\sqrt{\hat{\omega}} - 1\right)^2, \left(\sqrt{\hat{\omega}} + 1\right)^2\right)$.

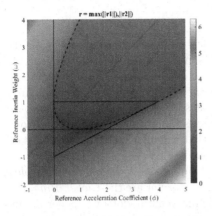
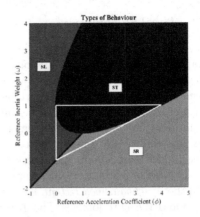

Fig. 3. On the left, magnitude of the dominant root. Settings inside red triangle ensure convergence ($r < 1$). On the right, *Sectors* for three *Types of Behaviour* in CPSO: black region is *Oscillatory*, dark grey region is *Monotonic*, and light grey region is *Zigzagging*.

4.2 Stochastic Features

The random weights in (1) affect the trajectory of a particle towards the overall attractor whilst also affecting its generation as a stochastic convex combination of the individual and the social attractors, as shown in (4). These two features are decoupled here. The *Stochastic Features* are concerned only with the former.

Stochastic Scaling. This refers to whether the stochastic variables in (5) are sampled once per particle position update (*vector scaling*) or resampled anew per dimension as well (*component scaling*). The former is often used by mistake.

Stochastic Sampling. In classical PSO, $\omega = \hat{\omega}$ (deterministic) whereas the probability distribution of ϕ results from the sum of two stochastic terms sampled from uniform distributions: $\phi = \iota + \sigma$ as in (3). If they are sampled from the same interval, the resulting distribution of ϕ is triangular. Otherwise, it is trapezoidal. In RePSO, the user is allowed to choose any distribution for (ω, ϕ).

Trajectory Coefficients Sampling Settings. Once the distributions have been chosen, the parameters defining them must be set. For example, $(\phi_{\min}, \phi_{\max})$ for a uniform distribution, or the standard deviation for a normal distribution.

5   Social Behaviour Features

These are the features of the algorithm which control the social behaviour of a particle. Despite being SBFs, they are defined as *Particle Attributes* in RePSO. A particle's social behaviour is governed by its access to other particles' memories (*Local Sociometry*) and by how it handles this information (social influence).

5.1 Local Sociometry

In classical PSO, the sociometry is a global feature. It can be defined as a regular graph, or irregulary by defining one connection at a time. In the latter case, the structure cannot be automatically generated nor is it scalable. In RePSO, a *Local Sociometry* is defined for each particle, with the *Global Sociometry* resulting from their assembly. This has the advantange that sociometry is a particle attribute, facilitating object-oriented implementation. Also that different social behaviours can be exhibited by different particles, and that irregular global sociometries are possible without renouncing automation or scalability.

The Local Sociometry is generated by defining the *Neighbourhood Topology* and the *Neighbourhood Extent*. Examples of the former are the *Global, Ring, Forward* and *Wheel* topologies. The *Topology* defines a methodology to generate connections from the particle informed to its informers. The *Extent* defines the neighbourhood size (number of neighbours, distance of influence). An example of an unstructured neighbourhood is shown in Fig. 4, where the Local Sociometry of particle 1 is the *Global* topology whilst that of particle 2 is the *Ring* topology. Other aspects may be considered, such as whether a particle's memory is part of its neighbourhood (X in the connectivity matrix in Fig. 4).

	1	2	3	4	5	6	7	8
1	X	1	1	1	1	1	1	1
2	1	X	1	0	0	0	0	0
3	1	1	X	1	1	0	0	0
4	0	0	1	X	1	0	0	0
5	0	0	0	0	X	1	1	0
6	0	0	0	0	1	X	1	0
7	1	1	1	1	1	1	X	1
8	1	0	0	0	0	0	1	X

(a) Sociometry   (b) Connectivity Matrix

Fig. 4. Unstructured sociometry emerging from local sociometries.

5.2 Current Information Update

Any particle holds two types of information: *current* and *memorised*. The update of the former takes place by gathering information, generating an overall attractor using the information gathered, and applying the trajectory equation. A particle may access the information currently held, the one memorised, or both from its neighbours (*Information Gathering*). This is an extension to classical formulations, where a particle can only access their memorised information.

5.3 Memorised Information Update

This controls the update of a particle's memory when it accesses new information. This is performed directly rather than through a trajectory equation. The question is what *Type of Information* is accessible to a particle's memory.

Another feature affecting this update is the *Synchrony*, which defines whether a particle's memory is updated immediately after its currently held information is updated (asynchronous) or only after the currently held information of every particle is updated (synchronous). Typically, the update is synchronous.

RePSO also proposes to include the CHTs here. Thus, different particles may have different CHTs, and therefore may value a given location differently.

6 Conclusions

A general framework has been proposed aiming to encompass many variants of the PSO algorithm under one umbrella so that different versions may be posed as settings within the proposed unified framework. In addition, some extensions to the classical PSO method have been made such as the decoupling of the stochasticity that affects both the acceleration coefficient (ϕ) and the generation of the overall attractor; an extended treatment of the swarm initialisation; the particle trajectory closed forms; the identification of three types of deterministic behaviour to inform the setting of the control coefficients; and the global sociometry resulting from assembling local sociometries defined as particle attributes. Due to space constraints, most of these features are discussed only superficially.

References

1. Blackwell, T., Kennedy, J.: Impact of communication topology in particle swarm optimization. IEEE Trans. Evol. Comput. **23**(4), 689–702 (2019)
2. Bonyadi, M., Michalewicz, Z.: Impacts of coefficients on movement patterns in the particle swarm optimization algorithm. IEEE Trans. Evol. Comput. **21**, 378–390 (2017)
3. Campana, E.F., Fasano, G., Pinto, A.: Dynamic analysis for the selection of parameters and initial population, in particle swarm optimization. J. Global Optim. **48**, 347–397 (2010)
4. Cleghorn, C.W., Engelbrecht, A.P.: Particle swarm variants: standardized convergence analysis. Swarm Intell. **9**(2–3), 177–203 (2015)
5. Clerc, M., Kennedy, J.: The particle swarm - explosion, stability, and convergence in a multidimensional complex space. IEEE Trans. Evol. Comput. **6**(1), 58–73 (2002)
6. Coello Coello, C.A.: Use of a self-adaptive penalty approach for engineering optimization problems. Comput. Ind. **41**(2), 113–127 (2000)
7. Dhal, K.G., Das, A., Sahoo, S., Das, R., Das, S.: Measuring the curse of population size over swarm intelligence based algorithms. Evol. Syst. (2019)
8. Eberhart, R., Kennedy, J.: A new optimizer using particle swarm theory. In: Proceedings of the Sixth International Symposium on Micro Machine and Human Science, MHS 1995, pp. 39–43 (1995)
9. Fernández Martínez, J.L., García Gonzalo, E.: The PSO family: deduction, stochastic analysis and comparison. Swarm Intell. **3**(4), 245 (2009)
10. García-Gonzalo, E., Fernández-Martínez, J.L.: Convergence and stochastic stability analysis of particle swarm optimization variants with generic parameter distributions. Appl. Math. Comput. **249**, 286–302 (2014)
11. Helwig, S., Wanka, R.: Theoretical analysis of initial particle swarm behavior. In: Rudolph, G., Jansen, T., Beume, N., Lucas, S., Poloni, C. (eds.) PPSN 2008. LNCS, vol. 5199, pp. 889–898. Springer, Heidelberg (2008). https://doi.org/10.1007/978-3-540-87700-4_88

12. Hu, X., Eberhart, R.: Solving constrained nonlinear optimization problems with particle swarm optimization. In: Proceedings of the 6th World Multi-conference on Systemics, Cybernetics and Informatics (SCI 2002) (2002)

13. Innocente, M.S., Afonso, S.M.B., Sienz, J., Davies, H.M.: Particle swarm algorithm with adaptive constraint handling and integrated surrogate model for the management of petroleum fields. Appl. Soft Comput. **34**, 463–484 (2015)

14. Innocente, M.S., Sienz, J.: Particle swarm optimization with inertia weight and constriction factor. In: Proceedings of the 2011 International conference on swarm intelligence (ICSI 2011). pp. id-1–id-11 (2011)

15. Innocente, M., Sienz, J.: Pseudo-adaptive penalization to handle constraints in particle swarm optimizers. In: Proceedings of the Tenth International Conference on Computational Structures Technology. Civil-Comp Press

16. Jordehi, A.R.: A review on constraint handling strategies in particle swarm optimisation. Neural Comput. Appl. **26**(6), 1265–1275 (2015)

17. Kadirkamanathan, V., Selvarajah, K., Fleming, P.: Stability analysis of the particle dynamics in particle swarm optimizer. IEEE Trans. Evol. Comput. **10**(3), 245–255 (2006)

18. Kazimipour, B., Li, X., Qin, A.K.: A review of population initialization techniques for evolutionary algorithms. In: IEEE Congress on Evolutionary Computation (CEC). IEEE (2014)

19. Kazimipour, B., Li, X., Qin, A.K.: Why advanced population initialization techniques perform poorly in high dimension? In: Dick, G., et al. (eds.) SEAL 2014. LNCS, vol. 8886, pp. 479–490. Springer, Cham (2014). https://doi.org/10.1007/978-3-319-13563-2_41

20. Kennedy, J., Eberhart, R.: Particle swarm optimization. In: Proceedings of the IEEE International Conference on Neural Networks, vol. 4, pp. 1942–1948 (1995)

21. Kwok, N., Liu, D., Tan, K., Ha, Q.: An empirical study on the settings of control coefficients in particle swarm optimization. In: Proceedings of the 2006 IEEE Congress on Evolutionary Computation (CEC 2006), pp. 823–830 (2006)

22. Liu, J., Liu, H., Shen, W.: Stability analysis of particle swarm optimization. In: Huang, D.-S., Heutte, L., Loog, M. (eds.) ICIC 2007. LNCS (LNAI), vol. 4682, pp. 781–790. Springer, Heidelberg (2007). https://doi.org/10.1007/978-3-540-74205-0_82

23. Liu, Q., Wei, W., Yuan, H., Zhan, Z.H., Li, Y.: Topology selection for particle swarm optimization. Inf. Sci. **363**, 154–173 (2016)

24. Lynn, N., Ali, M.Z., Suganthan, P.N.: Population topologies for particle swarm optimization and differential evolution. Swarm Evol. Comput. **39**, 24–35 (2018)

25. Ozcan, E., Mohan, C.: Particle swarm optimization: surfing the waves. In: Proceedings of the IEEE Congress on Evolutionary Computation, vol. 3 (1999)

26. Piotrowski, A.P., Napiorkowski, J.J., Piotrowska, A.E.: Population size in particle swarm optimization. Swarm Evol. Comput. **58**, 100718 (2020)

27. Poli, R.: Mean and variance of the sampling distribution of particle swarm optimizers during stagnation. IEEE Trans. Evol. Comput. **13**(4), 712–721 (2009)

28. Shi, Y., Eberhart, R.: Empirical study of particle swarm optimization. In: Proceedings of the IEEE Congress on Evolutionary Computation, vol. 3 (1999)

29. Shi, Y., Eberhart, R.C.: A modified particle swarm optimizer. In: Proceedings of the IEEE International Conference on Evolutionary Computation (1998)

30. Trelea, I.C.: The particle swarm optimization algorithm: convergence analysis and parameter selection. Inf. Process. Lett. **85**(6), 317–325 (2003)

Ant Colony Optimization

On One Bicriterion Discrete Optimization Problem and a Hybrid Ant Colony Algorithm for Its Approximate Solution

Yurii A. Mezentsev[✉] and Nikita Y. Chubko

Novosibirsk State Technical University,
Prospekt Karla Marksa 20, Novosibirsk, Russia

Abstract. The bicriteria optimization problem of many projects developments' schedules with many competitive constraints on resources and interval constraints on the execution time and cost of operations is formulated in this article. Optimization is carried out according to the maximizing performance and the total cost of project execution criteria. The problem is NP-hard MILP and an efficient hybrid parametric algorithm that combines the critical path algorithm and ant colony optimization has been developed for its approximate solution. The actual performance and solutions' quality of the hybrid algorithm's software implementation have been compared with the results of IBM CPLEX on test problems. The effectiveness of the toolkit is confirmed experimentally by testing.

Keywords: Schedules' optimization · Multi-project development · MILP · Hybrid algorithm · Ant colony optimization

1 Introduction

Currently, there is a rapid development of the project approach to planning production activities. With the increase in the scale and complexity of projects being implemented among software developers, production departments of industrial enterprises and real estate developers it is becoming increasingly important to solve problems of efficient use of resources while simultaneously implementing a multitude of competing on resources projects.

Formalization and development of an algorithm for an approximate solution to one of these problems are the subject of this article. Briefly, it can be designated as the problem of optimal management in multi-project developments (OMMPD). The problem has a significant background. A brief description of its modifications and an overview of publications on this topic are presented next.

There is a set of projects, each contains many interdependent operations with a certain order of execution within the project, known intervals of execution time

---

The research is supported by Ministry of Science and Higher Education of Russian Federation (project No. FSUN-2020-0009).

Y. Tan and Y. Shi (Eds.): ICSI 2021, LNCS 12689, pp. 289–300, 2021.
https://doi.org/10.1007/978-3-030-78743-1_26

and corresponding intervals of the execution cost. Each operation consumes one or many resources. All available resources are limited and some of them can not be divided between operations; therefore, operations involving such a resource cannot be executed simultaneously. In a number of such formulations [1], the minimization criterion of the total execution time of all projects is applied, which requires a determination of an execution order of operations that use the same resources.

The availability of resources can be represented both as a binary value (the resource is fully utilized when performing an operation) and as an additive value (the resource is considered to be continuously shared and consumed when several operations are performed simultaneously). All continuously shared resources can be aggregated and taken into account by applying interval constraints on the execution time and cost of operations [10,11]. The presence of interval constraints on the execution time and cost of operations defines the application of two criteria, minimizing total completion time and cost of project implementation. In this case, the problem has many Pareto-optimal solutions. The bicriterial formulation of OMMPD is applied in this article.

It can be shown that in most cases the problem is NP-hard and does not have effective algorithms for the exact solution. Therefore, at the moment, the most promising tool for the OMMPD problem are effective heuristic algorithms that are able to obtain approximate solutions with polynomial dependence of the computation time on the dimension.

The idea of an ant colony algorithm application for solving the problem of managing the execution of a single project has already been researched [2] in the following formulation. The project consists of many operations, the execution time and used resources are known for each operation. The operations are interdependent, their technological order of execution is known. Resources are limited and reusable after the completion of operations. At any given time, the sum of the resources used to perform operations should not exceed their available volume. It is necessary to determine the execution order of operations so that the project execution time is minimal.

Constraint programming (CP) is also seen as a promising approach to solving the problem of optimal control of project implementation. For the problem in the above formulation [2], a constrained programming model was developed in the CHIP V5 software environment [3].

The topic of the evolutionary algorithms application for the problem of optimal management in multi-project developments was studied in [4,5] with the formulation simular to [2]. A similar formulation of the problem was suggested in one of the resent works, in which the use of the algorithm based on multi-agent systems and problem decomposition is proposed [6].

Studies of the effectiveness of various heuristic algorithms for solving this problem are partially presented in [7]. Based on the results of the analysis, a genetic algorithm was identified as promising, but the ant colony algorithm was not included in the comparison.

Despite the numerous works on this problem in different formulations, it is still relevant for research. In one of the latest works, the application of the meta-heuristic algorithms for the project scheduling optimization was considered in formulation similar to [1], but with the criteria of contractor's Net present value maximization. A comparison of the efficiency was provided for the genetic algorithm (GA), particle swarm optimization (PSO) and simulated annealing (SA) on the automatically generated problems. The results show that GA has better performance than SA and PSO but SA needs less time to solve the problem than GA and PSO [8].

Mixed-integer linear programming (MILP) is one of the classical solving tools for the considered problem. In its common form, it is barely applicable for real-life high dimensional problems, which is confirmed by test results presented in part 6 of this paper. However, in one of the latest works [9], an effective parallel cutting plane algorithm for the problem in formulation similar to [1] was presented. This new algorithm is based on MILP and uses five additional types of cuts: lifted precedence and cover cuts, cliques, odd-holes and strengthened Chvatal-Gomory cuts. According to the presented test results, the parallel cutting plane algorithm is much more efficient than the classical MILP, but the authors admit that it still demands further improvement.

Based on the analysis of previous studies, we can conclude that the most promising tools for solving the problem of scheduling multi-project developments are hybrid algorithms based on random search and modern metaheuristics. In some formulations, ready-made software complexes, for example, IBM ILOG CP Optimizer or CHIP V5, are also able to find solutions to the problem in question. However, CP does not guarantee the optimality of the obtained solutions, especially for high-dimensional problems. And it does not generate an effective solution algorithm, only partially removing the dimensionality problem. For large-scale OMMPD, this toolkit is barely applicable. Expert estimates determine a substantional increase in the admissible dimension for CP in comparison with exact methods with an uncertain estimate of the accuracy of solutions.

2   Substantial Problem Statement

The problems and algorithms for optimal control of the execution of individual projects have been studied for a long time. In most cases, to formalize and solve them, the network planning and management (NPM) approach is used [11]. Initially, the problems of the NPM under consideration were mostly polynomially solvable and consisted in determining the time characteristics of the project while observing the constraints on resources, most often reflected by the cost characteristics of their expenditure [10].

As noted above, computational difficulties have increased during the attempts of accounting for non-shared or discretely shared resources (equipment, labour, for example). At the same time, it turned out that the emergence of such resource constraints translates the NPM problems into the class of intractable ones. The generalization of the problem of management in single project development to multi-project developments leads to a significant complication which makes new problem unsolvable for exact methods in real-life conditions.

A set of projects is considered, the execution of which requires a range of resources. Each project from the entire set contains a finite set of operations connected by precedence-succession relations, for the execution of which a finite set of resources are consumed. Arguably this resources can be categorized in two types.

The first type is continuously shared (stockpiled and non-stockpiled) resources. The intensity of their use can be taken into account through the estimates of spending per unit of time. For any operation of any project, such an estimate will be the cost of execution for a given time. Based on the common idea of the OMMPD tasks, we consider the estimates of the cost and performance time of individual operations in normal and maximum intensive modes as known. And we also assume that the unit cost of accelerating the operation on the entire set of modes of execution of any project (from normal to the most intensive) is constant.

Consumable resources of the second type (non-shared or discretely shared) will be assumed to be used exclusively. The case of their discrete separation is not considered in this work. The exclusive use condition immediately leads to the execution of any operation of any project without interruption. The latter means that such a resource, consumed by any operation of any project, cannot be transferred until this operation completion to perform another operation. In turn, exclusive use leads to conflicts of operations on resources of the second type. And the resolution of such conflicts becomes the most time-consuming procedure for finding solutions, regardless of the formulation and algorithms used.

Management efficiency measures should take into account the efficiency of using both types of resources. In this case, the efficiency of using resources of the first type will be measured by means of cost characteristics, and the efficiency of using resources of the second type - by means of time characteristics. Thus, we obtain two criteria: minimizing the cost of implementing all projects and minimizing the total implementation time of all projects.

It is quite simple to show that, in this formulation, the OMMPD problem belongs to the NP class. Indeed, with the utmost simplification of the structures of the entire set of projects to sequential chains, limiting the modes of operations to the only normal one, considering the set of devices as resources of the second type, and not taking into account the resources of the first type at all, excluding the criterion of minimizing the total cost of operations, one of the scheduling theory classical problems is obtained - the job shop problem (JSP). The JSP has been proven to belong to the NP class. For it, there are also no approximate algorithms with a proven a priori accuracy of approximations to the optima.

3   Formal Problem Statement

There are I projects containing J operations in total. For each operation $j = \overline{1, J}$ it is known:

t_j^n - execution time in normal mode;
t_j^c - limit execution time with maximum acceleration;
C_j^n - cost of execution in normal mode;
C_j^c - cost of execution with maximum acceleration;
e_j - number of the resource involved in the execution;
p_j - project number.

The technological order of operation execution in projects is known. If the start of operation i is possible only after the end of operation j, then $d_{ij} = 1$, otherwise 0, for $i = \overline{1, J}$, $j = \overline{1, J}$.

Operations that involve the same resource cannot be executed simultaneously. If the same resource is used to perform operation i and j ($e_i = e_j$ and $i \neq j$), then if operation i precedes operation j, then $w_{ij} = 1$ otherwise 0, for $i = \overline{1, J}$, $j = \overline{1, J}$.

It is necessary to find a set of Pareto-optimal solutions to the problem with the following criteria:

1. the minimum cost of performing all operations;
2. minimum completion time for all projects.

In this case, the formal statement of the problem is:
Objective function:

$$Z = \sum_{j=1}^{J} (\Delta_j * x_j + C_j^n) \to min \tag{1}$$

$$D \in [T_k^n; T_k^c] \tag{2}$$

$$T_k \to min \tag{3}$$

Constraints:

$$T_k \leq D \tag{4}$$

$$T_j + t_j^n - x_j \leq T_i \quad \text{if } d_{ij} = 1 \text{ with } i = \overline{1, J}, j = \overline{1, J} \tag{5}$$

$$T_j + t_j^n - x_j \leq T_k \quad \text{with } j = \overline{1, J} \tag{6}$$

$$T_j \geq 0 \quad \text{with } j = \overline{1, J} \tag{7}$$

$$\begin{cases} T_j - T_i - B * w_{ij} \leq -(t_i^n - x_i) \\ T_i - T_j + B * w_{ij} \leq B - (t_j^n - x_j) \end{cases} \quad \text{if } e_i = e_j, i \neq j, d_{ij} = 0, d_{ji} = 0 \tag{8}$$

$$0 \leq x_j \leq t_j^n - t_j^c \quad \text{with } j = \overline{1, J} \tag{9}$$

where:

T_j - start time of operation j;

x_j - value of acceleration of operation j;

$\Delta_j = \frac{C_j^c - C_j^n}{t_j^n - t_j^c}$ is the unit cost of accelerating operation j;

T_k - completion time of the last of the projects;

T_k^n - time of completion of all projects in normal mode;

T_k^c - time of completion of all projects with maximum acceleration;

D - directive time of completion of all projects.

4   Hybrid Algorithm

The developed hybrid algorithm is based on the use of the ant colony algorithm to find the execution order of operations that using the same resources and the critical path method to find solutions to the problem with the acceleration of projects. A variant of the Max-min Ant System algorithm [12] was chosen as the basis for the implementation of the ant colony algorithm. The ant colony algorithm is a parametric iterative algorithm, at each iteration of the algorithm Ψ ants are created, each ant determines the execution order of operations in a random way, depending on the probability of their following. For the developed hybrid algorithm, the following parameters are set:

ι - number of iterations;

Ψ - is the number of ants;

α - coefficient of significance of the start time;

β - pheromone significance coefficient;

ϕ_{max} - maximum pheromone level;

ϕ_{min} - minimum pheromone level;

ρ - coefficient of pheromone weathering.

If operations i and j use the same resource, then the probability of the execution of operation j following operation is calculated by the formula:

$$p_{ij} = \frac{F(i,j)^\alpha * \phi_{ij}^\beta}{F(i,j)^\alpha * \phi_{ij}^\beta + \frac{1}{F(i,j)^\alpha} * \phi_{ji}^\beta} \tag{10}$$

$$F(i,j) = \begin{cases} 2, & \text{if } T_j > T_i \\ 1, & \text{if } T_j = T_i \\ 0.5, & \text{if } T_j < T_i \end{cases} \tag{11}$$

where:

ϕ_{ij} - pheromone level corresponding to the operation j following after operation i;

After determining the sequence of each pair of operations, the start time of all operations is recalculated. After determining the succession of all pairs of operations involving the same resources by each of the ants, the process of weathering of pheromones occurs according to the formula:

$$\phi_{ij} = max((1-p) * \phi_{ij}; \phi_{min}) \tag{12}$$

At the end of each iteration, the concentration of pheromones is increased according to the best solution S_{min} found for the entire time, which is described by the formula:

$$\begin{cases} \phi_{ij} = min((\phi_{max} - \phi_{min}) * p + \phi_{ij}; \phi_{max}), & \text{if } T_j > T_i \\ \phi_{ij} = min((\phi_{max} - \phi_{min}) * p + \phi_{ji}; \phi_{max}), & \text{if } T_j < T_i \end{cases} \quad i,j = \overline{1,J}, e_i = e_j \tag{13}$$

After passing through all the iterations, the best sequence of operations S_{min} with the total execution time of all projects T_k from those obtained at all iterations is selected. The cost of performing operations is calculated using the formula:

$$C = \sum_{j=1}^{J} C_j^n \tag{14}$$

To find a set of accelerated solutions, the critical path method is used:

1. The value of the discrete step ε is set.
2. The new directive execution time of project is determined:

$$T_d = T_k - \varepsilon \tag{15}$$

3. All critical paths are found in the current solution.
4. If at least one critical path cannot be accelerated, then go to point 9.
5. The cost of acceleration is determined for each of the operations included in the found set of critical paths by the formula:

$$\Delta_j^k = \frac{\Delta_j}{k}, \quad \text{if } x_j < t_j^n - t_j^c \tag{16}$$

where:
k - the number of critical paths that include operation j.

6. The operation j with the lowest acceleration cost Δ_j^k is selected and accelerated in the amount calculated by the formula:

$$\sigma = T_k - T_d \text{ and } x_j = x_j + \sigma \tag{17}$$

7. The total time T_k and the total costs C for the implementation of all projects are determined, the solution is fixed:

$$C = \sum_{j=1}^{J} (\Delta_j * x_j + C_j^n) \tag{18}$$

8. If $T_k \leq T_d$ then go to item 3, otherwise to item 2.
9. The end of the algorithm, a set of accelarated solutions have been found.

The hybrid algorithm has polynomial complexity. The approximate computation time of a problem can be calculated by the formula:

$$ct = N * \Psi * \Pi * \mu + A * K * \mu \qquad (19)$$

where:

N - number of iterations;
Ψ - number of ants;
Π - number of operation pairs where $e_i = e_j, i \neq j, d_{ij} = 0, d_{ji} = 0$ with $i = \overline{1, J}, j = \overline{1, J}$;
μ - time of the problem's network graph values calculation;
A - total acceleration of all projects completion time;
K - middle number of critical paths in all accelerated solutions.

5   Example Problem "data-j8-p2-r4"

The number of projects $I = 2$, the number of operations $J = 8$, data on operations are presented in Table 1.

Table 1. Initial data of the problem "data-j8-p2-r4"

Operation	Depend on	Project	Resource	t^n	t^c	C^n	C^c
1	-	2	4	18	5	17	32
2	-	1	2	10	9	18	41
3	2	1	2	14	6	14	29
4	1	2	1	20	12	19	34
5	1	2	3	25	11	35	49
6	1	2	2	10	6	20	39
7	2,3	1	3	11	8	20	36
8	4,1	2	4	9	8	14	48

The problem "data-j8-p2-r4" is presented in the form of a network diagram (see Fig. 1). At the top of the node, we can see "operation number/project number/resource number". The execution time of operation is at the bottom of the node.

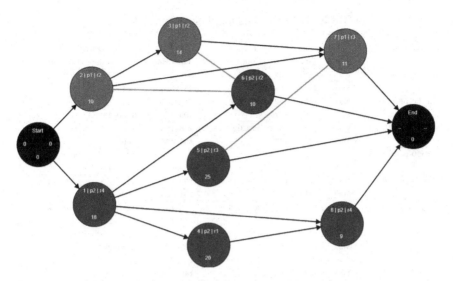

Fig. 1. Problem "data-j8-p2-r4" as a network diagram.

The solutions of the problem "data-j8-p2-r4" received by IBM ILOG CPLEX and a hybrid algorithm are presented on the first line of the Table 3. The hybrid algorithm is based on the ant algorithm for constructing solutions and the critical path method for obtaining accelerated solutions.

The normal execution time of all projects is 54 with a price of 157. The maximum accelerated execution time of all projects is 25 with a price of 265 (prices rounded off).

The part of the set of Pareto-optimal solutions found by IBM ILOG CPLEX is presented in Table 2. The same solutions have been found by the hybrid algorithm.

Table 2. Solutions of the problem "data-j8-p2-r4"

T1	T2	T3	T4	T5	T6	T7	T8	Tk	x1	x2	x3	x4	x5	x6	x7	x8	w26	w36	w57	C
0	0	21	18	18	35	43	38	**54**	0	0	0	0	0	0	0	0	1	1	1	**157**
0	0	28	18	18	18	42	44	**53**	0	0	0	0	1	0	0	0	1	0	1	**158**
																				...
0	0	10	5	5	16	16	17	**26**	13	0	8	8	14	0	1	0	1	1	1	**221.33**
0	0	10	5	5	16	16	17	**25**	13	0	8	8	14	1	2	1	1	1	1	**265.42**

6   Test Results

The test results for all sample problems are presented in Table 3. The calculation of the solutions with the hybrid algorithm is carried out 5 times since the algorithm is based on the generation of random numbers. The number of calculation attempts of the solutions with the hybrid algorithm has been chosen empirically. The maximum duration of the task calculation is 6 h. For the

Table 3. Test results for all sample problems

Problem name	Accel.	CPLEX			Hybrid Algorithm		
		Time	Cost	Comput. Time	Time Range	Cost Range	Comput. Time
data-j8-p2-r4	No	54	157	00:00:02	54–54	157	00:00:00
	Max	25	265		25–25	265–265	
data-j50-p5-r10—1	No	146	1228	00:00:26	155–161	1228	00:00:11
	Max	105	1446		109–117	1480–1533	
data-j50-p5-r10—2	No	186	1308	00:13:24	186–186	1308	00:00:15
	Max	126	1677		138–138	1609–1615	
data-j50-p5-r10—3	No	156	1213	00:43:32	156–156	1213	00:00:18
	Max	86	1775		98–98	1767–1779	
data-j50-p5-r10—4	No	152	1172	00:03:26	152–159	1172	00:00:14
	Max	101	1449		101–104	1508–1592	
data-j50-p5-r10—5	No	191	1240	00:00:26	191–191	1240	00:00:18
	Max	113	1473		114–121	1465–1546	
data-j100-p10-r20—1	No	173	2437	04:36:43	178–185	2437	00:00:47
	Max	110	2812		127–132	2779–2957	
data-j100-p10-r20—2	No	204	2343	over 6 h	214–223	2343	00:01:18
	Max	202	2346		143–155	2887–2990	
data-j100-p10-r20—3	No	229	2476	over 6 h	229–235	2476	00:01:07
	Max	203	2509		148–166	2896–3225	
data-j100-p10-r20—4	No	167	2445	over 6 h	175–177	2445	00:00:54
	Max	154	2473		126–132	2888–3069	
data-j100-p10-r20—5	No	166	2656	over 6 h	176–183	2656	00:01:02
	Max	155	2682		131–141	2987–3064	
data-j150-p10-r30—1	No	184	3646	over 6 h	215–220	3646	00:02:33
	Max	150	3767		149–149	4343–4364	
data-j150-p10-r30—2	No	196	3799	over 6 h	202–210	3799	00:02:54
	Max	163	3850		131–145	4393–4734	
data-j150-p10-r30—3	No	?	?	over 6 h	203–212	3506	00:02:25
	Max	?	?		149–151	4060–4095	
data-j150-p10-r30—4	No	182	3668	over 6 h	212–212	3668	00:02:44
	Max	169	3696		141–142	4545–4571	
data-j150-p10-r30—5	No	181	3695	over 6 h	202–205	3695	00:02:46
	Max	170	3705		137–143	4289–4354	
data-j200-p30-r30—1	No	277	4864	over 6 h	277–277	4864	00:06:34
	Max	277	4864		183–192	5544–5665	
data-j200-p30-r30—2	No	208	4816	over 6 h	237–242	4816	00:07:33
	Max	207	4816		162–165	5719–5805	
data-j200-p30-r30—3	No	213	5093	over 6 h	213–217	5093	00:09:15
	Max	211	5094		140–150	5978–6046	
data-j200-p30-r30—4	No	?	?	over 6 h	229–248	4799	00:09:57
	Max	?	?		156–161	5605–5608	
data-j200-p30-r30—5	No	?	?	over 6 h	264–264	4875	00:09:34
	Max	?	?		156–184	5631–5814	

problems, all solutions of which were not found in 6 h, the solutions found in the allotted time are presented.

According to the test results for the "data-j8-p2-r4" problem, consisting of 8 works, 2 projects and 4 resources, (see illustrative example above), the hybrid algorithm is able to find the entire set of Pareto-optimal solutions in all counting attempts.

Analysing the results obtained for the medium-dimensional problems, it is clear that for the examples "data-j50-p5-r10—2" and "data-j50-p5-r10—4" the hybrid algorithm is able to optimal solutions without projects execution acceleration in all tests. It should be noted that for the problems of average dimension "data-j50-p5-r10—x" (50 operations, 5 projects and 10 resources), the hybrid algorithm is not able to find a complete set of Pareto-optimal solutions, since the application of the critical path method for the acceleration of the operations' execution conflicts with the possibility of changing their execution order. However, the deviation of solutions obtained with the hybrid algorithm, both in terms of projects' execution time and the cost of executing from the optimal solutions does not exceed 10%. At the same time, the calculation time of solutions with the hybrid algorithm within the same dimension varies slightly from problem to problem and does not exceed 18 s, while the time to find solutions in IBM ILOG CPLEX can range from 26 s to more than 43 min.

In high-dimensional test problems, the hybrid algorithm demonstrates similar accuracy of the obtained solutions relative to IBM ILOG CPLEX. In some problems, it can even find optimal solutions without acceleration. The computing time for problems "j100-p10-r20—x" does not exceed 1.5 min, for problems "j150-p10-r30—x" does not exceed 3 min and for problems "j300-p30-r30—x" does not exceed 10 min. In comparison, IBM ILOG CPLEX can not find the whole set of Pareto optimal solutions for more than 6 h and for some problems it can not find even solutions without acceleration by this amount of time.

Analyzing the results obtained, it can be concluded that the hybrid algorithm is promising in real-time project planning systems. In a dynamically changing situation, it is necessary to quickly search for optimal or close to optimal solutions, which are not able to provide accurate optimization algorithms.

7 Conclusions

The article deals with the problem of optimal management in multi-project developments. A review of scientific works on this topic is made, a substantial and formal statement of the problem of optimal control in multi-project developments is presented. It is shown that this problem belongs to the NP class.

The effective hybrid algorithm presented in the work is able to find close to optimal solutions for the considered problem of optimal control in multi-project developments quickly. The hybrid algorithm is based on modifications to the ant colony algorithm to determine the execution order of operations and the critical path method to find a set of accelerated solutions close to Pareto-optimal solutions based on cost and performance criteria.

The efficiency of the algorithm has been confirmed empirically by comparing the speed of problem solving and the quality of solutions obtained with the hybrid algorithm and the solutions obtained with the implementation of integer linear programming tools in the IBM ILOG CPLEX software product on sets of test problems of different dimensions. In a sample test problem "data-j8-p2-r4", the hybrid algorithm is able to find the entire set of Pareto-optimal solutions. In medium-dimension and high-dimension test problems, the hybrid algorithm is able to find solutions approximate to the solutions from the set of Pareto-optimal ones.

However, the great advantage of the developed hybrid algorithm is the stable high speed of finding solutions. For medium-dimensional problems, finding solutions takes less than 20 s, while finding optimal solutions in IBM ILOG CPLEX can take up to 43 min. In high-dimensional problems, the time to find solutions is less than 10 min, while finding optimal solutions in IBM ILOG CPLEX can take more than 6 h, which is unacceptable for practical use.

Considering the advantages and disadvantages of the hybrid algorithm, we can predict its effective application in decision support systems in the field of project planning in real-time.

References

1. Oleinikova, S.A.: Matematicheskaya model i optimizacionnaya zadacha sostavleniya raspisaniya dlya multiproektnoi sistemi s vremennimi i resursnimi ogranicheniyami i kriteriem ravnomernoi zagruzki. Vestnik Voronejskogo gosudarstvennogo tehnicheskogo universiteta 6(3) (2013)
2. Merkle, D., Middendorf, M., Schmeck, H.: Ant colony optimization for resource-constrained project scheduling. IEEE Trans. Evol. Comput. 6(4), 333–346 (2002)
3. Trojet, M., H'Mida, F., Lopez, P.: Project scheduling under resource constraints: application of the cumulative global constraint. In: 2009 International Conference on Computers and Industrial Engineering, pp. 62–67 IEEE. Troyes, France (2009). https://doi.org/10.1109/ICCIE.2009.5223894
4. Yassine, A., Meier, C., Browning, T.: Multi-Project Scheduling Using Competent Genetic Algorithms. University of Illinois Department of Industrial and Enterprise Systems Engineering, Illinois (2007)
5. Gonçalves, J.F., Mendes, J.J.M., Resende, M.G.C.: A genetic algorithm for the resource constrained multi-project scheduling problem. Eur. J. Oper. Res. 189(3), 1171–1190 (2008)
6. Li F., Xu Z. : A multi-agent system for distributed multi-project scheduling with two-stage decomposition. PloS One 13(10) (2018). https://doi.org/10.1371/journal.pone.0205445
7. Hanchate, D.B., Thorat, M.Y.A., Ambole, M.R.H.: Review on multimode resource constrained project scheduling problem. Int. J. Comput. Sci. Eng. Technol. 3(5), 155–159 (2012)
8. Zaree, M., et al.: Project scheduling optimization for contractor's Net present value maximization using meta-heuristic algorithms: a case study. J. Ind. Eng. Manag. Stud. 7(2), 36–55 (2020). https://doi.org/10.22116/JIEMS.2020.221672.1342
9. Araujo, J.A.S., et al.: Strong bounds for resource constrained project scheduling: preprocessing and cutting planes. Comput. Oper. Res. 113 (2020)
10. Taha, H.A.: Operations Research: An Introduction, 8th edn. Upper Saddle River, New Jersey (2007)
11. Phillips, D.T., Garcia-Diaz, A.: Fundamentals of Network Analysis. Wiley Periodicals, Englewood Cliffs (2007)
12. Dorigo, M., Birattari, M., Stutzle, T.: Ant colony optimization. IEEE Comput. Intell. Mag. 1(4), 28–39 (2006)

Initializing Ant Colony Algorithms by Learning from the Difficult Problem's Global Features

Xiangyang Deng[✉], Limin Zhang, and Ziqiang Zhu

Institute of Information Fusion, Naval Aeronautical University, Yantai, China
xavior2012@aliyun.com

Abstract. Deception, which stems from the tackled problem instance and algorithmic structure, has a tremendous negative impact on the algorithmic performance. An improved ACO called GFL-ACO with a global feature learning strategy is proposed to process the algorithmic initialization. The strategy consists of two parts: a greedy random walking of ant colony and a mean value approach. With the former part, some initialized ants are launched to step forward by a greedy rule till finished a tour. A statistical manner of edge-based relative frequency is used to initial pheromone trails and ants' starting positions. With the latter part, a mean value calculated from edge-based relative frequency is used to generate ant population size. The experiments on the TSPLIB benchmark show that GFL-ACO can achieve a rather better performance on the standard benchmark.

Keywords: Ant colony optimization · Deception · Algorithmic difficulty · Global feature · Parameter initialization

1 Introduction

Traveling Salesman Problem (TSP), especially Large-scale TSP, is a well-known NP-hard problem, which is an often-used model of a series of combinatorial optimization problems. There are considerable researchers employ ant colony optimization (ACO) to solve it all the time, because ACO has a positive feedback mechanism and is intrinsic parallel, self-organizing and adaption, etc. [1]. For example, Kaplar et al. improved an agent-based ACO to solve large-scale TSP with the use of distributed computing [2]. LIAO et al. fused the density peaks clustering algorithm with an ACO and proposed a hierarchical hybrid algorithm for TSP [3]. In addition, for the larger instances, scientists gave some strategies of hybrid multi-populations [4], Cooperative Co-evolutionary Metaheuristics [5], Co-Evolution Mechanism [6], etc. The above methods are all concentrating on the improvement of algorithm but not on the problem features. In fact, a difficultly solved problem, often called a deceptive problem, is usually resulting in the disability of algorithms.

Deception is a critical problem of meta-heuristic algorithms all the time, because it plays a key role in the algorithmic performance and brings the algorithms difficulty. ACO algorithms are without exception [7]. D. Merkle et al. firstly discussed the bias phenomenon and showed that the behavior of an ACO algorithm is strongly influenced by

© Springer Nature Switzerland AG 2021
Y. Tan and Y. Shi (Eds.): ICSI 2021, LNCS 12689, pp. 301–310, 2021.
https://doi.org/10.1007/978-3-030-78743-1_27

the pheromone model. Moreover, it was shown that the bias may decrease performance of an ACO algorithm during a run, because in general this worsens the probability of finding better and better solutions [8]. After that, a comprehensive discussion on deception of ACO algorithms was given by Dorigo [9], which defined the deception by modeling an ACO algorithm applied in a problem instance, and proposed the concepts of first-order deception system (FODS) and second-order deception system (SODS). Moreover, it gave an example of SODS and considered that the SODS would be the most important issue to be investigated in the future ACO algorithm design. And then, they provided a way to distinguish fair and unfair competitions between solution components, and presented a competition balanced system to avoid construction bias caused by second-order deception effects [10]. For better describing second-order deception effects, Montgomery et al. introduced two types of bias caused by the structural aspects of a problem instance, and studied different pheromone mechanisms to achieve better performance [11]. The above researches indicate that the deception is the root cause of the difficulty of problems, and an effective artificial pheromone mechanism can lead to a better solution.

As an important component of ACO algorithms, the artificial pheromone mechanism without a doubt plays a critical role in a specific ant colony algorithm [12]. It includes mainly two parts: static pheromone structure and dynamic pheromone structure. The static pheromone structure often contains the pheromone trail graph and their initial values which respectively represent the acquired experiences and the prior knowledge. The pheromone trails are often updated by some best iteration elite ants in the ant colony's searching procedure. They are commonly combined with heuristic information, which is derived from the tackled problem instance, to bias the ants' solution constructing processes. The dynamic pheromone structure usually contains some updating rules. Most of ACO variations predominantly pay attention to improvements on the above pheromone mechanism, proved having a great effect on the algorithmic characteristics and solution construction performance.

Usually, when the pheromone trail graph is selected associated with tackled problem instance, the ACO algorithmic structure is basically determined. Except for the pheromone initialization, in the solution construction steps, the pheromone trails as a kind of numeric information as heuristic information are used to calculate the transition probability between two neighbor cities. The pheromone mechanisms are mainly activated in the iteratively searching procedure. In this paper, the pheromone initialization belongs to the first phase of an ACO algorithm referred as algorithmic initialization procedure (AIP phase), and other pheromone-related issues belong to the second phase referred as algorithmic running procedure (ARP phase).

As another important numeric information, heuristic not only forms the basis of pheromone mechanisms, but also represents the specific structure of a problem instance. Similar to the pheromone mechanism, the heuristic information is also more often employed at the ARP phase. Except participating in the ant individual one step moving decision, the heuristic information is widely used to generate neighbor structures, which can be well coupled with the global update rule to obtain high-quality algorithmic solution. The neighbor structure is substantially a kind of local searching structure, which is often directly used to construct a more efficient partial solution because of its best utilization of heuristic information. The iterated local search approach introduced in [13] utilized a simple rule of conducting iteratively perturbation steps to improve the locally optimal solution, and it could progressively obtain an optimized neighborhood. Karapetyan et al. [14] dealt with traveling salesman problem (TSP) and generalized TSP on behave of local heuristic information algorithms. In fact, ACO algorithms were proved to the best solution for a number of combinatorial optimization problems, when coupled with local search methods [15]. Duan et al. [16] utilized the natural niche ideology to generate a reachable cities array for each node, which could create a kind of local optimization approach.

A large number of researches have indicated that the heuristic information has a wide influence on the algorithmic performance. But, most of the time, the heuristic information is coupled with pheromone trails at the ARP phase, while there is rarely utilization of heuristic information at the AIP phase. Even though the literature [13] showed that it can be used to generating an initial solution, it only referred the heuristic information as a local neighborhood, but not as a representation of global features of the tackled problem instance. In this paper, we conduct a greedy random walking of ant colony at the beginning to process the global structure of heuristic information, so that the ant colony can learn from the global features of the heuristic of tackled problem instance to perform a highly efficient algorithmic initialization. With the greedy random walking, ant colony takes a statistical samples of the global solution space, and an edge-based relative frequency matrix is generated used to calculate the initial pheromone values. In addition, with a mean value approach based on the relative frequency matrix, a certain amount of important solution components is selected to initialize the ant colony and their initial positions. Giving an example based on the standard TSP bench, combined with iteration-best update (IB-update) rule, a serious of experimental tests with an improved ACO algorithm abbreviated as GFL-ACO are carried out, and demonstrate high efficiency.

2 Learning from the Global Features

2.1 The Global Features of Solution Space

Travelling salesman problem (TSP) is a common model of enormous practical and theoretical problems. The solution is a Hamiltonian tour of minimal length labeled as $\pi = \{\pi_1, \ldots, \pi_i, \ldots, \pi_n\}^t$ an all permutation of the n nodes, where π_i is the i th component of the solution at iteration t. A feasible solution is obtained by a tour completed ant of visiting each city exactly once. When solved by an ACO algorithm, it should be modeled as a graph $G = (N, E)$ is given with $n = |N|$ nodes, a set E of edges fully connecting the nodes, and the distances between the nodes are given by a distance matrix $D = \{d_{ij}\}$ (d_{ij} is the distance between node i and j), which represent the linking relationships between nodes. Generally, for two nodes of a tackled problem instance, the larger the value of d_{ij} is, the closer the relationship of node i and j gets. When they have an extraordinary weak relationship, the d_{ij} is absent or an infinite value that means the two nodes are independent of each other.

In the graph G, the edges linking to a node i are denoted as $C = \{c_j^i\}$, $j \in N \setminus \{i\}$, which represents its nearest neighborhood. If j represents one of the one-jump reaching nodes of node i, C represents a first order neighborhood. When it is one of the second-jump reaching nodes of node i, C represents a second order neighborhood. It can be showed in Fig. 1.

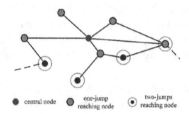

Fig. 1. The central node has five one-jump reaching nodes marked yellow, and four two-jump reaching nodes marked deep blue. (Color figure online)

In most cases, only the first order neighborhood is used to construct a local optimization strategy, because a first order neighbor node sometime can not only represent a short term dependency showed as in Fig. 1, but also a long term dependency on one solution instance. It can be showed in Fig. 2.

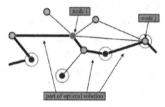

Fig. 2. In partial optimal solution $\pi_p = \{\pi_{i-2}, \pi_{i-1}, \pi_i, \pi_{i+1}, \pi_{i+2}, \pi_j\}$, the node j is a three jumps node of the central node i, while it is a first order neighborhood node at the time.

That is to say, a normal first order neighborhood is not always only a representation of local connection relations, but also occasionally a representation of global connection relations. The global features of a tackled problem instance are implied in a more complex connection map of nodes.

For a first order neighborhood C^1 of node i, the distance subset $D^1 = \{d_{ij} | j \in C^1\}$ can only be seen as unchangeable heuristic information of the nearest neighbor nodes, and they are determined at problem's modeling phase. Though a first order neighborhood can indicate a local connection relation at the same time a global connection relation, its numeric descriptions D^1 can only provide a short term heuristic representation. What's more, for a second order neighborhood or a higher order neighborhood, the finite representative capability of distance matrix D can't provide a better expression of complex correlativity, even though D is created by some more complex distance structures such as Hausdorff distance [17], geodesic distances defined between two points on a topological manifold [18], etc. In ACO algorithms, the pheromone mechanism provides a more effective solution that can represent a global features of the complex connection map, via an indirect communication mechanism of ant colony individuals. The pheromone trails are updated by ant colony's iteratively searching behaviors gradually integrating the lower-order and higher-order correlativity of different edges, and conversely affect the ant colony's searching behaviors. By means of the relative pheromone depositing on the edges belonging to an iteration-best path, pheromone trails can express the complex global relationships of different nodes. The integrating effect can be shown in Fig. 3.

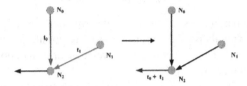

Fig. 3. Pheromone on an edge deposited coupled with several relative edges stores the searching behaviors of ants.

In Fig. 3, the pheromone on the edge out from node N_2 is generated by the ants entering N_2 along the edge N_0N_2 and N_1N_2. The pheromone should be deposited on the edge N_0N_2 and N_1N_2 would also be relatively deposited on the node N_2, making the changes of pheromone trails on the node N_2 are more obvious. At the same time, the mutual effect among the searching behaviors of ant colony is closer.

2.2 Edge-Based Relative Frequency

To study the communication of ant colony, Deneubourg et al. [19] ever designed a double-branch bridge experiment to demonstrate ants' decisions of selecting a branch (Fig. 4), and they came to a conclusion that the pheromone density on a branch is in direct proportion to the number of ant individuals which passed the branch. And then, the following ant individuals select the branch based on the pheromone density (the more pheromones there are on a branch, the more possible the ants will select the branch).

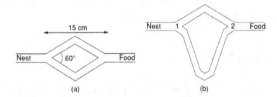

Fig. 4. Double-branch bridge experiment.

They proposed an approximate model to describe it. Suppose the short branch is A, the long branch is B. A_m and B_m represent the number of ants which have passed the short branch and those which have passed the long branch respectively. If the number of ants which have passed branch A is m, the next ant will select branch A with the probability as follows:

$$P_{A_m} = \frac{(A_m + t)^\alpha}{(A_m + t)^\alpha + (B_m + t)^\alpha}$$

where α and t are parameters to match the experimental data. The model indicates that the more ant individuals passed a branch, the more possible it is for the branch to be selected. That is to say the number of ants traversed a branch denotes its importance of constructing a complete tour.

Considering the solution space model of graph G of a particular instance, we specify a numeric value s_{ij} for each edge $e_{ij} \in E$, used to count the traversed ant individuals. When an ant crosses the edge e_{ij}, s_{ij} pluses one. If there is an ant colony walking on the graph G randomly or with another specific rule, for example greedy rule. After a while, a counter matrix S composed of elements $\{s_{ij}\}$ can be obtained, and then is normalized by the following formulas:

$$S_{norm} = \frac{S+1}{sum(S+1)}$$

where S_{norm} is the normalized counter matrix. Because it is possible that there are some nodes have no ants traversing it, conduct a plus one process can avoid appearing zero valued node. In addition, for each edge e_{ij}, the corresponding element s_{ij}^{norm} of matrix S_{norm} multiplies the counter s_{ij} as following:

$$rf_{ij} = s_{ij}^{norm} \times (1 + s_{ij})$$

where rf_{ij} denotes the edge-based relative frequency of an edge, and accordingly obtain an edge-based relative frequency matrix $RF = \{rf_{ij}\}$. According to the Good-Turing Estimate [20], if there is a quite big number of ant colony, and iterates enough times, the above plus one process corresponds to distribute a very small probability to the zero valued edges from the probability mass.

3   Initializing GFL-ACO

GFL-ACO is a successor of Ant Colony System (ACS) which was proposed by Dorigo and Gambardella [21]. With a TSP instance, the main steps of G-ACS are as follows:

- Initializing algorithmic parameters.
- Conducting a greedy-random walking of ant colony. At the beginning, place an ant at each node, the ants move from one node to another with a tabu rule and a greedy rule.
- Initializing the pheromone trails.
- Initializing the ant colony and their positions.

- Begin main iterative procedure. The ants use a pseudo-random proportional rule to select an edge and move to the next node.
- Repeat selecting and moving until perform a complete tour.
- Evaluate the ant colony and select out the iteration-best path according to the evaluation function.
- Update the pheromone trails by IB-update rule.
- Complete or transfer to step 5).
- End the algorithm.

At the step 3, the initialization of pheromone trails is conducted by following:

$$phromone_{ij} = L_{rbest} \times rf_{ij}$$

where L_{rbest} denotes the shortest path produced by the random walking ant colony. At the step 4, firstly, a mean value m of the counter matrix S is calculated by:

$$m = mean(S + 1)$$

Second, a subset of edges E' included in E is selected if the counter $s_{ij} \in E'$ satisfies $s_{ij} > m$. When the iteration starts, the nodes belonging to the edges included in E' will be placed by an ant, whose next node is the other node of the same edge.

At the step 5, if p_{ij}^k represents the state transition probability of ant k transferring from node i to node j:

$$p_{ij}^k = \begin{cases} \dfrac{\tau_{ij}^\alpha \times \eta_{ij}^\beta}{\sum_{l \in allowned} \left[\tau_{il}^\alpha \times \eta_{il}^\beta \right]}, & if \ j \in allowned \\ 0, & otherwise \end{cases}$$

where α is the information heuristic factor, representing the relative importance of the trajectory, and β is the desired heuristic factor, representing the relative importance of the visibility. τ_{ij} is the pheromone density on edge e_{ij}, and η_{ij} is the value of the heuristic function on edge e_{ij}, and is often equal to $1/d_{ij}$.

At the step 8, update the pheromone trails at the end of each iteration according to the following rules:

$$\tau_{ij} = (1 - \rho) \times \tau_{ij} + \rho \times \frac{1}{L_{iteration\_best}}$$

where ρ represents the pheromone evaporation coefficient, and $L_{iteration\_best}$ is the length of the best path of the iteration, and $1/L_{iteration\_best}$ represents the pheromone increment on specific edges belongs to the best iterative path.

4 Experimental Tests

In order to test the validity of GFL-ACO, a standard TSP bench set is used to evaluate it, which contains a total of 111 instances and their so-far best solutions. As the global optimum of some TSP instances is uncertain, a lower bound is used instead. The tested TSP instances include ulysses22.tsp, att48.tsp, eil51.tsp, berlin52.tsp, eil76.tsp, pr124.tsp, ch150.tsp, and gr666.tsp.

GFL-ACO was implemented in MATLAB R2014a, and all codes were executed on a personal computer with an Intel Pentium 2.5 GHz processor and 4GB RAM. To verify the effectivity of the algorithm, there are eight parametric combinations are discussed as follows (Table 1):

Table 1. The parametric combinations

ID	α	β	m	q_0	ρ	ID	α	β	m	q_0	ρ
1	2	1	30	1	0.9	5	3	2	35	0.8	0.9
2	2	2	30	1	0.9	6	3	2	35	0.9	0.8
3	2	2	30	1	0.85	7	3	3	40	0.8	0.8
4	3	2	30	0.9	0.85	8	3	3	40	0.6	0.75

q_0 refer to a ratio of a fixed value as the initialized pheromone concentration. Each combination is tested 5 times, then they are ranked by the mean values of 5 tests. After that, the best one is selected, which is marked as: $\alpha = 3$, $\beta = 2$, m = 35, $q_0 = 0.9$, and $\rho = 0.8$. In the final experiment, each TSP instance iterates 500 times, and the results were averaged over 10 trials. The results are list in the Table 2, and the eight TSP instances are respectively demonstrated in Fig. 5.

Table 2. The experimental results

TSP instances	Best	Opt	Mean	Convergence
ulysses22.tsp	75.59	70.13	75.59	59
att48.tsp	34801	–	34805	49
eil51.tsp	426	426	427	86
berlin52.tsp	3123.43	–	3127.6	76
eil76.tsp	538	538	539.7	87
pr124.tsp	59083.1	59030	59108.45	79
ch150.tsp	6543.3	6528	6549.3	71
gr666.tsp	3129.30	2943.58	3183.28	498

The experimental tests show that GFL-ACO with each tested TSP instance has a quick exploiting procedure and achieve convergence steadily in the rather shorter time. The main improvement of the greedy random walking of ant colony plays a critical role in gaining the important edges and keeping them cross the different generations.

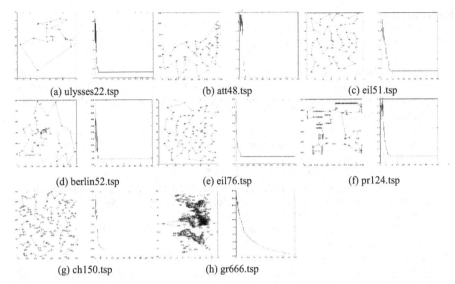

(a) ulysses22.tsp   (b) att48.tsp   (c) eil51.tsp

(d) berlin52.tsp   (e) eil76.tsp   (f) pr124.tsp

(g) ch150.tsp   (h) gr666.tsp

Fig. 5. The algorithm-best solution and the iteration-best fitness value curve of all TSP instances.

The greedy random walking of ant colony can be described as a population parallel sampling procedure, which can help the ant colony gain a global perception of the tackled problem instance. By means of heuristic information, a statistical approach extracts the long term relationships, equivalent to a high order correlativity, and stores them in the pheromone trails, so that an edge-based relative frequency matrix can be obtained at the end. With the matrix, GFL-ACO can achieve a better balanced condition than before ACO algorithms, and find a best equilibrium point of exploring and exploiting. Furthermore, GFL-ACO can obtain a better solution in a shorter time.

5   Conclusion

The paper focus on reducing the neglect impact of the problem instance's deception on the ACO based algorithmic performance. By means of autonomous learning the global heuristic structure of the tackled problem, and applying it in the algorithmic initialization of pheromone trails and ant colony and their beginning points, we obtain good performance of a new novel ant colony optimization algorithm (GFL-ACO). This new feature makes the initial pheromone trails become more balanced and meanwhile find the important edges. Moreover, we can gain a more meaningful amount of ant colony and initialize them. With the higher efficiency initialization, GFL-ACO achieves a good balance of exploring ability and exploiting ability.

If can be combined with some local optimization technology, GFL-ACO can gain a better performance in the real engineering situations. About some large scale optimization problems, finding more fundamental global structure to couple with local searching approaches is a feasible way in the future.

References

1. López-Ibánez, M., Stützle, T., Dorigo, M.: Ant Colony Optimization: a Component-Wise Overview (2015)
2. Kaplar, A., Vidakovic, M., Luburic, N., Ivanovic, M.: Improving a distributed agent-based ant colony optimization for solving traveling salesman problem. In: 2017 40th International Convention on Information and Communication Technology, Electronics and Microelectronics (MIPRO). IEEE (2017)
3. Liao, E., Liu, C.: A hierarchical algorithm based on density peaks clustering and ant colony optimization for traveling salesman problem. IEEE Access **6**, 38921–38933 (2018)
4. Deng, W., Xu, J., Zhao, H.: An improved ant colony optimization algorithm based on hybrid strategies for scheduling problem. IEEE Access **7**, 20281–20292 (2019)
5. Chen, J., Wang, Y., Xue, X., Cheng, S., El-Abd, M.: Cooperative co-evolutionary meta-heuristics for solving large-scale TSP art project. In: 2019 IEEE Symposium Series on Computational Intelligence (SSCI). IEEE (2019)
6. Zhang, H., You, X.: Multi-population ant colony optimization algorithm based on congestion factor and co-evolution mechanism. IEEE Access **7**, 1 (2019)
7. Blum, C., Sampels, M.: When model bias is stronger than selection pressure. In: Guervós, J.J.M., Adamidis, P., Beyer, H.-G., Schwefel, H.-P., Fernández-Villacañas, J.-L. (eds.) PPSN 2002. LNCS, vol. 2439, pp. 893–902. Springer, Heidelberg (2002). https://doi.org/10.1007/3-540-45712-7_86
8. Merkle, D., Middendorf, M.: Modeling the dynamics of ant colony optimization. Evol. Comput. **10**(3), 235–262 (2002)
9. Blum, C., Dorigo, M.: Deception in ant colony optimization. In: Ant Colony Optimization and Swarm Intelligence, pp. 118–129. Springer, Heidelberg (2004). https://doi.org/10.1007/978-3-540-28646-2_11
10. Blum, C., Dorigo, M.: Search bias in ant colony optimization: on the role of competition-balanced systems. IEEE Trans. Evol. Comput. **9**(2), 159–174 (2005)
11. Montgomery, J., Randall, M., Hendtlass, T.: Structural advantages for ant colony optimisation inherent in permutation scheduling problems. In: Innovations in Applied Artificial Intelligence, pp. 218–228. Springer, Heidelberg (2005). https://doi.org/10.1007/11504894_31
12. Montgomery, J., Randall, M., Hendtlass, T.: Automated selection of appropriate pheromone representations in ant colony optimization. Artif. Life **11**(3), 269–291 (2005)
13. Lourenço, H.R., Martin, O.C., Stützle, T.: Iterated Local Search. Springer, Heidelberg (2003). https://doi.org/10.1007/0-306-48056-5_11
14. Karapetyan, D., Gutin, G.: Efficient local search algorithms for known and new neighborhoods for the generalized traveling salesman problem. Eur. J. Oper. Res. **219**(2), 234–251 (2012)
15. Dorigo, M., Stützle, T.: Ant Colony Optimization. MIT Press, Cambridge (2004)
16. Haibin, D., Daobo, W., Xiufen, Y.: MAX-MIN meeting ant colony algorithm based on cloud model theory and niche ideology. J. Jilin Univ. **36**(5), 803–808 (2006)
17. Dubuisson, M.P., Jain, A.K.: A modified Hausdorff distance for object matching. In: Proceedings of the 12th IAPR International Conference on Pattern Recognition, Vol. 1-Conference A: Computer Vision & Amp; Image Processing 1994, vol. 1. IEEE (1994)
18. Donoho, D.L., Grimes, C.: Hessian eigenmaps: locally linear embedding techniques for high-dimensional data. Proc. Natl. Acad. Sci. **100**(10), 5591–5596 (2003)
19. Deneubourg, J.-L., et al.: The self-organizing exploratory pattern of the argentine ant. J. Insect Behav. **3**(2), 159–168 (1990)
20. Gale, W.A., Sampson, G.: Good-turing frequency estimation without tears*. J. Quant. Linguist. **2**(3), 217–237 (1995)
21. Dorigo, M., Gambardella, L.M.: Ant colony system: a cooperative learning approach to the traveling salesman problem. IEEE Trans. Evol. Comput. **1**(1), 53–66 (1997)

An Ant Colony Optimization Based Approach for Binary Search

N. K. Sreelaja$^{(\boxtimes)}$ and N. K. Sreeja

PSG College of Technology, Coimbatore, India

Abstract. Search is considered to be an important functionality in a computational system. Search techniques are applied in file retrievals and indexing. Though there exists various search techniques, binary search is widely used in many applications due to its advantage over other search techniques namely linear and hash search. Binary search is easy to implement and is used to search for an element in a large search space. The worst case time complexity of binary search is O (log $_2$ n) where n is the number of elements (search space) in the array. However, in binary search, searching is performed on the entire search space. The complexity of binary search may be further reduced if the search space is reduced. This paper proposes an Ant Colony Optimization based Binary Search (ACOBS) algorithm to find an optimal search space for binary search. ACOBS algorithm categorizes the search space and the key element is searched only in a specific category where the key element can exist thereby reducing the search space. The time complexity of ACOBS algorithm is O (log $_2$ c) where c is the number of elements in the reduced search space and c < n. The proposal is best suited for real time applications where searching is performed on a large domain.

Keywords: Ant colony optimization · Binary search · Optimal search space

1 Introduction

Swarm Intelligence [2], is an algorithm that models the collective behavior of autonomous agents. An autonomous agent may be regarded as a subsystem that interacts with its environment consisting of other agents, but acts relatively independent of the other agents. The autonomous agent does not follow commands from a leader, or some global plan [3]. Nature-inspired algorithms are based on Swarm Intelligence, which in turn forms the foundation of metaheuristics [11]. Swarm intelligence algorithms includes Genetic Algorithms (GAs), Ant Colony Optimization (ACOs) [1], Particle Swarm Optimization (PSO) [4], cuckoo search [5], firefly algorithm (FA) [6], bee algorithm [7], fish schooling search (FSS) [8], fireworks algorithm (FWA) [10], brain storm optimization (BSO) [9]. PSO is widely used for real-parameter optimization while ACO has been successfully applied to solve combinatorial optimization problems.

Ant System is a Swarm Intelligence algorithm to solve optimization problems. Artificial Ants [3] have some characteristics which do not find counterparts with real ants. The ants live in a discrete world and the moves consist of transitions from discrete state

© Springer Nature Switzerland AG 2021
Y. Tan and Y. Shi (Eds.): ICSI 2021, LNCS 12689, pp. 311–321, 2021.
https://doi.org/10.1007/978-3-030-78743-1_28

to discrete states. They have an internal state which contains the memory of the ant agent's past action. They deposit a particular amount of pheromone, which is a function of the quality of the solution found. An Artificial Ant's timing in pheromone deposition is problem dependent and often does not reflect real ant's behavior.

The ant agent moves by applying a stochastic local decision policy based on two parameters, called trails and attractiveness. The solution is constructed incrementally by the ant agent while moving. The ant computes the solution either during the construction phase of the solution or after completing the solution. The trail value on the components of the solution is modified by the ant agent when the evaluation of the solution is complete. In addition, an ACO algorithm includes two more mechanisms such as trail evaporation and, optionally, daemon actions. Trail evaporation reduces all trail values over time, in order to avoid unlimited accumulation of trails over some component [1].

Search is considered to be an important functionality in a computational system. Search techniques are applied in file retrievals, indexing etc. Though there exists various search techniques, binary search is widely used in many applications due to its advantage over other search techniques namely linear and hash search. Binary search is easy to implement and is used to search for an element in a large search space. The worst case time complexity of binary search is $O(\log_2 n)$ where n is the number of elements in the array (Search space). However, in binary search, searching is performed on the entire search space. The complexity of binary search may be further reduced if the search space is reduced.

Zeeshan et al. [12] have proposed a binary search algorithm based on checkpoint. The drawback is that it performs badly in a worst case when compared to binary search algorithm. Mehmood et al. [13] have proposed ASH search. ASH search works only for numbers and to search a string, it needs to be converted into numbers using a hash function which increases the computational complexity.

This paper proposes an Ant Colony Optimization based approach to reduce the search space of binary search. In this proposal termed Ant Colony Optimization based Binary Search (ACOBS), the set of elements sorted in ascending order are categorized and the ant agent finds the reduced search space by computing the count and last positions of occurrence of elements belonging to each category. ACOBS algorithm reduces the search space of binary search thereby reducing the time complexity of binary search. The proposal is best suited for real time applications where searching is performed on a large domain. The proposal achieves better computational complexity than the existing search algorithms.

The paper is organized as follows. Section 2 describes the model of the system. Section 3 describes ACOBS algorithm. Section 4 discusses a case study. The experimental results are discussed in Sect 5. A comparison of ACOBS algorithm and other search mechanisms is discussed in Sect. 6. Section 7 discusses the Mathematical Model of the system. Section 8 discusses the computational complexity of ACOBS algorithm and Sect. 9 presents the concluding remarks.

2 Model of the System

The elements sorted in ascending order are categorized based on the nature of the elements. For instance, if the elements are numbers and are of varying length, then the categorization is based on the number of digits. If the elements are strings and are of varying length, then the categorization is based on the first varying digit. If all elements in the array are of the same length, then the elements are catrgorized based on the first varying digit. The ant agent stores the number of elements belonging to each category and the position of last occurrence of elements of each category in its tabu-list. To search for the key value, the ant agent finds the category of the search key. The ant agent deposits pheromone and chooses the position value and the count value from the tabu-list of the corresponding category and the reduced search space is found. A binary search is performed in this reduced search space. If the search space does not exist, the key value is not present and the process is stopped. Figure 1 shows the model of the system.

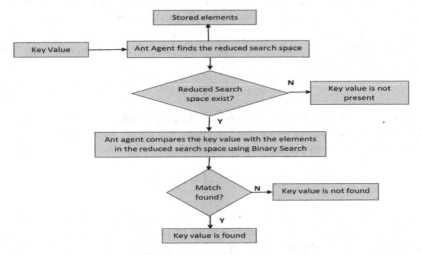

Fig. 1. Model of the system

3 Ant Colony Optimization based Binary Search

Let $X = [X_1, X_2....X_n]$ be a set of elements in ascending order. Let Ky be the key value to be searched. The elements are grouped based on a specific category. If the elements are numbers or strings of varying length, then the categorization is based on the length of the elements or based on the first varying digit respectively. If all elements in the array are of the same length, then the elements are categorized based on the first varying digit. The ant agent has a tabu-list denoting its memory. The tabu-list has a position list P and count list C. The number of the elements belonging to each category are found and stored in the count list as shown in Eq. (1).

$$C = \{C_1, C_2, C_3, ..., C_k\} \tag{1}$$

where C_i denotes the number of elements belonging to category 'i'. The position of last occurrence of the elements (P_i) belonging to each category is found using Eq. (2).

$$P_i = \begin{cases} \sum_{j=1}^{i} C_j & \text{if } C_j \neq 0 \\ 0 & \text{if } C_j \neq 0 \end{cases} \qquad (2)$$

The position list $[P_1, P_2, P_3, \ldots\ldots, P_k]$ is stored in the tabu-list of the ant agent.

The ant agent has a low position lp and a high position hp. Initially, the values of lp and hp are zero. The search space denotes the subset of elements in which the key value Ky is searched. To find an optimal search space, the ant agent deposits pheromone by choosing the position value P_i corresponding to the category 'i' to which Ky belongs. If P_i is zero, the search space is not found and the ant agent stops the process. If P_i is greater than zero, the count value C_i corresponding to the category 'i' of Ky is chosen from the count list. The position value P_i is stored in hp. The count value C_i is subtracted from the position value P_i and the subtracted value $(P_i - C_i) + 1$ is stored in lp of the ant agent as shown in Eq. (3).

$$lp = (P_i - C_i) + 1 \qquad (3)$$

The range [lp, hp] denotes the optimal search space in ich the key value Ky has to be searched. The pheromone deposition evaporates and the ant agent moves to the next trail. The ant agent deposits pheromone by computing the mid value as shown in Eq. (4).

$$midvalue = int\left(\frac{lp + hp}{2}\right) \qquad (4)$$

The ant agent chooses the element at the position denoted by the pheromone deposition. The ant agent computes the energy value by comparing the key value Ky with the element denoted by the pheromone deposition. The energy value is $+1$, if the Ky is less than the element at the position denoted by the pheromone deposition and the ant agent updates hp to $(midvalue - 1)$. The energy value is -1, if Ky is greater than the element at the position denoted by the pheromone deposition and the ant agent updates lp to $(midvalue + 1)$. The energy value is 0, if Ky is equal to the element at the position denoted by the pheromone deposition as shown in Eq. (5).

$$Energy(Ant\ agent) = \begin{cases} +1 & \text{if } Ky < X[\text{midvalue}] \text{ set } hp = midvalue - 1 \\ 0 & \text{if } Ky = X[\text{midvalue}] \\ -1 & \text{if } Ky > X[\text{midvalue}] \text{ set } lp = midvalue + 1 \end{cases} \qquad (5)$$

If the energy value of the ant agent is zero, the key value Ky is found. If the key value is not found, the pheromone evaporates and the ant agent moves to the next trail and the process continues until either a match occurs or lp > hp. lp > hp indicates Ky is not found. Figure 2 shows the pseudocode ACOBS algorithm.

4 Case Study

Consider an array of sorted numbers {1, 2, 10, 20, 22, 23, 34, 124, 148, 150, 1458, 2900, 3500, 10000}. Since the numbers are of variable length, the category is defined based on the number of digits in the number. Assuming the maximum number of digits in a number to be 10, the categories are classified as 1, 2, 3, 4, 5, 6, 7, 8, 9, 10. It is found that the count of the numbers having 1, 2, 3, 4, 5, 6, 7, 8, 9 and 10 digits are {2, 5, 3, 3, 1, 0, 0, 0, 0, 0} respectively. Therefore the count list C in the tabu-list of the ant agent contains {2, 5, 3, 3, 1, 0, 0, 0, 0, 0}. The position list (P) in the tabu-list of the ant agent contains the last positions of occurrence of the numbers belonging to each category. Therefore, P = {2, 7, 10, 13, 14, 0, 0, 0, 0, 0}. A case study is discussed for two different cases (i) Existence of a search space in which the key value may be found and (ii) Non-existence of a search space.

```
Procedure ACOBS (Ky, X[n], C, P)  // Ky is the key value to be searched in a sorted array X[n]
  C={C₁,C₂,C₃,....,Cₖ};
  P = { P₁, P₂, P₃,.......,Pₖ};
  lp=0; hp=0;
  Ant agent finds the category i of Ky;
  Ant agent deposits pheromone by choosing Pᵢ from the tabu-list;
  If (Pᵢ≠ 0)
     hp=Pᵢ;
     lp= Pᵢ −Cᵢ +1;
     while(lp ≤ hp)
         midvalue = int ((lp+hp)/2)
         Pheromone=midvalue;
         If (Ky < X [midvalue]) then Energy (Ant agent) = +1;  hp=midvalue-1;
         Else If (Ky >X [midvalue]) then Energy (Ant agent) = -1; lp=midvalue+1;
         Else If (Ky =X [midvalue]) then Energy (Ant agent) = 0;
         End
         If (Energy (Ant agent) = =0) then
            Return (midvalue);
            Exit();
         Else
            Return(Not Found);
         End;
     End;
  End;
End ACOBS()
```

Fig. 2. Pseudocode for ACOBS algorithm

4.1 Existence of a Search Space in Which the Key Value May Be Found

Let Ky = 146 be the key value to be searched. Since Ky is a 3 digit number, the category of Ky is 3. The ant agent deposits pheromone by choosing the position value $P_3 = 10$ corresponding to the category of Ky (i.e) 3 from the position list. Since P_3 is greater than 0, the ant agent chooses the count value $C_3 = 3$ corresponding to the category of Ky (ie) 3 from the count list C. The ant agent assigns the value in P_3 to hp and ($P_3 - C_3$ + 1) to lp. Hence the values in lp and hp are 8 and 10 respectively. Thus the optimal search space in which the key has to be searched is [8, 10]. The highlighted rows in Table 1 denotes the reduced search space. Table 2 shows the ant agent searching for the key value 146 in the reduced search space. It is found that the key value Ky does not occur in the reduced search space. It may be noted that out of 14 elements, only 3 elements are searched using ACOBS algorithm thereby reducing the number of searches.

Table 1. Ant agent finding the search space

Values	Count of values belonging to each category (C_i)	Position of last occurrence of values in a category (P_i)
1		
2	2	2
10		
20		
22		
23		
34	5	7
124		
148		
150	3	10
1458		
2900		
3500	3	13
10000	1	14

Table 2. Ant agent finding a match using Binary search in the reduced search space

Ant agent	Trail	Low position	High position	midvalue	Pheromone	Energy value
1	1	8	10	9	148	1
1	2	8	8	8	124	−1
1	3	9	8	−	−	−

4.2 Non-existence of a Search Space

Let Ky = 100034 be the key value to be searched. Since Ky is a 6 digit number, the category of Ky is 6. The ant agent deposits pheromone by choosing the position value $P_6 = 0$ corresponding to the category of Ky (ie) 6 from the position list. Since the value in P_6 value is 0, the search space does not exist and therefore Ky is not found in the array. Thus the number of searches using ACOBS is 1.

5 Experimental Results

Experiments were performed to search the information about a country based on the zip code. The experiment was performed using the dataset [15]. The dataset had 42522 zip codes in sorted order. The zip codes were categorized based on the length. The number of zip codes in the dataset of length 3, 4 and 5 are 194, 3475 and 38853 respectively.

Table 3 shows the position of the zip codes in the database and the number of searches required to locate the zip code in the database.

6 Comparison Between ACOBS and Search Techniques

6.1 Comparison Between ACOBS and Binary Search

Experiments were performed to show the efficiency of ACOBS algorithm in searching a dictionary dataset [16] which consisted of 370103 elements. The number of searches for every word in the dictionary dataset [16] was found. The words are in sorted order and are categorized based on the first letter in the word. Figure 3 shows a comparison of the total number of searches using ACOBS and binary search for searching all words beginning with the alphabets 'a' to 'z' with the dictionary dataset [16]. It is shown that ACOBS performs better compared to Binary Search. Figure 4 shows the comparison between the number of searches using ACOBS and binary search to compare each zip code in Table 3 with the zip codes in the dataset [15]. Figure 5 shows the total number of searches using ACOBS and binary search for searching all zip codes in the dataset [15].

6.2 Comparison Between ACOBS and Sequential Search

The set of elements {1, 2, 10, 20, 22, 23, 34, 124, 148, 150, 1458, 2900, 3500, 10000} used in Sect. 4 was chosen and a comparison was made for searching each key value from the set. It is observed from Fig. 6 that ACOBS performs better compared to Sequential Search.

6.3 Time Complexity of ACOBS and Other Search Techniques

The Time complexity of ACOBS algorithm and other existing search algorithms have been shown in Table 4. It may be noted from Table 4 that the time complexity of ACOBS algorithm is O(log c) where c is the number of elements in the reduced search space and $c < n$.

7 Mathematical Model of the System

The problem is modelled as an optimization problem. The optimization problem may be represented as a pair $O = (S, f)$ where S denotes the search space with $S \neq \emptyset$ and $f: S \rightarrow R$ is the objective function where R denotes the reduced search space. Let $(x_1, \ldots, x_n) \in S$ be a feasible solution of the optimization problem. The solution to the optimization problem (S, f) is to find a minimal search space $S_j \in S$ such that $f(S_j) < f(S_i) \, \forall \, S_i \in S$.

8 Computational Complexity

Let $X = [X_1, X_2, X_3, \ldots, X_n]$ denote a set of 'n' elements sorted in ascending order. The number of elements belonging to category j is denoted as C_j. The positions of the last occurrence of the elements in a particular category is denoted as P_j. Figure 7 shows the method of finding reduced search space to search a key value belonging to category 2.

Table 3. Number of searches using ACOBS

ZipCode	Position	Number of searches
501	1	8
794	108	6
795	109	8
9020	3254	10
5449	1885	9
24557	10267	14
33469	14639	14
33470	14640	15
44422	19161	12
48110	20969	15
99950	42522	15
796	NOT FOUND	8
999555	NOT FOUND	1
617	15	7
631	20	8
987	193	8

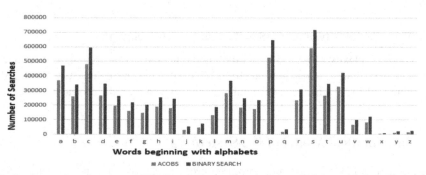

Fig. 3. Comparison between ACOBS and Binary Search for searching words in a dictionary dataset

8.1 Successful Search Space

Let Ky be the key value. The category j to which the key value belongs is found. The position P_j and the count value C_j corresponding to category j is retrieved. Hence the search space to find Ky is in the range $[P_j - C_j + 1, P_j]$. A binary search is performed in this search space. Thus the number of searches to compare a key value with the stored elements is $\log(C_j)$ where C_j is the number of elements belonging to a category j where $j < n$.

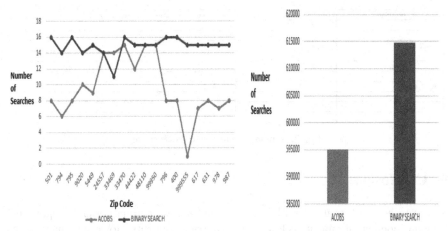

Fig. 4. Comparison between ACOBS and Binary Search for zip codes

Fig. 5. Comparison between total number of searches using ACOBS and Binary Search for zip codes

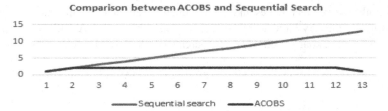

Fig. 6. Comparison between ACOBS and Sequential Search

Table 4. Time complexity of various search algorithms

Search algorithms	Input size	Time complexity	
		Worst case	Average case
Exponential Search	n	O(log n)	O(log n)
Fibonacci search	n	O(log n)	O(log n)
Ubiquitous Binary Search	n	O(log n) + 1	O(log n)
Hash Search	n	O(n)	O(1)
Ternary Search[14]	n	O(2 log $_3$ n)	-
ACOBS	n	**O(log c), c < n**	**O(log c), c < n**

8.2 Unsuccessful Search Space

Let Ky be the key value. The category j to which the key value belongs is found. If the position P_j is zero, the search space does not exist and the number of searches is 1.

Position	Elements	Number of elements belonging to a category
	X_1	
	X_2	
$P_1=C_1$	X_3	$C_1= P_1$
	X_4	
	X_5	
	X_6	
$P_2= P_1+ C_2$	X_7	$C_2= P_2- C_1$
	.	..
	.	
$P_n= P_{n-1}+ C_n$	X_n	$C_n= P_n- C_{n-1}$

Fig. 7. Finding the reduced search space

9   Conclusion

Search techniques are used in file retrievals and indexing. Binary search is preferred for many applications due to its low computational complexity. However, binary search algorithm works on the entire array (search space) to search for a key element. Reduction in search space would further reduce the time complexity of binary search. This paper proposes an Ant Colony Optimization based Binary Search (ACOBS) algorithm to find the optimal search space for binary search. The proposal has less time complexity compared to other search techniques and is best suited for applications in which searching is performed on a very large search space. It is also shown that ACOBS algorithm is efficient than sequential search when the search space has very few elements.

References

1. Dorigo, M., Stützle, T.: Ant Colony Optimization. MIT Press (2004)
2. Liu, Y., Passino, K.M.: Swarm Intelligence, Literature Overview, Dept. of Electrical Engineering. The Ohio State University (2000)
3. Padhy, N.P.: Artificial Intelligence and Intelligent Systems. Oxford University press (2005)
4. Kennedy, J.: Particle swarm optimization. In: Encyclopedia of Machine Learning, pp. 760–766. Springer (2011)
5. Yang, X.-S., Deb, S.: Cuckoo search via lévy flights. In: Proceedings of the Nature & Biologically Inspired Computing (NaBIC 2009) World Congress, pp. 210–214 (2009)
6. Yang, X.: Firefly algorithm, stochastic test functions and design optimization. Int. J. Bio-Inspired Comput. **2**(2), 78–84 (2010)
7. Pham, D.T., Ghanbarzadeh, A., Koc, E., Otri, S., Rahim, S., Zaidi, M.: The Bees Algorithm. Technical Note, Manufacturing Engineering Centre, Cardiff University, UK (2005)
8. Bastos Filho, C.J., de Lima Neto, F.B., Lins, A.J., Nascimento, A.I., Lima, M.P.: A novel search algorithm based on fish school behavior. In: Systems Man and Cybernetics, pp. 2646–2651 (2008)
9. Shi, Y.: Brain storm optimization algorithm. In: Proceedings of the International Conference in Swarm Intelligence, pp. 303–309. Springer (2011). https://doi.org/10.1007/978-3-642-21515-5_36
10. Tan, T, Zhu, Y.: Fireworks algorithm for optimization. In: International Conference in Swarm Intelligence (2010)
11. Yang, X.-S., Deb, S., Fong, S., He, X., Zhao, Y.X.: Swarm intelligence to metaheuristics: nature-inspired optimization algorithms. Computer **49**, 52–59 (2016)

12. Zeeshan, M., Tripathi, A., Khan, S.: An alternate binary search algorithm based on variable checkpoint. Int. J. Eng. Res. Technol. (IJERT) **4** (09), 459–462 (2015)
13. Mehmood, A.: ASH search: binary search optimization. Int. J. Comput. Appl. **178**(15), 0975–8887 (2019)
14. Bajwa, M.S., Agarwal, A.P., Manchanda, S.: Ternary search algorithm: improvement of binary search. In: 2nd International Conference on Computing for Sustainable Global Development (INDIACom), pp. 1723–1725 (2015)
15. https://edelalon.com/blog/2013/09/zipcode-to-city-state-excel-spreadsheet/
16. https://raw.githubusercontent.com/dwyl/english-words/master/words_alpha.txt

A Slime Mold Fractional-Order Ant Colony Optimization Algorithm for Travelling Salesman Problems

Ziheng Rong[1(✉)], Xiaoling Gong[2], Xiangyu Wang[1], Wei Lv[1], and Jian Wang[1(✉)]

[1] College of Science, China University of Petroleum (East China), Qingdao, Shangdong 266580, China
{lvwei,wangjiann1}@upc.edu.cn
[2] College of Control Science and Engineering, China University of Petroleum (East China), Qingdao 266580, Shangdong, China
gongxiaoling@s.upc.edu.cn

Abstract. In this paper, a novel algorithm of slime mold fractional-order ant colony optimization (SMFACO) for travelling salesman problems (TSPs) is proposed. The newly developed algorithm, SMFACO, takes full use of the long-term memory characteristics of the fractional calculus to balance exploration and exploitation. In addition, it considers the property of the slime mold model, which retains the critical path to avoid trapping into the local optima. To evaluate the performance of the SMFACO, we conduct comprehensive experiments on various data sets. According to the experimental results, the proposed algorithm outperforms its peer algorithms on solution quality, search efficiency and convergence speed.

Keywords: Ant colony optimization · Slime mold · Fractional-order calculus · Traveling salesman problems

1 Introduction

Travelling salesman problems (TSPs), one of the most classical combinatorial optimization problems, have been attracting considerable interests since the 1970s [1,2]. However, deterministic traditional methods are less competitive, due to the NP-hard nature of TSPs [3,4]. Meta-heuristic algorithms are proposed to find the optimal solution within a reasonable time and escape the need of infinitely exploring all combinations of a problem [5–7]. Meanwhile, meta-heuristic algorithms have been intensively researched and successfully applied to a great number of areas [8–10]. In the filed of meta-heuristic algorithms, ant colony optimization (ACO) is a powerful tool in dealing with TSPs [11,12]. A number of ACO variants have been developed to balance between exploration and exploitation, which can be roughly classified into: adjustment of parameters,

© Springer Nature Switzerland AG 2021
Y. Tan and Y. Shi (Eds.): ICSI 2021, LNCS 12689, pp. 322–332, 2021.
https://doi.org/10.1007/978-3-030-78743-1_29

modification of pheromone updates, and integration with other search technologies [13,14]. Although these variants performs well, there still exists some problems such as premature convergence and weak robustness still exist. Recently, fractional-order ACO algorithms have been proposed in [15,16], and shown a good balance between fast convergence and global search ability.

Most recently, slime mold (SM), a single-celled organism which resembles an amoeba, has attracted researchers' attention due to its unique biological mechanism, as well as its intelligent behavior with the strong ability to design networks and find paths [17–21]. In SM, the positive feedback mechanism and the characteristic of preserving critical path are major contributors to find the shortest path. When the protoplasmic flow continues increasing, the tube becomes thicker; otherwise, the tube becomes thinner or even disappears. Ultimately the critical paths are remained. Recently, researchers attempt to find more applications of SM, such as graph-optimization problem [22], community mining [23], route optimization [24], the user equilibrium traffic assignment problem [25], supply chain network design [26,27], and the dark matter network prediction between galaxies [28].

After reviewing the previous researches of the slime mold, we find that it is particularly suitable for tackling shortest-path-finding-related problems, which is accorded with the main target of TSPs. Therefore, the slime mold algorithm is supposed to be a good candidate for addressing TSPs. Inspired by the fractional ant colony optimization algorithm and the intelligent behavior of SM, in this paper, we put forward a modified ACO algorithm, slime mold fractional-order ant colony optimization (SMFACO), which takes advantage of slime mold and fractional calculus in pheromone updating strategy. In addition, the fractional state transition probability is used to improve the search accuracy. The main contributions of this paper are summarized as follows.

A) We modify the classic slime mold model with multi-pair inlet and outlet, which can overcome the shortcoming of ignoring some crucial tube connections in single-entry-outlet models.
B) An algorithm called SMFACO is proposed for solving TSPs. In order to obtain long term memory and preserve critical paths, the Grnwald-Letnikov fractional difference and protoplasm flow of SM is used in updating the pheromone formula. In addition, a fractional transition probability is developed to determine the transition to the next city.
C) The substantial experiments are conducted, and experimental results indicate the superior performance of the proposed algorithm. Numerical experiments and comparisons tested on a series of standard TSP datasets demonstrate the validity and rationality of the proposed algorithm.

The rest of this paper is organized as follows. In Sect. 2, we briefly introduce ACO, fractional-order calculus, and the conventional slime mold model. The details of the modified SM model and the proposed SMFACO algorithm are presented in Sect. 3. Section 4 discusses the simulation results in comparison with other peer algorithms. The conclusions are drawn in Sect. 5.

2 Related Work

In this section, we briefly review the framework of ACO, the relevant background of fractional calculus, and the mathematical model of classic SM.

2.1 Ant Colony Optimization Algorithm

Hypothesizing the number of cities and ants are N and M, respectively. Ant a $(a = 1, 2, \ldots, M)$ in city i selects the next arriving city j according to the probability of state transition, which is defined as:

$$p_{ij}^a = \begin{cases} \dfrac{[\tau_{ij}]^\alpha [\eta_{ij}]^\beta}{\sum\limits_{u \in J_i^a} [\tau_{iu}]^\alpha [\eta_{iu}]^\beta}, & \text{if } j \in J_i^a, \\ 0, & \text{otherwise,} \end{cases} \tag{1}$$

where τ_{ij} is the pheromone concentration, $\eta_{ij} = \frac{1}{d_{ij}}$ is the heuristic information; α and β are weight coefficients related to heuristic information and pheromone concentration, respectively; J_i^a represents an optional set of the next cities.

After each iteration, ants release pheromones according to the length of the constructed path. Considering the evaporation of pheromones in practice situation, the updating formula is described as follows:

$$\tau_{ij} = (1 - \rho) \cdot \tau_{ij} + \sum_{a=1}^M \Delta \tau_{ij}^a, \tag{2}$$

where

$$\Delta \tau_{ij}^a = \begin{cases} (l^a)^{-1}, & \text{if } (i, j) \in r^a, \\ 0, & \text{otherwise,} \end{cases} \tag{3}$$

where ρ represents the rate of pheromone evaporation, $0 < \rho < 1$; $\Delta \tau_{ij}^a$ is the amount of pheromone increment, which is released by the ant a on its visited edge; l^a is a function related to the length of the path constructed by the ant a.

2.2 Fractional-Order Calculus

The Fractional-order calculus is a generalization of the integral calculus, and its order can be any complex number, which can achieve a continuum of the calculus orders. As a new tool, it has attracted researchers' attention in many application fields. In this paper, we use the fractional-order calculus in the form of Grünwald-Letnikov [29]. The fractional derivative of order v is defined as:

$$_a^{G-L} D_x^v h(x) = \lim_{H \to \infty} \left\{ \frac{\left(\dfrac{x-a}{H} \right)^{-v}}{\Gamma(-v)} \sum_{l=0}^{H-1} \frac{\Gamma(l-v)}{\Gamma(l+1)} h\left[x - l\left(\frac{x-a}{H} \right) \right] \right\}, \tag{4}$$

where $\Gamma(\alpha) = \int_0^\infty e^{-x} x^{\alpha-1} dx$ is the Gamma function, $\frac{x-a}{H}$ is the sampling step, $_a^{G-L}D_x^v$ is a fractional differential operator, and $[a, x]$ denotes the domain of x. Let $\Delta x = \frac{x-a}{H}$, in domain $[x - H\Delta x, x]$, then (4) is derived as:

$$
\begin{aligned}
_a^{G-L}Diff_x^v h\,(x) &= \frac{1}{(\Delta x)^v} \sum_{l=0}^{H-1} \frac{\Gamma(l-v)}{\Gamma(-v)\Gamma(l+1)} h(x - l\Delta x) \\
&= \frac{1}{(\Delta x)^v} \left[h(x) + \sum_{l=1}^{N-1} \frac{\Gamma(l-v)}{\Gamma(-v)\Gamma(l+1)} h(x - l\Delta x) \right],
\end{aligned}
\tag{5}
$$

when $v = 0$, the first-order difference expression is obtained:

$$
_a^{G-L}Diff_x^1 h\,(x) = \frac{1}{\Delta x} \left[h(x) - h(x - \Delta x) \right].
\tag{6}
$$

The comparison between (5) and (6) indicates that the fractional calculus has the characteristic of long-term memory.

2.3   Slime Mold Model

In SM model, the fluid that flows in a network tube is defined as Hagen-Poiseuille flux [30]. Therefore, the fluid Q_{ij} is written as:

$$
Q_{ij} = \frac{\pi r_{ij}^4}{8\omega} \frac{p_i - p_j}{L_{ij}} = \frac{p_i - p_j}{L_{ij}} D_{ij},
\tag{7}
$$

where ω is the viscosity coefficient of the flux, $D_{ij} = \pi r_{ij}^4/8\omega$ is called conductivity, and p_i is pressure.

According to the Kirchhoff's law [31], the flux in the network must be conserved, which satisfies the following expression:

$$
\sum_i \frac{D_{ij}}{L_{ij}} (p_i - p_j) = \begin{cases} -I_0, & \text{for } j = entry, \\ I_0, & \text{for } j = outlet, \\ 0, & \text{otherwise,} \end{cases}
\tag{8}
$$

where I_0 is the fixed flow from entry to outlet in the entire network.

By setting $p_{outlet} = 0$, all pressure values are calculated by (8), then Q_{ij} is derived from (7). The adaptive formation process of the network is described by the following expression:

$$
\frac{d}{dt} D_{ij} = f\left(|Q_{ij}|\right) - \gamma D_{ij},
\tag{9}
$$

where $f\left(|Q_{ij}|\right)$ denotes a monotonic increasing function with $f(0) = 0$, and γ represents the decline rate of the tube.

3   Algorithm Description

3.1   Modified Slime Mold Model

Referring to [32], the classical single-entry-outlet model is modified to obtain a more suitable multi-entry-exit slime mold to deal with TSPs. The core idea of the modified SM model is to utilize each pair of nodes in the network as an entrance/exit to form a sub-network, and divide-and-conquer. Therefore, the pressure of each node is calculated with the Poisson equation:

$$\sum_{i \neq j} \frac{D_{ij}}{L_{ij}} (p_i - p_j) = \begin{cases} \frac{-I_0}{F}, & \text{for } j = \text{entry}, \\ \frac{I_0}{F}, & \text{for } j = \text{outlet}, \\ 0, & \text{otherwise}, \end{cases} \tag{10}$$

where F and I_0 are the number of tubes and the initial flux flowing in the network, respectively. The flow Q_{ij} is expressed as:

$$Q_{ij} = \sum_{f=1}^{F} q_{ij}^f, \quad q_{ij}^f = \frac{D_{ij}}{L_{ij}} (p_i - p_j). \tag{11}$$

The conductivity of the next moment can be derived as:

$$D_{ij}(t+1) = \sum_{f=1}^{F} d_{ij}^f(t+1), \tag{12}$$

where

$$d_{ij}(t+1) = f\left(|q_{ij}(t)|\right) + (1 - \gamma)d_{ij}(t), \tag{13}$$

where $f\left(|q_{ij}(t)|\right) = \phi|q_{ij}(t)|$; ϕ and γ are coefficients that control the influence of q_{ij} and the decline rate of d_{ij}, respectively.

3.2   SMFACO State Transition Probability

The traditional ACO state transition probability as known in (1) only considers the information of next optimal. In our work, the fractional calculus is considered in the path selection, since its long-term memory can make full use of neighboring information of the current terrain. By considering a series of unselected city combinations, it can improve the shortcoming of trapping into local optima. The fractional state transition probability is defined as:

$$^v p_{ij}^a(t) = \frac{1}{C} \begin{cases} p_{ij}^a(t) + \sum_{k=1}^{N_1-1} |\frac{\Gamma(k-v)}{\Gamma(-v)\Gamma(k+1)}| p_{(j+k-1)(j+k)}(t), & \text{if } j \in J_i^m(t), (j+k) \in J_i^m(t), \\ 0, & \text{if } j \notin J_i^m(t), \end{cases} \tag{14}$$

where $C = \sum_{k=0}^{N_1-1} \left|\frac{\Gamma(k-v)}{\Gamma(-v)\Gamma(k+1)}\right|$ is a normalization component; $\frac{\Gamma(k-v)}{\Gamma(-v)\Gamma(k+1)}$ is a nonlinear decreasing function over k; $(N_1 - 1)$ denotes the number of optional

---

Algorithm 1. SMFACO Algorithm

Input: Distance Matrix D of TSP; The maximum number of iterations T_{max};
Output: The optimal solution S_{min};
 1: $t = 0$;
 2: Initialization parameter, and place each ant in n cities randomly;
 3: **while** $Termminal\ condition$ is not met **do**
 4:    Calculate fraction-order state transition probability;
 5:    Each ant completes the whole travel;
 6:    Use 3-Opt algorithm to local optimize;
 7:    Computer and rank path length, find the optimal solution;
 8:    Apply modified SM algorithm;
 9:    Update conductivity;
10:    **for** each edge **do**
11:       According to SMFACO pheromone update rule to updating pheromone;
12:    **end for**
13:    $t = t + 1$;
14: **end while**
15: Use 3-Opt algorithm to local optimize;
16: Return shortest travel path.

---

cities near to the city j; $p_{ij}^a(t)$ and $p_{(j+k-1)(j+k)}^a(t)$ follow the definition (1). When $k > 1$, ant a uses the linear combination probability of N_1 cities to carry out the next city transfer. Therefore, it can be seen that the fractional-order addition allows the algorithm to make full use of the neighborhood information. The fractional-order state transition probability has the nature of foresight by utilizing the information of next $(N_1 - 1)$ steps, which achieves a good balance between exploration and exploitation.

3.3   SMFACO Pheromone Updating Rule

The traditional pheromone updating formulas (2) and (3) only considers the increase of elitist ants pheromone, which causes the rapid growth of pheromones in some paths, leading to premature convergence. In this work, the pheromone is updated by using the long-term memory of fractional calculus and the critical path preservation of slime mold.

After $t - th$ iteration, we sort all paths visited by ants as follows:

$$L^1(t) \leq \cdots \leq L^a(t) \leq \cdots \leq L^{N_3}(t) \leq \cdots \leq L^{O_a}(t), \tag{15}$$

where O_a represents the number of ants, and $L^a(t)$ is the total length of the visited tour of ant a in iteration t.

Then, the SMFACO pheromone updating formula is performed as follows:

$$\tau_{ij}(t+1) = (1-\rho)\tau_{ij}(t) + \sum_{a=1}^{N_3} \left| \frac{\Gamma(a-v-1)}{\Gamma(-v)\Gamma(a)} \right| \Delta\tau_{ij}^a + \sigma(t)Q_{ij}(t), \qquad (16)$$

where

$$\Delta\tau_{ij}^a = \begin{cases} (l_a)^{-1}, & \text{if } (i,j) \in r^a, \\ 0, & \text{otherwise}, \end{cases} \qquad (17)$$

where N_3 $(1 < N_3 < O_a)$ is the number of elite ants; $\sigma(t) = 1 - [1/(1+1.1^{\frac{T_{max}}{4}-(t+1)})]$ is a control factor, which is used for regulating the effect of protoplasm flow in SM on pheromone. Q_{ij} is a stream of protoplasm that flows in SM. From (16), it can be seen that the pheromone renewal takes into account the pheromone volatilization, the historical information of the N_3 elite ants, and the pheromone released by the slime molds.

Compared with (2), it is clear that pheromone updating formula (16) increases the pheromone of elite ants N_3, and improves the global search ability and fast convergence. In addition, the protoplasm flowing in the slime mold is regarded as pheromone. Since the slime mold can retain critical paths efficiently, the pheromone on important paths increases, and the convergence speed of the SMFACO is accelerated.

With the aforementioned descriptions and definitions, the pseudocode of SMFACO algorithm is given in Algorithm 1. In addition, 3-Optimization (3-Opt) technology [33] is used to locally optimize paths constructed by all ants in each iteration.

4   Experiments

4.1   Experimental Settings

In order to fairly appraise the performance of the proposed algorithm, the minimum solution (Min), the average solution (Ave), the root mean squared error (RMSE), and the relative error (RE) are recorded throughout the whole experiments. The experiment is conducted 20 runs on eight datasets selected from the standard TSPs, including att48, eil51, eil101, berlin52, st70, pr76, pr144, and rat99. The size of population is set to be equivalent to the number of cities. The parameters α, β and ρ are set to be 1, 5, 0.2, respectively, referring to [34]. As for the other parameters in SMFACO, the tube decline rate γ is 0.55, ϕ is set to 0.8, N_1 and N_3 are both equal to 8, v and T_{max} are respectively set to be 0.8 and 300.

4.2   Experimental Results and Analysis

To test the performance of the proposed SMFACO, four meta-heuristic algorithms and two state-of-the-art ACO algorithms are chosen to compare with

Table 1. Comparisons of SMFACO algorithm with others.

	Algorithms	Datasets							
		att48	eil51	eil101	berlin52	st70	pr76	pr144	rat99
	BKS	33522	426	629	7542	675	108159	58537	1211
Min	MMAS	**33522**	**426**	**629**	**7542**	**675**	**108159**	**58537**	1212
	ACO-Taguchi	-	**426**	640	**7542**	-	108785	-	-
	HA	**33522**	427	633	**7542**	678	108979	**58537**	1213
	FPSO	**33522**	427	630	**7542**	**675**	**108159**	**58537**	**1211**
	[15]	**33522**	-	**629**	-	**675**	**108159**	-	**1211**
	FACO	**33522**	**426**	**629**	**7542**	**675**	**108159**	**58537**	**1211**
	SMFACO	**33522**	**426**	**629**	**7542**	**675**	**108159**	**58537**	**1211**
Ave	MMAS	33576.4	428.1	636.1	7542.0	682.6	109646.0	58560.3	1214.5
	ACO-Taguchi	-	435.4	655.0	7635.4	-	110420.0	-	-
	HA	33612.5	430.8	638.9	7617.7	684.4	109898.0	58653.0	1217.3
	FPSO	33585.7	430.5	636.5	**7542.0**	682.3	109470.5	58679.3	1215.2
	[15]	33575.1	-	636.3	-	680.7	110420.0	-	1218.4
	FACO	33544.7	427.4	635.6	**7542.0**	680.1	109272.0	**58537.0**	**1213.0**
	SMFACO	**33533.9**	**427.1**	**634.0**	**7542.0**	**678.1**	**108666.7**	**58537.0**	1215.0
RMSE	MMAS	72.03	2.30	8.03	**0.00**	8.90	1588.68	23.95	4.76
	ACO-Taguchi	-	-	-	-	-	1617.78	-	-
	HA	100.46	5.88	10.69	86.99	10.14	1820.42	131.37	7.60
	FPSO	33522	5.47	8.91	**0.00**	8.75	1445.70	148.51	4.75
	[15]	65.65	-	3.61	-	4.59	1617.78	-	7.87
	FACO	37.01	1.61	7.64	**0.00**	6.67	1285.59	**0.00**	**2.10**
	SMFACO	**24.23**	**1.34**	**3.55**	**0.00**	**2.04**	**513.40**	**0.00**	4.44
RE(%)	MMAS	0.16	0.49	1.13	**0.00**	1.13	1.38	0.04	**0.29**
	ACO-Taguchi	-	4.13	2.21	1.24	-	1.50	-	-
	HA	0.27	1.13	1.57	0.10	1.39	1.21	0.20	0.52
	FPSO	0.19	1.06	1.19	**0.00**	1.08	1.21	0.24	0.35
	[15]	0.16	-	1.16	-	0.84	2.09	-	0.61
	FACO	0.07	0.33	1.05	**0.00**	0.76	1.03	**0.00**	0.33
	SMFACO	**0.04**	**0.25**	**0.64**	**0.00**	**0.46**	**0.47**	**0.00**	0.33

SMFACO : MMAS (2002) [12], ACO-Taguchi (2013) [35], HA (2015) [36], FPSO (2016) [37], Literature [15] (2020), FACO (2021) [16]. The comparison results with six other algorithms on eight TSP datasets are shown in Table 1. In Table 1, the results which are not found in references are denoted by '-', and the best results are in bold, and BKS represents the best known solution.

First of all, it is easily observed that in terms of the minimum path length, our algorithm and FACO construct the optimal solutions on all TSP instances, which shows that the proposed algorithm is effective in finding the optimal path. Then, results reveal that the optimum searching capabilities of the ACO-Taguchi and HA algorithms are relatively poor. For the eigeht TSP datasets, the MIN, Ave, RMSE, and RE are clearly higher than those of other optimization algorithms. Furthermore, SMFACO generates better solutions than six other intelligence algorithms except TSP dataset rat99 in term of AV and RMSE. Particularly, in term of the average solution, SMFACO has improved 0.03%, 0.24%, 0.29%, and 0.56% on the instances att48, eil101, st70, and pr76 compared with the suboptimum algorithm, respectively. Finally, the RE of these tours found by the SMFACO are minimal for all instances except rat99, which implies that the SMFACO can obtain solutions with higher accuracy.

Overall, among all performance evaluation indexes, compared with other algorithms, SMAFCO obtains the minimum value on all data sets, except for rat99, indicating that the optimized performance of SMFACO is relatively the best. Furthermore, the proposed algorithm SMFACO outperforms the other intelligence algorithms in 87.5% on 8 instances. Therefore, experimental results indicate that SMFACO can effectively solve TSPs with higher quality solutions and stronger robustness.

5   Conclusion

In this paper, we propose an meta-heuristic optimization algorithm termed SMFACO, which is based on ACO and two attractive technologies to address TSPs. The fractional calculus and slime mold model are applied to updating the pheromone, which makes the algorithm has long-term memory, and the ability of retaining key information. The fractional state transition probability takes full use of neighbouring informations. The proposed algorithm SMFACO is tested on eight standard TSP instances, and the simulation results show that SMFACO algorithm performs well in terms of all evaluation metrics compared with the classical meta-heuristics algorithms and state-of-the-art algorithms. In the future work, we will investigate applications of SMFACO on lager scale TSP instances and optimize the proposed algorithm.

Acknowledgment. This work was supported in part by the National Natural Science Foundation of China (No. 51722406, 51874335, and 51674280), the Natural Science Foundation of Shandong Province (No. ZR2015AL014, JQ201808, ZR201709220208) and the Fundamental Research Funds for the Central Universities (No. 18CX02036A, 18CX02097A, 20CX05002A), the National Science and Technology Major Project of China under Grant (No. 2016ZX05025001-006), the Major Scientific and Technological Projects of CNPC under Grant (No. ZD2019-183-008), the Science and Technology Support Plan for Youth Innovation of University in Shandong Province under Grant (No. 2019KJH002), the National Science and Technology Major Project of China under Grant (2016ZX05025001-006).

References

1. Garey, M.R., Johnson, D.S.: Computers and intractability: a guide to the theory of NP-completeness. **2**(23), 555–565 (1979)
2. Gutin, G., Punnen, A.: The traveling salesman problem and its variations. Paradigms Comb. Optim. Probl. **4**(2), 193–205 (2007)
3. Arigliano, A., Calogiuri, T., Ghiani, G.: A branch-and-bound algorithm for the time-dependent travelling salesman problem. Networks **72**(3) (2018)
4. Hernández-Pérez, H., Salazar-González, J.J.: An exact algorithm for the split-demand one-commodity pickup-and-delivery travelling salesman problem. In: Lee, J., Rinaldi, G., Mahjoub, A.R. (eds.) ISCO 2018. LNCS, vol. 10856, pp. 241–252. Springer, Cham (2018). https://doi.org/10.1007/978-3-319-96151-4_21

5. Wang, H.Q., Huang, D.S., Wang, B.: Optimisation of radial basis function classifiers using simulated annealing algorithm for cancer classification. Electron. Lett. **41**(11), 630–632 (2005)
6. Guo, L., Huang, D.S., Zhao, W.: Combining genetic optimisation with hybrid learning algorithm for radial basis function neural networks. Electron. Lett. **39**(22), 1600–1601 (2003)
7. Wang, G.G.: Improving metaheuristic algorithms with information feedback models. IEEE Trans. Cybern. **99**, 1–14 (2017)
8. Chen, G., Zhang, K., Zhang, L.: Global and local surrogate-model-assisted differential evolution for waterflooding production optimization. SPE J. **25**(1), 105–118 (2020)
9. Ma, X., Zhang, K., Yao, C.: Multiscale-network structure inversion of fractured media based on a hierarchical-parameterization and data-driven evolutionary-optimization method. SPE J. **25**(5), 2729–2748 (2020)
10. Zhao, M., Zhang, K., Chen, G.: A classification-based surrogate-assisted multiobjective evolutionary algorithm for production optimization under geological uncertainty. SPE J. **25**(5) (2020)
11. Dorigo, M.: Optimization, learning and natural algorithms. Ph.d. thesis Politecnico Di Milano (1992)
12. Stutzle, T., Hoos, H.: MAX-MIN Ant System and local search for the traveling salesman problem. In: IEEE International Conference on Evolutionary Computation (ICEC 97). IEEE (2002)
13. Dahan, H.E., Mathkour: Dynamic flying ant colony optimization (DFACO) for solving the traveling salesman problem. Sensors **19**(8) (2019)
14. Hgarwal, P., Sourabh, M., Sachdeva, R.: Recommending Optimal Tour for Groups Using Ant Colony Optimization. IEEE Computer Society (2018)
15. Gong, X., Rong, Z., Gao, T.: An improved ant colony optimization algorithm based on fractional order memory for traveling salesman problems. In 2019 IEEE Symposium Series on Computational Intelligence, SSCI (2020)
16. Pu, Y.F., Siarry, P., Wang, J., Zhang, N.: Fractional-order ant colony algorithm: a fractional long term memory based cooperative learning approach. Swarm Evol. Comput. (2021)
17. Nakagaki, T., Iima, M., Ueda, T.: Minimum-risk path finding by an adaptive amoebal network. Phys. Rev. Lett. **99**(6), 068–104 (2007)
18. Tero, A., Kobayashi, R., Nakagaki, T.: A mathematical model for adaptive transport network in path finding by true slime mold. J. Theor. Biol. **244**(4), 553–564 (2007)
19. Nakagaki, T., Yamada, H.: Tóth.: Maze-solving by an amoeboid organism. Nature **407**, 6803 (2000)
20. Atsushi, T., Seiji, T., Tetsu, S.: Rules for biologically inspired adaptive network design. Science **327**(5964), 439–442 (2010)
21. LiuY., Feng, X., Yu, H., Luo, L.: Physarum Dynamic Optimization Algorithm Based on Energy Mechanism (2017)
22. Zhang, X., Gao, C., Deng, Y., Zhang, Z.: Slime mould inspired applications on graph-optimization problems. In: Adamatzky, A. (ed.) Advances in Physarum Machines. ECC, vol. 21, pp. 519–562. Springer, Cham (2016). https://doi.org/10.1007/978-3-319-26662-6_26
23. Liang, M., Gao, C., Li, X., Zhang, Z.: A *Physarum*-inspired ant colony optimization for community mining. In: Kim, J., Shim, K., Cao, L., Lee, J.-G., Lin, X., Moon, Y.-S. (eds.) PAKDD 2017. LNCS (LNAI), vol. 10234, pp. 737–749. Springer, Cham (2017). https://doi.org/10.1007/978-3-319-57454-7_57

24. Zhang, X., Zhang, Z., Zhang, Y.: Route selection for emergency logistics management: a bio-inspired algorithm. Saf. Sci. **54**, 87–91 (2013)
25. Jiang, S., Wen, S.: A modified Physarum-inspired model for the user equilibrium traffic assignment problem. Appl. Math. Modelling (2018)
26. Gao, C., Chen, S., Li, X.: A physarum -inspired optimization algorithm for load-shedding problem. Appl. Soft Comput. **61** (2017)
27. Zhang, X., Chan, F.T.S., Adamatzky, A.: An intelligent physarum solver for supply chain network design under profit maximization and oligopolistic competition. Int. J. Prod. Res. **55**(1), 224–263 (2016)
28. Burchett, J., Elek, O.: Slime Mold Simulations Used to Map Dark Matter Holding Universe Together (2020)
29. Oldham, K.B., Spanier, J.: The fractional calculus. Math. Gazette **56**(247), 396–400 (1974)
30. Wang, Y., Xu, J., Yang, C.: Fluid inhomogeneity within nanoslits and deviation from Hagen-Poiseuille flow. AIChE J. (2016)
31. Robitaille, P.M.: On the validity of Kirchhoff's law of thermal emission. IEEE Trans. Plasma Sci. **316**, 1263–1267 (2003)
32. Qian, T., Zhang, Z., Gao, C., Wu, Y., Liu, Y.: An ant colony system based on the *Physarum* network. In: Tan, Y., Shi, Y., Mo, H. (eds.) ICSI 2013. LNCS, vol. 7928, pp. 297–305. Springer, Heidelberg (2013). https://doi.org/10.1007/978-3-642-38703-6_35
33. Gülcü, A., Mahi, M.: A parallel cooperative hybrid method based on ant colony optimization and 3-Opt algorithm for solving traveling salesman problem. Soft Computing A Fusion of Foundations Methodologies (2018)
34. Tuani, A.F., Keedwell, E., Collett, M.: Heterogenous adaptive ant colony optimization with 3-opt local search for the travelling salesman problem. Appl. Soft Comput. **97** (2020)
35. Peker, M., En, B., Kumru, P.Y: An efficient solving of the traveling salesman problem: the ant colony system having parameters optimized by the Taguchi method. Turkish J. Electr. Eng. Comput. Sci. **21**, 2015–2036 (2013)
36. Gündüz, M., Kiran, M.S., Özceylan, E.: A hierarchic approach based on swarm intelligence to solve the traveling salesman problem. Mathematics **23**(1), 215–235 (2015)
37. Couceiro, M., Sivasundaram, S.: Novel fractional order particle swarm optimization. Appl. Math. **283**, 36–54 (2016)

Ant Colony Optimization
for K-Independent Average Traveling
Salesman Problem

Yu Iwasaki and Koji Hasebe[✉]

Department of Computer Science, University of Tsukuba, 1-1-1, Tennodai,
Tsukuba 305-8573, Japan
iwasaki@mas.cs.tsukuba.ac.jp, hasebe@cs.tsukuba.ac.jp

Abstract. In this paper, we propose a K-independent average traveling salesman problem (KI-Average-TSP) extended from the TSP. This
is an optimization problem that minimizes the weighted sum of the average and standard deviation of K circuits' costs, with mutually independent edges. As a method to solve the KI-Average-TSP, we propose K-independent average ant colony optimization (KI-Average-ACO)
extended from the original ACO. KI-Average-ACO moves K ants simultaneously using the following two heuristics to prevent different circuits
from sharing the same edge. The first heuristic uses a degree of possible
options representing the number of vertices that an ant can reach from
its current vertex. The destination of ants is stochastically determined
by this value to reduce the circuit construction failure rate. The second
heuristic, named 2-best-opt, uses a greedy algorithm in reconstructing a
better path to obtain K circuits if circuit construction fails. Comparison
results between the approximate solution obtained using KI-Average-
ACO and the solution obtained using a quadratic programming method
for a binary search showed that the number of circuits for KI-Average-
ACO was higher, and KI-Average-ACO obtained a better approximate
solution than the quadratic programming method.

Keywords: Ant colony optimization · Traveling salesman problem ·
Heuristics

1 Introduction

One of the common combinatorial optimization problems is the traveling salesman problem (TSP) [6]. Given distances (edges) connecting cities, the TSP finds
the shortest routes to visit all cities. The TSP is applied to various problems, such
as vehicle routing and job-shop scheduling [5]. However, optimization problems
in the real world are considered more complicated than the TSP. For example,
in a transportation company's delivery plans, even if the company constructs
the shortest circuits to access cities, these routes may become inaccessible due
to road damage or accidents.

© Springer Nature Switzerland AG 2021
Y. Tan and Y. Shi (Eds.): ICSI 2021, LNCS 12689, pp. 333–344, 2021.
https://doi.org/10.1007/978-3-030-78743-1_30

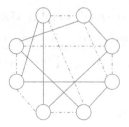

Fig. 1. An example of K-Independent paths (with $K = 2$), where multiple paths do not share the same edge in $N = 8$ complete graph.

In this study, we consider constructing mutually independent circuits with no shared edges to improve reliability and propose a K-independent average TSP (KI-Average-TSP) that minimizes the weighted sum of the average and standard deviations of K circuits' costs, where the circuits are mutually independent, that is, there are no shared edges among the circuits. Compared to a study to find multiple independent Hamiltonian paths in a graph [12], this study minimizes the cost by considering the standard deviation in a complete graph so that the K circuits act as backup routes. Figure 1 shows an example of $K = 2$ circuits in a complete graph of $N = 8$ vertices.

To solve the problem, we propose an ant colony optimization (ACO)-based K-independent average ACO (KI-Average-ACO). ACO [2,7] is known as a meta-heuristic solution to the TSP using ant swarm characteristics and simulates the pheromone communication of ants on a graph to find the approximate shortest path. In our optimization algorithm, K ants move simultaneously, making it possible for K ants to use equally favorable edges and reducing the standard deviation. However, as the ants move, the number of reachable vertices for the ants decreases, and the circuit construction failure rate increases. Therefore, we introduce two heuristics to reduce the failure rate of circuit construction. The key concept of the first heuristic is a degree of possible options that represents the number of vertices an ant can reach from its current vertex. The destination of ants is stochastically determined by this number to reduce the circuit construction failure rate. The second heuristic, called 2-best-opt, is an algorithm based on the idea of 2-opt [3,6]. It uses a greedy algorithm in reconstructing a better path to obtain K circuits if circuit construction fails.

In this paper, we evaluated our proposed method by comparing the approximate solution obtained using KI-Average-ACO with the solution obtained using a quadratic programming method for a binary search. Comparison results showed that the number of circuits for KI-Average-ACO was higher, and KI-Average-ACO obtained a better approximate solution than the quadratic programming method.

Related Work. ACO is a search algorithm that is inspired by the process by which ants use pheromones to discover the shortest path to food [2]. In particular, it is known as metaheuristics for finding approximate solutions to shortest path problems, as typified by the TSP. An application of ACO is the vehicle routing problem [11], which delivers resources from a depot to customers through delivery vehicles. Another application is the multiple TSP [4], which builds a partial traveling circuit in which multiple salesmen share each other's visits to cities from a depot.

On the other hand, a few studies have been conducted on algorithms to find multiple independent circuits in a complete graph. Teng [12] reported properties such as the conditions for establishing multiple Hamiltonian paths in a given graph. However, algorithms for constructing circuits that are independent of each other have not yet been investigated.

Paper Organization. The organization of this paper is as follows. Section 2 defines KI-Average-TSP and a related problem named KI-Total-TSP. Section 3 introduces our optimization algorithm named KI-Average-ACO. Section 4 presents experimental results. Finally, Sect. 5 concludes the paper and presents future work.

2   Problem Description

In this section, we give the definition of our target problem named K-independent average traveling salesman problem (KI-Average-TSP). In addition, although not directly dealt with in this study, we also define K-independent total traveling salesman problem (KI-Total-TSP), which is another optimization problem related to KI-Average-TSP. The former is the problem of finding the K-independent circuits that minimize the weighted sum of average and standard deviation in a given complete graph, while the latter is the problem that removes the term of standard deviation from the objective function in KI-Average-TSP and minimizes only the total cost of K-independent circuits.

Here, let $G = (V, E, d)$ (with $|V| = N, |E| = \frac{N(N-1)}{2}$) be a weighted undirected complete graph, where d_{ij} is the weight of edge (i, j) and N is the number of cities.

2.1   K-Independent Average TSP

KI-Average-TSP is a problem to minimize the weighted sum of the average and standard deviations of K independent circuits' cost in a graph G. The definition is as follows.

Definition 1. *KI-Average-TSP is a problem to perform the following optimization in graph $G = (V, E)$.*

$$\textbf{min} \qquad \text{cost}_{\text{avg}} + \gamma \cdot \text{cost}_{\text{sd}}^{\theta} \tag{1}$$

$$\textbf{subject to} \qquad \sum_{k \in K} x_{ijk} \leq 1 \qquad (\forall i, j \ (i \neq j)) \tag{2}$$

$$\sum_{j \in V} x_{ijk} = 1 \qquad (\forall i, k) \tag{3}$$

$$\sum_{j \in V} x_{jik} = 1 \qquad (\forall i, k) \tag{4}$$

$$u_{ik} + 1 - (N-1)(1 - x_{ijk}) \leq u_{jk} \qquad (\forall i, j, k) \tag{5}$$

$$x_{ijk} \in \{0, 1\} \tag{6}$$

$$0 \leq u_{ik} \leq N - 1 \tag{7}$$

where

$$\text{cost}_{\text{avg}} = \frac{1}{K} \text{cost}_{\text{sum}}, \tag{8}$$

$$\text{cost}_{\text{sd}} = \sqrt{\frac{1}{K} (\sum_{k \in K} (\sum_{i \in V} \sum_{j \in V} d_{ij} \cdot x_{ijk} - \frac{1}{K} (\sum_{i \in V} \sum_{j \in V} \sum_{k' \in K} d_{ij} \cdot x_{ijk'}))^2)}. \tag{9}$$

The value x_{ijk} represents the probability of ant k using the edge connecting vertex i to vertex j. The value u_{ik} is the arc-constraint to excludes subtours based on the Miller–Tucker–Zemlin formulation [8]. Hereafter, the total cost of the K circuits is expressed as cost_{sum}. The weighted sum is represented as $\text{cost}_{\text{ssd}} = \text{cost}_{\text{avg}} + \gamma \cdot \text{cost}_{\text{sd}}^{\theta}$, where cost_{avg} and $\text{cost}_{\text{sd}}^{\theta}$ respectively represent the average and standard deviation of K circuits' costs. Variables γ, θ are parameters for weighting the average and standard deviation respectively, and the constraints are the same as in KI-Total-TSP.

2.2 K-Independent Total TSP

The KI-Total-TSP is a problem to minimize the total cost in K circuits among the combinations of K independent circuits in the graph G. The definition is as follows.

Definition 2. *KI-Total-TSP is a problem to perform the following optimization in graph $G = (V, E, d)$.*

$$\textbf{min} \qquad \sum_{i \in V} \sum_{j \in V} \sum_{k \in K} d_{ij} \cdot x_{ijk} \tag{10}$$

with the same constraint conditions as in the KI-Average-TSP (i.e., Eqs. 2–7).

We would like to note that the problems introduced above are complementary to each other. That is, the solution of KI-Average-TSP is useful when finding K circuits with similar utility values. On the other hand, KI-Total-TSP is useful when finding K circuits with ranked utility values. Specifically, the former is a case, where multiple packets are sent simultaneously through K routes, while the latter is a case, where spare routes should be prepared for a failure of the current route.

3 K-Independent Average ACO

3.1 Overview

In this section, we explain the proposed K-independent average ant colony optimization (KI-Average-ACO) algorithm for solving KI-Average-TSP. Considering that it is difficult to calculate the exact solution to KI-Average-TSP in a feasible time, we propose KI-Average-ACO to obtain an approximate solution.

Unlike the original ACO, KI-Average-ACO averages the cost of K circuits by repeatedly moving K ants along one edge at a time. However, because the construction failure rate increases when K ants move simultaneously, we use two heuristics. The first heuristic uses a degree of possible options, which indicates the feasible vertices the ant can reach. Ants move to vertices with fewer destinations using this index, putting off many potential movable vertices. The second is 2-best-opt, which searches efficiently by reconstructing failed circuits greedily using 2-opt. Using these heuristics, it is possible to reduce the construction failure rate while averaging the moving cost of K circuits, rather than repeating ACO. The pseudocode of KI-Average-ACO is presented in Algorithm 1.

3.2 Simultaneous Movement of Ants

KI-Average-ACO differs from the original ACO in moving K ants along one edge at a time. In the original Ant System [1] and Max-Min Ant System [10], some ants construct a path. If these algorithms are applied to KI-Average-TSP repeatedly, some ants construct a circuit using preferable edges greedily. Consequently, the cost of the circuit in the latter half of the construction increases, the shape becomes complicated, and the averaging cannot be satisfied. In contrast, in Line 17 in the pseudocode, KI-Average-ACO moves K ants along one edge at a time, so that all ants can use their preferred edges. In Line 19, ants are arranged in descending order of moving cost so far after every movement, and the next ants move in this order. As a result, it is possible to perform the averaging of the cost in a greedy manner, because ants, which have consumed bigger moving costs so far, can move to smaller-cost and pheromone-rich edges more preferentially. We would like to note that the cost of an edge used becomes infinite and the pheromone value becomes zero to ensure that it is not used as much as possible again.

3.3 Heuristic with Degree of Possible Options

KI-Average-ACO moves K ants simultaneously. As a result, close to the K-th movement, there are possibilities that ants may reuse edges used by other ants, thereby increasing the construction failure. Therefore, to increase the number of successes, we introduce the heuristic with the degree of possible options. This is incorporated into the transition probability equation in Line 17 in the pseudocode.

Algorithm 1. KI-Average-ACO

1: **function** ki_average_aco(G, N, K)
2:     aco(G)   ▷ init G's pheromone with Ant System
3:     ants = [ ]
4:     **for** $i = 1$ to K **do**
5:         ants.append(Ant())
6:     **end for**
7:     **for** $t = 1$ to T **do**
8:         make_tsps(G, N, K, ants)
9:         2_best_opt(G, K, ants)
10:         pheromone_update(G, ants)
11:     **end for**
12: **end function**
13:
14: **function** make_tsps(G, N, K, ants)
15:     **for** $i = 1$ to N **do**
16:         **for** $j = 1$ to K **do**
17:             ants[j].move_one_edge(G)   ▷ use the degree of possible options
18:         **end for**
19:         ants.sort(key=ant.cost$_{sum}$, reverse=true)   ▷ sort ants in descending order
20:     **end for**
21: **end function**
22:
23: **function** 2_best_opt(G, N, K, ants)
24:     **for** $i = 1$ to K **do**
25:         **if** ants[i].path has duplicated edge **then**
26:             ant = ants[i]
27:             alts = [ ]
28:             **for** $j = 1$ to N **do**
29:                 **for** $k = 1$ to N **do**
30:                     at = ant.2_opt(ant.path[j], ant.path[k])
31:                     **if** at.path has no contradiction **then**
32:                         alts.append(at)
33:                     **end if**
34:                 **end for**
35:             **end for**
36:             alts.sort(key=ant.cost$_{sum}$)
37:             ants[i] = alts[0]   ▷ use best swap reducing cost
38:         **end if**
39:     **end for**
40: **end function**
41:
42: **function** pheromone_update(G, ants)
43:     **if** ants has no duplicated edge **then**
44:         update(G, ants)
45:     **end if**
46: **end function**

Assume that each of the K ants has already moved t times out of N times, and the set of vertices visited by ant h is U_h. Here, we define $R_h^t(x) \subseteq V$ as a function that returns a set of vertices where ant h can move consistently from vertex x to vertex y. The word "consistent" averages that vertex $y \in R_h^t(x)$ satisfies $y \notin U_h$ and the edge (x, y) is not yet used by other ants $1, 2, \ldots, h - 1, h + 1, \ldots, K$.

At this time, transition probability equation P_{ij}^h that ant h selects the next vertex j from the vertex i is defined by Eq. 11.

$$P_{ij}^h = \frac{[\tau_{ij}]^\alpha [\eta_{ij}]^\beta}{\sum_{u \in N_h^t(i)} [\tau_{iu}]^\alpha [\eta_{iu}]^\beta} \times \frac{1}{|R_h^t(j)|}, \tag{11}$$

$$\eta_{ij} = \frac{1}{d_{ij}} \tag{12}$$

where τ_{ij} is the pheromone quantity of the edge (i, j) and η_{ij} is the heuristic value. $N_h^t(i)$ is a set of vertices where an ant h can move from vertex i in the t-th move. In Eq. 11, the transition probability is divided by the number of vertices $|R_h^t(j)|$ that ant h can move from vertex j. Using this operation, ants can preferentially move to vertices that have little non-affordably movable vertices. This reduces the construction failure rate. The time complexity of KI-Average-ACO with this heuristic is $O(KN^3)$, while that without this heuristic is $O(KN^2)$. Although the time complexity is increased by $O(N)$ during the moving process, the construction failure rate is reduced.

3.4   2-best-opt

In Line 9, we use the heuristic called 2-best-opt to improve paths after constructing the circuits to further increase the success probability of constructing independent circuits and minimizing cost$_{\text{ssd}}$. Procedures of the 2-best-opt are depicted from Line 23 to 40.

Assume that in the K paths after the construction, an edge $e = (a, b)$ is redundantly used in multiple paths of F (> 1) ants. At this time, 2-best-opt is performed for each of the $l_1, l_2, \ldots, l_F$ paths of F ants. 2-best-opt is the following operation and is shown in Fig. 2 and from Line 23 to 40.

Consider a case where an edge $e = (a, b)$ is redundantly used by other paths of a certain path l and other $N - 1$ edges $e' = (c, d)$ of the path l are exchanged by 2-opt. At this time, if the two new edges $e_1 = (a, c)$ and $e_2 = (b, d)$ are not yet used for any K paths, the number of use of edges can be reduced without contradiction, and the edge e' is added to the replacement candidate set S in Line 30 to 33. Then, among the exchange candidates of these edges, an edge $e' \in S$ is selected and swapped by e in 2-opt, so that the moving cost of the path l becomes the smallest by exchanging with the edge e in Line 36 and 37.

The time complexity of KI-Average-ACO with 2-best-opt is $O(KN^2)$, however, experimental results described in Sect. 4 show that the running time of 2-best-opt is smaller than KI-Average-ACO without this heuristic. Using this

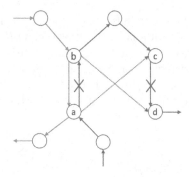

Fig. 2. The example of 2-best-opt which is trying to swap $e = (a, b)$ and $e' = (c, d)$ because the edge e is used twice. Swapped edges $e_1 = (a, c)$, $e_2 = (b, d)$ can reduce usage count in $e = (a, b)$.

2-best-opt, the overlapping edges causing the failure can be corrected greedily and the construction failure rate and cost_{ssd} can be reduced.

3.5   Pheromone Update

After performing 2-best-opt, in Line 10, if K paths are reconstructed and are independent of each other, the pheromone update equation, Eq. 13, is executed.

$$\tau_{ij}(t+1) = \rho \cdot \tau_{ij}(t) + \sum_{h=1}^{K} \Delta_{ij}^{h}, \tag{13}$$

$$\Delta_{ij}^{h} = \begin{cases} \frac{1}{C_h + \text{cost}_{\text{sd}}^{\theta}} & ((i, j) \in l_h) \\ 0 & (otherwise) \end{cases} \tag{14}$$

where ρ is the retention rate of the pheromone, C_h is the cost of the circuit constructed by ant h, l_h is the path of ant h, and θ is equal to θ in Eq. 1. However, if the K paths are not independent of each other, the updating equation for the pheromone on the graph and the evaporation of pheromone are not performed from Line 43 to 45. This tries to centralize searching by updating.

4   Empirical Study

4.1   Parameters and Settings

This section presents two experiments to evaluate our algorithm. In the first experiment, the performance of the two heuristics used in KI-Average-ACO was evaluated. In the second experiment, KI-Average-TSPs were solved using KI-Average-ACO and a combinatorial optimization method to compare their solutions and the time taken to obtain these solutions.

Table 1. Parameter settings.

Parameter	Value
α (pheromone rate)	1
β (heuristic rate)	3
ρ (pheromone residual rate)	0.97
Number of ants	N
AT (number of the cycles in Ant System)	200
KT (number of the cycles in KI-Average-ACO)	1000
LT (number of trials)	10

The parameters in the experiments are as shown in Table 1. Here, AT represents the number of cycles to initialize the pheromone using the Ant System on the graph before starting KI-Average-ACO. KT represents the number of cycles that KI-Average-ACO executes to build K paths. LT represents the number of experimental trials performed.

4.2   Performance Evaluation of Heuristics

To evaluate the performance of the heuristics used in KI-Average-ACO, we considered four cases with and without each heuristic and compared them by solving KI-Average TSP for each case. In every case, the pheromone was always updated.

As the graphs used for the optimization problems, we selected three graphs ulysses22, bays29, and att48, which have a different number of vertices from TSPLIB [9], the dataset often used for performance evaluations of TSP solution algorithms.

We attempted to construct 6 circuits in each graph. Here, we set K to this value because it is about half of 10 ($= \lfloor \frac{22-1}{2} \rfloor$), which is the maximum number of independent paths for the smallest graph, ulysses22. We measured the weighted cost cost$_{ssd}$, execution time, and construction failure rate. Even if only one edge is duplicated, this is considered as a construction failure. For example, if the construction failure rate is 0.48, this means that one or more edges have been used in duplicates in 480 of 1,000 trials. The results of the above experiments are shown in Table 2. Here, DPO, 2BO, DPO+2BO, and NONE represent cases, where only the heuristic with degree of possible options was used, only 2-best-opt was used, both two heuristics were used, and neither of the two was used, respectively.

Table 2 shows the comparison results of the heuristic performance in KI-Average-ACO. These results show that 2-best-opt, in particular, improves the circuit construction failure rate in all three graphs. Moreover, the execution time of 2-best-opt is not long, so this heuristic would be feasible. On the other hand, heuristic with the degree of possible options did not contribute to reduce the cost of the solution even though the execution time was longer than that of 2-best-opt. This is because the execution time of this heuristic takes $O(N)$, and costly edges

Table 2. Performance of heuristics in KI-Average-ACO.

Problem	Heuristics	Cost of solution	Required time	Failure rate
ulysses22	NONE	6.39×10^4	14	0.999
	DPO	$\mathbf{5.22 \times 10^4}$	55	0.999
	2BO	5.33×10^4	**16**	**0.0**
	DPO+2BO	5.84×10^4	57	**0.0**
bays29	NONE	1.15×10^4	32	0.994
	DPO	1.01×10^4	126	0.970
	2BO	$\mathbf{8.97 \times 10^3}$	**34**	**0.0**
	DPO+2BO	9.83×10^3	126	**0.0**
att48	NONE	2.96×10^5	70	0.989
	DPO	4.12×10^5	488	0.964
	2BO	$\mathbf{2.91 \times 10^5}$	**72**	**0.0**
	DPO+2BO	3.43×10^5	489	**0.0**

were also selected to give priority to the reduction of the circuit construction failure rate. However, for ulysses22, the cost of solution was the smallest when heuristic with the degree of possible options was used. This suggests that this heuristic may also be useful depending on the problem type.

4.3   Performance Evaluation of KI-Average-ACO

We evaluated the performance of KI-Average-ACO. Specifically, we compared the costs of solutions obtained using KI-Average-ACO to that obtained using a combinatorial optimization algorithm. In the experiments, we used the graph gr17 with $N = 17$ as a problem to solve. The weighted parameters γ and θ of the KI-Average-TSPs were set as 1 and 2, respectively. These parameter settings in Eq. 1 minimized the weighted sum of average and variance.

In general, it is difficult to find the exact solution for KI-Average-TSP. Indeed, in our preliminary experiments, we observed that exact solutions could be found only for problems, where the size of the graph is $N < 8$ and the number of circuits is $K < 3$ in a feasible time. Therefore, we evaluated the performance of KI-Average-ACO and the combinatorial optimization algorithm by comparing the costs of approximate solutions instead of exact solutions. The combinatorial optimization algorithm used as the comparison target is as follows. Since the standard deviation can be calculated from K circuits, a binary search was used to determine whether the maximum difference d of costs between the K circuits could be less than or equal to a certain threshold value. Repeating this operation, while gradually lowering the threshold value within a predetermined time limit, minimized the maximum difference in the costs of K circuits (thus, the standard deviation was also approximately minimized). In this case, the time limit was set to 300 s.

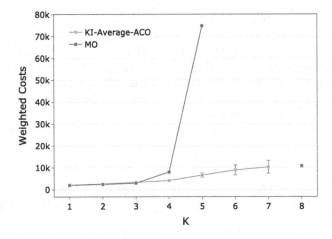

Fig. 3. Costs of solutions for KI-Average-TSP.

Figure 3 shows the experimental results. The horizontal and vertical axes of the graph represent the K number of circuits in the problem and the total costs of the solutions, respectively. "KI-Average-ACO" and "MO" represent the results obtained using our algorithm and the mathematical optimization algorithm, respectively. Here, the plots of MO for $K = 6, 7$ are lost because MO did not find any solution within the time limit. This figure shows that for $K = 1, 2, 3$, the total cost of the solutions obtained by the proposed algorithm was almost the same as that of MO. Furthermore, for $K = 4, 5, 6, 7$, our algorithm obtained better solutions. We would like to remark on the result when $K = 8$. It is considered that the reason why MO obtained a solution, in this case, is that the solution has to use all edges, so it is no longer necessary to decide whether or not to use edges in the solution. On the other hand, this did not bring any benefit to the solution of our algorithm even though it took more time to calculate as the problem became more complicated. As a result, no solution could be found. However, this is a special case, and overall, we have observed that it is useful, especially when the problems are complicated compared to the mathematical optimization algorithm.

5   Conclusions and Future Work

In this study, we proposed two problems named KI-Average-TSP and KI-Total-TSP, which were extensions of the TSP. We also proposed KI-Average-ACO, an optimization algorithm to solve KI-Average-TSP. The idea behind our algorithm is to move K ants simultaneously. However, to reduce the failure rate of circuit construction, we introduced two heuristics with the degree of possible options and 2-best-opt, a heuristic based on 2-opt. We evaluated the performance of our algorithm and the effectiveness of the heuristics. In the experiments, we observed that 2-best-opt significantly contributed to reducing solution costs and construction failure rates. In addition, the solution cost of KI-Average-ACO was reduced when the circuit to be constructed was larger compared to the solution cost of the mathematical optimization algorithm for a binary search.

One of the important future directions is to apply our algorithm to realistic problems. In particular, we would like to generalize KI-Average-TSP to formulate an optimization problem that allows $m < K$ edges to be shared between circuits and to find its solution algorithm.

References

1. Dorigo, M., Maniezzo, V., Colorni, A.: Ant system: optimization by a colony of cooperating agents. IEEE Trans. Syst. Man Cybern. Part B (Cybern.) **26**(1), 29–41 (1996)
2. Dorigo, M., Stützle, T.: Ant colony optimization: overview and recent advances. In: Gendreau, M., Potvin, J.Y. (eds.) Handbook of Metaheuristics, vol. 146, pp. 311–351. Springer, Boston (2019). https://doi.org/10.1007/978-1-4419-1665-5_8
3. Johnson, D.S., McGeoch, L.A.: The traveling salesman problem: a case study in local optimization. Local Search Comb. Optim. **1**(1), 215–310 (1997)
4. Pan, J., Wang, D.: An ant colony optimization algorithm for multiple travelling salesman problem, pp. 210–213, January 2006. https://doi.org/10.1109/ICICIC.2006.40
5. Lenstra, J.K., Kan, A.R.: Some simple applications of the travelling salesman problem. J. Oper. Res. Soc. **26**(4), 717–733 (1975)
6. Lin, S., Kernighan, B.W.: An effective heuristic algorithm for the traveling-salesman problem. Oper. Res. **21**(2), 498–516 (1973)
7. Matai, R., Singh, S.P., Mittal, M.L.: Traveling salesman problem: an overview of applications, formulations, and solution approaches. In: Traveling Salesman Problem, Theory and Applications, vol. 1 (2010)
8. Pataki, G.: Teaching integer programming formulations using the traveling salesman problem. SIAM Rev. **45**(1), 116–123 (2003)
9. Skorobohatyj, G.: MP-TESTDATA - the TSPLIB symmetric traveling salesman problem instances. http://elib.zib.de/pub/mp-testdata/tsp/tsplib/tsp/
10. Stützle, T., Hoos, H.H.: Max-min ant system. Futur. Gener. Comput. Syst. **16**(8), 889–914 (2000)
11. Tan, W.F., Lee, L.S., Majid, Z.A., Seow, H.V.: Ant colony optimization for capacitated vehicle routing problem. J. Comput. Sci. **8**(6), 846–852 (2012)
12. Teng, Y.H., Tan, J.J., Ho, T.Y., Hsu, L.H.: On mutually independent Hamiltonian paths. Appl. Math. Lett. **19**(4), 345–350 (2006). https://doi.org/10.1016/j.aml.2005.05.012. http://www.sciencedirect.com/science/article/pii/S0893965905002387

Differential Evolution

Inferring Small-Scale Maximum-Entropy Genetic Regulatory Networks by Using DE Algorithm

Fu Yin[1]($\boxtimes$) (iD), Jiarui Zhou[2], Zexuan Zhu[3], Xiaoliang Ma[3], and Weixin Xie[1]($\boxtimes$)

[1] College of Electronics and Information Engineering, Shenzhen University, Shenzhen, China
{fuyin,wxxie}@szu.edu.cn
[2] School of Biosciences, University of Birmingham, Birmingham, UK
[3] College of Computer Science and Software Engineering,
Shenzhen University, Shenzhen, China

Abstract. Maximum-entropy genetic regulatory networks (GRNs) have been increasingly applied to infer pairwise gene interactions from biological data. Most maximum-entropy GRNs inferring methods estimate the inverse covariance matrix based on the assumption that the network is sparse and the problem can be approximated via convex optimization. However, the assumption might not be true in reality. To address this issue, in this paper, we propose an adaptive differential evolution (DE) algorithm to directly infer the maximum-entropy GRNs, which is formulated as a constrained optimization problem with the maximum entropy being the objective function and the first and second moments being two penalty terms. A GRN inferred by DE is a fully connected network that can reflect the gene regulatory relations. The experimental results on both simulated and real data suggest that the proposed method is robust in inferring the small-scale maximum-entropy GRNs.

Keywords: Maximum-entropy · Genetic regulatory networks · Constrained optimization · DE algorithm

1 Introduction

In recent years, a large number of methods have been proposed for inferring gene regulatory networks (GRNs) from gene expression data. Correlations and other statistical measures that group genes by profile similarity identify functionally related groups of genes [1, 2]. Much effort has been devoted to inferring GRNs using varies modeling approaches, ranging from simple Boolean networks to dynamical models of cellular processes [3, 4]. However, correlation measures do not provide direct insight into the identification of the gene interactions that give rise to the observed expression patterns [5]. For this reason, pairwise maximum-entropy probability models have been introduced to infer the GRNs [6]. The logic of such methods is to determine the probability distribution governing the microarray data where the entropy-reducing constraint their pairwise correlations is faithfully encoded [6]. Consequently, the real-valued maximum-entropy

© Springer Nature Switzerland AG 2021
Y. Tan and Y. Shi (Eds.): ICSI 2021, LNCS 12689, pp. 347–357, 2021.
https://doi.org/10.1007/978-3-030-78743-1_31

distribution given first and second moments is found as a Boltzmann-like distribution, which is determined by the mean and the covariance matrix C, and the inverse covariance matrix M (also known as the precision or concentration matrix) [7].

Statistical inference methods using partial correlations in the context of Gaussian graphical models (GGMs) have led to similar results. By assuming that the precision matrix is sparse and the data samples are drawn independently from the same distribution, the most commonly used method to infer the maximum-entropy networks are spectral decomposition [6] and graphical lasso [8].

Although the above methods have been successfully used to estimate the regulatory relationships among genes, their performance may be limited in some areas. The inferring performance of the spectral decomposition method is not good enough when the samples are very few. Although the graphical lasso is better than spectral decomposition on small samples, its GRNs can not reflect gene regulatory relations (expression and repression) and it is difficult how to choose the right lasso penalty to fit the sparseness is very difficult [9].

To address the above problems, in this paper, we proposed a new way to infer the maximum-entropy GRNs, which is formulated as a constrained optimization problem, using a differential evolution (DE) algorithm. DE has achieved widely successes on various complex constrained optimization problems [10]. We set maximum entropy as the objective function and its subject to the constraint of first and second moment as the penalty functions based on the pairwise maximum-entropy probability models. To demonstrate the performance of the proposed method, the method is compared with other state-of-the-art methods on two synthetic datasets and four real-world datasets. The GRNs obtained by the DE are fully connected networks that reflect gene regulatory relations to identify GRNs involved in diverse cellular processes. Experiment results demonstrate that our method outperforms the other two state-of-the-art inferring maximum-entropy GRNs methods on synthetic datasets. In the meantime, the real data results suggest that the proposed approach is robust to inferring small-scale GRNs.

The rest of this paper is organized as follows. In the Sect. 2, we introduce the background of the maximum-entropy GRNs. In the Sect. 3, we present our proposed framework in detail. In the Sect. 4, we describe the performance of our method on synthetic and real-world datasets. Finally, Sect. 5 concludes this work.

2 Maximum-Entropy GRNs

Pairwise associations between genes can be determined by gene expression and are commonly estimated by the sample Pearson correlation coefficient computed for each pair of genes. However, the Pearson correlation is a misleading measure for direct dependence as it only reflects the association between two genes while ignoring the influence of the remaining ones. Therefore, the relevance network approach is not suitable to deduce direct interactions from a dataset [11].

To address these problems, maximum-entropy GRNs is proposed. It relies on Boltzmann's concept of entropy maximization to support statistical inference with minimal reliance on the form of missing information, which can remove the variational effect due to the influence of the remaining variables.

Let the state vector $x = (x_1, ..., x_N)$ denote the expression levels of the N genes that are probed in a microarray experiment, and a series of T measurements then has associated with it T distinct state vectors. Let $\rho(x)$ denote the probability that the genome is in the arbitrary state x. We determine $\rho(x)$ by maximizing the Shannon entropy.

$$S = -\rho(\vec{x}) \, ln(\vec{x}) \tag{1}$$

subject to the $\rho(x)$ is normalized

$$\sum_{\vec{x}} \rho(\vec{x}) = 1 \tag{2}$$

first moment, $<x_i>$, and second moment, $<x_i, x_j>$

$$<x_i> = \sum_{\vec{x}} \rho(\vec{x}) x_i = \frac{1}{T} \sum_{k=1}^{T} x_i^k \tag{3}$$

$$<x_i, x_j> = \sum_{\vec{x}} \rho(\vec{x}) x_i x_j = \frac{1}{T} \sum_{k=1}^{T} x_i^k x_j^k \tag{4}$$

Equation (2) provides the normalization condition that the probabilities of all observable states sum to 1. Equations (3) and (4) ensure that the distribution $\rho(x)$ preserves the mean expression level of each gene and the correlations between genes. This procedure leads to a Boltzmann-like distribution:

$$\rho(x) \sim e^{-H}$$

where

$$H = \frac{1}{2} \sum_{ij} x_i M_{ij} x_j$$

Note that, because $<x_i, x_j> = <x_j, x_i>$, the number of constraints is $1 + N + N(N + 1)/2$. In the same reason $M_{ij} = M_{ji}$, the number of M_{ij} should be estimated is $N(N + 1)/2$.

The elements of the matrix M are the effective pairwise gene interactions that reproduce the gene profile covariances exactly while maximizing the entropy of the system. The intensity and type of an element M_{ij}: a positive value denotes expression (facilitation) and a negative value denotes repression while a zero (0) value implies that there is no interaction between i and j [6, 11].

The matrix of M can be obtained by inverting the matrix of their covariances C. However, in the high dimensional setting where the number of features p is larger than the number of observations n, the empirical covariance matrix C is singular and so can not be inverted to yield an estimate of M. If $p \approx n$, then even if C is not singular the estimate for C will suffer from very high variance [5].

Spectral decomposition and graphical lasso are proposed to get around this problem by estimating the inverse covariance matrix based on the assumption that the network is sparse and the problem can be approximated via convex optimization. However, the assumption might not be true in reality. The performance of spectral decomposition is not good enough at solving the small sample problem. Although the graphical lasso has better inferring performance, its GRNs cannot reflect the gene regulatory relations (expression and repression). Also, it is difficult to choose a right lasso penalty to control the sparseness of the inferred networks [9].

3 Method

To address the above problems, in this paper, we proposed a new way to infer the maximum-entropy GRNs, a constrained optimization problem, by using an adaptive differential evolution (DE) algorithm. DE as a nature-inspired method has become a more feasible and popular choice among researchers due to their competitive performance on complex search spaces to address the constrained optimization problems [10].

However, the performance of the classic DE is still entirely dependent on control parameters and mutation strategies to both experimental studies and theoretical analyses [12]. The adaptive and self-adaptive DE algorithms have shown faster and more reliable convergence performance than the classic DE algorithms for many benchmark problems.

For this reason, the main objectives of this work are three-fold. First, we set maximum entropy as the objective function and its subject to the constraint of first and second moment as the penalty functions. Second, the Probability Matching (PM) method is integrated into DE to implement the adaptive strategy selection. Third, the JADE [13] is used to set controls mutation factor F and crossover probability CR in an adaptive manner. Details behind algorithm are elucidated as follows.

3.1 Problem Formulation

The general form of the constrained optimization problem will be expressed as follows:

$$\min f(x)$$
$$\text{s.t. } g_i(x) \leq 0, \ i = 1, 2, \cdots, j$$
$$h_i(x) = 0, \ i = j+1, j+2, \cdots, m \quad (5)$$

where $x = (x_1, x_2, ..., x_n)$ are the decision variables of the objective function $f(x)$, g_i is an inequality constraint describing the variable, which role of the inequality constraint is to form the search area in the feasible domain. h_i is equality constraint that forms a boundary value condition in the feasible domain, which role is to control the boundary of the search area. Normally, we define the objective function as $\min f(x)$ and penalty function as

$$G_i(x) = \begin{cases} \max\{0, g_i(x)\}, & 1 \leq i \leq j \\ \max\{0, |h_i(x) - \delta|\}, & j+1 \leq i \leq m \end{cases}$$

$$G(x) = \sum_{i=1}^{m} G_i(x) \tag{6}$$

where δ is a small positive tolerance value. The final fit function would be like

$$\text{Fit} = f(x) + \sigma G(x) \tag{7}$$

where σ is the punitive coefficient.

In this paper, Eq. (1) is set to the objective function and its subject to the constraint of first and second moment Eqs. (2–4) are set to the penalty functions. Then the optimization problems (1–4) can convert into the optimization problem (7) that will be minimized by DE. The initial population $\{x_i = (x_{1,i,0}, x_{2,i,0}, ..., x_{D,i,0}) | i = 1, 2, ..., NP\}$ is randomly generated according to a uniform distribution $[-1, 1]$, where $D = N(N + 1)/2$ (the number of M_{ij}) is the dimension of the problem and NP is the population size.

3.2 Strategy Selection: Probability Matching

Suppose there are $K > 1$ strategies in the pool $A = \{a_1, \cdots, a_K\}$ and a probability $P(t) = \{p_1(t), \cdots, p_k(t)\}(\forall t : p_{min} \leq p_i(t) \leq 1; \sum_{i=1}^{K} p_i(t) = 1)$. In this work, the PM technique is used to adaptively update the probability $p_a(t)$ of each strategy a based on its known performance and updated by the rewards received. Denote $r_a(t)$ as the reward that a strategy a receives after its application at time t. $q_a(t)$ is the empirical estimate of a strategy a, that is updated as follows [14]:

$$q_a(t + 1) = q_a(t) + \alpha[r_a(t) \cdot q_a(t)] \tag{8}$$

where $\alpha \in (0, 1]$ is the adaptation rate. Based on this quality estimate, the PM method updates the probability $p_a(t)$ of applying each operator as follows:

$$p_a(t + 1) = p_{min} + (1 - K \cdot p_{min}) \frac{q_a(t+1)}{\sum_{i=1}^{K} q_i(t+1)} \tag{9}$$

where $p_{min} \in (0, 1)$ is the minimal probability value of each strategy, used to ensure that no operator gets lost [13].

In order to assign the credit for each strategy, we adopt the relative fitness improvement η_i proposed in [12] as follows:

$$\eta_i = \frac{\delta}{cf_i} \cdot |pf_i - cf_i| \tag{10}$$

where $i = 1, \cdots, NP$. δ is the fitness of the best-so-far solution in the population. pf_i and cf_i are the fitness of the target parent and its offspring, respectively. If no improvement is achieved, a null credit is assigned.

Denote S_a as the set of all relative fitness improvements achieved by the application of a strategy a $(a = 1, \cdots, K)$ during generation t. At the end of the generation, a unique reward is used to update the quality measure kept by the PM method (Eq. 9). The credit assignment is as follows [14]:

$$r_a(t) = \frac{\sum_{i=1}^{|S_a|} S_a(i)}{|S_a|} \tag{11}$$

where $|S_a|$ is the number of elements in S_a. If $| S_a | = 0$, $r_a(t) = 0$.

In DE, many schemes have been proposed, applying different mutation strategies and/or recombination operations in the reproduction stage [15]. In order to constitute the strategy pool used in this work, we have chosen four strategies: 'DE/rand/1', 'DE/rand/2', 'DE/rand-to-best/1' and 'DE/current-to-rand/1'.

3.3 Parameter Adaptation

The parameter adaptation is similar to JADE. At each generation g, the crossover probability CR_i of each individual xi is independently generated according to a normal distribution of mean μ_{CR} and standard deviation 0.1 as

$$CR_i = \text{randn}_i(\mu_{CR}, 0.1) \tag{12}$$

and then truncated to [0, 1] [13]. Denote S_{CR} as the set of all successful crossover probabilities CR_i's at generation g. The mean μ_{CR} is initialized to be 0.5 and then updated at the end of each generation as

$$\mu_{CR} = (1 - c) \cdot \mu_{CR} + c \cdot \text{mean}_A(S_{CR}) \tag{13}$$

where c is a positive constant between 0 and 1 and $\text{mean}_A(\cdot)$ is the usual arithmetic mean.

Similarly, at each generation g, the mutation factor F_i of each individual x_i is independently generated according to a Cauchy distribution with location parameter μ_F and scale parameter 0.1 as:

$$F_i = randn_i(\mu_F, 0.1) \tag{14}$$

and then truncated to be 1 if $F_i \geq 1$ or regenerated if $F_i \leq 0$ [13]. Denote S_F as the set of all successful mutation factors in generation g. The location parameter μ_F of the Cauchy distribution is initialized to be 0.5 and then updated at the end of each generation is as follows:

$$\mu_F = (1 - c) \cdot \mu_F + c \cdot \text{mean}_L(S_F) \tag{15}$$

where $\text{mean}_L(\cdot)$ is the Lehmer mean [13].

3.4 Optimization Work Flow

The probability matching method and JADE are used respectively to select the mutate strategy and set the parameter adaptively. In Algorithm 1, the use of our adaptive DE for inferring Maximum-Entropy GRNs is illustrated.

Algorithm 1 The DE algorithm with adaptive strategy selection and JADE parameter adaptation based on probability matching

---

Input: search space [-1, 1] , objective function f Eq.(1), penalty function G Eqs.(2-4)
Output: optimal solution
  1: Generate the initial population
  2: Evaluate the fitness for each individual
  3: For each strategy a, set $q_a(t) = 0$ and $p_a(t) = 1/K$
  4: **while** The halting criterion is not satisfied **do**
  5:    **for** $i = 1$ to NP **do**
  6:        Select the strategy SI_i based on its probability
  7:        Select uniform randomly $r_1 \neq r_2 \neq r_3 \neq r_4 \neq r_5 \neq i$
  8:        $j_{rand} = \text{randn}(1, D)$
  9:        Using Eqs. (12), (14) generating F_i^a and CR_i^a
10:        **for** $j = 1$ to D **do**
11:            **if** randj $[0, 1) < CR_i^a$ or $j = j_{rand}$ **then**
12:                Using strategy SI_i generating u_{ij}
13:            **end if**
14:        **end for**
15:    **end for**
16:    **for** $i = 1$ to NP **do**
17:        Evaluate the offspring u_i
18:        **if** $f(u_i) \geq f(x_i)$ **then**
19:            Calculate η_i using Eq.(10)
20:            Replace x_i with u_i
21:        **else**
22:            Set $\eta_i = 0$
23:        **end if**
24:        $S_{SI_i} \leftarrow \eta_i$
25:    **end for**
26:    Calculate the reward $r_a(t)$ for each strategy using Eq.(11)
27:    Update the quality $q_a(t)$ for each strategy using Eq.(8)
28:    Update the probability $p_a(t)$ for each strategy using Eq.(9)
29:    Update the F_i^a and CR_i^a using Eqs.(13),(15)
30:    $t = t + 1$
31: **end while**

---

4 Experimental Results

Let θ_{ij} and $\hat{\theta}_{ij}$ denote the elements in the true GRNs and the inferred GRNs, respectively. Whether the absolute value of a particular element is 0 or 1 can be evaluated by a threshold defined for the purpose of inclusion of an interaction in a GRN. An edge can be characterized into four types: true positive (TP), false positive (FP), true negative (TN), and false negative (FN), with their definitions as follows:

TP: if $\theta_{ij} = 1$ and $\hat{\theta}_{ij} = 1$; TN: if $\theta_{ij} = 0$ and $\hat{\theta}_{ij} = 0$.
FP: if $\theta_{ij} = 0$ and $\hat{\theta}_{ij} = 1$; FN: if $\theta_{ij} = 1$ and $\hat{\theta}_{ij} = 0$.

Then the metrics based on which the proposed methodology can be evaluated. (1) True Positive Rate (TPR)/Recall: this signifies the fraction of the total number of existing edges in the original network, correctly predicted in the inferred GRNs; (2) False Positive Rate (FPR)/Complimentary Specificity: this signifies the fraction of the total number of nonexistent edges, incorrectly predicted in the inferred GRNs; (3) Positive Predictive Value (PPV)/Precision: this signifies the fraction of the total number of inferred edges, which is correct. (4) F-Score: this signifies the harmonic mean of the precision and recall.

4.1 Simulation Studies

We first build a random ER random network denoted by its adjacency binary matrix M with non-zero element substituted by a uniform distribution value on $[-0.6, -0.3] \cup [0.3, 0.6]$. To ensure the positive definiteness of the covariance matrix, the real precision matrix Θ is set as

$$\Theta = M + \sigma I$$

σ is the absolute value of the eigenvalues of M, and I is an identity matrix. After this procedure, the synthetic gene expression data could be generated with zero means and covariance $C = \Theta^{-1}$. In order to test the performance of our method with the other two state-of-art method which can deal with the small sample problem ($p \approx n$). We generate two small-scale groups of samples (group 1 with n = 5 samples and p = 5 genes; group 2 with n = 10 samples and p = 10 genes) to simulate the small-scale GRNs. 10 random datasets are generated for the above two groups. The empirical covariance matrix C in each dataset is singular and so can not be inverted to yield an estimate of M.

The gene interaction network comprising the genes showing the strongest couplings is highly interconnected. For this reason, we choose the top 20% strongest pairwise interaction to identify the most consistent predicted edges for the construction of the final GRNs.

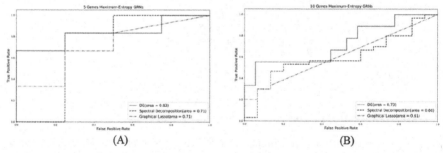

Fig. 1. The experiment results on two small-scale groups of samples: (A) 10 datasets of 5 genes network with 5 samples. (B) 10 datasets of 10 genes network with 10 samples.

Figure 1 presents the average performance on two different scale networks datasets. For graphical lasso, its sparsity-controlling parameter is chosen automatically by cross-validation. In particular, we run 10 times of the DE on each dataset and take the best optimization result as the final inferring result.

We can find that our method dominates the other two methods on inferring maximum-entropy GRNs. As the number of genes increases, there is a degradation on the performance of all three methods, our method could still achieve competitive performance with the other two comparative methods. The results suggest that our approach can effectively solve the small sample problem while meantime reflecting the gene regulatory relations.

4.2 Real Data Analysis

In this section, the proposed method for inferring maximum-entropy GRNs has been employed to identify the causal relationships among the genes from an in vivo (experimental) microarray dataset. The said dataset summarizes the dynamics of the well illustrated transcriptional network involved in the SOS DNA repair mechanism of E. coli studied experimentally by Ronen et al. [16]. The study included eight genes heavily involved in the SOS repair mechanism: recA, lexA (the master repressor), uvrA, uvrD, uvrY, umuD, ruvA, and polB. The original network has been shown in Fig. 2.

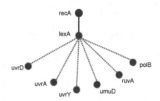

Fig. 2. The original structure of the SOS DNA repair transcriptional network of E.coli. The solid black lines denote activation, and the dashed red lines denote repression.

We choose the absolute value of $M_{ij} > 0.7$ as the inferred Maximum-Entropy GRNs for the 4 datasets. Table 1 displays a comparison of the statistical properties of the inferred GRNs with those presented in recent investigative work [17–19] for different experimental datasets. Table 2 shows the top 3 genes in our inferred GRNs.

Table 1. Comparison of results obtained from the E.coli experiments with those presented in a recent investigative work.

Dataset	Precision				Recall				F-score			
	[17]	[18]	[19]	DE	[17]	[18]	[19]	DE	[17]	[18]	[19]	DE
1	0.23	0.36	0.44	**0.50**	0.43	0.71	1	0.71	0.30	0.48	**0.61**	0.59
2	**0.58**	0.26	0.30	0.45	1	0.57	1	0.71	**0.73**	0.36	0.46	0.55
3	0.31	0.38	0.41	**0.56**	0.57	0.71	1	0.71	0.40	0.50	0.58	**0.63**
4	0	0.27	0.25	**0.43**	0	0.43	**0.57**	0.43	0	0.33	0.35	**0.43**
Mean	0.28	0.32	0.35	**0.50**	0.5	0.61	**0.9**	0.64	0.36	0.42	0.49	**0.55**

Experiment results show that our method performs better in Precision than the other methods in all experiments except the method [17] in experiment 2. However, the method [17] fails to identify any true positive in experiment 4.

We have to concede that the method [19] has a higher Recall than our GRNs, but its Precision is significantly less than our method. When viewed from the aspect of F-score, our method performs better by comprehensive considering of the Precision and Recall in all 4 experiments.

In Table 2, it should be noticed that lexA (the master gene) is the node with the highest degree in our inferred GRNs in all four experiments, so our GRNs find the master gene correctly. In the meantime, the lexA—uvrY and lexA—polB are not predicted in our GRNs except experiment 2.

Table 2. Top 3 nodes with the highest degree in our inferred GRNs

Dataset	Rank1	Rank2	Rank3
1	lexA	uvrA	recA
2	lexA	uvrA	recA
3	lexA	uvrA	uvrD
4	lexA	recA	ruvA

5 Conclusion

In this paper, we propose a DE based inferring method that can effectively estimate maximum-entropy GRNs. Unlike the other inferring methods of inverse the covariance we consider the inferring maximum-entropy GRNs as a constrained optimization problem and the best individuals searched by our method is the inferred maximum-entropy GRNs.

First, we assume that the maximum-entropy distribution is a Boltzmann-like distribution. Under this assumption, we set maximum entropy as the objective function and its subject to the constraint of first and second moment as the penalty functions. Then the probability matching method and JADE are used respectively to select the mutate strategy and set the parameter adaptively to improve the success rate of the algorithm.

The GRNs resulting from the DE is a fully connected network that fulfills the maximum-entropy GRNs reflecting gene regulatory relations (expression and repression), which graphical lasso can not. For this reason, we can identify connections between genes involved in diverse cellular processes by choosing the different degrees of pairwise interactions.

It outperforms the other two state-of-the-art inferring maximum-entropy GRNs methods on synthetic datasets. In the meantime, the real data results suggest that it can find the master gene, so the proposed approach is robust to inferring small-scale GRNs.

The performance of nature-inspired algorithms often deteriorates rapidly as the dimensionality of the problem increases. Small-scale and large-scale constrained optimization are two completely different problems. There are too few true predictions and a large number of incorrect predictions [19]. Thus, the methodology implemented in this paper needs to be enriched further by studying its performance in larger networks. This provides a vital scope for further research.

References

1. Saldanha, A.J., Brauer, M.J., Botstein, D.: Nutritional homeostasis in batch and steady- state culture of yeast. Mol. Biol. Cell **15**, 4089–4104 (2004)
2. Perou, C.M., et al.: Molecular portraits of human breast tumours. Nature **406**, 747–752 (2000)
3. Shmulevich, I., Dougherty, E.R., Kim, S., Zhang, W.: Probabilistic Boolean networks: a rule-based uncertainty model for gene regulatory networks. Bioinformatics **18**, 261–274 (2002)
4. Akutsu, T., Miyano, S., Kuhara, S.: Algorithms for identifying Boolean networks and related biological networks based on matrix multiplication and fingerprint function. J. Comput. Biol. **7**, 331–343 (2000)
5. Danaher, P., Wang, P., Witten, D.M.: The joint graphical lasso for inverse covariance estimation across multiple classes. J. Roy. Stat. Soc. Ser. B Stat. Methodol. **76**, 373 (2014)
6. Lezon, T.R., Banavar, J.R., Cieplak, M., Maritan, A., Fedoroff, N.V.: Using the principle of entropy maximization to infer genetic interaction networks from gene expression patterns. Proc. Natl. Acad. Sci. **103**, 19033–19038 (2006)
7. Stein, R.R., Marks, D.S., Sander, C.: Inferring pairwise interactions from biological data using maximum-entropy probability models. PLoS Comput. Biol. **11**, e1004182 (2015)
8. Friedman, J., Hastie, T., Tibshirani, R.: Sparse inverse covariance estimation with the graphical lasso. Biostatistics **9**, 432–441 (2008)
9. Wu, N., et al.: Weighted fused pathway graphical lasso for joint estimation of multiple gene networks. Front. Genet. **10**, 623 (2019)
10. Noman, N., Iba, H.: Inferring gene regulatory networks using differential evolution with local search heuristics. IEEE/ACM Trans. Comput. Biol. Bioinform. **4**, 634–647 (2007)
11. De Martino, A., De Martino, D.: An introduction to the maximum entropy approach and its application to inference problems in biology. Heliyon **4**, e00596 (2018)
12. Qian, W.: Adaptive differential evolution algorithm for multiobjective optimization problems. Appl. Math. Comput. **201**, 431–440 (2008)
13. Zhang, J., Sanderson, A.C.: JADE: adaptive differential evolution with optional external archive. IEEE Trans. Evol. Comput. **13**, 945–958 (2009)
14. Thierens, D.: An adaptive pursuit strategy for allocating operator probabilities. In: Proceedings of the 7th Annual Conference on Genetic and Evolutionary Computation, pp. 1539–1546 (2005)
15. Price, K., Storn, R.M., Lampinen, J.A.: Differential Evolution: A Practical Approach to Global Optimization. Springer, Heidelberg (2006). https://doi.org/10.1007/3-540-31306-0
16. Ronen, M., Rosenberg, R., Shraiman, B.I., Alon, U.: Assigning numbers to the arrows: parameterizing a gene regulation network by using accurate expression kinetics. Proc. Natl. Acad. Sci. **99**, 10555–10560 (2002)
17. Kentzoglanakis, K., Poole, M.: A swarm intelligence framework for reconstructing gene networks: searching for biologically plausible architectures. IEEE/ACM Trans. Comput. Biol. Bioinform. **9**, 358–371 (2011)
18. Xu, R., Wunsch, D., II., Frank, R.: Inference of genetic regulatory networks with recurrent neural network models using particle swarm optimization. IEEE/ACM Trans. Comput. Biol. Bioinform. **4**, 681–692 (2007)
19. Khan, A., Mandal, S., Pal, R.K., Saha, G.: Construction of gene regulatory networks using recurrent neural networks and swarm intelligence. Scientifica **2016** (2016)

Variable Fragments Evolution
in Differential Evolution

Changshou Deng[1], Xiaogang Dong[1,2(✉)], Yucheng Tan[3], and Hu Peng[1]

[1] School of Computer and Big Data Science, JiuJiang University,
Jiujiang 332005, Jiangxi, China
dengtju@aliyun.com
[2] School of Information and Management, Jiangxi university of finance
and economics, Nanchang 330077, Jiangxi, China
[3] School of Scinece, JiuJiang University, Jiujiang 332005, Jiangxi, China

Abstract. The crossover operator plays an important role in Differential Evolution. However, the choice of proper crossover operator and corresponding parameters is dependent on the features of the problems. It is not easy for practitioners to choose the right crossover operator and associated parameter value. In the newly proposed method, a novel evolution scheme called Variable Fragments Evolution was presented. During the evolution, the roughly fixed fragments of genes of all individuals were selected in a population for directional variation. Variable Fragments Evolution was compared with commonly used binomial crossover. Experimental results show that Variable Fragments Evolution exhibits better performance than the binomial crossover. Thus it can serve as an alternative evolution scheme for Differential Evolution.

Keywords: Differential evolution · Binomial crossover · Variable fragments evolution · Crossover-free

1 Introduction

Differential evolution (DE) is a simple yet efficient algorithm for global optimization problems in continuous domain [1]. Due to its simplicity, effectiveness and robustness, DE has drawn the attention of many researchers all over the world and it has been widely used in various scientific and engineering fields [2]. The performance of DE mainly depends on control parameters, mutation strategies, and crossover operators [3]. Many studies related to the evolutionary operators of DE have focused on the mutation operator [4]. Compared with

Supported by the National Natural Science Foundation of China (No. 61763019, 61364025, 62041603), Natural Science Foundation of Jiangxi Province (No. 20202BABL202036), Science and Technology Research Project of Education Department of Jiangxi Province (No. GJJ201808), and The "Thirteenth Five-Year Plan" of Education Science of Jiangxi Province for 2017 (No. 17YB211) as well.

Y. Tan and Y. Shi (Eds.): ICSI 2021, LNCS 12689, pp. 358–367, 2021.
https://doi.org/10.1007/978-3-030-78743-1_32

mutation operator, there are less studies related to crossover operator in differential evolution [5]. Previous studies on the crossover operator in DE can be classified into two categories: parameter setting and crossover scheme. There are empirical suggestions for setting parameter for crossover operator; however they are lack of sufficient experimental justifications. Based on the analysis in [6], DE with low values of Cr (near 0) results in very small exploratory moves that are orthogonal to the current axes, while DE with high values of Cr (near 1) makes large exploratory moves that are at angles to the search axes. In [7], the authors draw a conclusion that A low value of Cr = 0.1 was often the best chosen. In [8], a pool of Cr values was taken from the range of [0.1, 0.9]. It is still hard to set proper parameter for the crossover operator in DE due to lack of theory analysis.

In this study, a new scheme name variable fragments evolution (VFE) was proposed and then it was applied in DE. With variable fragments evolution, DE does not need to depend on crossover operator to search the optimum only more. During iteration, VFE only needs to select specific gene fragments to participate in the mutation. Each individual's genetic fragments involved in the mutation are roughly the same. In first intention, its aim is to find out whether the new scheme VFE has adverse effects on the performance of DE, rather than to propose a new, betterperforming algorithm. For this reason, DE with VFE will be compared solely to original DE with the binomial crossover, and not to any other state-of-the-art DE variants.

2 Differential Evolution

This section will give the description of the original DE [1]. To clarify the notation used in this study, It is supposed that we are going to find the minimization of the objective function, where x is a vector of n decision variables in a space D.

2.1 Generation of Initial Population

The DE algorithm starts with the initial population $X = (x_{ij})_{NP*n}$ with the size of NP and the dimension of n, which is generated by the following way.

$$x_{ij}^G = x_j^l + rand(0,1) * (x_j^u - x_j^l) \tag{1}$$

where $G = 0; i = 1, 2, ..., NP; j = 1, 2, ..., n;$ x_j^u and x_j^l denotes the upper constraints and the lower constraints respectively.

2.2 Mutation Operator

In DE/rand/bin/1 scheme, for each target vector, a mutant vector is produced by

$$v_i^{G+1} = x_{r1}^G + F * (x_{r2}^G - x_{r3}^G) \tag{2}$$

where $i, r1, r2, r3 \in \{1, 2, ..., NP\}$ are randomly chosen and must be different from each other. And F is the scaling factor for the difference between the individual x_{r2} and x_{r3}. Several variants of mutation operator can be referred in [1].

2.3 Crossover Operator

DE employs the crossover operation to add the diversity of the population. The commonly used binomial approach is given by (3).

$$u_{ij}^{G+1} = \begin{cases} v_{ij}^{G+1}, & if \ rand < CR \ or \ j = rand(i) \\ x_{ij}^{G}, & otherwise \end{cases} \tag{3}$$

where $i = 1, 2, ..., NP; j = 1, 2, ..., n; CR \in [0, 1]$ is the crossover probability and $rand(i) \in (1, 2, ..., NP)$ is the randomly selected number. The crossover operator can ensure at least one component of the trial individual comes from the mutation vector.

2.4 Selection Operator

Selection operation decides whether the trial individual u_i^{G+1} should be a member of the next generation, it is compared to the corresponding x_i^G. The selection operation is based on the survival of the fitness among the trial individual and the corresponding one such that:

$$x_i^{G+1} = \begin{cases} u_i^{G+1}, & if \ f(u_i^{G+1}) < f(x_i^G) \\ x_i^{G}, & otherwise \end{cases} \tag{4}$$

3 Analysis of Crossover Operator in DE

The crossover operator plays an important role in DE. The binomial operator is frequently employed in most DE variants and applications while the exponential crossover operator has been demonstrated to outperform binomial operator when solving hard high dimensional problems [9]. In [9], the authors draw a conclusion that the classical exponential crossover operator does not scale with scaling of dimension. Thus, when solving a practical problem, it is not easy to determine which crossover should be used.

In DE, the parameter CR is associated with the crossover. CR is used to control the way that the components will be inherited from the vectors which are produced by the mutation operator. Several researchers attempted to set the proper value of CR to enhance the performance of DE. In [10], the authors suggest that A small value of CR (e.g. $CR \leq 0.2$) is more appropriate for the separable functions, while a large CR (e.g. $CR > 0.9$) value for non-separable functions is recommended. Montgomery and Chen [11] analyzed how the value of CR would influence the exploratory moves of DE. They found that DE with low values of Cr (near 0) results in very small exploratory moves that are orthogonal to the current axes, while DE with high values of Cr (near 1) makes large exploratory moves that are at angles to the search space's axes [11]. In order to set the parameter CR manually, several adaptation and selfadaptation techniques have been developed [12].

Although many researchers focused on setting the value of parameter CR, we can find that they have different views and there are still lack of sufficient theoretical and experimental justifications. As the authors in [5] the authors concluded that the choice of the proper crossover method and its associated parameters is dependent on the features of the problems. Thus, when tackling complex black-box optimization problems, the choice of crossover operator and its associated parameter CR value is still a hard nut to track. This motivates us to design a new evolution mechanism in DE which does not need crossover anymore.

4   Variable Fragments Evolution in DE

4.1   Variable Fragments Evolution

In DE algorithm, the binomial operator is used to produce a trial vector from a pair of target and mutant vectors. However, the binomial operator ignores the relationship between different variables. Thus DE is relationship-blind. Although DE can solve the non-separable functions with a high value of CR, DE with a high CR value may cause premature convergence. In addition, each individual in DE evolves randomly and independently during every generation. However, Independent evolution is not conducive to solving non-separable problems.

Essentially, during DE evolution, each individual also selects several coordinates to mutate at a time. This is similar to the Block-coordinate descent (BCD) method [13]. In BCD, the coordinates are partitioned into N blocks. At each iteration, local minimum of the problem is found with respect to one of the coordinate blocks while the other coordinates are held fixed.

Similar to BCD, during one generation evolution of the population, each individual chooses roughly the same gene bits to evolve. But each individual's chosen gene bits are also somewhat different.

Firstly a group of variables called fragment was determined. This group of variables is just as the fragment of genes which correspond to some coordinates. Then a variation operator was applied to change the size of the determined fragment. Each time, the selected fragment will be increased or decreased by curtain step size. In our experiments, the step size is set to one. In this way, the main body of the selected fragments will remain unchanged. Lastly, all individuals in the current population only evolve based on the selected fragment while keep the other variables unchanged. Figure 1 presents the difference between binomial crossover and VFE. It can be seen clearly from Fig. 1 that during one generation of evolution, with binomial crossover, the individual independently chooses variables to be mutated. Unlike binomial crossover, with VFE, several individuals choose same variables to be mutated simultaneously.

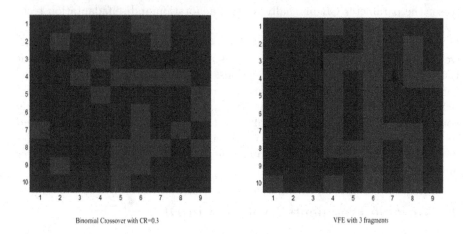

Binomial Crossover with CR=0.3   VFE with 3 fragments

Fig. 1. Binomial crossover with CR = 0.3 v.s. VFE with 3 fragments.

4.2   DE with Variable Fragment Evolution

In this section, we use variable fragment evolution to construct a new crossover-free DE variant. The details of DE with Variable Fragment Evolution (DE-VFE) are presented as follows.

5   Experimental Study

5.1   Experimental Setup

To investigate the performance of the proposed DEVFE, thirteen classic benchmark functions [14]are used as test bed. Among the thirteen functions, there are unimodal problems and multimodal problems. The details of the problems can be referred in appendix of [14].

In order to make comprehensive comparisons, traditional DE/ran/bin/1 with different crossover rate CR is used as compared method. In this study, CR is set to 0.1,0.3,0.5,0.7 and 0.9 respectively. In order to make fair comparisons, for each method and each test problem, 25 independent runs were conduced with 5000*D as maximum number of function evaluations. The scaling factor of mutation operator was set to 0.5.

Algorithm 1. DE-VFE

1: Set mutation operator Parameter F, Population size NP; Maximum number of function evaluations MaxFEs.
2: Generation of Initial Population using formula (1)
3: Evaluate the objective function value f for each individuals
4: FEs = NP
5: **Shuffle the decision variable series**
6: **Group the variable series into several fragments**
7: while FEs ≤ MaxFEs do
8:     **Choosing one fragment randomly**
9:     **Variation of the selected fragment**
10:    for i=1:NP do
11:        Generation of a trial vector U_i^{G+1} according to formula (2).
12:        Evaluation of the trial vector U_i^{G+1}.
13:        Execution of Selection Operator according to formula (4).
14:    end for
15:    FEs = NP+FEs
16: end while
17: output the individual with smallest objective function value.

5.2   Results on Benchmark Functions

The statistical results of the experiment are given in Table 1. We recorded the best, worst, median, mean, and standard deviation (Std.) values of solutions achieved by each method in 25 independent runs. The better values in terms of Best, Worst, Median, Mean and STD between the compared algorithms are highlighted in boldface. In Table 1, DE (X), X representing the CR value of 0.1, 0.3, 0.5, 0.7 and 0.9 respectively. From Table 1, we can find that DE-VFE significantly outperforms the corresponding DE algorithm with different CR values in all compared terms except for functions f3, f5 and f6. For f3, DE(0.9) is the best one in all terms considered among the methods. For f5, DE(0.9) wins in term of Best, while DE(0.3) wins the remainder indexes. For f6, the performance of DE-VFE equals to that of DE(X) in all terms. Due to limited space, we only present the convergent curves of the even problems. Figure 2 shows the evolutionary process of the representative ones. Comparing to DE(X), it is clear that DE-VFE performed significantly better.

Table 1. The statistical results of DE-VFE and DE WITH different CR VALUES

Problem	Methods	Best	Worst	Median	Mean	Std
f1	DE(0.1)	6.72E-20	1.42E−19	1.15E−19	1.11E−19	1.73E−20
	DE(0.3)	3.00E−12	8.78E−12	5.95E−12	6.02E−12	1.38E−12
	DE(0.5)	2.88E−05	6.58E−05	4.63E−05	4.61E−05	1.10E−05
	DE(0.7)	5.23E−06	2.59E−05	1.15E−05	1.40E−05	6.69E−06
	DE(0.9)	2.50E−18	2.72E−17	7.92E−18	9.89E−18	6.63E−18
	DE-VFE	**1.73E−48**	**3.75E−30**	**1.86E−47**	**1.50E−31**	**7.50E−31**
f2	DE(0.1)	2.03E−12	3.62E−12	2.73E−12	2.70E−12	3.43E−13
	DE(0.3)	6.56E−08	9.99E−08	8.00E−08	8.13E−08	9.43E−09
	DE(0.5)	1.62E−03	3.24E−03	2.22E−03	2.22E−03	3.86E−04
	DE(0.7)	2.30E−03	9.09E−03	4.85E−03	4.88E−03	1.59E−03
	DE(0.9)	1.60E−10	7.86E−10	4.12E−10	4.06E−10	1.36E−10
	DE-VFE	**2.28E−28**	**4.57E−26**	**1.23E−27**	**4.11E−27**	**9.13E−27**
f3	DE(0.1)	1.03E+05	1.66E+05	1.44E+05	1.44E+05	1.25E+04
	DE(0.3)	1.57E+05	2.39E+05	2.05E+05	2.07E+05	1.69E+04
	DE(0.5)	1.77E+05	2.55E+05	2.18E+05	2.18E+05	1.83E+04
	DE(0.7)	1.56E+05	2.40E+05	2.04E+05	2.01E+05	2.00E+04
	DE(0.9)	**5.38E+03**	**1.67E+04**	**1.01E+04**	**1.05E+04**	**3.05E+03**
	DE-VFE	8.52E+04	1.52E+05	1.09E+05	1.11E+05	1.66E+04
f4	DE(0.1)	2.90E+00	3.64E+00	3.23E+00	3.25E+00	1.67E-01
	DE(0.3)	1.98E+01	2.32E+01	2.13E+01	2.13E+01	8.64E-01
	DE(0.5)	3.96E+01	4.79E+01	4.35E+01	4.39E+01	2.25E+00
	DE(0.7)	1.49E+01	2.82E+01	2.07E+01	1.99E+01	3.26E+00
	DE(0.9)	1.29E+01	2.53E+01	1.93E+01	1.89E+01	3.35E+00
	DE-VFE	**2.42E-01**	**8.73E-01**	**3.14E-01**	**3.64E-01**	**1.51E-01**
f5	DE(0.1)	9.40E+01	9.62E+01	9.54E+01	9.53E+01	6.20E-01
	DE(0.3)	9.38E+01	**9.48E+01**	**9.41E+01**	**9.41E+01**	**1.93E-01**
	DE(0.5)	1.08E+02	1.69E+02	1.25E+02	1.26E+02	1.37E+01
	DE(0.7)	9.42E+01	9.62E+01	9.53E+01	9.53E+01	5.45E-01
	DE(0.9)	**8.58E+01**	1.98E+02	1.43E+02	1.38E+02	3.92E+01
	DE-VFE	9.18E+01	2.05E+02	9.55E+01	1.12E+02	2.98E+01
f6	DE(0.1)	**0.00E+00**	**0.00E+00**	**0.00E+00**	**0.00E+00**	**0.00E+00**
	DE(0.3)	**0.00E+00**	**0.00E+00**	**0.00E+00**	**0.00E+00**	**0.00E+00**
	DE(0.5)	**0.00E+00**	**0.00E+00**	**0.00E+00**	**0.00E+00**	**0.00E+00**
	DE(0.7)	**0.00E+00**	**0.00E+00**	**0.00E+00**	**0.00E+00**	**0.00E+00**
	DE(0.9)	**0.00E+00**	**0.00E+00**	**0.00E+00**	**0.00E+00**	**0.00E+00**
	DE-VFE	**0.00E+00**	**0.00E+00**	**0.00E+00**	**0.00E+00**	**0.00E+00**
f7	DE(0.1)	4.81E−02	7.08E−02	6.04E−02	5.90E−02	6.38E−03
	DE(0.3)	6.76E−02	9.27E−02	8.13E−02	8.14E−02	7.29E−03
	DE(0.5)	1.20E−01	1.84E−01	1.50Ev01	1.45E−01	1.62E−02
	DE(0.7)	4.68Ev02	9.45E−02	7.02E−02	7.02E−02	1.38E−02
	DE(0.9)	2.08E−02	4.12E−02	3.33E−02	3.25E−02	4.68E−03
	DE-VFE	**1.70E−02**	**3.28E−02**	**2.51E−02**	**2.54E−02**	**4.15E−03**

(continued)

Table 1. (*continued*)

Problem	Methods	Best	Worst	Median	Mean	Std
f8	DE(0.1)	**−4.19E+04**	**−4.19E+04**	**−4.19E+04**	**−4.19E+04**	7.16E−08
	DE(0.3)	−1.97E+04	−1.78E+04	−1.86E+04	−1.86E+04	4.18E+02
	DE(0.5)	−1.48E+04	−1.34E+04	−1.40E+04	−1.41E+04	3.93E+02
	DE(0.7)	−1.24E+04	−1.07E+04	−1.14E+04	−1.15E+04	4.41E+02
	DE(0.9)	−1.49E+04	−9.31E+03	−1.12E+04	−1.17E+04	1.80E+03
	DE-VFE	**−4.19E+04**	**−4.19E+04**	**−4.19E+04**	**−4.19E+04**	**1.49E−11**
f9	DE(0.1)	2.30E+02	2.72E+02	2.59E+02	2.55E+02	1.14E+01
	DE(0.3)	5.92E+02	6.56E+02	6.28E+02	6.26E+02	1.54E+01
	DE(0.5)	7.63E+02	8.29E+02	8.03E+02	8.01E+02	1.68E+01
	DE(0.7)	8.06E+02	8.97E+02	8.55E+02	8.54E+02	2.03E+01
	DE(0.9)	2.12E+02	6.94E+02	5.77E+02	5.21E+02	1.40E+02
	DE-VFE	**0.00E+00**	**0.00E+00**	**0.00E+00**	**0.00E+00**	**0.00E+00**
f10	DE(0.1)	3.85E−11	5.44E−11	4.47E−11	4.43E−11	3.41E−12
	DE(0.3)	2.85E−07	4.11E−07	3.48E−07	3.54E−07	3.07E−08
	DE(0.5)	8.13E−04	1.50E−03	1.12E−03	1.10E−03	1.64E−04
	DE(0.7)	4.49E−04	1.07E−03	6.56E−04	6.73E−04	1.57E−04
	DE(0.9)	2.23E−10	1.19E−09	4.86E−10	5.80E−10	2.60E−10
	DE-VFE	**7.99E−15**	**1.51E−14**	**1.15E−14**	**1.20E−14**	**2.96E−15**
f11	DE(0.1)	0.00E+00	0.00E+00	0.00E+00	0.00E+00	0.00E+00
	DE(0.3)	2.22E−12	9.83E−12	3.63E−12	3.96E−12	1.51E−12
	DE(0.5)	1.95E−05	4.14E−05	2.84E−05	2.86E−05	5.68E−06
	DE(0.7)	3.21E−06	1.92E−05	6.63E−06	8.03E−06	3.60E−06
	DE(0.9)	**0.00E+00**	2.21E−02	0.00E+00	1.48E−03	4.76E−03
	DE-VFE	**0.00E+00**	**0.00E+00**	**0.00E+00**	**0.00E+00**	**0.00E+00**
f12	DE(0.1)	1.59E−20	4.97E−20	2.85E−20	3.04E−20	8.46E−21
	DE(0.3)	1.84E−08	2.99E−07	7.95E−08	9.54E−08	6.94E−08
	DE(0.5)	5.90E+00	1.98E+01	1.03E+01	1.10E+01	3.93E+00
	DE(0.7)	2.10E−05	1.42E−03	2.54E−04	4.18E−04	4.05E−04
	DE(0.9)	3.56E−19	3.11E−02	5.68E−17	2.49E−03	8.61E−03
	DE-VFE	**4.71E−33**	**6.65E−33**	**4.71E−33**	**4.90E−33**	**5.01E−34**
f13	DE(0.1)	1.05E−19	2.73E−19	1.94E−19	1.92E−19	4.57E−20
	DE(0.3)	1.03E−08	6.91E−08	3.71E−08	3.94E−08	1.50E−08
	DE(0.5)	6.87E+00	8.38E+01	3.99E+01	4.04E+01	2.31E+01
	DE(0.7)	2.33E−04	2.22E−02	1.77E−03	3.10E−03	4.46E−03
	DE(0.9)	2.48E−17	1.60E+00	1.99E−13	6.43E−02	3.19E−01
	DE-VFE	**1.35E−32**	**1.04E−30**	**1.35E−32**	**6.40E−32**	**2.04E−31**

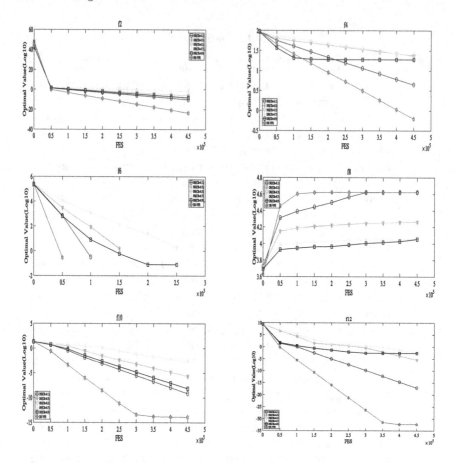

Fig. 2. Convergence figure

6 Conclusions

In order to reduce the task of choosing the crossover scheme of DE and it's associated parameter, in this work, a new evolution scheme, which named Variable Fragments Evolution, was proposed. And it was applied in DE to construct a completely new crossover-free DE. To evaluate the performance of DE-VFE, it was compared with conventional DE with several CR. Experimental results of thirteen commonly used benchmark functions show that the performance of DE-VFE is better than that of conventional DE with different CR values in terms of quality in most cases. Thus DE-VFE can serve as an alternative for the traditional DE.

In the future, VFE will be investigated in other DE variants and other population-based nature-inspired optimization algorithms, particularly, for large scale optimization problems.

References

1. Storn, R., Price, K.V.: Differential evolution–a simple and efficient heuristic for global optimization over continuous spaces. J. Glob. Optim. **11**(4), 341–359 (1997)
2. Das, S., Mullick, S.S., Suganthan, P.N.: Recent advances in differential evolution–an updated survey. Swarm Evol. Comput. **27**, 1–30 (2016)
3. Guo, S.M., Yang, C.C.: Enhancing differential evolution utilizing eigenvector-based crossover operator. IEEE Trans. Evol. Comput. **19**(1), 31–49 (2015)
4. Qin, A., Huang, V., Suganthan, P.: Differential evolution algorithm with strategy adaptation for global numerical optimization. IEEE Trans. Evol. Comput. **13**(2), 398–417 (2009)
5. Lin, C., Qing, A., Feng, Q.: A comparative study of crossover in differential evolution. J. Heurist. **17**(6), 675–703 (2011)
6. Qiu, X., Tan, K.C., Xu, J.-X.: Multiple exponential recombination for differential evolution. IEEE Trans. Cybern. **47**(4), 995–1006 (2017)
7. Mezura-Montes, E., Veluez-Reyes, J., Coello, C.: Modified differential evolution for constrained optimization. In: Proceedings of the Congress on Evolutionary Computation, pp. 332–339. IEEE Press, Sheraton Vancouver Wall Centre Hotel, Vancouver (2006)
8. Mallipeddi, R., Suganthan, P., Pan, Q., Tasgetiren, M.: Differential evolution algorithm with ensemble of parameters and mutation strategies. Appl. Soft Comput. **11**(2), 1679–1696 (2011)
9. Weber, M., Neri, F.: Contiguous binomial crossover in differential evolution. In: Rutkowski, L., Korytkowski, M., Scherer, R., Tadeusiewicz, R., Zadeh, L.A., Zurada, J.M. (eds.) EC/SIDE -2012. LNCS, vol. 7269, pp. 145–153. Springer, Heidelberg (2012). https://doi.org/10.1007/978-3-642-29353-5_17
10. Rönkkönen, J., Kukkonen, S., Price, K.: Real-parameter optimization with differential evolution. In: The 2005 IEEE Congress on Evolutionary Computation, vol. 1, pp. 506–513 (2005)
11. Montgomery, J., Chen, S.: An analysis of the operation of differential evolution at high and low crossover rates. In: 2010 IEEE Congress on Evolutionary Computation (CEC), pp. 1–8 (2010)
12. Brest, J., Greiner, S., Boskovic, B., Mernik, M., Zumer, V.: Self-adapting control parameters in differential evolution: a comparative study on numerical benchmark problems. IEEE Trans. Evol. Comput **10**(6), 646–657 (2006)
13. Tseng, P.: Convergence of a block coordinate descent method for nondifferentiable minimization. J. Optim. Theory Appl. **109**(3), 475–494 (2001)
14. Yao, X., Liu, Y., Lin, G.: Evolutionary programming made faster. IEEE Trans. Evol. Comput. **3**(2), 82–102 (1999)

The Efficiency of Interactive Differential Evolution on Creation of ASMR Sounds

Makoto Fukumoto$^{(\boxtimes)}$ (iD)

Fukuoka Institute of Technology, Fukuoka, Japan
fukumoto@fit.ac.jp

Abstract. Autonomous Sensory Meridian Response (ASMR) is a popular movie content among Internet users. It is a kind of entertainment content, and the users enjoy positive feelings caused by its binaural sounds in terms of reality. By referring to previous proposals creating ASMR sounds based on Interactive Evolutionary Computations (IECs), this study constructed a system of the Interactive Differential Evolution (IDE) creating ASMR sounds suited to the preference of each user. The purpose of this study is to investigate the efficiency of the IDE, which is one of IEC: its subjective evaluation is based on the user's paired comparison of the ASMR sounds. A listening experiment was conducted to fundamentally investigate the efficiency of the IDE. The ASMR sounds were composed of six natural sounds. Each of the nine subjects participated in the listening experiment, and they repeatedly compared two ASMR sounds afforded by the IDE system. As a result of the search process, a shrink in the search space was observed in accordance with generations. After the repetitive comparisons, the subjects scored two representatives ASMR sounds picked up from the 0th and the 10th generations respectively. With statistical analysis, a marginal increase in the fitness values was observed.

Keywords: Differential Evolution · Interactive Evolutionary Computation · Sound · Autonomous Sensory Meridian Response · Paired comparison · Preference

1 Introduction

We enjoy the many contents of various media types in our daily life. Especially, advances in the internet progress of this tendency. With the internet, we can easily find content and enjoy them. As one of the trends of internet content, ASMR content is popular among users. ASMR is the abbreviation word of Autonomous Sensory Meridian Response, and it is also known as the contents name of the movie: you can easily find them on the internet. Previous studies investigated the psycho-physiological effects of the ASMR contents [1–3].

One of the important points of the ASMR is to use the binaural listening of the contents via headphones. With the binaural listening, the users can feel strange and interesting sounds as if they are existing with the movie contents of ASMR. From this point of view, Miyazaki et al. proposed an interesting approach that creates sounds of

© Springer Nature Switzerland AG 2021
Y. Tan and Y. Shi (Eds.): ICSI 2021, LNCS 12689, pp. 368–375, 2021.
https://doi.org/10.1007/978-3-030-78743-1_33

ASMR with the binaural recording [4]. This approach manually treats multiple binaural sounds composing ASMR sounds with the aim of creating much effective ASMR sounds for the users.

Referring to the previous study [4], previous studies proposed a method for creating ASMR sounds for each user by using Interactive Genetic Algorithm (IGA) and Interactive Differential Evolution (IDE) [5, 6]. IGA is one of Interactive Evolutionary Computation (IEC) which is a well-known search method creating media content suited to each user's preference and feelings. IEC applies an ability of search of evolutionary computation [7, 8]. Most of the target of IEC studies were computer graphics, and the second candidate for the media type was related to a sense of hearing [9–14].

In the previous studies [5, 6], the ASMR sound was composed of several sound sources, and the set of sound sources was the target of optimization (Fig. 1). By listening to the ASMR sound via headphones, the user feels the sound sources existing around the user. In the ASMR sounds, a mechanism of binaural recording is an important factor for establishing the existence of virtual sound, and no other IEC studies treated ASMR sounds or binaural sounds as optimization target were found. As an evaluation method of the ASMR sound, the user scored each of them in the IGA [5]. With the IDE, the user compared two sounds and selected a better one [6], however, the efficiency of the search with the IDE was not investigated. Differential Evolution [15, 16] is a relatively recent evolutionary algorithm and is known as having a higher ability of search [17]. Additionally, the subjective comparison by the user in the evaluation process is expected to an easier evaluation for the users than scoring.

The purpose of this study is to investigate the efficiency of the IDE creating ASMR sounds as an application of swarm intelligence for media creation. A listening experiment was conducted in this study. To have the listening experiment, a basic system based on the IDE was constructed by referring to the previous study [5]. In the listening experiment, the subjects listened to ASMR sounds created by the IDE system for searching for good solutions for the subjects' preference.

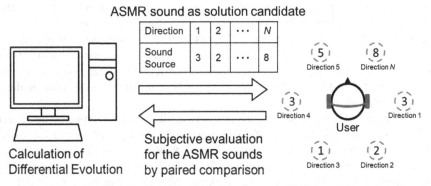

Fig. 1. A scheme of the search of ASMR sounds with Interactive Differential Evolution. The user listens to two ASMR sounds and selects a better one.

2   Differential Evolution and Interactive Differential Evolution

This section describes DE algorithm and IDE with a flow chart. They are the basis of the proposed approach described in the next section.

2.1   Differential Evolution (DE)

DE is a relatively recent evolutionary algorithm having a simple scheme, and many variants have been proposed by previous studies. This study employs one of the fundamental DEs, which is called DE/rand/1/bin [15]. Figure 2 shows a typical flow of DE algorithm. As same as other evolutionary algorithms, DE's search is performed with many solution candidates in the same generation. In DE, the solution candidates in the current generation are called as target vectors, which have N-variables as a target of optimization. The start of the search of DE is initializing the variables of target vectors with random numbers in a certain range.

The evolutionary process for searching better and/or the best solutions is performed by creating a new vector and comparing it with the target vector. The new vector is called a trial vector which also has N-variables same as the target vector. Fitness values are obtained for each of the target and the trial vectors with a certain mathematical function, and the better one survives as the target vector in the next generation. To create the trial vector, variables of some target vectors in the same generation are used. In this process, a differential vector between two target vectors in the same generation is used with a parameter F which changes the length of the differential vector in DE/rand/1/bin. Crossover is also used to create the trial vector with another parameter Cr. Detailed descriptions of DE algorithm are explained in a book [16].

2.2   Interactive Differential Evolution (IDE)

As described above, the evolutionary process of DE is performed by repetitive comparisons of the target vector and the trial vector. The selection process in Fig. 2 means the paired comparison based on the fitness values of the vectors. IDE is an interactive type of DE, therefore, the human users subjectively evaluate the vectors instead of mathematical functions. With the subjective evaluation by each of the users, obtaining media contents suited to each user's preference is expected: the effectiveness of the adjustment for each user's preference was clarified in the previous study [11]. The evaluation can be done by the user's scoring.

As an effective IDE, the paired comparison-based IDE [18] was proposed by Takagi et al., and it has become the basic IDE. The strong point of the paired comparison-based IDE is the subjective comparison of target and trial vectors by the user. Evaluating each of the vectors by scoring seems to be a more difficult task for human users than comparing two vectors. Most of the previous IDEs employed the paired comparison-based IDE.

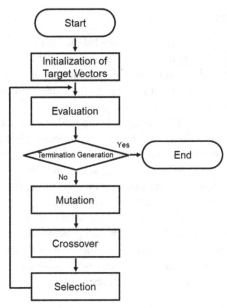

Fig. 2. A typical flow of DE. The selection process is applied for each of the target vectors. In the IDE, the evaluation process is done by the human user.

3 IDE Creating ASMR Sounds

The IDE creating ASMR sounds was proposed in the author's previous study [6]. As the target of optimization, the sound set composing ASMR sound is treated in this method. As shown in Fig. 1, ASMR sound is composed of several sound sources located in different directions for the user. Each of the source sounds was made its location for the user by using a sound effector, after that, ASMR sound was composed by combining them. The number of the sound sources is described as N, and the number corresponds to N-variables of the target and the trial vectors of DE.

The main purpose of this study is to investigate the efficiency of the proposed IDE in terms of good ASMR sounds for each user with a listening experiment described in the next section. A concrete system based on the IDE was constructed based on the paired comparison-based IDE. Therefore, the user listens to two ASMR sounds sequentially presented from the IDE system: the sequence of two sounds corresponding to the target and the trial vectors is randomized by the system. After listening, the user defines a better one from the two sounds and inputs the decision to the system.

4 Experimental Method

To investigate the efficiency of the IDE, the listening experiment was conducted. Nine persons participated in the experiments as subjects. The listening experiment included two steps, a search experiment and an evaluation experiment.

4.1 Search Experiment

In the search experiment, the subjects repeatedly listened to two ASMR sounds presented from the IDE system via headphones. After the listening, the subjects selected a better one from a perspective of their preference. The subjects could control the loudness of the sounds by themselves and have a rest during the experiment freely when they felt fatigued.

As shown in Fig. 1, the ASMR sound was composed of six sound sources. Via headphones, each subject felt that these sound sources were played from different directions with the technique of binaural sounds. Ten natural sounds such as bird songs, and water flow, were employed as the sound sources: the selection of the sound sources referred to popular contents of ASMR on the Internet. Thus, the target vector had six variables, and the range of the variable was from 0 to 9 in integer.

As a set of the IDE, eight target vectors were included in each generation. As the experiment, ten generations from the 0th to the 9th generations were performed. Therefore, the subjects continuously compared two sounds eighty times. The variables of the target vectors in the 0th generation were defined with random integers. The parameters of DE were defined as $Cr = 0.6$ and $F = 0.9$, respectively.

4.2 Evaluation Experiment

With only the search experiment, we cannot understand the efficiency of the IDE enough, because the fitness values were not obtained in the search experiment where the repetitive comparisons were performed by the user.

In the evaluation experiment, the subjects evaluated the two representatives ASMR sounds and made scoring them by the Semantic Differential method with a 7-point scale. 7 meant extremely like, and 1 meant extremely dislike. Each of the two representative sounds was selected from the 0th and 10th generations: note that after the comparisons in the 9th generation, the target vectors of the 10th generation were already obtained in the search experiment. In each of the 0th and the 10th generations, the representative target vector was selected in terms of having the smallest Euclidean distance between target vectors by referring to the previous studies of IDE [11, 14].

5 Experimental Results

5.1 Result of Search Experiment

As a result of the search experiment, Fig. 3 shows the progress of a summation of the Euclidean distance between the eight target vectors. The summation of the Euclidean distance was obtained by calculating the Euclidean distances of all combinations of two target vectors in each generation. As a convergence of the search space, the distance of the solution candidates often decreases in the successful search in general evolutionary computations. As shown in Fig. 3, the gradual decrease in the distance was observed in accordance with the progress of the generations. Besides, by comparing the distance in the 0th and the 10th generations, the smaller distance in the 10th generation was observed in all nine subjects.

5.2   Result of Evaluation Experiment

Figure 4 shows the mean and standard deviation of subjective fitness values in each of the 0th and the 10th generations. The trend of the increase in the fitness value was observed by the mean fitness value. A larger standard deviation was observed in the 0th generation. A statistical test was performed, and a marginal difference was observed between these generations ($P = 0.055$).

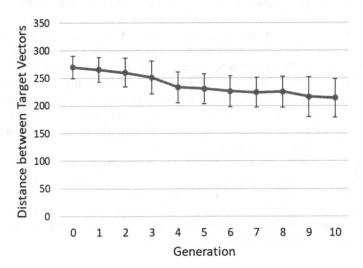

Fig. 3. The progress of the summation of Euclidean distances in the search experiment.

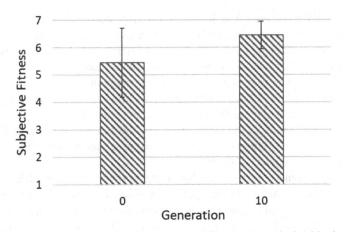

Fig. 4. Mean and standard deviation of the subjective fitness values obtained in the evaluation experiment.

6 Discussion

By referring to the previous IDE studies, the results of the listening experiment were analyzed. The results of the search experiment showed a gradual decrease in the distance, which is often observed in the successful search in general evolutionary computation. Therefore, in the search with the IDE, a successful search in terms of the convergence of the search space seems to be performed.

As the result of the evaluation experiment, the trend of increase in terms of mean fitness value was observed as the marginal difference of the statistical test. This result means that the proposed IDE has a possibility to search the good combinations of source sounds from a random selection of sounds in terms of establishing ASMR sounds. To find better ASMR sounds by the search with the IDE, the performance of the search should be resolved with longer search periods: the search with 10 generations is general in IEC, however, the number of the generations is shorter than general swarm optimization treats global searches. The previous study proposed a continuous search with IDE [14]. The IDE may be improved its search for finding better ASMR sounds by employing the continuous search and other variants of DE.

Both results in the listening experiment are considered as showing the efficiency of the IDE limitedly. By having further experiments, we will gather many samples for showing the definite efficiency of the IDE. Adding other source sounds to the ten sounds used in the IDE system and making these sounds move around the user as the binaural sounds may effective to find better solutions for the users. For example, the previous study uses whispers as a trigger for eliciting an embodied affective response [3].

7 Conclusion

In this study, the IDE creating ASMR sounds was investigated with the listening experiments composed of the search and the evaluation experiments. In the process of the search for good solutions with the IDE, the users listen to two ASMR sounds sequentially and select a better one. A concise evaluation with scoring media contents seems to be difficult for human users, therefore, the comparison in the IDE is expected to be an easier and concise way of evaluation especially time-domain media such as sound. The experimental results showed the obvious decrease in the distance between the target vectors as the convergence of the search space and the marginal increase in the preference from the 0th to the 10th generations. By comparing these results, this study could limitedly show the efficiency of the IDE.

Further experiments are needed to show better performance of the IDE in terms of showing higher fitness value in the final generation. These experiments will be conducted with psycho-physiological measurements as ASMR responses, after improving the IDE by employing other source sounds and a new variant of DE. The superiority of the IDE should be shown by comparing the performance of search of IECs with other evolutionary algorithms, e.g., GA.

References

1. Poerio, G.L., Blakey, E., Hostler, T.J., Veltri, T.: More than a feeling: autonomous sensory meridian response (ASMR) is characterized by reliable changes in affect and physiology. PLoS One **13**(6), e0196645 (2018)
2. Fredborg, B.K., Clark, J.M., Smith, S.D.: Mindfulness and autonomous sensory meridian response (ASMR). PeerJ **6**, e5414 (2018)
3. Smith, N., Snider, A.-M.: ASMR, affect and digitally-mediated intimacy. Emot. Space Soc. **30**, 41–48 (2019)
4. Miyazaki, H., Minamizawa, K.: Music composition based on ASMR to influence the human body. Thesis of Graduate School of Keio University (2016, in Japanese)
5. Fukumoto, M., Hijikuro, K.: Optimization of sound of autonomous sensory meridian response with interactive genetic algorithm. In: Proceedings of SCIS&ISIS 2020, pp.7580 (2020)
6. Fukumoto, M.: Creation of ASMR sounds based on interactive differential evolution. In: Proceedings of ISET 2020, p. 24 (2020)
7. Dawkins, R.: The Blind Watchmaker. Penguin Books, USA (1986)
8. Takagi, H.: Interactive evolutionary computation: fusion of the capabilities of EC optimization and human evaluation. Proc. of the IEEE **89**(9), 1275–1296 (2001)
9. Miki, M., Orita, H., Wake, S.H., Hiroyasu, T.: Design of sign sounds using an interactive genetic algorithm. In: 2006 Proceedings of IEEE Systems, Man, and Cybernetics, vol. 4, pp. 3486–3490 (2006)
10. Takagi, H., Ohsaki, M.: Interactive evolutionary computation-based hearing aid fitting. IEEE Trans. Evol. Comput. **11**, 414–427 (2007)
11. Fukumoto, M.: An efficiency of interactive differential evolution for optimization of warning sound with reflecting individual preference. IEEJ Trans. Electr. Electron. Eng. **10**(S1), S77–S82 (2015)
12. Liang, R., Guo, R., Xi, J., Xie, Y., Zhao, L.: Self-fitting algorithm for digital hearing aid based on interactive evolutionary computation and expert system. Appl. Sci. **7**(3), 272 (2017)
13. Inoue, A., Kidera, D., Fukumoto, M.: Creation of ideal voice with continuous sounds using interactive differential evolution and UTAU. In: Proceedings of ISIS 2019 & ICBAKE 2019, pp.152–157 (2019)
14. Fukumoto, M., Hanada, Y.: Investigation of the efficiency of continuous evaluation-based interactive evolutionary computation for composing melody. IEEJ Trans. Electr. Electron. Eng. **15**(2), 235–241 (2020)
15. Storn, R., Price, K.V.: Differential evolution - a simple and efficient adaptive scheme for global optimization over continuous spaces. Institute of Company Secretaries of India, Chennai, Tamil Nadu. Technical report, TR-95-012 (1995)
16. Price, K.V., Storn, R., Lampinen, J.: Differential Evolution - A Practical Approach to Global Optimization. Springer, Germany (2005)
17. Vesterstrøm, J., Thomson, R.: A comparative study of differential evolution, particle swarm optimization, and evolutionary algorithms on numerical benchmark problems. In: Proceedings of 2004 IEEE Congress on Evolutionary Computation, vol. 2, pp. 1980–1987 (2004)
18. Takagi, H., Pallez, D.: Paired comparison-based interactive differential evolution. In: Proceedings of World Congress on Nature and Biologically Inspired Computing, pp. 375–380 (2009)

Genetic Algorithm and Evolutionary Computation

Genetic Algorithm Fitness Function Formulation for Test Data Generation with Maximum Statement Coverage

Tatiana Avdeenko$^{(\boxtimes)}$ and Konstantin Serdyukov

Novosibirsk State Technical University, 20, Karl Marx Avenue, Novosibirsk, Russia
avdeenko@corp.nstu.ru

Abstract. In present paper we solve an urgent problem of generating the optimal set of test data that provides maximum statement coverage of the code when it is used in the software white box testing process. Formulation of a fitness function containing two terms, and, accordingly, two versions for implementing genetic algorithm (GA) have been proposed. The first term of the fitness function is responsible for the complexity of the code statements executed on the path generated by the current individual test case (current set of statements). The second term formulates the maximum possible difference between the current set of statements and set of statements covered by the remaining test cases in the population. Using only the first term does not make it possible to obtain 100% statement coverage by generated test cases in one population, and therefore implies repeated launch of GA with changed weights of the code statements which requires recompiling the code under test. By using both terms of the proposed fitness function, we obtain maximum statement coverage in one launch of the GA.

Keywords: Genetic algorithm · Test data generation · Fitness function

1 Introduction

Classic software engineering lifecycle includes such important stages as requirements engineering, design of the software architecture, implementation (or coding), testing and maintenance. In this sequence the software testing is a process of investigation of the software product aimed at checking the correspondence between actual behavior of the program code and its expected behavior on a special set of tests (the so-called test cases) selected in a certain way. Testing stage is a very costly taken up to 40–60% of the total software development time.

The goal of testing is to ensure accordance of the developed program with the specified requirements, compliance with logic while data processing and obtaining the correct final results. There are two major testing techniques allowing to check the software under test (SUT) for errors with different levels of access to the code. The latter approaches are black-box testing and white-box testing [1]. The black-box testing considers the software as a "black box" investigating functionality without seeing the source code.

© Springer Nature Switzerland AG 2021
Y. Tan and Y. Shi (Eds.): ICSI 2021, LNCS 12689, pp. 379–389, 2021.
https://doi.org/10.1007/978-3-030-78743-1_34

On the contrary, the white box testing considers the internal code structure and behavior of SUT. The tester chooses inputs to exercise paths through the code and determine the appropriate outputs. In some cases, the test data is already available, but, in most cases, it is required to be generated.

Test data generation is a complex and time-consuming process which needs a lot of effort and budget. Therefore, automation of this process, at least partially, is an urgent research problem, the solution of which could improve the efficiency of the software testing. One of the goals of the automatic test data generation is to create such a multitude of test data that would ensure a sufficient level of quality of the final product by checking most of the various code paths, i.e. would provide maximum code coverage to satisfy some criteria (for example, statement or branch coverage).

There are different approaches to solving the problem of automating test data generation. So, in paper [2], it was proposed to use a constraint-based algorithm for the Mort system, which uses the so-called error testing in which test data is selected in such a way that to determine the presence or absence of certain errors. In the work [3] they proposed using Constraint Logic Programming and symbolic execution to solve the problem. In paper [4] Constraint Handling Rules are used to help in manual verification of problem areas in the computer program.

Many researchers use heuristic approach to automate the software testing process using the Data-flow diagram. Studies of automation methods using this kind of diagrams were carried out in papers [5, 6]. Some of the researchers suggest using hybrid approaches. For example, an approach proposed in [7] combines Random Strategy, Dynamic Symbolic Execution, and Search Based Strategy. The paper [8] proposes a hybrid approach based on Memetic Algorithm for generating test data. The work [9] compares different methods for generating test data, including genetic algorithms, random search, and other heuristic methods.

UML diagrams are also used while generating test data, for example, it is proposed [10, 11] to use genetic algorithms to generate triggers for UML diagrams, which allow finding the critical path in the program. The paper [12] proposes an improved method based on genetic algorithm to select test data for many parallel paths in UML diagrams.

In addition to UML diagrams, the code can be displayed in the form of Classification-Tree Method [13]. The problem of constructing the trees was considered and an integrated classification tree algorithm was proposed [14] and the developed ADDICT prototype (AutomateD test Data generation using the Integrated Classification-Tree methodology) for an integrated approach was studied [15].

As follows from the above, many researchers focus on evolutionary approaches to solving this problem, in particular, on the genetic algorithm and its hybrid modifications. However, it should be noted that traditionally genetic algorithm is used to find the most fitted chromosome, which is a set of test data that ensures passage along the most complex (long) path in the Control Flow Graph [16]. Many data sets that provide maximum code coverage can be found by repeating this procedure multiple times with preliminary zeroing of the code operation weights corresponding to the chromosomes found earlier [17]. So, the fitness function of the genetic algorithm has a simple form, but the process of finding all the data sets is quite long and non-optimal. In present paper, we use the idea of an Improved Genetic Algorithm for Multiple Paths Automatic Software Test

Case Generation proposed when an additional term responsible for the greatest possible difference in the paths of the population, along with a term responsible for the complexity of each path, is included into the fitness function [18]. We investigated this approach, identified its shortcomings, and propose an improved form of the fitness function, as well as changes in the selection method, allowing us to achieve a more uniform increase in the percentage of code coverage. Our research confirmed greater effectiveness of the proposed approach compared to the original version.

The paper is organized as follows. Section 1 gives introduction to the problem and literature review. Section 2 discusses theoretical issues of the research including description of the algorithm's basic version. In Sect. 3 we describe case study and results of the research. Section 4 provides the conclusions.

2 Theoretical Background

2.1 Genetic Algorithm for Test Data Generation

Genetic Algorithm (GA) borrows its idea and terminology from the biological world. In such a way, it uses different representations for potential solutions referred to as chromosomes, genetic operators such as crossover and mutation used to generate new child solutions, and also selection and evaluation mechanisms derived from the nature.

With regard to the problem considered here, a set of generated test data, which best contributes to the software testing process, can serve as potential solutions. Depending on the values of the input variables supplied to the SUT input, the code execution process can follow various paths determined by the sequence of statements, among which there can be both linear statements following one after another, conditional statements (IF, CASE) and loops (WHILE, FOR), leading to branching of computations. It is the latter that ultimately determines the variety of paths of the code execution.

In this paper we assume that input variables $var_1, var_2, \ldots, var_N$ of the SUT can take continuous values from the certain intervals. So, it is the most reasonable to use continuous (real-valued) GA (unlike the binary GA) where the values of input variables are the genes included in the chromosomes that determine potential solutions to the problem of generating input test data. Denoting chromosomes by x_i, we obtain test data population, consisting of m individuals each containing N values of the input variables

$$\{x_1, x_2, \ldots, x_m\}, \text{ where } x_i = \left[var_{1,i}, var_{2,i}, \ldots, var_{N,i}\right]. \tag{1}$$

The foundation of white box techniques is to execute every part of the SUT at least once in order to achieve a previously defined percentage of code coverage. Testing theory distinguishes between the following types of code coverage: statement coverage, branch coverage, conditions coverage and path coverage. In this research we consider statement coverage as the quality criterion for the generated test cases population (1) the purpose of which is to execute as many statements of the program as possible in comparison with the total number of statements. Thus, the GA fitness function for a certain chromosome x_i has to be formulated to take into account statement coverage requirement. That is, test case corresponding to the most fitted chromosome traverses the most loaded (more complex) path containing as many SUT statements as possible.

A complementary approach to the formulation of the fitness function is the requirement for maximum coverage not only by one test case, but also by multiple test cases at once (preferably 100% coverage by the chromosome population). The latter leads to the possibility of obtaining the final solution in one GA run, and can be heuristically provided by the inclusion of special terms into the fitness function ensuring as much variety of individuals x_i and distance between them in the population (1) as possible.

The genetic algorithm includes the following main stages:

1. *Initialization.* The initial population is formed randomly taking into account constraints on the values of input variables.
2. *Population evaluation.* Each of the chromosomes is evaluated by a fitness function.
3. *Selection.* The best 20% chromosomes are selected for the next generation directly, the rest 80% chromosomes are obtained as a result of crossover.
4. *Crossover.* Crossover occurs through the random choice of a certain *l*-th gene in the two random parent chromosomes and subsequent blending where single offspring gene comes from a linear combination of the two corresponding parent genes $var_{l,offspring} = \beta \cdot var_{l,mother} + (1 - \beta) \cdot var_{l,father}$, $\beta \in [0, 1]$, [19]. Remaining genes of the offspring are chosen randomly from one of the two parents.
5. *Mutation.* In random order, a gene can change a value randomly. The main goal of mutations is to obtain solutions that could not be obtained from existing genes.

After all the stages have been carried out, it is assessed whether the population has reached the desired coverage of the solution, or has come to a limit on the number of populations M.

2.2 Formulation of the Fitness Function for Maximum Statement Coverage

In this section, we will formulate the fitness function of the genetic algorithm in such a way that to maximize the coverage of SUT statements by both individual test cases and the whole test cases population.

The first step of white-box testing is to translate the source code into a Control Flow Graph (CFG). In the CFG, the statements are represented as nodes (boxes) and the control flows between the statements is represented as edges. Denote the set of nodes of the CFG by $\{v_1, v_2, \ldots, v_n\}$, where v_j is a separate node of CFG (corresponding to one or more statements of the code). Note that the order of execution of separate nodes v_j may differ depending on various input data, since the program code contains conditional statements when computations are branched along several paths. Thus, different initial data of the program leads to traversing along different paths of the CFP, ensuring the execution of only quite specific statements of the program. Let us denote $g(x_i)$ a vector that is an indicator of the graph nodes coverage with a path initiated by a specific set of the test case x_i:

$$g(x_i) = \big(g_1(x_i), g_2(x_i), \ldots, g_n(x_i)\big), \text{ where}$$

$$g_j(x_i) = \begin{cases} 1, & \text{if path initiated by } x_i \text{ traverses through the node } v_j; \\ 0, & \text{otherwise} \end{cases}$$

Assigning weights to edges of the CFG one can take into account the fact that different paths of executing program code have different complexity. More weights are assigned to statements that are critical, being a part of the more error-prone paths. Following the procedure proposed in [19] an initial credit is taken (for example, 100 or 10), if CFG is dense i.e. large numbers of statements are there than initial credit should be taken as 100 and if CFG is sparse (small code) then it can be taken as 10. At each node of CFG the incoming credit (sum of the weights of all the incoming edges) is divided and distributed to all the outgoing edges of the node. For the conditional and loops statements we have used an 80–20 rule: 80% of weight of the incoming credit is given to loops and branches and the remaining 20% of the incoming credit is given to the edges in sequential path. If we encounter a conditional statement with two or more conditions, fulfillment of each one leads to the execution of certain following statements, the weight of such a statement is divided by the number of the outgoing edges.

Let us denote by $\{w_1, w_2, \ldots, w_n\}$ the weights assigned to all the statements in accordance with the above described method. Then the fitness function for the individual chromosome x_i can be formulated as follows.

$$F_1(x_i) = \sum_{j=1}^{n} w_j g_j(x_i). \qquad (2)$$

Indeed, the more is the sum of weighted statements covered by a path initiated with the test case x_i, the more fit is the chromosome x_i.

On the other hand, the use of formula (2) for the fitness function will lead to a situation where the most adapted and capable of reproduction will always be individuals that lead to the most complex pieces of the code, to the detriment of the diversity of individuals in the population, since the population aspect in this formula not taken into account. As a result of using GA with such a fitness function, we get the most fitted individuals, however, if we evaluate the fitness of the resulting population as a whole, it will not provide maximum code coverage, since the chromosomes of the population will generate very similar paths.

To ensure a greater diversity of the population, it is necessary to introduce into the fitness function a term that gives preference to chromosomes that provide the greatest possible distance from each other all the paths that are generated by test cases of the population's chromosomes.

The developed fitness function is based on the idea given in paper [18]. We correct some inconsistencies in the formulas and propose more balanced relation of terms in the final formula of the fitness function.

In order to calculate the j - th similarity coefficient $sim_j(x_{i_1}, x_{i_2})$ of the two chromosomes x_{i_1} and x_{i_2} we compare if the node v_j of the CFG is covered or uncovered by both paths initiated by these two test cases

$$sim_j(x_{i_1}, x_{i_2}) = g_j(x_{i_1}) \oplus g_j(x_{i_2}), j = \overline{1, n}. \qquad (3)$$

The more matching bits are there between the two paths, the greater is the similarity value between the chromosomes. The following formula takes into account weights of corresponding CFG nodes

$$sim(x_{i_1}, x_{i_2}) = \sum_{j=1}^{n} w_j \cdot sim_j(x_{i_1}, x_{i_2}). \qquad (4)$$

The value of similarity between the chromosome x_i and the rest of the chromosomes in the population is calculated as

$$f_{sim}(x_i) = \frac{1}{(m-1)} \sum_{\substack{s=1 \\ s \neq i}}^{m} sim(x_s, x_i). \tag{5}$$

Now we can determine the maximum value of path similarity in the whole population.

$$\overline{f_{sim}} = \max_{i=\overline{1,m}} f_{sim}(x_i). \tag{6}$$

So, we can formulate the term of fitness function responsible for the diversity of paths in a population. It is.

$$F_2(x_i) = \overline{f_{sim}} - f_{sim}(x_i). \tag{7}$$

Thus, the fitness function for the chromosome x_i is calculated by the formula

$$F(x_i) = F_1(x_i) + k \cdot F_2(x_i), \tag{8}$$

where $F_1(x_i)$ and $F_2(x_i)$ are defined by formulas (2) and (7). The first term $F_1(x_i)$ determines the complexity of the path initialized by the chromosome x_i, and the second term $F_2(x_i)$ determines the remoteness of this path from other paths in the population. The constant k determines relation between the two terms and is chosen depending on the number of different paths in the SUT.

3 Research

To investigate the GA work with the proposed fitness function (8), a code for testing was developed containing six conditional statements and two cycles, in such a way determining sufficient number of different paths of the program code. Figure 1 shows a block diagram of this code.

The number inside the blocks contains the number of linear statements. Cycle 1 contains most of the statements and conditions, so they will be executed multiple times. Conditions A, B and C are checked sequentially and require different test cases to execute. Condition F will only be executed if both D and E are true and then Cycle 2 is completed. So, the code has different approaches to representing conditions, so the proposed method will generate data under different circumstances.

In the course of our research, we examined two versions of GA, using formula (8) to calculate the fitness function for the number of individuals in the population $m = 100$. In the first version, we put $k = 0$ in formula (8). Since for this version complete code coverage was never achieved in one population with a single application of GA, each application of it was used to find one best-fit chromosome. Further, the statements covered by the graph path initiated by the test case found in the previous step received zero weight, and the process of searching for the next best fit chromosome continued in a similar way. The results of studies by this method are presented in Table 1. A total of five studies were carried out, in each of which we received four test cases that completely covered all the statements of the program code. However, these solutions were not obtained in an optimal way, since we had to run the GA four times consecutively (single path at a time), achieving with each new test case more and more coverage. The coverage indicators of the graph nodes, colored green, correspond to the nodes already covered at the moment, either with the current test case, or with the test cases found in the previous steps.

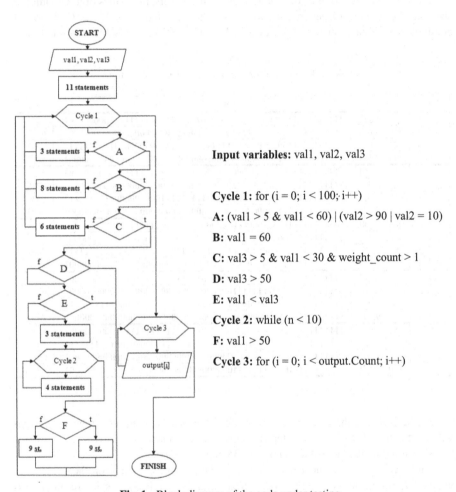

Input variables: val1, val2, val3

Cycle 1: for (i = 0; i < 100; i++)

A: (val1 > 5 & val1 < 60) | (val2 > 90 | val2 = 10)

B: val1 = 60

C: val3 > 5 & val1 < 30 & weight_count > 1

D: val3 > 50

E: val1 < val3

Cycle 2: while (n < 10)

F: val1 > 50

Cycle 3: for (i = 0; i < output.Count; i++)

Fig. 1. Block diagram of the code under testing

Table 2 shows the results of studying the GA work with a nonzero value of $k = 1$ in formula (8) for the fitness function with the same $m = 100$, that is, with the presence of both terms. In the five trials, it was possible to achieve 100% coverage of program statements in one population, and, as a result, in one pass of the genetic algorithm. However, this required not four, but five test cases. Therefore, the improvement of the form of fitness function and other stages of GA remains relevant.

To study the effect of the constant k in (8) on the results, the values of the population size and the number of generations were specially selected $m = M = 35$ for which complete 100% statement coverage of the SUT given in Fig. 1 is achieved quite rare.

Table 1. Results for the multiple launch GA-algorithm.

#	#	Test sets	Statement coverage	%
1	1	[1, 82,87]	11111111111000000000000000000111111111111111111110000000001	52%
	2	[60,44,60]	11111111111000111111111000000000000000000000000000000000001	67%
	3	[4, 85, 97]	11111111111000000000000111111111111111000000000111111111111	94%
	4	[11,52,51]	11111111111111000000000000000000000000000000000000000000001	100%
2	1	[83,12,99]	11111111111000000000000000000111111111111111111110000000001	52%
	2	[60,40,44]	11111111111000111111111000000000000000000000000000000000001	67%
	3	[5, 84, 97]	11111111111000000000000111111111111111000000000111111111111	94%
	4	[39,14,78]	11111111111111000000000000000000000000000000000000000000001	100%
3	1	[68,14,98]	11111111111000000000000000000111111111111111111110000000001	52%
	2	[60, 9, 33]	11111111111000111111111000000000000000000000000000000000001	67%
	3	[2, 4, 93]	11111111111000000000000111111111111111000000000111111111111	94%
	4	[28,81,48]	11111111111111000000000000000000000000000000000000000000001	100%
4	1	[69,80,90]	11111111111000000000000000000111111111111111111110000000001	52%
	2	[60, 2, 76]	11111111111000111111111000000000000000000000000000000000001	67%
	3	[0, 49, 94]	11111111111000000000000111111111111111000000000111111111111	94%
	4	[83,99,89]	11111111111111000000000000000000000000000000000000000000001	100%
5	1	[81, 6, 93]	11111111111000000000000000000111111111111111111110000000001	52%
	2	[5, 17, 58]	11111111111000000000000111111111111111000000000111111111111	80%
	3	[54,47,65]	11111111111111000000000000000000000000000000000000000000001	85%
	4	[60,15,17]	11111111111000111111111000000000000000000000000000000000001	100%

Figure 2 shows the average value of the achieved statement coverage for various values of k from 0 to 50, calculated from 40 GA runs, each time carried out with new random initial populations and maximum 35 generations.

Thus, we see a non-linear dependence of the average coverage on the value of k, which determines the ratio between the terms F_1 and F_2 in the expression for the fitness function. First, as k grows, the statement coverage increases, reaching its maximum for $k = 10$. After that, the value of the fitness function begins to decline, as excessive attention begins to be paid to F_2, which is responsible for the diversity of paths in the population at the expense of the coverage for each path.

Table 2. Results for the single launch GA-algorithm.

#	#	Test sets	Statement coverage	%
1	1	[41,11,35]	1111111111111100000000000000000000000000000000000000000001	100%
	2	[2, 85, 86]	1111111111100000000000011111111111111110000000001111111111	
	3	[72, 9, 96]	1111111111100000000000000000011111111111111110000000001	
	4	[79, 42, 67]	1111111111100000000000000000000000000000000000000000000000	
	5	[60, 88, 48]	1111111111100011111111100000000000000000000000000000001	
2	1	[90, 91, 72]	1111111111111100000000000000000000000000000000000000000001	100%
	2	[3, 75, 48]	1111111111100000000000000000000000000000000000000000000000	
	3	[60, 70, 16]	1111111111100011111111100000000000000000000000000000001	
	4	[4, 74, 81]	1111111111100000000000011111111111111110000000001111111111	
	5	[67, 70, 78]	1111111111100000000000000000011111111111111110000000001	
3	1	[2, 19, 65]	1111111111100000000000011111111111111110000000001111111111	100%
	2	[61, 92, 12]	1111111111111100000000000000000000000000000000000000000001	
	3	[2, 79, 5]	1111111111100000000000000000000000000000000000000000000000	
	4	[85, 59, 90]	1111111111100000000000000000011111111111111110000000001	
	5	[60, 50, 37]	1111111111100011111111100000000000000000000000000000001	
4	1	[15, 37, 33]	1111111111100000000000000000000000000000000000000000000000	100%
	2	[81, 84, 24]	1111111111100011111111100000000000000000000000000000001	
	3	[69, 84, 86]	1111111111100000000000000000011111111111111110000000001	
	4	[60, 58, 59]	1111111111100011111111100000000000000000000000000000001	
	5	[3, 4, 84]	1111111111100000000000011111111111111110000000001111111111	
5	1	[61, 91, 60]	1111111111111100000000000000000000000000000000000000000001	100%
	2	[88, 38, 29]	1111111111100000000000000000000000000000000000000000000000	
	3	[3, 62, 86]	1111111111100000000000011111111111111110000000001111111111	
	4	[81, 17, 85]	1111111111100000000000000000011111111111111110000000001	
	5	[60, 38, 72]	1111111111100011111111100000000000000000000000000000001	

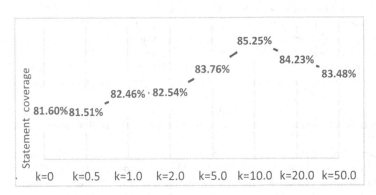

Fig. 2. Average value of the achieved statement coverage of final population

4   Conclusion

The method considered in present paper permits to generate test data based on two terms - the complexity of the source code path for a particular test case and the achievement of the greatest variety of paths covered with different test cases in one population. This allows obtaining test cases for many different code paths within a single run of the genetic algorithm. In the future, it seems promising for increasing the convergence rate to consider the option of dynamically changing the ratio between both terms of the fitness function in the process of approaching to optimal solution. Also, a niche GA seems promising for the task of generating test data, which can also allow combining the goals of the most complete code coverage with a variety of niches in the population.

Acknowledgments. The research is supported by Ministry of Science and Higher Education of Russian Federation (project No. FSUN-2020-0009). The research is supported RFBR, project №. 19-37-90156.

References

1. Spillner, A., Linz, T., Schaefer, H.: Software Testing Foundations: A Study Guide for the Certified Tester Exam. 4th edn. Rocky Nook (2011)
2. Richard, A.D., Jefferson, A.O.: Constraint-based automatic test data generation. IEEE Trans. Softw. Eng. **17**(9), 900–910 (1991)
3. Meudec, C.: ATGen: automatic test data generation using constraint logic programming and symbolic execution. Softw. Test. Verif. Reliabil. **11**, 81–96 (2001)
4. Gerlich, R.: Automatic test data generation and model checking with CHR. In: 11th Workshop on Constraint Handling Rules (2014)
5. Girgis, M.R.: Automatic test data generation for data flow testing using a genetic algorithm. J. Univ. Comput. Sci. **11**(6), 898–915 (2005)
6. Khamis, A., Bahgat, R., Abdelaziz, R.: Automatic test data generation using data flow information. Dogus Univ. J. **2**, 140–153 (2011)
7. Liu, Z., Chen, Z., Fang, C., Shi, Q.: Hybrid test data generation. state key laboratory for novel software technology. In: ICSE Companion 2014 Companion Proceedings of the 36th International Conference on Software Engineering, pp. 630–631 (2014)
8. Harman, M., McMinn, P.A.: Theoretical and empirical study of search-based testing: local, global, and hybrid search. IEEE Trans. Softw. Eng. **36**(2), 226–247 (2010)
9. Maragathavalli, P., Anusha, M., Geethamalini, P., Priyadharsini, S.: Automatic test-data generation for modified condition. Decision coverage using genetic algorithm. Int. J. Eng. Sci. Technol. **3**(2), 1311–1318 (2011)
10. Doungsa-ard, C., Dahal, K., Hossain, A.G., Suwannasart, T.: An automatic test data generation from UML state diagram using genetic algorithm, pp. 47–52. IEEE Computer Society Press (2007)
11. Sabharwal, S., Sibal, R., Sharma, C.: Applying genetic algorithm for prioritization of test case scenarios derived from UML diagrams. IJCSI Int. J. Comput. Sci. **8**(3(2)), 433–444 (2011)
12. Doungsa-ard, C., Dahal, K., Hossain, A., Suwannasart, T.: GA-based automatic test data generation for UML state diagrams with parallel paths. In: Yan, X.T., Jiang, C., Eynard, B. (eds.) Advanced Design and Manufacture to Gain a Competitive Edge: New Manufacturing Techniques and Their Role in Improving Enterprise Performance, pp. 147–156. Springer, Heidelberg (2008). https://doi.org/10.1007/978-1-84800-241-8_16
13. Grochtmann, M., Grimm, K.: Classification trees for partition testing. Softw. Test. Verif. Reliabil. **3**(2), 63–82 (1993)
14. Chen, T.Y., Poon, P.L., Tse, T.H.: An integrated classification-tree methodology for test case generation. Int. J. Softw. Eng. Knowl. Eng. **10**(6), 647–679 (2000)

15. Cain, A., Chen, T.Y., Grant, D., Poon, P.-L., Tang, S.-F., Tse, T.H.: An automatic test data generation system based on the integrated classification-tree methodology. In: Ramamoorthy, C.V., Lee, R., Lee, K.W. (eds.) SERA 2003. LNCS, vol. 3026, pp. 225–238. Springer, Heidelberg (2004). https://doi.org/10.1007/978-3-540-24675-6_18

16. Praveen, R.S., Tai-hoon, K.: Application of genetic algorithm in software testing. Int. J. Softw. Eng. Appl. 3(4), 87–96 (2009)

17. Serdyukov, K., Avdeenko, T.: Investigation of the genetic algorithm possibilities for retrieving relevant cases from big data in the decision support systems. In: CEUR Workshop Proceedings, vol. 1903, pp. 36–41 (2017)

18. Zhu, E., Yao, C., Ma, Z., Liu, F.: Study of an improved genetic algorithm for multiple paths automatic software test case generation. In: Tan, Y., Takagi, H., Shi, Y. (eds.) ICSI 2017. LNCS, vol. 10385, pp. 402–408. Springer, Cham (2017). https://doi.org/10.1007/978-3-319-61824-1_44

19. Haupt, R.L., Haupt, S.E.: Practical Genetic Algorithms, 2nd edn. Wiley, Hoboken (1998)

A Genetic Algorithm-Based Ensemble Convolutional Neural Networks for Defect Recognition with Small-Scale Samples

Yiping Gao, Liang Gao, Xinyu Li$^{(\boxtimes)}$, and Cuiyu Wang

State Key Laboratory of Digital Manufacturing Equipment and Technology, Huazhong University of Science and Technology, Wuhan, China
lixinyu@mail.hust.edu.cn

Abstract. In modern manufacturing, defect recognition is an important technology, and using recent advances, such as convolutional neural networks (CNNs) to help defect recognition have addressed many attentions. However, CNN requires large-scale samples for training. In industries, large-scale samples are usually unavailable, and this impedes the wide application of CNNs. Ensemble learning might be a feasible manner for the small-scale-sample problem, But the weight for different CNNs needs explicit selection, and this is complex and time-consuming. To overcome this problem, this paper proposes a genetic algorithm (GA)-based ensemble CNNs for small-scale sample defect recognition problem. The proposed method uses an ensemble strategy to combinate several CNN models to solve the small-scale-sample problem in defect recognition, and use GA to optimize the ensemble weights with 5-fold cross-validation. With these improvements, the proposed method can find the optimal ensemble weight automatically, and it avoids the complex and explicit parameter selection. The experimental results with different trainable samples indicate that the proposed method outperforms the other defect recognition methods, which indicates that the proposed method is effective for small-scale sample defect recognition tasks. Furthermore, the discussion results also suggest that the proposed method is robust for noise, and it indicates that the proposed method has good potential in defect recognition tasks.

Keywords: Convolutional neural network · Defect recognition · Genetic algorithm · Ensemble learning

1 Introduction

In modern manufacturing, defect recognition is an important technology [1]. A good defect recognition can not only ensure the product quality, but also provide a gist to optimize the process parameters [2]. Traditionally, defect recognition was performed manually. But the recognition speed is too slow to satisfy modern manufacturing, and the results are also unstable. As a replacement, using machine vision to help defect recognition has become a research hotspot [3]. Machine vision-based defect recognition employs computer vision techniques to collect and recognize defect images. Comparing

© Springer Nature Switzerland AG 2021
Y. Tan and Y. Shi (Eds.): ICSI 2021, LNCS 12689, pp. 390–398, 2021.
https://doi.org/10.1007/978-3-030-78743-1_35

with manual recognition, machine vision-based defect recognition is cheap for deployment, and has fast and stable recognition results. Based on these advantages, machine vision-based defect recognition has been widely used, including steel [4], welding [5], and fabric [6].

Recently, since some new technologies, such as IoT, digital twin and big data have developed rapidly, defect collection is fast and convenient in machine vision-based defect recognition [2, 7]. Furthermore, the developments of the hardware, such as GPU, also bring some conveniences for defect recognition. Thus, most of the research is focused on improving recognition results.

In machine vision-based defect recognition, machine learning is one of the common methods to recognize defect types, such as support vector machine [8], and artificial neural network [9]. However, most of these methods require an explicit feature extraction, and the recognition results highly rely on the feature representation. A good feature representation will lead to a good recognition result, while the inappropriate representation might cause poor results. The common feature extractors include local binary pattern (LBP) [10], grey level co-occurrence matrix (GLCM) [11] and wavelet transformation [12]. But the extractor selection processing is complex and time-consuming, and it requires explicit knowledge. This impedes the generalization greatly. Recently, deep learning (DL) has become a research hotspot. With the outstanding performance on image recognition, using DL, especially convolutional neural networks (CNNs), for defect recognition has driven many attentions. Gao et al. [2] proposed a semi-supervised CNN model to recognize steel surface defects. Niu et al. [13] used a generative adversarial network to generate some fake samples and improve the recognition results. Jiang et al. [14] developed a CNN-based defect recognition method for welding defects. The most merit of CNNs is the automatic feature extraction, and it can avoid the explicit selection processes. However, the automatic feature extraction needs large-scale samples, otherwise, the CNN might not perform as expected due to the lack of useful information. In defect recognition tasks, since the defect occurs rarely, it is difficult to collect large scale samples, and only a few samples are available for model training. Therefore, defect recognition is a typical small-scale-sample problem, and this limits the application of CNNs.

To overcome the small-scale-sample problem, ensemble learning, which builds and combines several models for better results, is a feasible manner. But how to develop ensemble learning into CNN is still underdeveloped, and the biggest problem is to find the optimal ensemble weight for each model. On the one hand, the CNNs are too large to train together. Thus, ensemble strategies, such as boost and Adaboost might not be feasible for this situation [15]. On the other hand, setting the weight manually is impracticable and time-consuming. CNNs with different initializations perform differently so that the weight is also different. And this is not conducive for generalization. To overcome this problem, this paper proposes a genetic algorithm (GA)-based ensemble CNNs for defect recognition. In the proposed method, five CNNs are built and trained individually. After that, each CNN calculates the recognized results, and a GA is used to optimize the ensemble weight for each CNN with 5-fold cross-validation. With this improvement, the proposed method can find the optimal weight automatically, which avoids manual weight selection and requires less computation source. To evaluate the performances, the proposed method is tested on a steel surface defect recognition dataset. The experimental results suggest that the proposed method has better recognition results with different trainable samples. This result indicates that the proposed method is effective for small-scale-sample defect recognition tasks. Furthermore, the discussion result shows that the proposed method is robust for noise, this result also indicates that the proposed method has good application potential.

The rest of this paper is organized as follows. Section 2 presents the proposed method. Section 3 gives the experimental results of the proposed method. Section 4 is the discussion and Sect. 5 is the conclusion and future work.

2   Proposed GA-Based Ensemble CNNs

To overcome the small-scale sample problem and improve the recognition result of CNN, this paper proposes a GA-based ensemble CNNs for defect recognition. In the proposed method, five CNN models are built and trained individually. After that, the recognition results of training samples are used to optimize the ensemble weight with 5-fold cross-validation. And this optimization is performed by GA. More detail is discussed below.

2.1   Basic CNN Model

In the proposed method, five CNN model is built and trained individually. These models are used as the basic models for ensemble learning. CNN is a feedforward neural network, which can extract the feature automatically. A CNN is usually composed of convolutional layers, pooling layer and classification layer. Convolutional layer performs a convolution operation that uses sliding windows to map the input into feature maps. And the sliding windows are also known as convolutional kernels. After the sliding windows, an activation is used to map the feature into a non-linear space, and it might make the feature more discriminative. Pooling layer performs an un-sampling to reduce the dimension and avoid over-fitting. Convolutional layers and pooling layers are stacked alternately, and the combination of them is also known as feature extractor. After the feature extractor, a classification layer is connected to recognize the feature. Classification usually uses multilayer perceptron with softmax activation function to calculate the probabilities that the defect belongs to each type. A typical CNN architecture is shown in Fig. 1.

In the proposed method, five CNNs are built and trained as the basic models. The architectures of these CNNs are the same as Fig. 1, which composes 3 convolutional layers, 3 pooling layers and a classification layer. The convolutional layer uses 32, 64, and 128 3 * 3 convolutional kernels individually, and uses ReLU, which $f(x) = \max(0, x)$, as activation functions. The pooling layers use the max-pooling strategy to extract the max value of a 2 * 2 non-overlapped sliding window, and the dimensions will be reduced by a quarter. This will release the computation source and avoid over-fitting. The classification layer uses a 3-layer perceptron with softmax to calculate the probabilities. The first two layers use 512 units and ReLU as activation function, while the last one has m units, where m means the number of defect types.

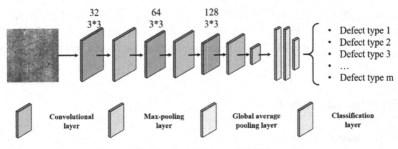

Fig. 1. Architecture of CNN

All the five models use cross-entropy as loss functions. Assuming y is the ground truth type and y' is the recognized type, cross-entropy loss function L is defined as:

$$L = -(y log y' + (1 - y) log(1 - y'))$$ (1)

The loss function L is optimized by Adam with a mini-batch. Each model is trained individually with different initializations. Furthermore, a dropout technique is used to improve the generalization of the model, and a global average pooling layer is added for vectorization.

2.2 GA for Ensemble Weight Optimization

How to find the optimal weight for different models is one of the biggest challenges to develop ensemble learning into CNNs. CNNs are too large for self-adaption ensemble strategies, and constant weight is also unfeasible because different CNNs perform differently. Therefore, the proposed method uses GA to find the optimal weight automatically. Assuming y_i' denotes the recognized probabilities in model i, w_i is the corresponding weight, the proposed method uses the accuracy of 5-fold cross-validation as fitness value f.

With this fitness, the proposed method initiates 50 populations, and uses GA to find the optimal weight w. The optimization involves four steps with 50 iterations. Step 1: Initialization. This step initiates 50 populations randomly in the range of [0, 1]. Step 2: Selection. This step selects two populations randomly, and save the population with better fitness value as the new population for the next generation. Step 3: Crossover. This step also selects two populations randomly, and exchange some points with p_{cross}. Step 4: Mutation. This step chooses a population and re-initiates some point randomly with p_m. Step 2–4 are performed iteratively until meeting the stop criterion. After optimization, the optimal ensemble weight w is found to combinate the five CNN models, and the ensemble model can be deployed for defect recognition.

2.3 Application

The ensemble weight w can be regarded as confidence for each CNN model, and the final recognition result is voted by each model with this confidence. For example, in a binary classification problem, the five CNNs give five recognition probabilities [0.9, 0.1], [0.4, 0.6], [0.2, 0.8], [0.3, 0.7], [0, 1.0], and the weight w is [0.5, 0.4, 0.3, 0.2, 0.1]. The overall recognition result with w is [0.73, 1.22]. And the re-normalized result is [0.374, 0.626], therefore, this sample should belong to the second type.

3   Experimental Results

3.1   Experimental Setting

Defect recognition is a small-scale-sample problem, and this paper proposes a GA-based ensemble CNNs to solve this problem. In order to evaluate the performances, the proposed method is tested on a public defect recognition dataset, NEU [16]. The dataset contains six types of hot-rolled steel strip, including crazing (Cr), inclusion (In), patches (Pa), pitted surface (PS), rolled in scale (RS), and scratches (Sc). Each defect type contains 300 images. The examples of NEU dataset are shown in Fig. 2. In this experiment, the NEU dataset is divided into a training set and a testing set. Each set contains 150 images for each defect type, and totally has 900 images. In order to simulate the situation of the small-scale sample, in the training set, this experiment chooses different numbers of trainable samples randomly. The numbers include 50, 100, and 150 per defect.

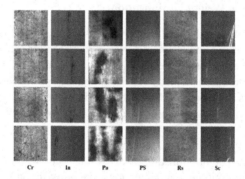

Fig. 2. Examples of NEU dataset [17]

The experiment contains two parts. The first part is to evaluate if the GA-based ensemble strategy has better performances than the other strategies or the individual model. In the second part, the proposed method is compared with the other defect recognition methods, including the traditional machine learning methods and deep learning methods. In this experiment, the proposed method uses the CNN architecture in Fig. 1 as the basic models, and uses the GA described in Sect. 2.2 to find the optimal ensemble weight. Each CNN model is trained individually and optimized by Adam. The batch size is 32 and each model iterates 100 epochs. All the methods run 10 times and calculate the average accuracy to evaluate the performances. All the images are resized into 64 * 64, and no extra data augmentation is used. The experimental results are discussed below.

3.2 Experimental Results

The experiment contains two parts. The first part is to evaluate if the GA-based ensemble strategy has better performances than the other strategies or the individual models. In this part, this paper compares the proposed method with the individual basic model and average ensemble strategy, and the results are presented in Table 1.

Table 1. Accuracy compared with the other ensemble strategy and individual model

Methods	50	100	150
Individual CNN	97.37	98.55	99.06
Average ensemble weight	97.65	98.84	99.42
Proposed method	**98.06**	**99.07**	**99.57**

From these results, the proposed method has better results. Comparing with the individual CNN models, the recognition results are improved greatly by the proposed method. This result indicates that the ensemble CNNs is more suitable for small-scale sample defect recognition tasks. Comparing with the average ensemble strategy, the proposed method also has better results. This result suggests that the proposed method, which uses GA to find the optimal ensemble weight, is effective. This result also explains why the average ensemble weight is not suitable for CNN. This is because different CNNs with different initializations might perform differently, some CNNs might be stronger, while the other might be weaker. If it set an average weight, the weaker CNNs might mislead the recognition result. Therefore, the proposed method uses GA to find the optimal ensemble weight.

The second part is the comparison with the conventional defect recognition methods, including support vector machine (SVM) [16], nearest neighbor classifier (NNC) [16], Bayes classifier [8], Alexnet [17] and Decaf [18]. SVM, NNC and Bayes classifier are conventional machine learning methods for defect recognition, and Alexnet and Decaf are DL-based defect recognition methods. The experimental results are presented in Table 2, and all the comparison results are from the related literature.

Table 2. Comparison with the other defect recognition method

Methods	50	100	150
SVM	–	–	98.93
NNC	–	–	97.93
Bayes classifier	–	–	97.42
Alexnet	89.83	94.21	95.29
Decaf	–	–	99.27
Proposed method	**98.06**	**99.07**	**99.57**

From these results, the proposed method has the best recognition results. Comparing with the machine learning-based defect recognition methods, the recognition results are improved greatly, and comparing with the DL-based models, the proposed method also performs better. These results indicate that the proposed method is more suitable for small-scale-sample defect recognition tasks.

4 Discussion

This section discusses the performances of the proposed method with noisy defect images. Since noise is an unavoidable problem, this section evaluates the proposed method under different noise to show its potential for wide applications.

This discussion adds some binary noise to the defect images both on the training set and testing set, and gives the recognition results under those noisy images. The noise rates include [0.01, 0.05, 0.1, 0.2, 0.3, 0.4], and all the experimental set is as same as Sect. 3. The examples of the noisy defect images are shown in Fig. 3, and the experimental results are shown in Table 3.

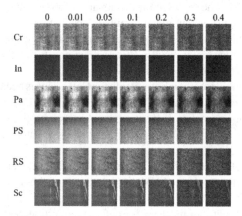

Fig. 3. Examples of the noisy defect images

From the results, the proposed method has declining performances with the increasing of noise rates. For the 150 samples per defect, it could provide acceptable recognition results. While For the 100 samples per defect, it can only work as expected with small noise rates. Once with a large noise rate, the recognition result is declined obviously. For the 50 samples, the proposed method performs a little poor. This is because the proposed method cannot learn useful information with such few samples and distributions. All the discussion results suggest that with a small noise rate, increasing the number of trainable samples will make acceptable results. While for a large noise rate, it suggests that using some techniques to rebuild the model or augment the data.

Table 3. Accuracy with different noise rates

Noise rates	50	100	150
0	98.06	99.07	99.57
0.01	95.86	97.53	98.57
0.05	92.59	95.9	96.87
0.1	91.23	95.18	96.37
0.2	89.46	94.29	95.83
0.3	87.00	93.61	95.13
0.4	85.72	92.61	94.81

5 Conclusion and Future Work

Defect recognition is a small-scale sample problem, and developing ensemble learning into CNN is a feasible manner to solve this problem. However, the ensemble weight is difficult to select. To overcome this limitation, this paper proposes a GA-based ensemble CNNs. The proposed method builds several CNNs, and uses GA and 5-fold cross-validation to find the optimal ensemble weight. With these improvements, the proposed method can find the optimal ensemble weight automatically. It can avoid explicit weight selection, and require less computation source. The experimental results also indicate the proposed method has better performances than the other ensemble strategy and defect recognition methods. And it also shows the robustness for noise, which suggests that the proposed method has good potential for application.

The limitation of this paper contains two aspects. One is the recognition speed. Because five CNNs are used, the recognition speed might be a little slow. Another is the recognition results still need to improve further. Therefore, the future work of this paper will focus on two directions. One is to find a new strategy with fewer models to accelerate recognition speed. Another one is to use new techniques to improve the recognition results of the proposed method.

Acknowledgements. This research work is supported by the National Key R&D Program of China under Grant No. 2018AAA0101700, and the Program for HUST Academic Frontier Youth Team under Grant No. 2017QYTD04.

References

1. Liu, Y.C., Hsu, Y.L., Sun, Y.N., et al.: A computer vision system for automatic steel surface inspection. In: Proceedings of the 2010 5th IEEE Conference on Industrial Electronics and Applications, ICIEA 2010, pp. 1667–1670 (2010)
2. Gao, Y., Gao, L., Li, X., Yan, X.: A semi-supervised convolutional neural network-based method for steel surface defect recognition. Robot. Comput. Integr. Manuf. **61**, 101825 (2020)
3. Xie, X.: A review of recent advances in surface defect detection using texture analysis techniques. ELCVIA Electron. Lett. Comput. Vis. Image Anal. **7**, 1–22 (2008)

4. Xu, K., Liu, S., Ai, Y.: Application of shearlet transform to classification of surface defects for metals. Image Vis. Comput. **35**, 23–30 (2015)
5. Liu, T., Bao, J., Wang, J., Zhang, Y.: A coarse-grained regularization method of convolutional kernel for molten pool defect identification. ASME J Comput Inf Sci Eng **20**, 021005 (2020)
6. Bi, M., Sun, Z.: Fabric defect detection using undecimated wavelet transform. Inf. Technol. J. **10**, 1701–1708 (2011)
7. Leng, J., Zhang, H., Yan, D., Liu, Q., Chen, X., Zhang, D.: Digital twin-driven manufacturing cyber-physical system for parallel controlling of smart workshop. J. Ambient Intell. Hum. Comput. **10**(3), 1155–1166 (2018). https://doi.org/10.1007/s12652-018-0881-5
8. Xiao, M., Jiang, M., Li, G., Xie, L., Yi, L.: An evolutionary classifier for steel surface defects with small sample set. EURASIP J. Image Video Process. **2017**(1), 1–13 (2017). https://doi.org/10.1186/s13640-017-0197-y
9. Gaja, H., Liou, F.: Defect classification of laser metal deposition using logistic regression and artificial neural networks for pattern recognition. Int. J. Adv. Manuf. Technol. **94**(1–4), 315–326 (2017). https://doi.org/10.1007/s00170-017-0878-9
10. Luo, Q., Sun, Y., Li, P., et al.: Generalized completed local binary patterns for time-efficient steel surface defect classification. IEEE Trans. Instr. Meas. **68**, 667–679 (2019)
11. Yang, S.-W., Lin, C.-S., Lin, S.-K., Chiang, H.-T.: Automatic defect recognition of TFT array process using gray level co-occurrence matrix. Optik (Stuttg) **125**, 2671–2676 (2014)
12. Hu, H., Peng, G., Wang, X., Zhou, Z.: Weld defect classification using 1-D LBP feature extraction of ultrasonic signals. Nondestruct. Test Eval. **33**, 92–108 (2018)
13. Niu, S., Li, B., Wang, X., Lin, H.: Defect image sample generation with GAN for improving defect recognition. IEEE Trans. Autom. Sci. Eng. **17**(3), 1611–1622 (2020)
14. Jiang, H., Hu, Q., Zhi, Z., et al.: Convolution neural network model with improved pooling strategy and feature selection for weld defect recognition. Weld World (2020)
15. Chen, W., Gao, Y., Gao, L., Li, X.: A new ensemble approach based on deep convolutional neural networks for steel surface defect classification. Proc. CIRP **72**, 1069–1072 (2018)
16. Song, K., Yan, Y.: A noise robust method based on completed local binary patterns for hot-rolled steel strip surface defects. Appl. Surf. Sci. **285**, 858–864 (2013)
17. Gao, Y., Gao, L., Li, X., Wang, X.V.: A multilevel information fusion-based deep learning method for vision-based defect recognition. IEEE Trans. Instr. Meas. **69**, 3980–3991 (2020)
18. Ren, R., Hung, T., Tan, K.C.: A generic deep-learning-based approach for automated surface inspection. IEEE Trans. Cybern. **48**, 929–940 (2018)

Biased Random-Key Genetic Algorithm for Structure Learning

Baodan Sun and Yun Zhou[✉]

Science and Technology on Information Systems Engineering Laboratory,
National University of Defense Technology, Changsha, China
{sunbaodan,zhouyun}@nudt.edu.cn

Abstract. The structure learning of Bayesian networks is a NP-hard problem, which cannot be easily solved since it is usually a complex combination optimization problem. Thus, many structure learning algorithms using evolutionary techniques are investigated recently to obtain a reasonable result. However, evolutionary algorithms may suffer from a low accuracy and restricts their applications. In this paper, we apply the Biased Random-Key Genetic Algorithm to solve Bayesian network structure learning problem since this framework is novely designed to solve conventional combination optimization problems. Also, we use a local optimization algorithm as its decoder to improve the performance. Experiments show that our method achieves better performances on the real-world networks than other state-of-art algorithms.

Keywords: Bayesian networks · Structure learning · Genetic Algorithms

1 Introduction

As an important probabilistic graphical model, Bayesian networks (BN) have gained a lot of attentions in the past two decades, and are broadly applied in machine learning [4], data fusion [8] and risk analysis [14]. The model of Bayesian networks contains the structure and parameters, which means that the learning algorithms of BN can be divided into two parts: structure learning and parameter learning. As the basis of parameter learning, structure learning takes an important role in Bayesian networks constructions. The structure of Bayesian networks is represented by directed acyclic graphs (DAGs), and it is a NP-hard problem [9] to learn a good DAG from the data only.

The conventional structure learning strategy can be divided into three types: score-based approach, constraint-based approach and hybrid approach. The score-based approach uses scoring functions, such as BIC, BDe, MDL, or Structural Hamming Distance (SHD), to search the solution space and find out DAGs

This work is supported by National Natural Science Foundation of China (No. 61703416) and Training Program for Excellent Young Innovators of Changsha (No. KQ2009009).

© Springer Nature Switzerland AG 2021
Y. Tan and Y. Shi (Eds.): ICSI 2021, LNCS 12689, pp. 399–411, 2021.
https://doi.org/10.1007/978-3-030-78743-1_36

with best scores. The constraint approach uses CI tests to determine the independent relations between two nodes in a graph. The hybrid approach combines both of them, which uses the constraint approach to determine part of the structure and uses the score-based approach to search the remaining solution space. Besides these classic methods, some researches tried to utilize loss functions to evaluate DAGs, such as works in [21] and [22].

Many researches have been working on Bayesian network structure learning (BNSL), which is a non-convex optimization problem that cannot be solved easily. Recent researches have tried more algorithms to get a solution closer to the exact one. de Campos et al. [3] used parameter constraints and structure constraints to reduce search space and applied the branch and bound to find an exact solution. Jaakkol et al. [15] proposed a method to construct BNSL as a linear optimization problem, and used the branch and bound to iteratively tighten the outer bound of this problem. Alovaro et al. [7] proposed a pruning method that can calculate the upper bounds for BDeu score to help conducting the exact BNSL. Ye et al. [21] proposed the regularized Cholesky score combining Simulated Annealing algorithm to search over permutations to optimize the BNSL problem. Bryon et al. [1] proposed a fast concave penalized estimation for large-scale BNs. Zheng et al. [22] proposed a method to convert the BNSL problem into a continuous optimization problem to avoid the combination optimization process. Gu et al. [13] proposed a penalized estimation of DAGs. Schmidt et al. [17] learned DAGs using L1-regularization with MDL score. Silander et al. [18] used to use local scores to find the best sink for variable sets.

However, as a non-convex optimization problem, BNSL cannot be solved very easily and heuristic algorithms is an effective approach to get a reasonable solution. Constantinou et al. [5] used a heuristic algorithm called Saiya to obtain a reliable DAG. There are also many researches on using heuristic algorithms to solve the BNSL problem, such as Simulated Annealing [16], Particle Swarm Optimization (PSO) [11], Genetic Algorithms (GA) [6] and so on.

In this paper, we firstly utilized a genetic algorithm called Biased Random-Key Genetic Algorithm (BRKGA) [12] to solve the BNSL problem, which is a general framework used to solve combination optimization problems. The overall mechanism of BRKGA is similar to the original GA, but it contains a decoder to connect the random initial solutions for the optimization problem and it will help the solver to find a more reliable solution to BNSL than other random searching algorithms. It is understandable that the decoder takes a very important role in BRKGA, and we employed an algorithm called NO TEARS to decode the initial solutions as it can obtain a local minimum of BNSL problem. By combining both of them, we can find a more reliable solution to BNSL than the other heuristic algorithms. It should be noticed that the whole searching space is continuous and BNSL is actually a discrete problem so that the proposed method will convert the continuous values into discrete values (0 or 1 for Bayesian networks) at the end of the searching process.

The paper is organized as follows. In Sect. 2, we introduce the basic knowledge of Bayesian networks and BRKGA. In Sect. 3, we introduce some details for using BRKGA to solve BNSL, especially for the decoder designed to relate random generated solutions to BNSL problem. Section 4 show the experiment results of the proposed algorithm and its comparing to two state-of-art heuristic algorithms. Section 5 is the conclusion.

2   Background

BRKGA is an improved random-key genetic algorithm (RKGA). Random-key genetic algorithm (RKGA) was firstly introduced by Bean [2] and it is designed for solving combination optimization problem. In RKGA, random keys are vectors consisting of randomly generated real numbers in the interval [0,1] corresponding to the chromosomes in Genetic Algorithms. Different from the general Genetic Algorithm, RKGA requires a component called decoder to interpret the random keys as initial solutions to the original combination optimization problem so that fitness values can be computed. The other components of RKGA are the same as GA, which include mutation operator and crossover operator. The mutation operator is a vector generated with the same strategy used to generate initial solutions, and it is designed to avoid the local optimum obtained by GA. The crossover operator of RKGA is designed to keep the elite solutions unchanged and copied directly to the next generation. Genetic algorithm with random keys can achieve better performance than the standard genetic algorithm and the details can be seen in the previous work [10].

During the searching process, BRKGA searches the continuous n-dimensional unit hypercube instead of the original solution space, and uses a decoder to map solutions from the hypercube to the original solution space [10]. It should be noticed that the fitness values of solutions to the combination optimization problem are evaluated in the original solution space. The decoder in RKGA is different from the decoding operation at the end of GA, which is a component relating the random keys to the optimization problem. It can be designed according to different optimization problems and it also can be a local optimizer. For example, Bean used the decoder to sort random keys and took their indices as a sequence [2]. And BRKGA is different from RKGA in ways of selecting individuals to conduct crossover. To be specific, RKGA randomly selects two individuals randomly in the population while BRKGA selects one parent in the elite individuals with better fitness value and the other in the non-elite individuals or the whole population. Although it seems that BRKGA changes very slightly, its performance can be improved significantly [10]. Main steps for using BRKGA to solve BNSL problem and the details for solving process will be listed in the following part.

As we can see in Fig. 1, the framework of BRKGA can be divided into two blocks: the problem-dependent block and the problem-independent block. The problem-dependent block is corresponding to the decoder, and the problem-independent block is corresponding to the other operations shown in Fig. 1. Since BRKGA is a general framework, we can only design the decoder according to the

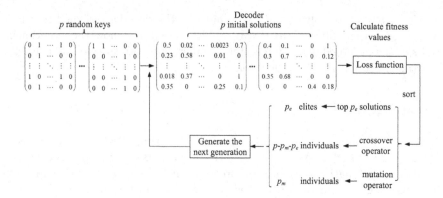

Fig. 1. The flowchart of using BRKGA solve Bayesian network structure learning.

unsolved problem and the other operations can be kept the same. The most characteristic part of BRKGA is that we only need to adjust the decoder according to different combination problems and the other parts are generally used.

3   Bayesian Network Structure Learning

3.1   Problem Definition

In this paper, we will firstly define the mathematical model of Bayesian networks. Given a DAG $G = \langle V, E \rangle$, V represents the set of nodes in the DAG and E represents the set of edges between these nodes. The nodes in V are corresponding to random variables, $X = \{X_1, X_2, \ldots, X_p\}$ and $p = |V|$ is the number of nodes. According to the implicit independence hypothesis in the structure, given its parents nodes, X_i is conditionally independent of its non-children nodes, and the joint probability distribution can be decomposed into the product of multiple conditional probability distributions:

$$P(X_1, X_2, \ldots, X_p) = \prod_{j=1}^{p} P(X_j | Pa(X_j)) \tag{1}$$

where, $P(X_j | Pa(X_j))$ represents the conditional distribution for X_j given its parents $Pa(X_j)$ with directed edges from each node in $Pa(X_j)$ to X_j in G.

In this paper, the structure of a Bayesian network actually represents the conditional independence property between any two nodes in the graph and the nodes in DAGs represent random variables. In the traditional methods, a adjacency matrix $A = \{a_{ij}\}^{n \times n}$ is usually used to represent a DAG. If there is an edge from i to j, the corresponding a_{ij} and a_{ji} in the adjacency matrix are set to 1 and 0, respectively. It should be noticed that the elements in the diagonal are 0 since it is acyclic. One important property of the adjacency matrix is that elements in the diagonal of the power function of the adjacency matrix should be 0. We will use the property to check and modify the final results.

NO TEARS algorithm [22] provides a way to take a new look at BNSL problem, which firstly uses a loss function to describe it and proposes a new way to define acyclicity constraint. Then, it uses classic optimization method to solve it. It should be noticed that BNSL is a non-convex optimization problem so that NO TEARS can only obtain a local minimum rather than the global exact solution.

In NO TEARS, it sets a real matrix $W = (w_{ij}) \in \mathbb{R}^{d \times d}$ as a collection of parameters satisfying $A(W) \in \{0,1\}^{d \times d}$ such that the elements in $A(W)$ are set to 1 if $w_{ij} \neq 0$ and 0 otherwise [22]. Thus, $A(W)$ is a adjacency matrix of a directed acyclic graph. By this way, we can achieve a continuous optimization with BRKGA since BNSL is originally a discrete optimization problem. In traditional approaches, the structure of BN is evaluated with scoring functions, which calculates the likelihood of the estimated DAG and data. A higher value of scoring functions means that the estimated structure is better. In NO TEARS, a loss function is proposed to evaluate the estimated DAG rather than scoring functions, which can re-construct the BNSL problem as the equality constrained problem to simplify solving process. The BNSL problem can be written as [22]:

$$min \; \ell(W; X) \quad s.t. \; A(W) \in DAGs \tag{2}$$

where, ℓ is the loss function and the constraint represents that $A(W)$ is the adjacency matrix of DAGs. This equation means that we want to find the minimum of the loss function defined by a real matrix W and data matrix X. The constraint illustrates that the adjacency matrix $A(W)$ converted from W is corresponding to a directed acyclic graph.

The evaluation criterion used to test the performance of BNSL algorithms can vary with different learning strategies. As mentioned above, one can use scoring functions, such as BIC, BDe, MDL or Structural Hamming Distance (SHD). In recent years, loss functions have been received more attention than before in Bayesian networks and some loss functions have been proposed and applied to structure learning algorithms, such as regularized Cholesky score [21]. This description seems to be very simple because it is based on matrix operations. We can not use traditional scoring functions in this way because scoring functions are based on instances in observation data and calculate their probabilities of taking certain values.

In this paper, we also try to use a loss function in the execution process of structure learning algorithms to find out better DAGs with more exact structures. To examine the performance of the proposed learning algorithm, we will use SHD to evaluate the final results of the learned networks. The details for the loss function used in this paper are listed in the following section.

3.2   Implementation Process

Decoder. As mentioned above, the most important component of BRKGA is the decoder of random keys and it is designed according to the specific optimization problem. For example, Bean [2] uses the decoder to sort random keys and uses their sorted indexes to represent a sequence. In this paper, we use NO TEARS algorithm [22] as the decoder since it can generate initial solutions and obtain a local minimum, simultaneously. Therefore, it is not only a decoder but also a local optimizer which can effectively improve the performance of GA.

In the above section, we have already shown the equality constrained problem (ECP) of BNSL. In NO TEARS, the constraint in (1) can be replaced by matrix exponential as followings [22]:

$$min \ \ell(W; X) = \frac{1}{2n}\|\mathbf{X} - \mathbf{X}W\|_F^2 \quad s.t. \ h(W) = 0 \tag{3}$$

$$h(W) = tr(e^{W \circ W}) - d \tag{4}$$

where, $\mathbf{X}$ is the data matrix, and n is the sample size. $W \circ W$ represents the Hardmard product and $e^{W \circ W}$ represents the matrix exponential. $h(W) = 0$ guarantees the acyclicity of DAGs, which actually derivates from the property of the adjacency matrix: the n-th power of adjacency matrix a_{ij} means that there are n steps from i to j. Then, this optimization problem can be solved by augmented Lagrangian method with an augmented quadratic penalty [22]:

$$min \ \ell(W; X) + \frac{\rho}{2}|h(W)|^2 \quad s.t. \ h(W) = 0 \tag{5}$$

Then the dual problem can be written as [22]:

$$D(\alpha) = min \ L^\rho(W, \alpha) \tag{6}$$

$$min \ L^\rho(W, \alpha) = \ell(W; X) + \frac{\rho}{2}|h(W)|^2 + \alpha h(W) \tag{7}$$

$$\alpha \leftarrow \alpha + \rho h(W_\alpha^*) \tag{8}$$

where, W_α^* is a local minimum, α is the Lagrange multiplier and ρ is the step size. W_α^* can be easily obtained by numerical algorithms, and L-BFGS is used in NO TEARS. We should make it clear that all the equations above and its derivation process are cited from [22] and the demonstration of NO TEARS and its further explanation can be seen in [20].

Although the above equations seem quite concise and easily understood, we should notice that the original BNSL is a combination optimization problem and its constraint is non-convex even if one can design a convex loss function. Actually, BNSL problem is a non-convex optimization problem and can be not find the exact solution by the above process. In this way, we need to find more possible solutions and BRKGA is utilized for this purpose. The above process can be seen as a decoder since NO TEARS can achieve a local minimum to improve the totally stochastic process happened in heuristic algorithms.

Mutation and Crossover. Before introducing the mutation and crossover operators in BRKGA, we must explain some basic concepts involved in GA. At the start of GA, we generate a certain number of solutions making up a population, the members of the population are called individuals and an individual has a corresponding chromosome that encodes the solution. The members consisting of a chromosome are called genes. The crossover operation and the mutation operator are important components of Genetic Algorithms, which are designed to search the solution space and avoid being stuck in the local minimum of the optimization problem. The basic principle of the crossover operator is exchanging several genes between two chromosomes according to some strategies. And the basic principle of mutation operator is randomly picking up a chromosome and changing its value.

In this paper, we exploit the parameterized uniform crossover [19], which generates a new offspring through comparing to a vector consisting of random numbers in the interval $[0, 1]$. And there is a pre-defined threshold ρ_e illustrating the probability of an offspring inheriting from the elite parent. Let n represent the number of genes in a chromosome and the parameterized uniform crossover first generates a vector of random numbers of size n. For the i-th element of the vector $v(i)$ comparing to ρ_e, if it is no bigger than ρ_e, the new offspring inherits the element $e(i)$ in the elite parent; otherwise, the new offspring inherits the element $e'(i)$ in the non-elite parent. The pseudo code of this process is shown in Algorithm 1.

Algorithm 1. Parameterized Uniform Crossover

1: **Input:** threshold ρ_e, the size of genes n, elite parent e, non-elite parent e'
2: **for** $i = 0$ to n **do**
3:     Initialize the new generation $newpop$
4:     **if** $v(i) <= \rho_e$ **then**
5:         $newpop[i] = e(i)$
6:     **else**
7:         $newpop[i] = e'(i)$
8:     **end if**
9: **end for**
10: **Output:** $newpop$

The mechanism of mutation operation is the same as that of generating initial solutions at the start of BRKGA, which generates p_m vectors of n random numbers in the interval $[0, 1]$ and decodes them as initial solutions to the optimization problem. After executing the crossover and mutation operations, a new population is thus generated. The whole steps for BRKGA solving BNSL can be concluded in Algorithm 2. The first step for solving BNSL with BRKGA is to generate p vectors of random keys of size n. Each random key is in the real interval $[0, 1]$ and random keys are the input of the decoder. The decoder interprets random keys as initial solutions to the optimization problem and the fitness values are then calculated using loss function defined in the next section. We sort the fitness values of the population and divide it into two part: $p_e = 0.2 * p$ elite individuals and $p - pe$ non-elite individuals. To search the solution space, the mutation operator and the crossover operator are needed. The mechanism of mutation operator is mentioned above and p_m mutants are generated. The elite individuals are directly copied to the next generation and the crossover operator is executed. Next, these new individuals are combined together to form a new generation and their fitness values are re-calculated. The process will be executed iteratively until the algorithm reaches the maximum iteration, which is a pre-defined number by users.

Algorithm 2. BRKGA for Solving BNSL

1: **Input:** the population size p, maximum iteration max_iter, the elite population p_e, the mutant population p_m
2: Initialize p vectors of random keys of size n
3: Use the decoder to decode random keys into initial solutions to BNSL
4: **repeat**
5:     Calculate fitness values of all the solutions according to (3) and sort them
6:     Select $p_e = 0.2 * p$ elite individuals and copy them to the next generation
7:     **for** $i = 1$ to $p - p_e - p_m$ **do**
8:         Execute the crossover operator
9:     **end for**
10:     **for** $p - p_m + 1$ to p **do**
11:         Execute the mutation operator
12:     **end for**
13:     **for** $p_e + 1$ to p **do**
14:         Use the decoder to recalculate local solutions to BNSL
15:     **end for**
16: **until** max_iter
17: Execute post-processing process
18: **Output:** W

Thresholding and Acyclicity. After the execution of our algorithm, the obtained adjacency matrix is not always representing a DAG. Firstly, it is because the returned result of our algorithm is a matrix of continuous values, which usually are not 0 or 1. Since then, we need to convert these continuous values into discrete values. In BNSL, we usually define an indicator function to deal with this problem. In this paper, we pre-defined a threshold ω: if the elements in W_star are bigger than ω, the elements are set to 1; otherwise, the elements are set to 0. In this way, we can obtain the adjacency matrix of a BN. ω is chosen to be small enough that can preserve the sparsity of Bayesian networks.

Secondly, after post-processing, the 0–1 matrix cannot ensure the acyclicity of the directed graph. Hence, we need to design an algorithm to delete the cycles contained in the graph. Here, to ensure the acyclicity of Bayesian networks, we use an important property of DAGs: the n-th power of adjacency matrix a_{ij} means that there are n steps from i to j. The first step for our algorithm is to calculate the trace of the adjacency matrix, A. If the trace of the adjacency matrix is not equal to zero, we randomly choose two nodes V_x, V_y corresponding to the non-zero elements of the adjacency matrix and we delete the corresponding edges or reverse them. We repeat the recursive procedure until the trace of the adjacency is equal to zero. The details is shown in Algorithm 3.

Algorithm 3. Acyclicity of DAGs

1: **Input:** adjacency matrix, A
2: **repeat**
3:   initialize $C = A$
4:   **if** the diagonal of C does not contain non-zero elements **then**
5:     $C = C * A$
6:     $i = i + 1$
7:   **else**
8:     randomly choose two nodes V_x, V_y corresponding to the non-zero elements of C, delete the corresponding edges or reverse the edges in A
9:   **end if**
10: **until** $i = n$ & there is no non-zero elements in the diagonal of C
11: **Output:** A

---

4   Experiment

4.1   Experimental Parameters

In our experiment, we implement our algorithm in R and execute the above algorithm on realistic networks downloaded from Bayesian Network Repository[1]. The details for networks utilized in this paper are listed in Table 1. The sample sizes of these networks are 100, 500, 1000. The population size p is set to 50, and the maximum iteration is 100. The sizes of elite individuals and mutant individuals are $p_m = 0.2 * p$ and $p_e = 0.2 * p$, respectively. ρ_e is set to 0.7. All the results are the averages of 10 times experiments. SHD (Structural Hamming Distance) is used to compare the estimated DAG to the true graph and a smaller SHD means that two directed acyclic graphs are more similar. All the parameters sensitivity analysis is given in the previous work [10].

4.2   Experimental Results

In this section, we list the experimental results of our algorithm conducting on these Bayesian networks in Table 1 with sample sizes of 100, 500 and 1000. We also compare our algorithm to the original NO TEARS algorithm and the standard Genetic Algorithm. The details for NO TEARS are given in Sect. 3. For NO TEARS, we set the maximum iteration $t = 100$, tolerance $\epsilon = 1e{-}8$, $c = 0.25$. The population size of the standard Genetic Algorithm is 50, and the crossover probability is 0.9, and the mutation probability is 0.1. Figure 2 shows

---

[1] https://www.bnlearn.com/bnrepository/.

an example of CHILD network to compare the experimental results with the original network. In the figure, the left network is the original CHILD network and the right network is our estimated result. The experimental results are shown in the Table 1. The smallest SHD values are presented in bold text.

Table 1. The experimental results of three BN Learning Algorithms on 9 standard networks.

Network	Nodes	Arcs	Samples	NO TEARS	GA	BRKGA
CANCER	5	4	100	**2.6**	6.6	4.2
			500	**2.9**	7.1	4.9
			1000	**2.7**	6.8	5.2
EARTHQUAKE	5	4	100	**6.3**	6.5	**6.3**
			500	**6.0**	6.2	6.5
			1000	**5.9**	6.3	6.4
SURVEY	6	6	100	9.2	8.4	**8.2**
			500	10.1	9.3	**8.4**
			1000	10.4	9.4	**7.4**
ASIA	8	8	100	12.4	12.4	**12.3**
			500	12.8	13.0	**12.2**
			1000	12.9	13.3	**12.6**
SACHS	11	17	100	27.7	22.1	**22.0**
			500	28.1	22.9	**21.2**
			1000	27.1	23.8	**22.7**
CHILD	20	25	100	37.7	40.2	**33.3**
			500	38.5	41.4	**32.9**
			1000	38.7	39.4	**32.9**
INSURANCE	27	52	100	80.3	71.9	**68.2**
			500	82.9	72.1	**67.2**
			1000	84.4	72.6	**67.1**
ALARM	37	46	100	80.2	74.0	**64.0**
			500	81.9	78.3	**63.8**
			1000	83.2	81.1	**63.9**
HAILFINDER	56	66	100	100.2	117.0	**95.2**
			500	**98.9**	118.6	**98.9**
			1000	**98.2**	117.7	98.9

4.3   Analysis

The table shows 9 representative Bayesian Networks, and lists their nodes and arcs. These networks are corresponding to small networks (<20 nodes), medium

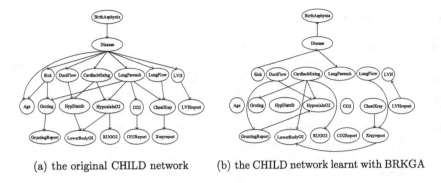

(a) the original CHILD network   (b) the CHILD network learnt with BRKGA

Fig. 2. The learnt structure of CHILD network.

networks (20–50 nodes) and large networks (>50 nodes). As Table 1 shows, SHD increases with the number of arcs in the networks. We can also notice that the gap of SHD values of comparison tests and our algorithm increases with the nodes of these networks. In the experiments, we can see that our algorithm achieves smaller SHD values than the other algorithms on these Bayesian networks except the CANCER and EARTHQUAKE network, which means that our algorithm can obtain a DAG closer to the real structure than the other two algorithms on these networks. The table shows that NO TEARS achieves smaller SHD values on CANCER network and EARTHQUAKE network than standard GA and BRKGA. The table also shows that the performance of NO TEARS is better than GA on CANCER, EARTHQUAKE, ASIA, CHILD, and ALARM network. Also, NO TEARS achieves better SHD values than BRKGA on CANCER network, EARTHQUAKE network and HAILFINDER network with the sample size of 1000. Comparing to the standard GA, our algorithm achieves better performance on all the networks.

When the networks are small, we notice that NO TEARS can achieve better or similar SHD values than our algorithm. It may be the reason that NO TEARS has already find the local best solution near to the global solution. However, with the increases of nodes, NO TEARS tends to be more and more difficult to find a better solution than our algorithm. We must point out that our algorithm is designed to get a continuous solution and discretize it with an indicator function. So even if the best solution obtained by our algorithm achieves a smaller loss value, their adjacency matrixes may be the same. In a word, although BRKGA only adds a decoder and generates random keys, it significantly enhances the performance of the standard GA, which can be obviously seen from Table 1. As for the decoder, the most significant improvement is that it is a local optimizer and interprets random keys as initial solutions to the optimization problem at the same time.

5   Conclusion

Bayesian network structure learning is a non-convex optimization problem. In this paper, we use an evolutionary algorithm, BRKGA, to solve Bayesian network structure learning problem. Firstly, we introduce the overall framework of BRKGA and its basic principle. Then, we apply the NO TEARS algorithm as the local optimization method to decode random keys randomly generated in the interval $[0, 1]$ into initial solutions to the optimization problem. Next, we utilize the parameterized uniform crossover and mutation operator for BRKGA. Finally, we conduct experiments on real-world networks and compare our algorithm to other structure leaning algorithms. The experiments compare different sizes of real-world networks and all the involved parameters are given in the context. The experimental results show that our algorithm achieves a good performance than GA and the original NO TEARS, which is effective in solving BNSL problem.

In the future, we will extend our research to reduce the randomness of our algorithm and import structure priors to improve the performance of our algorithm. Another inspiration is that we only use a simple indicator function to discretize the solution of our algorithm. In future work, we will try to find a more reliable discretization method trying to keep more structural information.

References

1. Aragam, B., Qing, Z.: Concave penalized estimation of sparse Gaussian Bayesian networks. J. Mach. Learn. Res. **16**, 2273–2328 (2015)
2. Bean, J.C.: Genetic algorithms and random keys for sequencing and optimization. ORSA J. Comput. **6**, 154–160 (1994)
3. de Campos, C.P., Zeng, Z., Ji, Q.: Structure learning of Bayesian networks using constraints. In: Proceedings of the 26th Annual International Conference on Machine Learning, ICML 2009, pp. 113–120. Association for Computing Machinery (2009)
4. Chen, X., Yuan, Y., Orgun, M.A.: Using Bayesian networks with hidden variables for identifying trustworthy users in social networks. J. Inf. Sci. **46**(5), 600–615 (2020)
5. Constantinou, A.C.: Learning Bayesian networks with the Saiyan algorithm. ACM Trans. Knowl. Discov. Data **14**(4), 1–21 (2020)
6. Contaldi, C., Vafaee, F., Nelson, P.C.: Bayesian network hybrid learning using an elite-guided genetic algorithm. Artif. Intell. Rev. **52**(1), 245–272 (2018). https://doi.org/10.1007/s10462-018-9615-5
7. Correia, A.H.C., Cussens, J.: On pruning for score-based Bayesian network structure learning. In: Proceedings of the Twenty Third International Conference on Artificial Intelligence and Statistics (AISTATS 2020), vol. 108, pp. 2709–2718 (2020)
8. Costa, P.C., Yu, B., Atiahetchi, M., Myers, D.: High-level information fusion of cyber-security expert knowledge and experimental data. In: 2018 21st International Conference on Information Fusion, pp. 2322–2329 (2018)
9. Chickering, D.M., Heckerman, D., Meek, C.: Large-sample learning of Bayesian networks is NP-hard. J. Mach. Learn. Res. **5**(1999), 1287–1330 (2004)

10. Fernando, J., Mauricio, G.: Biased random-key genetic algorithms for combinatorial optimization. J. Heuristics **17**(5), 487–525 (2011)
11. Gheisari, S., Meybodi, M.R.: BNC-PSO: structure learning of Bayesian networks by Particle Swarm Optimization. Inf. Sci. **348**, 272–289 (2016)
12. Gonçalves, J., Almeida, J.: A hybrid genetic algorithm for assembly line balancing. J. Heuristics **8**, 629–642 (2002)
13. Gu, J., Fu, F., Zhou, Q.: Penalized estimation of directed acyclic graphs from discrete data. Stat. Comput. **29**(1), 161–176 (2018). https://doi.org/10.1007/s11222-018-9801-y
14. He, R., Li, X., Chen, G., Wang, Y., Jiang, S., Zhi, C.: A quantitative risk analysis model considering uncertain information. Process Saf. Environ. Prot. **118**, 361–370 (2018)
15. Jaakkola, T., Sontag, D., Globerson, A., Meila, M.: Learning Bayesian network structure using LP relaxations. J. Mach. Learn. Res. Proc. Track **9**, 358–365 (2010)
16. Lee, S., Kim, S.: Parallel simulated annealing with a greedy algorithm for Bayesian network structure learning. IEEE Trans. Knowl. Data Eng. **32**(6), 1157–1166 (2020)
17. Schmidt, M., Niculescu-Mizil, A., Murphy, K.: Learning graphical model structure using L1-regularization paths. In: Proceedings of the National Conference on Artificial Intelligence, vol. 2, pp. 1278–1283 (2007)
18. Silander, T., Myllymäki, P.: A simple approach for finding the globally optimal Bayesian network structure. In: Proceedings of the 22nd Conference on Uncertainty in Artificial Intelligence, UAI 2006, pp. 445–452 (2006)
19. Spears, W.M., DeJong, K.A.: On the virtues of parameterised uniform crossover. In: International Conference on Genetic Algorithms, pp. 230–236 (1991)
20. Wei, D., Gao, T., Yu, Y.: DAGs with no fears: a closer look at continuous optimization for learning Bayesian networks (2020)
21. Ye, Q., Amini, A., Zhou, Q.: Optimizing regularized Cholesky score for order-based learning of Bayesian networks. IEEE Trans. Pattern Anal. Mach. Intell. (2020). https://doi.org/10.1109/TPAMI.2020.2990820
22. Zheng, X., Aragam, B., Ravikumar, P., Xing, E.P.: DAGs with no tears: continuous optimization for structure learning. In: Advances in Neural Information Processing Systems, vol. 2018-Decem, pp. 9472–9483 (2018)

Fireworks Algorithms

Performance Analysis of the Fireworks Algorithm Versions

Ira Tuba, Ivana Strumberger⊙, Eva Tuba⊙, Nebojsa Bacanin⊙,
and Milan Tuba⁽⊠⁾⊙

Singidunum University, Danijelova 32, 11000 Belgrade, Serbia
`tuba@ieee.org`

Abstract. In the last decades, swarm intelligence algorithms have become a powerful tool for solving hard optimization problems. Nowadays numerous algorithms are proved to be good for different problems. With the overwhelming number of algorithms, it became hard for a common user to choose an appropriate method for solving a certain problem. To provide guidelines, it is necessary to classify optimization metaheuristics according to their capabilities. Deep statistical comparison represents a novel method for comparing and analyzing optimization algorithms. In this paper, the deep statistical comparison method was used for comparing different versions of the widely used fireworks algorithm. The fireworks algorithm was developed and improved in the last ten year, and this paper provides a theoretical analysis of five different versions, a cooperative framework for FWA, bare bones FWA, guided FWA, loser-out tournament based FWA, and dynamic search FWA. Based on the obtained results, the loser-out tournament based FWA has the best performance in the term of the solution quality, while the dynamic search FWA is the best in term of the solutions distribution in the search space.

Keywords: Swarm intelligence · Fireworks algorithm · Deep statistical comparison · Performance analysis

1 Introduction

Solving optimization problems is one of the most important tasks in various applications. Almost any problem that can be defined by mathematical function can be described as an optimization problem. Nowadays, there are various mathematical methods for solving optimization problems, but the class of problems that remains unsolvable (or unsolvable in a reasonable time with the available technology) is the class of NP-hard problems. Problems in this class are the most interesting since the majority of the real-life optimization problems are in it. It is important to have a good heuristic that can be used for finding a solution for these problems. In the last decades, numerous methods have been proposed and class of algorithms that provided good results are swarm intelligence algorithms.

Swarm intelligence (SI) algorithms proved to be efficient for finding acceptable or optimal results for different hard optimization problems in a relatively

© Springer Nature Switzerland AG 2021
Y. Tan and Y. Shi (Eds.): ICSI 2021, LNCS 12689, pp. 415–422, 2021.
https://doi.org/10.1007/978-3-030-78743-1_37

short time. The general idea is to use a swarm of simple agents that exchange information about the quality of the results and move toward better solutions according to some rules. Two main parts of every SI algorithm are exploration or global search and exploitation or local search. It is very important to examine the whole search space to find the promising areas where a more detailed search should be done. Particle swarm optimization [5] and ant colony optimization [1] are among the first swarm intelligence algorithms that were proposed. After the promising results that were obtained, various nature and non-nature phenomena were translated into the SI optimization algorithms. In one period, finding new inspirations and proposing novel optimization algorithms was a hot research topic and that resulted in large number of SI algorithms where the main focus was on explaining translation from phenomena to exploitation and exploration mechanisms. Comparison of the results obtained by different algorithms was provided, but the theoretical (mathematical) comparison of the used operators was rarely considered. Moreover, the algorithms were compared by only one statistic such as mean or median. This method provides a certain comparison between the algorithms, but it cannot provide a deeper analysis of the exploration and exploitation operators and sometimes it can differentiate algorithms that are not significantly different. In order to overcome this problem, deep statistical comparison (DSC) was proposed [3]. The rankings by DSC are created based on the distributions of solutions from multiple runs which is less sensitive to outliers and insignificant differences than the rankings by one statistic.

In this paper, the DSC was used for comparing and analyzing five different versions of the fireworks algorithm [11], i.e. the last four versions, bare bones fireworks algorithm (BBFWA), guided fireworks algorithm (GFWA), loser-out tournament based fireworks algorithm (LoTFWA) and cooperative framework for fireworks algorithm (CoFWA) and the version that obtained good results for different problems, dynamic search fireworks algorithm (dynFWA).

The rest of this paper is organized as follows. A short description of the fireworks algorithm and compared versions is given in Sect. 2. Section 3 presents the main idea of the deep statistical analysis. A comparison of five versions of the FWA algorithm is presented in Sect. 4. The paper is concluded in Sect. 5.

2   Fireworks Algorithm

Fireworks algorithm (FWA) is a swarm intelligence algorithm proposed by Tan et al. in 2010 [11]. The fireworks algorithm (FWA) was inspired by the explosion of the fireworks and nowadays there are several upgraded and modified versions of the algorithm. The FWA and its modified version were successfully used for solving optimization problems in various applications in the field of wireless sensor networks [17], image processing [12,16,18], machine learning [13–15], etc.

The general idea of the FWA is to generate certain number of new solutions around the previous best solutions and to save the best solution from each group for the next iteration. Search space around each solution is controlled by the exploding amplitude and the mechanism for generating solutions is different in the different version. The exploration is done by spreading the population around the search space. The space around the each solution where the new solution will be generated is controlled by the quality of the solution and the iteration number. Exploitation is implemented through adjusting the size of that search space around the solutions from the population. In different versions, how and how many solutions are generated around each solution in each iteration is changed with aim to improve the balance between the exploration and the exploitation as well as the quality of these operators.

The dynamic search fireworks algorithm (dynFWA) was proposed as the improved version of the enhanced fireworks algorithm (EFWA) [19]. The dyn-FWA does not generate solution based on the Gaussian distribution which reduce the complexity of the algorithm. The number and position of the new solutions is determined in the same way as in the EFWA for all previous solutions except for the best solution. In the dynFWA, the size of the search space around the best solution, named core firework (CF) where the sparks, i.e. new solutions, will be generated depends on the improvements of the best solution. If the fitness function value of the best solution was improved, the search space around it will be increased. On the other hand, if the best solution was not changed, the size of the search space around it where the new solution will be generated is decreased. Additionally, the check for the minimal size of the search space around the previous solutions was removed in the dynFWA.

A cooperative framework for fireworks algorithm (CoFWA) summed up all the collected knowledge up till then about the performance of the algorithm and modified operators to overcome noticed drawbacks [20]. The main modification was introduction of the independent selection method. In the previous versions, in each generation, new solutions were generated around the solutions from the previous generation. The selection process for the next generation was done over all current solutions and each solution was chosen with the probability that is determined based on the solution quality. On the other hand, in the CoFWA only the best solutions were saved for the next iteration. This reduces the complexity and also enhances the convergence. In order to ensure diversity of solutions, crowdness-avoiding mechanism was introduced: if one solution comes too close to the best solution of that generation, it will be reinitialized to random solution.

The bare bones fireworks algorithm (BBFWA) represents the least computationally expensive version of the FWA [9]. The idea is to save only the best solution in one iteration as well as the information about the change of the best solution. Similarly to the dynFWA, the search space around the best solution where new solutions will be generated is controlled based on the fact did the best solution change or not. In the BBFWA the number of solution that are generated in each iteration is fixed unlike to the previous versions. The complexity of the BBFWA was reduced compared to the other FWA versions since there is no calculation of the number of solutions and only one explosion amplitude, i.e. size of the search space around the saved solution is calculated.

The guided fireworks algorithm (GFWA) was proposed by Li, Zheng and Tan [8]. In the GFWA the idea of exploiting the local best solution was implemented.

In each generation, new group of solutions are generated around each solution saved from the previous iteration. In each group of solutions, the best one is marked as the centroid of the cluster. The best and the worst centroids are used to calculate the guiding vector which is further used for generating new solution based on the previous best solution in the population. The number of solutions that will be generated around the previously saved solution as well as the search space size where they will be generated depend on the quality of the solution regarding to the current best solution in the population, same as in the EFWA, the CoFWA and the dynFWA.

The loser-out tournament based FWA (LoTFWA) was proposed in 2018 [7]. The idea of the fireworks algorithm was based on the cooperation of several solutions in the population. The LoTFWA introduces the change where the competition between solutions is proposed. Instead of treating each solution separately and just saving the best or one among the best solutions generated around the previous solution, in the LoTFWA, the progress of each solution is followed. If the progression of the quality of one solution is not satisfying, i.e. the quality of the solution is not competitive with the current best solution according to the quality and its progress rate, the solution will be considered as a loser in the tournament and it will be reinitialized randomly. This mechanism enhances the exploration ability of the algorithm which reduces the probability of getting stacked in a local minimum.

3   Deep Statistical Comparison

Deep Statistical Comparison (DSC) represents a novel method for providing a statistical comparison of stochastic optimization algorithms [3]. The comparison is based on solutions obtained in multiple runs on benchmark problems. The main difference to the commonly used comparison based on one statistic is that DSC uses a distribution of the solutions from multiple runs instead of just mean or median. The rankings provided by the DSC method are less sensitive to outliers and minor differences between data because the rankings for each benchmark optimization problem have been also tested for statistical significance.

The DSC compares fitness function values with the two-sample Anderson-Darling test. This comparison can provide the algorithm rankings. In order to further analyze the algorithms, extended version of the DSC (eDSC) was proposed [2]. The eDSC was used for comparing the distribution of the obtained solutions and not the fitness function values for these solutions.

Based on the results, combination of the DSC and eDSC rankings, it is possible to better understand exploration and exploitation abilities of the compared algorithms. When comparing two algorithms (A and B) several scenarios could occur. If the algorithm A has better DSC and eDSC rankings, it indicates that it has better exploration powers, but nothing can be said about exploitation since poor exploration of the algorithm B can influence its DSC ranking. If the algorithm A has better DSC ranking, but worse eDSC ranking it means that we are most probably dealing with the multimodal problem with many local optima and similar performances. In this case, the algorithm A has better exploration and exploitation abilities. If the algorithm A has worse DSC ranking, but better eDSC ranking it means that the algorithm is often stuck in some local optima. This indicates a poor exploration abilities, but nothing can be said about the exploitation abilities. If the algorithm A has worse DSC and eDSC rankings it indicates we are dealing with a problem with one obvious global optimum, and the algorithm A has poor exploration powers. We cannot say anything about exploitation, since poor exploration can influence algorithm's B DSC ranking. There are more combinations. For further information please refer to paper [6].

4 Fireworks Algorithms Evaluation

Five versions of the FWA algorithm were tested on the CEC2013 benchmark set which contains 28 functions [10]. The parameters of algorithms were set based on the results reported in the original papers since the same set of function was used and the best combination of parameter's values were determined. Each algorithm was tested for dimensions 10 and 30. The maximal fitness function evaluation number was set to 10000*dimension. Each algorithm was started 30 times for each problem and dimension. Rankings were provided based on these results. All experiments were performed by the web service based e-Learning tool - DSCTool [4].

Table 1. DSC Rankings for the FWA versions

(a) 10D

	BBFWA	CoFWA	dFWA	GFWA	LoTFW
f1	5.0	2.0	2.0	2.0	4.0
f2	2.0	4.0	5.0	2.0	2.0
f3	3.0	5.0	1.0	3.0	3.0
f4	1.5	4.5	3.0	1.5	4.5
f5	4.0	1.0	2.0	3.0	5.0
f6	3.0	3.0	5.0	3.0	1.0
f7	2.0	5.0	4.0	3.0	1.0
f8	4.0	3.0	1.0	5.0	2.0
f9	4.0	4.0	2.0	4.0	1.0
f10	3.0	3.0	5.0	3.0	1.0
f11	4.5	2.5	1.0	4.5	2.5
f12	3.0	3.0	5.0	3.0	1.0
f13	2.0	4.0	5.0	3.0	1.0
f14	4.5	2.0	1.0	4.5	3.0
f15	4.0	4.0	2.0	4.0	1.0
f16	2.0	4.0	5.0	3.0	1.0
f17	4.5	2.0	1.0	4.5	3.0
f18	5.0	3.0	2.0	4.0	1.0
f19	4.5	1.5	3.0	4.5	1.5
f20	3.0	3.0	5.0	3.0	1.0
f21	3.0	1.0	4.5	4.5	2.0
f22	4.5	2.0	1.0	4.5	3.0
f23	3.0	4.0	2.0	5.0	1.0
f24	3.0	3.0	5.0	3.0	1.0
f25	3.0	3.0	5.0	3.0	1.0
f26	4.0	3.0	1.0	5.0	2.0
f27	4.0	2.5	5.0	2.5	1.0
f28	2.0	5.0	4.0	3.0	1.0
avg	3.39	3.11	3.13	3.5	1.86

(b) 30D

	BBFWA	CoFWA	dFWA	GFWA	LoTFW
f1	3.0	3.0	3.0	3.0	3.0
f2	3.0	4.0	1.0	2.0	5.0
f3	5.0	4.0	3.0	1.5	1.5
f4	2.0	4.0	3.0	1.0	5.0
f5	4.0	2.0	1.0	3.0	5.0
f6	5.0	3.0	1.0	4.0	2.0
f7	3.0	4.0	5.0	3.0	1.0
f8	3.0	2.0	4.0	5.0	1.0
f9	2.5	4.0	5.0	2.5	1.0
f10	1.0	4.0	2.0	4.0	4.0
f11	4.5	4.5	3.0	1.5	1.5
f12	2.5	4.0	5.0	2.5	1.0
f13	4.5	4.5	3.0	1.5	1.5
f14	4.5	2.0	3.0	4.5	1.0
f15	4.0	4.0	2.0	4.0	1.0
f16	3.0	5.0	4.0	2.0	1.0
f17	5.0	3.0	4.0	2.0	1.0
f18	4.5	4.5	3.0	2.0	1.0
f19	4.0	4.0	2.0	4.0	1.0
f20	2.0	4.0	1.0	5.0	3.0
f21	3.0	2.0	4.5	4.5	1.0
f22	4.5	2.0	3.0	4.5	1.0
f23	4.0	4.0	2.0	4.0	1.0
f24	2.0	4.0	5.0	3.0	1.0
f25	2.0	4.0	5.0	3.0	1.0
f26	1.0	5.0	2.0	4.0	3.0
f27	2.5	4.0	5.0	2.5	1.0
f28	4.0	3.0	1.0	5.0	2.0
avg	3.32	3.59	3.05	3.16	1.88

The DSC rankings for dimensions 10 and 30 are presented in Table 1. The p-value from the Friedman test was 0.00, and since the statistical significance was set to 0.05 the null hypothesis was rejected which means that there is a statistical significance between the performance of the algorithms. The last row in Table 1 represents the average rankings over all 28 functions of each algorithm. As it can be seen from the results, the LoTFWA algorithm was the best overall ranked algorithm. For the functions f1 and f5 it was the worst ranked algorithm, while the f4 ended up before the BBFWA. All other algorithms ended up with a similar overall rank. In order to find where the significance occurred, the pairwised comparison between each algorithm and control algorithm was performed. The control algorithm was the LoTFWA because it had the lowest overall rank. Based on the pairwise comparison, the LoTFWA algorithm was statistically significantly different from the CoFWA, the GFWA and the BBFWA, while there is no significant difference to the dynFWA. A similar situation is obtained for dimension 30.

Table 2. eDSC Rankings for the FWA versions

(a) 10D

	BBFWA	CoFWA	dFWA	GFWA	LoTFWA
f1	5.0	3.0	1.0	2.0	4.0
f2	3.0	5.0	1.0	2.0	4.0
f3	4.0	5.0	1.0	3.0	2.0
f4	2.5	4.5	1.0	2.5	4.5
f5	4.0	2.0	1.0	4.0	4.0
f6	4.0	4.0	1.0	4.0	2.0
f7	3.5	5.0	1.0	3.5	2.0
f8	3.5	3.5	1.0	3.5	3.5
f9	3.5	3.5	1.0	3.5	3.5
f10	3.5	3.5	1.0	3.5	3.5
f11	3.5	3.5	1.0	3.5	3.5
f12	3.0	5.0	1.0	4.0	2.0
f13	3.0	5.0	1.0	4.0	2.0
f14	3.5	3.5	1.0	3.5	3.5
f15	3.5	3.5	1.0	3.5	3.5
f16	3.5	3.5	1.0	3.5	3.5
f17	5.0	2.0	1.0	4.0	3.0
f18	3.5	3.5	1.0	3.5	3.5
f19	3.5	3.5	1.0	3.5	3.5
f20	4.0	4.0	1.0	4.0	2.0
f21	3.0	4.0	1.0	2.0	5.0
f22	5.0	3.0	1.0	4.0	2.0
f23	3.5	3.5	1.0	3.5	3.5
f24	3.0	5.0	1.0	4.0	2.0
f25	4.0	4.0	1.0	4.0	2.0
f26	2.5	4.5	1.0	2.5	4.5
f27	4.0	4.0	1.0	4.0	2.0
f28	3.0	3.0	1.0	3.0	5.0
avg	3.59	3.82	1.0	3.41	3.18

(b) 30D

	BBFWA	CoFWA	dFWA	GFWA	LoTFWA
f1	1.0	2.0	5.0	3.5	3.5
f2	3.5	3.5	1.0	3.5	3.5
f3	5.0	4.0	1.0	2.5	2.5
f4	3.0	4.0	1.0	2.0	5.0
f5	3.5	3.5	1.0	3.5	3.5
f6	5.0	2.0	1.0	4.0	3.0
f7	4.0	4.0	1.0	4.0	2.0
f8	3.5	3.5	1.0	3.5	3.5
f9	3.5	3.5	1.0	3.5	3.5
f10	4.0	5.0	1.0	2.0	3.0
f11	3.5	3.5	1.0	3.5	3.5
f12	4.0	5.0	1.0	3.0	2.0
f13	3.0	4.0	1.0	2.0	5.0
f14	3.5	3.5	1.0	3.5	3.5
f15	3.5	3.5	1.0	3.5	3.5
f16	3.5	3.5	1.0	3.5	3.5
f17	5.0	4.0	1.0	3.0	2.0
f18	4.5	4.5	1.0	2.5	2.5
f19	4.0	5.0	1.0	3.0	2.0
f20	2.0	4.0	1.0	5.0	3.0
f21	4.5	3.0	2.0	4.5	1.0
f22	4.0	5.0	1.0	3.0	2.0
f23	4.0	4.0	1.0	4.0	2.0
f24	4.0	4.0	1.0	4.0	2.0
f25	3.0	3.0	1.0	5.0	3.0
f26	2.0	5.0	1.0	3.0	4.0
f27	4.0	3.0	1.0	5.0	2.0
f28	3.5	3.5	1.0	3.5	3.5
avg	3.62	3.78	1.18	3.44	2.96

Table 2 shows the results of the eDSC rankings where the algorithms were compared regarding to the distribution of the solutions instead of the fitness function values. The algorithms were tested and ranked for problem dimensions 10 and 30. The eDSC rankings depend on the solution diversity where solutions clustered in the search space are preferred. If the application prefer sparse solutions in the search space, then the best rank is the highest number. The obtained rankings were analyzed by the Friedman test. For dimension 10, the p-value is 0.00, so the null hypothesis is rejected and there is a statistical difference between the distributions of the solutions in the search space of the tested versions of the FWA algorithm. The best ranked algorithm was the dynFWA, i.e. the dynFWA has the most clustered solutions. The other four version of the FWA algorithm were with the similar average ranking. Based on the rankings for each test function, it can be concluded that the LoTFWA is dealing better with modal and composite functions than with the unimodal functions (f1-f5) in comparison to the other FWA versions. The further analysis included pair-wise analysis with the best ranked dynFWA. The result is that the dynFWA has the multivariate significant statistical different performance in term of the solution distribution.

The similar rankings were also obtained for dimension 30. The LoTFWA algorithm achieved slightly better average ranking than the BBFWA, the CoFWA and the GFWA, while the dynFWA remains the best overall ranked algorithm. The additional pair-wise comparison of the algorithms with the dynFWA, the best ranked version, showed that the dynFWA is significantly different to other four versions of the FWA regarding the solution distribution in the search space. In conclusion, the dynFWA has the multivariate significant statistical different performance to all other versions when considering solutions distribution in both cases, for dimensions 10 and 30.

5 Conclusion

The state-of-the-art swarm intelligence algorithms have to be theoretically analyzed in order to determine their drawbacks and to improve the quality of the algorithms. On the other hand by a deeper understanding of the algorithm, it is possible to find the quality of each algorithm for different types of hard optimization problems. In this paper, deep statistical comparison and extended deep statistical comparison were used for comparing different versions of the FWA algorithm. It can be concluded that dynamic search fireworks algorithm has the best diversity of the solutions while the loser-out tournament fireworks algorithm outperformed other versions in the term of the solution quality. Future research should include more SI algorithms to provide clusters of algorithms with similar performance and analysis of the quality of the algorithm for different types of optimization problems.

Acknowledgement. The authors thank Tome Eftimov and Peter Korošec for sharing the DSC tool and providing the statistical results.

References

1. Dorigo, M., Gambardella, L.: Ant colony system: a cooperative learning approach to the traveling salesman problem. IEEE Trans. Evol. Comput. **1**(1), 53–66 (1997)
2. Eftimov, T., Korošec, P.: A novel statistical approach for comparing meta-heuristic stochastic optimization algorithms according to the distribution of solutions in the search space. Inf. Sci. **489**, 255–273 (2019)
3. Eftimov, T., Korošec, P., Seljak, B.K.: A novel approach to statistical comparison of meta-heuristic stochastic optimization algorithms using deep statistics. Inf. Sci. **417**, 186–215 (2017)

4. Eftimov, T., Petelin, G., Korošec, P.: DSCTool: a web-service-based framework for statistical comparison of stochastic optimization algorithms. Appl. Soft Comput. **87** (2020)

5. Kennedy, J., Eberhart, R.: Particle swarm optimization. In: Proceedings of the IEEE International Conference on Neural Networks, vol. 4, pp. 1942–1948 (1995)

6. Korošec, P., Eftimov, T.: Insights into exploration and exploitation power of optimization algorithm using DSCTool. Mathematics **8**(9), 1–11 (2020)

7. Li, J., Tan, Y.: Loser-out tournament-based fireworks algorithm for multimodal function optimization. IEEE Trans. Evol. Comput. **22**(5), 679–691 (2018). https://doi.org/10.1109/TEVC.2017.2787042

8. Li, J., Zheng, S., Tan, Y.: The effect of information utilization: introducing a novel guiding spark in the fireworks algorithm. IEEE Trans. Evol. Comput. **21**(1), 153–166 (2017). https://doi.org/10.1109/TEVC.2016.2589821

9. Li, J., Tan, Y.: The bare bones fireworks algorithm: a minimalist global optimizer. Appl. Soft Comput. **62**, 454–462 (2018). https://doi.org/10.1016/j.asoc.2017.10.046

10. Liang, J., Qu, B., Suganthan, P., Hernández-Díaz, A.G.: Problem definitions and evaluation criteria for the CEC 2013 special session on real-parameter optimization. Computational Intelligence Laboratory, Zhengzhou University, and Nanyang Technological University, Singapore, Technical report 201212 (2013)

11. Tan, Y., Zhu, Y.: Fireworks algorithm for optimization. In: Tan, Y., Shi, Y., Tan, K.C. (eds.) ICSI 2010. LNCS, vol. 6145, pp. 355–364. Springer, Heidelberg (2010). https://doi.org/10.1007/978-3-642-13495-1_44

12. Tuba, E., Jovanovic, R., Beko, M., Tallón-Ballesteros, A.J., Tuba, M.: Bare bones fireworks algorithm for medical image compression. In: Yin, H., Camacho, D., Novais, P., Tallón-Ballesteros, A.J. (eds.) IDEAL 2018. LNCS, vol. 11315, pp. 262–270. Springer, Cham (2018). https://doi.org/10.1007/978-3-030-03496-2_29

13. Tuba, E., Jovanovic, R., Hrosik, R.C., Alihodzic, A., Tuba, M.: Web intelligence data clustering by bare bone fireworks algorithm combined with k-means. In: Proceedings of the 8th International Conference on Web Intelligence, Mining and Semantics, p. 7. ACM (2018)

14. Tuba, E., Strumberger, I., Bacanin, N., Jovanovic, R., Tuba, M.: Bare bones fireworks algorithm for feature selection and SVM optimization. In: 2019 IEEE Congress on Evolutionary Computation (CEC), pp. 2207–2214. IEEE (2019)

15. Tuba, E., Tuba, M., Beko, M.: Support vector machine parameters optimization by enhanced fireworks algorithm. In: Tan, Y., Shi, Y., Niu, B. (eds.) ICSI 2016. LNCS, vol. 9712, pp. 526–534. Springer, Cham (2016). https://doi.org/10.1007/978-3-319-41000-5_52

16. Tuba, E., Tuba, M., Dolicanin, E.: Adjusted fireworks algorithm applied to retinal image registration. Stud. Inform. Control **26**(1), 33–42 (2017)

17. Tuba, E., Tuba, M., Simian, D.: Wireless sensor network coverage problem using modified fireworks algorithm. In: 2016 International Wireless Communications and Mobile Computing Conference (IWCMC), pp. 696–701. IEEE (2016)

18. Tuba, E., Tuba, M., Simian, D., Jovanovic, R.: JPEG quantization table optimization by guided fireworks algorithm. In: Brimkov, V.E., Barneva, R.P. (eds.) IWCIA 2017. LNCS, vol. 10256, pp. 294–307. Springer, Cham (2017). https://doi.org/10.1007/978-3-319-59108-7_23

19. Zheng, S., Janecek, A., Li, J., Tan, Y.: Dynamic search in fireworks algorithm. In: IEEE Congress on Evolutionary Computation (CEC), pp. 3222–3229. IEEE (2014)

20. Zheng, S., Li, J., Janecek, A., Tan, Y.: A cooperative framework for fireworks algorithm. IEEE/ACM Trans. Comput. Biol. Bioinf. **14**(1), 27–41 (2015). https://doi.org/10.1109/TCBB.2015.2497227

Using Population Migration and Mutation to Improve Loser-Out Tournament-Based Fireworks Algorithm

PengCheng Hong[1,2] and JunQi Zhang[1,2(✉)]

[1] Department of Computer Science and Technology, Tongji University,
Shanghai, China
{1933056,zhangjunqi}@tongji.edu.cn
[2] Key Laboratory of Embedded System and Service Computing,
Ministry of Education, Shanghai, China

Abstract. The fireworks algorithm (FWA) is a newly proposed swarm intelligence algorithm inspired by the phenomena of fireworks explosion and has solved many real-world optimization problems successfully. A loser-out tournament-based fireworks algorithm (LoTFWA) is a new baseline in the development of FWA due to its outstanding independent framework and competition mechanism for multimodal optimization. Under this framework, each firework calculates its expected fitness improvement compared with the best fitness to determine whether to be reinitialized. Although LoTFWA achieves the best performance among the variants of FWA, it lacks of comprehensive consideration of the fireworks' cooperation and hence weakens the algorithm's power. This paper improves the cooperation of fireworks in LoTFWA based on the idea of population migration and mutation in biogeography-based optimization (BBO). The proposed mechanism not only promotes fireworks' exploration ability but also enhances their exploitation ability greatly. Experimental results show that the proposed algorithm attains superior performance than the state-of-the-art fireworks algorithm in both unimodal and multimodal functions.

Keywords: Biogeography-based optimization · Evolutionary algorithms · Fireworks algorithm · Swarm intelligence · Population migration

1 Introduction

As an emerging field, swarm intelligence (SI) algorithm has attracted the attention of researchers in many disciplines since its appearance in the 1980s, and has become a hot and frontier field in artificial intelligence, economics, society, and biology. The missions completed by a single complex individual can also be accomplished by a group of large numbers of simple individuals, and the latter tends to have more robustness, flexibility and economic advantages.

© Springer Nature Switzerland AG 2021
Y. Tan and Y. Shi (Eds.): ICSI 2021, LNCS 12689, pp. 423–432, 2021.
https://doi.org/10.1007/978-3-030-78743-1_38

Swarm intelligence provides new ways to complex problems without centralized control and global model [5]. Therefore, by direct or indirect interaction among agents with the environments [3], swarm behavior can be stimulated to help simple agents approach or search the target. Recently, more and more stochastic and population-based swarm intelligence (SI) algorithms have been proposed such as Particle Swarm Optimization (PSO) [2], Ant Colony Optimization [1], Biogeography-Based Optimization [13], Artificial Bee Colony [4] and Magnetic Optimization Algorithm [15].

As a new type of SI algorithm inspired by the natural phenomena of fireworks explosion in the night, Fireworks Algorithm (FWA) is fisrt proposed in 2010 by Tan etc. [14]. FWA has achieved a lot of progress since proposed. Its algorithm framework has changed from a centralized search to a distributed one, which greatly improves the global search performance of the fireworks algorithm. Among these variants, the most influential one is LoTFWA, which has become a new baseline of FWA. LoTFWA completely adopts an independent distributed search framework where each firework population searches independently and no longer has a cooperative mechanism. That is, the number of explosion sparks generated from fireworks will not be dynamically allocated according to fireworks' fitness, and the explosion range (amplitude) of each firework is adjusted dynamically and independently based on its own search results. In addition, LoTFWA innovatively introduces a loser-out tournament mechanism to maintain the competition between the fireworks.

Although LoTFWA achieves the best performance among the variants of FWA, it lacks of comprehensive cooperation among fireworks and hence weakens the power of algorithm. This paper proposes an improved LoTFWA based on the idea of population migration and mutation in biogeography-based optimization (BBO). The expected fitness improvement in each firework is divided into four degrees and each degree triggers a corresponding search pattern. Specifically, fireworks with a higher degree of expected fitness improvement migrate to the best firework for exploitation. While fireworks with a lower degree of expected fitness improvement perform mutation to increase the exploration ability of the population and avoid fast convergence.

The rest of this paper is organized as follows: Sect. 2 introduces the related work about the framework and operations of LoTFWA. Section 3 elaborates the proposed algorithm. Experimental results are shown in Sect. 4 to validate the performance of the proposed method. Section 5 concludes this paper.

2   Related Work

In this section, we introduce the related work about the framework and competition mechanism of LoTFWA [6] in detail.

2.1   Explosion Operation

In each generation, a certain number of explosion sparks are generated around the fireworks within a certain explosion amplitude. Different from previous variants [7,8,16–18], the explosion operation in LoTFWA adopts power law distribution to allocate the explosion sparks. That is,

$$\lambda_i = \bar{\lambda} \cdot \frac{r_i^{-\alpha}}{\sum\limits_j (r_j^{-\alpha})} \tag{1}$$

where r represents the fitness rank of firework X_i, α is a parameter to control the distribution of fireworks' fitness rank. The larger α is, the more explosion sparks that good fireworks generate. LoTFWA adopts equilibrium (i.e., $\alpha = 0$) to maintain effective search performance on multimodal functions.

In LoTFWA, a completely independent dynamic explosion amplitude is adopted in each firework. It is calculated as:

$$A_i^g = \begin{cases} A_i^1 & g = 1 \\ C_a A_i^{g-1} & f(X_i^g) < f(X_i^{g-1}) \\ C_r A_i^{g-1} & f(X_i^g) = f(X_i^{g-1}) \end{cases} \tag{2}$$

where A_i^g is the explosion amplitude of firework X_i in generation g, C_a and C_r are two coefficients to dynamically control the explosion amplitude by amplification and reduction, respectively.

After λ_i and A_i in each firework are calculated, its explosion sparks are generated within a hypercube uniformly. The center of the hypercube is the position of the firework. The radius of the hypercube is the explosion amplitude. Besides, LoTFWA adopts the guiding spark mechanism proposed in [8] as its mutation operation.

2.2   Selection Operation

After explosion and mutation sparks are generated, a selection operation is performed to choose the next fireworks population. Different from centralized selection operation in the previous variants of FWA [7,8,16,17], LoTFWA uses an independent selection operation where each firework in next generation is selected from its own firework population. That is,

$$X_i^{g+1} = \arg\min\{f(X_i^g), f(s_{ij}), f(R_i)\}. \tag{3}$$

2.3   Loser-Out Tournament-Based Fireworks Algorithm

Although the independent selection framework improves information inheritance among generations, it reduces interaction between fireworks. Therefore, LoTFWA innovatively introduces a competition mechanism to improve fireworks' interaction in which the fireworks are compared with each other not only according to their current status but also according to their expected fitness improvement. The improvement of the i-th firework in generation g is calculated as follows:

$$I_i^g = f(X_i^{g-1}) - f(X_i^g). \tag{4}$$

The firework X_i with the expected fitness improvement in the final generation g_{max} is calculated as:

$$f(\widehat{X_i^{g_{max}}}) = f(X_i^g) - (g_{max} - g) \cdot I_i^g. \tag{5}$$

The competition mechanism in LoTFWA is based on the loser-out tournament strategy which conducts the fitness comparison between the expected fitness improvement of firework X_i and the current best one. If a firework's expected fitness improvement cannot exceed the best one, i.e., $f(\widehat{X_i^{g_{max}}}) > \min_j\{f(X_j^g)\}$, it is considered as a loser and reinitialized.

3   The Proposed Algorithm

To further improve the fireworks cooperation in LoTFWA, this paper proposes an improved interactive mechanism based on the idea of population migration and mutation from biogeography-based optimization (BBO).

3.1   Biogeography-Based Optimization

BBO [13] is a recently proposed optimization algorithm inspired by the science of biogeography which indicates that habitats with a high HSI (Habitat Suitability Index, which is equivalent to good fitness solutions) tend to have a large number of species, while those with a low HSI have a small number of species. Generally, high HSI habitats have a high emigration rate and a low immigration rate, vice versa for low HSI habitats. Therefore, lots of species in high HSI habitats emigrate to low HSI habitats. When a population X_i is selected with an immigration rate λ, it will be modified by a population X_j with an emigration rate u_j. The above population migration in [11] can be expressed as:

$$X_i = X_i + rand(0, 1) \cdot (X_j - X_i). \tag{6}$$

Population mutation operation is determined by the species count probabilities. In general, very high HSI solutions (species-rich) and very low HSI solutions (species-poor) are equally rare. They are likely to mutate to other solutions due to the population instability.

Inspired by the above two operations in BBO, an improved interaction mechanism is proposed based on the expected fitness improvement in LoTFWA. A firework with a relatively higher expected fitness improvement migrates to the best firework and a lower one performs mutation within a certain range. In the following, the description of the proposed algorithm is given in detail.

3.2   ILoTFWA

In LoTFWA, If a firework's expected fitness improvement cannot exceed the best one, i.e., $f(\widehat{X_i^{g_{max}}}) > \min_i\{f(X_i^g)\}$, it is considered as a loser and reinitialized. Although loser-out tournament strategy promotes the exploration ability of fireworks, it needs to maintain some useful information to enhance exploitation ability. Therefore, a reasonable division of the expected fitness improvement of fireworks enables the information to be effectively utilized. To realize it, the fitness difference between current firework X_i and best firework $\min_i\{f(X_i^g)\}$ is defined as follows:

$$\Delta_i = f(X_i) - \min_j\{f(X_j^g)\}. \tag{7}$$

According to the Δ_i, the expected fitness improvement of each firework in the final generation g_{max} (i.e., $(g_{max} - g) \cdot I_i$) is divided into four degrees: D_1 : $(+\infty, \Delta_i], D_2 : (\Delta_i, \Delta_i/2], D_3 : (\Delta_i/2, \Delta_i/4], D_4 : (\Delta_i/4, 0]$.

Each degree triggers corresponding mechanism to change firework's search pattern.

The firework X_i with the expected fitness improvement in the final generation g_{max} (i.e., $f(\widehat{X_i^{g_{max}}})$) is divided into following four cases: $C_1 : (-\infty, \min_j \{f(X_j^g)\}], C_2 : (\min_j\{f(X_j^g)\}, \min_j\{f(X_j^g)\} + \Delta_i/2], C_3 : (\min_j\{f(X_j^g)\} + \Delta_i/2, \min_j\{f(X_j^g)\} + 3\Delta_i/4], C_4 : (\min_j\{f(X_j^g)\} + 3\Delta_i/4, f(X_i)]$. If a firework with the expected fitness improvement is in C_1, it is considered as a promising one and retained to ensure the stability of the fireworks population. If the one is in C_2, it migrates to the best firework X_b to enhance the exploitation ability on the basis of its existing useful information. The migration operation is calculated as:

$$X_i = X_i + rand(0, 1) \cdot (X_b - X_i). \tag{8}$$

In the meantime, the explosion amplitude of the firework is updated according to the distance between X_b and X_i as follows:

$$A_i = (1 - \theta)A_i + \theta\|X_b - X_i\|. \tag{9}$$

where θ is a parameter to control the influence of migration distance on explosion amplitude.

If the one is in C_3, it mutates in a certain range to enhance exploration ability. The mutation operation is calculated as:

$$X_i = \frac{rand(-1, 1) \cdot (L - U)}{10} + X_i. \tag{10}$$

where L and U represent the lower bound and the upper bound of the search space. The explosion amplitude of the firework X_i still holds the line. The firework will be reinitialized if it is predicted in C_4.

Algorithm 1 shows the improved interactive mechanism based on the idea of population migration and mutation. Algorithm 2 shows the complete process of ILoTFWA.

4   Experiments

In order to test the performance of the proposed algorithm, numerical experiments are conducted on the CEC 2013 benchmark suite [10] including 28 functions and CEC 2015 benchmark suite [12] including 15 functions. According to

---

Algorithm 1. Improved Interactive Mechanism

INPUT: maximal generation number g_{max}, current generation g, explosion amplitude parameter θ.

1: **for** each firework X_i **do**
2:     **if** $f(X_i^g) < f(X_i^{g-1})$ **then**
3:         $I_i^g = f(X_i^{g-1}) - f(X_i^g)$.
4:     **end if**
5:     $\Delta_i = f(X_i) - \min_j\{f(X_j^g)\}$.
6:     **if** $f(\widehat{X_i^{g_{max}}})$ is in C_1 **then**
7:         Retain the firework X_i.
8:     **else if** $f(\widehat{X_i^{g_{max}}})$ is in C_2 **then**
9:         Execute migration of firework X_i by (8).
10:        Update explosion amplitude of firework X_i by (9).
11:    **else if** $f(\widehat{X_i^{g_{max}}})$ is in C_3 **then**
12:        Execute mutation of firework X_i by (10).
13:    **else**
14:        Reinitialize the firework X_i.
15:    **end if**
16: **end for**

Algorithm 2. ILoTFWA

1: Initialize N fireworks randomly in a search space and evaluate their fitness values.
2: **while** termination criteria are not met **do**
3:     Calculate the number of explosion sparks by (1).
4:     Calculate the explosion amplitudes by (2).
5:     **for** each firework **do**
6:         Generate explosion sparks within the explosion amplitude uniformly.
7:         Generate guiding sparks.
8:         Evaluate all fitness values of sparks and fireworks.
9:         Select a best one from its own firework population as the firework in next generation.
10:    **end for**
11:    Perform the improved interactive mechanism according to Algorithm 1.
12: **end while**
13: **return** The position and the fitness of the best individual

---

the instructions of the benchmark suites, all the test functions are repeated for 51 times, and the number of dimensions of all the test functions is set to $D=30$. The maximal number of fitness evaluations is $10000D$ in each run. All the experiments are carried out using MATLAB R2019b on a PC with Intel(R) Core(TM) i7-8550U running at 3.10GHz with 8G RAM. In the following, we briefly introduce the parameter settings in LoTFWA and related parameter in our proposed algorithm.

4.1   Experimental Settings

Multimodal function optimization problems require algorithms to keep a balance between exploration and exploitation. Generally, a small number of fireworks N generates more sparks to exploit the feasible space better, while a large one generates fewer sparks to explore more areas. In the proposed algorithm ILoTFWA, we follow the suggestion in LoTFWA [6] and set the number of fireworks $N = 5$. The amplitude coefficients C_r and C_a are two important parameters for dynamic search. In this paper, we follow the suggestion in [16] and set the two coefficients to 0.9 and 1.2, respectively. The parameter σ proposed in GFWA [8] is set to 0.2. The parameter α and λ is set to 0 and 300 respectively as suggested in LoTFWA.

The parameter θ proposed in this paper is to control the impact of migration distance on the explosion amplitude. A fine-tuned θ is given based on a set of experiments illustrated in Fig. 1. The Average Rank of each parameter θ in Fig. 1 is calculated by averaging fitness rank in each benchmark function among different θ. The best parameter $\theta = 0.1$ is choosed for following experiments.

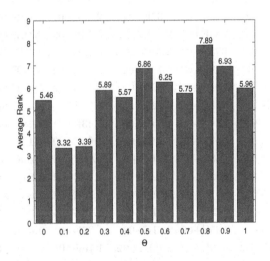

Fig. 1. A set of experiments on CEC2013 benchmark suite is illustrated to show the influence of parameter θ where $\theta = 0.1$ performs best.

4.2   Experimental Results

In this part, we compared our proposed method with two up-to-date FWA variants including LoTFWA, MSCFWA [9] on CEC 2013 benchmark suite. The mean errors, standard deviations of experimental results are presented in Table 1 and Wilcoxon signed-rank test is used to validate the performance

Table 1. Accuracy Results about MSCFWA, LoTFWA and ILoTFWA on CEC 2013 benchmark suite

Function	MSCFWA		LoTFWA		ILoTFWA	
	Mean	Std.	Mean	Std.	Mean	Std.
1	6.82E-13	6.07E−13	**0.00E+00**	0.00E+00	**0.00E+00**	0.00E+00
2	9.76E+05	4.93E+05	1.19E+06	4.27E+05	**8.64E+05**	5.05E+05
3	1.80E+07	2.03E+07	2.23E+07	1.91E+07	**4.57E+06**	5.48E+06
4	1.89E+03	7.09E+02	2.13E+03	8.11E+02	**5.62E+02**	1.57E+02
5	4.00E−03	6.19E−04	3.55E−03	5.01E−04	**2.13E−03**	5.99E−04
6	1.52E+01	5.89E+00	1.45E+01	6.84E+00	**1.29E+01**	3.40E+00
7	4.08E+01	1.27E+01	5.05E+01	9.69E+00	**2.68E+01**	8.85E+00
8	**2.09E+01**	5.14E−02	**2.09E+01**	6.14E−02	2.09E+01	6.39E−02
9	1.70E+01	1.82E+00	1.45E+01	2.07E+00	**1.08E+01**	2.76E+00
10	3.49E−02	2.31E−02	4.52E−02	2.47E−02	**2.39E−02**	1.88E−02
11	8.23E+01	1.62E+01	6.39E+01	1.04E−01	**3.14E+01**	9.43E+00
12	7.84E+01	1.52E+01	6.82E+01	1.45E+01	**3.46E+01**	9.86E+00
13	1.46E+02	2.79E+01	1.36E+02	2.30E+01	**5.96E+01**	1.82E+01
14	2.76E+03	3.24E+02	2.38E+03	3.13E+02	**2.10E+03**	3.81E+02
15	2.75E+03	3.22E+02	**2.58E+03**	3.83E+02	2.77E+03	2.27E+02
16	1.87E−01	7.19E−02	5.74E−02	2.13E−02	**5.45E−02**	2.14E−02
17	1.34E+02	2.01E+01	6.20E+01	9.45E+00	**5.66E+01**	8.77E+00
18	1.37E+02	1.78E+01	6.12E+01	9.56E+00	**5.83E+01**	6.03E+00
19	5.03E+00	1.14E+00	3.05E+00	6.43E−01	**2.79E+00**	4.49E−01
20	1.27E+01	1.03E+00	1.33E+01	1.02E+00	**1.14E+01**	9.89E−01
21	2.18E+02	3.83E+01	**2.00E+02**	2.80E−03	2.20E+02	4.22E+01
22	3.40E+03	4.62E+02	3.12E+03	3.79E+02	**2.81E+03**	3.98E+02
23	3.42E+03	4.07E+02	3.11E+03	5.16E+02	**2.85E+03**	5.00E+02
24	2.44E+02	8.73E+00	2.37E+02	1.20E+01	**2.21E+02**	1.78E+01
25	2.78E+02	6.35E+00	2.71E+02	1.97E+01	**2.68E+02**	6.82E+00
26	**2.00E+02**	2.06E−02	**2.00E+02**	1.76E+01	**2.00E+02**	1.04E−02
27	7.95E+02	5.23E+01	6.84E+02	9.77E+01	**6.00E+02**	1.72E+02
28	2.80E+02	5.99E+01	**2.65E+02**	7.58E+01	2.80E+02	6.32E+01
A.R.	2.43		2.04		**1.11**	

improvement (with confidence level at least 95%). A.R. is the average ranking value. The better results are marked in bold. According to the results, ILoTFWA performs significantly better than LoTFWA and MSCFWA on 22 ($f_2 - f_7, f_9 - f_{14}, f_{16} - f_{20}, f_{22} - f_{25}, f_{27}$) out of 28 test functions. Additionally, ILoTFWA is worse than the contenders on merely 3 (f_{15}, f_{21}, f_{28}) out of 28 functions. In all, ILoTFWA shows excellent performance on both unimodal and multimodal functions.

Table 2. Accuracy Results about LoTFWA and ILoTFWA on CEC 2015 benchmark suite

Function	LoTFWA		ILoTFWA	
	Mean	Std.	Mean	Std.
1	1.1097E+06	6.2634E+05	**8.7910E+05**	3.2667E+05
2	1.6949E+03	1.7226E+02	**1.5105E+03**	1.1089E+01
3	**1.5200E+03**	1.9981E−05	**1.5200E+03**	1.0982E−04
4	1.5631E+03	1.0018E+01	**1.5303E+03**	5.9840E+00
5	3.5896E+03	2.3758E+02	**3.0778E+03**	4.6273E+02
6	2.6784E+04	1.1232E+04	**2.0096E+04**	1.0212E+04
7	1.5119E+03	1.3659E+00	**1.5110E+03**	2.4589E+00
8	2.1660E+04	1.3702E+04	**1.8835E+04**	1.1098E+04
9	1.6038E+03	2.3134E−01	**1.6031E+03**	2.5798E−01
10	4.5436E+04	2.2027E+04	**2.4947E+04**	1.1543E+04
11	**1.8038E+03**	8.5392E−01	1.8179E+03	4.7949E+01
12	1.6078E+03	9.4638E−01	**1.6058E+03**	7.9294E−01
13	**1.5001E+03**	2.5096E−02	**1.5001E+03**	3.1067E−02
14	**3.2932E+04**	1.1173E+02	3.3244E+04	9.6429E+02
15	**1.5000E+03**	2.2201E−11	**1.5000E+03**	5.6499E−12
A.R.	1.67		**1.13**	

To further validate our proposed method, we compare it with LoTFWA on CEC 2015 bechmark suite. The experimental results are shown in Table 2. According to the results, ILoTFWA outperforms LoTFWA on 10 ($f_1 - f_2, f_4 - f_{10}, f_{12}$) out of 15 functions.

5 Conclusion

In this paper, an improved interaction mechanism inspired by the idea of population migration and mutation in BBO is proposed to further improve the LoTFWA's performance. Under the independent selection framework in LoTFWA, the proposed fireworks interaction mechanism is based on the division of fireworks' expected fitness improvement. When a firework is predicted with a relatively higher fitness improvement, it migrates to the best firework for exploitation. While the one is predicted with a lower fitness improvement, it mutates in a certain range to increase exploration ability. The experimental results show the proposed algorithm attains superior performance than the state-of-the-art fireworks algorithm in both unimodal and multimodal functions.

Acknowledgement. This work was supported by Innovation Program of Shanghai Municipal Education Commission (202101070007E00098). This work was also supported in part by the National Natural Science Foundation of China (51775385,

61703279, 62073244, 61876218) and the Shanghai Innovation Action Plan under grant no. 20511100500.

References

1. Dorigo, M., Birattari, M., Stutzle, T.: Ant colony optimization. IEEE Comput. Intell. Mag. **1**(4), 28–39 (2006)
2. Eberhart, R., Kennedy, J.: A new optimizer using particle swarm theory. In: MHS 1995. Proceedings of the Sixth International Symposium on Micro Machine and Human Science, pp. 39–43. IEEE (1995)
3. Engelbretch, A.: Fundamentals of Computational Swarm Intelligence, pp. 5–129. Wiley, London (2005)
4. Karaboga, D., Gorkemli, B., Ozturk, C., Karaboga, N.: A comprehensive survey: artificial bee colony (ABC) algorithm and applications. Artif. Intell. Rev. **42**(1), 21–57 (2014). https://doi.org/10.1007/s10462-012-9328-0
5. Kennedy, J.: Swarm intelligence. In: Zomaya, A.Y. (ed.) Handbook of Nature-Inspired and Innovative Computing, pp. 187–219. Springer, Heidelberg (2006). https://doi.org/10.1007/0-387-27705-6_6
6. Li, J., Tan, Y.: Loser-out tournament-based fireworks algorithm for multimodal function optimization. IEEE Trans. Evol. Comput. **22**(5), 679–691 (2018)
7. Li, J., Zheng, S., Tan, Y.: Adaptive fireworks algorithm. In: IEEE Congress on Evolutionary Computation (CEC), pp. 3214–3221 (2014)
8. Li, J., Zheng, S., Tan, Y.: The effect of information utilization: introducing a novel guiding spark in the fireworks algorithm. IEEE Trans. Evol. Comput. **21**(1), 153–166 (2017)
9. Li, Y., Tan, Y.: Multi-scale collaborative fireworks algorithm. In: 2020 IEEE Congress on Evolutionary Computation (CEC), pp. 1–8 (2020)
10. Liang, J.J., Qu, B.Y., Suganthan, P.N., Hernández-Díaz, A.G.: Problem definitions and evaluation criteria for the CEC 2013 special session on real-parameter optimization. Technical report 201212, Zhengzhou Univ., China and Nanyang Technol. Univ., Singapore (2013)
11. Ma, H., Simon, D.: Blended biogeography-based optimization for constrained optimization. Eng. Appl. Artif. Intell. **24**(3), 517–525 (2011)
12. Qu, B.Y., Liang, J.J., Suganthan, P.N., Chen, Q.: Problem definitions and evaluation criteria for the CEC 2015 competition on single objective multi-niche optimization (2016)
13. Simon, D.: Biogeography-based optimization. IEEE Trans. Evol. Comput. **12**(6), 702–713 (2008)
14. Tan, Y., Zhu, Y.: Fireworks algorithm for optimization. In: Tan, Y., Shi, Y., Tan, K.C. (eds.) ICSI 2010. LNCS, vol. 6145, pp. 355–364. Springer, Heidelberg (2010). https://doi.org/10.1007/978-3-642-13495-1_44
15. Tayarani-N, M.H., Akbarzadeh-T, M.R.: Magnetic optimization algorithms a new synthesis. In: 2008 IEEE Congress on Evolutionary Computation (IEEE World Congress on Computational Intelligence), pp. 2659–2664 (2008)
16. Zheng, S., Janecek, A., Li, J., Tan, Y.: Dynamic search in fireworks algorithm. In: IEEE Congress on Evolutionary Computation (CEC), pp. 3222–3229 (2014)
17. Zheng, S., Janecek, A., Tan, Y.: Enhanced fireworks algorithm. In: IEEE Congress on Evolutionary Computation (CEC), pp. 2069–2077 (2013)
18. Zheng, S., Li, J., Janecek, A., Tan, Y.: A cooperative framework for fireworks algorithm. IEEE/ACM Trans. Comput. Biol. Bioinf. **14**(1), 27–41 (2017)

Region Selection with Discrete Fireworks Algorithm for Person Re-identification

Xuan Li, Tao Zhang$^{(\boxtimes)}$, Xin Zhao, and Shuang Li

School of Electrical and Information Engineering, Tianjin University,
No. 92 Weijin Road, Nankai District, Tianjin 300072, China
zhangtao@tju.edu.cn

Abstract. Various hand-crafted features with metric learning methods have improved the person re-identification (Re-ID) accuracy. Metric learning methods for person Re-ID mean to match the features acquired from different persons. However, not all information of the features is valid for metric learning. Compared to these metric learning methods, the region selection with discrete fireworks algorithm (RS-DFWA) is proposed in this paper for hand-crafted feature designing. RS-DFWA uses the fireworks algorithm after discretization to select the effective regions of the feature maps at the metric learning stage. RS-DFWA has a faster convergence speed and a better optimization accuracy so that the noise regions such as background features would be ignored. RS-DFWA optimizes the fitness of the discrete fireworks algorithm while training the deep networks for person feature learning. The method we proposed is validated on the CUHK03 dataset, region selection with discrete fireworks algorithm for the deep features achieve favorable accuracy. For example, on the CUHK03 dataset in single query mode, an improvement of mAP = +4.6% is obtained by RS-DFWA compared to the Baseline model.

Keywords: Discrete fireworks algorithm · Feature selection · Deep learning

1 Introduction

The fireworks algorithm (FWA) [3,18,19] is one of the most popular Swarm Intelligence (SI) algorithms [11–17,26]. FWA shows its strong capability and convergence speed while applied to many real-world optimization problems. FWA is inspired by the natural fireworks explosion phenomenon, which exchanges information among different fireworks by controlling the resource allocation and the search manner dynamically.

The Person re-identification (Re-ID) [8–10,24,25] task aims to retrieve a specific pedestrian from disjoint camera views with pedestrian visual features [23]. The metric learning method is an excellent method for person Re-ID, which uses distance measure of feature matrix obtained from deep convolutional networks

© Springer Nature Switzerland AG 2021
Y. Tan and Y. Shi (Eds.): ICSI 2021, LNCS 12689, pp. 433–440, 2021.
https://doi.org/10.1007/978-3-030-78743-1_39

to predict the particular image identity. However, there are some challenges for person Re-ID because of the differences among disjoint camera views. The background and viewpoints exactly interfere with the feature representations acquired from the metric learning method. Figure 1 shows the different backgrounds in the images with the particular pedestrian.

Fig. 1. The different backgrounds in the images with the particular pedestrian

In addressing the problem described above, the region selecting with discrete fireworks algorithm (RS-DFWA) is proposed in this paper. RS-DFWA selects the effective regions on feature maps, not including the background regions. The process is implemented via the discrete fireworks algorithm. Firstly, RS-DFWA implements the fireworks algorithm after discretization to optimize the effective regions on feature maps. Secondly, RS-DFWA takes the distance metric of the effective feature regions as the evaluation of the different sparks. In the meantime, RS-DFWA evaluate the loss function of the person Re-ID network structure according to the effective regions selected by the discrete fireworks algorithm.

The remainder of this paper is organized as follows. Section 2 introduces some related work. Section 3 describes the framework of RS-DFWA. In Sect. 4, experimental results are presented to validate the performance of the RS-DFWA. Section 5 concludes the paper.

2   Related Work

Ying Tan et al. [1] inspired by the emergent swarm behavior of fireworks, and proposed Fireworks Algorithm (FWA) as a novel swarm intelligence algorithm. The loser-out tournament-based FWA (LoTFWA) for multimodal optimization is designed by [2]. The LoTFWA proposed the competitive mechanism, the fireworks compete with each other and the losers will be forced to restart from a new location. Haoran Luo et al. [4] applied FWA to traveling salesman problem and propose a discrete fireworks algorithm DFWA-TSP. [4] exploited 2-opt and 3-opt as the basic operation for generating sparks in the fireworks explosion. Adaptive strategy and mutation method are also used for DFWA-TSP. Linzi Qu et al. [5] designed a new network – CycleNet to extract handicraft features of image regions. CycleNet would assign a more accurate representative for every pixel. Xiang Bai et al. [6] learns highly discriminative features for person Re-ID according to Long Short-Term Memory (LSTM). [6] applied LSTM in an end-to-end way to model the pedestrian, seen as a sequence of body parts from head to foot.

3 Method

RS-DFWA implements the FWA iterating process during the training phase of the network structure. RS-DFWA interchange information to dynamically control the each generation of the SI algorithm and the hyper-parameter of the network structure for person Re-ID.

3.1 A Subsection Sample

The DFWA implemented for RS-DFWA follows the general principle of FWA. DFWA searches for better feature regions by the iterations of the explosion and selection operation. Besides, the Loser-Out Tournament (LoT) [2] mechanism is applied to RS-DFWA.

Initialization. The random selection of feature regions initializes each firework. Each firework is represented with the binary matrix, where 1 represents the current corresponding feature point is effective, while 0 represents that the current corresponding feature point should be ignored.

Explosion. The number of explosion sparks and explosion amplitude is two important parameters in the explosion step. The number of explosion sparks represents the amounts of sparks that the corresponding firework generates. For each firework i, the number of explosion sparks is calculated by formula Eq. (1). Where $\hat{\lambda}$ is a constant parameter to control the total number of explosion sparks in each generation. The function f stands for the fitness calculation, which is the distance metric among different pedestrian features. $max_j\{f(X_j)\}$ and $f(X_i)$ are the worst fitness and the $i-th$ firework fitness respectively. n is the number of the firework in the current generation. μ is a const small number to avoid the denominator to be zero. The explosion amplitude represents the difference existing between the firework and the corresponding sparks. The explosion amplitude is represented as formula Eq. (2). A_{max} and ξ represents the maximum explosion amplitude and const parameter respectively.

$$\lambda_i = \hat{\lambda} * \frac{max_j\{f(X_j)\} - f(X_i)}{\sum_n (max_j\{f(X_j)\} - f(X_n)) + \mu}. \tag{1}$$

$$A_i = A_{max} * \frac{f(X_k) - f_{min} + \xi}{\sum_k (f(X_k) - fmin) + \xi}. \tag{2}$$

Mutation. There might existing local optimal solution during the iterations of SFWA. In order to avoid this problem, specific fireworks are required to generate mutation sparks. In this step, the mutation sparks are generated randomly, then the distance matrix between different pedestrians would be given a random value. In the next generation, the fireworks would explode sparks as the explosion process.

Selection. During the iterations of DFWA, the firework in the nest generation should be selected from the last generation. Define each firework along with its own offspring as an independent set, and the firework should be selected from its own set independently. For RS-DFWA, the best individual in each set would be selected to be the firework of the next generation.

Loser-Out Tournament. The best position selection of the fireworks could be considered as a problem of time series forecasting [7]. When the difference between the best individual generated from neighboring generations is large, it means the corresponding local area might contain some potential solutions, so DFWA is better to put some effort into searching in the current local area. In this paper, we follow the elitism selection mechanism [2].

3.2   Region Selecting with Discrete Fireworks Algorithm

The whole strcture of RS-DFWA is shown in Fig. 2. RS-DFWA iters DFWA while training the network backbone for original feature maps extraction. Each individual of DFWA stands for the selections of the effective feature regions, which is represented by a binary matrix. Each final feature after region selection is obtained by multiplying the corresponding original feature map and the best individual of DFWA.

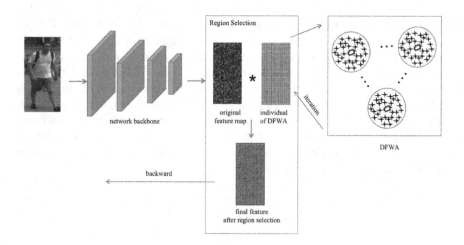

Fig. 2. The whole strcture of RS-DFWA

For RS-DFWA, P identities and K instances are randomly sampled for each mini-batch is fed into the network backbone. The loss function of network training is represented as Eq. (3). N is the size of mini-batch in training process, W_k is the weight vector of class k. y_i is the ground truth identity of the sample i. f_i is the i-th learned feature, I_b is the best individual of DFWA. s_p and s_n are the within-class similarity scores and between-class similarity scores respectively. γ and α are the margin hyperparameters.

$$L = -\sum_{i=1}^{N} log \frac{e^{W_{y_i}^T (f_i * I_b)}}{\sum_{m=1}^{M} e^{W_m^T(f_i*I_b)}} - log(1 + \sum_{j=1}^{P} exp(\gamma(s_n^j + \alpha)) \sum_{n=1}^{K} exp(\gamma(-s_p^n))).$$

(3)

4   Experiment

In this section, RS-DFWA is demonstrated on CUHK03 datasets. Here, ResNet-50 is used as the network backbone for person Re-ID. The details and results of the experiments have been analyzed.

CUHK03 consists of 767 identities for the training set and 700 identities for the testing set. Manually labeled pedestrian bounding boxes and DPM-detected bounding boxes are provided in the dataset as annotations. In this paper, the DPM-detected bounding boxes are used in the experiments. The new training/testing protocol following [22] is adopted in this paper. In this protocol, 767 identities are used for training and the remaining for testing. During the training phase, the mini-batch size is 96, which is sampled with randomly selected 12 identities and randomly sampled 8 images for each identity from the training set. The Baseline model represents the ResNet-50 structure without the region selection strategy we proposed.

The performance of mean average precision (mAP) and Cumulative Matching Characteristic (CMC) curve are evaluated in the experiments. CMC is reported at rank-1, rank-5 and rank-10, and mAP is reported on all the candidate datasets. Table 1 shows the comparison of results on ResNet-50 and RS-DFWA. RS-DFWA achieves Rank-1/mAP = 51.4%/51.6% on CUHK03 detected setting, which outperforms the Baseline model. Figure 3 shows the mAP comparison of Baseline

Table 1. Comparison between RS-DFWA and other advanced algorithms on CUHK03.

	mAP	Rank1	Rank5	Rank10
SVDNet-ResNet50 [21]	37.3%	41.5%	–	–
HA-CNN [9]	38.6%	41.7%	–	–
Baseline	47.0%	46.0%	68.4%	77.1%
MLFN [20]	47.8%	52.8%	–	–
RS-DFWA	51.6%	51.4%	71.6%	80.6%

model and RS-DFWA. RS-DFWA gets better results about the training speed. The results demonstrate that the region selection with RS-DFWA is efficient to person Re-ID task. The redundant might be ignored when matching the features in the feature retrieval process. Figure 4 shows the fitness of RS-DFWA, the fitness curve indicates the DFWA has the ability to search the better feature regions as expected.

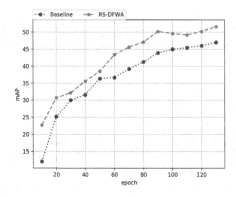

Fig. 3. The mAP comparison of ResNet-50 and RS-DFWA

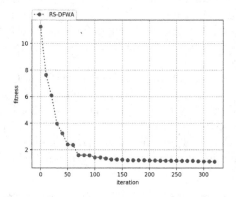

Fig. 4. The fitness of RS-DFWA

5   Conclusion

In this work, an excellent DFWA is applied to feature region selection. RS-DFWA is proposed for person Re-ID and achieves satisfying results. DFWA is designed with explosion operation, selection operation, and LoT strategy. RS-DFWA searches the better feature regions while training the network for feature extraction. Numerical experiments show that RS-DFWA has a high performance for person Re-ID.

In the future, there are several research directions along with this topic. Firstly, several evolutionary and swarm algorithms might be considered to apply to feature region selection, such as evolution strategy, particle swarm optimization, the memetic algorithm, Etc. Secondly, RS-DFWA could use some other network backbones to learn the original features in order to improve the learning ability of RS-DFWA.

References

1. Tan, Y., Zhu, Y.: Fireworks algorithm for optimization. In: Tan, Y., Shi, Y., Tan, K.C. (eds.) ICSI 2010. LNCS, vol. 6145, pp. 355–364. Springer, Heidelberg (2010). https://doi.org/10.1007/978-3-642-13495-1_44
2. Li, J., Tan, Y.: Loser-out tournament-based fireworks algorithm for multimodal function optimization. IEEE Trans. Evol. Comput. **22**(5), 679–691 (2017)
3. Liu, Z., Nan, Z., Qiu, C., et al.: A discrete fireworks optimization algorithm to optimize multi-matching selective assembly problem with non-normal dimensional distribution. Assem. Autom. (2019)
4. Luo, H., Xu, W., Tan, Y.: A discrete fireworks algorithm for solving large-scale travel salesman problem. In: 2018 IEEE Congress on Evolutionary Computation (CEC), pp. 1–8. IEEE (2018)
5. Qu, L., He, L., Ke, J., et al.: Learning more accurate features for semantic segmentation in CycleNet.In: Proceedings of the Asian Conference on Computer Vision (2020)
6. Bai, X., Yang, M., Huang, T., et al.: Deep-person: learning discriminative deep features for person re-identification. Pattern Recognit. **98**, 107036 (2017)
7. Chatfield, C.: Time-Series Forecasting. CRC Press, Boca Raton (2000)
8. Sun, Y., Zheng, L., Yang, Y., Tian, Q., Wang, S.: Beyond part models: person retrieval with refined part pooling (and a strong convolutional baseline). In: Ferrari, V., Hebert, M., Sminchisescu, C., Weiss, Y. (eds.) ECCV 2018. LNCS, vol. 11208, pp. 501–518. Springer, Cham (2018). https://doi.org/10.1007/978-3-030-01225-0_30
9. Li, W., Zhu, X., Gong, S.: Harmonious attention network for person re-identification. In: CVPR (2018)
10. Wang, C., Zhang, Q., Huang, C., Liu, W., Wang, X.: Beyond part models: person retrieval with refined part pooling (and a strong convolutional baseline). In: Ferrari, V., Hebert, M., Sminchisescu, C., Weiss, Y. (eds.) ECCV 2018. Mancs: A multi-task attentional network with curriculum sampling for person re-identification, vol. 11208, pp. 384–400. Springer, Cham (2018). https://doi.org/10.1007/978-3-030-01225-0_23
11. Chakraborty, A., Kar, A.K.: Swarm intelligence: a review of algorithms. In: Patnaik, S., Yang, X.-S., Nakamatsu, K. (eds.) Nature-Inspired Computing and Optimization. MOST, vol. 10, pp. 475–494. Springer, Cham (2017). https://doi.org/10.1007/978-3-319-50920-4_19

12. Zhao, X., Wang, C., Su, J., et al.: Research and application based on the swarm intelligence algorithm and artificial intelligence for wind farm decision system. Renew. Energy **134**, 681–697 (2019)

13. Brezočnik, L., Fister, I., Podgorelec, V.: Swarm intelligence algorithms for feature selection: a review. Appl. Sci. **8**(9), 1521 (2018)

14. Mavrovouniotis, M., Li, C., Yang, S.: A survey of swarm intelligence for dynamic optimization: algorithms and applications. Swarm Evol. Comput. **33**, 1–17 (2017)

15. Thrun, M.C., Ultsch, A.: Swarm intelligence for self-organized clustering. Artif. Intell. **290**, 103237 (2020)

16. Zedadra, O., Guerrieri, A., Jouandeau, N., et al.: Swarm intelligence-based algorithms within IoT-based systems: a review. J. Parallel Distrib. Comput. **122**, 173–187 (2018)

17. Ertenlice, O., Kalayci, C.B.: A survey of swarm intelligence for portfolio optimization: algorithms and applications. Swarm Evol. Comput. **39**, 36–52 (2018)

18. Tuba, E., Tuba, M., Dolicanin, E.: Adjusted fireworks algorithm applied to retinal image registration. Stud. Inform. Control **26**(1), 33–42 (2017)

19. Cheng, R., Bai, Y., Zhao, Y., et al.: Improved fireworks algorithm with information exchange for function optimization. Knowl.-Based Syst. **163**, 82–90 (2019)

20. Chang, X., Hospedales, T.M., Xiang, T.: Multi-level factorisation net for person re-identification. In: Proceedings of the IEEE Conference on Computer Vision and Pattern Recognition, pp. 2109–2118 (2018)

21. Sun, Y., Zheng, L., Deng, W., et al.: SVDNet for pedestrian retrieval. In: Proceedings of the IEEE International Conference on Computer Vision, pp. 3800–3808 (2017)

22. Zhong, Z., Zheng, L., Cao, D., et al.: Re-ranking person re-identification with k-reciprocal encoding. In: Proceedings of the IEEE Conference on Computer Vision and Pattern Recognition, pp. 1318–1327 (2017)

23. Li, X., Zhang, T., Zhao, X., et al.: Guided autoencoder for dimensionality reduction of pedestrian features. Appl. Intell. **50**(12), 4557–4567 (2020). https://doi.org/10.1007/s10489-020-01813-1

24. Li, X., et al.: Learning fused features with parallel training for person re-identification. Knowl.-Based Syst. **220**, 106941 (2021)

25. Zhang, T., et al.: Image generation and constrained two-stage feature fusion for person re-identification. Appl. Intell. 1–11 (2021). https://doi.org/10.1007/s10489-021-02271-z

26. Zhang, T., Li, X., Liu, G.: An improved artificial bee colony algorithm for the task assignment in heterogeneous multicore architectures. In: Tan, Y., Shi, Y., Tang, Q. (eds.) ICSI 2018. LNCS, vol. 10941, pp. 179–187. Springer, Cham (2018). https://doi.org/10.1007/978-3-319-93815-8_18

Fireworks Harris Hawk Algorithm Based on Dynamic Competition Mechanism for Numerical Optimization

Wenyu Li, Ronghua Shi, Heng Zou, and Jian Dong[✉]

School of Computer Science and Engineering, Central South University, Changsha, China
dongjian@csu.edu.cn

Abstract. Harris Hawk Optimizer (HHO) is a new algorithm based on population, because of the diversity of its plunder strategy, it has good exploration ability, but there is still room for further improvement of exploitation ability. Because of its unique "explosion" mechanism, Fireworks Algorithm (FWA) has good exploitation ability. In order to make up for the shortcomings of HHO algorithm, this paper proposes an improved HHO algorithm, fireworks Harris hawk algorithm based on dynamic competition mechanism (DCFW-HHO). In the iterative process, taking the escape energy function of HHO algorithm as an index, different competition mechanisms and fireworks explosion operations are performed in different stages of the algorithm. In order to verify the performance of the proposed algorithm, the benchmark function of CEC2005 is optimized by DCFW-HHO, and compared with the marine predator algorithm (MPA), whale optimization algorithm (WOA), lightning search algorithm (LSA), water cycle algorithm (WCA), FWA and HHO, experiments show that the proposed DCFW-HHO algorithm has strong optimization ability.

Keywords: Harris Hawk Optimizer · Fireworks Algorithm · Dynamic competition mechanism · Swarm intelligence

1 Introduction

Heuristic algorithm is a mathematical optimization strategy for solving various life phenomena and natural laws, which is widely used to solve nonlinear complex function optimization problems and complex real problems [1]. Compared with the traditional mathematical methods, heuristic algorithm has the characteristics of high efficiency and low cost. As a classical meta heuristic algorithm, the universality of genetic algorithm [2] and differential evolution algorithm [7] has been proved by many researchers [3−6]. Heuristic algorithm includes genetic programming (GP) [8], biogeography-based optimizer [9], evolution strategy [10], etc.

In recent years, algorithms based on swarm intelligence (SI) [11] have been widely used. It is a branch of meta heuristic optimization algorithm based on population. Ant colony algorithm (ACO) [12], harris hawk optimizer (HHO) [13] and artificial bee colony algorithm (ABC) [14] are excellent meta heuristic algorithms. The Si algorithm based on

© Springer Nature Switzerland AG 2021
Y. Tan and Y. Shi (Eds.): ICSI 2021, LNCS 12689, pp. 441–450, 2021.
https://doi.org/10.1007/978-3-030-78743-1_40

random initialization has the following advantages: (1) it does not have a large number of parameter settings; (2) it can find the global optimum in most cases; (3) it does not require the continuity of the search space, the convexity and differentiability of the objective function.

Fireworks algorithm [15] is a new optimization algorithm inspired by fireworks explosion. FWA has been applied to solve all kinds of practical problems, and shows strong global optimization ability. The algorithm mainly uses explosion operation and selection operation to carry out heuristic search. In explosion operation, fireworks will produce many sparks in the range of explosion amplitude. Then, choose a new generation of fireworks from these sparks. In the previous work, Tan Ying proposed Loser-Out Tournament-Based Fireworks Algorithm [16], and effectively improved the performance of the firework algorithm. Competition is the cornerstone of the evolution of nature. Through this mechanism, the losers can be eliminated, which can effectively reallocate resources and improve the average quality of species. Harris hawk optimization algorithm (HHO) has four different plunder strategies. In different stages of iteration, different plunder strategies will be adopted. In order to further improve the exploitation ability of HHO, this paper introduces FWA exploitation strategy into HHO, and proposes a fireworks Harris hawk algorithm based on dynamic competition mechanism (DCFW-HHO).

The rest of this paper is organized as follows: The second section introduces the fireworks algorithm and Harris Hawk Algorithm, as well as their related work in the field. The third section introduces proposed algorithm. The fourth section gives the experimental results to illustrate the performance of the proposed algorithm. The fifth section summarizes this article.

2   Related Work

2.1   Harris Hawk Algorithm

HHO [13] is a novel meta heuristic algorithm based on population. The algorithm determines the exploration or exploitation stage of the algorithm by escaping energy E.

When $|E| > 1$, HHO algorithm is in the exploration stage, all agents are waiting and looking for an optimal solution. All agents position updated by:

$$X_i^{t+1} = \begin{cases} X_{rand}^t - r_1 \left| x_{rand}^t - 2 * r_2 * x_i^t \right|, q \geq 0.5 \\ \left(X_{prey} - X_{mean}^t \right) - r_3 * (lb + r_4 * (ub - lb)), q < 0.5 \end{cases} \tag{1}$$

where X_{rand}^t is a random Harris Hawk in the population of the t th iteration, X_{prey} is the optimal solution in the current population, and q, r_1, r_2, r_3, r_4 are random numbers in $(0, 1)$.

When $|E| \leq 1$, HHO algorithm will enter the exploitation stage. Next, we will introduce these four kinds of plunder strategies in detail.

Soft Besiege. When $r \geq 0.5$ and $|E| \geq 0.5$, The agent position is updated by:

$$\begin{cases} X(t+1) = \Delta X(t) - E|JX_{prey}(t) - X(t)| \\ \qquad J = 2(1 - r_5) \\ \qquad \Delta X(t) = X_{prey}(t) - X(t) \end{cases} \qquad (2)$$

where r_5 is a random number between $(0,1)$, $X(t)$ and $X(t+1)$ represent the current position and the next iteration position respectively.

Hard Besiege. When $r \geq 0.5$ and $|E| < 0.5$, The agent position is updated by:

$$X(t+1) = X_{prey}(t) - E|\Delta X(t)| \qquad (3)$$

where, the meaning of $\Delta X(t)$ is the same as the parameter in Eq. (2).

Soft Besiege with Progressive Rapid Dives. When $r < 0.5$ and $|E| \geq 0.5$, At this time, the agent position is updated by:

$$\begin{cases} Y = X_{prey}(t) - E|JX_{prey}(t) - X(t)| \\ \quad Z = Y + S \times Levy(D) \end{cases} \qquad (4)$$

where, J, $JX_{prey}(t)$ and $X(t)$ have the same meaning as parameters in Eq. (2), $S \in R_{1 \times D}$ is the random matrix between $(0, 1)$, $Levy$ is levy flight function.

$$X(t+1) = \begin{cases} Y, if \ F(Y) < F(X(t)) \\ Z, if \ F(Z) < F(X(t)) \end{cases} \qquad (5)$$

where, $F(X)$ is the fitness function. The other parameters in Eq. (5) are similar to Eq. (4).

Hard Besiege with Progressive Rapid Dives. When $r < 0.5$ and $|E| < 0.5$, at this time, Agent position is updated by:

$$\begin{cases} Y = X_{prey}(t) - E|JX_{prey}(t) - X_m(t)| \\ \quad Z = Y + S \times Levy(D) \end{cases} \qquad (6)$$

$$X(t+1) = \begin{cases} Y, if \ F(Y) < F(X(t)) \\ Z, if \ F(Z) < F(X(t)) \end{cases} \qquad (7)$$

in the formula, the parameters in Eq. (6) and (7) have the same meaning as Eq. (4) and (5). $X_m(t)$ is the average position of each dimension of the current population.

2.2 The Explosive Operation of Fireworks Algorithm

Fireworks algorithm is a novel meta heuristic algorithm proposed in 2010. It has been widely concerned by many scholars since it was proposed. Now it has been applied to clustering [17], privacy protection [18] and other practical applications.

Fireworks algorithm is inspired by the process of fireworks explosion. Its original "explosion" operation makes the algorithm have good exploitation ability. The explosion operation used in this paper is the same as in FWA [15].

3 Proposed Algorithm: DCFW-HHO

In this section, we will introduce the fireworks Harris algorithm based on dynamic competition mechanism, namely DCFW-HHO. First, we will propose a dynamic competition mechanism, which will perform different competition operations in different stages of the algorithm, so as to balance the exploitation and exploration of the algorithm.

3.1 Dynamic Competition Mechanism

In HHO algorithm, different exploitation methods will be performed according to the different escaping energy E. So, we set different competition modes based on resource recovery to adapt to the mechanism of HHO algorithm. In the competition mechanism, the population is divided into winner group and loser group. We make E_{group} equal to the average of $|E|$ for each individual of the population. When $E_{group} \geq 1$, the algorithm is still in the exploration stage. We use the 1-to-1 competition model, in which the individuals with lower adaptation value are divided into the winner group, and the others are divided into the loser group. The resources of the losers will be deprived and allocated to the winners. When $0.5 < E_{group} < 1$, the algorithm begins to enter the exploitation stage, at this time, the same competition mechanism as the previous stage is still adopted, but the difference is that the resources deprived by the loser have changed. These resources will be given to the best individual in the current population to speed up the exploitation ability of the algorithm for the optimal solution. When $E_{group} \leq 0.5$, the algorithm has entered the final stage, and the population position tends to be stable. Only the best individual in the current population will be assigned to the winner group, and the rest will be assigned to the loser group, resources of the losers will be deprived and allocated to the winner to enhance the exploitation of the global optimal solution. The framework of Dynamic Competition Mechanism is shown in Algorithm 1.

```
Algorithm 1 - Dynamic competition mechanism

if E_gounp ≥ 1 then
    for i = 1 to N/2 then
        Choose the winner from X_i and X_{N-i}
        Deprive the resources of loser to the winner
else if  0.5 < E_group < 1  then
        Choose the winner from X_i and X_{N-i}
        Deprive the resources of loser to the best individ-
ual
else if E_group ≤ 0.5 then
        Choose the best individual as the winner
        Deprive the resources of others to the best indi-
vidual
```

3.2 Fireworks Harris Hawk Algorithm based on Dynamic Competition Mechanism (DCFW-HHO)

In order to enhance the exploitation ability of HHO, we add dynamic competition mechanism at the end of HHO. Next, we will give the detailed process of the algorithm.

```
Algorithm 2 - Pseudo-code of DCFW-HHO algorithm

Initialize population of the hawks X_i, and calculate fix(X_i)
for t=1 to t_max do
    Calculate the fitness values of hawks
    Set X_prey as the location of rabbit (best location)
    for (each hawk(X_i)) do
        Update the escaping energy E
        if |E| ≥ 1 then
            Execute exploration stage using Eq.(1)
        else if |E| < 1 then
            if r ≥ 0.5 and |E| ≥ 0.5 then
                Execute soft besiege using Eq.(2)
            else if r ≥ 0.5 and |E| < 0.5 then
                Execute hard besiege using Eq.(3)
        else if r < 0.5 and |E| ≥ 0.5 then
                Execute soft besiege with progressive rap-
id dives using Eq.(5)
        else if r < 0.5 and |E| < 0.5 then
                Execute hard besiege with progressive rap-
id dives using Eq.(7)
            end if
        end if
    end for
    Execute dynamic competition Mechanism using Alg.2
end for
return best solution X_prey and its fitness values fit(X_prey)
```

In the exploration and exploitation phase, we keep the mechanism of basic HHO, the dynamic competition mechanism will appear after the end of the four kinds of plunder mechanism. The loser will be eliminated and replaced by a firework produced by the winner. When $E_{group} \geq 1$, there will be winners (N/2 in total), and each individual will produce a firework to replace the loser (As shown in Algorithm 2). How about when $0.5 < E_{group} < 1$, the best individual will produce N/2 fireworks to replace the loser. In above two cases, the amplitude of fireworks explosion will also be dynamically adjusted with the number of iterations, which is updated by:

$$A(t) = K * exp(-a\frac{iter}{maxiter}) \tag{8}$$

where K and a are the difference between the upper and lower bounds and initial value respectively. *iter* is the current iteration and *maxiter* is the predefined maximum number of the iteration. When $E_{group} \leq 0.5$, the best individual will produce N-1 fireworks to replace the whole population, in order to further exploit the most promising area at present, we need to adjust the explosion amplitude of fireworks so that can focus more on the current area. At this point, a in Eq. (8) will be adjusted to $5a$.

The flowchart of the DCFW-HHO algorithm is presented in Algorithm 2.

4 Experiment and Result

In order to verify the performance of DCFW-HHO, DCFW-HHO is compared with marine predator algorithm (MPA), whale optimization algorithm (WOA), lightning search algorithm (LSA), water cycle algorithm (WCA), FWA and HHO based on CEC2005 benchmark functions.

Table 1. The parameter settings of algorithms

Algorithm	Parameters
DCFW-HHO	Hawks numbers = 42 Const a = 30
FWA	Number of fireworks = 5 Total number of sparks = 50 Const a = 0.04, const b = 0.8 Maximum explosion amplitude = 40
HHO	Hawks numbers = 42
WOA	Whales number = 42 A variable decrease linearly from 2 to 0 (Default) A2 variable decreases linearly from 2 to 0 (Default)
LSA	Projectiles number = 42 Channel time = 10
MPA	Elites number = 42 Preys number = 42
WCA	Raindrops number = 42 Number of rivers = 8 Minimum distance between a river and sea = 1E−03

4.1 Benchmark Functions and Parameter Setting

All functions are selected form CEC2005 benchmark F1–F3 are unimodal functions, F7 and F14 are multi-modal functions. F15 and F21–F23 are Fixed-dimension functions. For convenience, these functions are relabeled F1–F10. Each of experiment was independently run 30 times and the number of iterations is 500 in MATLAB 2019a. The parameter settings of DCFW-HHO and other algorithms are shown in Table 1.

Table 2. Results of benchmark functions

FUN	Item	FW	HHO	MPA	WOA	LSA	WCA	DCFW-HHO
F1	Ave	9.88E−90	1.3E−101	4.39E−23	1.52E−80	3.60E−09	1.10E−14	**0**
	Best	5.1E−133	1.3E−111	2.62E−24	7.47E−17	7.47E−17	6.04E−21	**0**
	Std	5.26E−89	4.3E−101	4.47E−23	8.28E−80	1.48E−08	3.70E−14	**0**
F2	Ave	3.58E−43	1.33E−52	3.51E−13	3.63E−53	0.04843	2.84E−09	**2.81E−276**
	Best	8.48E−66	5.10E−58	3.85E−14	6.42E−60	9.81E−06	4.62E−12	**2.239E−313**
	Std	1.96E−42	3.48E−52	2.45E−13	1.19E−52	0.112168	4.65E−09	**0**
F3	Ave	1.22E−63	6.74E−79	1.83E−4	27622.4	68.1722	0.001219	**0**
	Best	9.5E−100	9.5E−108	6.68E−07	2438.25	12.3834	1.74E−05	**0**
	Std	6.68E−63	2.55E−78	4.45E−04	10254	35.099	0.001917	**0**
F4	Ave	1.30E−03	1.69E−04	1.09E−03	2.02E−03	0.027350	0.012805	**1.14E−04**
	Best	1.16E−04	1..30E−05	3.04E−04	1.54E−05	0.01216	0.004921	**1.46E−06**
	Std	1.30E−03	2.08E−04	5.56E−04	2.61E−03	7.67E−03	4.01E−03	**8.67E−05**
F5	Ave	8.88E−16	8.88E−16	1.22E−12	3.85E−15	2.88389	0.117869	**8.88E−16**
	Best	8.88E−16	8.88E−16	7.19E−14	8.88E−16	1.34042	2.64E−11	**8.88E−16**
	Std	0	0	7.25E−13	2.81E−15	0.83796	0.453929	**0**
F6	Ave	0.998005	1.06427	0.998005	2.70203	1.32751	**0.998004**	**0.998004**
	Best	**0.998004**	**0.998004**	**0.998004**	**0.998004**	**0.998004**	**0.998004**	**0.998004**
	Std	2.45E−06	0.252192	1.62E−7	2.8902	1.07983	9.22E−17	**1.98E−18**
F7	Ave	4.60E−04	4.21E−04	**3.07E−04**	8.15E−04	5.84E−04	3.69E−04	3.86E−04
	Best	3.15E−04	3.10E−04	**3.07E−04**	3.09E−04	3.07E−04	3.07E−04	3.09E−04
	Std	2.27E−04	3.09E−04	**8.53E−15**	5.30E−04	4.23E−04	2.32E−04	2.16E−04
F8	Ave	−10.1504	−5.71941	**−10.1532**	−8.77368	−7.54754	−8.63433	**−10.1532**
	Best	−10.1529	−10.138	**−10.1532**	−10.1526	**−10.1532**	**−10.1532**	**−10.1532**
	Std	2.90E−03	1.72613	6.05E−11	2.53463	3.13422	2.35964	**1.20E−15**
F9	Ave	−10.4002	−5.59269	**−10.4029**	−7.38462	−7.90151	−9.34675	**−10.4029**
	Best	−10.4028	−10.3896	**−10.4029**	−10.4025	**−10.4029**	**−10.4029**	**−10.4029**
	Std	1.80E−03	1.54735	4.80E−11	3.15558	3.40043	2.14851	**7.58E−16**
F10	Ave	−10.5341	−5.12741	**−10.5364**	−7.98994	−7.43648	−9.82164	**−10.5364**
	Best	−10.5363	−5.12846	**−10.5364**	−10.5363	**−10.5364**	**−10.5364**	**−10.5364**
	Std	2.07E−03	1.04E−03	5.11E−11	3.25577	3.67499	1.85346	**4.69E−14**
Number of best Ave		1	1	4	0	0	1	**9**

4.2 Numerical Experiment

The numerical test results are shown in Table 2. The best results are highlighted in bold. In the last line of the table, the number of times each algorithm gets the best average is counted.

4.3 Converging Curves of the Average Best Fitness

This section shows the average fitness value convergence curve of each algorithm, as shown in Fig. 1. As can be seen from the figure, DCFW-HHO is superior to other algorithms in performance, and its convergence speed is also significantly faster than other algorithms in many functions (F1, F2, F3, F5, F8, F9).

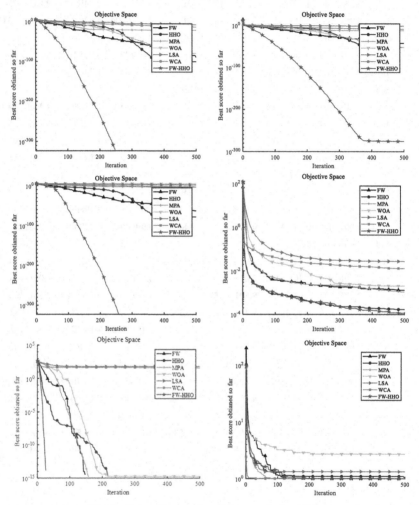

Fig. 1. Converging curves of the average best fitness

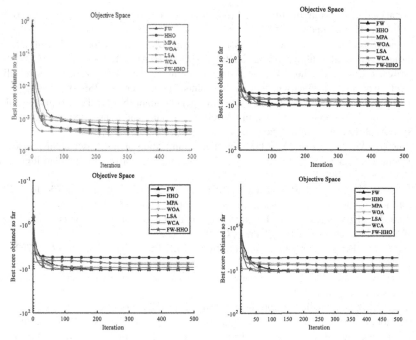

Fig. 1. (*continued*)

5 Conclusion

In this paper, a dynamic competition mechanism is proposed and combined with the explosion mechanism of fireworks algorithm, which is added into the HHO algorithm framework, namely DCFW-HHO, and effectively improves the exploitation ability of HHO. In the early stage of iteration, a relatively mild competition strategy is adopted to reallocate resources and improve the diversity of the algorithm. In the later stage of the algorithm, as the algorithm gradually tends to be stable, more cruel competition strategy is adopted. The test of 12 benchmark functions shows that DCFW-HHO has better performance and stability than FW, HHO, WPA, WOA, LSA, and WCA. In the future, this mechanism can be combined with more algorithms to improve the performance of the algorithm.

Acknowledgements. This research was funded in part by the National Natural Science Foundation of China under grant number 61801521 and 61971450, in part by the Natural Science Foundation of Hunan Province under grant number 2018JJ2533, and in part by the Fundamental Research Funds for the Central Universities under grant number 2018gczd014 and 20190038020050.

References

1. Dhiman, G., Kumar, V.: Spotted hyena optimizer: a novel bio-inspired based Metaheuristic technique for engineering applications. Adv. Eng. Softw. **114**, 48–70 (2017)

2. Bonabeau, E.: Swarm Intelligence: From Natural to Artificial Systems, vol. 1. Oxford University Press, London (1999)
3. Guijarro, F., Martínez-Gómez, M., Visbal-Cadavid, D.: A model for sector restructuring through genetic algorithm and inverse DEA. Expert Syst. Appl. **154**, Art. no. 113422 (2020)
4. Soares, L.C.R., Carvalho, M.A.M.: Biased random-key genetic algorithm for scheduling identical parallel machines with tooling constraints. Eur. J. Oper. Res. **285**(3), 955–964 (2020)
5. Yuan, S., Li, T., Wang, B.: A co-evolutionary genetic algorithm for the two-machine flow shop group scheduling problem with job-related blocking and transportation times. Expert Syst. Appl. **152**, Art. no. 113360 (2020)
6. Ding, H., Wang, Z., Guo, Y.: Multi-objective optimization of fiber laser cutting based on generalized regression neural network and non-dominated sorting genetic algorithm. Infr. Phys. Technol. **108**, Art. no. 103337 (2020)
7. Storn, R., Price, K.: Differential evolution—a simple and efficient heuristic for global optimization over continuous spaces. J. Global Optim. **11**(4), 341–359 (1997)
8. Koza, J.R., Koza, J.R.: Genetic Programming: On the Programming of Computers by Means of Natural Selection, vol. 1. MIT Press, Cambridge (1992)
9. Simon, D.: 'Biogeography-based optimization.' IEEE Trans. Evol. Comput. **12**(6), 702–713 (2008)
10. Beyer, H.-G., Schwefel, H.-P.: 'Evolution strategies—a comprehensive introduction.' Nat. Comput. **1**(1), 3–52 (2002)
11. Beni, G.: Swarm Intelligence, pp. 1–28. Springer, Heidelberg (2019)
12. Dorigo, M., Di Caro, G.: Ant colony optimization: a new metaheuristic. In: Proceedings of The 1999 Congress on Evolutionary Computation, vol. 2, pp. 1470–1477. IEEE (1999)
13. Heidari, A.A., Mirjalili, S., Faris, H., Aljarah, I., Mafarja, M., Chen, H.: Harris hawks optimization: algorithm and applications. Future Gener. Comput. Syst. **97**, 849–872 (2019)
14. Yang, X.S.: Engineering optimizations via nature-inspired virtual bee algorithms. In: Mira, J., Álvarez, J.R. (eds.) Artificial Intelligence and Knowledge Engineering Applications: A Bioinspired Approach. IWINAC 2005. LNCS, vol. 3562, pp. 317–323. Springer, Heidelberg (2005). https://doi.org/10.1007/11499305_33
15. Tan, Y., Zhu, Y.: Fireworks algorithm for optimization. In: Tan, Y., Shi, Y., Tan, K.C. (eds.) Advances in Swarm Intelligence. ICSI 2010. LNCS, vol. 6145, pp. 355–364. Springer, Heidelberg (2010). https://doi.org/10.1007/978-3-642-13495-1_44
16. Li, J., Tan, Y.: Loser-out tournament-based fireworks algorithm for multimodal function optimization. IEEE Trans. Evol. Comput. **22**, 679–691 (2018)
17. Yang, X., Tan, Y.: Sample index-based encoding for clustering using evolutionary computation. In: Tan, Y., Shi, Y., Coello, C.A.C. (eds.) Advances in Swarm Intelligence. ICSI 2014. LNCS, vol. 8794, pp. 489–498. Springer, Heidelberg (2014). https://doi.org/10.1007/978-3-319-11857-4_55
18. Rahmani, A., Amine, A., Hamou, R.M., Rahmani, M.E., Bouarara, H.A.: Privacy preserving through fireworks algorithm based model for image perturbation in big data. Int. J. Swarm Intell. Res. (IJSIR) **6**(3), 41–58 (2015)

Enhancing Fireworks Algorithm in Local Adaptation and Global Collaboration

Yifeng Li and Ying Tan[✉]

Key laboratory of Machine Perception (MOE), Department of Machine Intelligence,
School of Electronics Engineering and Computer Science, Peking University,
Beijing 100871, China
{liyifeng,ytan}@pku.edu.cn

Abstract. In order to improve the performance of fireworks algorithm, this paper carries out a comprehensive enhancement for its framework. Locally, the basic explosion operator is replaced by an efficient adaptation method in CMA-ES. Globally, the explosion range of all fireworks is effectively collaborated by search space partition. On the one hand, the proposed algorithm can quickly adapt to local landscape and improve the local exploitation efficiency significantly. On the other hand, it can collaborate the search ranges of multiple fireworks to form a seamless and non-overlapping partition of the search space, thereby ensuring the global search ability. Since the proposed framework evaluates one batch of a fixed large number of solutions in each iteration, it also achieves better computational efficiency in modern parallel hardware. The proposed algorithm is tested on the CEC 2020 benchmark functions with three different dimensions. The experimental results prove that those strategies improve fireworks algorithm significantly.

Keywords: Fireworks algorithm · Swarm intelligence · Optimization · Collaboration

1 Introduction

Modern optimization problem has changed drastically in recent years. On the one hand, more and more difficult objective functions have emerged in practical applications, which are usually multi-modal and high-dimensional. On the other hand, modern computing technologies, especially parallel technology, put forward new directions for the development of optimization algorithms.

The fireworks algorithm (FWA [12]) is a family of algorithms inspired by the phenomenon of firework explosion, which is very promising for solving such kind of problems effectively. During the optimization, each firework search a

This work is supported by the National Natural Science Foundation of China (Grant No. 62076010), and partially supported by Science and Technology Innovation 2030 - "New Generation Artificial Intelligence" Major Project (Grant Nos.: 2018AAA0102301 and 2018AAA0100302).

© Springer Nature Switzerland AG 2021
Y. Tan and Y. Shi (Eds.): ICSI 2021, LNCS 12689, pp. 451–465, 2021.
https://doi.org/10.1007/978-3-030-78743-1_41

local area by explosion. All fireworks collaborate their strategies for overall efficiency. Many variants of FWA have achieved competitive performance in standard benchmarks, such as EFWA [19], AFWA [7], dynFWA [18], GFWA [8] and LoTFWA [6]. FWA has also solved real-world problems like image processing [15], engineering [4] and resource scheduling [10].

However, in most variants of FWA, the efficiency of explosion operator based on uniform sampling is very limited. Their collaborative strategies also have little effect on the independent search of fireworks. At the same time, the parallel efficiency is obviously weakened by operators like mutation, because they requires an additional evaluation of a small batch of mutation sparks.

In this article, new strategies are proposed for both local explosion and global collaboration. For each firework, the basic explosion method is replaced by an adaptation strategy for a Gaussian distribution, which is able to fit the local landscape and target the extreme very fast. For global optimization, a collaboration method based on search space partition is proposed to arrange the search areas of fireworks, thus greatly reduce the probability of overlapping or omission. The restart strategy is also improved. Since all the evaluations in each iteration are done in one large batch, the proposed algorithm is also well adapted to large-scale parallel computing hardware.

The paper is organized as follows. It starts by introducing backgrounds in Sect. 2. In Sect. 3, the proposed strategies are described in detail. In Sect. 4, the proposed algorithm is evaluated and compared on benchmark problems. Finally, the proposed algorithm is discussed and analyzed in Sect. 4 and concluded in Sect. 5.

2   Backgrounds

2.1   Problem Definition

In this paper, we consider the general bound-constrained optimization problem which targets to find the optimal solution x^*:

$$x^* = \arg \min_{x \in S} f(\mathbf{x}) \tag{1}$$

where $f : \mathbb{R}^d \to \mathbb{R}$ is an unknown objective function (also called fitness function). $S = \left\{ x \in \mathbb{R}^d : lb_i < x_i < ub_i \right\}$ is the feasible space of f.

Optimization algorithms (or optimizers) are applied to approximate the optimal x^* or its value $f(x^*)$ by iterating the process of ask and tell. Since we consider complex objective functions with high time cost, the termination condition is a specific number of evaluations. At the same time, in order to maximize the computational efficiency, we hope the algorithm always provide a fixed number of solutions in each batch. The actual size of batch should be determined by the parallel computing devices.

2.2 Fireworks Algorithms

Fireworks algorithm is a novel optimization framework that adopts multiple collaborative isomorphic subgroups. Among all the novel implementations of fireworks algorithm, LoTFWA [12] has achieved the most significant global optimization performance with extremely simple mechanisms. In LoTFWA, each firework optimize its local area by an uniform explosion within dynamic amplitudes. A guided mutation spark is generated for each firework to accelerate its local exploitation. Then, some unpromising fireworks are detected and restarted to avoid waste of resources.

There are two major weaknesses in LoTFWA which are improved in the proposed algorithm. First, the local search efficiency of the explosion operator and mutation operator is limited by a basic uniform trust region scheme. Second, the collaboration method is too weak because the restart mechanism is rarely triggered and it can only save limited resources rather than guide fireworks to cooperate.

2.3 Related Works

A great number of Evolutionary Algorithms (EAs) and Swarm Intelligence Optimization Algorithms (SIOAs) have been proposed for similar optimization problems, but their ideas are fundamentally different from the proposed algorithm.

The idea of adopting multiple sub-populations for optimization is implemented in a large number of recent research of EAs and SIOAs. In most cases, different sub-populations evolve under different strategies in order to combine their advantages and obtain efficient hybrid algorithm. For example, EBOwith-CMAR [5] uses three sub-populations which apply Effective Butterfly Optimizer or Covariance Matrix Adapted Retreat method respectively, and achieved outstanding performance in the competition of CEC2017 [16]. Some optimizers use the same algorithm with different parameters in sub-populations. For example, BIPOP-CMA-ES [1] adopts multi-restart populations with different sizes. In IMODE [11], the winner of CEC2020 competition [17], different sub-populations with dynamic sizes evolve under different DE parameters. There are also many algorithms like SHADE [13] that utilizes archive strategy to collect an elite population in order to enhance the optimization efficiency.

The essential difference between those methods and the proposed algorithm is that we analytically defined the ranges of sub-populations according to the principle of search space partition. And the sub-populations are diversified and cooperated in different local areas instead of different strategies.

3 Proposed Strategies

The proposed algorithm is improved in both local exploitation and global collaboration. Locally, CMA-ES [3] is introduced to accelerate the optimization of each firework. Globally, the explosion distributions are collaborated to form a seamless and non-overlapping partition of the search space. The framework of the proposed algorithm is described in Algorithm 1.

Algorithm 1. Framework of Proposed Algorithm

Initialize each firework $\mathbf{X}_i$
while termination conditions are not satisfied **do**
    // 1. Adaptation
    for each firework $\mathbf{X}_i$ **do**
        generate λ_i sparks by explosion
    end for
    Gather and estimate all sparks
    for each firework $\mathbf{X}_i$ **do**
        update states of $\mathbf{X}_i$
    end for
    // 2. Restart
    Examine and restart fireworks
    // 3. Collaboration
    for each pair of fireworks $\mathbf{X}_i$ and $\mathbf{X}_j$ **do**
        Determine their collaborative search boundaries
    end for
    for each firework $\mathbf{X}_i$ **do**
        Fit search boundary towards the collaboration result
    end for
end while

3.1 Adaptation

In order to enhance the local optimization efficiency, the uniform explosion is replaced by a self-adaptive Gaussian distribution. With strategies introduced from CMA-ES [2], it is able to estimate the local fitness landscape and generate more effective sparks.

In the g-th generation, the k-th explosion spark $\mathbf{x}_k^{(g+1)}$ is generated from a Gaussian distribution:

$$\mathbf{x}_k^{(g+1)} \sim \mathbf{m}^{(g)} + \sigma^{(g)} \times \mathcal{N}(\mathbf{0}, C^{(g)}) \qquad (2)$$

where $\mathbf{m}$ and C is the mean and co-variance matrix. $\sigma^{(g)}$ is the overall step size. In the proposed algorithm, each firework generate the same number of λ sparks.

After evaluation of all sparks $\mathbf{x}^{(g+1)}$, the explosion distribution is adapted according to the strategies in CMA-ES. The complete adaptation algorithm is provided in supplementary A. And a detailed explanation and parameter setting of CMA-ES can be found in [2].

3.2 Restart

Since the adaptation accelerates local optimization significantly, several conditions are proposed to ensure timely restart of fireworks that are not promising to improve the global optimal.

Three restart conditions are determined by the search status of the firework individual:

1. **Low Value Variance:** var $\left[f(x_{1:\lambda}^{(g+1)}) \right] \leq \epsilon_v$
2. **Low Position Variance:** $\sigma^{(g+1)} \times \left\| C^{(g+1)} \right\| \leq \epsilon_p$
3. **Not improving:** Not improved for $I_{max\_not\_improve}$ iterations.

One more restart condition is determined by the relationship between fireworks:

1. **Covered by Better:** More than 85% of the firework's sparks are covered by a better firework's explosion range.

3.3 Collaboration

The explosion boundary of a firework X with parameters $(\mathbf{m}, C, \sigma)$ is defined as:

$$\left\{ \mathbf{x} \middle| \left\| C^{-\frac{1}{2}} (\frac{\mathbf{x} - \mathbf{m}}{\sigma}) \right\| = E \left\| \mathcal{N}(\mathbf{0}, \mathbf{I}) \right\| \right\} \tag{3}$$

Obviously, it is a elliptical shell and covers the majority of X's explosion sparks. The proposed strategy is designed according to two core ideas:

1. The explosion scopes tends to form a segmentation within the global optimization area.
2. The better fireworks tend to search independently, and the worse fireworks tend to search collaboratively.

The first idea is helpful to avoid overlapping or omission of search scopes, so the overall efficiency of fireworks can be improved in collaboration. The second idea ensures the local optimization of leading fireworks will not be severely affected by collaboration. Based on these ideas, the proposed algorithm conducts collaboration by the following steps:

a) Compare Fireworks. A fuzzy comparison between each pair of fireworks is introduced to estimate their relative optimization progress, which is described in Algorithm 2.

b) Compute Dividing Points. The dividing point for each pair of fireworks is obtained, which specifies where the search range of both fireworks are divided. Figure 1 gives examples of the collaboration method in 4 possible situations.
The following steps are conducted to calculate the dividing point:

1. Calculate the distance d_{ij} between X_i and X_j
2. Calculate the radius $r_{ij} = |X_i A_i|$ and $r_{ji} = |X_j A_j|$ on line $X_i X_j$
3. Determine the situation (See Fig. 1) according to r_{ij}, r_{ji} and d_{ij}
4. Calculate the position of A_i and A_j
5. If the optimization of X_i is ahead of X_j, A_i is the dividing point. If X_j is ahead of X_i, A_j is the dividing point. Otherwise, the midpoint B of $A_i A_j$ is the dividing point.

Algorithm 2. Fuzzy Comparison of Fireworks

Require: Fireworks $\mathbf{X}_i$ and $\mathbf{X}_j$ with sparks $\mathbf{x}_{i,1:\lambda}^{(g+1)}$ and $\mathbf{x}_{j,1:\lambda}^{(g+1)}$ (if not restarted)
  if Both $\mathbf{X}_i$ and $\mathbf{X}_j$ are just restarted **then**
   return $\mathbf{X}_i$ and $\mathbf{X}_j$ are similar
  end if
  if $\mathbf{X}_i$ is restarted **then**
   return $\mathbf{X}_j$ is ahead of $\mathbf{X}_i$
  end if
  ... #vice versa
  if $\min \mathbf{x}_{i,1:\lambda}^{(g+1)} > \max \mathbf{x}_{j,1:\lambda}^{(g+1)}$ **then**
   return $\mathbf{X}_j$ is ahead of $\mathbf{X}_i$
  end if
  ... #vice versa
  return X_i and X_j are similar

Before fitting the boundary to obtained dividing points of X_i, two additional operations are required. First, only the closest N (the dimension of objective function) dividing points are kept, so the collaboration is conducted locally. Second, the distance of X_i to its dividing points with X_j is clipped within $[0.5r_{ij}, 2r_{ij}]$, so there won't be too drastic changes after collaboration.

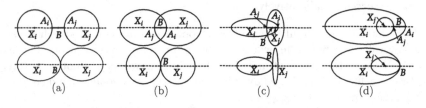

Fig. 1. Four cases of collaboration between two fireworks. A_i and A_j are the closer intersections of line X_iX_j with their boundaries. The actual dividing point could be any point on A_iA_j. The second row shows the collaboration results when taking the midpoint B of A_iA_j as dividing point.

c) Fit Dividing Points. The boundary of firework $X(\mathbf{m}, C, \sigma)$ is adapted to fit its dividing points. For each dividing point P_k, a new covariance matrix C_k is calculated. On the direction of XP_k, P_k lies right on the boundary. On the conjugate directions, the radius of boundary is not changed. The mathematical calculation for fitting a single split point is given in the Appendix B. The mean of all adapted covariance matrix $\frac{1}{K}\sum_{k=1}^{K} C_k$ is taken as the overall collaborated results of X.

Algorithm 3 outlines the framework of the proposed collaboration strategy:

Algorithm 3. Framework of Fireworks Collaboration

Require: n fireworks X_i and parameters $(\mathbf{m}_i, \mathbf{C}_i, \sigma_i)$ in N dimensional feasible space
Ensure: Collaborated parameters of fireworks
    for each pair of fireworks X_i and X_j **do**
        Compare the progress of X_i and X_j
        Calculate $d_{ij} = |X_iX_j|$, expected sample distance r_{ij} and r_{ji} on X_iX_j
        Calculate the dividing point $P_{ij}\ (= P_{ji})$
    end for
    for each firework X_i **do**
        Gather $K = \min(N, n - 1)$ closest dividing points $P_{i,j_{1:K}}$
        Clip the length of $X_iP_{ij_k}$ within $[0.5r_{ij_k}, 2r_{ij_k}]$
        for $k \leftarrow 1 : K$ **do**
            Fit P_{ij_k} on the boundary of X_i and obtain $\mathbf{C}_{ij_k}$
        end for
        $\mathbf{C}_i \leftarrow \frac{1}{K}\sum_{k=1}^{K}\mathbf{C}_{ij_k}$
    end for

3.4 Experiments

The performance of proposed algorithm is tested on objective functions from the CEC 2020 benchmark test suit [17]. According to the settings of the bound-constrained single-objective optimization competition, each function is tested for 30 repetitions with 10, 15, 20 dimensions. The termination condition is a maximum of 1,000,000, 3,000,000 or 10,000,000 evaluations for 10, 15 or 20 dimensions, respectively.

For the generalization ability of the proposed strategies, there is few additional parameters introduced. In the restart conditions, ϵ_v and ϵ_p are both $1E-6$, and the maximum number of unimproved iteration $I_{max\_unimprove}$ is 20. Its basic settings are the same as LoTFWA, which includes 5 fireworks and 300 sparks in each iteration. The parameters of local adaption is also set to be the same as CMA-ES. As we can see, there is no parameter selection according to the target problems.

In order to prove the effectiveness of our proposed strategies, the proposed algorithm is compared with two baselines. LoTFWA is the most efficient one of the main variants of the firework algorithm. CMAFWA is a compromise between LoTFWA and the proposed algorithm, whose fireworks use the local search strategy of CMA-ES but are collaborated by the loser-out tournament strategies from LoTFWA.

The statistical test results of the three algorithms are shown in the Table 1, Table 2 and Table 4 for 10, 15 and 20 respectively. Their fitness curves are shown in supplementary C.

As can be seen from the experimental results, the proposed algorithm outperforms LoTFWA significantly on all objective functions. CMAFWA improves on uni-modal (1), basic functions (2, 3, 4) and hybrid functions (5, 6, 7) compared with LoTFWA, but becomes worse in complex functions (8, 9, 10) due to ineffective collaboration. The proposed algorithm is overall better than CMAFWA,

Table 1. Wilcoxon signed-rank test on 10D problems. ($\alpha = 0.05$. Statistical test is conducted against the proposed method. '+' means the proposed method is significantly better. '−' means the proposed method is significantly worse. '=' means the two algorithm performs similarly.)

F.	LoTFWA			CMAFWA			Proposed	
	Mean	Std		Mean	Std		Mean	Std
1	9.123E+05	2.579E+05	+	0.000E+00	0.000E+00	=	0.000E+00	0.000E−00
2	3.947E+02	2.131E+02	+	2.558E+01	3.445E+01	−	1.427E+02	1.606E+02
3	3.629E+01	7.296E+00	+	1.147E+01	6.350E−01	−	1.295E+01	3.144E+00
4	3.456E+00	6.189E−01	+	6.900E−01	1.427E−01	+	0.000E+00	0.000E+00
5	8.592E+03	7.521E+03	+	2.227E+02	1.166E+02	+	3.110E+01	1.643E+01
6	1.367E+02	4.205E+01	+	8.365E−01	3.917E−01	=	7.231E−01	4.031E−01
7	4.532E+03	4.710E+03	+	7.656E+00	2.204E+01	=	5.257E+00	6.804E+00
8	9.747E+01	2.689E+01	+	2.240E+02	3.200E+01	+	9.507E+01	1.845E+01
9	3.022E+02	8.871E+01	+	3.305E+02	9.224E−01	+	1.616E+02	8.019E+01
10	4.140E+02	2.155E+01	+	4.313E+02	2.004E+01	+	3.978E+02	1.015E−01
Rank	2.60			2.00			1.20	

Table 2. Wilcoxon signed-rank test on 15D problems. ($\alpha = 0.05$)

F.	LoTFWA			CMAFWA			Proposed	
	Mean	Std		Mean	Std		Mean	Std
1	1.444e+06	2.522e+05	+	0.000e+00	0.000e+00	=	0.000e+00	0.000e−00
2	1.095e+03	3.681e+02	+	8.932e+01	5.050e+01	−	9.387e+02	4.298e+02
3	5.343e+01	5.794e+00	+	1.652e+01	2.682e−01	−	3.617e+01	1.679e+01
4	7.060e+00	1.108e+00	+	7.677e−01	1.449e−01	+	6.257e−01	3.998e−01
5	1.060e+05	8.527e+04	+	2.967e+02	1.062e+02	+	1.217e+02	3.851e+01
6	3.769e+02	9.960e+01	+	7.248e−01	1.722e−01	−	4.624e+01	2.497e+01
7	5.507e+04	3.426e+04	+	1.982e+00	9.683e−01	−	3.834e+01	4.806e+01
8	1.103e+02	5.193e−01	+	2.298e+02	1.095e+01	+	1.000e+02	1.666e−07
9	3.099e+02	1.458e+02	+	3.905e+02	2.175e−01	+	1.583e+02	7.640e+01
10	4.385e+02	7.625e+01	+	5.228e+02	8.684e+01	+	4.000e+02	4.451e−07
Rank	2.60			1.80			1.40	

especially on composition functions (8, 9 and 10) and problems that have relatively simple local landscape (4, 5). But it failed to improve on problems with a large number of local areas with insignificant overall trend (2, 3) or related hybrid problems when the dimension becomes large. The most possible reason could be that the limited number of fireworks are not able to form an effective partition of the huge search space when dimension grows. On the other hand, linking the ranges of limited local search sometimes might leads to inefficient local exploitation (Table 3).

Table 3. Wilcoxon signed-rank test on 20D problems. ($\alpha = 0.05$)

F.	LoTFWA			CMAFWA			Proposed	
	Mean	Std		Mean	Std		Mean	Std
1	1.798e+06	4.388e+05	+	0.000e+00	0.000e+00	=	0.000e+00	0.000e-00
2	1.454e+03	3.986e+02	+	5.772e+01	1.833e+01	−	4.299e+02	1.681e+02
3	6.751e+01	1.126e+01	+	2.316e+01	5.063e−01	−	6.181e+01	2.962e+01
4	1.017e+01	1.274e+00	+	1.985e+00	1.113e−01	+	1.867e+00	6.521e-01
5	2.564e+05	1.808e+05	+	7.899e+02	1.829e+02	+	1.891e+02	4.939e+01
6	5.239e+02	1.968e+02	+	1.947e+00	2.190e+01	−	1.594e+02	5.865e+01
7	9.663e+04	6.730e+04	+	5.185e+00	3.104e+00	−	1.005e+02	4.884e+01
8	1.001e+02	1.945e+01	=	2.694e+02	1.855e+01	+	1.000e+02	2.272e-07
9	4.446e+02	1.994e+01	+	4.005e+02	1.476e+00	+	2.112e+02	9.651e+01
10	4.255e+02	1.695e+01	+	4.063e+02	4.547e−13	+	4.024e+02	5.840e+00
Rank	2.70			1.50			1.40	

The proposed algorithm is also compared with LoTFWA, IPOP-CMA-ES [9] and LSHADE [14], which have been the most famous EA or SIOA in recent years, in the Table 1 on CEC 2020 benchmark test suits with 20 dimensions. The proposed algorithm outperforms LoTFWA and IPOP-CMA-ES in all problems. It achieved better performance on composition functions but is not as good as LSHADE on basic functions and hybrid functions of CEC 2020 test suits.

Table 4. Comparison with classic algorithms on 20D problems of CEC 2020

F.	LoTFWA		IPOP-CMA-ES		LSHADE		Proposed	
	Mean	Std	Mean	Std	Mean	Std	Mean	Std
1	1.80e+06	4.39e+05	0.00e+00	0.00e+00	0.00e+00	0.00e+00	0.00e+00	0.00e−00
2	1.45e+03	3.99e+02	2.16e+03	2.41e+01	2.39e+00	1.38e+00	4.30e+02	1.68e+02
3	6.75e+01	1.13e+01	5.43e+01	7.97e+00	2.08e+01	5.23e−01	6.18e+01	2.96e+01
4	1.02e+01	1.27e+00	2.32e+00	2.78e−01	4.70e−01	4.66e−02	1.87e+00	6.52e−01
5	2.56e+05	1.81e+05	1.23e+03	2.83e+02	5.51e+01	6.01e+01	1.89e+02	4.94e+01
6	5.24e+02	1.97e+02	4.91e+02	2.19e+00	3.48e−01	8.05e−02	1.59e+02	5.87e+01
7	9.66e+04	6.73e+04	7.18e+02	2.10e+02	8.13e−01	1.33e−01	1.00e+02	4.88e+01
8	1.00e+02	1.95e+01	2.48e+03	1.85e+02	1.00e+02	1.00e−03	1.00e+02	2.27e−07
9	4.45e+02	1.99e+01	4.32e+02	1.48e+00	4.03e+02	1.06e+00	2.11e+02	9.65e+01
10	4.26e+02	1.70e+01	4.30e+02	4.55e−01	4.14e+02	1.47e−02	4.02e+02	5.84e+00
Rank	3.7		3.0		1.2		1.7	

There are also some highly efficient variants of classic algorithms in the CEC 2020 bound-constrained single-objective competition. The proposed algorithm has certain advantages in the competition, especially on composition functions.

But it is still insufficient to compete with the best algorithms. We do not compare with these algorithms for several reasons: a) Many of them improve their performance based on too delicate strategies and tricks, like applying additional optimizer in certain stage of optimization. b) Almost all of them applied dynamic population size, which violates our assumption on parallel computing devices. c) Most of them are designed and fine-tuned for the specific problems of CEC 2020 instead of general problems.

4   Discussions

The collaboration strategy plays an important role for the proposed algorithm in two ways.

Globally, the collaboration strategy tends to link the explosion ranges of separated fireworks. Therefore, fireworks naturally fill their vacancy even when searching in the same direction. It also help the poor fireworks to expand their search ranges and get closer to the better fireworks.

Locally, the collaboration strategy helps to avoid overlapping explosion ranges of different fireworks. Even when multiple fireworks fall into a same convex area, they tends to form a segmentation of the local area and search together, instead of overlapping and conduct similar searches independently.

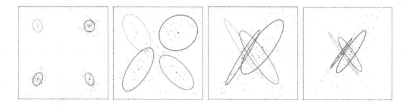

Fig. 2. A simple example of the collaboration of 4 fireworks.

Figure 2 gives a simple example of the collaboration of 4 fireworks in a single-modal problem. In the early stage of optimization, the explosion ranges expand and connect each other quickly. While in the later stage, four explosion ranges collaboratively search around the optimal, just like a single Gaussian distribution with larger population size.

5   Conclusion

This paper proposed a novel fireworks algorithm which is enhanced in both local adaptation and global collaboration. The uniform explosion method is replaced by a self-adaptive Gaussian distribution with strategy introduced from CMA-ES. The fireworks are effectively collaborated by the idea of search space partition.

The experimental results show that the proposed algorithm has better performance compared to former FWA variants.

The proposed algorithm is developed based on a theoretical thinking of firework algorithm. There are still plenty of details could be improved. For example, the balancing between local adaptation and global collaboration is extremely valuable for an in-depth study.

Appendix

A. Covariance Matrix Adaption

The local adaption of firework is done independently by the strategies from CMA-ES.

For firework X with parameters $(\mathbf{m}^{(g)}, C^{(g)}, \sigma^{(g)})$ and explosion sparks $\mathbf{x}_{1:\lambda}^{(g+1)}$. First, a recombination weight $\mathbf{w}$ is applied to μ best sparks for updating the mean:

$$\mathbf{m}^{(g+1)} = \mathbf{m}^{(g)} + c_m \sum_{i=1}^{\mu} w_i (\mathbf{x}_i^{(g+1)} - \mathbf{m}^{(g)}) \tag{4}$$

where c_m is the learning rate. $w_i \geq 0$ and $\sum w_i = 1$.

For the adaption of covariance matrix, a combined rank-μ update and rank-one update is applied in CMA-ES:

$$C^{(g+1)} = (1 - c_1 - c_\mu \sum w_j) C^{(g)}$$
$$+ c_\mu \sum_{i=1}^{\lambda} w_i \mathbf{y}_i^{(g+1)} (\mathbf{y}_i^{(g+1)})^T \tag{5}$$
$$+ c_1 \mathbf{p}_c^{(g+1)} (\mathbf{p}_c^{(g+1)})^T$$

where

- c_1 and c_μ are learning rates.
- $\mathbf{y}_i^{(g+1)} = (\mathbf{x}_i^{(g+1)} - \mathbf{m}^{(g)})/\sigma^{(g)}$.
- $\mathbf{p}_c^{(g+1)}$ is the evolution path, which is intiallized as $\mathbf{0}$ and updated by Eq. 6

$$\mathbf{p}_c^{(g+1)} = (1 - c_c) \mathbf{p}_c^{(g)} + \sqrt{c_c (2 - c_c) \mu_{\text{eff}}} \frac{\mathbf{m}^{(g+1)} - \mathbf{m}^{(g)}}{\sigma^{(g)}} \tag{6}$$

For the adaptation of scale σ, a conjugate evolution path $\mathbf{p}_\sigma^{(g)}$ is initialized as $\mathbf{0}$ and updated in each iteration:

$$\mathbf{p}_\sigma^{(g+1)} = (1 - c_\sigma) \mathbf{p}_\sigma^{(g)} + \sqrt{c_\sigma (2 - c_\sigma) \mu_{\text{eff}}} C^{(g)-\frac{1}{2}} \frac{\mathbf{m}^{(g+1)} - \mathbf{m}^{(g)}}{\sigma^{(g)}} \tag{7}$$

In general CMA-ES, the rank-1 update plays a significant role in rapidly moving towards a better local position at the initial stage of search. However, we'd like the firework to focus more around its initial position. According to experiments, the proposed algorithm performs much better without rank-1 update, that is:

$$C^{(g+1)} = (1 - c_\mu \sum w_j) C^{(g)} + c_\mu \sum_{i=1}^{\lambda} w_i \mathbf{y}_i^{(g+1)} (\mathbf{y}_i^{(g+1)})^T \tag{8}$$

Finally, the scale $\sigma^{(g+1)}$ is updated by comparing the length of $\|\mathbf{p}_\sigma^{(g+1)}\|$ with its expected length $E \|\mathcal{N}(\mathbf{0}, \mathbf{I})\|$:

$$\ln \sigma^{(g+1)} = \ln \sigma^{(g)} + \frac{c_\sigma}{d_\sigma} \left(\frac{\|\mathbf{p}_\sigma^{(g+1)}\|}{E \|\mathcal{N}(\mathbf{0}, \mathbf{I})\|} \right) \tag{9}$$

B. Fitting Single Dividing Point

Here, we fit a diving point $\mathbf{x}$ on the boundary (defined in Eq. 3) of a Gaussian distribution $\mathcal{N}(\mathbf{m}, C)$ and overall sample scale σ.

First, a linear transformation $f(\mathbf{x}) = C^{-\frac{1}{2}} (\mathbf{x} - \mathbf{m})/\sigma$ is conducted to the entire space, so the normal distribution is transformed to $\mathcal{N}(\mathbf{0}, I)$. Assume diving point $\mathbf{x}$ is projected to $\mathbf{z}$.

In the transformed space, the boundary should only be changed on the direction of $\mathbf{z}$. So we can assume the adapted covariance matrix C_x in the transformed space is $aI + b\mathbf{z}\mathbf{z}^T$.

Extend $\mathbf{z}$ into a set of linear bases $B = \{\mathbf{z}, \mathbf{z}_1, ..., \mathbf{z}_{N-1}\}$. Assume all $\mathbf{z}_i$ is on the boundary of $\mathcal{N}(\mathbf{0}, I)$. Since the sample distance on the conjugate directions of $\mathbf{z}$ should not be changed for C and C_x, they are also on the boundary of $\mathcal{N}(\mathbf{0}, aI + b\mathbf{z}\mathbf{z}^T)$. So we have:

$$\left\| (aI + b\mathbf{z}\mathbf{z}^T)^{-\frac{1}{2}} \mathbf{y} \right\| = E \|\mathcal{N}(\mathbf{0}, \mathbf{I})\|, \forall \mathbf{y} \in B \tag{10}$$

Let $d = E \|\mathcal{N}(\mathbf{0}, \mathbf{I})\|$, it is equivalent to:

$$\mathbf{y}^T (aI + b\mathbf{z}\mathbf{z}^T)^{-1} \mathbf{y} = d^2, \forall \mathbf{y} \in B \tag{11}$$

According to the Woodbury Matrix Identity (Eq. 13), the equations can be solved to obtain a and b.

$$(A + UCV)^{-1} = A^{-1} - A^{-1} U (C^{-1} + VA^{-1}U)^{-1} VA^{-1} \tag{12}$$

Finally, the adapted matrix in original space is :

$$\begin{aligned} C_x &= C^{\frac{1}{2}} \left(aI + b\mathbf{z}\mathbf{z}^T \right) C^{\frac{1}{2}} \\ &= aC + b(\mathbf{x} - \mathbf{m})(\mathbf{x} - \mathbf{m})^T / \sigma^2 \end{aligned} \tag{13}$$

C. Fitness Curves

Here we provide the fitness curves of LoTFWA, CMAFWA and the proposed algorithm on the CEC 2020 benchmark problems (Fig. 3).

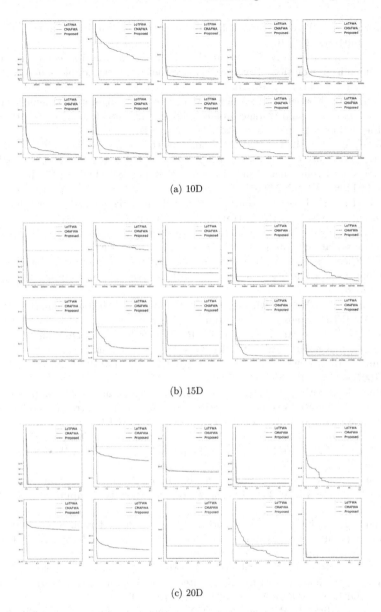

(a) 10D

(b) 15D

(c) 20D

Fig. 3. Fitness curves on CEC2020 problems.

References

1. Hansen, N.: Benchmarking a BI-population CMA-ES on the BBOB-2009 function testbed. In: Proceedings of the 11th Annual Conference Companion on Genetic and Evolutionary Computation Conference: Late Breaking Papers, pp. 2389–2396 (2009)

2. Hansen, N.: The CMA evolution strategy: a tutorial. arXiv preprint arXiv:1604.00772 (2016)
3. Hansen, N., Müller, S.D., Koumoutsakos, P.: Reducing the time complexity of the derandomized evolution strategy with covariance matrix adaptation (CMA-ES). Evol. Comput. **11**(1), 1–18 (2003)
4. Imran, A.M., Kowsalya, M.: A new power system reconfiguration scheme for power loss minimization and voltage profile enhancement using fireworks algorithm. Int. J. Electr. Power Energy Syst. **62**, 312–322 (2014)
5. Kumar, A., Misra, R.K., Singh, D.: Improving the local search capability of effective butterfly optimizer using covariance matrix adapted retreat phase. In: 2017 IEEE Congress on Evolutionary Computation (CEC), pp. 1835–1842 (2017). https://doi.org/10.1109/CEC.2017.7969524
6. Li, J., Tan, Y.: Loser-out tournament-based fireworks algorithm for multimodal function optimization. IEEE Trans. Evol. Comput. **22**(5), 679–691 (2017)
7. Li, J., Zheng, S., Tan, Y.: Adaptive fireworks algorithm. In: 2014 IEEE Congress on evolutionary computation (CEC), pp. 3214–3221. IEEE (2014)
8. Li, J., Zheng, S., Tan, Y.: The effect of information utilization: introducing a novel guiding spark in the fireworks algorithm. IEEE Trans. Evol. Comput. **21**(1), 153–166 (2016)
9. Loshchilov, I.: CMA-ES with restarts for solving CEC 2013 benchmark problems. In: 2013 IEEE Congress on Evolutionary Computation, pp. 369–376. IEEE (2013)
10. Reddy, K.S., Panwar, L.K., Kumar, R., Panigrahi, B.K.: Distributed resource scheduling in smart grid with electric vehicle deployment using fireworks algorithm. J. Mod. Power Syst. Clean Energy **4**(2), 188–199 (2016). https://doi.org/10.1007/s40565-016-0195-6
11. Sallam, K.M., Elsayed, S.M., Chakrabortty, R.K., Ryan, M.J.: Improved multi-operator differential evolution algorithm for solving unconstrained problems. In: 2020 IEEE Congress on Evolutionary Computation (CEC), pp. 1–8. IEEE (2020)
12. Tan, Y., Zhu, Y.: Fireworks algorithm for optimization. In: Tan, Y., Shi, Y., Tan, K.C. (eds.) ICSI 2010. LNCS, vol. 6145, pp. 355–364. Springer, Heidelberg (2010). https://doi.org/10.1007/978-3-642-13495-1_44
13. Tanabe, R., Fukunaga, A.: Success-history based parameter adaptation for differential evolution. In: 2013 IEEE Congress on Evolutionary Computation, pp. 71–78. IEEE (2013)
14. Tanabe, R., Fukunaga, A.S.: Improving the search performance of shade using linear population size reduction. In: 2014 IEEE Congress on Evolutionary Computation (CEC), pp. 1658–1665. IEEE (2014)
15. Tuba, M., Bacanin, N., Alihodzic, A.: Multilevel image thresholding by fireworks algorithm. In: 2015 25th International Conference Radioelektronika (RADIOELEKTRONIKA), pp. 326–330. IEEE (2015)
16. Wu, G., Mallipeddi, R., Suganthan, P.N.: Problem definitions and evaluation criteria for the CEC 2017 competition on constrained real-parameter optimization. National University of Defense Technology, Changsha, Hunan, PR China and Kyungpook National University, Daegu, South Korea and Nanyang Technological University, Singapore, Technical report (2017)
17. Yue, C., et al.: Problem definitions and evaluation criteria for the CEC 2020 special session and competition on single objective bound constrained numerical optimization. Computational Intelligence Laboratory, Zhengzhou University, Zhengzhou China And Technical Report, Nanyang Technological University (2019)

18. Zheng, S., Janecek, A., Li, J., Tan, Y.: Dynamic search in fireworks algorithm. In: 2014 IEEE Congress on Evolutionary Computation (CEC), pp. 3222–3229. IEEE (2014)
19. Zheng, S., Janecek, A., Tan, Y.: Enhanced fireworks algorithm. In: 2013 IEEE Congress on Evolutionary Computation, pp. 2069–2077. IEEE (2013)

Brain Storm Optimization Algorithm

Multi-objective Brainstorming Optimization Algorithm Based on Adaptive Mutation Strategy

Yali Wu[1(✉)], Yulong Wang[1,2(✉)], and Xiaoxiao Quan[1,2]

[1] School of Automation and Information Engineering,
Xi'an University of Technology, Xi'an 710048, China
yliwu@xaut.edu.cn

[2] Shaanxi Province Key Laboratory of Complex System Control and Intelligent Information
Processing, Xi'an 710048, China

Abstract. Multi-objective Problems (MOP) is a classic combinatorial optimization problem. A brainstorming optimization algorithm based on multiple adaptive mutation methods in multiple regions of the population (DE_MOBSO) is proposed in this paper to solve the MOP. Firstly, the algorithm uses differential mutation to evolve the population, which can improve the diversity of population. Secondly, an adaptive mutation learning factor is introduced on the mutations to enhance the search efficiency of the algorithm considering the characteristics of the MOP. The effectiveness and practicability of the algorithm are verified by a set of simulation example. The results show that the proposed algorithm has better performance in solving large-scale MOP.

Keywords: Brainstorming optimization algorithm · Adaptive · Clustering · Multi-group crossover

1 Introduction

Multi-objective optimization problem is a typical complex optimization problem, which is focused on by many scholars and experts. Multi-objective optimization problems have been applied in our daily life and engineering production. In the path planning problem, it is necessary to consider the shortest driving distance and the minimum number of vehicle arrangements [1]. In machine learning, the minimization of learning error and the lowest computational complexity should be considered in the supervised learning problem [2]. With the continuous development of intelligent optimization algorithms, multi-objective optimization problems have gradually developed in the direction of multi-modality, large-scale, high-dimensionality, etc. How to use efficient intelligence

Shaanxi Key R&D Program "Research and Application of Intelligent Service Platform for Complex Heavy Equipment Based on Industrial Internet", project number: 2020ZDLGR07-06; National Key R&D Program of the Ministry of Science and Technology: "R&D of a Network Collaborative Manufacturing Platform for Customized Manufacturing of Complex Heavy Equipment" 2018YFB1703000.

Y. Tan and Y. Shi (Eds.): ICSI 2021, LNCS 12689, pp. 469–478, 2021.
https://doi.org/10.1007/978-3-030-78743-1_42

optimizing algorithms to solve hot issues in daily life has become a major trend in the study of multi-objective problems.

For the common optimization problems, many optimization methods have been proposed. The weighted summation method was early proposed by Zaden [3], whose idea is to convert multi-objective optimization into single-objective optimization by assigning different weights to different objective functions, and then use single-objective solution ideas to obtain the optimal solution. Many intelligent optimization algorithms have been widely used in the field of multi-objective optimization due to their simple structure and powerful search capabilities [4]. Such as genetic algorithm (GA) [5], particle swarm optimization algorithm (PSO) [6], brainstorm optimization algorithm (BSO) [7],differential evolution algorithm (DE), etc. Through learning good way from the parents, the mutation and selection parameters were been made to adaptively change by Zhang [8]. Besides, the disturbance threshold is added to the algorithm, which expands the search range of the algorithm. The combination of PSO algorithm and greedy random adaptive search strategy was proposed by Marinakis [9], which enhances the search ability of the algorithm. The algorithm's clustering target was changed from the decision space to the target space by Xue [10], who also introduced an elite strategy to speed up the convergence speed of the algorithm. An improved algorithm based on multi-objective BSO, which replaced the original kemans clustering in the BSO algorithm with DBSCAN clustering and replaced the original Gaussian mutation with differential mutation to make the algorithm's convergence accuracy and convergence speed be improved, was proposed by Xie [11].

The above-mentioned improved algorithms, to a certain extent, have improved the optimization ability of multi-objective problems. But when solving some specific problems, there are still the phenomenon of low convergence efficiency and easy to fall into local optimum. For this reason, a hybrid algorithm DE_MOBSO based on the combination of differential evolution algorithm and brainstorming optimization algorithm is proposed in this paper. The idea of differential vector is introduced into BSO, which speeds up the search efficiency of the algorithm. According to the different stages of the iterative evolution of the algorithm, the learning factor is adaptively changed, which enhances the learning efficiency of the algorithm and achieves a balance between the convergence and diversity of the algorithm. And the effectiveness of the algorithm is verified by different target types of related test functions.

The arrangement of other sections of this article is as follows: Some basic knowledge of multi-objective optimization problems is introduced in Sect. 2, such as BSO algorithm. In the third section, a detailed introduction of the proposed DE_MOBSO algorithm is given. In the fourth section, the DE_MOBSO algorithm and other optimization algorithms are tested experimentally, and the experimental results are discussed and analyzed. Finally, the conclusion and future development direction of the algorithm are given in the fifth section.

2   The Basic Problem Description

2.1   Multi-objective Optimization Problem

There are generally two types of solutions to multi-objective problems: traditional optimization algorithms and intelligent optimization algorithms.

Traditional optimization algorithms are generally deterministic algorithms and are usually aimed at structured problems, which usually has the best overall advantage. Its idea of solving multi-objective problems is relatively simple, whose core is to convert multi-objective problems into a single-objective problem through certain steps, solve the single-objective problem and get the optimal value. Intelligent optimization algorithms are mostly heuristic algorithms.

Most of them are based on random characteristics [12, 13]. Optimal solutions can be found through constant iterations, and the problems they deal with are more universal. Common intelligent optimization algorithms include genetic algorithm, particle swarm algorithm, and artificial fish swarms algorithm and brainstorming optimization algorithms [14], etc. There is no definite solution to the multi-objective problem. Every possible solution is a non-inferior solution. All the non-inferior solutions together form a set of non-inferior solutions, which is called the non-inferior frontier. So the performance of intelligent optimization algorithms is usually better than traditional optimization algorithms when solving the multi-objective optimization problem.

2.2   Brainstorming Optimization Algorithm

The Brainstorming Optimization Algorithm (BSO) is a new type of intelligent optimization algorithm inspired by human conferences. It was proposed by professor Shi Yuhui [15] at the second international swarm intelligence conference in 2011. The BSO algorithm uses clustering operations to find the local optimal, and then compares the local optimal to find the global optimal. Meanwhile, it strives to balance the exploration and development in the optimization process through the idea of aggregation and dispersion. BSO adopts way of mutation to enhance the diversity of the optimization individual, so the search results can jump out of the local optimal solution. The specific process is shown in Table 1:

Table 1.   The process of BSO

The process of BSO
Step1: Generate an initial population;
Step2: Calculate individual fitness values and cluster;
Step3: Discuss the population between groups;
Step4: Update population and cluster center;
Step5: Output the optimal individual if the maximum number of iterations is reached, otherwise go to **Step2**

3 Multi-objective Brainstorming Optimization Algorithm Based on Adaptive Mutation Strategy

The basic multi-objective brainstorming optimization algorithm is characterized by poor population diversity and being easy to fall into the local optimum. When the number of targets increases, the optimal result cannot be found in some function test sets. In order to solve these problems, in this paper, a new hybrid multi-objective optimization algorithm based on the combination of differential evolution algorithm and multi-objective brainstorming optimization algorithm (DE_MOBSO) is proposed.

3.1 Population Mutation

The mutation is an important operation of the optimization algorithm. Gaussian mutation method is usually adopted in the classical MOBSO algorithm during individual mutation. The specific method is as follows:

$$X_{new}^d = X_{select}^d + \xi(\mu, \sigma). \tag{1}$$

$$\xi = \log sig((IterationMax/2 - Iteration)/K)^* rand. \tag{2}$$

where X_{select}^d is the d-th dimension of the selected individual; X_{new}^d is the d-th dimension of the newly generated individual; $\zeta(\mu, \sigma)$ is the Gaussian variation function, and logsig is an S-type logarithmic transfer function.

The range of variation produced by Gaussian mutation is fixed and the information of the parent individuals is not fully utilized. Gaussian mutation includes the operation of S-type transfer function, random distribution generation and the four arithmetic operations, which makes this mutation method has high computational complexity [16]. Therefore, this paper adopts an individual mutation generation method based on differential evolution algorithm. After the parent population is clustered, the next generation population adopts a mutation strategy of different regions to select different methods, which effectively enhances individual diversity. The excellent information of the parent individual has also been fully utilized. The specific variation method is as follows:

$$n\_p = Clu1(p1) + w^*P1^*(Clu1(p2 - p3)) + (1 - w)^*P1^*(Clu1(p4 - p5)). \tag{3}$$

$$n\_p = Clu2(p1) + P1^*Clu2(p2 - p3). \tag{4}$$

$$n\_p = p\_best + w^*P1^*Clu3(p1 - p2) + (1 - w)^*P1^*Clu3(p3 - p4). \tag{5}$$

$$n\_p = Clu4(p1) + P1^*(Clu4(p1) - p\_best). \tag{6}$$

When n_p is the newly generated individual, Clui are the four cluster groups, p_best is the best individual in the parent population, P1 is the learning factor, w is the probability factor, pi are the different parent individuals in the cluster group.

The first quarter of the population adopts the mutation method of formula 5 to mutate, and the second quarter adopts the mutation method of formula 6 to mutate..., and so on, the whole population adopts 4 mutation methods. This mutation method effectively expands the diversity of the population, which is conducive to the newly mutated individuals to approach the optimal frontier.

3.2 Adaptation of Learning Factors

The DE_MOBSO algorithm proposed in this paper adopts a dynamic adaptive learning factor, and uses different learning factors according to the different evolutionary periods of the population. The specific adaptive transformation is as follows:

$$P1 = P1_{max} - (P1_{max} - P1_{min})^* \frac{Iter}{Iter_{max}}. \tag{7}$$

Where $P1_{max}$ is the maximum; $P1_{min}$ is the minimum values; Iter is the current iteration number; $Iter_{max}$ is the maximum iteration number.

In the early stage of the algorithm search, the value of P1 is larger and the algorithm learning ability is stronger. When the individual mutates, the information of the good parent can be quickly learnt and the convergence speed can be accelerated. In the later stage of the search, the value of P1 gradually decreases; the learning ability decreases, and the optimization of learning in nearby areas is enhanced.

4 Experiment

In order to test the proposed algorithm, in this paper, ZDT data set and DTLZ data set are used to verify the effectiveness of the algorithm in solving MOP and MaOP, and GD, SP, and DM are used to evaluate the diversity and convergence of the algorithm.

4.1 Testing Proplems

In order to verify the effectiveness of DE_MOBSO algorithm, the specific test functions selected in this paper are ZDT1–ZDT4 and ZDT6, and the decision space dimension is 30. They are used to verify algorithms' performance in the optimization of 2 objectives. In addition, the test functions DTLZ1–DTLZ7 are also selected to test the optimization performance of the algorithm in 3 objectives and 5 objectives.

4.2 Parameter Setting

This experiment was done on MATLAB R2017b with Inter Core i5-9400F CPU, 16 GB RAM, and Win10 operating system. For the sake of comparison, we let the difficulty coefficient of DTLZ1 be 5, the difficulty coefficient of DTLZ2–DTLZ6 10, and the difficulty coefficient of DTLZ7 20, and the other parameter settings are shown in Table 2:

Table 2. Parameter settings

P.1max	P.1min	P.2	w	Pop_Size
0.9	0.1	0.5	0.5	100

P.1 is the learning weight of individual variation mode, and P.2 is the selection probability of individual crossover mode, the number of Pop_Size is 100.

Three evaluation indicators GD, SP, and DM are used to verify the effectiveness of the algorithm in this paper. GD is used to evaluate the degree of approximation to the optimal frontier. The smaller the GD value, the better the convergence of the algorithm; SP is used to evaluate the uniformity of the algorithm, the smaller the SP, the better the uniformity of the optimal value found by the algorithm; DM is used to evaluate the breadth of the algorithm distribution, the larger the DM, the wider the optimal value is distributed in space, and the better the algorithm.

4.3 Experimental Results and Analysis

In order to reduce the randomness error of the test, the number of iterations of each algorithm is 100,000. Each algorithm test is run 30 times continuously, and finally the average value is taken as the evaluation result.

In order to verify the effectiveness of the proposed algorithm, in this paper, the DE_MOBSO algorithm is compared with other improved MOBSO algorithm. The MMBSO in literature [15] is an improved multi-objective brainstorming optimization algorithm.

Table 3 shows the GD, SP, and DM indicators of several algorithms in the ZDT test set. The results of bolding and darkening indicate the best performance in the algorithm comparison. It can be seen from Table 3 that for the problem of two objectives, in the five test sets of the ZDT, the DE_MOBSO algorithm shows good performance. For the test functions ZDT1–ZDT2 and ZDT6, from the perspective of convergence, the DE_MOBSO algorithm shows better performance. In the five types of test problems, the optimization rate has reached 100%. From the perspective of diversity, the optimization ability of DE_MOBSO algorithm has reached 100%. In the five test functions, the performance of DE_MOBSO is the best. From the perspective of the distribution of non-inferior solutions, the distribution of non-inferior solutions found by the MMBSO algorithm is even better. In general, although the breadth of optimization distribution of

Table 3. Two-objective experiment data

Test function	Evaluation index	ZDT1	ZDT2	ZDT3	ZDT4	ZDT5
DE_MOBSO	GD	**9.5078e−04**	**5.6983e−05**	**5.6252e−05**	**2.0653e−04**	**2.5000e−03**
	SP	**1.9000e−03**	**5.3109e−05**	**4.7000e−03**	**3.5000e−03**	**1.0400e−02**
	DM	4.4500e−02	3.2700e−02	2.5460e−01	**8.3270e−01**	**8.6400e−01**
MMBSO	GD	8.3000e−03	1.7900e−02	1.7500e−02	3.2400e−02	6.0400e−02
	SP	6.3000e−03	1.6800e−02	2.0100e−02	1.3900e−02	1.3190e−01
	DM	**5.2800e−02**	**5.9220e−01**	**9.4640e−01**	5.0770e−01	7.8180e−01

DE_MOBSO algorithm is not the best, it is still relatively strong in terms of the three indicators.

Table 4 and Table 5 shows the optimization capabilities of two algorithms in testing the DTLZ data set three objectives. It can be seen from Table 4 and Table 5 that from the perspective of convergence, DE_MOBSO's optimization capability is optimal, and from the perspective of diversity indicators, the DE_MOBSO's optimization capability is also better. It can be seen that as the number of objectives increases and the difficulty upgrades, the DE_MOBSO algorithm can jump out of the local optimum faster and improve the convergence speed and performance.

Table 4. Three-objective experiment data

Test function	Evaluation index	DTLZ1	DTLZ2	DTLZ3	DTLZ4
DE_MOBSO	GD	**6.2943e−03**	**5.0440e−04**	**4.6983e−04**	**2.7000e−03**
	SP	**2.0700e−02**	**8.2300e−02**	**6.6300e−02**	**7.9400e−02**
	DM	1.6610e−01	3.1640e−01	1.5200e−01	6.1600e−02
MMBSO	GD	4.1983e+00	2.2800e−02	3.0392e+01	1.9900e−02
	SP	2.8140e+00	9.8400e−02	2.3152e+01	1.0920e−01
	DM	**9.4000e−02**	**7.4780e−01**	**4.8700ev02**	**4.7880e−01**

In order to further verify the performance of the algorithm proposed in this paper, the DE_MOBSO algorithm is compared with other popular algorithms, MOBSO_G is a classical multi-objective brainstorming optimization algorithm based on Gaussian mutation [17], and the literature [18] SMOBSO is an adaptive multi-objective brainstorming optimization algorithm.

Table 5. Three-objective experiment data

Test function	Evaluation index	DTLZ5	DTLZ6	DTLZ7
DE_MOBSO	GD	**4.5533e−04**	4.8143e−06	**4.2900e−03**
	SP	**2.8700e−02**	2.7600e−02	**5.9400e−02**
	DM	2.0390e−01	1.0500e−01	2.4850e−01
MMBSO	GD	1.3100e−02	**9.1904e−07**	7.8000e−03
	SP	3.8000e−02	**8.7000e−03**	1.0820e−01
	DM	**6.3180e−01**	**8.6200e−01**	**8.9670e−01**

Table 6. Five-objective experiment data

Test function	Evaluation index	DE_MOBSO	MMBSO	MOBSO_G	SMOBSO
DTLZ1	GD	**1.7000e−03**	5.6483e+00	4.6387e+00	1.8400e−01
	SP	**3.2500e−02**	7.4311e+00	7.1213e+00	9.5100e−01
	DM	1.3540e−01	**9.7600e−01**	1.5540e−01	5.2220e−01
DTLZ2	GD	**6.7000e−03**	1.5570e−01	1.3670e−01	1.5190e−01
	SP	**2.1150e−01**	4.0620e−01	5.1490e−01	3.9330e−01
	DM	1.7370e−01	5.8150e−01	5.5960e−01	**5.8490e−01**
DTLZ3	GD	**3.5720e−03**	9.9109e+01	1.0371e+02	9.5012e+01
	SP	**8.3100e−01**	1.3610e+02	1.2093e+02	1.1880e+02
	DM	2.4290e−01	**2.9800e−01**	1.5180e−01	3.1800e−02
DTLZ4	GD	**9.7827e−04**	1.2470e−01	1.4320e−01	1.2340e−01
	SP	**1.2200e−01**	3.2150e−01	3.8060e−01	3.3270e−01
	DM	5.9700e−02	2.8220e−01	**4.8620e−01**	2.8180e−01
DTLZ5	GD	**2.9000e−03**	2.4600e−01	2.3750e−01	2.4140e−01
	SP	**7.9400e−02**	4.0170e−01	4.2100e−01	3.9560e−01
	DM	1.4940e−01	2.7530e−01	**2.9150e−01**	2.7610e−01
DTLZ6	GD	**1.4911e−06**	1.1752e+00	1.2668e+00	1.2049e+00
	SP	**6.0900e−02**	1.7395e+00	2.1211e+00	1.8324e+00
	DM	**7.4610e−01**	1.1360e−01	8.6600ev02	1.2600e−01
DTLZ7	GD	**7.2000e−03**	6.2730e−02	3.7440e−01	6.9300e−02
	SP	**1.5400e−02**	1.8470e−01	2.6460e−01	2.6220e−01
	DM	2.2040e−01	4.0180e−01	5.4040e−01	**6.9460e−01**

It can be seen from Table 6, with the gradual increase of the number of targets in the optimization problem, the advantages of DE_MOBSO algorithm gradually become obvious. It can be seen that DE_MOBSO has better performance. This also shows that the DE_MOBSO algorithm has stronger stability when dealing with optimization problems with different target numbers, and is more suitable for solving large-scale multi-objective problems.

On the whole, in various types of MaOP problems, DE_MOBSO has good processing performance. When it is compared with several other improved MOBSO algorithms, DE_MOBSO has better competitiveness. Especially for problems with a large number of targets, DE_MOBSO shows better performance Performance.

5 Conclusion

In this paper, Brain Storm Optimization Algorithm based on multiple adaptive mutation methods in multiple regions (DE_BSO) for MOP was proposed and was compared with other algorithms by testing on different scale experiences. The differential mutation is used to evolve the population to enhance convergence performance of DE_MOBSO. Taking the characteristics of the MOP into account, the adaptive mutation learning factor is used to enhance the information interactions capability and to prevent the algorithm from jumping into local optimum. The experimental results demonstrated that the DE_MOBSO generally performs better than others to solve accuracy for MOP and performs well enough for large-scale MOP. But there are still some problems that computation time is longer as the problem scale increases. So the direction of the next research is how to reduce computation time on solving large-scale.

References

1. Montoya-Torres, J.R., Faranco, J.L., Isaza, S.N., et al.: A literature review on the vehicle routing problem with multiple depots. Comput. Ind. Eng. **79**, 115–129 (2015)
2. Jin, Y., Sendhoff, B.: Pareto-based multibojective machine learning: an overview and case studies. IEEE Trans. Syst. Man Cybern. Part C **38**(3), 397–415 (2008)
3. Zadeh, L.: Optimality and non-scalar-valued performance criteria. IEEE Trans. Autom. Control **8**, 59–60 (1963)
4. He, D.H., Li, Y.X., Gong, W.Y., et al.: An adaptive differential evolution algorithm for constrained optimization problem. Acta Electron. Sin. **44**(10), 2535–2542 (2016)
5. Gao, Y., Shi, L., Yao, P.J.: Study on multi-objective genetic algorithm. In: Proceedings of the 3rd World Congress on Intelligent Control and Automation, pp. 646–650 (2000)
6. Cheng, R., Jin, Y.C.: A social learning particle swarm optimization algorithm for scalable optimization. Inf. Sci. **291**(C), 43–60 (2015)
7. Wu, Y.L., Jiao, S.B.: Brain Storm Optimization Algorithm Theory and Application. Science Press, Beijing (2017)
8. Zhang, Q., Zou, D.X., Geng, N., et al.: Adaptive differential evolution algorithm based on multiple mutation strategies. J. Comput. Appl. **38**(10), 2812–2821 (2018)
9. Wan, L.X., Xue, L.M., Mei, Q.A.,et al.: an enhanced differential evolution algorithm based on multiple mutation strategies. Comput. Intell. Neurosci. 285730 (2015)
10. Xue, J., Wu, Y., Shi, Y., Cheng, S.: Brain storm optimization algorithm for multi-objective optimization problems. In: Tan, Y., Shi, Y., Ji, Z. (eds.) ICSI 2012. LNCS, vol. 7331, pp. 513–519. Springer, Heidelberg (2012). https://doi.org/10.1007/978-3-642-30976-2_62

11. Xie, L., Wu, Y.: A modified multi-objective optimization based on brain storm optimization algorithm. In: Tan, Y., Shi, Y., Coello, C.A.C. (eds.) ICSI 2014. LNCS, vol. 8795, pp. 328–339. Springer, Cham (2014). https://doi.org/10.1007/978-3-319-11897-0_39
12. Shi, X.D.: Research on swarm intelligence algorithm based on particle swarm optimization and chicken swarm optimization. Ningxia University, Yinchuan (2018)
13. Lei, Y., Jiao, L.C., Gong, M.G., et al.: Improved NNIA algorithm for solving multi-objective examination timetable problem. J. Xidian Univ. **43**(2), 157–161 (2015)
14. Ma, X.M., Liu, N.: Adaptive visual field artificial fish school algorithm to solve the shortest path problem. J. Commun. **35**(01), 1–6 (2014)
15. Shi, Y.H.: Brain storm optimization algorithm. In: Tan, Y., Shi, Y., Chai, Y., Wang, G. (eds.) Advances in Swarm Intelligence. ICSI 2011. LNCS, vol. 6728, pp. 303–309. Springer, Heidelberg (2011). https://doi.org/10.1007/978-3-642-21515-5_36
16. Wang, R., Zhou, Z., Ishibuchi, H., et al.: Localized weighted sum method for many-objective optimization. IEEE Trans. Evol. Comput. **22**(1), 3–18 (2018)
17. Xie, C.W.: Multi-target Group Intelligent Optimization Algorithm. Beijing Institute of Technology Press, Beijing (2020)
18. Guo, X., Wu, Y., Xie, L., Cheng, S., Xin, J.: An adaptive brain storm optimization algorithm for multiobjective optimization problems. In: Tan, Y., Shi, Y., Buarque, F., Gelbukh, A., Das, S., Engelbrecht, A. (eds.) ICSI 2015. LNCS, vol. 9140, pp. 365–372. Springer, Cham (2015). https://doi.org/10.1007/978-3-319-20466-6_39

Brain Storm Optimization Algorithm Based on Formal Concept Analysis

Fengrong Chang[1], Lianbo Ma[1(✉)], Yan Song[2(✉)], and Aoshuang Dong[1]

[1] College of Software, Northeastern University, Shenyang, China
malb@swc.neu.edu.cn
[2] School of Physics, Liaoning University, Shenyang, China

Abstract. The brain storm optimization (BSO) algorithm is an excellent swarm intelligence paradigm, inspired from the behaviors of the human process of brainstorming. The design of BSO is characterized by the clustering mechanism. However, this mechanism is inefficient to deal with complex large-scale optimization problems. In this paper, we propose a high-dimensional BSO algorithm based on formal concept analysis (FCA), called HBSO, for dealing with large-scale optimization problems. In HBSO, two new procedures are developed, i.e., relationship analysis of individuals and adaptively determine the number of clusters. Relationship analysis is used to judge the similarity of individuals in the population. The FCA is used to determine the size of k in the original clustering algorithm, in order to alleviate the evolution stagnation of clusters. Experiments are conducted on a set of the CEC2017 benchmark functions and the results verify the effectiveness and efficiency of HBSO on the benchmark problems.

Keywords: Brain storm optimization · Pearson correlation coefficient · Swarm intelligence · Formal concept analysis

1 Introduction

Swarm intelligence (SI), is an effective global optimization technology, originated from the simulation of the intelligent behavior of social insects or animals in the ecosystem. The most famous examples include Ant Colony Optimization (ACO) [1, 2], Particle Swarm Optimization (PSO) [3, 4] and Artificial Bee Colony Algorithm (ABC) [5, 6]. In these SI models, various learning strategies have been usually applied to the exchange of information between individuals in the population to generate cooperative intelligence. A population of interacting individuals search in the decision space to minimize or maximize a function [7–11].

The social behaviors of creatures such as ants, birds, and insects have shown the characteristics of division of labor and collaboration, and how to simulate biological behaviors with higher intelligence and higher social collaboration is still of great significance. In 2011, Y [12] proposed the Brain Storm Optimization (BSO) algorithm based on human thinking and behavior. It simulates the creative problem-solving method of human beings: brainstorming. The BSO has shown strong robustness, fast convergence

© Springer Nature Switzerland AG 2021
Y. Tan and Y. Shi (Eds.): ICSI 2021, LNCS 12689, pp. 479–491, 2021.
https://doi.org/10.1007/978-3-030-78743-1_43

ability, and strong global search ability. Different from other classic SI algorithms that imitate the cooperative behavior of simple insects or animals, the BSO aims to simulate the brainstorming process of humans to solve complex problems [13]. From the perspective of knowledge growth and learning ability, BSO has a greater potential to benefit from the learning mechanism of collective individuals [14]. Recently, a set of new BSO improvements have been made. For example, MBSO [15] modified the clustering of the algorithm and generated new individual operations, simplified the calculation load of the algorithm and improved the efficiency; PPBSO [16] can jump out of the local optimum in solving the optimization problem of the DC brushless motor, and accurately find the global optimal value; CLBSO [17] successfully solved the two-impulse control multi-satellite formation reconfiguration problem; QBSO [18] solved the solenoid optimization problem. The above improvement strategies enhance the performance of the algorithm to a certain extent.

For SI algorithms, the exploration and exploitation [8] are two important operations to be balanced. In BSO, there are two new operations including convergent operation and divergent operation for the exploration and exploitation [12, 13]. In the convergent operation, a clustering method is first used to group all individuals into a set of clusters, and each cluster has a center and a number of ordinary individuals. The most commonly used clustering method is the k-means method in the original BSO. The k-means algorithm is relatively simple and has low time complexity. However, when the dimension of problems increases, the algorithms are apt to perform worse due to the ineffectiveness of the clustering based on learning mechanism. In addition, the k-means is more sensitive to the setting of initial value k and may lead to cessation of clusters evolution. For this drawback, we propose a new method to enhance the convergence performance and alleviate the evolution stagnation of clusters.

The main novelties of the proposed algorithm are as follow:

1) The similarity determination strategy is introduced into BSO. Different from existing strategies, we use Pearson correlation coefficient to judge the similarity of individuals in the population, with the purpose of improving the convergence of the population. The Pearson correlation coefficient is a method for judging the similarity of the two users in collaborative filtering.

2) The number of clusters can be determined adaptively. We use FCA technique to determine the size of k in the original k-means algorithm with the goal of improving the distribution of the population, and then update all individuals using the original BSO strategy. This method avoids the defect that k-means clustering is sensitive to the value of k. It can dynamically obtain several subpopulations according to the characteristics of different problems.

The rest is organized as follows. Section 2 presents the related work. In Sect. 3, the HBSO, which is suitable for high-dimensional (e.g., 100-dimensional) search space, is proposed. Experiments on benchmark functions and discussions of experimental results are given in Sect. 4. Finally, the conclusion is given in Sect. 5.

2 Related Work

2.1 Original Brain Storm Optimization Algorithm

BSO simulates the creative problem-solving method of human beings: brainstorming. In the brainstorming process, there are three kinds of individuals: the moderator, some problem owners and a population of brainstormers. The moderator is responsible for guiding the brainstorming process smoothly without prejudice. The problem owners collect better ideas from each generation of ideas. These ideas are generated by brainstormers. In BSO algorithm, a person (an individual) represents an idea, which in turn represents a potential solution to the problem to be solved. The procedure of the original BSO is listed in the Algorithm 1 [12, 14].

Algorithm 1: Procedure of the brain storm optimization algorithm

1 **Population Initialization**: Randomly generate n potential solutions (individuals), and evaluate the n individuals;

2 **While** have not reached the determined maximum number of iterations **do**

3   **Clustering**: Cluster n individuals into m clusters with a clustering algorithm;

4   **New individuals' generation**: Randomly select one or two cluster(s) to generate new individuals;

5   **Selection**: The newly generated individual is compared with the existing individual with the same individual index; the better one is kept and recorded as the new individual;

6   Evaluate the n individuals;

In original BSO, similar to other swarm intelligence algorithms, a random method is used to initialize the population. Note that, OSBSO [19] uses an orthogonal experimental design to initialize the population, which obtains satisfactory experimental results. In the main loop of the algorithm, the population of individuals will be evaluated according to a known evaluation function. The n individuals will then be clustered into m clusters with the best individual in each cluster mimicking a better idea picked up by a problem owner. The clustering algorithm is the k-means clustering algorithm. A new individual can be generated based on one or two individuals in the cluster. The new individuals are generated according to the Eq. (1), Eq. (2) and Eq. (3) [14, 20]. The selection strategy is utilized to keep good solutions in all individuals.

$$x_{new}^i(t+1) = x_{old}^i(t) + \xi(t) \times \text{rand}() \tag{1}$$

where x_{new}^i represents the i th dimension of the newly generated individual, and x_{old}^i represents the i th dimension of the selected individual based on the current population of individuals.

$$x_{old}^i(t) = \begin{cases} x_{old1}^i(t) \\ x_{old1}^i(t) \times rand() + x_{old2}^i(t) \times (1 - \text{rand}()) \end{cases} \tag{2}$$

where x_{old1}^i and x_{old2}^i represent two individuals selected from the current population of individuals. Function rand () returns a random value within the range (0, 1). The coefficient $\xi(t)$ is the step size which weights the contribution of the Gaussian random value to the new generated value.

$$\xi(t) = \log \text{sig}\left(\frac{0.5 \times T - t}{c}\right) \times \text{rand}()$$

(3)

where log sig() is a logarithmic sigmoid transfer function, T is the maximum number of iterations, and t is the current iteration number, c is for changing log sig() function's slope.

2.2 Formal Concept Analysis

Formal concept analysis (FCA) is a powerful analysis tool for data analysis [21], which can reveal the relation information between objects and attributes in a formal context. The extent and intent of the formal context show a deeper understanding of the objective world.

In FCA, a formal concept consists of two parts: the extent, which is the collection of all objects belonging to this formal context, and the intent, which is the collection of attributes shared by all these objectives. In a nutshell, the formal concept represents the relationship between objects and attributes in the domain [22, 23]. Then, the relationship can be represented in the form of a concept lattice. The details are as follows:

Definition 1 (Formal Context). A formal context is defined as a triple $K = (U, A, I)$, where $U = \{x_1, x_2,..., x_n\}$ is the collection of objects, $A = \{a_1, a_2,..., a_m\}$ is the collection of attributes, and I is the binary relation between U and A. $(x_i, a_j) \in I$ denotes that object x_i has attribute a_j, and $(x_i, a_j) \notin I$ denotes that object x_i does not have attribute a_j, where $x_i \in U$ and $a_j \in A$. Let "1" denote $(x_i, a_j) \in I$ and "0" denote $(x_i, a_j) \notin I$, then the formal context is an information system that only contains "0" or "1", as shown in Table 1.

Table 1. Formal context K.

U/A	a_1	a_2	a_3	a_4	a_5	a_6	a_7
x_1	1	1	1	0	0	0	1
x_2	1	1	1	1	0	0	0
x_3	1	1	1	0	0	0	1
x_4	0	0	0	1	1	0	0

Definition 2. For a formal context $K = (U, A, I)$, the makers $\uparrow$ and $\downarrow$ are formula as [24–27]:

$$X^\uparrow = \{a \in A | \forall x \in X, (x, a) \in I\}$$
$$B^\downarrow = \{x \in U | \forall a \in B, (x, a) \in I\}$$

(4)

where $X \subseteq U$ and $B \subseteq A$. In addition, we set $\{x\}^{\uparrow} = x^{\uparrow}, \forall x \in U$, and $\{a\}^{\downarrow} = a^{\downarrow}$, $\forall a \in A$.

Definition 3 (Concept). For a formal context $K = (U, A, I)$, if (X, B) satisfies $X^{\uparrow} = B$ and $B^{\downarrow} = X$, (X, B) is called as a concept. X is the extent of the concept. B is the intent of the concept. $X^{\uparrow}$ is called as the intent of X and $B^{\downarrow}$ is termed as the extent of B.

Definition 4. The set $C(K)$ of all concepts of the formal context K together with the partial order $(X_1, B_1) \leq (X_2, B_2) \Leftrightarrow X_1 \subseteq X_2$ (which is equivalent to $B_1 \supseteq B_2$) is called as the concept lattice of K [25].

According to the formal context K, we can construct a concept $C(K)$ as shown in Fig. 1. In this figure, each node represents a concept, and all the concepts of K include: $(\emptyset, \{a_1, a_2, a_3, a_4, a_5, a_6, a_7\})$, $(\{x_1, x_3\}, \{a_1, a_2, a_3, a_7\})$, $(\{x_2\}, \{a_1, a_2, a_3, a_4\})$, $(\{x_4\}, \{a_2, a_4, a_5\})$, $(\{x_1, x_2, x_3\}, \{a_1, a_2, a_3\})$, $(\{x_2, x_4\}, \{a_2, a_4\})$, $(\{x_1, x_2, x_3, x_4\}, \emptyset)$. $(\{x_1, x_2, x_3, x_4\}, \emptyset)$ and $(\emptyset, \{a_1, a_2, a_3, a_4, a_5, a_6, a_7\})$ are two special concepts, which are able to ensure the integrity of the partial order relationship.

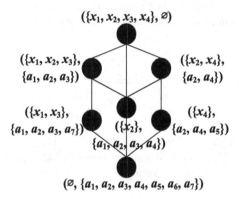

Fig. 1. Concept $C(K)$ of formal context K.

3   The Proposed Method

3.1   Framework of HBSO

The framework of HBSO is presented in Algorithm 2, which includes the following procedures:

1) Population Initialization. The population initialization plays a key role in maintaining the diversity of solutions and improving the search convergence for SI algorithms [28]. We use the orthogonal initialization strategy [19] to initialize n clustering centers and evaluate the fitness values of n individuals.

2) Individual similarity analysis. In this process, we analyze the similarity between individuals in order to prepare for gathering similar individuals together and improve the convergence of the population.
3) Adaptively determine the number of clusters. In this section, we use formal concept analysis technique to determine the value of k in the k-means algorithm. Formal concept analysis technology dynamically realizes individual clustering, avoiding the shortcomings of k-means method.

The new individuals' generation, selection and evaluation use the original BSO strategy.

3.2 Individual Similarity Analysis

Pearson correlation coefficient is widely used to measure the degree of correlation between two variables. It is also used to calculate the relationship between users in the collaborative filtering recommendation algorithm, which is more complicated than the calculation of Euclidean distance evaluation. Pearson correlation evaluation can give better results when the scoring data is not standardized. In this paper, we use it to analyze the similarity between individuals. Its mathematical description is as follows:

$$p(X,Y) = \frac{\left| \sum_{i=1}^{D} (X_i - \overline{X})(Y_i - \overline{Y}) \right|}{\sqrt{\sum_{i=1}^{D} (X_i - \overline{X})^2} \sqrt{\sum_{i=1}^{D} (Y_i - \overline{Y})^2}} \tag{5}$$

where D is the dimension of the decision space, X_i is the value of individual X in the i-th dimension, $p(X, Y)$ is the similarity between individuals X and Y. The two individuals are considered to have a strong similarity, when the $p(X, Y)$ value exceeds a certain threshold.

Algorithm 2: Framework of HBSO

---
1 **Population Initialization**: Initialize n clustering centers by the orthogonal initialization strategy [19] and evaluate the fitness values of n individuals;
2 **Individual similarity analysis:** Use Pearson correlation coefficient to analyze the similarity of n individuals in the population.;
3 **Adaptively determine the number of clusters:** Integrate the similarity of individuals and use FCA divide n individuals into m clusters;
4 **While** have not reached the determined maximum number of iterations **do**
5   **Clustering**: Input the obtained value m into the clustering algorithm;
6   **New individuals' generation**: Randomly select one or two cluster(s) to generate new individuals based on dimensionality reduction information;
7   **Selection**: The newly generated individual is compared with the existing individual with the same individual index; the better one is kept and recorded as the new individual;
8   Evaluate the n individuals;

3.3 Adaptively Determine the Number of Clusters

Before clustering the populations, we use Pearson correlation coefficient to analyze the similarity between the individuals. Then, we store the similarity information in Table 2.

From definition 1, the population relation formal context can be formulated as a combination of decision variables and their relationships. Specifically, a triple can be defined as $K = (Q_1, Q_2, I)$, where $Q_1 = \{q_1, q_2, ..., q_n\}$ is the collection of variables, $Q_2 = Q_1 = \{q_1, q_2, ..., q_n\}$, and I is the interaction between Q_1 and Q_2. $(q_i, q_j) \in I$ denotes that variable q_i is strong similarity with q_j, $(q_i, q_j) \notin I$ denotes that variable q_i and q_j are not strong similarity with each other, where $q_i \in Q_1$, $q_j \in Q_2$. The variable relation formal context is shown in Table 2. $I(q_1, q_2) = 1$ means that q_1 is strong similarity with q_2, and $I(q_1, q_4) = 0$ means that q_1 is not strong similarity with q_4.

Figure 2 shows the concept lattice for the population relation formal context in Table 2. Since formal concept analysis gathers similar objects into concepts, concepts with the same extent and intent (i.e., red nodes) have a higher degree of similarity. The red nodes represent the three subpopulations (clusters), respectively.

Table 2. Population relation formal context K.

Q_1/Q_2	q_1	q_2	q_3	q_4	q_5	q_6	q_7	q_8	q_9	q_{10}
q_1	1	1	1	0	0	0	0	0	0	0
q_2	1	1	1	1	0	0	0	0	0	0
q_3	1	1	1	0	0	0	0	0	0	0
q_4	0	1	0	1	1	1	1	0	0	0
q_5	0	0	0	1	1	1	1	0	0	0
q_6	0	0	0	1	1	1	1	0	0	0
q_7	0	0	0	1	1	1	1	1	0	0
q_8	0	0	0	0	0	0	1	1	1	1
q_9	0	0	0	0	0	0	0	1	1	1
q_{10}	0	0	0	0	0	0	0	1	1	1

Compared with other clustering approaches, the HBSO has two advantages: 1) It can adaptively divide the population into several subpopulations according to the characteristics of the population, which solves the defect of k-means method relying on subjective consciousness. 2) The uniformity of individuals in a cluster can be improved by the quantization of Eq. (5). Given the above, the method is an effective way to enhance the exploration performance, which can locate the global optima region quickly.

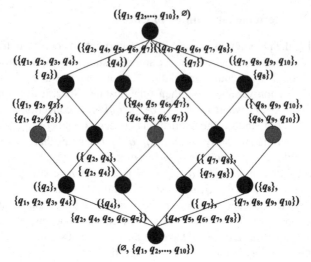

Fig. 2. Concept $C(K)$ of population relation formal context K. (Color figure online)

4   Experiments and Results

4.1   Parameter Settings and Test Functions

To evaluate the performance of HBSO, we use a set of 16 benchmark functions from the CEC2017, covering unimodal function F1, multimodal functions F4, F5, F6, F7, F8, F9, F10, hybrid functions F13, F14, F15, F17, F18, F19, F20, and composition functions F23. The composition function F23 is difficult to be optimized, because it merges the properties of the subfunctions better and maintains continuity around the global and local optima.

The HBSO is compared against several state-of-the-art BSOs, including BSO [12], PPBSO [16], MBSO [15], and QBSO [18]. All comparison algorithms use the same population size n and the same number of cluster m, where n is set to 100 and m is set to 5. The μ and σ for the Gaussian function are 0 and 1. Their other parameters (e.g., the number of clusters of comparison algorithms) refer to the default settings of their original references [12, 16–18]. For the HBSO, the population relevance threshold is set to 0.1. The other parameters for the HBSO are the same as for the original BSO. For a fair comparison, all the algorithms run 30 times on each benchmark function with 100-dimension. The maximum number of function evaluations is set to 100,000.

4.2   Result and Discussion

Table 3 reports the statistical results obtained by the algorithms on 100-dimensional test functions. We can observe that all the algorithms can obtain satisfactory performances. However, in these comparison algorithms, HBSO still has the best overall performance, among which 12 out of 16 test functions won the first place. HBSO is superior to other algorithms for the unimodal function F1. This is mainly due to that the formal concept analysis strategy can gather several clusters to make the generated individuals evenly distributed, thereby enhancing the exploration ability for the global optimal solution. HBSO performs the best on 5 instances (i.e., F5, F6, F8, F9 and F10) and does the third best on 2 instances (i.e., F4 and F7) for the multimodal functions F4–F10. In these 100-dimensional test functions, the superiority of HBSO over other algorithms is attributed to the clustering strategy of non-specified number of clusters, which can help the algorithm avoid falling into the local optimum and quickly locate the global optimum. HBSO still achieves satisfactory performance on most hybrid functions and composition functions.

Table 3. Results of HBSO, origin BSO and other BSO variants algorithm with 100D

Function	Stats	HBSO	BSO	MBSO	PPBSO	QBSO
F1	Mean	**1.21E+07**	3.14E+07	3.95E+09	3.06E+07	2.36E+11
	Std	**4.27E+06**	1.66E+07	4.04E+08	1.46E+07	9.02E+09
	Rank	**1**	3	4	2	5
F4	Mean	1.93E+03	9.19E+02	3.36E+03	**9.15E+02**	6.27E+04
	Std	3.11E+02	5.09E+01	3.50E+02	**1.82E+01**	8.22E+03
	Rank	3	2	4	**1**	5
F5	Mean	**1.12E+03**	1.22E+03	1.49E+03	1.27E+03	1.94E+03
	Std	**6.22E+01**	6.22E+01	6.32E+01	4.43E+01	9.23E+01
	Rank	**1**	2	4	3	5
F6	Mean	**6.55E+02**	6.57E+02	6.75E+02	6.60E+02	6.97E+02
	Std	**2.31E+00**	4.17E+00	3.23E+00	3.73E+00	4.87E+00
	Rank	**1**	2	4	3	5
F7	Mean	3.57E+03	3.87E+03	**3.02E+03**	3.48E+03	4.54E+03
	Std	6.27E+02	3.20E+02	**3.01E+02**	2.84E+02	1.32E+02
	Rank	3	4	**1**	2	5
F8	Mean	**1.59E+03**	1.62E+03	1.88E+03	1.69E+03	2.41E+03
	Std	**6.59E+01**	8.31E+01	1.03E+02	7.94E+01	5.69E+01
	Rank	**1**	2	4	3	5
F9	Mean	**2.17E+04**	2.26E+04	5.49E+04	3.02E+04	7.18E+04
	Std	**1.51E+03**	1.41E+03	4.73E+03	4.25E+03	4.81E+03
	Rank	**1**	2	4	3	5
F10	Mean	**1.58E+04**	1.64E+04	2.21E+04	1.62E+04	3.33E+04
	Std	**7.45E+02**	2.06E+03	1.17E+03	3.08E+02	8.02E+02
	Rank	**1**	3	4	2	5
F13	Mean	**9.34E+04**	9.95E+04	2.83E+07	9.80E+04	3.54E+10
	Std	**3.31E+04**	3.43E+04	7.12E+06	3.99E+04	7.66E+09
	Rank	**1**	2	4	3	5
F14	Mean	1.84E+05	**1.77E+05**	2.62E+06	2.03E+05	3.49E+07
	Std	1.01E+05	**1.32E+05**	1.52E+06	4.22E+04	2.13E+07
	Rank	2	**1**	4	3	5
F15	Mean	**5.16E+04**	5.79E+04	7.50E+06	7.06E+04	1.58E+10
	Std	**1.93E+04**	2.28E+04	2.94E+06	1.19E+04	1.63E+09

(continued)

Table 3. (*continued*)

Function	Stats	HBSO	BSO	MBSO	PPBSO	QBSO
	Rank	**1**	2	4	3	5
F17	Mean	**5.21E+03**	5.26E+03	6.27E+03	5.47E+03	2.98E+04
	Std	**5.56E+02**	4.30E+02	5.70E+02	5.06E+02	8.44E+03
	Rank	**1**	2	4	3	5
F18	Mean	**2.57E+06**	1.56E+06	1.69E+07	2.25E+06	3.66E+08
	Std	**1.21E+06**	8.32E+05	3.24E+06	1.67E+06	4.65E+07
	Rank	**1**	2	4	3	5
F19	Mean	**2.15E+06**	5.65E+06	3.30E+07	3.37E+06	1.40E+10
	Std	**8.95E+05**	2.38E+06	1.64E+07	1.45E+06	2.51E+09
	Rank	**1**	3	4	2	5
F20	Mean	**5.00E+03**	5.05E+03	5.08E+03	5.19E+03	7.46E+03
	Std	**4.65E+02**	2.48E+02	4.06E+02	5.26E+02	3.52E+02
	Rank	**1**	2	3	4	5
F23	Mean	1.03E+04	1.09E+04	7.00E+03	**7.73E+03**	1.90E+04
	Std	1.31E+03	5.66E+02	2.09E+03	**3.52E+02**	7.73E+02
	Rank	3	4	2	1	5

Especially for hybrid functions F13, F15, F17, F18, F19 and F20, HBSO obtains the best solutions. These observations show that the formal concept analysis strategy does improve the performance of HBSO in complex single-objective optimization.

Figure 3 compares the evolution of the algorithm on 100 dimensions F6, F8, F15 and F19. It further verified the effectiveness of HBSO. It can be seen that HBSO has obtained a better solution after a few iterations. Taking function F6 as an example, when the number of function evaluations is 10,000, HBSO has reached a better solution than the comparison algorithm. In addition, when the number of functional evaluations is 50,000, the optimization process of the comparative BSO almost stalls, while HBSO still finds a better solution.

From the above results, it can be clearly seen that the formal concept analysis strategy has enhanced the algorithmic ability to solve high-dimensional problems, and the effectiveness and efficiency of HBSO have also been verified through experiments.

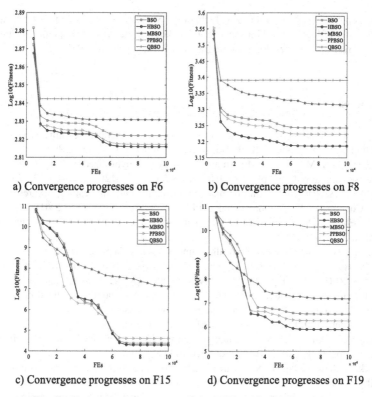

a) Convergence progresses on F6

b) Convergence progresses on F8

c) Convergence progresses on F15

d) Convergence progresses on F19

Fig. 3. Convergence progresses of the BSOs with 100 dimensions

5 Conclusion

In this paper, a new BSO variant HBSO based on FCA is proposed. FCA is a powerful data analysis technique used to analyze potential connections between data. In HBSO, two strategies are developed, i.e., Pearson correlation coefficient and cluster number adaptive. Pearson correlation coefficient is used to analyze the similarity between individuals. The number of clusters is adaptive through formal concept analysis technology. These operations can alleviate the stagnation of cluster evolution.

Experiments have been conducted on a set of the CEC2017 benchmark functions where HBSO is compared with several BSO algorithms. Experimental results demonstrate that the HBSO generally performs better than other BSO algorithms in terms of the accuracy and convergence.

In the future, the HBSO will be compared with more state-of-the-art SI algorithms on the latest higher-dimensional test functions. In addition, applying the HBSO algorithm to solve practical engineering problems is also the next research focus.

Acknowledgments. This work was supported by the National Natural Science Foundation of China (61773103), the Intelligent Manufacturing Standardization and Test Verification Project "Time Sensitive Network (TSN) and Object Linking and Embedding Unified Architecture for

Industrial Control OPC UA Fusion Key Technology Standard Research and Test Verification" project, Ministry of Industry and Information Technology of the People's Republic of China, and National key research and development program of China, No. 2018YFB1700103.

References

1. Dorigo, M., Gambardella, L.M.: Ant colony system: a cooperative learning approach to the traveling salesman problem. IEEE Trans. Evol. Comput. 1(1), 53–56 (1997)
2. Gambardella, L.M., Dorigo, M.: An ant colony system hybridized with a new local search for the sequential ordering problem. INFORMS J. Comput. 12(3), 237–255 (2000)
3. Eberhart, Y.S.: Particle swarm optimization: developments, applications and resources. In: IEEE Congress on Evolutionary Computation, vol. 1, no. 1, pp. 81–86 (2001)
4. Shi, Y., Eberhart, R.C.: Empirical study of particle swarm optimization. IEEE Congress Evol. Comput. 3, 101–106 (1999)
5. Karaboga, D.: Artificial Bee colony algorithm. Scholarpedia 5(3), 6915 (2010)
6. Ma, L., Hu, K., Zhu, Y., Chen, H.: Cooperative artificial bee colony algorithm for multi-objective RFID network planning. J. Netw. Comput. Appl. 42, 143–162 (2014)
7. Ma, L., Huang, M., Yang, S., Wang, R., Wang, X.: An adaptive localized decision variable analysis approach to large-scale multi-objective and many-objective optimization. IEEE Trans. Cybern. (2021). https://doi.org/10.1109/TCYB.2020.3041212
8. Thrun, M.C., Alfred, U.: Swarm intelligence for self-organized clustering. Artif. Intell. 290 (2021). https://doi.org/10.1016/j.artint.2020.103237
9. Slowik, A., Kwasnicka, H.: Nature inspired methods and their industry applications—swarm intelligence algorithms. IEEE Trans. Industr. Inf. 14(3), 1004–1015 (2018)
10. Ma, L., Cheng, S., Shi, Y.: Enhancing learning efficiency of brain storm optimization via orthogonal learning design. IEEE Trans. Syst. Man Cybern.: Syst. (2020). https://doi.org/10.1109/TSMC.2020.2963943
11. Cheng, J., Chen, J., Guo, Y., Cheng, S.: Adaptive CCR-ELM with variable length brain storm optimization algorithm for class-imbalanced learning. Nat. Comput. 20, 11–22 (2021)
12. Shi, Y.: Brain storm optimization algorithm. In: Tan, Y., Shi, Y., Chai, Y., Wang, G. (eds.) ICSI 2011. LNCS, vol. 6728, pp. 303–309. Springer, Heidelberg (2011). https://doi.org/10.1007/978-3-642-21515-5_36
13. Xue, J., Wu, Y., Shi, Y., Cheng, S.: Brain storm optimization algorithm for multi-objective optimization problems. In: Tan, Y., Shi, Y., Ji, Z. (eds.) ICSI 2012. LNCS, vol. 7331, pp. 513–519. Springer, Heidelberg (2012). https://doi.org/10.1007/978-3-642-30976-2_62
14. Shi, Y.: Brain storm optimization algorithm in objective space. In: IEEE Congress on Evolutionary Computation (CEC), Sendai, Japan, pp. 1227–1234 (2015)
15. Zhan, Z., Zhang, J., Shi, Y., Liu, H.: A modified brain storm optimization. In: IEEE Congress on Evolutionary Computation, pp. 1–8 (2012)
16. Duan, H., Li, S., Shi, Y.: Predator–prey brain storm optimization for DC brushless motor. IEEE Trans. Magn. 49(10), 5336–5340 (2013)
17. Sun, C., Duan, H., Shi, Y.: Optimal satellite formation reconfiguration based on closed-loop brain storm optimization. IEEE Comput. Intell. Mag. 8(4), 39–51 (2013)
18. Duan, H., Li, C.: Quantum-behaved brain storm optimization approach to solving Loney's solenoid problem. IEEE Trans. Magn. 51(1), 1–7 (2015)
19. Wang, R., Ma, L., Zhang, T.: Brain storm optimization algorithm based on improved clustering approach using orthogonal experimental design. In: IEEE Congress on Evolutionary Computation, pp. 262–270 (2019)

20. Arsuaga-Ríos, M., Vega-Rodríguez, M.A.: Cost optimization based on brain storming for grid scheduling. In: 2014 Fourth International Conference on Innovative Computing Technology, pp. 31–36 (2014)
21. Ganter, B., Wille, R.: Formal Concept Analysis: Mathematical Foundations. Springer, Heidelberg (1999). https://doi.org/10.1007/978-3-642-59830-2
22. Du, N., Wu, B., Pei, X.: Community detection in large-scale social networks. In: The 9th WebKDD and 1st SNA-KDD 2007 Workshop on Web Mining and Social Network Analysis, pp. 16–25 (2007)
23. Tang, P., Hui, S., Fong, A.: A lattice-based approach for chemical structural retrieval. Eng. Appl. Artif. Intell. **39**, 215–222 (2015)
24. Li, K., Du, Y., Xiang, D., Chen, H., Liao, Z.: A method for building concept lattice based on matrix operation. In: Huang, D.-S., Heutte, L., Loog, M. (eds.) ICIC 2007. LNCS (LNAI), vol. 4682, pp. 350–359. Springer, Heidelberg (2007). https://doi.org/10.1007/978-3-540-74205-0_39
25. Hao, F., Yau, S.S., Min, G., Yang, L.T.: Detecting K-balanced trusted cliques in signed social networks. IEEE Internet Comput. **18**(2), 24–31 (2014)
26. Rui, M.: An algorithm for knowledge acquisition of uncertain decision-making based on rough sets theory. J. Bohai Univ. (2017). http://en.cnki.com.cn/Article_en/CJFDTotal-JZSF201704014.htm
27. Hao, F., Min, G., Pei, Z., Park, D.S., Yang, L.T.: K-clique community detection in social networks based on formal concept analysis. IEEE Syst. J. **11**(1), 250–259 (2017)
28. Kazimipour, B., Li, X., Qin, K.: A review of population initialization techniques for evolutionary algorithms. In: IEEE Congress on Evolutionary Computation, Beijing, China, pp. 2585–2592 (2014)

An Improved Brain Storm Optimization Algorithm Based on Maximum Likelihood Estimation

Junfeng Chen[1]([✉]) [iD], Xingsi Xue[2] [iD], and Bulgan Ninjerdene[1]

[1] College of IOT Engineering, Hohai University, Changzhou 213022, Jiangsu, China
ninjerdene@hhu.edu.cn
[2] Fujian Key Lab for Automotive Electronics and Electric Drive,
Fujian University of Technology, Fuzhou 350118, Fujian, China

Abstract. Brain Storm Optimization (BSO) is a relatively new swarm intelligence algorithm. It employs clustering, creating, and selecting operators, all connected and significantly impacting the optimization performance. However, with the increase of the problem dimension and the offset of the optimal value, the performance of the basic BSO algorithm becomes worse. This paper designs the double grouping operator, which employs k-means clustering in the horizontal and differential grouping in the vertical. A new creating operator is designed based on maximum likelihood estimation for the mean and variance of the Gaussian distribution. The numerical experiments are carried out to amplify and highlight the performance of the proposed algorithm artificially. Experimental results show that the proposed algorithm achieves satisfactory results on shifted and rotated benchmark functions.

Keywords: Brain storm optimization · Double grouping · Maximum likelihood estimation · Mixed selection strategy

1 Introduction

Brain Storm Optimization (BSO) is a newly developed swarm intelligence algorithm, which is inspired by the problem-solving process of human brainstorming [1–3]. As with the other metaphor-based swarm algorithms, the BSO algorithm does not need to assume or model optimization problems and solves a problem through a population of solutions rather than a single one. In addition, BSO algorithm does not require that the optimization problem is differentiable, which makes BSO algorithm a very effective method to solve the problem in the real society. The BSO algorithm employs clustering, creating and selecting operators, which are all connected and have great impacts on the optimization performance. In recent years, many scholars have conducted preliminary research on the BSO algorithm. In addition to the research on the theory of BSO algorithm, many people also made some improvements to the algorithm. They proposed some variants of the algorithm and applied them to various optimization problems

© Springer Nature Switzerland AG 2021
Y. Tan and Y. Shi (Eds.): ICSI 2021, LNCS 12689, pp. 492–501, 2021.
https://doi.org/10.1007/978-3-030-78743-1_44

and practical problems in social life such as wireless sensor networks deployment [4], DC Brushless Motor [5], Reactive Power Dispatch Problem [6], electric power dispatch problems [7], design problems in aeronautics field [8], and optimization problems in finance [9].

In this paper, for the clustering strategy, we proposed a horizontal and vertical grouping strategy. The differential grouping was used to group the dimensions, while k-means clustering was used to group different individuals. This allows the extraction of row and column information for the entire population. Then for the creating strategy a method based on maximum likelihood estimation for the mean and variance of the Gaussian distribution was proposed in the paper. In order to make the population diverse, this paper also designed four generation methods. In the end, for the selecting strategy, a mixed selection strategy was introduced in this paper. At the beginning of iteration, the proportional selection method was used, and at the later stage, we used the competitive selection.

The rest of the article is organized as follows. The horizontal and vertical grouping strategy is introduced in Sect. 2. The creating strategy based on Maximum Likelihood Estimation is discussed in Sect. 3. Next, experiments are carried out to artificially amplify and highlight the performance of the strategy proposed in this paper in Sect. 4. Finally, conclusions are presented in Sect. 5.

2   Double Grouping

Clustering operator in BSO is a sticking point, affecting the results of the follow-up selecting & creating operator indirectly. The original BSO and most of its variants employ k-means clustering, which is just a clustering of individuals. With the increase of dimension, there is some correlation information between each dimension of each individual. Without any knowledge of the underlying structure, the subcomponents should be formed according to the interaction pattern of the decision variables so that the interactions between the subcomponents are kept to a minimum. K. Weicker and N. Weicker [10] proposed a CC technique to identify interacting variables. It is the first attempt at automatic formation of subcomponents in a CC framework. The decomposition strategy used in this paper is differential grouping [11]. The differential grouping can identify and group interacting variables. The underlying interactive structure of decision variables is found by the grouping function and then the variables can be separated into separable and non-separable subcomponents such that the interdependence between them is kept to a minimum. Therefore, double grouping strategy is proposed in this paper including k-means clustering in the horizontal direction and differential grouping in the vertical direction. Through this operation, we not only extract the information between each individual, but also extract the information between each variable dimension.

2.1   Interaction Structure of the Decision Variables

In practice, without prior knowledge about the problem, it is not clear how the problem should be decomposed. In this paper, we used an automatic decomposition strategy called differential grouping that can uncover the underlying interaction structure of the decision variables and form subcomponents.

Differential grouping comes from the definition of partially additively separable functions. These types of functions conveniently represent the modular nature of many real-world problems which always have high dimensions. The problem can be considered as partially additively separable functions if it has the following form:

$$f(\vec{x}) = \sum_{i=1}^{m} f_i(\vec{x}_i) \tag{1}$$

where $\vec{x}_i$ denote mutually exclusive decision vectors of function f_i, $\vec{x} = (x_1, \cdots, x_n)$ is a global decision vector which has n dimensions, and m is the number of independent subcomponents. If all independent subcomponent functions are 1-D, then it is called completely additively separable or fully separable for short.

Theorem 1. Let $f(\vec{x})$ be an additively separable function. $\forall a, b_1 \neq b_2, \delta \epsilon \Re, \delta \neq 0$, if the following condition holds, then x_p and x_q are non-separable.

$$\Delta_{\delta,x_p}[f](\vec{x})|_{x_p=a,x_q=b_1} \neq \Delta_{\delta,x_p}[f](\vec{x})|_{x_p=a,x_q=b_2} \tag{2}$$

$$\Delta_{\delta,x_p}[f](\vec{x}) = f(\cdots, x_p+\delta, \cdots) - f(\cdots, x_p, \cdots) \tag{3}$$

where x_p and x_q are two mutually exclusive decision variables, δ is the interval. Δ_{δ,x_p} refers to the forward difference of f with respect to variable x_p with interval δ.

As defined in *Theorem* 1, if two variables x_p and x_q are non-separable, it will have different results when evaluated with any two different values for x_q. On the contrary, if two variables x_p and x_q are separable, it will have the same results when evaluated with any two different values for x_q.

Take a non-separable objective function $f(x_1, x_2) = x_1^2 + \lambda x_1 x_2 + x_2^2, \lambda \neq 0$ as an example. According to Eq. 2:

$$\Delta_{\delta,x_1}[f] = [(x_1+\delta)^2+\lambda(x_1+\delta)x_2+x_2^2]-[x_1^2+\lambda x_1 x_2+x_2^2] = \delta^2+2\delta x_1+\lambda\delta x_2 \tag{4}$$

It can be seen that the difference equation $\Delta_{\delta,x_1}[f]$ is a function of both x_1 and x_2. Therefore, evaluating $\Delta_{\delta,x_1}[f]$ for two different values of x_2 does not give the same answer. So, according to *Theorem 1*, we conclude that x_1 and x_2 interact (they are non-separable). Note that λ reflects the strength of non-separability. Setting λ to zero makes the function fully separable.

2.2 Double Grouping Strategy

In this paper, the differential grouping strategy will be added to the clustering strategy. The original BSO algorithm employs k-$means$ clustering as its clustering operator. The k-$means$ clustering operator groups a set of candidate solutions into several different clusters that solutions in the same cluster are more similar to each other than to those in other clusters. In this paper, differential groups will be added before k-$means$ clustering which can find the correlation information between different dimensions of each variable. The whole Algorithm 1 is as follows.

Algorithm 1. Pseudocode of double grouping

Initialize parameters: a set of solutions $i \neq j$, where each solution is a m-dimensional real vector; clustering number $k = 2$; separable group $seps = \{\}$; all the subconponents $allgroups = \{\}$; dimension vector $dims = \{1, 2, 3, \cdots, m\}$

//**differential grouping**

for $i = 1$ to m **do**

  set vector $group = \{i\}$;

  for $j = 1$ to m and $i \neq j$ **do**

    $\vec{p_1} = lbound * ones(1, n)$, $\vec{p_2} = \vec{p_1}$, $\vec{p_2} = ubound$

    $\Delta_1 = func(\vec{p_1}) - func(\vec{p_2})$

    $\vec{p_1}(j) = 0$, $\vec{p_2}(j) = 0$

    $\Delta_2 = func(\vec{p_1}) - func(\vec{p_2})$

    if $|\Delta_1 - \Delta_2| > \varepsilon$ **then**

      $group = group \bigcup j$

    end if

  end for

  $dims = dims - group$

  if $length(group) = 1$ **then**

    $seps = seps \bigcup group$

  else

    $allgroups = allgroups \bigcup \{group\}$

  end if

end for

$allgroups = allgroups \bigcup \{seps\}$

// **k-means Clustering**

Partition n individuals into k clusters, then every cluster are divided as $allgroups$

As shown in Algorithm 1, the differential grouping first checks the interaction between the first decision variable with the other decision variables by calculating the paired relationship in Theorem 1. If the algorithm finds that the first decision variable interacts with other variables, it deletes it from the set of all decision variables and then puts it in a subpart. The algorithm will go on until all the variables that interact with the first variable are detected and then these variables make up the first subcomponent. If no interaction is detected, then this variable is considered as a separable variable. The remaining variables are also detected according to this process. The algorithm will not end until there are no remaining decision variables.

During the algorithm all variables are initialized to the lower bound of the function, denoted by vector p_1. In order to check the interaction between the ith dimension and the jth dimension, the vectors p_2 and p_1 are set identically, but the ith dimension is different. The ith dimension of p_2 is set as the upper bound. The value of delta1 can be calculated in this way. Then, the jth dimension of p_2 is set to the center of the search space for that dimension, and the value of Δ_2 is calculated. If the difference between Δ_1 and Δ_2 is greater than a small value, then it is considered that the ith and jth dimensions interact with each other. Then the jth dimension is removed from the set of decision variables and placed in the same subcomponent as the ith dimension. All the variables will be compared with the ith dimension and then continue to the $(i+1)$th dimension.

After all the variables have been grouped in the appropriate subcomponent, the clustering operator groups a set of candidate solutions into several different clusters so that solutions in the same cluster are more similar to each other than to those in other clusters.

3   Creating Strategy Based on Maximum Likelihood Estimation

As for the creating operator, the algorithm proposed in this paper employs Maximum Likelihood Estimation (MLE) based on Gaussian Probability Density Function [12], which is more efficiency and productivity, especially compared with the one by one mode in the original version.

It's also worth mentioning that the basic creating operator can produce an idea in four patterns by using the Gaussian random strategy. The formulas for generating new candidate solutions are given as follows.

$$x_{new} = x_{old} + \xi \times G(m, \sigma) \qquad (5)$$

where x_{new} and x_{old} represent the new and the selected solution from a cluster or two clusters, respectively. $G(m, \sigma)$ is Gaussian random function with mean m and standard derivation σ.

However, the distribution of random numbers generated by different means and variances varies greatly. The expected value $m_{ML} = \begin{bmatrix} 0 \\ 0 \end{bmatrix}$ and variance $S_{ML} = \begin{bmatrix} \sigma_1^2 & \sigma_{12} \\ \sigma_{12} & \sigma_2^2 \end{bmatrix}$, the parameter σ_{12} appears as the angle of rotation of the symmetry axis of the random number distribution, while σ_1^2 and σ_2^2 denotes the ellipses distribution of random numbers and the larger one is the semimajor axis of the ellipse.

In addition, we can also produce more complex distribution of data, for example, to generate a random data subject to multiple probability density distribution. Consider a mixture of two probability density distributions. The expected values are $m_1 = \begin{bmatrix} 1 \\ 2 \end{bmatrix}$, $m_2 = \begin{bmatrix} 2 \\ 3 \end{bmatrix}$ and variances are $S_1 = \begin{bmatrix} 0.5 & -0.05 \\ -0.05 & 0.1 \end{bmatrix}$, $S_2 = \begin{bmatrix} 0.2 & 0 \\ 0 & 0.2 \end{bmatrix}$.

However, at the beginning of the algorithm, it is often unknown what statistical distribution the data obeys. Therefore, the maximum likelihood estimation method is needed for parameter estimation. The usual way to handle function estimation is to assume that the probability density function is known, but the parameter values of the distribution function are unknown. In the original BSO algorithm, new individuals are produced by a Gaussian mutation, but its mean or covariance matrix is unknown and is set manually in the program. Different values of mean or covariance matrix will make a great impact on the new solutions to be generated. Therefore, we need to find an effective and reasonable method to determine the value of the parameter.

Maximum likelihood estimation method is a practical method. For the Gaussian distribution, we assume that the number of data is N, $x_i \epsilon R^l$, $i = 1, 2, \cdots , N$. The expected value and covariance matrix of the data are obtained according to the following formula.

$$m_{ML} = \frac{1}{N} \sum_{i=1}^{N} x_i \tag{6}$$

$$S_{ML} = \frac{1}{N} \sum_{i=1}^{N} (x_i - m_{ML})(x_i - m_{ML})^T \tag{7}$$

where N is usually taken as $N-1$, so as to ensure that the expected value m_{ML} and variance S_{ML} are unbiased estimates.

4   Experimental Results and Analysis

4.1   Complex Offset Test Functions and Parameter Settings

Numerical Experiments have been carried out in this paper to test the performance of the proposed algorithm. We chose 8 test functions for the experiment. Table 1 shows the mathematical expressions of these test functions. As discussed in [13], many benchmark numerical functions commonly used to evaluate and compare optimization algorithms may suffer from two problems. First, global optimum lies at the center of the search range. Second, local optima lie along the coordinate axes or no linkage among the variables/dimensions exists. To solve these problems, we can shift or rotate the conventional benchmark functions. For benchmark functions suffering from the first problem, we may shift the global optimum to a random position so that the global optimum position has different numerical values for different dimensions. For the second problem, we can rotate the function using an orthogonal rotation matrix to avoid local optima lying along the coordinate axes while retaining the properties of the test function. We shift eight commonly used benchmark functions $f1, f2, \cdots , f8$ where

$x = z - o$, and further rotate four functions $f5, f6, f7, f8$ where $z = M(x - o)$. $o = (o_1, o_2, \cdots, o_D)$ is the shifted global optimum, M is an orthogonal matrix. Other parameters involved in these algorithms are listed in Table 2. In order to obtain a more complete comparison, each experiment was tested 30 times under the conditions. In addition, in order to reduce the impact of the initial solution on the performance of the algorithm, the initial value settings of each algorithm remain the same.

Table 1. Benchmark functions.

Name	Mathematical expressions	Global optimum
Shifted sphere function	$f_1(x) = \sum_{i=1}^{D} z_i^2$	-450
Shifted Schwefel's Problem 1.2	$f_2(x) = \sum_{i=1}^{D}(\sum_{j=1}^{i} z_j)^2$	-450
Shifted Schwefel's Problem 1.2 with noise in fitness	$f_3(x) = (\sum_{i=1}^{D}(\sum_{j=1}^{i} z_j)^2)(1 + 0.4\|N(0,1)\|)$	-450
Shifted Rosenbrock's Function	$f_4(x) = \sum_{i=1}^{D}(100(z_i^2 - z_{i+1})^2 + (z_i - 1)^2)$	390
Shifted rotated High Conditioned Elliptic Function	$f_5(x) = \sum_{i=1}^{D}(10^6)^{\frac{i-1}{D-1}} z_i^2$	-450
Shifted rotated Griewank's function	$f_6(x) = \sum_{i=1}^{D} \frac{z_i^2}{4000}$	-180
Shifted rotated Ackley's function2	$f_7(x) = -20\exp(-0.2\sqrt{\frac{1}{D}\sum_{i=1}^{D} z_i^2}) - \exp(\frac{1}{D}\sum_{i=1}^{D}\cos(2\pi z_i)) + 20 + e$	-140
Shifted rotated Rastrigin's function	$f_8(x) = \sum_{i=1}^{D}(z_i^2 - 10\cos(2\pi z_i) + 10)$	-330

Table 2. Parameters involved in the BSO algorithms.

N	$Iter_{max}$	p_{one}	$p_{1center}$	$p_{2center}$	K	ω_1	ω_2
50	1000	0.5	0.2	0.3	20	0.3	0.4

4.2 Experimental Comparison

Experiments were conducted on a suite of 8 numerical functions to evaluate the algorithms proposed in this paper and were compared with the basic BSO algorithm with covariances of 1 and 10 respectively. The problem dimensions in Table 3 and Table 4 are 10 and 30 respectively. For the convenience of the following description, the algorithm proposed in this paper is referred to as BSO-DG algorithm for short.

Table 3. Dim = 10.

Name	Basic BSO ($\sigma = 1$)	Basic BSO ($\sigma = 10$)	BSO-DG
f_1	−4.499317e+02	−4.498768e+02	**−4.500000e+02**
f_2	−4.152201e+02	−4.498251e+02	**−4.500000e+02**
f_3	9.338284e+03	−4.497097e+02	**−4.500000e+02**
f_4	2.823552e+03	3.757654e+03	**3.911866e+02**
f_5	1.136462e+05	**8.352151e+04**	8.698848e+04
f_6	6.493108e+02	**−1.789498e+02**	5.185952e+02
f_7	−1.193785e+02	−1.192944e+02	**−1.199291e+02**
f_8	−2.588920e+02	−2.950397e+02	**−3.180605e+02**

Table 4. Dim = 30.

Name	Basic BSO ($\sigma = 1$)	Basic BSO ($\sigma = 10$)	BSO-DG
f_1	1.429155e+04	−4.476180e+02	**−4.500000e+02**
f_2	1.068291e+04	1.433885e+03	**−4.439227e+02**
f_3	4.004918e+04	2.332795e+04	**7.524117e+03**
f_4	4.027146e+08	1.114580e+03	**4.192215e+02**
f_5	2.619072e+07	**4.670158e+06**	7.014877e+06
f_6	3.803106e+03	**9.792736e+02**	3.566663e+03
f_7	−1.188855e+02	−1.189145e+02	**−1.194512e+02**
f_8	−5.135351e+01	−7.470952e+00	**−2.374401e+02**

In addition, during the experiments we found that the basic BSO algorithm has poor optimization effect on these functions with offset which can be seen at Basic BSO ($\sigma = 1$) in Table 3. That's because when it generates a new solution, it just adds a small Gaussian random value near the original solution which works well when global optimum lies at the center of the search range. Once the optimal points are transferred to a random position, this generation strategy will have little chance of detecting points in other locations. That's because in the basic BSO algorithm, the mean and covariance are fixed at 0 and 1. We found that fixed mean and covariance will bring two problems. One is that the generation of new individuals is limited to certain regions, and the other is that the excessive number of clusters will lead to the overlap of new individuals. This will make the area detected by the algorithm very limited. Once the optimal solution of the function is shifted, the effect of the basic BSO algorithm is obviously reduced, and almost no optimal solution can be found.

In the experiment, we were surprised to find that increasing the standard deviation of Gaussian distribution in the early stage of search would improve the experimental results, which was due to expanding the distribution of data. The results can be seen at Basic BSO ($\sigma = 10$) in Table 3. However, the results are not satisfactory, and the proposed method can effectively solve the test function with offset. As can be seen from Table 3 and Table 4, compared with the basic BSO algorithm, the performance of the algorithm proposed in this paper has improved a lot, and the global optimal solution can be found.

5   Conclusion

In this paper, the horizontal and vertical grouping was adopted in the algorithm which employs *k-means* clustering in the horizontal and differential grouping in the vertical. Through this operation, we not only extract the information between each individual, but also extract the information between each variable dimension. While for the creating operator, it is often unknown what statistical distribution the data obeys. Therefore, a method based on maximum likelihood estimation for the mean and variance of the Gaussian distribution was introduced in this paper. Meanwhile, this paper also designed a mixed selection strategy for exploration and exploitation. An improved BSO algorithm based on differential grouping and maximum likelihood estimation was then proposed. Finally, the proposed algorithm was applied to numerical optimization problems in comparison with the basic BSO. The boxplots and statistical results show that the proposed method can identify the regions with high quality solutions in the search space quickly and obtains satisfactory solutions on the optimization of offset problems and increased dimensions. Meanwhile, the evolutionary iteration diagram shows that the proposed BSO algorithm also can improve the convergence rate.

Acknowledgement. This work is supported by the National Key R&D Program of China (No. 2018YFC0407101), the Fundamental Research Funds for the Central Universities (No. 2019B22314), and the Natural Science Foundation of Fujian Province (No. 2020J01875).

References

1. Shi, Y.: Brain storm optimization algorithm. In: Tan, Y., Shi, Y., Chai, Y., Wang, G. (eds.) ICSI 2011. LNCS, vol. 6728, pp. 303–309. Springer, Heidelberg (2011). https://doi.org/10.1007/978-3-642-21515-5_36
2. Shi, Y.: An optimization algorithm based on brainstorming process. In: Emerging Research on Swarm Intelligence and Algorithm Optimization, pp. 1–35. IGI Global (2015)

3. Shi, Y.: Developmental swarm intelligence: developmental learning perspective of swarm intelligence algorithms. Int. J. Swarm Intell. Res. (IJSIR) **5**(1), 36–54 (2014)
4. Chen, J., Cheng, S., Chen, Y., Xie, Y., Shi, Y.: Enhanced brain storm optimization algorithm for wireless sensor networks deployment. In: Tan, Y., Shi, Y., Buarque, F., Gelbukh, A., Das, S., Engelbrecht, A. (eds.) ICSI 2015. LNCS, vol. 9140, pp. 373–381. Springer, Cham (2015). https://doi.org/10.1007/978-3-319-20466-6_40
5. Duan, H., Li, S., Shi, Y.: Predator-prey brain storm optimization for DC brushless motor. IEEE Trans. Magn. **49**(10), 5336–5340 (2013)
6. Lenin, K., Reddy, B.R., Kalavathi, M.S.: Brain storm optimization algorithm for solving optimal reactive power dispatch problem. Int. J. Res. Electron. Commun. Technol. **1**(3), 25–30 (2014)
7. Jadhav, H., Sharma, U., Patel, J., Roy, R.: Brain storm optimization algorithm based economic dispatch considering wind power. In: 2012 IEEE International Conference on Power and Energy (PECon), pp. 588–593. IEEE (2012)
8. Duan, H., Li, C.: Quantum-behaved brain storm optimization approach to solving Loney's solenoid problem. IEEE Trans. Magn. **51**(1), 1–7 (2014)
9. Sun, Y.: A hybrid approach by integrating brain storm optimization algorithm with grey neural network for stock index forecasting. In: Abstract and Applied Analysis, Hindawi, vol. 2014 (2014)
10. Weicker, K., Weicker, N.: On the improvement of coevolutionary optimizers by learning variable interdependencies. In: Proceedings of the 1999 Congress on Evolutionary Computation-CEC99 (Cat. No. 99TH8406), vol. 3, pp. 1627–1632. IEEE (1999)
11. Omidvar, M.N., Li, X., Mei, Y., Yao, X.: Cooperative co-evolution with differential grouping for large scale optimization. IEEE Trans. Evol. Comput. **18**(3), 378–393 (2013)
12. Coretto, P., Hennig, C.: Maximum likelihood estimation of heterogeneous mixtures of gaussian and uniform distributions. J. Stat. Plann. Inference **141**(1), 462–473 (2011)
13. Liang, J.-J., Suganthan, P.N., Deb, K.: Novel composition test functions for numerical global optimization. In: 2005 Proceedings of IEEE Swarm Intelligence Symposium, SIS 2005, pp. 68–75. IEEE (2005)

Bacterial Foraging Optimization Algorithm

Reorganized Bacterial Foraging Optimization Algorithm for Aircraft Maintenance Technician Scheduling Problem

Ben Niu[1,2], Bowen Xue[1,2], Tianwei Zhou[1,2(✉)], Churong Zhang[1,2], and Qinge Xiao[1,2]

[1] College of Management, Shenzhen University, Shenzhen 518060, China
tianwei@szu.edu.cn
[2] Great Bay Area International Institute for Innovation,
Shenzhen University, Shenzhen 518060, China

Abstract. This paper studies the problem of aircraft maintenance technician scheduling problem. Aircraft maintenance companies often need to allocate aircraft maintenance technicians in advance according to maintenance orders before carrying out maintenance work, with the aim of maximizing the company's benefits. In order to solve the aircraft maintenance technician scheduling problem, we propose a reorganized bacterial foraging optimization algorithm (RBFO), which introduces the individual information transmission mechanisms among each individual in the bacterial swarm, and reorganizes the structure of the original bacterial foraging algorithm. The experimental results verify the applicability of the proposed algorithm in the specific constructed model, and give the optimal task-technician allocation scheme based on the numerical example data. The performance of RBFO is high-lighted through comparative experiments.

Keywords: Aircraft maintenance · Technician assignment · Bacterial foraging optimization

1 Introduction

With the increase of flight routes and the decrease of travel costs, the proportion of air transportation in the world GDP is higher and higher, which also stimulates the growth of the demand for Aircraft Maintenance, Repair and Overhaul (MRO) [1, 2]. At present, most airlines adopt the mode of outsourcing MRO business to aircraft maintenance companies [3].

This paper focuses on the aircraft maintenance technician scheduling problem under the aircraft maintenance outsourcing mode. Aircraft maintenance companies need to match aircraft maintenance tasks with maintenance technicians when accepting maintenance orders from airlines. In recent years, in the literature of personnel scheduling problem in aviation industry, most papers pay more attention to the crew scheduling problem [4–6], while the research on aircraft maintenance technician scheduling problem is relatively rare. Both Qin et al. [2] and Permatasari et al. [7] used linear programming

© Springer Nature Switzerland AG 2021
Y. Tan and Y. Shi (Eds.): ICSI 2021, LNCS 12689, pp. 505–512, 2021.
https://doi.org/10.1007/978-3-030-78743-1_45

algorithm to get the optimal solution of technician scheduling with minimum maintenance cost of aircraft maintenance company. However, those papers only consider minimizing the cost of aircraft maintenance, without considering whether the workload allocation of aircraft maintenance technicians is fair and reasonable. Considering the high turnover rate of aircraft maintenance technicians, this is a factor worthy of in-depth discussion.

In this paper, a concrete NP-hard problem with regard to the dimensions of aircraft, shift, task and technician is considered. Heuristic algorithm has been widely used to solve NP hard scheduling problems, such as crew scheduling [8], nurse scheduling [9] and so on. As a representative heuristic algorithm, BFO has excellent performance in solving such problems [10]. Based on the traditional bacterial foraging optimization (BFO) [11] and bacterial colony optimization [12], we propose a reorganized bacterial foraging optimization (RBFO) algorithm which is suitable for solving the aircraft maintenance technician scheduling problem by integrating the ideas of reorganization of original BFO and information transmission mechanism within a colony.

The reminder of this paper is structured as follows. Section 2 states aircraft maintenance technician scheduling problem. Section 3 describes the proposed reorganized bacterial foraging optimization. Section 4 presents the coding mechanism and the computational results based on the comparative experiments. Section 5 concludes the paper and points out future directions.

2   Model of Aircraft Maintenance Technician Scheduling Problem

This section introduces the assignment model of aircraft maintenance technicians. Definitions of variables are listed in Table 1. First, in Subsect. 2.1, aircraft maintenance technician scheduling problem is described in detail and related variables are defined. Then, Subsect. 2.2 gives the objective function and constraints with explanation of practical significance.

2.1   Problem Description

Each aircraft parked in the hangar waiting for maintenance has a series of maintenance tasks with sequence. Following Gang et al. [13], a maintenance task is supposed to be assigned to only one aircraft maintenance technician, and there are precedence relations among a series of maintenance tasks. Besides, the license requirement of maintenance tasks limits the assignment of maintenance technicians. To provide the aircraft maintenance technicians with sufficient rest time, technicians are not allowed to work in two or more consecutive work shifts. A work shift usually lasts for eight hours and there are three consecutive shifts in a day [2]. To tackle this problem, a task-technician assignment solution should be given with the aim of realizing the minimization of total costs.

Table 1. Definition of variables.

Variables	Meaning of variables
A	Number of aircrafts
M	Number of aircraft maintenance technicians
T	Number of maintenance shifts
S_{it}	Number of maintenance tasks
λ_m	Cost of technician m in a shift
$d_{mt,is}$	Time spent by technician m to finish task s of aircraft i in shift t
g	Average working time of all technicians
NC_m	The number of times technician m participates in continuous shifts
sd_{it}	Delivery time of aircraft i in shift t
n_m	Normal working hours of technician m
PS_{is}	Pre-tasks of task s on aircraft i
ws_m	Working state of technician m
q_m	License level of technician m, $q_m \in \{1, 2, 3\}$
A_{qs}	Task s can be assigned to technicians with license q
$a_{mt,is}$	Whether technician m is assigned to task s of aircraft i in shift t
t_{ist}	Whether task s of aircraft i can be implemented in shift t
ow_m	Whether technician m works overtime
f_{is}	Whether task s of aircraft i is complicated

2.2 Objective Function and Constraints

Objective Function

$$
\min \left\{ \sum_{m \in M} \sum_{t \in T} \sum_{s \in S} a_{mt,is} \cdot \lambda_m + p_1 \cdot \left[\frac{1}{m} \sum_{m \in M} \left(\sum_{t \in T} \sum_{s \in S} a_{mt,is} \cdot d_{mt,is} - g \right)^2 \right] \right.
$$

$$
+ p_2 \cdot \sum_{m \in M} NC_m + p_3 \cdot \sum_{t \in T} \max \left\{ \sum_{m \in M} \sum_{s \in S} a_{mt,is} \cdot d_{mt,is} - sd_{it}, 0 \right\} \tag{1}
$$

$$
\left. + p_4 \cdot \sum_{m \in M} ow_m \cdot \max \left\{ \sum_{t \in T} \sum_{s \in S} a_{mt,is} \cdot d_{mt,is} - n_m, 0 \right\} \right\}
$$

The optimization objective of this paper consists of manpower cost and other four penalty costs, including (i) penalty of unfair distribution of workload; (ii) penalty of participating in two consecutive shifts; (iii) penalty cost of a shift in which the completion time of all tasks exceeds the specified end time of the shift; (iv) penalty of working time of a technician in the whole maintenance cycle exceeds the time stipulated in the labor contract. p_1, p_2, p_3, p_4 represent the penalty coefficients of the above four types of costs.

Constraints

$$t_{ist} \leq \frac{1}{|PS_{is}|} \cdot \sum_{s' \in PS_{is}} f'_{is}, \forall i \in A, \forall s \in S, \forall t \in T \tag{2}$$

$$\sum_{m \in M} a_{mt,is} = 1, \forall i \in A, \forall t \in T, \forall s \in S \tag{3}$$

$$\sum_{m \in M} \sum_{s \in S} a_{mt,is} \cdot d_{mt,is} \leq sd_{it}, \forall i \in A, \forall t \in T \tag{4}$$

$$\sum_{s \in S} a_{mt,is} \cdot \sum_{s \in S} am(t+1), is = 0, \forall i \in A, \forall t \in T, \forall m \in M \tag{5}$$

$$\sum_{i \in A} \sum_{t \in T} \sum_{s \in S} a_{mt,is} \cdot d_{mt,is} \leq n_m, \forall m \in M \tag{6}$$

$$a_{mt,is} \leq ws_m, \forall i \in A, \forall t \in T, \forall m \in M, \forall s \in S \tag{7}$$

$$a_{mt,is} \leq q_m A_q s, \forall i \in A, \forall t \in T, \forall m \in M, \forall s \in S \tag{8}$$

Constraints (2)–(3) indicate that each aircraft maintenance request is decomposed into a series of sub tasks with sequence, and each sub task is completed by only one maintenance technician. Constraint (4) is the regulation set to avoid the delay of subsequent aircraft maintenance tasks. Constraints (5)–(6) impose that maintenance technicians have enough rest time. Constraint (7) prescribes that only idle maintenance personnel can be assigned to task s to be performed on the aircraft i. Constraint (8) enables tasks to be assigned to maintenance technicians who meet their maintenance license requirements.

3   Reorganized Bacterial Foraging Optimization Algorithm

We mainly improve the bacterial foraging optimization [11] in the structure and information transmission mechanism of the algorithm, respectively.

3.1   Structural Recombination

Chemotaxis, reproduction and elimination are three operators in original BFO [11], which are represented by three nested loops in the algorithm. However, this kind of complex structure often brings high time complexity and space complexity, resulting in excessive computing cost. Therefore, in this paper, we reconstruct three operators and let them execute in order, so as to simplify the algorithm to a certain extent.

3.2 Information Transmission Mechanism

Biological information includes physical information, chemical information, behavioral information and nutritional information. Information transmission is a common way for species to communicate in biological world, including information generation, transmission and reception.

In the original bacterial foraging optimization algorithm, bacteria have the characteristics of global clustering [11], and the decision-making behaviors are closely related to information of itself and other individuals. For instance, in a bacterial swarm of D individuals, θ_d represents the location of the individual currently being optimized and θ_d^i represents the location of ith individual. When receiving attraction signals $d_{attract}$ and $w_{attract}$, the individual will swim to the center of the bacterial swarm; when receiving repulsion signals $h_{attract}$ and w_{repell}, the individual will keep distance with others. Consequently, an individual's influence of signal transmission among a bacterial swarm is:

$$Jcc = \sum_{i=1}^{Np} [-d_{attract} \exp(-w_{attract} \sum_{d=1}^{D} (\theta_d - \theta_d^i)^2) + h_{repell} \exp(-w_{repell} \sum_{d=1}^{D} (\theta_d - \theta_d^i)^2)] \quad (9)$$

In addition, there is no lack of communication mechanism between an individual and the optimal individual. We divide the optimal individuals in a bacterial swarm into two categories: self-historical optimal and swarm optimal. Self-historical optimal refers to the individuals that obtain the optimal objective value of the specific individual in the cumulative iteration process. Swarm optimal refers to the individuals obtain the optimal objective value among a bacterial swarm in all iterations. After each iteration, both self-historical optimal and swarm optimal might be updated according to the present optimization results. In order to improve the optimization ability of the algorithm and enhance the diversity of the search process, we also introduce random individuals for information transmission among individuals in the bacterial swarm.

In consequence, each individual's information transmission process includes three parts: information transmission with the self-historical optimal, the current swarm optimal, and a random individual. Therefore, the information transmission mechanism of each individual in a swarm is:

$$L_i = (1 - \alpha - \beta) \cdot L_i + \alpha \cdot L_h + \beta \cdot L_r \quad (10)$$

L_i is the location of ith individual, L_h is the location of self-historical optimal individual of ith individual, and L_r is the location of a random individual. α and β are two learning factors of L_h and L_r, respectively.

4 Experiments and Results

4.1 Encoding Scheme

BFO is a continuous optimization algorithm, whereas the personnel scheduling problem is a discrete problem. Therefore, in the coding scheme, how to realize the conversion from continuous coding to discrete coding is the key to solve the problem. Table 2 is a continuous coding scheme in the process of iterative optimization using RBFO algorithm. What we need to achieve is to select a position in the corresponding column of each task to represent the selected maintenance technician. In this process, we need to determine which positions cannot be selected from according to the constraints. For example, in Table 2, the parts filled with blue indicate that this part of the technicians does not meet the requirements of the maintenance license level for this task, while the red number indicates that the maintenance technicians are working and should not be assigned to complete other tasks. Finally, we select the largest number from the remaining numbers in each column as the selected maintenance technicians, and the results are shown in Table 3. In Table 3, the first maintenance task is assigned to the tenth maintenance technician, and the second and third maintenance tasks are assigned to the ninth maintenance technician.

Table 2. Continuous encoding scheme.

Aircraft index	Technician index	Shift t /8h		
		Task 1	Task 2	Task 3
	1	0.51	0.72	0.45
	2	0.21	0	0.22
	3	0.13	0.18	0.11
	4	0.41	0.35	0.4
	5	0.65	0.36	0.29
1	6	0.13	0	0.56
	7	0.24	0.49	0
	8	0.57	0.52	0.04
	9	0.86	0.91	0.19
	10	0.97	0.04	0
	11	0.47	0.55	0.15

Table 3. Discrete encoding scheme.

Aircraft index	Shift t/8h		
	Task 1	Task 2	Task 3
1	10	9	9

4.2 Parameter Settings

The relevant data of aircrafts, tasks and technicians used in the experiment are randomly generated on the basis of consulting a large number of reference materials. In this paper, the number of aircrafts is $A \in \{1, 2, 3, 4\}$, the number of maintenance technicians $M = 11$, and the number of shifts $T = 3$.

In order to test and highlight the excellent performance of RBFO in solving this aircraft maintenance technician scheduling model, we also set up comparative experiments to compare this algorithm with other heuristic algorithms, including BFO, PSO, and GA. The population size of all algorithms is 30, and the fitness evaluation time is 30000. In RBFO and BFO, the elimination probability P_{ed} is 0.25 and the length of swim $N_s = 4$, $C_{start} = 0.2$, $C_{end} = 0.01$. In PSO, the learning factors are set to 2. In GA, the crossover probability is 0.95 and mutation probability is 0.1.

4.3 Experimental Results

The experiments are carried out five times and the convergence of each algorithm on the average optimal fitness value is shown in Fig. 1. With the increasing number of aircrafts, the total maintenance cost of each algorithm grows. Among them, the incremental cost of BFO algorithm is the largest, while that of RBFO algorithm is the smallest. In addition, compared with other algorithms, the final optimal solution of RBFO algorithm always corresponds to the lowest total maintenance cost in the four cases with different number of aircrafts. Moreover, RBFO has stronger convergence performance than the other three algorithms.

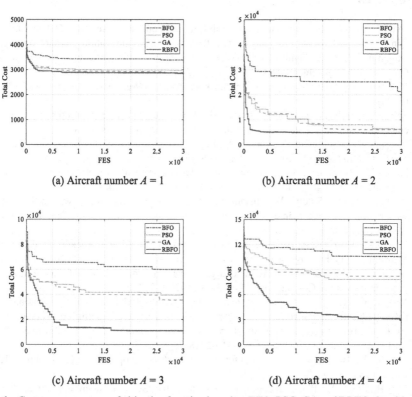

Fig. 1. Convergence curves of objective function based on BFO, PSO, GA and RBFO algorithms.

5   Conclusions and Future Directions

In this paper, we propose RBFO algorithm and apply it to solve the improved model for aircraft maintenance technician scheduling problem. Experiments verify the superiority of the proposed RBFO and optimal task-technician allocation scheme can be obtained with the lowest cost.

In the future, building multi-objective optimization model on the basis of RBFO algorithm is an important development direction. In addition, application of the proposed algorithm to other types of scheduling problems is also an interesting direction, including aircraft maintenance tools scheduling, crew scheduling and so on.

Acknowledgement. This work is supported in part by the National Natural Science Foundation of China under Grant 71971143, and in part by Guangdong Basic and Applied Basic Research Foundation under Grant 2019A1515110401, and in part by Key Projects of Colleges and Universities in Guangdong Province under Grant 2019KZDXM030.

References

1. IATA Economics. https://www.iata.org/publications/economics/. Accessed 26 Feb 2021
2. Qin, Y., Zhang, J., Chan, F., Chung, S., Qu, T.: A two-stage optimization approach for aircraft hangar maintenance planning and staff assignment problems under MRO outsourcing mode. Comput. Ind. Eng. **146**, 106607 (2020)
3. Marcontell, D.: MRO's offshore edge shrinking. Aviation Week Space Technol. **175**(22), 56 (2013)
4. Salazar-Gonzalez, J.: Approaches to solve the fleet-assignment, aircraft-routing, crew-pairing and crew-rostering problems of a regional carrier. Omega **43**, 71–82 (2014)
5. Quesnel, F., Desaulniers, G., Soumis, F.: Improving air crew rostering by considering crew preferences in the crew pairing problem. Transp. Sci. **54**(1), 97–114 (2019)
6. Zhang, Z., Zhou, M.C., Wang, J.: Construction-based optimization approaches to airline crew rostering problem. IEEE Trans. Autom. Sci. Eng. **17**(3), 1399–1409 (2020)
7. Permatasari, C.I., Sutopo, W., Hisjam, M.: Aircraft maintenance manpower shift planning with multiple aircraft maintenance licenced. IOP Conf. Ser.: Mater. Sci. Eng. **495**, 012023 (2019)
8. Garcia, J., Altimiras, F., Pena, A., Astorga, G., Peredo, O.: A binary cuckoo search big data algorithm applied to large-scale crew scheduling problems. Complexity **2018**, 1–15 (2018)
9. Gutjahr, W.J., Rauner, M.S.: An ACO algorithm for a dynamic regional nurse-scheduling problem in Austria. Comput. Oper. Res. **34**(3), 642–666 (2007)
10. Niu, B., Wang, C., Liu, J., Gan, J., Yuan, L.: Improved bacterial foraging optimization algorithm with information communication mechanism for nurse scheduling. In: Huang, D.-S., Jo, K.-H., Hussain, A. (eds.) ICIC 2015. LNCS, vol. 9226, pp. 701–707. Springer, Cham (2015). https://doi.org/10.1007/978-3-319-22186-1_69
11. Passino, K.: Biomimicry of bacterial foraging for distributed optimization and control. IEEE Control Syst. Mag. **22**(3), 52–67 (2002)
12. Niu, B., Wang, H.: Bacterial colony optimization. Discrete Dyn. Nature Soc. **2012**, 698057 (2012)
13. Gang, C., Wen, H., Lawrence, C., Tan, L., Han, Y.: Assigning licenced technicians to maintenance tasks at aircraft maintenance base: a bi-objective approach and a Chinese airline application. Int. J. Prod. Res. **55**, 19–20 (2017)

A Bacterial Foraging Optimization Algorithm Based on Normal Distribution for Crowdfunding Project Outcome Prediction

Yingsi Tan, Shilian Chen, and Shuang Geng[(✉)]

College of Management, Shenzhen University, Shenzhen 518060, China
gs@szu.edu.cn

Abstract. Crowdfunding is a concept that raising fund for different individual or organization to conduct creative projects and it has gained more and more popularity during these years. Fund used for projects can reach to billions of dollars, so it's very significant to perfectly predict multiple crowdfunding ads. To improve the accuracy of crowdfunding project outcome prediction, a modified Bacterial Foraging Optimization Algorithm (NBFO) through population initialization, reproduction and elimination-dispersion was proposed to cooperate with Light Gradient Boosting Machine (LightGBM). This paper used normal distribution through the period of population initialization and elimination-dispersion. Moreover, during reproduction, selective probability was introduced to enhance the performance of bacteria. Experiments used 5561 valid data collected from Kickstarter from June 2017 to February 2018, and compared the predictive power of LightGBM incorporated with Particle Swarm Optimization (PSO), Bee Colony Optimization (BCO) and Evolutionary Strategy (ES). Results showed that the performance of NBFO surpasses all comparative algorithms. The performance of LightGBM incorporated with other swarm intelligent algorithms and evolutionary algorithm are discussed. Findings in this study contribute to the study of crowdfunding, Light Gradient Boosting Machine, swarm intelligent algorithm and evolutionary algorithm.

Keywords: Crowdfunding · Bacterial foraging optimization · Light gradient boosting machine

1 Introduction

Crowdfunding, as a new and innovative financing method through the Internet, helps a large number of entrepreneurs get investment help from various online personnel, thus effectively providing economic support for enterprise projects or venture capital. Especially in recent years, the crowdfunding industry has flourished on a global scale [1], which has greatly stimulated scholars, operators of various platforms, entrepreneurs and investors to pay attention to it.

The novel and innovative financing method of crowdfunding can effectively solve the huge difficulties and forward development challenges for small-and medium-sized

© Springer Nature Switzerland AG 2021
Y. Tan and Y. Shi (Eds.): ICSI 2021, LNCS 12689, pp. 513–522, 2021.
https://doi.org/10.1007/978-3-030-78743-1_46

enterprises (SMEs) in the initial stage, and prevent enterprises and projects with strong development prospects from failing or ending ahead of schedule. At the same time, with the recent outbreak of COVID-19 in 2020, the crowdfunding market has grown more rapidly, especially donating crowdfunding to support and help communities, people and many organizations to fight this epidemic. According to Market Data Forecast's estimates, in 2019, the estimated size of the global crowdfunding market is 14.2 billion US dollars. When it reaches 2025, it will have a great possibility to reach 28.8 billion US dollars, and the compound annual growth rate from 2020 to 2015 is calculated to be 16% [2].

However, although crowdfunding has such a vigorous development prospect, the main problems of crowdfunding in these years are still information asymmetry between crowdfunding promoters and investors, low financing success rate and unacceptable high financing risks for investors [3]. Although there are many researches that can effectively help alleviate the information gap between investors and crowdfunding [4], the quality of crowdfunding projects, the authenticity of information and whether the final project is real and practical will still cause great obstacles for investors to choose projects. Some people who initiate crowdfunding sometimes register multiple crowdfunding platform accounts or hire a large number of platform users to comment on his projects, thus pretending that the society shows high enthusiasm and interest in his crowdfunding projects. Finally, unsuspecting investors are deceived to invest in their crowdfunding projects. Such behavior is very unfavorable to investors. At the same time, some crowdfunding projects cannot achieve the expected return on income, which makes many investors disappointed. Such behavior has caused an increase in the degree of distrust between the two sides, thus jeopardizing the sustainable development of the crowdfunding market. Therefore, it is of great significance and urgent need for investors to predict the results of crowdfunding projects effectively.

In recent years, some researchers have adopted machine learning methods, such as Light Gradient Boosting Machine (LightGBM) [5], to analyze the characteristics and factors of crowdfunding projects to predict and judge crowdfunding results (success, survival and failure). What's more, swarm intelligent algorithms, like bacterial foraging optimization (BFO) [6], particle swarm optimization (PSO) [7], bee colony optimization (BCO) [8] and evolutionary strategy (ES) [9], have gradually become the new favorite of complex problems for prediction because they are simple and effective. Up to now, although multiple search methods have been used in crowdfunding project outcome prediction, less studies applied swarm intelligent algorithms in machine learning method to enhance the predictive ability. In this study, our investigation is based on a popular machine learning method Light Gradient Boosting Machine and a swarm intelligent algorithm BFO. The goals of this research are shown as follows:

1. Normal distribution is introduced into the process of population initialization and elimination – dispersion of BFO to empower of predictive ability.
2. Redesign the reproduction mechanism of BFO with selective probability to empower of predictive ability.
3. Compare the accuracy in crowdfunding project outcome prediction of different swarm intelligent algorithms (BFO, improved BFO, PSO and BCO) and evolutionary algorithm (ES) incorporated with LightGBM.

4. Measure the advancement of accuracy in crowdfunding project outcome prediction of LightGBM with improved BFO.

The structure of our research paper is arranged as follows: Sect. 2 introduces the basic method: LightGBM Method and standard BFO. The Enhanced LightGBM framework with improved BFO will be held in Sect. 2.3. Section 3 illustrates the details of crowdfunding project dataset and parameter settings, then reporting the experiment results and finally, Sect. 4 reaches a conclusion and discusses future work.

2 Methodology

2.1 Light Gradient Boosting Machine

Light gradient boosting machine (LightGBM) is an evolutionary version based on GBDT, which is an algorithm model developed by Microsoft Corporation in 17 years [10]. We chose LightGBM as the basis of our optimization problem because it only needs low calculation cost, but its results have high efficiency and accuracy, feature classification ability and prediction ability, and have achieved good results in the application of large data sets. Different from other hierarchical constraints, LightGBM saves computing power and improves maximum effective branches by limiting the maximum number of leaves in decision-tree structure.

Controlling the training mode of data in LightGBM is accomplished by selecting several hyperparameters. In addition to the traditional manual adjustment and grid search, the method of adjusting these hyperparameters can also use optimization algorithm. Through the combination of different feasible solutions, the most suitable and best solution is finally obtained as the parameter selection of LightGBM.In our work, we choose multiple optimization algorithms and build multiple integration frameworks to compare the optimization results of the algorithms. We choose seven hyperparameters including the maximum number of leaves in tree structure, the bagging's frequency and fraction, regularization L1 and L2, fraction of feature, the value of the minimum number of samples on each leaf in LightGBM as the solution set of swarm intelligence or evolutionary algorithm, and compare the accuracy of LightGBM running results under different optimization algorithms.

2.2 Bacterial Foraging Optimization

Inspired by Escherichia coli eating food in the human gut, Passino [11] proposed a biological heuristic simulation algorithm, Bacterial Foraging Optimization Algorithm (BFO). For the reason that it has several advantages such as parallel searching and skipping local optimality, it has been used for feature selection and prediction.

When looking for food, bacteria use its flagellum to move. Flagellum has two functions: tumbling and swimming. Tumbling helps change direction while swimming means walking in the changed direction. In a D-dimensional environment, θ represents the position of the bacteria, and $J(\theta)$ represents the function value. We use i to represent every bacterium. Each bacterium will turn in a random vector $\Delta(i)$ and used Eq. (1) to update its position. $\theta^i(j, k, l)$ represent Jth chemotaxis, Kth reproduction and Lth elimination - dispersion. $C(i)$ represents the step of moving.

$$\theta^i(j+1, k, l) = \theta^i(j, k, l) + C(i)\frac{\Delta(i)}{\sqrt{\Delta^T(i)\Delta(i)}} \tag{1}$$

When bacteria have obtained enough nutrient and appropriate temperature, each of them starts to reproduce, forming two new bacteria, that is, replace the position of the bottom 50% of the bacteria with that of the top 50% of the bacteria according to their fitness value. If the environment suddenly became hostile, some bacteria may be eliminated and others may be dispersed to a new place, that is, update the position of part of bacteria randomly.

2.3   Enhanced LightGBM Framework with Improved BFO

We applied LightGBM in crowdfunding project outcome prediction because of its faster training speed and less memory footprint. To better its outcome prediction, we proposed an enhanced LightGBM framework that deployed an improved BFO algorithm to optimize its hyperparameters. Seven hypermeters were chosen for comparison purpose with other parameter turning methods, such as Particle Swarm Optimization [5], that is, the maximum depth of the tree, minimum number of records that a lead may have (minimum child sample), the proportion of randomly selected features per iteration (feature fraction), the proportion of randomly selected data per iteration (bagging fraction), bagging frequency, specified regularization 1 and specified regularization 2. The default of parameter setting is 31, 20, 1.0, 1.0, 0, 0.0, 0.0 respectively.

Figure 1 illustrates the overall flow of the improved LightGBM framework. Generally, in BFO algorithm, bacteria initialize their positions through two method. The first is using the same default value for every position. The second is each position produced a random number. Considering that LightGBM framework has have a default number, we applied normal distribution in the period of position initialization and elimination-dispersion for five hyperparameters: the maximum depth of the tree, minimum child sample, bagging frequency, specified regularization 1 and specified regularization 2, using default value as mean value.

Compared with other algorithms such as BFO and BCO, NBFO with improved initialization process can find the optimal solution in data set faster, improve convergence speed and initial optimization ability, reduce waste of bacteria and improve optimization efficiency.

Then, the hyperparameters will be transferred into the LightGBM framework for model training together with selected features. The fitness value will be returned to the BFO for continued iteration. After chemotaxis, each bacterium will use Eq. (2) to calculate its selective probability $Ps(i)$. $\sum_{i=0}^{pN} J^i(\theta)$ describes the cumulative probability per iteration. Table 1 illustrate the process of reproduction. The process will continue until we have obtained enough bacteria. In this way, better bacteria have more probability to reproduce and speed up the convergence. On the other hand, bacteria at a temporary disadvantage also have the chance, thus help avoid local optimal solution. Finally, once

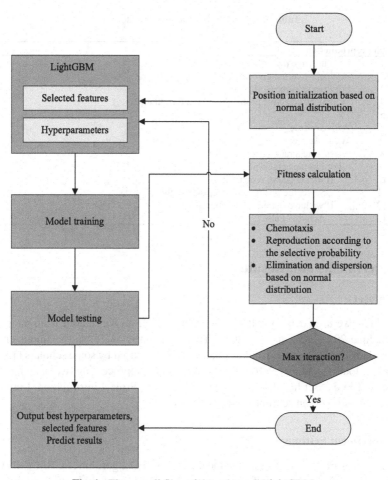

Fig. 1. The overall flow of the enhanced LightGBM.

BFO algorithm reach its max iteration, the method will output the best hyperparameters and accuracy.

$$Ps(i) = \frac{J^i(\theta)}{\sum_{i=0}^{pN} J^i(\theta)} \tag{2}$$

Table 1. The pseudo code of reproduction.

During reproduction	
1	For i in range (self.pN):
2	Calculate cumulative probability
3	For i range range (self.pN):
4	Calculate selective probability using formular (2)
5	
6	Active = True
7	While Active:
8	Generate a random number R
9	For i in range (self.pN):
10	If R < selective probability:
11	Select the position and step size of this bacteria
12	If we have obtain self.pN bacteria:
13	Active = False

3   Experiments and Results

3.1   Dataset

In this study, we used dataset collected by Yang [12] from Kickstarter from the period between June 2017 and February 2018. This platform is one of most famous crowd-funding platforms in the world and this dataset has been used by some scholars [13, 14]. The dataset totally contains 5916 projects. After data preprocessing, we obtained 5516 valid data. The dataset has three types of information: Project information. Linguistic features and Description sentiment and 31 features.

3.2   Experiment Settings

In order to measure the effectiveness of the improved BFO algorithm (LGBM_NBFO) in predicting the outcome of crowdfunding project, we incorporated LightGBM with other swarm intelligent algorithms (PSO and BCO) and evolutionary algorithm (ES). The parameter setting for LGBM, LGBM_PSO, LGBM_BCO, LGBM_ES, LGBM_BFO and LGBM_NBFO are reported in Table 2 and Table 3.

3.3   Experiment Results

The experiment was conducted in Python, using Accuracy (Accuracy = 1 – the error rate of classification) as evaluation criterion to assess the performance of the methods. The results are shown in Table 4 and Fig. 2. The results are range from 82.58% to 83.68%. LGBM_NBFO achieved the highest accuracy of 83.68%, followed by that of LGBM_BCO and LGBM_BFO, at 83.60% and 83.53% respectively. The numbers in accuracy of LGBM_PSO and LGBM_ES are very close, at 83.34% and 83.17% respectively. The accuracy of the original LGBM is 82.58%. In conclusion, LGBM_NBFO enhanced the prediction accuracy compared with LGBM, LGBM_PSO, LGBM_BCO, LGBM_BFO and LGBM_ES. Figure 3 reports the average outcome predictive accuracy of each algorithm on crowdfunding project.

Table 2. Algorithm parameter setting.

Method	Value
LGBM	num_leaves = 31 min_child_samples = 20 feature_fraction = 1 bagging_fraction = 1 bagging_freq = 0 lambda_l = 0.0 lambda_l2 = 0.0
LGBM_PSO	W (inertia weight) = 0.8 C1 (learning speed) = 2 C2 (learning speed) = 2 R1 (random constant) = 0.6 R2 (random constant) = 0.3 pN (number of particles) = 50 Dim = Feature number + parameter number Iteration = 50
LGBM_BCO	pN (number of bee) = 50 OnLooker (number of follow bees) = 50 L (upper bound of abandoning) = round(0.6*nVar*pN)) A(enlargement coefficient) = 1 Iteration = 50 nVar = 7
LGBM_ES	N_kid (number of offspring) = 25 pN (number of gene) = 50 Gene_size = Feature number + parameter number Generation = 50
LGBM_BFO LGBM_NBFO	pN (number of bacteria) = 50 Dim = Feature number + parameter number Nc (number of chemotaxis) = 24 Ns (limit of the swimming) = 4 Nre (number of reproduction) = 2 Ned (number of elimination) = 1 Iteration (Nc*Nre*Ned) = 48

Table 3. Normal distribution parameter setting in LGBM_NBFO population initialization

Parameter	Value
num_leaves	Mean = 31, standard deviation = 1
min_child_samples	Mean = 20, standard deviation = 10
feature_fraction	Value = 1
bagging_fraction	Value = 1
bagging_freq	Mean = 0, standard deviation = 1
lambda_l1	Mean = 0.0, standard deviation = 0.3
lambda_l2	Mean = 0.0, standard deviation = 0.5

Table 4. Classification accuracy of each algorithm.

Method	Accuracy
LGBM	0.825866
LGBM_PSO	0.833474
LGBM_BCO	0.836010
LGBM_ES	0.831784
LGBM_BFO	0.835320
LGBM_NBFO	**0.836855**

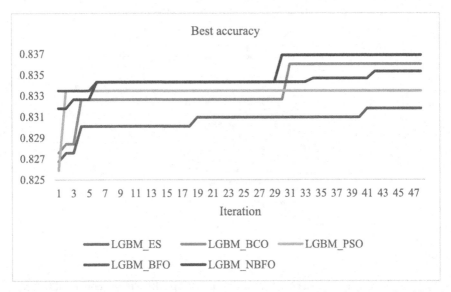

Fig. 2. Best accuracy of different swarm intelligent algorithms and evolutionary algorithm.

4   Conclusion and Future Work

To improve the accuracy of crowdfunding project outcome prediction, a modified BFO (NBFO) based on population initialization, reproduction and elimination-dispersion was proposed to cooperate with LightGBM. This paper used normal distribution through the period of population initialization and elimination-dispersion, and in order to better adapting to the dataset collected by Yang [12] from Kickstarter. Moreover, during reproduction, selective probability was introduced to enhance the performance of bacteria. Comparing with BCO, PSO, ES, BFO, the performance of NBFO surpasses all of them. The contribution of this paper are as follows: (1) We improved the initialization of data set adaptability of BFO, and modified the process of bacterial reproduction of BFO; (2) The proposed BFO algorithm incorporated with Light GBM enhanced the predictive accuracy of this crowdfunding project datasets compared with LightGBM method. (3)

We incorporated LightGBM with different swarm intelligent algorithms (BFO, PSO, BCO) and evolutionary strategy (ES) to turn hyperparameters, and we find that NBFO rank first in the best accuracy among these algorithms.

In our algorithm research and crowdfunding platform test, there are some limitations and our future research agenda. First of all, we need to test the standard deviation of the data set when initializing the Gaussian distribution, which takes a little time, but the rough result of the algorithm is very good, which can be reflected in the improved NBFO and BCO algorithms. Secondly, we have only tested our improved algorithm in Kickstarter's English crowdfunding data set, and the generalization ability of the algorithm in other data sets has yet to be done. However, from the perspective of improving our algorithm, it can expand the application scope very well, which is also one of our future research plans. Thirdly, the algorithm we compare only uses some classical optimization algorithms, and does not test in a large area. We will expand the experiment in the future to see if we can get richer conclusions and discoveries.

Acknowledgement. This study is supported by National Natural Science Foundation of China (71901150, 71702111, 71971143), the Natural Science Foundation of Guangdong Province (2020A1515010749), Guangdong Basic and Applied Basic Research Foundation (Project No. 2019A1515011392), Shenzhen University Teaching Reform Project (Grants No. JG2020119).

References

1. Ziegler, T., Shneor, R., Zhang, B.Z.: The global status of the crowdfunding industry. In: Shneor, R., Zhao, L., Flåten, B.-T. (eds.) Advances in Crowdfunding, pp. 43–61. Springer, Cham (2020). https://doi.org/10.1007/978-3-030-46309-0_3
2. Global Crowdfunding Market Research Report – Segmentation by Product (Awards-Based Crowdfunding, Crowdfunding Auctions, and others), End-users (Cultural Industries, Technology, Product, Healthcare, Others), Industry Analysis, Size, Share, Growth, Trends & Forecast To 2025
3. Miglo, A., Miglo, V.: Market Imperfections and Crowdfunding. Small Business Economics, Forthcoming (2016)
4. Courtney, C., Dutta, S., Li, Y.: Resolving information asymmetry: signaling, endorsement, and crowdfunding success. Entrep. Theory Pract. 41(2), 265–290 (2017)
5. Geng, S., Huang, M., Wang, Z.: A swarm enhanced light gradient boosting machine for crowdfunding project outcome prediction. In: Chen, X., Yan, H., Yan, Q., Zhang, X. (eds.) ML4CS 2020. LNCS, vol. 12488, pp. 372–382. Springer, Cham (2020). https://doi.org/10.1007/978-3-030-62463-7_34
6. Majhi, R., Panda, G., Majhi, B., Sahoo, G.: Efficient prediction of stock market indices using adaptive bacterial foraging optimization (ABFO) and BFO based techniques. Expert Syst. Appl. 36(6), 10097–10104 (2009)
7. Zhao, L., Yang, Y.: PSO-based single multiplicative neuron model for time series prediction. Expert Syst. Appl. 36(2), 2805–2812 (2009)
8. Zhang, Y., Wu, L.: Stock market prediction of S&P 500 via combination of improved BCO approach and BP neural network. Expert Syst. Appl. 36(5), 8849–8854 (2009)
9. Kang, H.I.: A fuzzy time series prediction method using the evolutionary algorithm. In: Huang, D.-S., Zhang, X.-P., Huang, G.-B. (eds.) ICIC 2005. LNCS, vol. 3645, pp. 530–537. Springer, Heidelberg (2005). https://doi.org/10.1007/11538356_55

10. Ke, G.M., et al.: LightGBM: a highly efficient gradient boosting decision tree. In: Advances in Neural Information Processing Systems, pp. 3146–3154, Morgan Kaufmann Publishers, San Mateo, USA (2017)
11. Passino, K.: Biomimicry of bacterial foraging for distributed optimization and control. IEEE Control Syst. Mag. **22**(3), 52–67 (2002)
12. Yang, K.L: Kickstarter crowdfunding projects dataset. Peking University Open Research Data Platform, V1 (2018)
13. Colombo, M.G., Franzoni, C., Rossi-Lamastra, C.: Internal social capital and the attraction of early contributions in crowdfunding. Entrep. Theory Pract. **39**(1), 75–100 (2015)
14. Butticè, V., Colombo, M.G., Wright, M.: Serial crowdfunding, social capital, and project success. Entrep. Theory Pract. **41**(2), 183–207 (2017)

Bacterial Foraging Optimization with Leader Selection Strategy for Bi-objective Optimization

Hong Wang, Yixin Wang, Yikun Ou$^{(\boxtimes)}$, and Ben Niu$^{(\boxtimes)}$

College of Management, Shenzhen University, Shenzhen 518060, China
ouyikun2019@email.szu.edu.cn

Abstract. Multi-objective problem (MOP) has long been a challenging issue. Many novel Swarm Intelligence (SI) method like Bacterial Foraging Optimization (BFO) has been extended to tackle MOPs recent years. To further improve the efficiency of BFO in multi-objective optimization, this paper proposes a novel BFO for Bi-objective optimization (abbreviated as BIBFO) with enhanced leader selection strategy. The leader selection strategy incorporating with the Density-Based Spatial Clustering of Applications with Noise (DBSCAN) method in comprehensive learning mechanism can direct evolution and enhances the search efficiency. Besides, the strategies of reproduction and elimination are improved using elitism strategy to enhance the collaboration between search group and the external archive, which can speed up the convergence and improve the search efficiency. In addition, the external archive control strategy is further applied to balance the convergence and the solution diversity. The effectiveness of BIBFO is demonstrated on six frequently used benchmarks, and comparative studies have been conducted among bacterial-based multi-objective optimization algorithms. Experimental results indicate that the proposed BIBFO performs well in generation distance (GD) and diversity (Δ) metrics of obtained Pareto front.

Keywords: Bacterial foraging optimization · Bi-objective optimization · Leader selection strategy · DBSCAN

1 Introduction

Many applications in real life often have a multi-objective property. For example, in the stock investment problem, we simply have two conflicting goals. One is spending minimization and the other is revenue maximization or risk minimization [1]. Generally, MOPs contain multiple contradictory objectives, and there is no unique global optimal solution. Therefore, MOPs are usually solved by finding a trade-off solution set. At the same time, MOPs also face more problems, such as computing complexity, dimensionality curse, discontinuous solution distribution, and so on.

Beginning in the 21st century, nature-inspired heuristic methods like evolutionary computing (EC) and swarm intelligence (SI) began to be widely used in MOPs [2]. Some well-known state-of-the-art Multi-objective Evolutionary Algorithms (MOEAs) include the Improving Strength Pareto Evolutionary Algorithm (SPEA2 [3]) and the

© Springer Nature Switzerland AG 2021
Y. Tan and Y. Shi (Eds.): ICSI 2021, LNCS 12689, pp. 523–533, 2021.
https://doi.org/10.1007/978-3-030-78743-1_47

Non-dominated Sorting Genetic Algorithm II or III (NSGA II [4], NSGA III [5]), Multi-objective Artificial Bee Colony Algorithm (MOABC[6]), Multi-objective Particle Swarm Optimization (MOPSO [7]), and so on. The population-based method has excellent global search capabilities [8], and naturally has the advantage of dealing with MOPs. MOEAs are usually able to cover the whole Pareto front in many benchmarks and thus are widely studied. In engineering applications, some MOEAs are proved to have the advantages of less computational burden [9], lower time-consumption [10], stronger robustness [11] and so on. Therefore, it is of great theoretical significance to develop more multi-objective heuristic algorithms.

Bacterial Foraging Optimization (BFO) is a type of swarm intelligence optimization algorithm simulating the foraging behavior of bacteria [12]. It is easy to describe bacterial foraging optimization framework for its simple bionic structure. As BFO has an inner potential to solve the multi-objective optimization algorithm, we design an enhanced BFO algorithm, named Bi-objective Bacterial Foraging Optimization (BIBFO), to fully excavate its optimal performance. In 2013, Wang et al. applied the BFO algorithm to a MOP for the first time (MBFO [13]). Since then, some BFO variants were proposed to solving the MOPs, like a novel MBFO based on a Multi-swarm Cooperative operation (MCMBFO [14]), Multi-objective Bacterial Colony Optimization (MOBCO [11]), Multi-objective BCO with Ring-topology (MORBCO [11]). From their experimental results, these bacterial-based multi-objective optimization algorithms are no less powerful than other swarm intelligence in multi-objective optimization.

Even so, the potential of BFO in MOPs has not been completely realized and it faces several problems like relatively low accuracy, complicated computation. Based on these, the BIBFO has been designed to have a comprehensive learning strategy and an improving process of the reproduction, elimination and dispersal. In addition, to improve the search diversity of the BFO in MOPs and to make the solution closer to the real Pareto front (PF),we presents a leader selection strategy with the basis of Density-Based Spatial Clustering of Applications with Noise (DBSCAN) [15].

The rest of this paper is organized as follows: Sect. 2 briefly describes the background of MOPs and conventional BFO. The extended BIBFO is introduced in Sect. 3. In Sect. 4, the experiments on well-known benchmarks are conducted, followed by an analysis of results obtained. Section 5 presents the conclusions and future works.

2   Related Background

2.1   Multi-objective Optimization

Multi-objective Optimization Problem (MOP) is abstracted from real life. Mathematically, a MOP can be defined as:

$$\text{Maximize/Minimize}\quad F(x) = (f_1(x), f_2(x), f_3(x), \ldots, f_m(x))$$
$$\text{Subject to:}\quad g_i(x) \leq 0, i = 1, 2, 3, \ldots, q \tag{1}$$

where $x \in \Re^n$ is a n dimensions decision variable including m objectives constrained by q constraint conditions $g(x)$. In fact, it is difficult to obtain the optimal effect on each objective. A solution may be optimal in one objective, but may not be superior in other objectives, which determines that the MOP is pursuing a compromise solution set instead of a certain optimal solution.

2.2 Pareto Optimality

As mentioned above, the goal of the MOP is to find out a relatively satisfactory solution set. Pareto optimality is just such a solution set that represents a balancing result among different objectives. The multi-objective optimization algorithm just tries to approach and cover the true Pareto optimality set. Before using algorithms to solve MOPs, we must understand several concepts below.

Dominance: Suppose the optimization problem is a minimization problem. A vector $\vec{u} = (u_1, u_2, u_3, \ldots, u_n)$ is said to dominate $\vec{v} = (v_1, v_2, v_3, \ldots, v_n)$ if and only if $u_i \leq v_i, \forall i \in \{1, 2, 3, \ldots, n\} \wedge u_j < v_j, \exists j \in \{1, 2, 3, \ldots, n\}$, denoted by $\vec{u} \prec \vec{v}$. When $\vec{u}$ is not dominated by any other vectors, so $\vec{u}$ is called a non-dominance solution, also known as a Pareto optimality.

Pareto optimality: For a MOP, a feasible solution $x \in \Re^n$ is called Pareto optimality if and only if $\nexists \tilde{x} \in \Re^n$ such that $F(\tilde{x}) \prec F(x)$.

Pareto Front: For a MOP, a solution set contained the whole Pareto optimality solution is called a Pareto front (PF), which is usually an equilibrium surface.

2.3 Bacterial Foraging Optimization

Passino [12] firstly proposed BFO in 2002, which is a novel Swarm Intelligence (SI) optimization algorithm simulating bacteria colony foraging behavior. Compared with the behavior of a single bacterium, the bacteria colony can produce swarming effect that helps the whole community gather effectively in areas with high nutrition. More information about BFO can refer to [12].

3   Bi-objective Bacterial Foraging Optimization

In this section, the conventional BFO is extended to a bi-objective optimization based on Pareto dominance and the external archive methods. In the proposed BIBFO, novel leader selection, swarm strategy for reproduction and elimination are introduced to fit the bi-objective optimization problem. The DBSCAN is adopted to select a global leader from external archive for chemotaxis in comprehensive learning, which is expected to direct evolution. Unlike the original BFO, the reproduction and elimination-dispersal are performed based on the external archive instead of the evolutionary group. Both reproduction and elimination are based on elitism expected to speed up convergence rate. The overall framework is shown in Fig. 1.

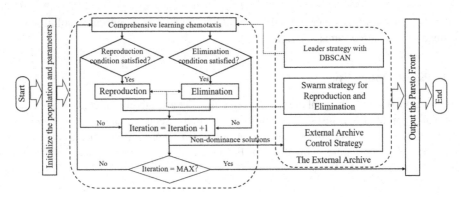

Fig. 1. The overall framework of BIBFO

3.1 Leader Selection Strategy

The Pareto front of bi-objective problems is usually a group of discrete points in a plane. As the number of non-dominance solutions increases, the distribution and density of the Pareto front also change. To enhance the uniformity of Pareto front, it is necessary to explore more latent solutions in some empty space of current Pareto front, which filled the gap and store more even-distributed Pareto optimal solutions. DBSCAN is a typical clustering method based on density distance, by which it can identify the data set distribution and determine different class label [15]. Meanwhile, it does not need to know the clustering number ahead of time and have good clustering ability for irregular sample distribution. Therefore, to improve the capability to search empty solution space, the DBSCAN is applied in the selection of a global optimal solution from the external archive in current iteration for comprehensive learning strategy.

Wang et al. applied a comprehensive strategy in bacterial colony optimization, which blend an operator learning from bacteria colony optimal solution in current iteration has shown great ability in global search and convergence speed [16]. The comprehensive learning mechanism is calculated as follows:

$$\theta_i^t = \theta_i^{t-1} + C(i) * \left[f_1 * \left(leader^t - \theta_i^{t-1} \right) + f_2 * \left(\theta_{best\,i} - \theta_i^{t-1} \right) \right] \tag{2}$$

where θ_i^t is the position of ith bacterium in tth iteration, the f_1 and f_2 are two weight parameters, and $\theta_{best\,i}$ denotes the history optimum of ith bacterium. $leader^t$ is considered as a leader in the direction of evolution.

For MOPs, it is important to note that the goal is to find out as many uniformly distributed Pareto optimality as possible. To search for a more even-distributed non-dominance solution set, current non-dominance solutions are clustered by the DBSCAN to several classes. In two adjacent categories with maximum gap, a bacterium that closest to the other category is selected to calculate the leader of current iteration. A virtual bacterium is introduced as a leader to direct evolution, it can be calculated as follows:

$$leader^t = \frac{1}{2} * \left(Position_1^t + Position_2^t \right) \tag{3}$$

where $Position^t_{1,2}$ is the bacterium selected from the 1st or the 2nd category in tth chemotaxis iteration.

3.2 Swarm Strategy

For fully improving the search ability, an adaptive chemotaxis step size is applied in the proposed BIBFO. The core idea is that the initialized bacterium needs a stronger exploration ability in the early stage of searching and more exploitation competence in the late search process [17]. Therefore, the bigger step size is given to initialized bacterium, the more significant the linear decline is with the increase of chemotaxis iteration. The formula is as follows:

$$C(i) = C_{min} + \left(\frac{\text{iteration}_{max} - \text{iteration}_t}{\text{iteration}_{max}} \right) * (C_{max} - C_{min}) \tag{4}$$

where C_{min} and C_{max} represent the minimal and the maximal chemotaxis step size predefined at the start of chemotaxis respectively, iteration_{max} is the maximal number of iterations, iteration_t represents the tth iteration.

To retain more excellent bacteria, the reproduction and elimination process were modification based on elitism idea. According to dominance rule, the bacteria of search group will be replaced by the non-dominated ones in external archive when meet the conditions for reproduction, that is, some non-dominance solutions will perform search function after reproduction.

The modified elimination process means that the bacteria will be replaced by the neighborhood of a randomly-chosen non-dominated solution in current iteration with a predefined probability.

3.3 External Archive Control

Colello [7] firstly applied an adaptive external archive to store the non-dominance solution in multi-objective particle swarm optimization. As the search progresses, an increasing number of non-dominance solution is found out while the external archive size is limited. Thus, it is necessary to apply some strategies to control the external archive to obtain high diversity. In the proposed BIBFO, the crowding distance method [4] is applied to identify the density of the non-dominance solution distribution. The strategy is that the bacteria that are in the low-density area have a better chance of being preserved than bacteria that are in a higher one. After calculating the crowding distance of each bacterium, the bacteria were sort in an order according to their crowding distance and the bacterium with the highest crowding distance will be deleted.

Aim to achieve the more uniformly-distributed Preto Front, the proposed BIBFO will not allow the dominated solutions with the same cost enter into the external archive. To be specific, there are serval bacteria may consume the same cost value due to the SI property that the search members will learn from the best one. For a Pareto method, the solutions with the same cost value are redundant and may decrease the diversity of final Pareto set. In order to avoid these adverse effects, only one in the solutions with the same cost value will be selected to preserve in external archive. The pseudo code of BIBFO is shown in the Table 1.

Table 1. The pseudo-code of BIBFO

BIBFO

1 Initialize: *npop, MaxIts, Ped, Cmin, Cmax,* f_1, f_2, *Ns, Minpts,* ε,etc.
2 **For** its = 1: the maximum number of chemotaxis *MaxIts*
3   **For** each bacterium
4   Updating position with chemotaxis operator using (2)
5   Updating the bacterium history best
6   **End For**
7   Updating the external archive, **do**
8   Adding non-dominance bacteria into the external archive
9   Controlling the external archive with crowding distance method
10   Updating the global optimum leader with DBSCAN clustering algorithm
11   **If** meet the reproduction condition, **do**
12   Reproduce operation
13   **If** meet elimination and dispersal condition, **do**
14   Eliminate operation
15   its ← its + 1
16 **End For**
17 Output: Pareto front

---

4 Experiments and Results

4.1 Problems and Algorithm Settings

Six well-known benchmarks including Zitzler studies (ZDT1 ~ 3 [18]), Schaffer (SCH1[19]), Fonseca (FON [20]) and Kursawe (KUR [21]), are chosen to test the proposed BIBFO, and all of them are bi-objective problems with no constraints. To verify that BIBFO improves the performance of traditional BFO extended to MOPs, 3 multi-objective optimization algorithms based on bacteria colony are selected for comparing experiments, including MORBCO [11], MCMBFO [14], MOBCO [11]. The parameters of the comparing algorithms were consistent with the cited literatures.

To evaluate the performance of a multi-objective optimization algorithm, the generation distance (GD) and the diversity (Δ) are introduced in this paper. *GD* is a distance-based measurement, which estimates the distance between the actual Pareto front and the current Pareto optimality set [22]. Diversity (Δ), is a metric reflecting the extent of the obtained solution set [4].

As for the proposed BIBFO, the parameters are as follows: $npop = 100$, $C_{min} = 0.05$, $C_{max} = 1.2$, $MaxIts = 300$, $f_1 = 3$, $f_2 = 1$, $Ped = 0.5$, $Ns = 5$. As the DBSCAN, the ε representing the neighbor threshold and *Minpts* describing the minimum number of samples in a class, are set 0.02 and 1 respectively. All of these comparing algorithms, the population size and the external archive size are 100, the maximum number of iterations is set as 1000. The tests were conducted 30 times independently. All of experiments were conducted in MATALAB R2018b, AMD Ryzen 7 4800H, 2.90 GHz under Windows 10 system.

4.2   Results and Analysis

The comparison results are shown in Table 2. It shows the performance scores of the test algorithms on the generation distance and diversity of each benchmark. The best results obtained by algorithms have been highlighted in bold. It can be concluded that the average performance of BIBFO do better than the other compared algorithms in terms of these benchmarks.

Table 2. Comparison of performance metrics on benchmarks

		distance (GD)				Diversity (Δ)			
		Best	Worst	Mean	Std.	Best	Worst	Mean	Std.
ZDT1	BIBFO	**3.47E−04**	**7.83E−04**	**4.89E−04**	**1.13E−04**	**1.56E−01**	**2.76E−01**	**2.08E−01**	**2.92E−02**
	MORBCO	1.37E−03	7.00E−03	3.60E−03	1.30E−03	4.75E−01	8.30E−01	6.26E−01	7.77E−02
	MCMBFO	7.90E−03	9.00E−03	8.40E−03	3.86E−04	6.09E−01	6.96E−01	6.54E−01	3.33E−02
	MOBCO	1.22E−01	5.55E−01	2.72E−01	9.91E−02	4.18E−01	9.24E−01	6.88E−01	1.18E−01
ZDT2	BIBFO	**4.00E−04**	**8.51E−04**	**5.39E−04**	**1.10E−04**	**1.52E−01**	**3.17E−01**	**2.63E−01**	3.70E−02
	MORBCO	1.05E−03	9.74E−03	3.86E−03	2.30E−03	5.94E−01	8.48E−01	6.80E−01	6.90E−02
	MCMBFO	8.80E−03	1.40E−02	1.18E−02	1.90E−03	6.06E−01	6.41E−01	6.21E−01	**1.37E−02**
	MOBCO	1.41E−02	5.68E−02	3.11E−02	1.03E−02	5.51E−01	8.39E−01	6.84E−01	7.03E−02
ZDT3	BIBFO	**7.15E−04**	**1.17E−03**	**9.40E−04**	**1.20E−04**	**3.33E−01**	**6.53E−01**	**4.72E−01**	8.48E−02
	MORBCO	3.45E−03	1.58E−02	6.70E−03	3.01E−03	5.60E−01	9.60E−01	7.32E−01	8.85E−02
	MCMBFO	6.30E−03	7.10E−03	6.70E−03	2.99E−03	5.58E−01	6.62E−01	6.23E−01	**4.40E−02**
	MOBCO	7.63E−02	2.53E−01	1.50E−01	4.77E−02	4.85E−01	8.36E−01	6.49E−01	8.74E−02
SCH1	BIBFO	**7.58E−04**	**1.08E−03**	**9.34E−04**	**7.21E−05**	**1.59E−01**	**2.29E−01**	**1.92E−01**	**1.68E−02**
	MORBCO	5.07E−03	8.46E−03	6.61E−03	9.11E−04	5.02E−01	6.32E−01	5.66E−01	3.56E−02
	MCMBFO	5.80E−03	7.20E−03	6.40E−03	5.75E−04	4.97E−01	6.40E−01	5.37E−01	4.16E−02
	MOBCO	5.13E−03	1.04E−02	7.00E−03	1.14E−03	5.03E−01	6.42E−01	5.64E−01	3.67E−02
FON	BIBFO	**2.92E−04**	**4.94E−04**	**3.89E−04**	**6.65E−05**	**1.60E−01**	**3.13E−01**	**2.22E−01**	3.98E−02
	MORBCO	1.31E−03	2.54E−03	1.98E−03	2.98E−04	5.40E−01	6.84E−01	5.98E−01	**3.66E−02**
	MCMBFO	3.30E−03	3.90E−03	3.60E−03	5.80E−04	5.32E−01	5.87E−01	5.62E−01	3.78E−02
	MOBCO	3.00E−03	4.17E−03	3.53E−03	2.98E−04	4.97E−01	6.86E−01	5.85E−01	4.31E−02
KUR	BIBFO	**7.36E−03**	**2.69E−02**	**1.23E−02**	4.47E−03	7.02E−01	9.59E−01	8.48E−01	6.13E−02
	MORBCO	1.74E−02	4.91E−02	2.73E−02	7.45E−03	**5.14E−01**	7.72E−01	6.48E−01	6.51E−02
	MCMBFO	2.38E−02	3.24E−02	2.89E−02	**3.70E−03**	6.67E−01	8.56E−01	7.61E−01	6.87E−02
	MOBCO	2.95E−02	6.39E−02	4.23E−02	8.43E−03	5.20E−01	**6.66E−01**	**5.99E−01**	**3.35E−02**

As we have seen from Table 2, whether it is diversity or generation distance, the performance metrics of BIBFO are much better than other algorithms, which can well reflect that the distance between the true Pareto front and the Pareto optimal set obtained by BIBFO is closer. Besides, the stability of BIBFO is also far superior to comparison algorithms. To our knowledge, these results indicate that the proposed BIBFO further improve the capability of BFO to tackle MOPs.

It is noted that the MOBCO is the weakest performance in any problems. On the contrary, the MORBCO, which introduced a ring topology for bacterial communication based on MOBCO, improved the performance to a certain extent. The MOBCO almost defeated the MCMBFO incorporated multi-swarm cooperative operation among six benchmarks. It can be concluded that effective communication strategy and collaboration strategy can greatly improve the performance of raw algorithm.

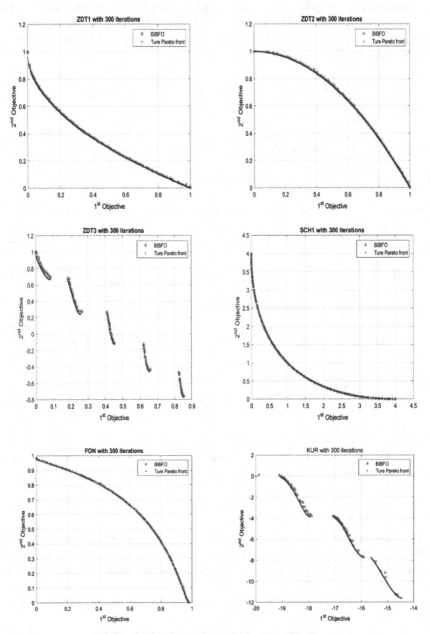

Fig. 2. The Pareto front obtained by BIBFO

Due to the space limitation, only the optimal Pareto fronts gained by BIBFO were displayed as Fig. 2. It can be observed that most the optimal Pareto fronts are close to the true Pareto front. For specific problem, the decision dimensions of SCH1, FON, and KUR are only 1 or 3, and the search range is relatively small. SCH1 and FON almost cover the true Pareto front fully in each comparing algorithm. However, note that the proposed algorithm performed poorly on the KUR function. The reason is that the true Pareto front of the KUR function is discontinuous, which makes BIBFO choose a wrong leader using the DBSCAN clustering method.

ZDT1 ~ 3 are relatively complicated, there are 30 dimensions in decision variable, the search space is relatively large. From the experimental results, the BIBFO can also achieve the expected results on ZDT1 ~ 3 and outperforms other algorithms. However, the performance of ZDT3 is slightly poor comparing to ZDT1 and ZDT2 for the partitioned Pareto front distribution.

5 Conclusions and Feature Work

In this paper, we proposed a bacterial foraging optimization algorithm with multi-strategy for bi-objective optimization. To be specific, leader selection operation using DBSCAN incorporated into comprehensive learning chemotaxis, helps the BIBFO clarify the evolution direction and thus speed up the convergence. Besides, the swarm strategy, including linear decreasing chemotaxis step size, modified reproduction and elimination based on elitism, plays the key role on enhancing the search capability. Comparing the other bacterial-based multi-objective algorithm, the modified external archive strategy of BIBFO further excavated the role of the external archive and improved the storage efficiency of non-dominated solutions.

Then the compared experiments were conducted and proved that the proposed BIBFO algorithm performs well on diversity and generation distance metrics of several bi-objective benchmarks, which achieved the expected improvement effect. Results proved that using BFO with multi-strategy are effective in enhancing the performance of solving bi-objective problems.

Even so, BIBFO itself has its limitations. Compared with other swarm intelligence algorithms, a big computation task cannot be ignored and it has multiple controllable parameters that need to be adjusted according to different problems. In future work, we will continue to improve the structure of the bacterial-based multi-objective algorithm and enhance the effectiveness of multi-strategy to solve more complex MOPs and applications.

Acknowledgment. This work is partially supported by The National Natural Science Foundation of China (Grants Nos. 71901152, 71971143), Natural Science Foundation of Guangdong Province (2020A1515010752), Natural Science Foundation of Shenzhen University (85303/00000155), and Scientific Research Team Project of Shenzhen Institute of Information Technology (SZIIT2019KJ022), Guangdong Basic and Applied Basic Research Foundation (Project No. 2019A1515011392).

References

1. Babaei, G., Bamdad, S.: A multi-objective instance-based decision support system for investment recommendation in peer-to-peer lending. Expert Syst. Appl. **150**, 113278 (2020)
2. Zhou, A., Qu, B.Y., Li, H., Zhao, S.Z., Suganthan, P.N., Zhangd, Q.: Multiobjective evolutionary algorithms: a survey of the state of the art. Swarm Evol. Comput. 1, 32–49 (2011)
3. Zitzler, E., Laumanns, M., Thiele, L.T.: SPEA2: improving the strength pareto evolutionary algorithm. In: Lect Notes Comput Sci (including Subser Lect Notes Artif Intell Lect Notes Bioinformatics). 8710 LNCS, pp. 35–46 (2001)
4. Deb, K., Pratap, A., Agarwal, S., Meyarivan, T.: A fast and elitist multiobjective genetic algorithm: nsga-ii. IEEE Trans. Evol. Comput. **6**, 182–197 (2002)
5. Yuan, Y., Xu, H., Wang, B.: An improved NSGA-III procedure for evolutionary many-objective optimization. In: GECCO 2014 - Proceedings of the 2014 Annual Conference on Genetic and Evolutionary Computation, pp. 661–668 (2014)
6. Zou, W., Zhu, Y., Chen, H., Zhang, B.: Solving multiobjective optimization problems using artificial bee colony algorithm. Discret Dyn. Nat. Soc. **2011**, 1–37 (2011)
7. Coello, C.A.C.: Handling multiple objectives with particle swarm optimization. IEEE Trans. Evol. Comput. **15**, 45–82 (2014)
8. Fister, I., Yang, X.S., Brest, J., Fister, D.: A brief review of nature-inspired algorithms for optimization. Elektroteh Vestnik/Electrotechnical Rev. **80**, 116–122 (2013)
9. Han, H., Lu, W., Qiao, J.: An Adaptive Multiobjective Particle Swarm Optimization Based on Multiple Adaptive Methods (2017)
10. Li, X., Wong, K.C.: Multiobjective patient stratification using evolutionary multiobjective optimization. IEEE J. Biomed. Health Inform. **22**, 1619–1629 (2018)
11. Niu, B., Liu, Q., Wang, Z., Tan, L., Li, L.: Multi-objective bacterial colony optimization algorithm for integrated container terminal scheduling problem. Nat. Comput. **20**(1), 89–104 (2020). https://doi.org/10.1007/s11047-019-09781-3
12. Passino, K.M.: Biomimicry of bacterial foraging for distributed optimization and control. IEEE Control Syst. Mag. **22**(3), 52–67 (2002)
13. Niu, B., Wang, H., Wang, J., Tan, L.: Multi-objective bacterial foraging optimization. Neurocomputing **116**, 336–345 (2013)
14. Niu, B., Liu, J., Tan, L.: Multi-swarm cooperative multi-objective bacterial foraging optimisation. Int. J. Bio-Inspired Comput. **13**, 21–31 (2019)
15. Ester, M., Kriegel, H.-P., Sander, J., Xu, X.: A density-based algorithm for discovering clusters in large spatial databases with noise. In: Proceedings of the 2nd International Conference on Knowledge Discovery and Data Mining, pp. 226–231 (1996)
16. Niu, B., Wang, H.: Bacterial colony optimization. Discret Dyn. Nat. Soc. **2012**, 1–28 (2012)
17. Niu, B., Fan, Y., Zhao, P., Xue, B., Li, L., Chai, Y.: A novel bacterial foraging optimizer with linear decreasing chemotaxis step. In: Proceedings of the 2010 2nd International Workshop on Intelligent Systems and Applications ISA 2010, pp. 1–4 (2010)
18. Van Veldhuizen, D.A., Lamont, G.B.: Multiobjective evolutionary algorithms: analyzing the state-of-the-art. Evol. Comput. **8**, 125–147 (2000)
19. Zitzler, E., Deb, K., Thiele, L.: Comparison of multiobjective evolutionary algorithms: empirical results. Evol. Comput. **8**, 173–195 (2000)
20. Schaffer, J.D.: Multiple objective optimization with vector evaluated genetic algorithms. In: Proceedings of the 1st International Conference on Genetic Algorithms, pp. 93–100 (1985).

21. Fonseca, C.M., Fleming, P.J.: Multiobjective optimization and multiple constraint handling with evolutionary algorithms - part i: a unified formulation. IEEE Trans. Syst. Man Cybern. Part A Syst. Hum. **28**, 26–37 (1998)
22. Kursawe, F.: A variant of evolution strategies for vector optimization. In: Schwefel, H.-P., Männer, R. (eds.) PPSN 1990. LNCS, vol. 496, pp. 193–197. Springer, Heidelberg (1991). https://doi.org/10.1007/BFb0029752

DNA Computing Methods

Stability and Hopf Bifurcation Analysis of DNA Molecular Oscillator System Based on DNA Strand Displacement

Tao Sun[1], Hui Lv[1(✉)], and Qiang Zhang[1,2(✉)]

[1] Key Laboratory of Advanced Design and Intelligent Computing, Ministry of Education, School of Software, Dalian University, Dalian 116622, China
lh8481@tom.com
[2] School of Computer Science and Technology, Dalian University of Technology, Dalian 116024, China
zhangq@dlu.edu.cn

Abstract. DNA molecular technology has gradually matured and has been widely used in the design of nanomaterials and chemical oscillators. In order to ensure the correct setting of DNA molecular oscillator, it is necessary to thoroughly study the dynamic behavior of system. This paper studies the dynamics system of DNA molecular oscillator based on DNA strand displacement. Modeling the reaction process transforms the reaction process into a specific mathematical model. The research results show that the influence of time delay is not considered in an ideal state. Stability near the equilibrium point of system is determined by initial reaction substrate concentration and reaction rate. Considering the time delay of separation of DNA double-stranded molecules in the reaction process, the time delay parameter is added to the system model. As the time delay increases, the system changes from a stable state to an unstable state and Hopf bifurcation occurs. At the same time, the study found that both Hopf bifurcation direction and the periodic solution are closely related to the time delay parameter. The result of numerical simulation proves the correctness of our conclusion.

Keywords: DNA molecular oscillator · Time delay · DNA strand displacement · Hopf bifurcation · Hopf bifurcation direction

1 Introduction

In recent years, the complex dynamic characteristics of inorganic oscillators [1, 2] have been known for a long time, but since they cannot be reprogrammed arbitrarily and achieved by a set of standard guidelines, new design ideas need to be sought. Because of the unique spontaneity [3], parallelism [4], programmability [5] and dynamic cascade of DNA strand displacement technology [6–8], it is widely used in various nanostructures [9, 10] device design and logic circuit [11] construction and DNA molecular oscillator [12, 13] design. Therefore, it is possible to select DNA strand displacement technology as a new idea of molecular oscillator design. The essence of DNA strand displacement

© Springer Nature Switzerland AG 2021
Y. Tan and Y. Shi (Eds.): ICSI 2021, LNCS 12689, pp. 537–546, 2021.
https://doi.org/10.1007/978-3-030-78743-1_48

reaction is the break of DNA double-strand molecule, in which a certain single-stranded DNA molecule combines with a new "invader" with complementary base pairs through foothold exchange. Different DNA molecules have different interaction forces. Invading strand DNA molecules with strong structural strength replace single-stranded DNA molecules with weak structural strength in the original double-stranded DNA molecules.

In order to better understand reaction process, it is necessary to establish a nonlinear system model based on chemical reaction equation. In the past research, biochemical modeling methods have been proposed [14, 15]. However, these models have shortcomings. They do not consider inevitable time delay effects in reality. A large number of studies have shown that time delay parameter is an important parameter for the graduated reaction kinetics. The state change of system depends not only on the current state of system, but also on the state of system in the past period of time. The state change of system is closely related to time delay parameter [16]. Bifurcation [17] is an important research field of biochemical reaction dynamics. The phenomenon that topological structure of each variable changes suddenly with the change of control parameters in a dynamic system is bifurcation. Hopf bifurcation has greater research value. There are many new methods [18] for analyzing the stability and Hopf bifurcation characteristics of time-delay biochemical systems.

In the process of designing DNA molecular oscillators, there are many reasons that may cause the results to not meet expectations. Therefore, this article will focus on analyzing the system model. Through the method of chemical reaction modeling, a molecular oscillator system model based on DNA strand replacement is established. According to some previous studies on DNA strand displacement reaction, it can be seen that it takes a certain time for the DNA duplex to separate and combine with the invading single strand. In order to describe system model more accurately, the time delay of DNA double-strand separation is introduced, and a nonlinear time-delay system model is constructed to study the stability of system. At the same time, Hopf bifurcation direction and bifurcation periodic solution of the model are analyzed. It is of great significance for the design of DNA molecular oscillator model and the follow-up research in related fields.

The main contributions of this article are as follows: (1) In order to understand the reaction process, a mathematical model based on the dynamics of DNA molecular oscillator was established. (2) In the light of actual situation, the reaction mechanism of DNA strand displacement is optimized to add time delay parameter to system model. (3) Through theoretical analysis and image simulation to study the stability of the system and the Hopf bifurcation phenomenon, so as to help researchers better understand the law of reaction.

2   Model Establishment

The reaction process of DNA molecular oscillator system based on DNA strand replacement is shown in Fig. 1. Among them, $Flux_{CAp}$, $Produce_{CApAq}$ and $RepA$ are substrates for the reaction, and $RepA$ is a fluorescent label chain for emitting fluorescent signals. When $Flux_{CAp}$ is added to the reaction vessel as an input strand, it reacts with $Produce_{CApAq}$ to form intermediates Ap and $Produceint_{CApAq}$. Finally, $RepA$ and the intermediate product Ap undergo a secondary cascade reaction to produce two final output chains.

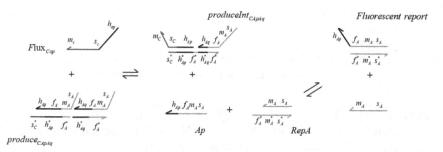

Fig. 1. DNA molecular oscillator system based on DNA strand displacement

To simplify writing, the entire reaction process is described by the following equation.

$$\begin{cases} A + B \xrightleftharpoons[K_{-1}]{K_1} C + D \\ D + E \xrightarrow{K_2} F + G \end{cases} \tag{1}$$

According to the conservation of mass, initial concentration of reactant is equal to the sum of remaining concentration of reactant and concentration of product. Therefore, the following relationships can be obtained.

$$\begin{cases} A_0 = A(t) + C(t) \\ A_0 = A(t) + D(t) + F(t) \\ B_0 = B(t) + C(t) \\ E_0 = E(t) + F(t) \end{cases} \tag{2}$$

where A_0, B_0 and E_0 represent initial concentration of reaction substrate $Flux_{CAp}$, $Produce_{CApAq}$ and $RepA$ respectively before the reaction starts.

Substituting the above quantitative relationship into the initial system, the following low-latitude system equation can be obtained.

$$\begin{cases} \dot{A}(t) = -k_1 A(t)[B_0 - A_0 + A(t)] + k_{-1}[A_0 - A(t)][A_0 - A(t) - F(t)] \\ \dot{F}(t) = k_2[A_0 - A(t) - F(t)][E_0 - F(t)] \end{cases} \tag{3}$$

3 Positive Boundedness of Solution

In this part, from the perspective of practical problems, the boundedness of solution will be proved.

Before reaction starts, the initial concentration of $A(t)$, $F(t)$ is $A_0 > 0$, $F_0 = 0$. $A(t)$ represents the initially added reactant, $F(t)$ represents the concentration of product. During the reaction, assume $t = t_1 > 0$, $A(t_1) = 0$ can be obtained from system (3). The reciprocal of $A(t_1)$ is $A'(t_1) = k_{-1}A_0[A_0 - F(t)] > 0$, which shows that $A(t) < 0$ for $t \in (t_1 - \delta, t_1)$. But $A_0 > 0$, δ is an arbitrarily small positive number. There is at least a $t_2 \in (0, t_1)$ ensures $A(t_2) = 0$. This contradicts to the hypothesis. So $A(t) > 0$. Select the function $W(t) = A(t) + F(t)$, which is derived as:

$$W'(t) = A'(t) + F'(t)$$

$$= k_{-1}A_0^2 + k_2A_0E_0 - [k_1(B_0 - A_0) + k_{-1}A_0 + k_2E_0]A(t)$$

$$- [k_{-1}A_0 + k_2(A_0 + E_0)]F(t) + (k_{-1} + k_2)A(t)F(t) + (k_{-1} - k_1)A^2(t) + k_2F^2(t)$$

$$< M - qN \qquad (4)$$

where $q = \min\{k_1(B_0 - A_0) + k_{-1}A_0 + k_2E_0, k_{-1}A_0 + k_2(A_0 + E_0)\}$.

Therefore $0 < A(t) < M/q + \delta, 0 \le F(t) < M/q + \delta$ are obtained from above. All of the solutions of nonlinear system (4) are positively bounded.

4 Dynamic Analysis of Systems Without Time Delay

In this section, the dynamic of system under ideal conditions with no time delay parameters will be studied.

First, by making all partial differential equations equal to zero.

$$-k_1A(t)[B_0 - A_0 + A(t)] + k_{-1}[A_0 - A(t)][A_0 - A(t) - F(t)] = 0$$
$$k_2[A_0 - A(t) - F(t)][E_0 - F(t)] = 0 \qquad (5)$$

The equilibrium points of system (5) are as follows

$$E_1 = (0, A_0), E_2 = (A_0 - B_0, B_0), E_3 = \left(\frac{-b + \sqrt{b^2 - 4ac}}{2a}, E_0\right)$$

where $a = k_{-1} - k_1, b = k_1(A_0 - B_0) - k_{-1}(2A_0 - E_0), c = k_{-1}A_0(A_0 - E_0)$.

The local stability of the above three equilibrium points will now be studied. Linearize the system at equilibrium point $\overline{E} = (\overline{A}, \overline{F})$, the following characteristic equation can be obtained.

$$\begin{vmatrix} \lambda + k_1(B_0 - A_0 + 2\overline{A}) + k_{-1}(A_0 - 2\overline{A} - \overline{F}) & k_{-1}(A_0 - \overline{A}) \\ k_2(E_0 - \overline{F}) & \lambda + k_2(A_0 - \overline{A} - 2\overline{F} + E_0) \end{vmatrix} = 0 \quad (6)$$

At equilibrium point $E_1 = (0, A_0)$, the characteristic Eq. (6) becomes

$$\lambda^2 + k_1(B_0 - A_0) + k_2(-A_0 + E_0)\lambda - k_{-1}A_0k_2(E_0 - A_0) = 0 \qquad (7)$$

According to Routh-Hurwitz Criteria, the necessary and sufficient conditions for the local asymptotic stability of the equilibrium point E_1 are as follows:

$$\begin{cases} k_1(B_0 - A_0) + k_2(-A_0 + E_0) > 0 \\ -k_{-1}A_0k_2(E_0 - A_0) > 0 \end{cases} \qquad (8)$$

In the same way, the necessary and sufficient conditions for stability at equilibrium points E_2, E_3 are as follows

$$\begin{cases} k_1(A_0 - B_0) - k_{-1}A_0 + k_2(E_0 - B_0) > 0 \\ k_{-1}B_0k_2(E_0 - B_0) > 0 \end{cases} \qquad (9)$$

$$\begin{cases} k_1(B_0 - A_0 + 2\frac{-b + \sqrt{b^2 - 4ac}}{2a}) + k_{-1}(A_0 - 2\frac{-b + \sqrt{b^2 - 4ac}}{2a} - E_0) > 0 \\ -k_2(A_0 - \frac{-b + \sqrt{b^2 - 4ac}}{2a}) > 0 \end{cases} \qquad (10)$$

5 Dynamic Analysis of Systems with Time Delay

In fact, it takes some time to complete DNA strand displacement reaction. Taking into account the time delay of the separation of DNA double-stranded molecules, a time delay parameter is added to the system model. The improved model is as follows:

$$
\begin{cases}
\dot{A}(t) = -k_1 A(t - \tau)[B_0 - A_0 + A(t - \tau)] \\
\qquad + k_{-1}[A_0 - A(t - \tau)][A_0 - A(t - \tau) - F(t)] \\
\dot{F}(t) = k_2[A_0 - A(t - \tau) - F(t)][E_0 - F(t)]
\end{cases}
\tag{11}
$$

Research the equilibrium point $E_* = (\bar{A}, \bar{F})$. Let $A^*(t) = A(t) - A^*$, $F^*(t) = F(t) - F^*$ be the disturbance variable, and linearize the system (11) to get the following form:

$$
\begin{cases}
\dot{A}^*(t) = [-k_1(B_0 - A_0 + 2\bar{A}) - k_{-1}(A_0 - 2\bar{A} - \bar{F})]A^*(t - \tau) - k_{-1}(A_0 - \bar{A})F^*(t) \\
\dot{F}^*(t) = -k_2(E_0 - \bar{F})A^*(t - \tau) - k_2(A_2 - \bar{A} - 2\bar{F} + E_0)F^*(t)
\end{cases}
\tag{12}
$$

Characteristic equation for system (12) is as following

$$
|\lambda e - J| = \lambda^2 - d_1\lambda + (a_1\lambda - a_1d_1 + b_1c_1)e^{-\lambda\tau} = 0
\tag{13}
$$

When $\tau \neq 0$ the change of τ value will cause corresponding change of characteristic root of equation, which will cause the stability change of system model near the equilibrium point. Suppose there is a τ_0 that makes the characteristic Eq. (13) of system have a pair of pure imaginary roots, denoted as $\lambda = i\omega(\omega > 0)$, substituting the characteristic Eq. (13), we can get

$$
\begin{cases}
(a_1d_1 - b_1c_1)\cos\omega\tau - a_1\omega\sin\omega\tau = -\omega^2 \\
a_1\omega\cos\omega\tau + (a_1d_1 - b_1c_1)\sin\omega\tau = -d_1\omega
\end{cases}
\tag{14}
$$

In the light of $\cos^2\theta + \sin^2\theta = 1$, it can be solved.

$$
f(\omega) = e_3\omega^6 + e_2\omega^4 + e_1\omega^2 + e_0 = 0
\tag{15}
$$

In line with Intermediate Value Theorem, we can see that because $\lim\limits_{x \to +\infty} f(z) = +\infty$, if $h_7 < 0$, then there at least one point $z_0 \in (0, +\infty)$ exists to make $f(z_0) = 0$ hold.

Condition (1) Eq. (13) has at least one positive root, then Eq. (13) has a positive follow ω, so that Eq. (11) has a pair of pure imaginary roots $\pm i\omega$ satisfying the following equation.

$$
\tau_0 = \frac{1}{\omega_0}\arccos\theta\frac{-b_1c_1\omega^2}{a_1^2\omega^2 + (a_1d_1 - b_1c_1))^2}
\tag{16}
$$

Derivation of Eq. (13) with respect to τ, one obtains

$$
\left(\frac{d\lambda}{d\tau}\right)^{-1} = -\frac{2d_1\lambda - d_1 - ae^{-\lambda\tau}}{(a_1\lambda - a_1d_1 + b_1c_1)\lambda e^{-\lambda\tau}} + \frac{\tau}{\lambda}
\tag{17}
$$

Substitute $\lambda = i\omega$ into the above formula, it derives that

$$
(\frac{d\lambda}{d\tau})^{-1}\big|_{\tau=\tau_0} = \frac{P+Qi}{M+Ni} + \frac{i\tau_0}{\omega_0}
\tag{18}
$$

where

$$
P = a_1 \cos \omega_0\tau, \cdot Q = 2\omega_0 d_1 + a_1 \sin \omega_0\tau, \cdot M = -a_1\omega_0^2 \cos \omega\tau - (a_1 d_1 - b_1 c_1)\omega_0 \sin \omega\tau
$$
$$
N = a_1\omega_0^2 \sin \omega\tau - (a_1 d_1 - b_1 c_1)\omega_0 \cos \omega\tau
$$

Condition (2) If $PM + QN \neq 0$, then $\text{Re}\left\{(\frac{d\lambda}{d\tau})^{-1}\big|_{\tau=\tau_0}\right\} = \frac{PM+QN}{M^2+N^2} \neq 0$ holds.

If conditions (1) and (2) are established, the following conclusions can be drawn.

Theorem 1

(1) When $\tau \in (0, \tau_0)$, the system (11) is locally asymptotically stable.
(2) When $\tau \geq \tau_0$, the system (11) loses its steady state at the equilibrium point and Hopf bifurcation occurs. The system switches between a stable equilibrium state and a limit cycle, where τ_0 is the critical parameter.

6 Hopf Bifurcation Direction

This section will use the central flow pattern and normal form theorem to study the bifurcation direction of Hopf bifurcation and the periodic nature of bifurcation periodic solutions. For calculation convenience, let $\tau = \tau_0 + \mu$, $\mu \in R$, and normalize the time delay $t = (t/\tau)$. Transform system (11) into a functional differential equation.

$$
\dot{x}(t) = L_\mu(x_t) + f(\mu, x_t), L_\mu(\phi) = (\tau_0 + \mu)[B_1\phi(0) + B_2\phi(-1)]
\tag{19}
$$

By Riesz Representation Theorem, there exists a function $\eta(\theta, \mu)$ of bounded variation for $\theta \in [-1, 0]$, such that

$$
L_\mu\phi = \int_{-1}^{0} d\eta(\theta, \mu)\phi(\theta)
\tag{20}
$$

In practical applications, choosing the following equation.

$$
\eta(\theta, \mu) = (\tau_0 + \mu)B_1\delta(\theta) - (\tau_0 + \mu)B_2\delta(\theta + 1)
\tag{21}
$$

For $\varphi \in [-1, 0]$, the define of $A(\mu)\phi$ and $R(\mu)\phi$ are:

$$
A(\mu)\phi = \begin{cases} \frac{d\phi(\theta)}{d\theta}, & \theta \in [-1, 0) \\ \int_{-1}^{0} d\eta(\theta, \mu)\phi(\theta), & \theta = 0 \end{cases}, R(\mu)\phi = \begin{cases} 0, & \theta \in [-1, 0) \\ f(\mu, \phi), & \theta = 0 \end{cases}
\tag{22}
$$

Then, define a bilinear inner product, for $\phi \in C^1([-1, 0], R^2)$, $\psi \in C^1([0, 1], (R^2)^*)$.

$$\langle \psi(s), \phi(\theta) \rangle = \overline{\psi}(0)^T \phi(0) - \int_{\theta=-1}^{0} \int_{\xi=0}^{\theta} \overline{\psi}^T (\xi - \theta) d\eta(\theta) \phi(\xi) d\xi \tag{23}$$

where $\eta(\theta) = \eta(\theta, 0)$, and satisfied $\langle \psi(s), A(0)\phi(\theta) \rangle = \langle A^*(0)\psi(s), \phi(\theta) \rangle$. Through calculation we can know

$$D = [1 + \gamma\overline{\gamma}^* + \tau_0 e^{i\omega_0 \tau_0} (A + C\overline{\gamma}^*)]^{-1} \tag{24}$$

Next, calculate the coordinates, which describes the center manifold C_0 at $\mu = 0$. Let x_t be the solution of (24), when $\mu = 0$, define

$$z(t) = \langle q^*, x_t \rangle, \quad W(t, \theta) = x_t - 2Re\{z(t)q(\theta)\} \tag{25}$$

On the center manifold C_0, $W(t, \theta)$ can be represented as

$$W(t, \theta) = W(z(t), \overline{z}(t), \theta) = W_{20}(\theta)\frac{z^2}{2} + W_{11}(\theta)z\overline{z} + W_{02}(\theta)\frac{\overline{z}^2}{2} + \cdots \tag{26}$$

where z and z^* are local coordinates for the center manifold C_0 in the direction vectors q and q^*. For the solution $x_t \in C_0$ and $\mu = 0$, it derives that

$$\dot{z}(t) = i\tau_0 w_0 z + \overline{q}^{*T}(0)f_0(z, \overline{z}) = i\tau_0 w_0 z + g(z, \overline{z}) \tag{27}$$

Through simple calculation, the following coefficient expressions that determine the properties of Hopf bifurcation can be obtained.

$$\begin{cases} c_1(0) = \frac{i}{2w_0\tau_0}\left(g_{11}g_{20} - 2|g_{11}|^2 - \frac{|g_{02}|^2}{3}\right) + \frac{g_{21}}{2}, & \beta_2 = 2Re\{c_1(0)\} \\ \mu_2 = -\frac{Re\{c_1(0)\}}{Re\{\lambda'(\tau_0)\}}, & T_2 = -\frac{Im\{c_1(0)\} + \mu_2 Im\{\lambda'(\tau_0)\}}{w_0\tau_0} \end{cases} \tag{28}$$

Theorem 2

(1) The sign of μ_2 determines the direction of Hopf bifurcation. If $\mu_2 > 0$, Hopf bifurcation is supercritical. If $\mu_2 < 0$, Hopf bifurcation is subcritical.
(2) The sign of β_2 determines stability of periodic solution. If $\beta_2 < 0$, periodic solution of bifurcation is stable; If $\beta_2 > 0$, periodic solution of bifurcation is unstable.
(3) If $T_2 > 0$, the period of the limit cycle is increasing. If $T_2 < 0$, the period of the limit cycle decreases.

7 Numerical Simulation

In this Section, the results of numerical simulation will verify correctness of previous theoretical analysis. Parameters of the system (4) is taken from [14], $A_0 = 0.22 \times 10^{-7}$, $B_0 = 0.44 \times 10^{-7}$, $E_0 = 1 \times 10^{-7}$, $k_1 = 1.2 \times 10^6$, $k_{-1} = 2.2 \times 10^5$, $k_2 = 7.4 \times 10^5$. After calculation, the critical value of the bifurcation control parameter is $\tau_0 = 27.716$.

When $\tau = 22 < \tau_0$, it can be obtained from the system state trajectory diagram in Fig. 2 that the system is locally stable at the equilibrium point. When $\tau = \tau_0 = 27.716$, the control parameter reaches the critical value, and the system state switches between stable equilibrium point and limit cycle. It can be seen from Fig. 3 that after shock, the system finally converged to one point. When $\tau = 29 > \tau_0$, time delay reaches critical value. From the system state trajectory diagram in Fig. 4, it can be seen that the system loses stability at equilibrium point and Hopf bifurcation occurs.

By calculating (33), the following results can be obtained:

$$\mu_2 = 1.252 \times e^{+23}, \quad \beta_2 = -1.479 \times e^{+15}, \quad T_2 = -4.027 \times e^{+20}$$

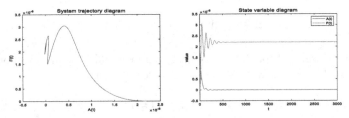

Fig. 2. System trajectory diagram and state variable diagram for time-delay $\tau = 22 < \tau_0$

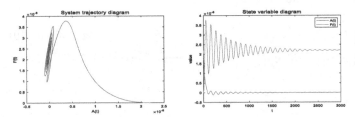

Fig. 3. System trajectory diagram and state variable diagram for time-delay $\tau = \tau_0 = 27.716$

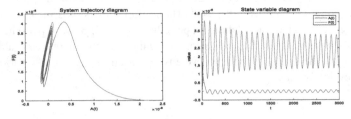

Fig. 4. System trajectory diagram and state variable diagram for time-delay $\tau = 29 > \tau_0$

It can be seen from the calculation result of (28) that $\mu_2 > 0$ $\beta_2 < 0$ and $T_2 < 0$. In the light of Theorem 2, the bifurcation of system model (11) is a supercritical bifurcation, the bifurcation phenomenon should occur when the control parameter exceeds the critical value. In connection with the state trajectory diagrams of the system in Fig. 2 and Fig. 4, the Hopf bifurcation occurs at $\tau \geq \tau_0$. This confirms our point of view. $\beta_2 < 0$ indicates that the periodic solution is stable, and the stable period of the state variable curve in the above figure verifies that the theory is correct. $T_2 < 0$ means that the periodic motion is reduced. It can be clearly seen from state variable diagram in Fig. 4 that the oscillation amplitude of each variable of system gradually decreases.

8 Conclusion

The dynamic characteristics of DNA molecular oscillator system based on DNA strand displacement reaction is the focus of this article. Research results show that under ideal conditions without considering the influence of time delay on this system. When the system reaches an equilibrium state, the stability of system is closely related to the initial concentration of reactants and the reaction speed. By studying a more realistic system model with time delay, it can be seen that the time delay of DNA double-strand separation cannot be ignored, and its change will often cause the stability of system model to change or even lose stability and occur Hopf bifurcation. Then, using paradigm theory and central manifold theorem, the direction of Hopf bifurcation and the stability of bifurcation periodic solution are studied in detail. This is conducive to a more comprehensive grasp of the dynamic characteristics of the system model. In the future, system stability control and Hopf bifurcation control will become important research directions.

Acknowledgments. This work is supported by the National Key R&D Program of China (No. 2018YFC0910500), National Natural Science Foundation of China (Nos. 61425002, 61751203, 61772100, 61972266, 61802040, 61672121, 61572093), Program for Changjiang Scholars and Innovative Research Team in University (No. IRT_15R07), Program for Liaoning Innovative Research Team in University (No. LT2017012), Natural Science Foundation of Liaoning Province (Nos. 2020-KF-14–05, 2019-ZD-0567), High-level Talent Innovation Support Program of Dalian City (Nos. 2017RQ060, 2018RQ75), Dalian Outstanding Young Science and Technology Talent Support Program (No. 2017RJ08), State Key Laboratory of Light Alloy Casting Technology for High-end Equipment (No.LACT-006) and Scientific Research Fund of Liaoning Provincial Education Department (No. JYT19051).

References

1. Yun, J., Cho, K., et al.: Dynamic electrical characteristics of low-power ring oscillators constructed with inorganic nanoparticles on flexible plastics. ACS Appl. Mater. Interfaces **87**(19), 3725–3728 (2012)
2. Kitagaki, B.T., et al.: Multivariate statistical analysis of chemical and electrochemical oscillators for an accurate frequency selection. Phys. Chem. Chem. Phys. **21**(30), 16423–16434 (2019)
3. Kim, W.J., et al.: DNA strand exchange stimulated by spontaneous complex formation with cationic comb-type copolymer. J. Am. Chem. Soc. **124**(43), 12676–12677 (2002)

4. Zhu, E., et al.: Biochemical logic circuits based on DNA combinatorial displacement. IEEE Access **8**, 34096–34103 (2020)
5. Wang, Y., Li, Z., et al.: Three-variable chaotic oscillatory system based on DNA strand displacement and its coupling combination synchronization. IEEE Trans. Nanobiosci. **19**(3), 434–445 (2020)
6. Zhang, D.Y., Winfree, E.: Control of DNA strand displacement kinetics using toehold exchange. J. Am. Chem. Soc. **131**(47), 17303–17314 (2009)
7. Haley, N.E.C., Ouldridge, T.E., et al.: Design of hidden thermodynamic driving for non-equilibrium systems via mismatch elimination during DNA strand displacement. Nat. Commun. **11**(1), 1–11 (2020)
8. Paulino, N.M.G., Foo, M., et al.: PID and state feedback controllers using DNA strand displacement reactions. IEEE Control Syst. Lett. **3**(4), 805–810 (2019)
9. Chen, R.P., Blackstock, D., et al.: Dynamic protein assembly by programmable DNA strand displacement. Nat. Chem. **10**(4), 474–481 (2018)
10. Surana, S., Shenoy, A.R., et al.: Designing DNA nanodevices for compatibility with the immune system of higher organisms. Nat. Nanotechnol. **10**(9), 741–747 (2015)
11. Zhao, J., Gao, J., et al.: Upconversion Luminescence-Activated DNA nanodevice for ATP sensing in living cells. J. Am. Chem. Soc. **140**(2), 578–581 (2018)
12. Ali, K.K., Cattani, C., et al.: Analytical and numerical study of the DNA dynamics arising in oscillator-chain of Peyrard-Bishop model. Chaos, Solitons Fractals **139**, 110089 (2020)
13. Srinivas, N., Parkin, J., Seelig, G., et al.: Enzyme-free nucleic acid dynamical systems. Science **358**(6369), eaal2052 (2017)
14. Eskov, V.V., Filatova, D.Y., et al.: Classification of uncertainties in modeling of complex biological systems. Mosc. Univ. Phys. Bull. **74**(1), 57–63 (2019)
15. Shu, Y., Huang, J., Dong, Y., et al.: Mathematical modeling and bifurcation analysis of pro-and anti-tumor macrophages. Appl. Math. Model. **88**, 758–773 (2020)
16. Guo, Q., Sun, Z., et al.: Bifurcations in a fractional birhythmic biological system with time delay. Commun. Nonlinear Sci. Numer. Simul. **72**, 318–328 (2019)
17. Qi, W., Kao, Y., et al.: Controller design for time-delay system with stochastic disturbance and actuator saturation via a new criterion. Appl. Math. Comput. **320**, 535–546 (2018)
18. Huang, C., Zhang, H., Cao, J., et al.: Stability and Hopf bifurcation of a delayed prey–predator model with disease in the predator. Int. J. Bifurcat. Chaos **29**(07), 1950091 (2019)

Dynamic Behavior Analysis of DNA Subtraction Gate with Stochastic Disturbance and Time Delay

Huiwen Li[1], Hui Lv[1(✉)], and Qiang Zhang[1,2(✉)]

[1] Key Laboratory of Advanced Design and Intelligent Computing, Ministry of Education, School of Software, Dalian University, Dalian 116622, China
lh8481@tom.com
[2] School of Computer Science and Technology, Dalian University of Technology, Dalian 116024, China
zhangq@dlu.edu.cn

Abstract. As one of the basic arithmetic gates of DNA circuits, the DNA subtraction gate plays an important role in the design and optimization of circuits. A nonlinear system with stochastic perturbations and delays is constructed to accurately describe the reaction process of DNA subtraction gates and comprehensively analyze the system dynamics. At the same time, enzyme recognition sites are added to the original basis of the DNA subtraction gate to increase the reaction rate. According to the law of conservation of quality, the dimensionality reduction of the system model with stochastic perturbation and time delay is performed, which greatly reduces the computational complexity. The properties of the solution of a DNA subtraction gate system are discussed, and the Lyapunov analysis proves that the model solution is global and unique. The properties of the solutions indicate that the constructed DNA subtraction gate system with stochastic perturbations and time delays is of practical significance. Through systematic ergodic analysis, it is found that the DNA subtraction gate system is distributed smoothly, which provides a theoretical basis for the realization of the DNA subtraction function. The results of numerical simulation show that the DNA subtraction gate can be implemented successfully under the influence of stochastic disturbance and time delay.

Keywords: DNA subtraction gate · Time delay · Stochastic perturbation · Stationary distribution · Ergodicity

1 Introduction

DNA strand displacement technology has been used to construct a variety of molecular circuits [1–5] and has been widely applied in fields of molecular computing such as intelligent drug delivery, molecular diagnosis, and treatment management. A DNA molecular circuit is designed according to the principle of DNA strand displacement, describing the input signal of the basic unit door using a DNA molecule to realize operation at that

© Springer Nature Switzerland AG 2021
Y. Tan and Y. Shi (Eds.): ICSI 2021, LNCS 12689, pp. 547–556, 2021.
https://doi.org/10.1007/978-3-030-78743-1_49

level [6–8]. The DNA subtraction gate, as a basic arithmetic operation gate, is the basic unit gate for building DNA circuits that execute specific instructions [9]. To realize the optimal design of a DNA subtraction gate, it is necessary to reasonably sequence the bases and master the dynamic law of the reaction process. When studying the dynamics of the system, it is crucial to accurately construct the complete nonlinear system model.

However, there are few studies on the dynamic analysis of DNA molecular circuits. Anshula et al. proposed to use three types of building blocks (propagators, connectors, and solution blocks) to construct a DNA-based calculator. Performing addition and subtraction operations through algorithmic self-assembly provides a potential platform for constructing various types of DNA algorithm crystals (such as flip-flops, encoders, and multiplexers) [10].

Considering the influence of random noise in the environment, constructing a DNA subtraction gate model with stochastic disturbance is more consistent with the real situation of the reaction. Scholars have recently considered the state change of double-well oscillators under the influence of white noise and sinusoidal excitation [11]. Thus, stochastic perturbation is a crucial reference factor for analyzing the dynamic behavior of a nonlinear system model. Stochastic disturbance and time delay interact in a subtle and complex way in a DNA subtraction gate, and the time delay is used as a vital parameter in establishing a mathematical model to better study its dynamic characteristics. This article studies the dynamic behavior changes of a DNA subtraction gate caused by a time delay under stochastic disturbance.

The DNA subtraction gate is the cornerstone of a large-scale cascaded circuit. The analysis of its dynamic behavior aids in the optimal design of a logic circuit. Based on the DNA subtraction gate reaction process and considering the influence of stochastic disturbance and time delay, a stochastic delay differential system is established in this article. The stochastic disturbance is environmental white noise, and the properties of the solution under the influence of white noise and time delay are explored. In addition, Lyapunov analysis proves that the solution of the system is positive and global, which verifies that the constructed model is realistic. Through dynamic behavior analysis, it is concluded that the DNA subtraction gate system is ergodic even at low noise intensity. Numerical simulation confirms our conclusions and indicates that the DNA subtraction gate reaction system can be well used.

2 Preparation

We modified the DNA strand in a DNA strand displacement reaction design subtraction gate [12] by adding an enzyme recognition site. This is because the enzyme can quickly catalyze the reaction of the substance and increase the reaction rate of the subtraction gate. The reaction flowchart is shown in Fig. 1. Considering the material transformation after adding the enzyme, the concentration change of substance A in this process is expressed by the Michaelis-Menten equation. In the DNA subtraction gate reaction process, A, B, E and G are reactants; C, D are intermediate products; F_1, F_2, H_1 and H_2 are products of the reaction; and $k_i(i = -1, 1, 2, 3)$ is the rate of reaction.

The entire reaction process is expressed as

$$A + B \underset{k_{-1}}{\overset{k_1}{\longleftrightarrow}} C + D \overset{k_2}{\rightarrow} F_1 + F_2, \ G + C \overset{k_3}{\rightarrow} H_1 + H_2 \tag{1}$$

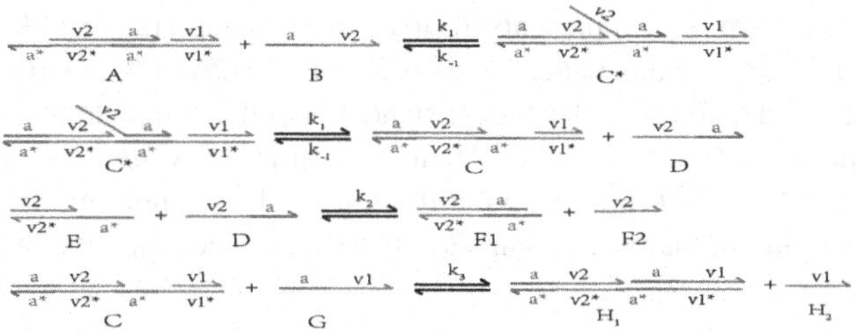

Fig. 1. DNA subtraction gate reaction process. C^* is the intermediate in the first step

Based on model (1), the equation of the reaction system is constructed as

$$\begin{cases} \dot{A}(t) = k_{-1}C(t)D(t) - k_1 A(t)B(t) \\ \dot{B}(t) = k_{-1}C(t)D(t) - k_1 A(t)B(t) \\ \dot{C}(t) = k_1 A(t)B(t) - k_{-1}C(t)D(t) - k_3 C(t)G(t) \\ \dot{D}(t) = k_1 A(t)B(t) - k_{-1}C(t)D(t) - k_2 D(t)E(t) \\ \dot{E}(t) = -k_2 E(t)D(t), \ \dot{F}_1(t) = k_2 E(t)D(t) \\ \dot{F}_2(t) = k_2 E(t)D(t), \ \dot{G}(t) = -k_3 H_1(t)H_2(t) \\ \dot{H}_1(t) = k_3 C(t)G(t), \ \dot{H}_2(t) = k_3 C(t)G(t) \end{cases} \tag{2}$$

From the law of conservation of quality in the chemical reaction process, the above system is expressed as

$$\begin{cases} A(t) = k_{-1}C(t)D(t) - k_1 A(t)B(t) \\ \dot{C}(t) = k_1 A(t)B(t) - k_{-1}C(t)D(t) - k_3 C(t)G(t) \\ \dot{E}(t) = -k_2 E(t)D(t) \end{cases} \tag{3}$$

At present, the DNA subtraction gate model is a deterministic system, and constructing a mathematical model that can fully describe the nature of the system is the focus of this article. The enzyme recognition site is added to the original DNA strand to increase the reaction rate. In order to more accurately simulate the reaction process of the DNA subtraction gate, a DNA subtraction gate model with stochastic disturbance and time delay is established, which is recorded as

$$\begin{cases} \dot{A}(t) = k_{-1}C(t)[A_0 - E_0 - A(t) + E(t)] - k_1 A(t)[B_0 - A_0 + A(t)] \\ \quad -v_{max}A(t)/(K_m + A(t)) + \sigma_1 A(t)dB_1(t) \\ \dot{C}(t) = k_1 A(t)[B_0 - A_0 + A(t)] - k_{-1}C(t)[A_0 - E_0 - A(t) + E(t)] \\ \quad -k_3 C(t-\tau)[H_0 - A_0 + A(t) + C(t)] + \sigma_2 C(t)dB_2(t) \\ \dot{E}(t) = -k_2 E(t)[A_0 - E_0 - A(t) + E(t)] + \sigma_3 E(t)dB_3(t) \end{cases} \tag{4}$$

In the above system, v_{max} represents the maximum reaction rate, and K_m is a characteristic constant of the enzyme, which is relatively constant. And $B_1(t)$, $B_2(t)$, $B_3(t)$ are Brownian motions defined by independent standards in the complete probability space $(\Omega, \mathcal{F}, P)$, and $\sigma_1^2 > 0$, $\sigma_2^2 > 0$, $\sigma_3^2 > 0$ are intensities of white noise. Let complete probability space $(\Omega, \mathcal{F}, \{\mathcal{F}_t\}_{t \geq 0}, P)$ with filtration $\{\mathcal{F}_t\}_{t \geq 0}$ approving the usual conditions, i.e., it is right continuous, and unless otherwise stated, $\mathcal{F}_0$ contains all P-empty sets. Let

$$\mathbb{R}_+^n = \{A \in \mathbb{R}^n : A_i > 0 \text{ for all } 1 \leq i \leq n\} \tag{5}$$

The initial value $A(t_0) = A_0 \in \mathbb{R}^n$, and $B(t) = (B_1(t), \ldots, B_m(t))^T$, $t \geq 0$ denotes m-dimensional standard Brownian motion defined on the above probability space.

3   Existence and Uniqueness of the Positive Solution

For any initial value, in order to get the only global positive solutions, the system (4) will not explode in a limited time. The requirement of the locally Lipschitz condition coefficient and linear growth condition [13], this project is nonlinear, coefficient (4) is apparently not keep linear growth condition, so explore system solution in a limited time. To solve this problem, Lyapunov analysis is used to prove that the solution of the system is positive and global [14].

Theorem 1 For the given initial value $\{(A(t), C(t), E(t)) : -\tau \leq t \leq 0 \in C([-\tau, 0]); \mathbb{R}_+^3\}$, the unique solution $(A(t), C(t), E(t))$ is defined for all $t \geq -\tau$, and the solution still exists in $\mathbb{R}_+^3$ with probability 1, i.e., $(A(t), C(t), E(t)) \in \mathbb{R}_+^3$ for $t \geq 0$ almost surely.

Proof Since the system is locally Lipschitz continuous for any initial value $\{(A(t), C(t), E(t)) : -\tau \leq t \leq 0 \in C([-\tau, 0]); \mathbb{R}_+^3\}$, DNA subtraction gate systems with stochastic disturbance and time delay are defined to have a unique local positive solution $(A(t), C(t), E(t))$ at $t \in [-\tau, \tau_e)$, where τ_e is the explosion time. If $\tau_e = \infty$ a.s., then the solution to the system is global. Let us make $n_0 \geq 0$ big enough to reach $A(t), C(t), E(t)$ within the interval $[1/n_0, n_0]$. For each positive integer $n \geq n_0$, define the stopping time:

$$\tau_n = \inf\{t \in [0, \tau_e) : \min\{A(t), C(t), E(t)\} \leq 1/n \text{ or } \max\{A(t), C(t), E(t)\} \geq n\}. \tag{6}$$

Throughout this article, we set $\inf \phi = \infty$, and as usual, ϕ denotes the empty set. According to the above conditions, τ_n is increasing as $n \to \infty$. Set $\tau_\infty = \lim\limits_{n \to \infty} \tau_n$, where $\tau_\infty \leq \tau_e$ a.s. Suppose $\tau_\infty = \infty$, a.s. holds. Then $(A(0), C(0), E(0)) \in \mathbb{R}_+^3$ for all $t \geq 0$ and $\tau_\infty = \infty$. This means that to complete the proof, all we require showing is that $\tau_\infty = \infty$, a.s. There is an integer $n_1 \geq n_0$ such that $P\{\tau_n \leq T\} > \varepsilon$, for all $n \geq n_1$.

Define a C^2 function $V(A, C, E) : \mathbb{R}_+^3 \to \mathbb{R}_+^3$ by

$$V = (A - 1 - \ln A) + (C - 1 - \ln C) + (E - 1 - \ln E) + 2k_3 \int_{t-\tau}^t C^2(s)ds$$
$$+ k_3 \int_t^0 \left| \tfrac{1}{2} A^2(s)(k_3 + k_3) + C^2(s)(2k_{-1} + \tfrac{1}{2}k_3) \right| ds \tag{7}$$

Calculate the differential operator of the above formula and simplify it to get

$$LV \leq k_1 A(t) + k_1(B_0 - A_0) + k_{-1}C(t) + \frac{v_{max}}{K_m + A(t)} - k_{-1}A(t) + k_{-1}E(t) - \frac{1}{2}k_2 E^2$$
$$- k_3 C(t - \tau)[H_0 - A_0 + A(t) + C(t)] + k_{-1}(A_0 - E_0) + k_3(H_0 - A_0)C(t - \tau)$$
$$- k_3 C^2(t - \tau) - k_2(A_0 - E_0)E(t) + \sigma_3(E - 1)dB_3(t) + k_2(A_0 - E_0) + \sigma_1(A - 1)dB_1(t)$$
$$+ \sigma_2(C - 1)dB_2(t) + k_2 E(t) - k_2 A(t) \leq K \tag{8}$$

where K is a positive constant. Integrate both sides of the inequality and take the expectation $\overline{E}V \leq V(A(0), C(0), E(0)) + \overline{E} \int_0^{\tau_n \wedge T} K dt \leq V(x(0), y(0)) + KT$.

Define $\Omega_n = \{\tau_n \leq T\}, n \leq n_1$. Then, by (4), $P(\Omega_n) \geq \varepsilon$. Note that for every $\omega \in \Omega_n$, there exists at least one $A(\tau_n, \omega)$, $E(\tau_n, \omega)$, or $C(\tau_n, \omega)$ that equals either n or $1/n$; $V(A(\tau_n), C(\tau_n), E(\tau_n))$ are no less than $1/n - 1 - \log 1/n = 1/n - 1 + \log n$ or $n - 1 - \log n$. Consequently, $V(A(\tau_n), C(\tau_n), E(\tau_n)) \geq (n - 1 - \log n) \wedge (\frac{1}{n} - 1 + \log n)$. It then follows from (9) that

$$V(A(0), C(0), E(0)) + KT \geq \overline{E}[1_{\Omega_n(\omega)} V(A(\tau_n), C(\tau_n), E(\tau_n))]$$
$$\geq \varepsilon[(n - 1 - \log n) \wedge (1/n - 1 + \log n)], \tag{9}$$

Where $1_{\Omega_n(\omega)}$ is the indicator function of Ω_n. Letting $n \to \infty$ leads to the contradiction that $\infty > V(A(0), C(0), E(0)) + KT = \infty$. Hence, there is $\tau_\infty = \infty$ a.s. This completes the proof.

4 Stationary Distribution and Ergodicity

Ergodicity is a hallmark of dynamic analysis of DNA subtraction gate systems. Ergodicity is a unique stationary distribution, and it can be predicted that the system will remain stable over time.

Let $A(t)$ be a homogeneous Markov process with stochastic differentiation in E_l (Euclidean l space) such that $dA(t) = b(A)dt + \sum_{r=1}^k g_r(A)dB_r(t)$. The diffusion matrix is $\Lambda(A) = (\lambda_{ij}(A), \lambda_{ij}(A)) = \sum_{r=1}^k g_r^i(A)g_r^j(A)$.

Lemma [15]. Suppose there is a bounded domain $U \subset E_l$ with regular boundaries Γ and the following properties:

(a.1) In the domain U and some vicinity thereof, the least eigenvalue of the diffusion matrix $\Lambda(A)$ is bounded away from zero (a.2) If $A \in E_l \backslash U$ is authentic, then the average time τ for the path from A to the set U is limited, and $\sup_{A \in K} E_A \tau < \infty$ for every compact subset $K \subset E_l$

Then the Markov process $A(t)$ has a stationary distribution $\mu(\cdot)$. Additionally, let $f(\cdot)$ be a function integrable with respect to the measure μ. For all $A \in E_l$

$$P_A \left\{ \lim_{T \to \infty} 1/T \int_0^T f(A(t)) dt = \int_{E_l} f(A) \mu(dA) \right\} = 1. \tag{10}$$

Remark 1. It is proved that there exists a stationary distribution $\mu(\cdot)$ of Eq. (4), and $\mathbb{R}_+^3$ is large enough for our whole space. To verify (a.1), proof is required that for any bounded domain D, there is a positive number M such that $\sum_{i,j=1}^k \lambda_{ij}(A) \xi_i \xi_j \geq M |\xi|^2, A \in \overline{D}, \xi \in \mathbb{R}^k$. To validate (a.2), it is sufficient to show that there exists a neighborhood U and a nonnegative C^2-function $V(A(t), C(t), E(t))$ such that $\mathcal{L}V$ is non-positive for any $E_l \backslash U$.

Definition. For any $0 < T < \infty, P \left\{ \sup_{0 \leq t \leq T} |X(t)| = \infty \right\} = 0$, A Markov process $A(t)$ is regular. If there is a bounded domain U such that $A \in E_l \backslash U$, then the regular process $A(t)$ with nonsingular diffusion matrix described by (4) is called recursive (i.e., the smallest eigenvalue of $\Lambda(x)$ is far from zero in each bounded domain in E_l): $P\{\tau_A < \infty\} = 1$, where $\tau_x = \inf\{t > 0 : X(0) = x, X(t) \in U\}$ is the striking time of U for $A(t)$.

Theorem 2. Suppose Theorem 1 is satisfied. For any initial value $(A(0), C(0), E(0)) \in \mathbb{R}_+^3$, there is a stationary distribution $\mu(\cdot)$ for nonlinear model (4) and it is ergodic.

Proof In order to prove the theorem, we first prove that (a.1) and (a.2) hold. There exists a positive constant $M = \min\{\sigma_1^2 A^2, \sigma_2^2 C^2, \sigma_3^2 E^2, (A, C, E) \in \overline{U}\} > 0$ such that

$$\sum_{i,j=1}^3 \lambda_{ij}(A, C, E) \xi_i \xi_j = \sigma_1^2 A^2 \xi_1^2 + \sigma_2^2 C^2 \xi_2^2 + \sigma_3^2 E^2 \xi_3^2 \geq K |\xi|^2 \text{ for all } \overline{U}, \xi \in \mathbb{R}^3. \text{ The}$$

equation provides favorable conditions to satisfy condition (a.1). After that, to verify (a.2) is essential. We construct a nonnegative C^2 function $V(A(t), C(t), E(t))$ and a closed set $U \in \mathbb{R}_+^3$ such that $\sup_{(A,C,E) \in \mathbb{R}_+^3 \backslash U} \mathcal{L}V(A, C, E) < 0$. This assures that (a.2) is satisfied. Define a C^2 function $h(A, C, E)$,

$$h(A, C, E) = l_1 A + l_2 C + E - l_3 E + \frac{1}{E} + \frac{1}{A} - \ln A - \ln C - \ln E, (A, C, E) \in \mathbb{R}_+^3 \tag{11}$$

Let $l_1 = \frac{1}{A_0}, l_2 = \frac{k_1 - k_2 A_0}{A_0(2k_1 + k_{-1})}, l_3 = \frac{1}{2} + \frac{k_{-1} l_2}{2k_2}$. Here $h(A, C, E)$ has a unique minimum point $(A, C, E)_{\min} = ((1 + \sqrt{1 + 4l_1})/2l_1, 1/l_2, (1 + \sqrt{1 + 4(1 - l_3)})/2(1 - l_3))$, and $\lim_{k \to \infty} \inf_{(A,C,E) \in \mathbb{R}_+^3 \backslash D_k} h(A, C, E) = +\infty$, where $D_k = (1/k, k) \times (1/k, k) \times (1/k, k)$. Define a C^2- positive function of the form $V(A, C, E) = h(A, C, E) - h(A, C, E)_{\min}$.

Then, $H = 2k_1(B_0 - A_0) + k_{-1}(A_0 - E_0) + 2k_2(A_0 - E_0) + k_2 + k_1 + \frac{1}{2}(\sigma_1^2 + \sigma_2^2 + \sigma_3^2)$.

$$\mathcal{L}V \leq H - (l_1 k_1(B_0 - A_0) - l_2 k_1(B_0 - A_0) - k_1 + k_{-1} + k_2)A - \frac{k_{-1}(A_0 - E_0)C}{A} - \frac{k_2 A}{E}$$

$$- [k_{-1}(l_2 - l_1)(A_0 - E_0) - k_{-1}]C - (k_2(1 - l_3)(A_0 - E_0) - k_2 - k_{-1})E - \frac{k_{-1}CE}{A^2} + H, \qquad (12)$$

where $\alpha = l_1 k_1(B_0 - A_0) - l_2 k_1(B_0 - A_0) - k_1 + k_{-1} + k_2$, $\beta = k_{-1}(l_2 - l_1)(A_0 - E_0) - k_{-1}$, the parameter χ is $\chi = k_2(1 - l_3)(A_0 - E_0) - k_2 - k_{-1}$.

Define a closed set, $U_{\varepsilon_1, \varepsilon_2, \bar{s}_3} = \{\varepsilon_1 \leq A \leq 1/\varepsilon_1, \varepsilon_2 \leq C \leq 1/\varepsilon_2, \varepsilon_3 \leq E \leq 1/\varepsilon_3\}$. In addition, $\varepsilon_1, \varepsilon_3$ is a higher-order infinitesimal of ε_2. Thus, $\varepsilon_1 = \varepsilon^2, \varepsilon_2 = \varepsilon^{1/2}$, $\varepsilon_3 = \varepsilon^3$, and ε is sufficiently small that

$$H - \alpha 1/\varepsilon^2 < -1, H - \beta \varepsilon^{-\frac{1}{2}} < -1, H - \chi 1/\varepsilon^3 < -1,$$

$$H - k_{-1}(A_0 - E_0)\varepsilon^{-\frac{3}{2}} < -1, H - k_2 1/\varepsilon < -1, H - k_{-1}\varepsilon^{-\frac{1}{2}} < -1. \qquad (13)$$

Set $\mathbb{R}_+^3 \backslash U_{\varepsilon_1, \varepsilon_2, \varepsilon_3} = D_1 \cup D_2 \cup D_3 \cup D_4 \cup D_5 \cup D_6$. For any $(A, C, E) \in \mathbb{R}_+^3 \backslash U$, denote $D_1 = \{A > 1/\varepsilon_1\}, D_2 = \{C > 1/\varepsilon_2\}, D_3 = \{E > 1/\varepsilon_3\}, D_4 = \{\varepsilon_2 \leq C \leq 1/\varepsilon_2, 0 < A < \varepsilon_1\}, D_5 = \{\varepsilon_1 \leq A \leq 1/\varepsilon_1, 0 < E < \varepsilon_3\}, D_6 = \{0 < A < \varepsilon_1, \varepsilon_2 \leq C \leq 1/\varepsilon_2, \varepsilon_3 \leq E \leq 1/\varepsilon_3\}$.

If $(A, C, E) \in D_1$, $\mathcal{L}V \leq H - \alpha A \leq H - \alpha \varepsilon^{-2}$; When D_2, $\mathcal{L}V \leq H - \beta C \leq H - \beta \varepsilon^{-1/2}$; And so on, the other four situations are similar, all available $\mathcal{L}V \leq -1$. The proof is completed.

5 Numerical Simulations

The rationality of the theory is verified by numerical simulation. Since the nonlinear stochastic differential system is too complex to be solved accurately, the Milstein Discrete method [16] is used to find an approximate solution.

Example 1. Take the initial values $A_0 = 4 \times 10^{-5}$, $E_0 = 5 \times 10^{-5}$, $B_0 = 3 \times 10^{-5}$, and set $G_0 = 2 \times 10^{-5}$, and the rate is set to $k_1 = 4 \times 10^4$, $k_2 = 0.9 \times 10^5$, $k_3 = 1.0 \times 10^5$, $v_{max} = 2 \times 10^{-6}$, $K_m = 2 \times 10^{-4}$, $\tau = 0.2$, $\sigma_3 = 0.3$, and $\sigma_1 = 0.25$, $\sigma_2 = 0.2$. The system equilibrium point is $P_1(0, 2 \times 10^{-5}, 1 \times 10^{-5})$. Thus, as Theorem 2 states, there is a stable distribution of DNA subtraction gates (see histogram on right side of Fig. 2). Through the sample trajectory of each substance, it can be concluded that the DNA subtraction gate model with stochastic disturbance and time delay has a solution, and the model is stable. The rationality of the theoretical results is verified. Red represents the solution of the perturbed system (4), blue represents the solution of the deterministic system (3), and the subgraph on the right is the density function of the stable distribution of the corresponding Brownian motion intensity.

Example 2. To illustrate the influence of Brownian motion and time delay on the DNA subtraction gate, all parameters remain unchanged except the time parameter, which is

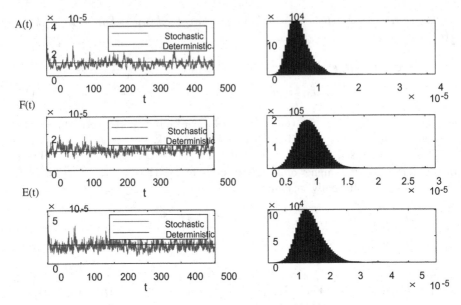

Fig. 2. Solution of stochastic system and its histogram.

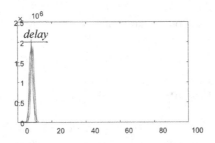

Fig. 3. The density function of C(t). As the time delay increases, the reaction process is delayed.

set to $\tau = 0.5, 3.5, 5.5$. It can be seen from Fig. 3 that with the passage of time, the impact of the system disturbance is delayed accordingly.

The sample trajectory of the image shows that the DNA subtraction gate model with stochastic disturbance and time delay has a stable distribution, and can be implemented smoothly under certain noise conditions.

6   Conclusions

We studied the dynamics of a DNA subtraction gate under the influence of stochastic perturbation and time delay. Firstly, the original strand that realizes the function of the DNA subtraction gate was improved. Based on the subtraction gate reaction, a nonlinear system equation with stochastic perturbation and time delay was constructed. To ensure that the system conforms to the actual situation, the existence of a globally unique positive solution was discussed. Secondly, Markov semigroup theory was used to prove that DNA subtraction gates are ergodic, i.e., the system has a stable distribution. Through theoretical analysis, it was found that the DNA subtraction gate system shows a stable state under the influence of stochastic disturbance and time delay. Finally, Numerical simulation results showed that nonlinear system equations with stochastic disturbances and time delays can be used to describe the dynamic characteristics of a DNA subtraction gate.

Acknowledgements. This work is supported by the National Key R&D Program of China (No. 2018YFC0910500), National Natural Science Foundation of China (Nos. 61425002, 61751203, 61772100, 61972266, 61802040, 61672121, 61572093), Program for Changjiang Scholars and Innovative Research Team in University (No. IRT_15R07), Program for Liaoning Innovative Research Team in University (No. LT2017012), Natural Science Foundation of Liaoning Province (Nos. 2020-KF-14-05, 2019-ZD-0567), High-level Talent Innovation Support Program of Dalian City (Nos. 2017RQ060, 2018RQ75), Dalian Outstanding Young Science and Technology Talent Support Program (No. 2017RJ08), State Key Laboratory of Light Alloy Casting Technology for High-end Equipment (No.LACT-006) and Scientific Research Fund of Liaoning Provincial Education Department (No. JYT19051).

References

1. Qian, L., Winfree, E.: Scaling up digital circuit computation with DNA strand displacement cascades. Science **332**(6034), 1196–1201 (2011)
2. Zhang, D., Winfree, E.: Control of DNA strand displacement kinetics using toehold exchange. J. Am. Chem. Soc. **131**(47), 17303–17314 (2009)
3. Rogers, W., Manoharan, V.: Programming colloidal phase transitions with DNA strand displacement. Science **347**(6222), 639–642 (2015)
4. Niu, Y., Han, F., Zhang, X., Zhou, Z.: A circuit simplification mechanism based on dna combinatorial strands displacement. Fund. Inform. **164**(2–3), 243–257 (2019)
5. Carbone, A., Seeman, N.C.: Circuits and programmable self-assembling DNA structures. Proc. Nat. Acad. Sci. **99**(20), 12577–12582 (2002)
6. Adleman, L.M.: Molecular computation of solutions to combinatorial problems. Science **266**(5187), 1021–1024(1994)
7. Liu, X., Parhi, K.K.: Molecular and DNA artificial neural networks via fractional coding. IEEE Trans. Biomed. Circuits Syst. **14**(3), 490–503 (2020)
8. De Silva, A.P.: Molecular logic gate arrays. Chem. Asian J. **6**(3), 750–766 (2011)
9. Coskun, A., Deniz, E., Akkaya, E.U.: Effective PET and ICT switching of boradiazaindacene emission: a unimolecular, emission-mode, molecular half-subtractor with reconfigurable logic gates. Org. Lett. **7**(23), 5187–5189 (2005)
10. Tandon, A., et al.: Demonstration of arithmetic calculations by DNA tile-based algorithmic self-assembly. ACS Nano **14**(5), 5260–5267 (2020)
11. Chang, R.J.: Cyclostationary gaussian and non-gaussian linearization on analyzing double-well nonlinear oscillators. Mech. Syst. Signal Proc. **142**, 106726 (2020)
12. Li, W., Yang, Y., Yan, H., Liu, Y.: Three-input majority logic gate and multiple input logic circuit based on DNA strand displacement. Nano Lett. **13**(6), 2980–2988 (2013)
13. Mao, X.: Stochastic Differential Equations and Applications. Elsevier, Amsterdam (2007)
14. Gray, A., Greenhalgh, D., Hu, L., Mao, X., Pan, J.: A stochastic differential equation SIS epidemic model. SIAM J. Appl. Math. **71**, 876–902 (2011)

15. Khasminskii, R.: Stochastic Stability of Differential Equations. vol. 66. Springer Science & Business Media, Berlin (2011)
16. Kahl, C., Schurz, H.: Balanced Milstein methods for ordinary SDEs. Monte Carlo Methods Appl. **12**(2), 143–170 (2006)

Modeling and Analysis of Nonlinear Dynamic System with Lévy Jump Based on Cargo Sorting DNA Robot

Hao Fu[1], Hui Lv[1(✉)], and Qiang Zhang[1,2(✉)]

[1] Key Laboratory of Advanced Design and Intelligent Computing, Ministry of Education,
School of Software, Dalian University, Dalian 116622, China
lh8481@tom.com
[2] School of Computer Science and Technology,
Dalian University of Technology, Dalian 116024, China
zhangq@dlu.edu.cn

Abstract. In this paper, a model of nonlinear dynamic system with Lévy jumps based on cargo sorting DNA robot is studied. Firstly, nonlinear biochemical reaction system based on cargo sorting DNA robot model is established. Considering the influence of external disturbances on the system, nonlinear biochemical reaction system with Lévy jump is built and its dimensionality is reduced. Secondly, in order to prove that the built system conforms to the actual meaning, the existence and uniqueness of the system solution is verified. Next, the sufficient conditions for the completion of cargo pick-up of cargo sorting DNA robot and the continued sufficiency are introduced, and the progress of cargo sorting DNA robot under different noise intensities is analyzed. Then, it is proved that the positive recursion of the reaction can better describe and show the persistence of the system. Finally, numerical simulations verify the correctness of the theoretical results. The results show that the end of cargo pick-up with DNA robots for cargo sorting is closely related to the intensity of noise.

Keywords: Cargo sorting DNA robot · Nonlinear system model · Lévy jump · Lyapunov function · Positive recursion

1 Introduction

In recent years, DNA nanotechnology has produced a variety of functional nanostructures, among which the programmability of DNA nanostructures makes it possible to provide conditions for nanorobots. Nanorobots can be used in biomedicine, military fields, etc., which have very good application prospects, and have become a hot spot in today's research. Nanorobots realize robot operations by programming data into the robot's environment. In [1], the working principles of various DNA nanomachines are described. Molecular robots to synthesize ion channels and DNA logic gates are introduced in [2]. In [3], a programmable and autonomous molecular robot driven by DNA hybridization are developed. Kabir et al. [4] discuss the latest development of swarm

© Springer Nature Switzerland AG 2021
Y. Tan and Y. Shi (Eds.): ICSI 2021, LNCS 12689, pp. 557–566, 2021.
https://doi.org/10.1007/978-3-030-78743-1_50

molecular robots, especially emphasize the effective use of biology and nanotechnology in swarm molecular robots, and introduce the importance of regulating the interaction between molecular robots in regulating their swarming. The latest developments in liposome-based molecular robots are introduced in [5]. Chang et al. [6] design a sorting and transporting robot and apply it to electrochemical biosensors to realize multiple detection of micro-ribonucleic acid through alkaline enzyme cutting that drives the robot to walk. Thubagere et al. [7] study cargo sorting DNA robot. DNA robots are also used in many fields of medicine. Taylor et al. [8] construct a DNA-based closed-loop device to manage diabetes molecular robots. Therefore, DNA nanotechnology is becoming more and more popular among researchers, and it also plays an important role in various fields.

In nature, most systems are nonlinear. In order to better analyze them, it can establish an appropriate mathematical model to express it more intuitively. Therefore, it can establish nonlinear system model [9, 10], and perform sensitivity analysis [11], stability analysis [12, 13], parameter estimation [14] and so on. Real life is full of randomness, and random disturbance is inevitable. Many scholars study infectious disease systems and population systems affected by Lévy noise. Lévy jump is often used in infectious disease models [15, 16], proving that the influence of Lévy noise can lead to the extinction of diseases. In [17], Lévy jump is added to the symbiosis model, and the sufficient conditions for the stability of the system's distribution are analyzed. In [18], Lévy jump is introduced into the predator system, and the sufficient conditions for the species' continued survival and extinction are analyzed. Gao et al. [19] add Lévy jumps to the multi-molecule biochemical reaction model, and analyze the conditions for the end and duration of the system reaction. Gaussian white noise is only an idealization of various random noises in reality, which can only describe small disturbances near the mean value, and cannot simulate large-scale random disturbances, while Lévy noise can describe large-scale random disturbances. In biochemical reaction system, there are few studies with Lévy noise. Therefore, adding disturbances such as Lévy jumps in the system can better understand the nature of the system.

Since the temperature will change during cargo pick-up process of cargo sorting DNA robot, resulting in a large random disturbance, this phenomenon needs to be described by a stochastic differential equation driven by Lévy noise. Focusing on the above problems, this article discusses nonlinear biochemical reaction system model with Lévy jump based on cargo sorting DNA robot. The main contributions of this research are as follows. For the first time, Lévy noise is introduced into DNA strand replacement reaction of cargo sorting DNA robot. The influence of noise intensity on the progress of cargo sorting DNA robot during cargo pick-up process is studied.

The rest of this article is organized as follows: In Sect. 2, nonlinear biochemical reaction model based on cargo sorting DNA robot with Lévy jump is established. In Sect. 3, the existence and uniqueness of the positive solution of the system are analyzed. In Sect. 4, the sufficient conditions for the end and the continuation of cargo picking process of cargo sorting DNA robot are analyzed, and the robot's progress under different noise intensities is analyzed. In Sect. 5, the positive recursion to better describe the continuity of the system is analyzed. In Sect. 6, numerical simulations are carried out to verify the above conclusions. Finally, conclusions are drawn in Sect. 7.

2 Modeling of Nonlinear Biochemical Reaction System with Lévy Jump Based on Cargo Sorting DNA Robot

2.1 Modeling of Nonlinear DNA Robot Reaction System

In this section, a mathematical model of nonlinear biochemical reaction system based on cargo sorting DNA robot will be established. The schematic diagram of cargo picking process of cargo sorting DNA robot [7] is shown in Fig. 1.

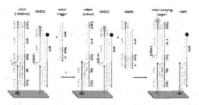

Fig. 1. Schematic diagram of cargo picking process of cargo sorting DNA robot.

In order to further study the impact of cargo sorting DNA robot on the robot's travel during cargo picking process, nonlinear biochemical reaction model based on cargo sorting DNA robot is built. According to Fig. 1, the net reaction equation of cargo loading process can be obtained as

$$\begin{cases} x + a \underset{k_{-1}}{\overset{k_1}{\rightleftharpoons}} b + c \\ b + d \xrightarrow{k_2} y + e, \end{cases} \tag{1}$$

where x represents robot (inhibited), a represents robot trigger, b represents robot (active), c represents waste, c represents cargo1, y represents robot carrying cargo1, e represents inert, and k_1, k_{-1} and k_2 represent the reaction rate. According to Eq. (1) and the mathematical modeling method, nonlinear model can be built as

$$\begin{cases} \dot{x}(t) = k_{-1}b(t)c(t) - k_1x(t)a(t) \\ \dot{a}(t) = k_{-1}b(t)b(t) - k_1x(t)a(t) \\ \dot{b}(t) = k_1x(t)a(t) - k_{-1}b(t)c(t) - k_2b(t)d(t) \\ \dot{c}(t) = k_1x(t)a(t) - k_{-1}b(t)c(t) \\ \dot{d}(t) = -k_2b(t)d(t) \\ \dot{y}(t) = k_2b(t)d(t) \\ \dot{e}(t) = k_2b(t)d(t) \end{cases} \tag{2}$$

where $x(t), a(t), b(t), c(t), d(t), y(t)$ and $e(t)$ respectively represent the concentration of x, a, y, b, c, d, and e at time t.

Based on Eq. (1), according to the law of conservation of mass, the relationship between the initial concentration of the reactant the product can be obtained as

$$\begin{cases} x_0 = x(t) + c(t) = x(t) + b(t) + y(t) \\ a_0 = a(t) + c(t) \\ d_0 = d(t) + y(t) \end{cases} \tag{3}$$

where x_0, a_0, d_0 represent the initial concentration of reactants x, a and d, respectively. According to Eq. (2) and Eq. (3), the following nonlinear biochemical reaction system model can be obtained

$$
\begin{cases}
\dot{x}(t) = \alpha_0 + \alpha_1 x(t) + \alpha_2 y(t) + \alpha_3 x^2(t) + k_{-1} x(t) y(t) \\
\dot{y}(t) = \beta_0 + \beta_1 x(t) + \beta_2 y(t) + k_2 y^2(t) + k_2 x(t) y(t)
\end{cases}
\tag{4}
$$

where $\alpha_0 = k_{-1} x_0^2, \alpha_1 = -2k_{-1}x_0 - k_1(a_0 - x_0), \alpha_2 = -x_0, \alpha_3 = k_1 + k_{-1}, \beta_0 = k_2 x_0 d_0,$ $\beta_1 = -k_2 d_0, \beta_2 = -k_2(x_0 + d_0)$.

2.2 Modeling of Nonlinear DNA Robot Reaction System with Lévy Jump

During operation, DNA robots for cargo sorting may experience sudden and severe disturbances during cargo loading, such as pressure shocks, temperature changes, and so on. These factors will cause large-scale random disturbances in cargo sorting DNA robot, and the resulting phenomenon cannot be accurately described by Eq. (4). Therefore, Lévy jump is added to the model, so that the model can more accurately describe the movement of the robot in cargo pickup. The following nonlinear biochemical reaction model with Lévy jump based on cargo sorting DNA robot is built.

$$
\begin{cases}
dx = \big(\alpha_0 + \alpha_1 x(t^-) + \alpha_2 y(t^-) + \alpha_3 x^2(t^-) + k_{-1} x(t^-) y(t^-)\big)dt \\
\quad -x(t^-)y(t^-)\big(\sigma dB(t) + \int_{\mathbb{Y}} \gamma(u)\tilde{N}(dt, du)\big) \\
dy = \big(\beta_0 + \beta_1 x(t^-) + \beta_2 y(t^-) + k_2 y^2(t^-) + k_2 x(t^-) y(t^-)\big)dt \\
\quad +x(t^-)y(t^-)\big(\sigma dB(t) + \int_{\mathbb{Y}} \gamma(u)\tilde{N}(dt, du)\big),
\end{cases}
\tag{5}
$$

where $B(t)$ is the standard one-dimensional Brownian motion, $\sigma^2 > 0$ are the intensity of white noise, $\tilde{N}$ is the compensated random measure defined by $\tilde{N}(dt, du) = N(dt, du) - \lambda(du)dt$, N is the Poisson counting measure, and λ is the characteristic measure of N, which is defined on the finite measurable subset $\mathbb{Y}$ of $(0, +\infty)$, $\lambda(\mathbb{Y}) < \infty$, $\gamma(u)$: $\mathbb{Y} \times \Omega \to \mathbb{R}$ are bounded continuous functions, and $|\gamma(u)| < l, l > 0$ are constants. Assume that B and N are independent.

Assumption 1. $|-\alpha\gamma(u)/k| \leq \delta < 1$ for any $u \in \mathbb{Y}$, where $\alpha = \max\{\alpha_1 + \beta_1, \alpha_2 + \beta_2\}$, $k = \max\{\alpha_3, k_2, 0.5(k_{-1} + k_2)\}$.

In addition, $\langle f(t) \rangle$ is the mean value of the function $f(t)$ on $[0, \infty)$, that is $\langle f(t) \rangle = t^{-1} \int_0^t f(s)ds$.

3 The Existence and Uniqueness of Positive Solutions

Theorem 1. If Assumption 1 holds, model (5) will have a unique solution at $t \geq 0$ for any given initial value $(x(0), y(0)) \in \mathbb{R}_+^2$, and the solution will be kept in $\mathbb{R}_+^2$ with probability 1, that is, $(x(0), y(0)) \in \mathbb{R}_+^2$ is almost surely $(a.s.)$ for all $t \geq 0$.

Proof. Since the coefficients of model (5) satisfy the local Lipschitz condition, for any given initial value $(x(0), y(0)) \in \mathbb{R}_+^2$, there is a unique local solution $(x(0), y(0))$ at $t \in [0, \tau_e)$, where τ_e represents the blasting time. Let $m_0 \geq 1$ be large enough so that all $(x(0), y(0))$ are in the interval $\left[\frac{1}{m_0}, m_0\right]$. For each integer of $m \geq m_0$, define.

$$\tau_m = \inf\left\{t \in [0, \tau_e] : \min\{x(t), y(t)\} \leq \frac{1}{m} \text{ or } \max\{x(t), y(t)\} \geq m\right\}.$$

Let $\tau_\infty = \lim\limits_{m \to +\infty} \tau_m$, thus $\tau_\infty \leq \tau_e$ a.s. Define a non-negative C^2 function V : $\mathbb{R}_+^2 \to \overline{\mathbb{R}}_+$ as follows: $V(x, y) = (x - 1 - \ln x) + (y - 1 - \ln y)$.

So we can get $LV(x, y) \leq \alpha_0 - \alpha_1 + \beta_0 - \beta_2 + \frac{\alpha^2}{k} + \frac{\sigma^2 \alpha^2}{2k^2} + \frac{\delta^2}{(1-\delta)^2}\lambda(\mathbb{Y}) := C$, where C is a constant. Then we can obtain

$$EV(x(\tau_m \wedge T), y(\tau_m \wedge T)) \leq V(x(0), y(0)) + CT. \tag{6}$$

Set $\Omega_m = \{\tau_m \leq T\}$ for $m \geq m_1$, we have $P\{\Omega_m\} \geq \varepsilon$. It can be seen from (6), $V(x(0), y(0)) + CT \geq \varepsilon\left[(m - 1 - \ln m) \wedge \left(\frac{1}{m} - 1 + \ln m\right)\right]$, Here $m \to \infty$ leads to the contradiction $\infty > V(x(0), y(0)) + CT = \infty$, so we must have $\tau_m = \infty$ a.s. This completes the proof.

4 Sufficient Conditions for the End and Continuation of the Reaction

4.1 Sufficient Conditions for the End of the Reaction

Theorem 2. Under Assumption 1, let $(x(t), y(t))$ be the solution of model (5) with any given initial value $(x(t), y(t)) \in \Gamma^*$. If one of the following two conditions holds.

$(a)\sigma'^2 > -\frac{k}{2(k_2+\beta_2)}$, or $(b)\sigma'^2 \leq -\frac{k^2}{\alpha}$ 和 $\frac{k_2\alpha}{k(\beta_2+k_2)} + \frac{\sigma'^2\alpha^2}{2k^2(\beta_2+k_2)} < 1$, then

$$\limsup_{t\to\infty} \frac{\ln y(t)}{t} \leq \frac{k}{2\sigma'^2} + \beta_2 + k_2 \text{ a.s. if } (a) \text{ holds},$$

$$\limsup_{t\to\infty} \frac{\ln y(t)}{t} \leq (\beta_2 + k_2)\left[\frac{k_2\alpha}{k(\beta_2+k_2)} - 1 + \frac{\sigma'^2\alpha^2}{2k^2(\beta_2+k_2)}\right] < 0 \text{ a.s. if } (b) \text{ holds},$$

where $\sigma'^2 = \sigma^2 + \int_{\mathbb{Y}} \frac{\gamma^2(u)}{(1+\delta)^2}\lambda(du)$, which means the reaction will end exponentially probability one.

Proof. From model (5), we have $\langle x(t^-)\rangle = \frac{\alpha_0+\beta_0}{\alpha_1+\beta_1} + \frac{\alpha_2+\beta_2}{\alpha_1+\beta_1}\langle y(t^-)\rangle + \varphi(t)$, in which $\varphi(t) = \frac{1}{\alpha_1+\beta_1}\left[\frac{x(t)-x(0)}{t} + \frac{y(t)-y(0)}{t}\right]$ satisfies $\lim\limits_{t\to\infty} \varphi(t) = 0$. And then,

$$\frac{\ln y(t) - \ln y(0)}{t} \leq \beta_2 + k_2 + k_2\langle x(t^-)\rangle - \frac{\sigma'^2}{2}\langle x(t^-)\rangle^2 + \frac{M_1(t)}{t} + \frac{M_2(t)}{t}$$

$$:= f(z) + \frac{M_1(t)}{t} + \frac{M_2(t)}{t}, \tag{7}$$

where $M_1(t) = \sigma \int_0^t x(s^-)ds$, $M_2(t) = \int_0^t \int_{\mathbb{Y}} \left[\ln\left(1 + \gamma(u)x(s^-)\right)\right]\tilde{N}(ds, du)$ are all martingale terms and $f : \left(0, \frac{-\alpha}{k}\right) \to \mathbb{R}$ is defined by

$$f(z) = -\frac{\sigma'^2}{2}\left(z - \frac{k}{\sigma'^2}\right)^2 + \frac{k}{2\sigma'^2} + \beta_2 + k_2, z = \langle x(t^-)\rangle \in \left(0, \frac{-\alpha}{k}\right). \tag{8}$$

Case 1: when $\sigma'^2 > -\frac{k}{2(k_2+\beta_2)}$, by (8), we can see that

$$\limsup_{t\to\infty} \frac{\ln y(t)}{t} \leq \frac{k}{2\sigma'^2} + \beta_2 + k_2 < 0 \, a.s. \tag{9}$$

Case 2: when $\sigma'^2 \leq -\frac{k^2}{\alpha}$ and $\frac{k_2\alpha}{k(\beta_2+k_2)} + \frac{\sigma'^2\alpha^2}{2k^2(\beta_2+k_2)} < 1$, from Eq. (7), it's easy to see that $\limsup_{t\to\infty} \frac{\ln y(t)}{t} \leq (\beta_2 + k_2)\left[\frac{k_2\alpha}{k(\beta_2+k_2)} - 1 + \frac{\sigma'^2\alpha^2}{2k^2(\beta_2+k_2)}\right] < 0 \, a.s.$

In summary, $\lim_{t\to\infty} y(t) = 0 \, a.s.$ This completes the proof.

4.2 Sufficient Conditions for Continuous Response

Definition 1. If $\liminf_{t\to\infty} \int_0^t y(s)ds > 0 \, a.s.$ holds, then the system (5) is persistent.

Assumption 2. $R_0^* := R_0 + \frac{\sigma''^2\alpha^2}{2k_2k^2} > 1$, where $\sigma''^2 = \sigma^2 + \int_{\mathbb{Y}} \frac{\gamma^2(u)}{(1-\delta)^2}\lambda(du)$.

Theorem 3. Let Assumption 1 and 2 hold, for any given initial value $(x(0), y(0)) \in \Gamma^*$, the solution $(x(t), y(t))$ of system (5) has the following property:

$$\liminf_{t\to\infty} \langle y(t^-)\rangle \geq \frac{\alpha_1+\beta_1}{\alpha_2+\beta_2}\left[\frac{-(k_2+\beta_2)}{k_2} - \frac{\sigma''^2\alpha^2}{2k_2k^2}\right] - \frac{\alpha_0+\beta_0}{\alpha_2+\beta_2} > 0.$$

Proof. By Eq. (7) and Eq. (8), we can get

$$\frac{\ln y(t)-\ln y(0)}{t} \geq \beta_2 + k_2\left[1 + \frac{\alpha_0+\beta_0}{\alpha_1+\beta_1} - \frac{\alpha_2+\beta_2}{\alpha_1+\beta_1}\langle y(t^-)\rangle + \varphi(t)\right] - \frac{\sigma''^2\alpha^2}{2k^2} + \frac{M_1(t)}{t} + \frac{M_2(t)}{t}.$$

Since $-\infty < \ln y(t) < \ln\left(-\frac{\alpha}{k}\right)$, we can get

$$\liminf_{t\to\infty} \langle y(t^-)\rangle \geq \frac{\alpha_1+\beta_1}{\alpha_2+\beta_2}\left[\frac{-(k_2+\beta_2)}{k_2} - \frac{\sigma''^2\alpha^2}{2k_2k^2}\right] - \frac{\alpha_0+\beta_0}{\alpha_2+\beta_2}.$$

Due to $R_0^* > 1$, $\liminf_{t\to\infty} \langle y(t^-)\rangle > 0$ can be obtained. This completes the proof.

5 Positive Recursion of Reaction

Since positive recursion can better describe and show the persistence of system (5) and give us a deeper understanding of how environmental noise affects the steady state of persistence. In this section, we will find a domain $D \in \Gamma^*$, which is positive recurrent for the process $(x(t), y(t))$.

Theorem 4. Let $(x(t), y(t))$ be the solution of system (5) with any initial value $(x(0), y(0)) \in \Gamma^*$. Under Assumption 1 and 2, solution $(x(t), y(t))$ is positively recursive in domain D, where $D = \{(x, y) \in \Gamma^* : x \geq \varepsilon, y \geq \varepsilon\}$, where ε is a sufficiently small normal number.

Proof. According to Theorem 1, for any initial value $(x(0), y(0)) \in \Gamma^*$, the solution of (5) is positive definite. Define a nonnegative C^2-function $\overline{V} : \Gamma^* \to \mathbb{R}_+$ as follows.

$$\overline{V}(x, y) = U(-\ln x - \ln y) - \ln x + 2U \ln\left(-\frac{\alpha}{k}\right) + \ln\left(-\frac{\alpha}{k}\right),$$

where $U > 0$ satisfies $-U\lambda - \alpha_1 + 0.5\sigma''^2 y^2 \leq -2$, where $\lambda = -k_2(R_0^* - 1) > 0$.
Let $\overline{V}(x, y) = U\overline{V}_1 + \overline{V}_2$, using Itô's formula for $-\ln x$ and $-\ln y$ to get.

$$L(-\ln x) \leq -\frac{\alpha_0}{x} - \alpha_1 + \frac{\sigma^2}{2}y^2 - \int_{\mathbb{Y}} \frac{y^2}{2(1-\delta)^2}\lambda(du), \quad L(-\ln y) \leq -\beta_2 + \frac{\sigma''^2}{2}\frac{\alpha^2}{k^2}.$$

So we get $L\overline{V} \leq U\left(-\alpha_1 - \beta_2 + \frac{\sigma^2}{2}y^2 - \int_{\mathbb{Y}} \frac{y^2}{2(1-\delta)^2}\lambda(du)\right) - U\lambda - \frac{\alpha_0}{x} - \alpha_1 + \frac{\sigma''^2}{2}y^2$.

Define a bounded closed set $D = \{(x, y) \in \Gamma^* : x \geq \varepsilon, y \geq \varepsilon\}$, where ε is a small enough normal number.

Let $(x(0), y(0)) \in \Gamma^*$, and then using Itô's formula, one can see that

$$E[\overline{V}(x(\tau_D), y(\tau_D))] - \overline{V}(x(0), y(0)) = E\int_0^{\tau_D} L\overline{V}(x(t), y(t))dt \leq -E(\tau_D).$$

Due to the positive definiteness of $\overline{V}$, $E(\tau_D) \leq \overline{V}(x(0), y(0))$. This completes the proof.

6 Numerical Simulation

In order to verify the conclusions obtained in this paper, the numerical simulation of the Levy jump of the system (5) is given next. Assuming the unit of time is minutes, the unit of reactant concentration is $mol/L \cdot min$, and the initial value $(x(0), y(0)) = (2.5 \times 10^{-6}, 0)$ is taken. Other parameters are as follows. $x_0 = 2 \times 10^{-6}, a_0 = 2.5 \times 10^{-6}, d_0 = 2 \times 10^{-6}, k_1 = 1.5 \times 10^4, k_{-1} = 1 \times 10^4, k_2 = 2 \times 10^4, \mathbb{Y} = (0, +\infty), \lambda(\mathbb{Y}) = 1$.

Case 1. Choose white noise intensity $\sigma = 0.85$ and jumping noise intensity $\gamma(u) = 0.5$, then Assumption 1 and $\sigma'^2 = 1.7225 > -0.625 = -0.5k/(k_2 + \beta_2)$ are satisfied. Therefore, the condition (a) in Theorem 2 is satisfied, and the reaction ends with a probability 1 index. The simulation result is shown in Fig. 2 (a).

Case 2. Choose white noise intensity $\sigma = 0.7$, jumping noise intensity $\gamma(u) = 0.2$, and set $\delta = 0.4$. Meets Assumption 1, $\sigma'^2 = 0.8501 \leq 7.1429 \times 10^9 = -k^2/\alpha$ and

$$\frac{k_2\alpha}{k(\beta_2 + k_2)} + \frac{\sigma'^2\alpha^2}{2k^2(\beta_2 + k_2)} = -1.75 \times 10^{-6} < 1.$$

Therefore, the condition (b) in Theorem 2 is satisfied, and the reaction ends with a probability 1 index. The simulation result is shown in Fig. 2 (b).

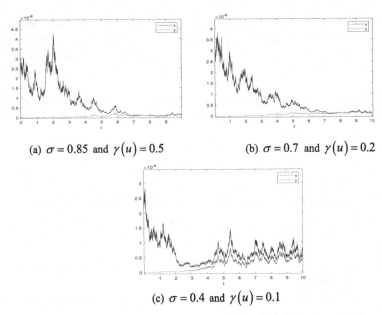

(a) $\sigma = 0.85$ and $\gamma(u) = 0.5$ (b) $\sigma = 0.7$ and $\gamma(u) = 0.2$

(c) $\sigma = 0.4$ and $\gamma(u) = 0.1$

Fig. 2. The state variable response diagram of system (5), in which the horizontal axis represents time and the vertical axis represents concentration.

Case 1 and case 2 show that when the above conditions are met, Lévy jump will force cargo sorting DNA robot to end cargo loading process. At this time, all the reactants in the system will be consumed, causing DNA robot to stop running in advance. This shows that when the above conditions are met, the operation of the DNA robot will end early due to the influence of noise, which will lead to the failure of the experiment.

Case 3. Choose white noise intensity $\sigma = 0.4$, jumping noise intensity $\gamma(u) = 0.15$, and set $\delta = 0.97$. Meets Assumption 1 and $R_0^* = 2.4233 > 1$. Therefore, according to Theorem 3, it can be known that cargo picking process of cargo sorting DNA robot will continue and the solution $(x(t), y(t))$ of system (5) is positive recurrent with respect to domain D in Γ^*. The simulation result is shown in Fig. 2 (c). At this time, the reactants in the system still remain, and DNA robot will continue to run in the system. This indicates that the DNA robot will continue to run during this process, so that all the goods will be picked up.

7 Conclusions

In this paper, nonlinear biochemical reaction system with Lévy jump based on cargo sorting DNA robot is studied. The existence and uniqueness of the positive solution of the system is analyzed. Next, it analyzes the sufficient conditions for the end of cargo sorting DNA robot under the influence of Lévy jump and the sufficient conditions for the reaction to continue. The positive recursion of the reaction is studied to better describe and show the persistence of the system. Finally, the conclusion is verified by numerical simulation. The results show that the end and continuation of cargo picking reaction of cargo sorting DNA robot is closely related to the intensity of Lévy noise, and Lévy jump has a significant impact on the nature of biochemical reaction system.

Acknowledgements. This work is supported by the National Key R&D Program of China (No. 2018YFC0910500), National Natural Science Foundation of China (Nos. 61425002, 61751203, 61772100, 61972266, 61802040, 61672121, 61572093), Program for Changjiang Scholars and Innovative Research Team in University (No. IRT_15R07), Program for Liaoning Innovative Research Team in University (No. LT2017012), Natural Science Foundation of Liaoning Province (Nos. 2020-KF-14–05, 2019-ZD-0567), High-level Talent Innovation Support Program of Dalian City (Nos. 2017RQ060, 2018RQ75), Dalian Outstanding Young Science and Technology Talent Support Program (No. 2017RJ08), State Key Laboratory of Light Alloy Casting Technology for High-end Equipment (No.LACT-006) and Scientific Research Fund of Liaoning Provincial Education Department (No. JYT19051).

References

1. Nummelin, S., Shen, B., Piskunen, P., Liu, Q., Kostiainen, M.A., Linko, V.: Robotic DNA nanostructures. ACS Synth. Biol. **9**(8), 1923–1940 (2020)
2. Kawano, R.: Synthetic ion channels and DNA logic gates as components of molecular robots. ChemPhysChem **19**(4), 359–366 (2018)
3. Muscat, R.A., Bath, J., Turberfield, A.J.: A programmable molecular robot. Nano Lett. **11**(3), 982–987 (2011)
4. Kabir, A.M.R., Inoue, D., Kakugo, A.: Molecular swarm robots: recent progress and future challenges. Sci. Technol. Adv. Mater. **21**(1), 323–332 (2020)
5. Shoji, K., Kawano, R.: Recent advances in liposome-based molecular robots. Micromachines (Basel). **11**(9), 788 (2020)
6. Chang, Y., Wu, Z., Sun, Q., Zhuo, Y., Chai, Y., Yuan, R.: Simply Constructed and Highly Efficient Classified Cargo-Discharge DNA Robot: A DNA Walking Nanomachine Platform for Ultrasensitive Multiplexed Sensing. Anal. Chem. **91**(13), 8123–8128 (2019)
7. Thubagere, A.J., Li, W., Johnson, R.F., Chen, Z., Doroudi, S., Lee, Y.L., et al.: A cargo-sorting DNA robot. Science. **357**(6356) (2017)
8. Taylor, S., Stojanovic, M.N.: Is there a future for DNA-based molecular devices in diabetes management? J. Diabetes Sci. Technol. **1**(3), 440–444 (2007)
9. Qian, H., Bishop, L.M.: The chemical master equation approach to nonequilibrium steady-state of open biochemical systems: linear single-molecule enzyme kinetics and nonlinear biochemical reaction networks. Int. J. Mol. Sci. **11**(9), 3472–3500 (2010)
10. Shindo, Y., Kondo, Y., Sako, Y.: Inferring a nonlinear biochemical network model from a heterogeneous single-cell time course data. Sci Rep. **8**(1), 6790 (2018)
11. Bashkirtseva, I., Ryashko, L., Zaitseva, S.: Stochastic sensitivity analysis of noise-induced transitions in a biochemical model with birhythmicity. J. Phys. A: Math. Theor. **53**(26), 265601 (2020)
12. Getz, M.C., Nirody, J.A., Rangamani, P.: Stability analysis in spatial modeling of cell signaling. Wiley Interdiscip Rev Syst Biol Med. **10**(1) (2018)
13. Cuba Samaniego, C., Giordano, G., Blanchini, F., Franco, E.: Stability analysis of an artificial biomolecular oscillator with non-cooperative regulatory interactions. J. Biol. Dyn. **11**(1), 102–120 (2017)

14. Sun, X., Medvedovic, M.: Model reduction and parameter estimation of non-linear dynamical biochemical reaction networks. IET Syst Biol. **10**(1), 10–16 (2016)
15. Liu, Y., Zhang, Y., Wang, Q.: A stochastic SIR epidemic model with Lévy jump and media coverage. Adv. Differ. Equ. **2020**(1), 1–15 (2020). https://doi.org/10.1186/s13662-020-2521-6
16. Caraballo, T., Settati, A., Fatini, M.E., Lahrouz, A., Imlahi, A.: Global stability and positive recurrence of a stochastic SIS model with Lévy noise perturbation. Phys. A **523**, 677–690 (2019)
17. Deng, M.: Stability of a stochastic delay commensalism model with Lévy jumps. Phys. A: Stat. Mech. Appl. **527**, 121061 (2019)
18. Liu, C., Liu, M.: Stochastic dynamics in a nonautonomous prey-predator system with impulsive perturbations and Lévy jumps. Commun. Nonlinear Sci. Numer. Simul. **78**, 104851 (2019)
19. Gao, M., Jiang, D.: Analysis of stochastic multimolecular biochemical reaction model with lévy jumps. Phys. A **524**, 601–613 (2019)

Stability and Hopf Bifurcation Analysis of Complex DNA Catalytic Reaction Network with Double Time Delays

Wei Chen[1], Hui Lv[1(✉)], and Qiang Zhang[1,2(✉)]

[1] Key Laboratory of Advanced Design and Intelligent Computing, Ministry of Education,
School of Software, Dalian University, Dalian 116622, China
lh8481@tom.com
[2] School of Computer Science and Technology,
Dalian University of Technology, Dalian 116024, China
zhangq@dlu.edu.cn

Abstract. DNA specific fragments are required in DNA computing. The fragments are usually obtained through DNA catalytic reactions. For achieving accurate regulation of DNA catalytic reaction network, toehold has been added into it. Due to the inevitable transcriptions and translations of DNA strands, the outcome of DNA catalytic reaction network using toehold may be affected by these operational delays. Based on this, a nonlinear differential model of complex DNA catalytic reaction network using toehold is proposed. Double time delays characterize delays of two DNA strands transcription in the reaction process. By assigning reactant concentrations and reaction rates, the stability of complex DNA catalytic reaction network system with double time delays is analyzed. The Hopf bifurcation at the equilibrium point is studied and the results of mathematical analysis are obtained. Finally, the correctness of theoretical analysis is verified by numerical simulation.

Keywords: DNA catalytic reaction network · Toehold · Double time delays · Stability analysis · Hopf bifurcation

1 Introduction

With the structure of DNA, DNA computing solves the problem by converting certain inputs into outputs. Due to the nanoscale size and high information density of DNA molecules, DNA computers can perform high-speed parallel calculations. Back in 1994, Adleman [1] used DNA molecules to solve the Hamilton Path problem, thereby revealing the computational power of DNA molecules. With the discovery of toehold [2], the speed of DNA reaction is accelerated, which will also accelerate the development of DNA computing. The researchers also use DNA strands to build logic gates [3–5] to carry out logical calculations, further promoting the development of DNA computing. Wang et al. [6] proposed a new DNA algorithm based on the Adleman-Lipton model, which solved the problem of vehicle routes in congested road sections. the practicability of DNA

© Springer Nature Switzerland AG 2021
Y. Tan and Y. Shi (Eds.): ICSI 2021, LNCS 12689, pp. 567–581, 2021.
https://doi.org/10.1007/978-3-030-78743-1_51

parallel algorithm was proved. Tian [7] proposed a DNA algorithm to solve the shop scheduling problem, which was proved to be superior to other heuristic algorithms by its computational complexity. The application of DNA cannot be separated from DNA strands and DNA strand reactions. Because there are too many uncertain factors in DNA reaction, it is easy to lead to the delay of DNA catalytic reaction, which affects the speed and result of DNA computing. If dynamic knowledge can be used to accurately analyze the delayed DNA catalytic reaction, it can provide a theoretical basis for the realization of the control reaction and ensure the sustainable development of DNA computing.

Time delay has always been the main research direction of dynamic [8–12]. In recent years, the study of time delay in biochemical reaction dynamics has also developed rapidly [13–17]. Du et al. [18] studied the dynamic system of an improved Leslie-Gower predator-prey system with double delay and diffusion. The stability of the system under the influence of double delay parameters at positive equilibrium was analyzed. The existence of Hopf bifurcations and double Hopf bifurcations are studied. The complex dynamic properties near positive equilibrium were also obtained. In medical research, an agestructured SEIRS model with time delay was analyzed [19] The agestructured SEIRS system was simplified to a nonlinear autonomous system with time delay. The existence of the equilibrium point of the model was studied and the local stability of the model at the equilibrium point was received. However, time delay analysis is still rare in DNA catalytic reaction network and the systems analyzed are still simple. If time-delayed dynamics can be used to study DNA catalytic reaction network, it will be more conducive to the overall development of DNA reaction dynamics.

Based on the above considerations, A three-dimensional mathematical model for the complex DNA catalytic reaction network is established for the first time according to the relationship between reactant concentration and rate constant. Law of conservation of mass of elements is used to reduce the dimensions of the mathematical model, a simplified mathematical model is finally obtained. In addition, double time delay generated by transcription and translation were substituted into the mathematical model of complex DNA catalytic reaction network for the first time to improve the accuracy. Then, by using Central Manifold Theorem, Routh Criterion, Euler Theorem, and Sheng Jin formula, the system states under the influence of different delay parameters are calculated. The Hopf bifurcation of the time-delay system at the equilibrium point is analyzed. Finally, the simulation results show that the process and results of DNA catalytic reaction network using toehold are affected by time delays.

The main contributions of this study are as follows:

(1) The differential equation of DNA catalytic reaction network is established, which transformed the complex biochemical reaction process into a multi-dimensional mathematical model for the first time.
(2) Time delays caused by the transcription of DNA strands are added into the dynamics model of DNA catalytic reaction network firstly. The dynamics characteristics of complex system are analyzed. The Hopf bifurcation of DNA catalytic reaction network with double time delays at the equilibrium point is obtained.
(3) The dynamics model of DNA catalytic reaction network with double time delays is simulated numerically. The results show that the size of the time-delay parameters does affect the system state of catalytic reaction network.

The rest of this paper is organized as follows: In Sect. 2, a mathematical model of DNA catalytic reaction network is established. Double time delays are added into the model to obtain a nonlinear time-delay model. In Sect. 3, the system states under the influence of different time delays are discussed. The theoretical analysis results are obtained. In Sect. 4, the system state diagrams and reaction trajectory diagrams under the influence of different time delays are received by using MATLAB functions and related data parameters, which verifies the authenticity of theoretical analysis.

2 Modelling and Analysis of Complex DNA Catalytic Reaction Network System

The following DNA catalytic reaction network is taken as an example (Fig. 1):

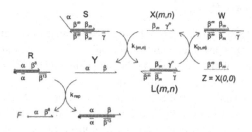

Fig. 1. DNA catalytic reaction network

The chemical reaction equation is

$$
\begin{cases}
X(m, n) + S \underset{k\{n,m\}}{\overset{k\{m,n\}}{\rightleftharpoons}} Y + L(m, n) \\[2mm]
Z + L(m, n) \underset{k\{m,n\}}{\overset{k\{n,m\}}{\rightleftharpoons}} X(m, n) + W \\[2mm]
Y + R \xrightarrow{k_{rep}} Q
\end{cases}
\tag{1}
$$

For convenience, the following symbols are used to refer to the concentrations. $A(t)$, $B(t)$, $C(t)$, $D(t)$, $E(t)$, $F(t)$, $G(t)$, $H(t)$, k_1, k_2, k_3 denote the concentrations of $X(m, n)$, $S, Y, L(m, n)$, Z, W, R, Q, $k\{m, n\}$, $k\{n, m\}$, k_{rep} at time t, respectively.

The Eq. (1) is rewritten as

$$
\begin{cases}
A(t) + B(t) \underset{k_2}{\overset{k_1}{\rightleftharpoons}} C(t) + D(t) \\[2mm]
E(t) + D(t) \underset{k_1}{\overset{k_2}{\rightleftharpoons}} A(t) + F(t) \\[2mm]
C(t) + G(t) \xrightarrow{k_3} H(t)
\end{cases}
\tag{2}
$$

2.1 System Modelling of DNA Catalytic Reaction Network Using Toehold

According to the relationship between reaction rate and time, Eq. (2) can be transformed into

$$
\begin{cases}
\dot{A}(t) = k_2 C(t)D(t) + k_2 E(t)D(t) - k_1 A(t)B(t) - k_1 A(t)F(t) \\
\dot{B}(t) = k_2 C(t)D(t) - k_1 A(t)B(t) \\
\dot{C}(t) = k_1 A(t)B(t) - k_2 C(t)D(t) - k_3 C(t)G(t) \\
\dot{D}(t) = k_1 A(t)B(t) + k_1 A(t)F(t) - k_2 C(t)D(t) - k_2 D(t)E(t) \\
\dot{E}(t) = k_1 A(t)F(t) - k_2 D(t)E(t) \\
\dot{F}(t) = k_2 D(t)E(t) - k_1 A(t)F(t) \\
\dot{G}(t) = -k_3 C(t)G(t) \\
\dot{H}(t) = k_3 C(t)G(t)
\end{cases}
\tag{3}
$$

The dimension of system (3) needs to be reduced because of too many parameters in it. Using the conservation law of elements in the biochemical reaction process to reduce the dimension, the calculation process can be simplified. The difficulty of calculation can be reduced and the accuracy isn't affected.

Let A_0, B_0, E_0, G_0 signify initial concentrations of $X(m, n), S, Z, R$, respectively. If F the concentration of $X(m, n)$ in the solution is $A(t)$ at time t, the concentration sum of F and Y is $A_0 - A(t)$ according to Eq. (1). The concentration sum of $L(m, n)$ and W is $A_0 - A(t)$ too. By analogy, the sum of concentration of Y and F is $B_0 - B(t)$, and the concentration sum of $L(m, n)$ and W is also $B_0 - B(t)$. Since reactant Z reacts only to form W and the reverse reacts to form Z, the concentration of W is $E_0 - E(t)$. And similarly, R only goes into Q, so the concentration of is $G_0 - G(t)$.

System (3) can be transformed into a three-dimensional model containing only three parameters. The simplified DNA catalytic reaction network model is

$$
\begin{cases}
\dot{A}(t) = k_2(A_0 - A(t) - H(t))(E(t) - A(t) + A_0 - E_0) \\
\quad - k_1 A(t)(E_0 - E(t) + A(t) + B_0 - A_0) + k_2 E(t)(E(t) - A(t) + A_0 - E_0) \\
\dot{E}(t) = k_1 A(t)(E_0 - E(t)) - k_2 E(t)(E(t) - A(t) + A_0 - E_0) \\
\dot{H}(t) = k_3(A_0 - A(t) - H(t))(G_0 - H(t))
\end{cases}
\tag{4}
$$

2.2 Double Time Delays System Modelling of DNA Catalytic Reaction Network

The established model (4) has been able to simply characterize the complex DNA catalytic reaction network. However, due to the transcription and translation processes inherent in the DNA catalytic reaction network, the reaction process will have a certain time delay. In order to more accurately describe the process of complex DNA catalytic reaction network, It's the first time that the two-time delay parameters are added to the three-dimensional mathematical model of complex DNA catalytic reaction network.

As mentioned above, objective regulators are added in system (4) artificially. Time delays τ_1 and τ_2 denote time delays of two transcription and translation in the reaction, respectively. On the premise of respecting objective facts, the biochemical reaction dynamic model with double time delays is obtained:

$$
\begin{cases}
\dot{A}(t) = k_2(A_0 - A(t - \tau_1) - H(t))(E(t - \tau_2) - A(t - \tau_1) + A_0 - E_0) \\
\quad - k_1 A(t - \tau_1)(E_0 - E(t - \tau_2)) + k_2 E(t - \tau_2)(E(t - \tau_2) - A(t - \tau_1) + A_0 - E_0) \\
\quad - k_1 A(t - \tau_1)(A(t - \tau_1) + B_0 - A_0) \\
\dot{E}(t) = k_1 A(t - \tau_1)(E_0 - E(t - \tau_2)) - k_2 E(t - \tau_2)(E(t - \tau_2) - A(t - \tau_1) + A_0 - E_0) \\
\dot{H}(t) = k_3(A_0 - A(t - \tau_1) - H(t))(G_0 - H(t))
\end{cases}
\tag{5}
$$

2.3 Model Simplification

The equilibrium point of system (5) can be obtained when all the equations of system (5) are equal to 0. Considering the following conditions:

1) If $A_0 - A(t) - H(t) = 0$, That is, $C(t) = 0$ and $\dot{E}(t) = 0$, so $A(t)B(t) = 0$ in $\dot{A}(t)$. If $A(t) = 0$ and $D(t)E(t) = 0$ in $\dot{E}(t)$, the equilibrium point $E_0 = (0, 0, A_0)$ if $E(t) = 0$ and the equilibrium point is $E_1 = (0, E_0 - A_0, A_0)$ if $D(t) = 0$ according to Eq. (5). If $B(t) = 0$, so $A(t) = A_0 - B_0$. It can be received from the data given in paper that $A_0 < B_0$, so $A(t)$ is negative. In biochemical reaction, the concentration of reactants must not be negative, so the calculated equilibrium points have no practical significance and will not be considered.

2) If $G_0 - H(t) = 0$, so $H(t) = G_0$. $k_2 C(t)D(t) - k_1 A(t)B(t) = 0$ and $k_1 A(t)F(t) - k_2 D(t)E(t) = 0$ because of $\dot{E}(t) = 0$ at this time. Due to the lack of additional information, the equilibrium point of system (5) cannot be calculated when $H(t) = G_0$.

As mentioned above, $E_1 = (0, E_0 - A_0, E_0)$ is chosen to analyze the dynamic state of system (5). E_1 is moved to the origin and system (6) after linearizing the above system is obtained as

$$
\begin{cases}
\dot{A}^*(t) = a_0 A^*(t - \tau_1) + a_1 E^*(t - \tau_2) \\
\dot{E}^*(t) = a_2 A^*(t - \tau_1) + a_1 E^*(t - \tau_2) \\
\dot{H}^*(t) = a_3 A^*(t - \tau_1) + a_3 H^*(t)
\end{cases}
\tag{6}
$$

in which $a_0 = k_2(E_0 - A_0) - k_1 B_0$, $a_1 = -k_2(E_0 - A_0)$, $a_2 = k_1 A_0 + k_2(E_0 - A_0)$, $a_3 = k_3(A_0 - G_0)$. The characteristic equation of system (6) can be gotten as

$$
|\lambda E - J| = (\lambda - a_3)[\lambda^2 - (a_0 e^{-\lambda \tau_1} + a_1 e^{-\lambda \tau_2}) + (a_0 a_1 - a_1 a_2)e^{-\lambda(\tau_1 + \tau_2)}]
\tag{7}
$$

3 Stability Analysis and Hopf Bifurcation of Complex DNA Catalytic Reaction Network System

The complex system (5) contains two uncertain time delays, namely τ_1 and τ_2. τ_1 and τ_2 represent the time delays generated by the two DNA translations in the reaction, respectively. Next, double delays will be divided into three categories. The complex DNA catalytic reaction network system will be analyzed in detail in five cases.

Case 1: $\tau_1 = \tau_2 = 0$.

When $\tau_1 = \tau_2 = 0$,there is no external influencing factor in the two reactions of DNA catalytic reaction network, which leads to the time delay of DNA strand displacement in the reaction network. In this case, system (5) is not affected by time delays.

Theorem 1. In dynamics, the sufficient and necessary condition for system stability is that all coefficients of the characteristic equation of the system have the same sign and all elements of the first column of Routh table are positive. Through calculation, it is known that all elements of the first column of Routh table are positive. System (5) is stable when $\tau_1 = \tau_2 = 0$.

Proof. The characteristic equation of system (5) is.

$$|\lambda E - J| = \lambda^3 - (a_0 + a_1 + a_2)\lambda^2 + (a_0a_1 - a_1a_2 + a_0a_3 + a_1a_3)\lambda - a_1a_3(a_0 - a_2) \tag{8}$$

Setting $\Delta_0 = -(a_0 + a_1 + a_2)$,

$$\Delta_1 = \begin{vmatrix} -(a_0 + a_1 + a_2) & -a_1a_3(a_0 - a_2) \\ 1 & (a_0a_1 - a_1a_2 + a_0a_3 + a_1a_3) \end{vmatrix}.$$

According to the Routh Criterion, the Routh table of the above equation is

$$\begin{array}{lll} \lambda^3 & 1 & a_0a_1 - a_1a_2 + a_0a_3 + a_1a_3 \\ \lambda^2 & -(a_0 + a_1 + a_2) & -a_1a_3(a_0 - a_2) \\ \lambda^1 & \Upsilon & 0 \\ \lambda^0 & -a_1a_3(a_0 - a_2) \end{array} \tag{9}$$

where $\Upsilon = a_0a_1 - a_1a_2 + a_0a_3 + a_1a_3 - \frac{a_1a_3(a_0-a_2)}{(a_0+a_1+a_2)}$.

By the values of parameters, $-(a_0 + a_1 + a_2) > 0$, $\Upsilon > 0$ and $-a_1a_3(a_0 - a_2) > 0$.

Case 2: $\tau_1 = 0, \tau_2 \neq 0$.

DNA helicase relies on ATP to unlock the double helix structure of DNA and RNA polymerase are used to generate messenger RNA to complete DNA transcription. In this case, due to the insufficient supply of ATP, the activity of DNA helicase near Z is low, which delays the process of DNA transcription. In this case, the system state of DNA catalytic reaction network system under the influence of τ_2 is mainly analysis.

Theorem 2. The first reaction in DNA catalytic reaction network proceeded normally, while the second reaction is delayed when $\tau_1 = 0, \tau_2 \neq 0$. When $\tau_2 < \tau_{20}$, the system is asymptotically stable at the equilibrium point E_1. When $\tau_2 > \tau_{20}$, the system is unstable. When $\tau_2 = \tau_{20}$, Hopf bifurcation appears in the system.

$$\tau_2 = \tau_{20} = \frac{1}{\omega_{20}} \cos^{-1} \frac{E_{11}E_{13} + E_{12}E_{14}}{E_{11}^2 + E_{12}^2} \tag{10}$$

Proof. When $\tau_1 = 0$, The characteristic equation of the system (5) is as

$$(\lambda - a_3)(\lambda^2 - (a_0 + a_1e^{-\lambda\tau_2})\lambda + (a_0a_1 - a_1a_2)e^{-\lambda\tau_2}) = 0 \tag{11}$$

$\pm i\omega (\omega > 0)$ is assumed to be a pair of pure imaginary roots of Eq. (11).
The following equation can be received through simple mathematical operation:

$$
\begin{cases}
\cos \omega\tau_2 = \dfrac{E_{11}E_{13} + E_{12}E_{14}}{E_{11}^2 + E_{12}^2} \\[3mm]
\sin \omega\tau_2 = \dfrac{E_{12}E_{13} - E_{11}E_{14}}{E_{11}^2 + E_{12}^2}
\end{cases}
\tag{12}
$$

in which $E_{11} = a_1\omega(a_0 + a_3 - a_2)$, $E_{12} = a_1(a_0a_3 - a_2a_3 - \omega^2)$, $E_{13} = \omega^3 - a_0a_3\omega$, $E_{14} = (a_0 + a_3)\omega^2$.

Adding the two expressions in the above equation by square. It can be gotten as

$$
aX^3 + bX^2 + cX + d = 0
\tag{13}
$$

where $X = \omega^2$, $a = 1$, $b = a_0^2 + a_3^2 - a_1^2$, $c = a_0^2a_3^2 + 2a_1^2a_3(a_0 - a_2) - a_1^2(a_0 + a_3 - a_2)^2$, $d = -a_1^2a_3^2(a_0 - a_2)^2$.

According to Sheng Jin Formula, if $d < 0$, Eq. (13) has at least one positive root. If $d \geq 0$, Eq. (13) has at least one positive root X^*, the root $X^* > 0$ makes $f'(X^*) = 0$ and $f''(X^*) \geq 0$. It is easily can be gotten that Eq. (13) has a unique positive root ω_{20}^2. The corresponding critical point τ_{2n} is

$$
\tau_{2n} = \frac{1}{\omega_{20}} \cos^{-1} \frac{E_{11}E_{13} + E_{12}E_{14}}{E_{11}^2 + E_{12}^2} + \frac{2n\pi}{\omega_{20}}, \, n = 0, 1, 2, \ldots\ldots
\tag{14}
$$

Supposing $\lambda(\tau_{2n}) = \pm i\omega_0$ are the roots of Eq. (11), the transversal condition can be obtained as

$$
\mathrm{Re}\left\{ \left[\frac{d\lambda}{d\tau} \right]_{\tau=\tau_{2n}}^{-1} \right\} = \mathrm{Re}\left\{ \frac{A_0 + B_0i}{C_0 + D_0i} \right\} = \frac{A_0C_0 + B_0D_0}{C_0^2 + D_0^2} > 0
\tag{15}
$$

where

$A_0 = (-3\omega^2 + a_0a_3)\cos\omega_0\tau_{2n} + (a_0 + a_1 + 2a_3)\omega\sin\omega_0\tau_{2n} + a_1(a_0 - a_2 + a_3)$,
$B_0 = [(-3\omega_0^2 + a_0a_3)\sin\omega_0\tau_{2n} - (a_0 + a_1 + 2a_3)\omega_0\cos\omega_0\tau_{2n} - 2a_1\omega_0]$,
$C_0 = a_1\omega_0^2$, $D_0 = a_1(a_0 - a_2)\omega_0$.

Thus $p'(\tau_{2n}) > 0$. This completes the proof.

Case 3: $\tau_2 = 0$, $\tau_1 > 0$.

In this case, a small amount of the inhibitor is involved in the reaction due to improper manipulation. Inhibitors act on the RNA polymerase on $X\{m, n\}$ resulting in partial alteration or loss of RNA polymerase activity. Only part of the RNA polymerase works properly, delaying the process of DNA transcription. The first reaction has a time delay in transcription while the second does not in Eq. (1). The effect of τ_1 on the state of DNA catalytic reaction network system is examined.

Theorem 3. In this situation, the system (5) is asymptotically balanced when $\tau_1 < \tau_{10}$. When $\tau_1 = \tau_{10}$, the system is in Hopf bifurcation. When $\tau_1 > \tau_{10}$, the system falls into an unstable state.

$$\tau_{10} = \frac{1}{\omega_{10}} \cos^{-1} \frac{E_{21}E_{23} + E_{22}E_{24}}{E_{21}^2 + E_{22}^2} \tag{16}$$

where $E_{21} = (a_0a_1 + a_0a_3 - a_1a_2)\omega$, $E_{22} = (a_0\omega^2 - a_0a_1a_3 + a_1a_2a_3)$, $E_{23} = \omega^3 - a_1a_3\omega$, $E_{24} = -(a_1 + a_3)\omega^2$.

Proof. The proof is similar to Theorem 2.

Case 4: $\tau_1 > 0$, $\tau_2 \in (0, \tau_{20})$, τ_{20} is a fixed value.

Due to the dual effects of inhibitor incorporation and ATP deficiency, time delays both exist in DNA catalytic reaction network using toehold when $\tau_1 > 0$, $\tau_2 \in (0, \tau_{20})$. Supposing τ_2 is a fixed value in $(0, \tau_{20})$ while τ_1 is uncertain. The effects of two nonzero delays on three-dimensional DNA catalytic reaction network are considered in this case. The properties of system states under the influence of indefinite τ_1 are mainly analyzed.

Theorem 4. If $\Delta_0 > 0$, $\Delta_1 > 0$, system (5) is asymptotically stable at equilibrium point E_1 when $\tau_2 \in (0, \tau_{20})$. System (6) is unstable when $\tau_2 > \tau_{20}$. Hopf bifurcation occurs when $\tau_2 = \tau_{20}$.

Proof. The characteristic equation of system (5) is

$$(\lambda - a_3)[\lambda^2 - (a_0e^{-\lambda\tau_1} + a_1e^{-\lambda\tau_2}) + (a_0a_1 - a_1a_2)e^{-\lambda(\tau_1+\tau_2)}] = 0 \tag{17}$$

τ_2 is a fixed value in $(0, \tau_{20})$. τ_1 is seen as a parameter. Supposing $\pm i\omega(\omega > 0)$ is roots of Eq. (17), The real and imaginary parts are separated.

It can be gained as

$$\begin{cases} \cos \omega\tau_1 = \dfrac{E_{31}E_{33} + E_{32}E_{34}}{E_{31}^2 + E_{32}^3} \\[2mm] \sin \omega\tau_1 = \dfrac{E_{32}E_{33} - E_{31}E_{34}}{E_{31}^2 + E_{32}^2} \end{cases} \tag{18}$$

in which

$E_{31} = (a_0 - a_2)a_1\omega \cos \omega\tau_2 + a_0a_3\omega + (a_0 - a_2)a_1a_3 \sin \omega\tau_2$,

$E_{32} = (a_0 - a_2)a_1a_3 \cos \omega\tau_2 - a_0\omega^2 - (a_0 - a_2)a_1\omega \sin \omega\tau_2$,

$E_{33} = \omega^3 + a_1\omega^2 \sin \omega\tau_2 - a_1a_3\omega \cos \omega\tau_2$, $E_{34} = a_3\omega^2 + a_1\omega^2 \cos \omega\tau_2 + a_1a_3\omega \sin \omega\tau_2$.

It can be gotten through the special properties of trigonometric functions:

$$\omega^6 + (a_1^2 + a_3^2 - a_0^2)\omega^4 + [a_1^2a_3^2 - a_1^2(a_0 - a_2)^2 - a_0^2a_3^2]\omega^2 - a_1^2a_3^2(a_0 - a_2)^2$$
$$+2a_1(\omega^5 + a_3^2\omega^3 - a_0(a_0 - a_2)\omega^3 - a_0a_3^2(a_0 - a_2)\omega) \sin \omega\tau_2 = 0 \tag{19}$$

The above equation can be rewritten as

$$\Psi_3 W^3 + \Psi_2 W^2 + \Psi_1 W + \Psi_0 + \Lambda_0 \sin \omega\tau_2 = 0 \tag{20}$$

Let $\omega_1^{(1)}$, $\omega_1^{(2)}$, $\omega_1^{(3)}$ and $\omega_1^{(4)}$ be four roots of Eq. (20). There is a ω_1^i ($i = 1, 2, 3, 4$) corresponding each $\tau_{1i}^{(j)}$.

$$\tau_{1i}^{(j)} = \frac{1}{\omega_1^i} \cos^{-1} \left(\frac{E_{31}E_{33} + E_{32}E_{34}}{E_{31}^2 + E_{32}^2} + 2j\pi \right)_{\omega_1 = \omega_1^j} , i = 1, 2, 3, 4; j = 0, 1, 2, \ldots.$$

$$(21)$$

Supposing $\tau_{10}' = \min\{\tau_{1i}^{(j)} | i = 1, 2, 3, 4; j = 0, 1, 2, \ldots\}$, ω_{10}' is the root of Eq. (20) when $\tau_{10} = \tau_{10}'$. When $\lambda = i\omega_{10}'$ is root of Eq. (17), it can be received as

$$\mathrm{Re}\left(\frac{d\lambda}{d\tau_1}\right)^{-1}_{\lambda=i\omega_{10}'} = \mathrm{Re}\left(\frac{A_1 + B_1 i}{C_1 + D_1 i}\right) = \frac{A_1 C_1 + B_1 D_1}{C_1^2 + D_1^2} > 0 \qquad (22)$$

where

$$A_1 = -3\omega^2 - a_0\omega(2 - \omega^2)\sin\omega\tau_{1n}' - a_1\omega(2 - a_3\tau_1)\sin\omega\tau_2 + a_0 a_3(1 + \omega^2)\cos\omega\tau_{1n}'$$
$$+ a_1(a_3 - \omega^2\tau_2)\cos\omega\tau_2 + a_1 a_3(a_0 - a_2)\tau_{1n}'\cos\omega(\tau_{1n}' + \tau_2) - a_1(a_0 - a_2)\omega\tau_{1n}'\sin\omega(\tau_{1n}' + \tau_2)$$

$$B_1 = -a_3\omega - a_0\omega(2 + \omega^2)\cos\omega\tau_{1n}' - a_1\omega(2 + a_3\tau_{1n}')\cos\omega\tau_2 - a_0 a_3(1 + \omega^2)\sin\omega\tau_{1n}'$$
$$+ a_1(\omega^2\tau_2 - a_3)\sin\omega\tau_2 - a_1(a_0 - a_2)\omega\tau_{1n}'\cos\omega(\tau_{1n}' + \tau_2) - a_1 a_3(a_0 - a_2)\tau_{1n}'\sin\omega(\tau_{1n}' + \tau_2)$$

$$C_1 = -a_1(a_0 - a_2)\omega^2\cos\omega(\tau_{1n}' + \tau_2) - a_1 a_3(a_0 - a_2)\omega\sin\omega(\tau_{1n}' + \tau_2)$$
$$+ a_0\omega^3\sin\omega\tau_{1n}' - a_2 a_3\omega^2\cos\omega\tau_{1n}'$$

$$D_1 = a_1(a_0 - a_2)\omega^2\sin\omega(\tau_{1n}' + \tau_2) - a_1 a_3(a_0 - a_2)\omega\cos\omega(\tau_{1n}' + \tau_2)$$
$$+ a_0\omega^3\cos\omega\tau_{1n}' + a_2 a_3\omega^2\sin\omega\tau_{1n}'$$

The transversality condition holds when $A_1 C_1 + B_1 D_1 \neq 0$. This completes the proof.

Case 5: $\tau_2 > 0$, $\tau_1 \in (0, \tau_{10})$, τ_1 is a fixed value

When $\tau_2 > 0$, $\tau_1 \in (0, \tau_{10})$, two delays exist in DNA catalytic reaction network because of inhibitor incorporation and ATP deficiency. It is assumed that the first delay τ_1 is fixed. τ_2 is treated as a parameter. The effects of different values of the second reaction time delay τ_2 on the dynamics of the system are investigated.

Theorem 5. If $\Delta_0 > 0$, $\Delta_1 > 0$, system (5) is asymptotically stable at equilibrium point E_0 when $\tau_1 \in (0, \tau_{10})$. When $\tau_1 > \tau_{10}$, system (5) is in oscillating. Hopf bifurcation occurs when $\tau_1 = \tau_{10}$. When $\tau_1 < \tau_{10}$, system (5) is in a stable state.

Proof. The proof method refers to Theorem 4, and the proof process is similar.

Remark 1. Routh Criterion is an important method to judge the stability of higher order linear systems. In order to avoid solving complex characteristic equation, the stability of the system can be judged by algebraic operation of the coefficient of characteristic equation. When the first column of the Routh table is all positive, the system is stable. In this paper, the system equation without time delay is solved and analyzed, which greatly reduces the difficulty of calculation. Euler's Formula trans-forms exponential function into trigonometric function with complex number. Combined with relevant knowledge of trigonometric function, through simple mathematical operation, the relationship between and time delay is gotten. Sheng Jin Formula is mainly used to solve cubic equations. In the above part, the complex higher-order function is transformed into a cubic equation by transforming the unknown quantity. The required solution intuitively and concisely is obtained through the relevant formulas of Sheng Jin Formula.

4 Numerical Simulation

System (5) of DNA catalytic reaction network with two delays will be simulated in this part. The system trajectory diagram and state variable diagram under the action of different double-delay parameter combinations are received in this part. By analyzing the trend of trajectory diagrams, the actual situation of reaction can also be intuitively verified.

Specific parameters are set as follows through the paper [20], $A_0 = 1\,\text{nm}$, $B_0 = 10\,\text{nm}$, $E_0 = 100\,\text{nm}$, $G_0 = 30\,\text{nm}$. $k_1 = 1 * 10^{-2}\,\text{nM/s}$, $k_2 = 4 * 10^{-4}\,\text{nM/s}$, $k_3 = 9 * 10^{-3}\,\text{nM/s}$. It can be received from Eq. (10) and Eq. (16) that $\tau_{10} = 17.36\,\text{s}$, $\tau_{20} = 22.00\,\text{s}$. $\tau_{10}' = 17.36\,\text{s}$, $\tau_{20}' = 21.25\,\text{s}$.

Case1
When $\tau_1 = \tau_2 = 0$, it is obviously that system (5) is stable from system trajectory diagram and state variable diagram (see Fig. 2). DNA catalytic reaction network reacts normally without delays. The results of images are consistent with Theorem 1.

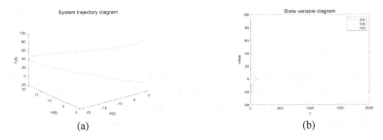

(a)   (b)

Fig. 2. System trajectory diagram and State variable diagram when $\tau_1 = \tau_2 = 0$.

Case2

The DNA catalytic reaction network is only affected by τ_2. When $\tau_2 = 19 < \tau_{20}$, Fig. 3(a) and Fig. 3(d) are in a certain fluctuation and eventually stabilizes. It is known from Fig. 3(a) that the reaction converges at the equilibrium point E_1. But it takes more time to complete the reaction. When $\tau_2 = \tau_{20} = 22$, the system is in a special state between a stable state and an unstable one. From Fig. 3(e), the curve is vibrating regularly. But

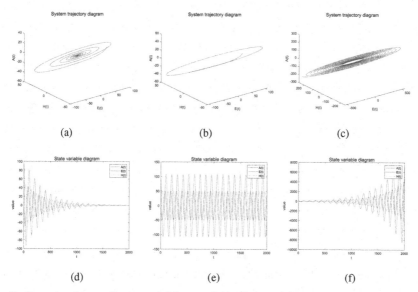

Fig. 3. System trajectory diagrams and State variable diagrams when $\tau_1 = 0$, $\tau_2 = 19, 22, 22.7$.

the curve does not converge at the equilibrium point E_1 in Fig. 3(b). The system should be experiencing Hopf bifurcation. From Fig. 3(f), it is shown clearly that the curves of state variables do not stabilize at last and fluctuate more and more violently. Also, the trajectories of the system in Fig. 3 (c) do not converge at the equilibrium point E_1. Judging from these, the system is unstable when $\tau_2 = 22.7 > \tau_{20}$. DNA catalytic reaction network using toehold does not work properly. Figure 3 is unified with mathematical calculation.

Case3
It is clearly known from Fig. 4(a) and Fig. 4(d) that the curve of system trajectory converges to a point, namely the equilibrium point E_1. The state variable curves become stable eventually, but the system takes more time to be stable. From Fig. 4(b) and Fig. 4(e), the system is in the critical state between a stable state and an unstable one. Hopf bifurcation occurs when $\tau_1 = \tau_{10}$. From Fig. 4(c) and Fig. 4(f), not only the system trajectory is unable converge to the equilibrium point E_1, but also the state variable diagram is not asymptotic to a value. It can be received that the system is in an unstable state when $\tau_1 = 19 > \tau_{10}$. The DNA catalytic reaction network using toehold goes wrong and the reaction fails.

Case4
When $\tau_1 = 2$, $\tau_2 = 18 < \tau'_{20} = 21.25$, the system is affected by τ_1 and τ_2. From Fig. 5(a), the curve converges to a point eventually. The oscillation in Fig. 5(d) gradually levels off. It can be seen clearly that system (5) is asymptotically stable when $\tau_1 < \tau'_{10}$. Required DNA fragments can also be received from the reaction. Figure 5(b) and Fig. 5(e) shows that system (5) is in an intermediate state between an unstable state and a stable one. Hopf bifurcation appears in the system (5) when $\tau_1 = 2$, $\tau_2 = \tau'_{20} = 21.25$ because

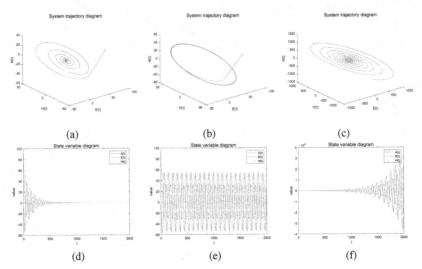

Fig. 4. System trajectory diagrams and State variable diagrams when $\tau_2 = 0$, $\tau_1 = 15, 17.36, 19$.

the state of this DNA catalytic reaction network delayed system changes. When $\tau_1 = 2$, $\tau_2 = 23 > \tau'_{20} = 21.25$, the system is unstable and cannot converge to a point from Fig. 5(c) and Fig. 5(f). DNA catalytic reaction network fails finally.

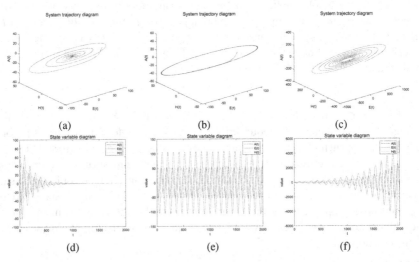

Fig. 5. System trajectory diagrams and State variable diagrams when $\tau_1 = 2$, $\tau_2 = 18, 21.25, 23$.

Case 5

When $\tau_1 = 14 < \tau'_{10} = 16.3$, $\tau_2 = 5$, the system (5) is affected by two delays τ_1 and τ_2. The influence of τ_1 on DNA catalytic reaction network is mainly analyzed. From

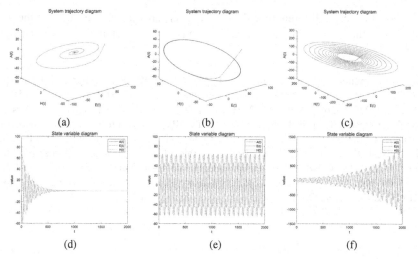

Fig. 6. System trajectory diagrams and State variable diagrams when $\tau_1 = 14$, 16.3, 17, $\tau_2 = 5$.

Fig. 6(a) and Fig. 6(d), the system (5) is asymptotically stable at the equilibrium point E_1. The system oscillates in a regular way from Fig. 6(e) and the system trajectory does not converge from Fig. 12(b). When $\tau_1 = \tau'_{10} = 16.3$, $\tau_2 = 5$, Hopf bifurcation arises in the system. When $\tau_1 = 17 > \tau'_{10} = 16.3$, $\tau_2 = 5$, the system is unstable. The system trajectory cannot converge to the equilibrium point E_1 from Fig. 6(c).

Remark 2. Through the simulation images above, the correctness of the mathematical analysis is verified. It is proved that the state of the biochemical system is influenced by time delays. When time delays are greater than critical values, the normal operation of DNA catalytic reaction network is seriously affected. Eventually, DNA catalytic reaction fails. When the values of delays are less than the thresholds, the delays do not make a huge impact on the reaction state, and the reaction is still normal. The critical values of delays are likely to be the limit of the change in the state of the system. In other words, Hopf bifurcation occurs at the critical value of the system.

5 Conclusion

The properties of complex DNA catalytic reaction network have been studied in this paper. The three-dimensional biochemical reaction dynamic model of DNA catalytic reaction network using toehold is established. To reflect the actual situation of DNA catalytic reaction network reaction using toehold more accurately and realistically, a new three-dimensional mathematical model with two delays is formed based on the original system for the first time. The central manifold theorem is used to linearize the system and the simplified model is obtained. By classifying the time delay, the system is analyzed in detail, and the stability of complex time delay system near the equilibrium point and the analysis results of Hopf bifurcation are gained. Finally, the state variable response diagrams and system trajectory diagrams of DNA catalytic reaction network under the influence of different time delay parameters are drawn. The values of the time delays affect the system state and reaction results of DNA catalytic reaction network system.

Acknowledgements. This work is supported by the National Key R&D Program of China (No. 2018YFC0910500), National Natural Science Foundation of China (Nos. 61425002, 61751203, 61772100, 61972266, 61802040, 61672121, 61572093), Program for Changjiang Scholars and Innovative Research Team in University (No. IRT_15R07), Program for Liaoning Innovative Research Team in University (No. LT2017012), Natural Science Foundation of Liaoning Province (Nos. 2020-KF-14–05, 2019-ZD-0567), High-level Talent Innovation Support Program of Dalian City (Nos. 2017RQ060, 2018RQ75), Dalian Outstanding Young Science and Technology Talent Support Program (No. 2017RJ08), State Key Laboratory of Light Alloy Casting Technology for High-end Equipment (No.LACT-006) and Scientific Research Fund of Liaoning Provincial Education Department (No. JYT19051).

References

1. Adleman, L.: Molecular computation of solutions to combinatorial problems. Science **266**(5187), 1021–1024 (1994)
2. Yurke, B., Turberfield, A., Mills, A., Simmel, F., Neumann, J.: A DNA-fuelled molecular machine made of DNA. Nature **406**, 605–608 (2000)
3. Zadegan, R., Jepsen, M., Hildebrandt, L., Birkedal, V., Kjems, J.: Construction of a fuzzy and Boolean logic gates based on DNA. Small **11**(15), 1811–1817 (2015)
4. Andrianova, M., Kuznetsov, A.: Logic Gates Based on DNA Aptamers. Pharmaceuticals **13**(11), 417 (2020)
5. Sami, P., Shen, C., Sani, M.: Ultra-fast all optical half-adder realized by combining AND/XOR logical gates using a nonlinear nanoring resonator. Appl. Opt. **59**(22), 6459–6465 (2020)
6. Wang, Z., Ren, X., Ji, Z., Huang, W., Wu, T.: A novel bio-heuristic computing algorithm to solve the capacitated vehicle routing problem based on Adleman-Lipton model. Biosystems **184**, 103997–104006 (2019)
7. Tian, X., Liu, X., Zhang, H., Sun, M., Zhao, Y.: A DNA algorithm for the job shop scheduling problem based on the Adleman-Lipton model. PLoS ONE **15**, e0242083 (2020)
8. Song, B., Zhang, Y., Park, J., Yang, Z.: Delay-dependent stability analysis of stochastic time-delay systems involving Poisson process. J. Franklin Inst. **358**(1), 1087–1102 (2021)
9. Kaslik, E., Neamţu, M., Vesa, L.: Global stability analysis of an unemployment model with distributed delay. Math. Comput. Simul. **185**(4), 535–546 (2021)
10. Cai, T., Cheng, P.: Stability Analysis of discrete-time stochastic delay systems with impulses. Mathematics **9**, 418 (2021)
11. Zhang, X., Wang, Y., Wu, L.: Analysis and design of delayed genetic regulatory networks. Studies in Systems, Decision and Control 2019, pp. 57-80. Springer, Warsaw (2017). https://doi.org/10.1007/978-3-030-17098-1
12. Abdulrashid, I.A.M., Han, X.: Stability analysis of a chemotherapy model with delays. Discrete Continuous Dyn. Syst. - B **24**(3), 989–1005 (2019)
13. Wang, J.-A., Fan, L., Wen, X.-Y.: Improved Results on Stability Analysis for Delayed Neural Network. Int. J. Control Autom. Syst. **18**(7), 1853–1862 (2020). https://doi.org/10.1007/s12 555-019-0536-0
14. Elaiw, A., Alshehaiween, S., Hobiny, A.: Global properties of a delay-distributed HIV dynamics model including impairment of B-Cell functions. Mathematics **7**(9), 837 (2019)

15. Khajanchi, S.: Chaotic dynamics of a delayed tumor–immune interaction model. Int. J. Biomathematics **13**(5), 2050009 (2020)

16. Prakash, M., Rakkiyappan, R., Manivannan, A., Cao, J.: Dynamical analysis of antigen-driven T-cell infection model with multiple delays. Appl. Math. Comput. **354**, 266–281 (2019)

17. Xie, B., Xu, F.: Stability analysis for a time-delayed nonlinear predator–prey model. Adv. Difference Equ. **2018**(1), 1–16 (2018). https://doi.org/10.1186/s13662-018-1564-4

18. Du, Y., Niu, B., Wei, J.: Two delays induce Hopf bifurcation and double Hopf bifurcation in a diffusive Leslie-Gower predator-prey system. Chaos **29**(1), 013101 (2019)

19. Yin, Z., Yu, Y., Lu, Z.: Stability analysis of an age-structured SEIRS model with time delay. Mathematics **8**(3), 455 (2020)

20. Zhang, D., Winfree, E.: Control of DNA strand displacement kinetics using toehold exchange. J. Am. Chem. Soc. **131**(47), 17303–17314 (2009)

Author Index

Abbass, Hussein II-168
Abramov, Evgeny II-230
Ahmadi, Taha II-533
Akhmedova, Shakhnaz I-174
Akimenko, Tatiana I-3
Alkilabi, Muhanad H. M. II-92
Avdeenko, Tatiana I-379, II-452

Bacanin, Nebojsa I-415
Bao, Weidong II-137
Basan, Elena I-26, II-230
Bureerat, Sujin I-38

Cai, Xiangyu II-563
Campbell, Benjamin II-168
Carletti, Timoteo II-92
Carolus, Timothy G. I-185
Chang, Fengrong I-479
Chang, Yatong II-58
Chen, Hao II-137
Chen, Jian II-263
Chen, Jinsong I-265
Chen, Junfeng I-492
Chen, Peibin II-511
Chen, Shilian I-513
Chen, Wei I-567
Chen, Yinnan II-3
Chen-Burger, Yun-Heh (Jessica) I-72
Cheng, Jian II-420
Cheng, Ruru II-553
Cheng, Shi II-73
Chu, Zhenzhong II-45
Chu, Zhugang II-85
Chubko, Nikita Y. I-289
Crane, Tyler I-232
Cui, Yuanzhe II-111, II-146

Dang, Sijie II-331
Deka, Ankur I-13
Deng, Changshou I-358
Deng, Kebo II-290
Deng, Libao I-244
Deng, Xiangyang I-301

Deng, Yimin II-195
Ding, Fei II-321
Dong, Aoshuang I-479
Dong, Jian I-83, I-441
Dong, Xiaogang I-358
Duan, Haibin II-195
Duan, Shihong II-129

El-Fiqi, Heba II-168
Engelbrecht, Andries I-232
Engelbrecht, Andries P. I-185, I-210
Ersoy, Okan K. II-45

Fan, Qinqin II-45
Fister Jr., Iztok II-243, II-381
Fister, Iztok II-243, II-381
Fournier-Viger, Philippe II-253
Fu, Hao I-557
Fukumoto, Makoto I-368

Gao, Jun II-300
Gao, Liang I-390
Gao, Yiping I-390
Gaona, Sebastián Soto II-533
Ge, Yunjiao I-155
Geng, Shuang I-513, II-440
Gong, Xiaoling I-322
Grigoryan, Karen I-26
Guan, Fei II-282
Guo, Jinyuan II-102, II-119
Guo, Jixiang II-331
Guo, Yinan II-420
Guo, Yuanjun I-140

Hamdan, Mohammad I-223
Han, Fei II-480
Han, Kai II-391
Han, Liyuan II-525
Hao, Zhi-yong II-500
Hasebe, Koji I-333, II-543
He, Wei II-182
He, Xiaofu II-440
Hong, Jiaming II-23

Hong, PengCheng   I-423
Hong, Yang   II-102
Hongzhen, Lei   II-563
Hou, Sibo   I-244
Hu, Renyuan   I-254
Huang, Canpeng   II-300
Huang, Chaomin   II-407
Huang, Kaishan   II-300
Huang, Lang   II-391
Huang, Xijie   II-300
Hunjet, Robert   II-168

Innocente, Mauro Sebastián   I-275
Iwasaki, Yu   I-333

Jayaraman, Elakiya   II-73
Ji, Falei   I-119, II-321
Jiang, Mingyan   I-119, I-130, II-321
Jiao, Botao   II-420
Jin, Daopeng   II-102, II-119
Juanli, Lan   II-563

Kang, Xuying   II-13
Kong, Lingjing   II-23

Lapina, Maria   I-26, II-230
Larkin, Eugene   I-3
Lee, Jinho   II-391
Lei, Hongtao   II-205
Lei, Tingjun   II-73
Li, Feng   I-58
Li, Huiwen   I-547
Li, Jiang   II-102, II-119
Li, Junya   II-407
Li, Ning   II-45
Li, Shuang   I-433
Li, Wanying   II-440
Li, Wenhua   II-205
Li, Wenyu   I-83, I-441
Li, Xiaofeng   I-58
Li, Xinyu   I-390, II-34
Li, Xiuzhi   II-218
Li, Xuan   I-433
Li, Yang   II-365
Li, Yifeng   I-451
Li, Yinghao   II-119
Li, Yuhao   I-155

Li, Zhen   II-282
Li, Zili   II-365
Liang, Rupeng   II-290
Lin, Shau-Ping   I-72
Lin, Xin   II-58, II-263
Liu, Fangcheng   II-391
Liu, Hsin-Ping   I-72
Liu, Jianhua   I-254
Liu, Ru   II-563
Liu, Shaopeng   II-23
Liu, Shicai   II-553
Liu, Wenyu   II-313
Long, Keping   II-182
Lu, Mingli   II-282
Luo, Chaomin   II-73
Luo, Wenjian   II-58
Luo, Yixuan   I-254
Lv, Hui   I-537, I-547, I-557, I-567
Lv, Wei   I-322

Ma, Li   II-137
Ma, Lianbo   I-479
Ma, Wei   II-290
Ma, Xiaoliang   I-347
Mao, Zexiang   II-290
Mecella, Massimo   I-26
Mezentsev, Yurii A.   I-289
Mudruk, Nikita   II-230
Murtazina, Marina   II-452

Nawaz, M. Saqib   II-253
Neri, Ferrante   II-472
NgoGia, Thao   II-119
Ni, Qingjian   II-13, II-272, II-462, II-491
Ninjerdene, Bulgan   I-492
Nishimura, Haruki   II-543
Niu, Ben   I-265, I-505, I-523

Olefirenko, Evgeniya   I-26
Ombuki-Berman, Beatrice   I-232
Onzo, Bernard-marie   II-472
Ou, Yikun   I-523

Pan, Zhen   II-352
Pasquier, Philippe   I-46
Pečnik, Luka   II-243, II-381
Peng, Hu   I-358

Peng, Wenqiang II-491
Phoa, Frederick Kin Hing I-72, I-106
Privalov, Aleksandr I-3

Qiao, Yanping I-58
Qiu, Guangyuan II-440
Qiu, Haiyun I-265
Quan, Xiaoxiao I-469

Rahimi, Shahram II-73
Rong, Ziheng I-322

Salimi, Mahsoo I-46
Serdyukov, Konstantin I-379
She, Zeneng II-58
Shen, Chenxin II-272, II-462
Shi, Jian II-282
Shi, Ronghua I-83, I-441
Shi, Yuhui II-155
Sleesongsom, Suwin I-38
Sleiman, Kamal Abubker Abrahim II-563
Song, Le I-244
Song, Wei II-407
Song, Yan I-479
Song, Yuanming II-205
Sreeja, N. K. I-311
Sreelaja, N. K. I-311
Stanovov, Vladimir I-174
Strumberger, Ivana I-415
Sun, Baodan I-399
Sun, Gaoji I-244
Sun, Meng II-253
Sun, Peng-ge II-500
Sun, Tao I-537
Sycara, Katia I-13

Tan, Chengming II-553
Tan, Ying I-451, II-58, II-511
Tan, Yingsi I-513
Tan, Yucheng I-358
Tang, Ke II-339
Tang, Qirong II-85, II-102, II-111, II-119,
    II-146
Tuba, Eva I-415
Tuba, Ira I-415

Tuba, Milan I-415
Tuci, Elio II-92

Uchida, Seiichi II-391

van Zyl, Jean-Pierre I-210

Wan, Jiawang II-129
Wan, Ruizhi II-3
Wang, Cuiyu I-390, II-34
Wang, Dan I-94
Wang, Hong I-523, II-300, II-430
Wang, Ji II-137
Wang, Jian I-322
Wang, Lin I-83
Wang, Rui II-205
Wang, Shijie II-420
Wang, Shuting II-34
Wang, Xiangyu I-322
Wang, Yihao II-45
Wang, Yihuai II-480
Wang, Yixin I-523, II-430
Wang, Yuhui II-272, II-462
Wang, Yulong I-469
Wang, Zihang I-254
Wang, Zixuan II-182
Wei, Qinglai II-525
Wu, Di II-282
Wu, Hang II-129
Wu, Meng II-137
Wu, Mingliang I-140
Wu, Xue I-163
Wu, Yali I-469

Xia, Shuang II-218
Xiang, Xinhao II-155
Xiao, Qinge I-505
Xie, Jun II-331
Xie, Weixin I-347
Xin, Miaomiao I-130
Xu, Benlian II-282
Xu, Cheng II-129
Xu, Pengjie II-111, II-146
Xu, Xiuyuan II-331
Xu, Zexi II-440

Xue, Bowen   I-505
Xue, Dongfan   II-491
Xue, Xingsi   I-254, I-492, II-313
Xue, Yu   II-472

Yan, Lijun   II-23
Yan, Xiaohui   II-430
Yan, Xiao-peng   I-199
Yang, Chaofan   II-313
Yang, Dongsheng   I-140
Yang, Jian   II-155
Yang, Peng   II-339
Yang, Qi   II-339
Yang, Wenfu   II-182
Yang, Zhicheng   II-282
Yang, Zhile   I-140
Yen, Pei-Chen   I-106
Yi, Zhang   II-331
Yin, Fu   I-347
Yin, Xiaoqing   II-365
Yu, Haiyan   I-130, II-321
Yu, Jun   I-155
Yu, Xin   II-491
Yu, Yueping   II-195
Yuan, Dongfeng   I-130, II-321
Yuan, Guowu   II-553
Yuan, Xia   I-83
Yuan, Yutong   II-137
Yubo, Wang   II-563
Yue, Guanghui   I-155

Zaghloul, Lina   I-223
Zaghloul, Rawan   I-223
Zeng, Li   II-365
Zhang, Chao   II-391
Zhang, Churong   I-155, I-505
Zhang, Cong   I-58
Zhang, Guo   II-205
Zhang, Haixian   II-352

Zhang, Jia-xu   I-199
Zhang, Jingtao   II-111, II-146
Zhang, JunQi   I-423
Zhang, Kun   II-111, II-146
Zhang, Limin   I-301
Zhang, Meng   II-272, II-462
Zhang, Min-Xia   I-163
Zhang, Qiang   I-537, I-547, I-557, I-567
Zhang, Tao   I-433, II-205
Zhang, Tian   II-218
Zhang, Tielin   II-525
Zhang, Xiangyin   II-218
Zhang, Xiaozhi   II-331
Zhang, Zhengwei   II-290
Zhang, Zili   I-94
Zhao, Donghui   II-155
Zhao, Shuai   II-13, II-272, II-462
Zhao, Xin   I-433
Zhao, Xinchao   II-3
Zheng, Jun   II-111
Zheng, Shaoqiu   II-290
Zheng, Yu-Jun   I-163
Zhong, Lou   II-85
Zhou, Hao   II-553
Zhou, Jiarui   I-347
Zhou, Tianwei   I-155, I-505
Zhou, Ying   II-23
Zhou, Yun   I-399
Zhou, Zheng   II-85
Zhou, Zhigang   I-58
Zhou, Zhuo   II-430
Zhu, Hai   II-313
Zhu, Jin   II-352
Zhu, Wenfeng   II-85
Zhu, Xiaomin   II-137
Zhu, Zexuan   I-347
Zhu, Ziqiang   I-301
Zou, Heng   I-441
Zou, Yao   II-182

Printed in the United States
by Baker & Taylor Publisher Services